Property Condition Assessments

ABOUT THE AUTHOR

Sam A. A. Kubba, Ph.D., is an award-winning architect whose practice includes projects in the United States, the United Kingdom, and the Middle East. He has more than 30 years of experience in all aspects of design, construction, and property condition assessments. A member of the American Institute of Architects, the American Society of Interior Designers and the Royal Institute of British Architects, he has lectured widely on architecture, interior design and construction. Dr. Kubba is the principal partner of The Consultants' Collaborative, a firm noted for its work in architecture, interior design, and project management. He is also the author of several books including *Mesopotamian Furniture* and *Space Planning for Commercial and Residential Interiors*.

Property Condition Assessments

Sam A. A. Kubba, Ph.D.

McGraw Hill

New York Chicago San Francisco Lisbon London Madrid
Mexico City Milan New Delhi San Juan Seoul
Singapore Sydney Toronto

The McGraw·Hill Companies

CIP Data is on file with the Library of Congress

McGraw-Hill books are available at special quantity discounts to use as premiums and sales promotions, or for use in corporate training programs. For more information, please write to the Director of Special Sales, McGraw-Hill Professional, Two Penn Plaza, New York, NY 10121-2298. Or contact your local bookstore.

1 2 3 4 5 6 7 8 9 0 FGR/FGR 0 1 3 2 1 0 9 8 7

ISBN 978-0-07-149841-8
MHID 0-07-149841-9

Sponsoring Editor
Joy Bramble
Acquisitions Coordinator
Rebecca Behrens
Editing Supervisor
David E. Fogarty
Project Manager
Jacquie Wallace
Copy Editor
Joseph Staples, Ph.D.
Proofreader
Alan Ingano
Indexer
Leona Woodson
Production Supervisor
Pamela A. Pelton
Composition
Lone Wolf Enterprises, Ltd.
Art Director, Cover
Jeff Weeks

This book is printed on acid-free paper.

This book is dedicated to
My mother and father,
Who bestowed on me the gift of life . . .
And to my wife and four children,
Whose love and affection inspired me on…

CONTENTS

CHAPTER 5: DEVELOPING A CONDITION EVALUATION PROGRAM & STRATEGY 67

CHAPTER 6: ELEMENTS OF PROPERTY CONDITION EVALUATIONS 75

CHAPTER 7: THE BUILDING SITE 89

CHAPTER 8: STRUCTURAL SYSTEMS 97

FOREWORD

Ever since the commercial mortgage back securitization (CMBS) market took off in the early 1990s in response to the Resolution Trust Corporation environment, conducting a Property Condition Assessment (PCA) has become common practice for real estate transactions. This is not to say that physical due diligence did not exist prior to this period, but such surveys became routine, standardized, and the demand for same increased substantially.

Since conducting physical due diligence was a CMBS underwriting requirement of the credit rating agencies, there was a need to establish procedures, the scope of a PCA, and to assist in developing a standard of care. In 1995, Standard & Poor's developed the "Structured Finance Ratings, Real Estate Finance, Property Condition Assessment Criteria," with the intent that this guide would be adopted by the CMBS industry. Prior to this, with the exception of procedures specifically developed for the use of Fannie Mae, national standards for conducting physical due diligence did not exist. Neither the engineering nor the architectural professional societies independently developed standards nor provided any focused support to their respective members who were involved within this fast growing field.

In 1999, the ASTM released "E 2018-99: Standard Guide for Property Condition Assessments: Baseline Property Condition Assessment Process," a document prepared by a consensual committee comprised of both users (clients) and providers (consultants) of commercial property due diligence services. This guide complemented the ASTM's "E1527-05: Standard Practice for Environmental Site Assessments: Phase I Environmental Site Assessment Process" for conducting environmental assessment due diligence, which is the industry's standard.

In developing the ASTM PCA standard guide, the committee identified what was commonly considered to be baseline practices, established a vocabulary, and determined a scope of services that could be reasonably provided by technically well-rounded individuals who were to conduct a PCA under the CMBS market's time and budget constraints. In years past, it was mostly thought that engineers exclusively conducted these eponymous "Engineering Reports." However, in the process of developing the ASTM Standard Guide, it was revealed that not only were there more architects than engineers conducting such surveys, but that the common technical knowledge base of the providers was limited.

The U.S. building surveying practice has a long way to go. In the U.K. such services are regulated under the auspices of the Royal Institute of Chartered Surveyors. The U.K. has a recognized, university level degreed program that specifically trains students to become certified building surveyors. In contrast, there are no formal education programs in the U.S., nor are practitioners of PCA services recognized as a distinctive, licensed or regulated profession. Furthermore, at the time of this writing, there are few PCA training seminars in the States. Those seminars that do exist are of short (two or three days) duration, and a domestic professional society consisting solely of PCA providers has yet to be formed. In the PCA field, while there are numerous books that focus on particular building systems, components, or building codes, there are relatively few books printed in the U.S. that are a "how to" guide for conducting PCAs of commercial buildings.

Since 2000, the profession has seen a convergence with respect to the format and presentation of the deliverable produced by consultants, methodology, and scope; much of this wrought by the ASTM Standard and market forces. Other factors that have molded the industry are the specific use the PCA is to serve, fees, and the U.S. litigation process.

Fee pressure has been intense. Our firm, Inspection & Valuation International, Inc., conducts approximately 4,000 PCAs annually, and we have seen a steady erosion of margin over the past 15 years. Fees have not risen with inflation, the compensation requirements of field observers, or professional liability insurance premiums. As a result, conducting PCAs for the CMBS market has now turned into a volume business. Insurance premiums and deductibles have increased substantially as more and more consultants are entangled by claims, most of which have plaintiffs claiming to be third party beneficiaries of the PCA. In insurance parlance, this business is low frequency and high severity. Claims are rare, maybe one out of every 6,000 assignments, but the amount of the claim could be in the millions, far exceeding the fee for the service.

Sam Kubba, R.A., has written an authoritative primer on the PCA due diligence process, which reads like a "How Buildings Work" book. The chapters on building systems go into much detail that would aid the knowledge base of the typical practitioner, field observer, or user of PCA services. Inasmuch as the scope of PCAs are dependent on such factors as the risk tolerance level of the user, budget, and time constraints, this book will help those in the practice to enhance and sharpen their technical skills. For those considering entering the PCA business, this book provides an excellent overview of building systems and makes the reader keenly aware of the knowledge scope that must be gleaned to deliver a professional service.

Carl de Stefanis, P.E., FRICS
President
Inspection & Valuation International, Inc.

ACKNOWLEDGMENTS

A book of this scope would not have been possible without the assistance and support of numerous individuals—friends, colleagues, architects/engineers and contractors who have contributed greatly to the formation and crystallization of my thoughts and insights on many of the topics and issues discussed during the writing of this book. I am also indebted to the innumerable people and organizations that have contributed ideas, comments, photographs, illustrations, and other items that have helped make this book a reality instead of a pipe-dream.

I must also clearly mention that without the unfailing enthusiasm, encouragement and wisdom of Mr. Roger Woodson, president of Lone Wolf Enterprises Ltd., and Ms. Cary Sullivan, senior editor with McGraw-Hill, this book may not have seen the light of day. It was both gratifying and a pleasure working with them. I also wish to thank Ms. Virginia Howe who edited the manuscript and provided much valued expertise. I must likewise acknowledge the wonderful work of Lone Wolf copy editor Joseph Staples, Ph.D., proofreader Alan Ingano, and layout and composition editor Ms. Jacquie Wallace for their unwavering commitment, under often difficult conditions.

The author especially wishes to express his profound appreciation to the distinguished consulting firm Inspection & Valuation International (IVI) and particularly to its president, Mr. Carl de Stefanis, for his untiring energy and steadfast support. Mr. de Stefanis graciously reviewed and commented on many of the chapters of this book and went out of his way to offer invaluable comments and suggestions for which I am indebted beyond words. I am also appreciative to Mr. Steve Millnick of Gerard Engineering for reviewing Chapters 10 and 13. His comments and suggestions were very beneficial. I also wish to thank Mr. Peter Hollander of Criterium Engineers, who kindly reviewed portions of the manuscript and provided a number of helpful comments.

Finally, I would like to thank my wife, Ibtesam, for her loving companionship and support and for helping me prepare some of the CAD and line illustrations. I also wish to record my gratitude to all those who came to my rescue during the final stretch of this work—the many nameless persons who kept me going with their enthusiasm, support, and technical expertise. I relied upon them in so many ways, and while no words can express my appreciation to all of the above for their assistance and advice, in the final analysis, I alone must bear responsibility for whatever mistakes, omissions or errors may have found their way into the text.

INTRODUCTION

All real estate is subject to the ravages of time. Choosing the right time to carry out repairs can help keep down maintenance costs, stave off expensive follow-up costs and avert warranty claims resulting from site owner liability. Institutions today are under increasing pressure to prioritize renewal and replacement dollars. Principal drivers have changed over the last two decades and today are comprised of existing and emerging regulations, the potential for third party litigation, and consumer and investor interests, which are increasingly focusing on social responsibility issues.

Furthermore, the economic recession in the U.S. and Europe during the late 1980s and early 1990s resulted in many organizations putting off scheduled maintenance of their physical plants and investments. This resulted in an unusually large deferred maintenance backlog that many companies have only recently started tackling.

Today, many of the central districts of large American cities have entered into advanced stages of decay. Detroit, for example, has one of the largest collections of pre-Depression skyscrapers in the world and in no other comparable urban area has the process of decay and abandonment advanced as far. Indeed, the place that invented planned obsolescence has itself become obsolescent.

Obsolete structures may not be able to accommodate new technologies—communication, building automation, or electrical systems. They may be inefficient in their use of energy. In some cases, they can even pose safety hazards like when they do not meet current standards of professional practice or building codes. These facilities may continue to be used, but their property value may decline as potential tenants and investors look to more modern facilities or demand lower rents. When users cannot move, the burdens of obsolescence eventually result in decreased efficiency, reduced output, and declining morale. Moreover, planned obsolescence is made more likely by making the cost of repairs comparable to the replacement cost.

The profession of evaluating existing building systems is only now emerging from its lethargic infancy. Since the 1980s, a number of due diligence firms have emerged that offer substantially different investigative approaches and documentation capabilities. In addition, the development of specialized integrated software packages proceeds unabated. These programs can take the building deficiency data collected during a physical inspection and combine it with other data such as cost spreadsheets, financial investment models and computer aided facilities management (CAFM) software. Such proprietary integrated software, which can also incorporate multimedia information, has become a powerful forecasting and strategic planning tool for management.

The Property Condition Assessment (PCA) is basically a methodology for collecting and recording relevant data for the "due diligence" analysis of commercial real estate investments. The PCA survey identifies physical deficiencies of the subject property. It is the intention of this handbook to present and analyze the many components of building systems evaluation in a manner that encourages understanding between those requesting and those performing the services. The handbook further expounds a standard procedure and methodology developed over years of field experience which has proven effective for this emerging field of property condition assessments (Figure I.1).

While the application of due diligence is considered a prerequisite for any prudent person prior to making a meaningful financial commitment, the process itself does not involve a decision or recommendation, but rather it confirms that requisite tasks pertaining to the property have been performed, pertinent issues addressed and critical information identified and disclosed. The due diligence investigation in essence attests compliance with designated standards, including acquisition policies and criteria, as well as legal and regulatory guidelines, and also that the decision process has been appropriately adhered to. Thus, performing a detailed evaluation of the property prior to the real estate transaction period ensures that the property is a good investment and will assuage fears of possible hidden costs or liabilities associated with facility operations or maintenance after purchase. It also provides mortgagees and buyers with an understanding of property operations prior to actual ownership. Indeed, most investors and real estate professionals have come to appreciate that due diligence of a prospective acquisition is crucial, irrespective of whatever investment strategy might be pursued.

However, for the greatest flexibility and power in accessing, analyzing and reporting the data, the deficiencies must be structured in a hierarchy of systems, subsystems and components. Field collection software should automatically offer appropriate recommendations for noted deficiencies. In addition, it should include search facilities within the reference knowledge database; a carry-forward feature to expedite data entry in the field; and the ability to catalog or inventory buildings, locations and equipment with related serv-

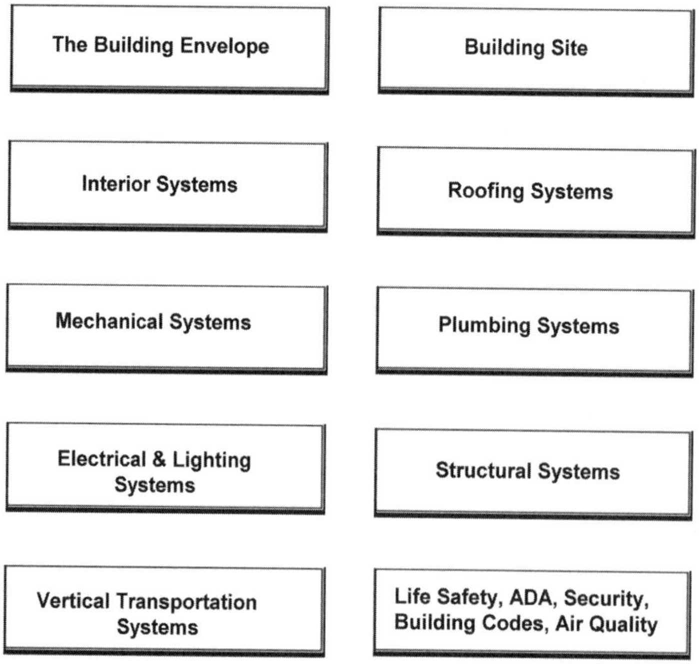

Figure I.1 Building systems and issues to be evaluated in a PCA inspection.

ice life information. Often a purchaser will use the PCA as a negotiating tool since PCAs are essentially directed at noting construction defects or components that seem to exhibit less than expected service life or that have been poorly maintained. They are not intended to develop detailed remedial plans for identified problems.

For this reason, in preparation for purchase or in planning a renovation or upgrade of any facility, it is important to fully understand the condition of the existing structure. The property condition assessment is an evaluation of the current condition of the building and its systems combined with an approximate cost estimate for deferred maintenance, needed repairs or upgrading, and sometimes a calculation of the reserve requirements for ongoing upkeep and replacement. It is a professional service to assist owners, purchasers and lenders to learn more about their facilities.

Typically, the PCA consists of a visual assessment of these systems and of components readily accessible, of the condition of the property elements, building(s), and related structures (i.e. structural and roofing systems, drainage, electrical/mechanical systems, paved areas, architectural finishes, fire protection, site improvements, etc). General code compliance and opinions on remaining useful life and the capacity of building systems to support planned modifications are customarily determined. Some clients also require anticipated capital needs for major replacements and repairs over the life of the mortgage or investment. This handbook clearly articulates most of the major physical condition assessment issues important to the financial analysis of investment opportunities. It may also assist investors and real estate professionals in understanding issues often overlooked by loan underwriters and originators.

Acquisition assessments typically include reviewing a facility for building deficiencies, which significantly affect the value or operation of the property. A limited acquisition survey (referred to as a "walk-through" survey) may include a general review of major systems, such as roofing and air conditioning, which tend to require more frequent repair or replacement. Comprehensive acquisition evaluations include a review of each building system and recommendations addressing any remedial work that will be required at the facility within the foreseeable future. A comprehensive survey is generally conducted by a team of specialists. The Property Condition Report (PCR) will provide the user with specific cost estimates on deficient systems or components requiring remediation immediately or in the upcoming years.

Depending on the position of the user, the PCR as a negotiation tool in the transaction can often result in the majority of the work recommended, or concerns identified in the evaluation, either being performed by the seller or the purchase price being decreased by the cost of these repairs. If the seller agrees to perform the work, it is important to take precautions to ensure that the work is done to acceptable standards. More times than not, the buyer and seller simply agree that the specified work needs to be done, and then the buyer finds that the work does not meet his or her qualitative or aesthetic standards. It is important to be very specific on negotiated work to be performed by the seller. This should include specificity on materials, construction methodology, location, quality and specifications.

This handbook is designed for anyone with an interest in real estate, architectural/engineering due-diligence providers, and facility and building managers in general. It can also be used by long-term real estate owners as a guide to making the most out of their facilities, both operationally and economically. It provides an effective tool to real estate investors by assisting in determining the financial and operational viability of a property or group of properties.

It should prove useful to A&E due-diligence providers, lenders, owners and investors, especially prior to the purchase, sale or refinancing of an asset, or by property managers wishing to ensure that the property elements, buildings and related structures are maintained by the tenants in accordance with their lease obligations.

The methodology detailed will enable executives and managers to establish evaluation programs in order to make informed decisions, based less on assumptions and guesses and more on real data and situations. It will also provide guidelines for on-line personnel to budget and expedite remedial facility repairs in a timely and organized manner. The results will be a more economical product of higher quality which serves the user more fully.

For students of the building profession, this handbook can also be used to provide an excellent source of knowledge and expertise, which up until this point has been unavailable in any single publication. By referencing the manual, building professionals will come away with a working knowledge of the major systems which comprise a facility, as well as an understanding of the value in and the methodology of building system evaluations.

No one handbook or course will provide all you need to know to evaluate building systems, but to the best of my knowledge, this is the best introduction and information source on the subject available at this time. Not only does it provide valuable technical information regarding multi-family and other commercial properties, its value is multiplied by providing invaluable tips on the whole assessment process. Building assessors cannot be specialists in every technical aspect of a property. Nevertheless, the assessment process requires that every system and feature of a property be evaluated with the same level of consistency and concern.

Finally, to assist the client in the ultimate evaluation of a property, it is necessary for the PCA consultant to follow the protocols agreed to with the client. Obviously there is a great deal to learn about assessing the physical condition of commercial properties, and this handbook, together with the field surveys, will help you in expanding your knowledge. I know that before joining IVI, I possessed over 30 years of experience as an international architect, and having won international and national architectural competitions, I felt confident that I knew all there was to know to enable me to carry out a proficient Property Condition Assessment. I was wrong. During my tenure with IVI I learned much that cannot be found in text books or which is outside the realm of normal architectural activity. This handbook is the fruit of this experience, plus the 30 years before and after.

Sam A. A. Kubba, Ph.D.

Property Condition Assessments

CHAPTER

1

Need for a Condition Assessment Program

1.1 GENERAL

Current due diligence engagements are conducted with far greater breadth and depth than those of the past. Facility managers are being plagued with requirements to save money. As such, benchmarking, downsizing, improving productivity and efficiency, streamlining supply, purchasing, and partnering are just a few of the initiatives ongoing in many facility departments today. The objective is to do more with less.

Inspect the property: Prospective buyers of real estate need to evaluate the condition and value of each property they intend to purchase. It is only prudent; certain evaluations or in-depth examinations of a property may reveal problems or potential problems that are not evident at first glance. As such, the buyer is given an opportunity to conduct independent evaluations, or Property Condition Assessments (PCAs). This process is known as "due diligence," and is an integral part of the buying process.

What PCAs do: Buyers have always been keen to make sure that they are getting good value for their money. No one likes to purchase a property only to find out they need a new roof, or the HVAC system needs to be replaced. That's where the building evaluation comes in. The PCA provides a record of a property's condition at the present moment, and forecasts what level of expense a buyer might expect to incur in order to maintain the property and keep it in compliance. Thus, a potential buyer can estimate not only current costs but what level of capital reserve is required for future expenses, including deferred maintenance.

When a consultant is hired to perform a PCA, the scope of services to be covered can be customized to address any special concerns or requirements the owner or prospective purchaser may have. Most assessments will typically examine the property from a variety of angles, including the following:

- The building envelope: its exterior size, type, and shape
- Fire, seismic, and flood hazards due to the location of the property
- Condition of interior systems (floors, roofs, walls, windows, stairs, and doors)
- Vertical transport systems, appliances, dock equipment, etc.
- HVAC, plumbing, electrical, roof, telephone, security, fire, and safety systems

- Outside concerns like landscape, lighting, fences, utilities, drainage, parking, pavement, and access
- Compliance issues (building codes, ADA).

Drawing on the expertise of the consultant, who may be an architect, engineer, construction and maintenance expert, etc., the PCA helps the buyer evaluate the risk of the purchase before committing. "We're in business to eliminate surprises," states Andrew Kuby III, Carlson Environmental's PCA consultant. The purpose of having a common, voluntary standard of assessment is to define good commercial and customary practice. "The standard is only a baseline," says Kuby. "Most assessments far exceed the baseline requirements by including many non-scope items or expanded coverage of specific areas." Prospective buyers need to be kept apprised of the possibility of new risks, and as times and situations change, inclusion of various non-scope issues in a typical PCA may increase or drop off.

The PCA is not only a tool for potential purchasers, it is also useful for facility managers, who suddenly found themselves in the awkward position where they had to become better versed in financial concepts in order to justify the financial benefit of the funding they sought. The PCA helps them do this. Today, managers have to think in terms of the active roles they can take in financial and budgeting matters, and the perspective afforded them by the PCA allows them to accomplish their responsibilities more effectively.

Useful life of a facility: All facilities have a finite useful life; they age, live, and breathe, and eventually they fall into disrepair and are either renovated or demolished to allow for new construction. If building systems are properly maintained and kept in good state of repair, their useful life is significantly extended, they are actually cheaper to maintain, and less possibility exists for building sickness.

The life expectancy of a facility today differs dramatically from what it was a couple of decades ago, or even a century ago. Much of the difference is due to changes in types of materials available or used. A hundred years ago, slate was a common material used for roofs. A slate roof, although expensive to install, has a 100-year life expectancy. Today however, other types of roof systems and materials are used. Mechanical systems were commercially introduced primarily after World War II (over 50 years ago). These systems have been redesigned and upgraded such that in some cases it may be cheaper to dispose of the system than to try to repair or rebuild it.

Because of these and other changes, the country is in the throes of an aging infrastructure. Over the last decade or so, "deferred maintenance" has become a well-known concept as building owners play catch-up with their facility renovations or upgrades, with large amounts of money being expended. Good preventive and predictive maintenance programs and a method of inspecting facilities are important steps to slow down deferred maintenance growth.

The renovations are either for modernization and upgrade reasons or for change of building use. Many of the renovations are limited in scope due to funding restraints and often result in cosmetic change with few or no infrastructure improvements. This fragmentation can lead to inefficiency of mechanical systems, customer complaints due to dissatisfaction with their facilities or environmental conditions, and eventually higher utility bills and maintenance costs. Consequently, recommissioning of the entire facility on a periodic basis (every few years) may be needed. The situation may warrant bringing in an in-house mechanical engineer, who, using checklists in this book, could conduct periodic inspections of entire facility systems. This information can then be used to feed into the deferred maintenance list.

Knowledge is power: The knowledge and information possessed by the facility manager gives him/her the power to transform a reactive maintenance program into a proactive one. A proactive maintenance organization is one that optimizes future benefits, i.e., it maximizes return on investment. Funding, therefore, has become the standard of performance; in other words, what value is the owner getting for the maintenance dollar? Because maintenance protects the capital investment of equipment, systems, and the physical plant, it should be considered an investment in the future. Furthermore, to maximize return on investment of physical plant assets, the facility manager requires accurate, sound and detailed information on the subject elements and status of the assets managed. A comprehensive inventory schedule of the physical plant's equipment, and the components that make up that equipment, is imperative and forms the basis for preventive maintenance, predictive maintenance, space utilization, and capital asset replacement analysis.

Equipment, systems, and structures inspections: Few facilities management activities have as much potential to influence facilities improvements and funding as formal scheduled inspections. Total building, equipment, and system inspections are an essential part of an overall facilities management plan. Formal inspections should not be considered as a replacement for other types of maintenance and operations processes, but rather as another process in the network of interdependent processes that make up the facilities management system. Data collection, deficiency reporting, and assessment activity for a piece of equipment is of very little value if the person performing the inspection does not understand how a specific piece of equipment fits into the system of which it is part. The various elements of mechanical equipment must all be part of an interdependent system that results in the temperatures, volumes, control, and automation that support the occupant's comfort and function. The same applies to the electrical, life safety, and structural components.

1.2 WHY A CONDITION ASSESSMENT PROGRAM

With older properties in particular, a prospective buyer would want to know the useful life of the existing roof, since replacing it would be a major expense. He would also want to know if the mechanical and electrical systems are working properly. The investor may feel that the time is right for a renovation or upgrade. But what needs to be upgraded and how much will it cost? Investors are often full of questions like these, and for answers, a full assessment of the facility and all of its parts is required (Figure 1.1).

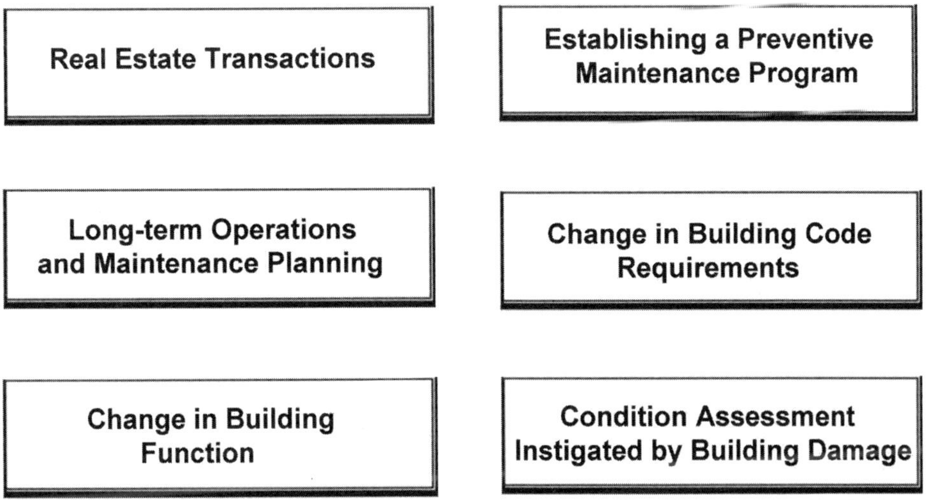

Figure 1.1 Property Condition Assessments (PCAs) are a necessary prerequisite for the real estate owner and investor.

Defining the Property Condition Assessment (PCA): Although known by many names (facilities assessment, facilities survey, conditions survey, facilities audit, or conditions audit), the facilities assessment is a holistic overview of a facility's condition by an appropriate team of professionals who assess the current condition of the building and its components.

Maintaining history: The repair or restoration of a historical building may necessitate investing in a historic structure report. This type of facilities assessment delves into the history of the building, original materials used, and how the building has evolved, changed or was altered through the years. In this report, the assessor uses history as a basis for making decisions concerning the future.

Assessing and planning: A master plan report is another type of facilities assessment. To complete this report, the assessor looks at the possible future space uses of the building. This report incorporates strategic planning aspects into the assessment.

Better planning: Investors can better apply their resources if they have a complete picture. Knowing the size and scope of a repair project assists with fundraising, planning, budgeting, scheduling and other aspects. Investors want to make the most of what they have. A facilities assessment lets you know where your property needs work. Thus if one knows what systems or parts of the building are in good condition, these systems or areas can be maintained with minimal effort so that the areas that need additional attention get it. The assessment allows the investor to be more time and cost efficient.

Ongoing assessment: Even well built, well designed buildings need regular maintenance and repair. Ongoing assessment involves checklists of needed tasks, keeping up on required maintenance, and being aware of emerging problems. Facility owners can save time and money by knowing their buildings and keeping up on the issues. A $1,000 problem can quickly escalate into a $10,000 problem or more if not addressed quickly.

Who does facilities assessment? Most facilities assessments are led by an architect or engineer, but are typically performed by a team of professionals with expertise in the areas of mechanical, plumbing and electrical systems, flooring, roofing systems, windows, structure systems, etc. The building assessor assigns the various components of the building to the person with the appropriate knowledge.

Finding a qualified consultant: An investor or building owner can tap numerous resources to help find a proficient consultant to conduct the PCA. It is usually safer to choose an assessor who has qualifications and experience conducting PCAs for buildings similar to the one in question.

Be prepared: The more information that is provided to the assessor, the less expensive and more complete the assessment will be. Any drawings or blueprints of the building or additions, maintenance records, historical documentation, photographs, records of renovation or restoration should be given to the assessor for review. No matter how old the documents, they are still helpful. If the information is not in hand, it may be available through the local historical society, previous contractors, state or county offices or denominational office. If enough historical or maintenance data is not available, architects may have to do "exploratory demolition." This involves breaking through the walls or roof or other areas to investigate what is going on within the structure. For this reason, it is worth spending additional time to retrieve necessary documentation.

Communicate: Keep the lines of communication open. The owner/investor needs to feel comfortable talking with the architect. A smooth give-and-take with the assessor makes his or her job easier and keeps everyone informed throughout the process.

Informing the owner: Upon completion of the assessment (including the report), the owner is informed of its contents—noted deficiencies, recommendations and cost estimates. The information may surprise the owner, and it may take some time to process it before being accepted and ready to proceed to the planning phase. The architect can answer questions and provide additional explanation if needed.

Plan of action: The final report usually includes phasing or staging the work needed based on the information the owner/investor provided about the availability and timing of funds. Once the owner/investor is comfortable with the scope and cost of the project, the consultant can develop a plan, help locate good contractors for the owner/investor to consider, and oversee the work once contracts are signed and the project begins.

File it in a Safe Place: The assessment report should be stored in a safe place for future reference. It will be helpful if work needs to be done at a later time, or as historical documentation for the next assessment.

A typical facilities assessment will include most of the following:

- Introduction
- Brief history of the property and maintenance programs, if any
- Executive summary
- Description of existing conditions
- Note of major deficiencies
- Recommendations and remarks
- Cost estimates
- Photographs, drawings, sketches or measurements
- Optional reports from various specialists, such as a structural engineer, mechanical or electrical engineer, etc.

1.3 RULES OF ENGAGEMENT

The contractual and legal obligations between a consultant and a user (and other parties, if any) are outside the scope of this handbook.

Communications: Communications shall be conducted in a professional and courteous manner at all times. Letters and other formal communications shall be issued only with the proper authority. Conversations, telephone calls, and other informal communications shall be conducted with the understanding that the consultant is acting in the interest of the client. The content of discussion held in official capacity shall be recorded in writing and made part of the appropriate file.

At times, the assessor may disagree with others. These disagreements should be handled with tact and should not be allowed to degenerate. A professional is expected to state opinions based on his training, knowledge, and judgment. The professional's opinion should be based on knowledge of the facts and issues, and should be defensible.

Regular client contact is important and helps to build trust and confidence. As a service organization it is vital that you understand a client's needs and concerns and to respond accordingly.

1.4 ORGANIZATION, ROLES AND RESPONSIBILITIES

The larger professional organizations use a team approach to deliver PCA services. The team typically comprises management, technical staff, administrative staff, and production staff. Each member of the team is vital to the delivery of the PCA services.

The Division Manager provides leadership and guidance to the PCA team, establishes policy, maintains client relations and develops new business. The Division Manager will make assignments, provide technical guidance, and establish quality control and assurance measures.

The Senior Project Managers provide leadership and technical guidance to other members of the PCA team, review and edit draft PCA reports, and enforce quality control measures. They may act as project managers and perform PCA assignments as required.

The Project Managers have overall responsibility to complete the work of the PCA, from assignment to the delivered report product, and to keep management and the client informed of progress.

The administrative staff provides support to management and the technical staff. They coordinate project assignments, travel plans, technical research, and report production. As members of the PCA team, they may also contribute to maintaining good client relations.

The production staff is an extension of the administration staff with the responsibility to produce and deliver the final report product.

User's Responsibilities according to the American Society for Testing and Materials (ASTM)

Access: User should arrange for the field observer to receive timely access, which is complete, supervised, and safe to the subject property's improvements (including roofs). In addition, the subject property's staff, vendors, and appropriate documents should be provided by owner, owner's representative, or made available by user. In no event should the field observer seek access to any particular location of the property, property management staff, vendors, tenants, or documents, if the owner, user, or occupant objects to such access or attempts to restrict the field observer from conducting any portion of the walk-through survey, research or interviews, or taking of photographs. Any conditions that significantly impede or restrict the field observer's walk-through survey or research, or the failure of the owner or occupant to timely provide access, information, or requested documentation shall be timely communicated by the consultant to the user. If such conditions are not remedied, the consultant is obligated to state within the PCR all such material impediments that interfered with conducting the PCA in accordance with this guide.

User disclosure: User should timely disclose all information in user's possession that may assist the consultant's efforts. The user should not withhold any pertinent information that may assist in identifying a material physical deficiency, including, but not limited to, (1) previously prepared property condition reports; (2) any study specifically prepared on a system or component of the subject property; (3) any knowledge of actual or purported physical deficiencies; or (4) any information, such as costs to remedy known physical deficiencies.

CHAPTER

2

Property Condition Assessments (PCA)

2.1 GENERAL

As outlined earlier, the Property Condition Assessment (PCA) essentially identifies physical deficiencies of a subject property's material systems, components, or equipment as observed at the time of the walk-through survey. The term physical deficiency refers to conspicuous defects or material deferred maintenance. The PCA is also often described as a methodology for collecting and reporting physical data important in the "due diligence" analysis of commercial real estate transactions. It is also designed to provide a professional opinion regarding future anticipated issues, which may result in a financial risk or liability to the client. The process includes a visual walk-through to observe existing conditions and a review of available public records, construction documentation, and current budgets. This information is then analyzed and presented with recommendations for repair or further detailed review (i.e., additional mechanical, structural or civil survey) if the issues cannot be determined through visual observation alone.

A PCA is usually performed prior to a real estate transaction for commercial properties. It is what any astute potential buyer or mortgagee would employ prior to making a meaningful financial commitment. The process does not involve a decision or recommendation, but rather is a confirmation that requisite tasks have been performed, pertinent issues have been addressed and critical information has been identified and disclosed. It further confirms that the decision process has been appropriately adhered to. Due diligence of prospective acquisitions is therefore crucial, irrespective of whatever investment strategy might be pursued.

The Property Condition Report (PCR) is extremely important in the due diligence process, and is often the basis for real estate financial decisions involving millions of dollars. It is essential that the PCA be conducted professionally, and that the report is comprehensive, informative, and accurate. Real estate transactions are normally conducted on a tight schedule, typically within 30 to 45 days, with success dependent on the timely performance of the various activities and consultants.

A PCA may be conducted for newly constructed or converted multi-family residential properties at the time the developer transfers the property over to the association. In the multi-family residential industry the assessment is commonly referred to as an Engineering/Developer Transition Study. The assessment typically identifies material and design defects, poor workmanship, and deviations from standard construction practices. This enables the association to pursue repairs or compensation from the developer for deficiencies that may exist.

2.2 THE PROPERTY CONDITION ASSESSMENT (PCA)

The Purpose and Function of the Property Condition Assessment is to:

1. Observe and define major components and sub-components
2. List observations of fact (observed conditions only) and label all relevant data by component category and location in the report
3. Identify and document major deficiencies (based upon the physical inspection)
4. Provide cost estimates of repair for major items identified. This represents the pertinent information the client seeks.
5. Identify, investigate and record in the report any observed unusual or hazardous conditions.

The Scope of the physical condition inspection is determined through agreement with the client but it typically consists of:

1. Visual inspection of readily accessible major components and systems
2. Operation of equipment using existing controls (upon agreement with client)
3. Review drawings, maintenance records and other documents including previous consultant's reports (regarded as an additional service and therefore requires payment)
4. Interview persons who can provide useful information, such as building owner, tenants, management, maintenance, service companies, fire marshal, building engineers, etc.
5. Disassemble and/or test for itemized components as/if agreed to in the inspection scope of works
6. Other action as called for by the specifics of the job.

The Limitations of a PCA are:

1. Not an exhaustive analysis of design or scientific testing
2. Not a compliance check for codes, laws, statues, Americans with Disabilities Act requirements, environmental, asbestos, fire protection, etc.
3. Not a bid or proposal to perform repair/construction work
4. May require list of specific exclusions in the report, anything not mentioned in the report is not to be inspected

5. Does not include tenant equipment or moving anything
6. Inclusion of an indemnity clause in the report is absolutely vital.

The Value and Benefit received by the client for fee paid for PCA includes:

1. It provides a permanent record
2. It provides valuable updated information for pre-purchase consideration
3. It can be utilized as a negotiating tool
4. It is a guide for maintenance and capital improvements (and possibly capital depreciation)
5. Report and physical inspection can be as complex and comprehensive in scope as the client wishes it to be and is willing to pay for.

Protocols for Building Condition Assessment: Sound property management involves regularly checking a building's health. But what should one look for and how does one know if a system needs attention? The NRC Institute for Research in Construction (NRC-IRC), a leading Canadian construction research agency is one of several agencies that provide a systematic approach to these and other issues. Their publication, Protocols for Building Condition Assessment also identifies problems at their earliest stages and helps to evaluate a building's future maintenance and repair needs.

The NRC-IRC publication deals with eight categories: building structure, building envelope, mechanical systems, electrical systems, interior finishes, life safety, elevators, and function. Each section has its own building assessment protocol which defines the scope of the audit for that category, describes the audit procedure, and identifies deliverables. Collectively, these eight protocols comprise the complete preliminary audit process.

Most major firms have their own check sheets, which highlight potential problem areas, and which are employed to assist in conducting the assessments and to ascertain the amount of work needed to repair areas requiring attention. Protocols should refer to national codes to guide the assessor in evaluating how well a given area or system complies with appropriate standards.

Standards for Property Condition Assessments: The industry is moving to a standard protocol for PCA services. The American Society for Testing and Materials (ASTM) has approved guidelines for conducting a PCA. ASTM's Standard Guide for Property Condition Assessments: Baseline Property Condition Assessment Process (E 2018-01) recognizes that there are numerous levels of physical due diligence that can be performed, but prescribes procedures, a methodology, and a scope of work for conducting a baseline PCA. An updated ASTM Standard is in development, but has yet to be adopted. Standard & Poor has adopted a protocol that is general in nature allowing for broad use. Other PCA users have established protocols that address their specific needs.

The main objectives in the development of the Standard Guide for Property Condition Assessments were to:

1. Define good commercial and customary practice for the PCA of primary commercial real estate
2. Facilitate consistent and pertinent content in producing Property Condition Reports (PCRs)
3. Develop practical and reasonable recommendations and expectations for site observations, document reviews and research associated with conducting a baseline PCAs and preparing PCRs
4. Formulate reasonable expectations for PCRs
5. Assist in developing an industry baseline standard of care for appropriate observations and research

6. Propose protocols for consultants to communicate observations, opinions, and recommendations in a manner meaningful to the user
7. Identify and communicate physical deficiencies to a user.

The ASTM Guide outlines procedures for conducting a walk-through survey to identify the subject property's material physical deficiencies, and recommends various systems, components, and equipment that should be observed by the field observer and reported in the PCR. The work product resulting from completing a Property Condition Assessment (PCA) in accordance with the guide is a PCR. The PCR incorporates the information obtained during the walk-through survey, the document review and interviews, and includes opinions of probable costs for suggested remedies of certain physical deficiencies identified. This information can be valuable in helping property owners and buyers understand operating and maintenance costs and helps to provide confidence to prospective purchasers that the transaction is solid.

The consultant works together with the client to determine the scope of the inspection services needed and is committed to providing outstanding client service and satisfaction. The consultant should at the very least adhere to the ASTM standards for performing a commercial property inspection.

2.3 THE FINANCIAL INDUSTRY, DUE DILIGENCE, & USE OF PCAS

Property Condition Assessment Reports offer the client a single document containing information crucial to assessing a project's feasibility relative to its physical condition. These reports are often the basis on which a decision to purchase a property is made. The reports should be clearly written in layman's terms, so that they can easily be understood by non-technical individuals. The financial industry utilizes the PCA report in different ways depending on the type of transaction that is to be made.

2.3.1 Securitization

The creation of a financial instrument, or security, based on the value potential of real property and/or property revenue stream has been termed the "securitization" of the property. Usually, a number of properties are consolidated within a security portfolio. The market eventually determines the value of the security and the meaning of individual property values is therefore lost. A high level of due diligence in this case may not have commensurate value.

Securitization/CMBS

The Commercial Mortgage-Backed Securities (CMBS) market emerged in the 1990s as an effective way to tap national and international capital markets for real estate finance, and is rapidly emerging as a pivotal component of the real estate debt market. CMBS transactions have not only influenced the entire debt market, but are also helping to provide greater underwriting due diligence and discipline to the flow of debt capital into real estate markets. Moreover, CMBS is providing enhanced portfolio diversification with better credit protection and stability compared to similar corporate bonds. The CMBS industry has grown from less than \$10 billion in the early 1990s to approximately \$600 billion today (Figure 2.1).

The Commercial Mortgage Securities Association (CMSA): This is an international trade organization for the commercial real estate capital markets consisting of 4,000 individuals representing over 300 member firms. The mission of the CMSA is to improve the liquidity of commercial real estate debt through access to the capital markets.

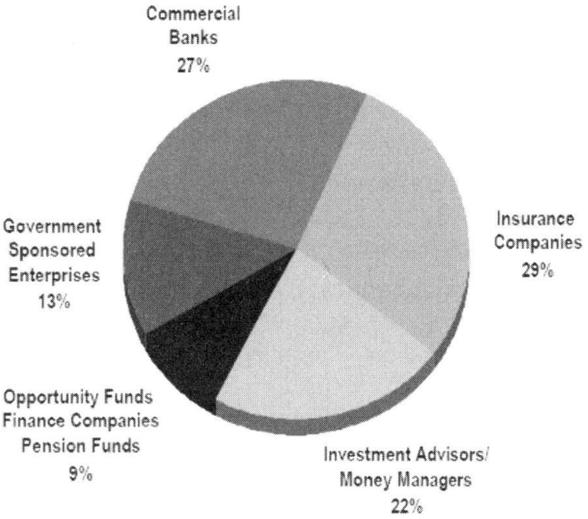

Figure 2.1 Purchasers of CMBS *(courtesy Morgan Stanley).*

The Participants in a Securitization

1. **Borrower:** The entity (individual, partnership, LLC, trust) owns real property, improvements, interests in leases and related property; all of which will be pledged to the lender to secure the borrower's loan repayment and performance obligations. The borrower retains ownership of the property securing the loan.
2. **Mortgage banker:** An intermediary between the borrower and the loan originator, may act as advisor to borrower or as a specialist for a specific capital source, may assist in selecting best execution for the borrower.
3. **Loan originators/loan sellers:** Lends money to the borrower, secured by a first priority lien on borrower's real property and related collateral. As the "owner" of the mortgage loan, enters into a mortgage loan purchase agreement (MLPA) to sell the loan to the securitization depositor.
4. **Issuer/depositor:** An entity that collects and pools the mortgage loans until sufficient collateral is obtained to begin the securitization process. The issuer/depositor is responsible for establishing the trust in which the mortgage loan collateral is deposited. The trust, which is the record owner of the commercial mortgage loans, holds the loans on behalf of the investors, and in turn issues the securities, which are subsequently sold to the CMBS investors. The cash proceeds are used to pay the mortgage loan sellers amounts due under each MLPA.
5. **Investment banker:** Has overall responsibility for structuring the securitization, bringing all the parties to the transaction, and selling the bonds/certificates (on behalf of the depositor) to investors. After the securitization closes, helps maintain a liquid secondary market for trading the bonds/certificates.
6. **Trustee:** The trustee holds legal title to the underlying security collateral for the benefit of the security holders. Pursuant to the PSA, the trustee is responsible for overall administration of the securities on behalf of and making payments to the investors.
7. **Investors:** Different investors with varying risk appetites purchase various certificates rated from AAA/Aaa (highest rated credit quality, lowest expected bond yield) to B/B (lowest rated credit quality, highest expected bond yield) and unrated certificates.
8. **Master servicer:** Pursuant to the Pooling and Servicing Agreement (PSA), the master servicer is responsible for servicing administration of all mortgage loans owned by the trust, which are not in default. These responsibilities include processing and, in most cases, approving borrower re-

quests, collecting debt service and escrow/reserve payments due from the borrowers, and compiling property and borrower information.

9. **Primary or sub servicer:** Will act on behalf of the master servicer as the main point of contact with the borrower and carry out related master servicer responsibilities. The primary or sub-servicer may be the originating mortgage bankers, typically hired by the master servicer.
10. **Special servicer:** Pursuant to the PSA, the special servicer is named at the issuance of the CMBS to be responsible for servicing any delinquent or sub-performing mortgage loans as well as the disposition of real estate owned that is obtained in foreclosure or similar action.
11. **Rating agency:** Hired by the investment banker and issuer to evaluate the underlying mortgage loans, the security structure of each security structure of each security class and the parties to the transaction—the rating agency then provides a credit rating based on these criteria. After the securitization funds, the rating agencies will continue to monitor performance of the trust's assets and certificates. Major rating agencies include: Moody's Investors Service, Standard and Poor's, Fitch Investor Services, Duff and Phelps Credit Rating Co., and Dun and Bradstreet.

Where the Money Goes (Figure 2.2)

Borrower

- Assigns mortgages and leases in return for loan from loan originator (at loan closing)
- Remits monthly debt service to servicer collection account

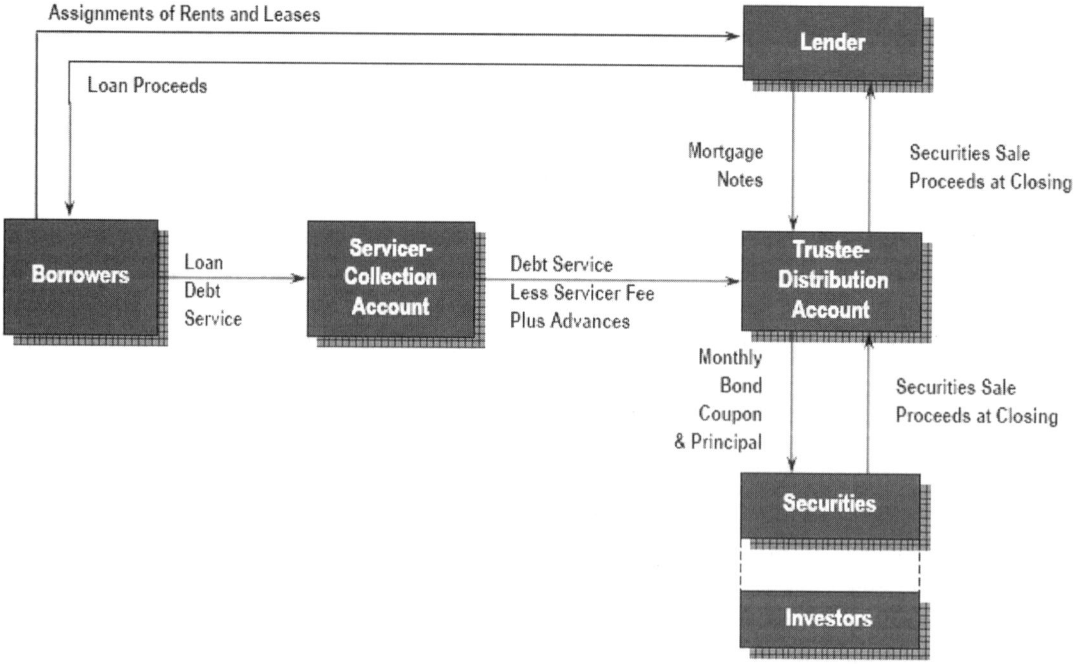

Figure 2.2 Diagram illustrating where the money goes *(courtesy CMSA)*.

Loan Originator/Loan Seller

- Deposits mortgage collateral in trust in return for issuance proceeds from the securitization, a portion of which is given to borrower in return for lien

Servicer

- Remits debt service (plus advances, less servicing fees) to trustee distribution account

Trustee

- Distributes to investors certificate interest and principal, as specified in the trust agreements, from trustee distribution account

Investors

- Purchase certificates and receive certificate interest and principal

Who is the Lender? (Post-Closing of CMBS)

1. In a conventional loan the lender is a single entity funding the loan, processing payments, processing any changes (such as assumptions, or releases), receiving all P&I payments and receiving early prepayments, working out a problem loan (Figure 2.3).
2. In a CMBS loan all those functions associated with a traditional lender are handled separately by different parties (i.e. the contact person to inform or process changes is not necessarily the same entity as the one which provided the funds for the loan).
3. At the loan closing, a borrower will be informed as to the interim servicer for the loan. After depositing the loan into the Real Estate Mortgage Investment Conduit (REMIC) Trust, a borrower will be informed as to the primary (or sub), master, and special servicers for the loan. The responsibilities of each servicing entity are governed by REMIC rules, the Pooling and Servicing Agreement (PSA), and the loan documents.

One of the most contentious areas of post-securitization is with respect to additional encumbrances (Figure 2.4). If a loan has subordinate debt, or if the loan documents provide that the borrower may incur subordinate debt in the future, Moody's will take this into account in its rating analysis. Once a loan is securitized, however, there is less latitude with respect to additional encumbrances if the loan documents prohibit such.

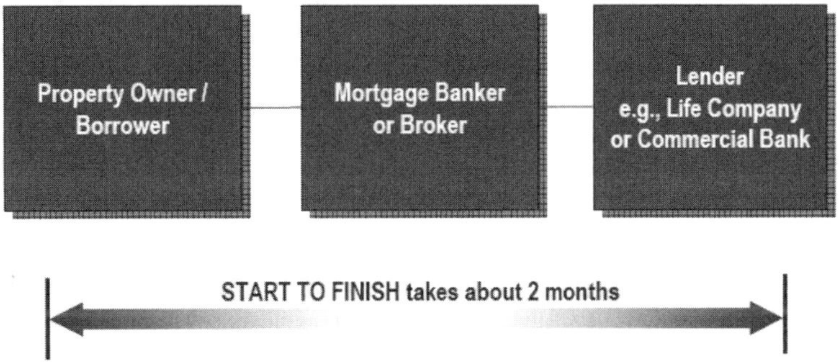

Figure 2.3 Participants in a conventional mortgage financing *(courtesy CMSA)*.

2.3.2 Refinancing

The refinancing of a loan on a property involves a certain level of diligence to determine the extent of the property's maintenance and

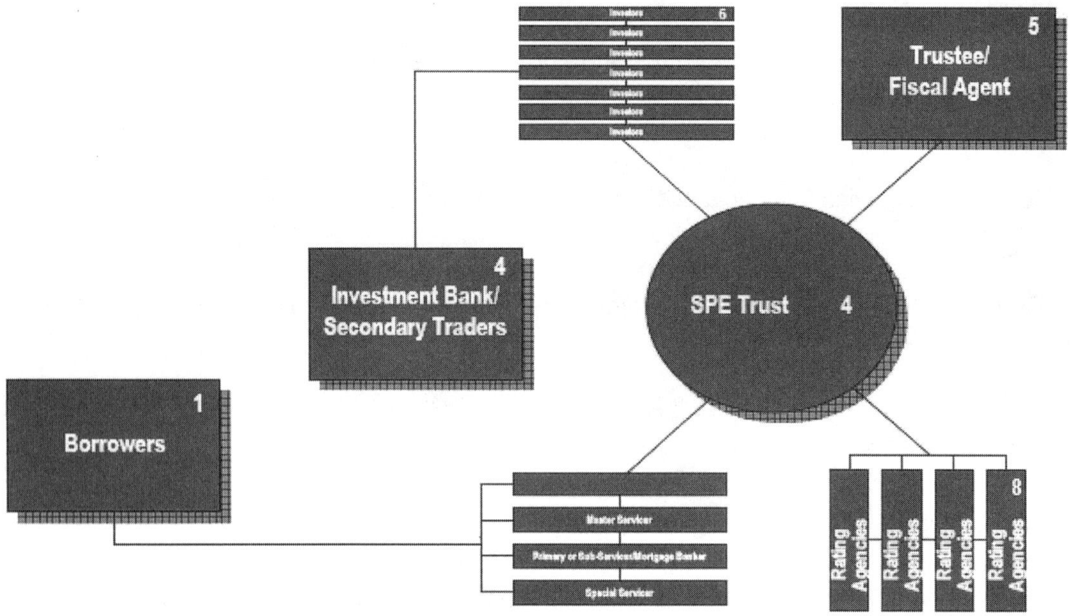

Figure 2.4 Participants after securitization is completed *(courtesy CMSA)*.

physical condition. Information should be more readily available on the property, making the effort to achieve this level of diligence on the property less than on one that is not known.

Refinancing of commercial property is basically a means to reduce high interest rates or get a longer term loan that is offering better provisions. One may also decide to obtain cash from the equity the property has built up. Note that if the capital is not reinvested in other commercial property, the interest paid on the new portion will not be tax deductible. If tracked to non-investment purchases, the cash-out portion is considered a consumer debt. Therefore the purpose defeats the tax deductible status of the entire loan.

In any real estate transaction, the type of loan should be carefully considered before making a commitment to a large amount for a lengthy repayment. Consider the options of fixed rate loans and variable interest rate loans when preparing to refinance commercial property. Check whether the variable rate loan has a cap and how often the rate is expected to vary. It is advisable to refinance with a lender that is willing to clarify its variable rates source and is able to help select one that varies with less volatility.

Commercial real estate owners also frequently want to refinance properties as an alternative to selling them outright or to replace credit lines that expire soon. However, just as with a house, the decision to refinance should be based entirely on the building's circumstances in order to make sense.

2.3.3 Underwriting

The underwriting of a loan requires a reasonable level of diligence to ensure that the property assets are known. This would include opining on the costs to remedy observed deficiencies. Most of real estate lending comes down to the results of three ratios:

- Debt Service Coverage Ratio (DSCR)
- Loan-To-Value Ratio
- Debt Ratio

The "processing" of a loan is merely an attempt to verify the numbers that go into the numerator and denominator of the above three ratios. The buyer needs to understand underwriting guidelines to determine available options when purchasing or refinancing a property. Some people are confused and misled by the terms—mortgage approval, mortgage pre approval, loan qualification, and pre-qualification.

Mortgage pre-approval (or loan pre-qualification) is in essence a pre-approval or pre-qualification based on information submitted before verification of all documentation. After documentation verification the file goes to a mortgage underwriter who again verifies the information. The underwriter may request other documentation deemed justified to strengthen the file. When the underwriter is satisfied, the borrower will receive an approval and clear to close. The actual closing can then be scheduled.

The loan-to-value (LTV) ratio is probably the most important of the three underwriting ratios. This is defined as: LTV Ratio = Total Loan Balances (1st mtg+2nd mtg+3rd mtg)/Fair Market Value of the Property.

Generally the fair market value of a property is determined by an appraisal. There is one important exception, however. When the proceeds of a mortgage loan are used to buy the same property that is securing the loan, then that mortgage is known as a "purchase money loan." If the appraisal comes in lower than the purchase price in a "purchase money" transaction, then the lender will use the lower of the purchase price or appraisal.

Loan-to-value ratios rarely exceed 80 percent on commercial loans, mainly because the lender almost always seeks some protection in case of default. Another ratio that lenders use when underwriting a loan is the debt ratio. This compares the amount of bills that the borrower is required to pay each month to the amount of earned monthly income. More precisely, the debt ratio is defined as: Debt Ratio = Monthly Debt Obligations/Monthly Income.

Commercial underwriting guidelines: Commercial financing is underwritten on a case by case basis. Every loan application is unique and has to be evaluated on its own merits, nevertheless there are some basal criteria lenders look for in a commercial loan package.

Financial analysis: A key component in making an underwriting evaluation is the debt coverage ratio (DCR). The DCR is defined as the monthly debt compared to the net monthly income of the investment property in question. Using a 1:1.10 DCR means that the lender is looking for $1.10 in net income for each $1.00 in mortgage payment. Typically they will determine the DCR ratio based on monthly figures, the monthly mortgage payment compared to the monthly net income. Most lenders will not go below a 1:1 ratio (a dollar of debt payment per dollar of income generated). Anything less then a 1:1 ratio will result in a negative cash flow situation which makes it less attractive for the lender because it ups the risk factor. DCRs are determined by property type and lender's perception of the risk. Today, apartment properties are considered to be the least risky category of investment lending. As such, lenders are inclined to accept smaller DCRs when evaluating a loan request.

Loan to value: Unlike residential lending, commercial investment properties are viewed more conservatively. Most lenders will require a minimum of 20 percent of the purchase price to be paid by the buyer. The remaining 80 percent can be in the form of a mortgage provided by either a bank or mortgage company. Some commercial mortgage lenders will require more than a 20 percent contribution toward the purchase from the buyer. What a bank/lender will do is subject to market conditions and the quality of the buyer and the property. Loan to value is the percentage calculation of the loan amount divided by purchase price.

Property analysis: Fair market value and fair market rent will be analyzed. Special use property may require additional underwriting. Age, appearance, local market, location, and accessibility are some other factors considered.

2.3.4 Disclosure

A PCA prepared on behalf of an owner for purposes of disclosure is intended to identify physical deficiencies that are expected to be discovered through buyer's due diligence in order to facilitate the deal. Appropriate efforts to identify physical deficiencies should be given, but usually no opinions are rendered in regard to probable costs to remedy the deficiencies identified. An opinion of cost in this case would not serve the best interest of the client, the seller.

User Disclosure (as recommended by ASTM): The ASTM guidelines explicitly state that the user should disclose in a timely manner all appropriate information in the user's possession that may assist the consultant's efforts including pertinent information that may assist in identifying a material physical deficiency, previously prepared property condition reports, any study specifically prepared on a system or component of the subject property, any knowledge of actual or purported physical deficiencies, or any information such as costs to remedy known physical deficiencies.

2.3.5 Acquisition

The utmost diligence should be exercised in property acquisitions. Existing deficiencies relate directly to the value of the property. Due to the complexity and/or age of some properties, a more comprehensive assessment of some or all building systems may be recommended. As a result, many clients (buyers) choose to enhance the ASTM's baseline survey by supplementing the consultant with specialty consultants, in which case the consultant will mobilize a team of construction professionals and other specialists to conduct the inspection of a proposed acquisition. The assessment should identify, locate, and quantify significant defects, deferred maintenance, required upgrades, and obvious code violations at the property as well as estimating the remaining useful life of major building components, and evaluating the property's physical condition.

The consultant reviews building department files in order to disclose any outstanding code violations and may conduct an abbreviated survey for ADA compliance. The consultant then prepares a thorough report with prioritized recommended repairs and replacements, and which includes cost estimates to remedy deferred maintenance and for necessary capital improvements.

Real estate transactions: Acquisition surveys typically include reviewing a facility for building deficiencies, which will significantly affect the value or operation of the property. A limited acquisition survey may include a general review of specific systems, such as roofing and air conditioning, which tend to experience more frequent repair or replacement. Comprehensive acquisition evaluations would typically include a review of each building system and recommendations to address any remedial work that is anticipated to be undertaken at the facility within the foreseeable future. The PCA report will provide the buyer with specific cost estimates on deficient systems or components requiring remediation immediately or in the upcoming years.

The use of the PCA report as a negotiation tool in the transaction can result in having most of the recommended remedial work in the evaluation either being performed by the seller or having the purchase price decreased by the estimated cost of these repairs. If the seller agrees to perform the work, it is important for precautions to be taken to ensure that the work is done to pertinent standards. It is important to be very precise on negotiated work to be performed by the seller. This should include specificity on materials, construction methodology and quality of work.

Phases of Structure	Level of Inspection	Frequency	Purpose	Skills (Duration)	Possible Actions
Acceptance	General	Once, before "in use" condition	• Calibration of parameters in service life models (durability design models) • Certification of performance	Engineer (h to d)	If performing according to service life calculations are not met, additional protective measures are required
In-use	Visual	1 to 3 years	Detection of obvious defects; especially important for the detection of unexpected defects due to irregularities during fabrication, unreported accidents or misuse of a structure	Technician (h)	• Short term repair on non-structural defects • Call for general inspection
	General	Flexible, according to development of condition state	• Determination of condition state • Calibration of parameters in service life models	Engineer (d)	• Set date for next inspection • Call for repair action • Call for structural assessment
	Structural assessment	On demand	Assessment of structural safety (static calculations, FEM analysis)	Engineer (d-w)	• Call for strengthening and repair • Temporary load restriction
Repair	General	During repair action	• Adaptation of MR&R extent • Calibration of service life models • Certification of performance	Engineer (d)	• Call for additional actions, if performance requirements are not fulfilled

Figure 2.5 Summary of various levels of inspections that are typically required to be conducted by a consultant *(courtesy Lifecon)*.

More and more, real estate sellers are performing evaluations during the preparation for the real estate transaction. These disclosure studies reveal to the potential buyer the quality of the property and alleviate some of the typical fears experienced in the transaction. The disclosure study can also result in third-party verification of the worth and quality of the building systems. For that reason, it is essential that the report is written objectively by a qualified independent consultant.

2.4 LEVELS OF DUE DILIGENCE

In order to meet the requirements of the financial industry and make the best use of resources, three levels of due diligence have been accepted for PCA use. The levels of diligence progress from a basal review of a property to a comprehensive study, depending on the requirements of the client (Figure 2.5). A study may include opinions of costs to remedy deficiencies and the development of replacement reserve schedules.

Replacement reserves are a way of identifying, quantifying and budgeting needed monies to fund future major building repairs and replacements. As properties age, expenditures for replacements and improvements are critical to maintaining the asset and its competitive position in the market. Not implementing needed repairs and replacements may result in significant physical deterioration, functional obsolescence, and impact the property's value.

Once the scope of the work is determined, the consultant can proceed to conduct the assessment. However, no two evaluations will be designed with the same diagnostic methodology. Each facility with its operations and combination of systems is unique, and an efficient evaluation warrants logistical coordination and scope delineation specific to that facility. A shopping mall or manufacturing facility is distinctly different from a high-rise office building. The size, the layout, the structure and the systems are all different and unique to the facility type, design, use, location and age. From the initial survey, it may become evident that a follow-up evaluation and study is necessary.

As discussed earlier, the scope and level of effort in a building assessment can vary tremendously depending on several factors. The time required to conduct an evaluation will also vary accordingly. If the survey is concentrated on a single system in an acquisition study, the time required in the planning, physical inspection and report preparation process will be significantly less than if the assessment constituted a comprehensive survey that examined the major systems in the facility. Where a Scoping is performed, the assessment process will again require much less time than if the evaluation consisted of a long-term equipment replacement program.

2.4.1 Level I Evaluation

The lowest level of due diligence, Level I, requires that a walk-through survey of the property be conducted and basic information related to the property be researched.

A Level I is used to form opinions on the likelihood, types and locations of issues affecting the condition of a property. Common issues range from the possible presence of hazardous building materials to visible cracks in a structural system. The information gathered by a Level I inspection can be used by owners, purchasers and lenders to make informed decisions regarding property management, acquisition and financing. A Level I would include records review, a site visit, interviews and an evaluation of all information by qualified assessors. It is important for the assessor to be fully conversant with the potential sources of information including government databases, archives, underwriters, etc. This first step in the assessment process is normally non-intrusive and non-destructive, but the consultant may try to enhance the program to meet the specific needs of the client or to address known concerns in a proactive, cost-efficient manner.

2.4.2 Level II Evaluation

The next level of due diligence, Level II, is more comprehensive and requires a higher level of investigation. Building components and systems are examined more carefully and more thoroughly. Material deficiencies are identified and opinions of cost to remedy the deficiencies provided. Reserve schedules are developed and noted in the report.

Oftentimes, an initial inspection brings to light a number of serious deficiencies. An example could be evidence of visible cracks in load-bearing brickwork or a major HVAC or roofing system deficiency. This strongly makes a case for the need of a more intensive evaluation. Additional evaluation may also be rec-

CRITERIA	EXAMPLE
Damage cause unknown	Cracks in the superstructure.
Proneness	Similar structures/components/systems suffered from know, but possibly imperceptible problems.
Damage of unknown extent	Chloride ingress, corrosion of re-bars.
Damage of large extent	Evaluation of secondary effects.
Damage which can not be sufficiently investigated by conventional (visual) methods	Mold, masonry cracks, structural deficiencies. Non-destructive testing possible to determine extent.
Development of damage, which deviates strongly from expected values	Chloride content or amount of cracks - increase rapidly and deviate from prognosis.
Damage development unknown	Collection of necessary input data.
Residual service life seems not sufficient	• high variance of data → increase of sample amount • models are too simple → use sophisticated models
High degree of statistical uncertainty	If the uncertainty is due to dispersed data and this can be reduced by additional sampling, such samples should be collected to an extent for which the additional inspection costs do not yet balance out the already achieved benefits.

Figure 2.6 Examples for criteria demanding for a more intensive inspection to be conducted by the consultant.

ommended if for example an issue is discovered during the field or documentation reviews that are outside the original scope of work. If upon review of a component in one building system, an adjacent system is seen from a different light or angle in a manner so as to indicate the presence of deficiencies warranting further investigation, additional evaluation should be performed.

The consultant may also recommend that additional study be conducted in the future for something other than a short-term issue. For example, if the consultant learns that in two years a planned annex to the facility is to be built and will necessitate increased requirements on the HVAC system, further studies would be recommended to maintain adequate service to the facility.

2.4.3 Level III Evaluation

The Level III due diligence requires a comprehensive evaluation of the property. Building components and systems are examined in detail, usually by specialists trained in specific areas. This level of assessment may involve testing programs and in depth research. Material deficiencies are identified in more detail and opinions of cost to remedy the deficiencies provided. Reserve schedules are also developed (Figure 2.6).

2.5 RISK & LIABILITY

The PCA is extremely important to real estate transactions, often involving substantial financial exposure to the parties. A contract agreement between the PCA services provider and a client binds the provider to perform the scope of work and implies that this work will be performed with a level of skill and care consistent with industry standards. The failure on the part of the service provider to perform the work in accordance with this agreement exposes the service provider to substantial liability, as well as damage to client relations and reputation.

The rise of third-party litigation continues to be a key factor in the due diligence process, as damage awards can and have crippled businesses. Due diligence firms should therefore take careful note and adequate precautions to prevent exposure that can lead to disastrous tort litigation. All practices and/or products that could possibly result in a firm's exposure and liability should be clearly identified.

2.5.1 Legal Overview

The consultant may be asked to provide expert assessments and litigation support to defendant or plaintiff law firms. These services may include, but are not limited to:

- Perform complex exposure reconstructions
- Analysis of structural or system failures
- Forensic analyses of equipment that may have contributed to an injury or death
- Investigations of suspected building-related illness
- Independent case review for arbitration.

The consultant may also be required to conduct complex sampling and testing protocols and sophisticated data analysis and interpretation, or to provide assessments of the strengths and weaknesses of cases, the potential data requirements to pursue a particular strategy, and the potential impact of recent technical and scientific findings.

One of the major issues in tort litigation is determining if exposures or failures may have occurred in the distant past, and whether those exposures or failures were sufficient to cause some effect either in individuals and/or buildings.

2.5.2 Legal Services

The most commonly requested legal services involve forensic engineering, exposure reconstruction, and assessments involving mold growth in buildings. Consultants are frequently asked to reconstruct exposures that occurred years ago or to identify probable sources and pathways for water intrusion that resulted in mold growth. Other issues include building envelope investigations, structural failure assessments, construction defect evaluations and even litigation by clients who have completely ignored the consultant's specific recommendation to carry out further investigation on an apparent system deficiency.

In addition to consulting and expert testimony services for both defendants and plaintiffs, the consultant may be asked to perform case evaluations, assist with settlements, and provide advice on avoiding litigation.

CHAPTER

3

Property Condition Assessments (PCA) Survey Guidelines

3.1 GENERAL

Upon initial client contact and expression of interest in the award of a project, a project file is created and a project number is assigned. This file will be maintained through the development and award of a contract.

The objective of a PCA survey is to observe and document pertinent information on the subject property to enable a proper assessment of the factors that are important to the "due diligence" process. A standard methodology is used to satisfy the intent of the due diligence. The use of standard forms and checklists is important to this process to ensure that all necessary observations have been made and recorded. It is recognized that real property is by nature unique and unforeseen situations arise. Therefore, the standard methodologies may require adjustment to meet the intent of the due diligence. The general PCA sequence and format is described in greater detail in Chapter 4.

3.1.1 Factors That Impact Time to Produce PCA

The amount of time that should be allocated to conduct a Property Condition Survey depends on a number of factors including:

Size of the facility: The size of the facility is one of the most discerning factors that determines the time required to make an evaluation, and therefore the greater a building's square footage the longer it will take to evaluate.

Age of the facility: As buildings grow older, so do their systems and they usually contain a greater number of deficiencies that need to be identified and diagnosed, which is not the case with newer construction. The more deficiencies there are, the more time needed to evaluate them.

Condition of the facility: Facilities which have been maintained properly require less time and effort to assess than those which have fallen into disrepair. Moreover, properties in good condition require less time for both the physical inspection and the report writing process.

Configuration and design of the facility: The configuration and design attributes of a facility can also impact the time needed to make an assessment. A facility with several floors all having similar interior finishes and layout will require less evaluation time than a facility where the floors have varied finishes and floor layouts.

Number of buildings: Often a project will consist of several buildings to be evaluated. The more buildings to be inspected, the more time needed to carry out the complete assessment.

Proximity of Buildings: The length of time required to inspect and evaluate multiple buildings is impacted by the physical location of each building relative to each another. Facilities with several buildings within a single complex will require less time than the same number of buildings scattered throughout a city or region.

Type of assessment: The kind of assessment, whether for acquisition or for establishing a preventive maintenance program, impacts the time required for an evaluation. The greater the depth and extensive nature of an inspection, the greater the time required.

Type of report: The type of report required in the assessment also affects the time required for an evaluation. If a letter report or short form is required, the evaluation process will need less time than for a fully bound report with color photographic documentation.

3.1.2 Categories of "Investment Grade" Real Estate

The main property types of investment grade real estate include:

1. Office buildings: High-rise, mid-rise, low-rise and single-story.
2. Hospitality: Hotels, motels, lodges and inns.
3. Multi-family, apartments and condominiums: High-rise, mid-rise and low-rise.
4. Retail Buildings: Shopping centers, malls, department stores, etc.
5. Industrial complexes, warehouses and flex-space buildings
6. Senior living facilities

3.1.2.1 Office Buildings

Office buildings are generally grouped into three categories: High-rise (overall height exceeds say, 75 feet or about six stories), mid-rise (generally from three to six or seven stories), and low-rise (single or two story). This part should be read in conjunction with the relevant sections of Chapters 2 and 4.

Standard & Poor's recommends in its Guidelines for Conducting Property Condition Assessments of office buildings that when conducting a property survey the field observer should: Observe property components, systems, and elements that are easily visible and readily accessible for the purposes of describing same, opining on their apparent physical condition, and identifying significant physical deficiencies. The consultant is not required to prepare detailed calculations, remove materials, operate equipment not typically operated by tenants, or conduct any exploratory probing or testing. This is a non-intrusive visual survey. However, the consultant is to make a reasonable attempt at discovery. The "law-of-reason" shall prevail.

The guidelines further state that survey procedures for office buildings will consist of:

- Walk-around visual survey
- Random operation of equipment, fixtures and systems, which are normally operated by tenants, on a sampling basis to determine system operability or operating characteristics
- Noting of material building code violations of items, systems, or inherent design that are readily apparent and discernible as a result of the "walk-through" survey
- The taking of measurements and system counts to adequately justify estimated costs to remedy physical deficiencies and to estimate replacement reserve expenditures. The basis for these costs must be substantiated by the consultant within the report.

The ASTM states that for complexes of buildings built in phases, each construction phase should be surveyed. For a subject property that contains a complex of multiple buildings, the concept of representative observations extends to each building individually and not to all buildings as a whole. Representative observations should include a mix of tenant (occupied and unoccupied) and common areas. Representative observations of the interiors of each construction phase should include a sufficient number of the top and bottom floors. If not specified in the agreement between consultant and user, the quantity of floor area and the number of components and systems surveyed in each construction phase should be sufficient to allow the field observer to develop an opinion with reasonable confidence regarding the present condition of the building systems. Such representative observations should be determined using the professional judgment and experience of the field observer at the time of the walk-through survey. The quantity of reported floor area, which is not available for occupancy, and the reasons it is reportedly not available, should be included in the PCR. The PCR should contain the consultant's rationale for determining the quantity of floor area surveyed and for selecting the specific floors that were surveyed.

This document should be used in conjunction with Standard & Poor's Guidance Document—Property Condition Assessment (PCA)—Base Document.

Special criteria or issues specific to high rise office buildings:

a. All water systems backflow preventers in place, or will be required soon?
b. Condition of balcony, other setbacks. Drainage issues.
c. Exterior Wall System
    i. Review condition of glazing, thermo seals, frames, sills, glazing stops
    ii. Review condition of masonry and joints
    iii. Note any applied films to glazing or coatings to anodized surfaces
    iv. Review adequacy of number and size of vertical and horizontal expansion joints
    v. Review adequacy of flashing and weep systems
    vi. Review of steel anchorages and lintels
    vii. Estimate remaining life of existing sealants, gaskets, sealed thermopanes and cost of replacement
    viii. Review interior water staining and history of leakage with tenants and maintenance personnel.
d. HVAC System
    i. Type, and remaining useful life. Comment on feasibility of modernization in the future to meet changing tenant requirements for ventilation, electricity, and data/communications.

ii. Ventilation standard (ASHRAE #) or building code (code and year) currently being met by the HVAC system. Note any indoor air quality concerns such as outdoor air intake locations, operation of outdoor air dampers, and condensate drain pan condition.
iii. Ask the property manager if there is now, or ever has been, an indoor air quality complaint. If yes, what was the nature of the complaint, and what was done to correct the problem.
iv. Availability and billing method for after hours air conditioning at tenant request
v. Average square feet served by single HVAC thermostat (also known as average zone area)
vi. CFC Issues—type of refrigerant contained in cooling equipment. Is a replacement plan in place.

e. Compare capital improvement budgets with your own findings
f. Parking area, location relative to the building, and condition. If parking structure exists contact lender for special instructions
g. Type of elevator control system. Will the elevators require upgrades to meet current ADA, fire safety, or tenant requirements?
h. Availability and capacity of emergency power system. Loading dock, and truck access.
i. Field verify approximate percentage of finished and unfinished space.

Following the World Trade Center tragedy, tenants have become increasingly concerned with security and safety. Features such as site lighting, entry security, and restriction of after-hours access have become normal corporate tenant prerequisites to leasing.

3.1.2.2 Hospitality Buildings

Hotels are an unusual investment product. Each hotel or chain has its own standard that defines the level of service that it is to provide. From a PCA standpoint, a hotel's furnishings, fixtures, and equipment are all considered chattels that fall under the lien of the mortgage loan.

Most guests consider the guestroom as the most important feature of a hotel (Figure 3.1 A). The room rate carries with it expectations of what sort of standard to expect. The amenities of the public areas are perhaps the next most important feature in a hotel. Security and life safety issues have also gained in importance in recent years. Furthermore, it should be recognized that items of functional obsolescence represent an ultimate liability to the property and reduce its current market value. The following section should be read in conjunction with the relevant sections of Chapters 2 and 4.

Standard & Poor's recommends in its Guidelines for Conducting Property Condition Assessments of Hospitality Buildings that when conducting a property survey the field observer should:

Observe property components, systems, and elements that are easily visible and readily accessible for the purposes of describing same, opining on their apparent physical condition, and identifying significant physical deficiencies. The consultant is not required to prepare detailed calculations, to remove materials, operate equipment not typically operated by guests, or conduct any exploratory probing or testing. This is a non-intrusive visual survey. However, the consultant is to make a reasonable attempt at discovery. The "law-of-reason" shall prevail.

Survey procedures will consist of:

- Walk-around visual survey

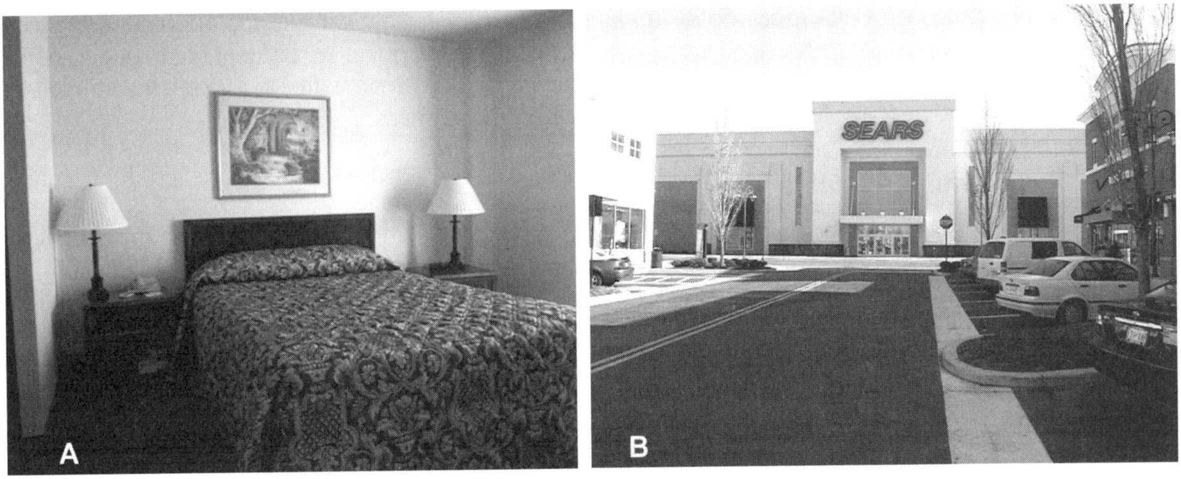

Figure 3.1 A,B A. A typical hotel bedroom interior reflects hotel standards. B. View of a typical anchor tenant (Sears) in a shopping center. Visibility is very important.

- Random operation of equipment, fixtures and systems which are normally operated by guests, on a sampling basis to determine system operability or operating characteristics. Support systems or amenities operated under concession to the hotel are excluded.
- Noting of material building code violations of items, systems, or inherent design that are readily apparent and discernible as a result of the "walk-through" survey.
- The taking of measurements and system counts to adequately justify estimated costs to remedy physical deficiencies and to estimate replacement reserve expenditures. The basis for these costs must be substantiated by the consultant within the report.

ASTM (with reference to representative observations) states that for complexes with multiple buildings, the exterior envelopes of all residential buildings should be surveyed, and for complexes built in phases, each construction phase should be surveyed. Representative observations of the interiors should include a mix of units, which are occupied, vacant, damaged, and under renovation or repair. Representative observations of the interiors of each construction phase should include a sufficient number of the top and bottom floors. If not specified in the agreement between consultant and user, the number of units, buildings, and components surveyed in each construction phase should be sufficient to allow the field observer to develop an opinion with reasonable confidence regarding the present condition of the building systems and should be determined using the professional judgment and experience of the field observer at the time of the walk-through survey. The number of reported units that are not available for occupancy and the reported reasons they are not available should be included in the PCR. The PCR should contain the consultant's rationale for determining the number of units surveyed and for selecting the units that are surveyed. In addition, the PCR should disclose the specific units surveyed.

Not every guest room needs to be surveyed. However, the common elements, and front and back-of-house areas should be. The consultant is required to survey a representative sampling of guest rooms to opine with confidence as to the typical pattern of deficiencies that may be encountered.

Based upon its opinion of a representative sampling, the consultant will extrapolate results to those guest rooms not surveyed for cost estimating purposes. As a general guide, 10 percent of the guest rooms are normally surveyed. It is the responsibility of the borrower or its representative to provide the consultant with supervised, timely access to guest rooms and back-of-house areas.

3.1.2.3 Multi-Family Buildings

Multi-family apartments and condominiums are the home and castle for the tenant. The most important features from a tenant's point of view is the unit's size, condition, layout and comfort (heating and cooling), as well as the general amenities offered. Security and dedicated parking have also become an important factor for tenants.

An investor's main concern is the durability and useful life of the building components. Frequent disruptions like water intrusion and elevator failure will lessen tenants' enthusiasm to renew their lease at the end of its term.

The following section should be read in conjunction with the relevant sections of Chapters 2 and 4.

Standard & Poor's recommends in its Guidelines for Conducting Property Condition Assessments of Multi-Family Buildings that when conducting a property survey the field observer should observe property components, systems, and elements that are easily visible and readily accessible for the purposes of describing same, opining on their apparent physical condition, and identifying significant physical deficiencies. The consultant is not required to prepare detailed calculations, to remove materials, operate equipment not typically operated by tenants, or conduct any exploratory probing or testing. This is a non-intrusive visual survey. However, the consultant is to make a reasonable attempt at discovery. The "law-of-reason" shall prevail.

The Standard & Pool's guidelines further state that survey procedures for multi-family buildings will consist of:

- Walk-around visual survey
- Random operation of equipment, fixtures and systems which are normally operated by tenants, on a sampling basis to determine system operability or operating characteristics
- Noting of material building code violations of items, systems or inherent design that are readily apparent and discernible as a result of the "walk-through" survey
- The taking of measurements and system counts to adequately justify estimated costs to remedy physical deficiencies and to estimate replacement reserve expenditures. The basis for these costs must be substantiated by the consultant within the report.

This section is to be used in conjunction with the Standard & Poor's Guidance Document—Property Condition Assessment (PCA)—Base Document.

Special criteria or issues specific to multi-family housing for acquisition:

a. Structural design, and construction workmanship
    i. Floors and toppings
    ii. Exterior balconies, decks, patios and stairs
    iii. Foundations—cracking and settlement, leakage
    iv. Roof trusses, floor joists and related sheathing
b. Through a combination of efforts using available building plans and physical measurement of the building during inspection, the consultant is to provide gross building areas for each build-

ing, the number of floors, the number of apartments, unit types per building, and the number of different building types.

The following information shall be provided for each building:

i. Gross square footage
ii. Number and type of units
iii. Number of floors
iv. Number of fireplaces
v. Number of exterior stairways
vi. Square footage of attached garages
vii Quantity and approximate square footage of patios
viii. Quantity and approximate square footage of balconies or wood decks

c. Number of parking spaces
   i. Unattached garages (type, number, and size)
   ii. Covered carport (type, number, and size)
   iii. Open lot parking (number and separate number for handicap spaces)
d. Amenities
   i. Pools, hot tubs and related filtering equipment (quantity and size)
   ii. Clubhouse, party or exercise rooms (gross square footage and description)
   iii. Tennis, racquetball, volleyball or basketball courts
   iv. Other common area/use facilities
e. Pest problems and control, termite protection
   i. Review maintenance records and certifications
   ii. Obtain a copy of and attach in appendix FHA approved "Wood Destroying Insect Infestation Report" (required by FHA and Fannie May Lenders)
   iii. Obtain costs for range of options for insect infestation control at perimeter of building from soil treatment and annual inspections with no guaranty to sealing foundation perimeter with feed spikes and 5-year guaranty including annual cost for maintenance
f. Attic
   i. Adequacy of ventilation
   ii. Access for maintenance of electrical and plumbing, etc.
   iii. Storage
g. Vertical dimensions
   i. Measured from the floor to the roof deck
   ii. Measured from the floor to the lowest structural member, or light, or other fixture
h. Landscaping and landscape irrigation systems
   i. Site—provide total site area in acres
   ii. Calculate housing density in units/acre
j. Fair Housing Act
   i. Discuss applicability and cost for compliance of the handicap section of the act as it relates to:

- Rental units—Include the cost to convert a single floor rental unit to be in full compliance with ADA in the level of detail as discussed in the base document
- Common areas/building—Include cost to convert common areas (not including rental unit building laundry rooms) to be in full compliance with ADA in the level of detail as discussed in the base document
- Site

Representative sampling: Not every rental unit must be surveyed. However, the common elements of each building shall be surveyed should more than one building exist. The consultant is required to survey a representative sampling of units to opine with confidence as to the typical pattern of Deficiencies to be encountered. If the Subject was constructed in various phases or the buildings consist of different construction systems, then a representative sampling should be conducted within each phase or building of different construction systems.

Based upon its opinion of a representative sampling, the consultant will extrapolate results to those units not surveyed for cost estimating purposes. As a guide, approximately 10 percent of the units should be surveyed within each phase of the subject if the subject was constructed of different building types or construction systems. It is the responsibility of the borrower or its representative to provide the consultant with supervised, timely access to units at the time of the consultant's site visit.

3.1.2.4 Retail Buildings

Whether we are discussing a shopping mall, or strip retail, the most hovering concern for a tenant is to please his customers and boost sales. For the customer, the most important features are easy access and ample and convenient parking. A pleasing storefront with prominent signage and good tenant mix are also important.

For the investor, tenant spaces should be flexible to allow reconfigurations of new tenants. Next in importance perhaps is the adequacy of the various systems (mechanical, electrical etc.). Older centers can be problematic if significant capital outlays are required to rectify existing deficiencies.

Malls and large shopping centers should be strategically located close to major highways or regional transportation routes. They should also be visible from major highways and approaches and the building entrances should be visible from the parking lot. Site access should be provided on as many sides of the site as possible.

All mall buildings and shopping centers must comply with the Title III provisions of the Americans with Disabilities Act (ADA): Public accommodations and commercial facilities shall be accessible for persons with disabilities from exterior public sidewalks, parking areas and entrances into the building. Handicapped parking spaces and proper curb cuts to the sidewalks are required. ADA issues are discussed in greater detail in Chapter 17.

Standard & Poor's recommends that the assessor of a retail building's property survey should observe property components, systems, and elements that are easily visible and readily accessible for the purposes of describing same, opining on their apparent physical condition, and identifying significant physical deficiencies. The consultant is not required to prepare detailed calculations, to remove materials, operate equipment not typically operated by tenants, or conduct any exploratory probing or testing. This is a non-intrusive visual survey. However, the consultant is to make a reasonable attempt at discovery. The "law-of-reason" shall prevail.

ASTM recommends that for complexes of retail buildings built in phases, each construction phase should be surveyed. For a subject property that contains a complex of multiple buildings, the concept of representative observations extends to each building individually and not to all buildings as a whole. Representative observations should include a mix of tenant (occupied and unoccupied) and common areas. Representative observations of the interiors of each construction phase should include a sufficient number of the top and bottom floors. If not specified in the agreement between consultant and user, the quantity of floor area and the number of components and systems surveyed in each construction phase should be sufficient to allow the field observer to develop an opinion with confidence as to the present condition of the building systems. Such representative observations should be determined using the professional judgment and experience of the field observer at the time of the walk-through survey. The quantity of reported floor area which is not available for occupancy, and the reasons it is reportedly not available, should be included in the PCR.

Standard & Poor's in its Guidelines for Retail Buildings further recommends that the field observer in conducting a property survey should:

- Conduct a walk-around visual survey
- Conduct random operation of equipment, fixtures and systems, which are normally operated by tenants, on a sampling basis to determine system operability or operating characteristics
- Note material building code violations of items, systems, or design that are readily apparent and discernible as a result of the "walk-through" survey
- Take measurements and system counts to adequately justify estimated costs to remedy physical deficiencies and to estimate replacement reserve expenditures. The basis for these costs must be substantiated by the consultant within the report.

The consultant is not required to survey the interior condition of shell-finish tenancies or the interior/base building conditions of anchor stores, unless included in the subject property.

Special criteria or issues specific to strip retail centers for acquisition:

a. Photo of center's monument sign
b. Metering method for all utilities—separate or billed by property manager
c. Responsible party for HVAC maintenance—tenant or building
d. Date of last canopy renovation
e. Visibility of signage from the road

Representative sampling: Not every tenant space need be surveyed. However, if more than one building exists, the Field Observer should survey the envelope of each building along with base building areas/systems.

3.1.2.5 Industrials and Flex Space Buildings

Tenants of Industrials and warehouses share common operational requirements, including minimum interior clearance heights (minimum 18 feet) within the buildings and specific needs regarding satisfactory truck access and loading areas (usually at rear of the building). Tenants look for convenient access and egress to the complex from and to major highways. Protection against stored material is also important and adequate precautions are a recognized requirement.

Flex space properties are typically multiple purpose buildings that are designed to meet the needs of both large and small tenant users. These buildings generally have many tenants of different sizes. Flex space tenants are often start-up companies with limited operating budgets. The main concern of investors of industrials and flex space properties is that of flexibility—to permit possible future reconfiguration of the space.

During a property survey of this building category, the assessor is required to observe property components, systems, and elements that are easily visible and readily accessible for the purposes of describing same, opining on their apparent physical condition, and identifying significant physical deficiencies. The consultant is not required to prepare detailed calculations, remove materials, operate equipment not typically operated by tenants, or conduct any exploratory probing or testing. This is a non-intrusive visual survey. Nevertheless, the consultant is to make a reasonable attempt at discovery.

Survey procedures will typically consist of:

- Walk-around visual survey
- Conducting random operation of equipment, fixtures and systems, which are typically operated by the tenant. This is done on a sampling basis to determine system operability or operating characteristics.
- Noting of material building code violations (if any) of items, systems, or inherent design that are readily apparent and discernible as a result of the "walk-through" survey
- The taking of measurements and system counts to adequately justify estimated costs to remedy physical deficiencies and to estimate replacement reserve expenditures. The basis for these costs must be substantiated by the consultant within the report.

Special criteria or issues specific to industrial warehouses for acquisition:

a. Maximum allowable storage height, by material type, per the local fire code or local governing body
b. Relative difficulty to convert from single to multi-tenant, or vice-versa
c. Floor and mezzanine loading capacities, flatness specification, and conditions
d. Minimum interior clear height:
    i. measured from the floor to the roof deck
    ii. measured from the floor to the lowest structural member, or light, or other fixture
e. Has the warehouse ever contained a manufacturing operation? If yes, are the tenant improvements for manufacturing above average for a warehouse? Please list items such as increased floor slab, HVAC, electric, parking pavement, etc.

Representative sampling: Not every tenant space needs to be surveyed. However, where more than one building exists, the envelope of each building along with base building areas/systems should be surveyed by the assessor.

3.1.2.6 Senior Living Facilities

The emergence of senior living facilities as a property category is fairly recent. A facility can consist of a single building or many buildings built in phases. The types of such facilities include:

- Independent living facilities
- Assisted living facilities with two levels of care, IADL and ADL
- Nursing homes
- Continuing care retirement communities

Nursing homes and continuing care retirement communities do not qualify as investment grade property. They provide care to the ill and infirmed and are therefore regulated by state government medical licensing statues. Their operational complexity makes it difficult to ascertain their appropriateness as an investment. Independent living facilities and assisted living facilities on the other hand do not offer medical services that are regulated. This puts them closer to traditional property investments.

Senior living accommodations should reflect a high standard of comfortable living, with tenants receiving an appropriate level of service and care in an environmentally pleasant residential atmosphere (Figure 3.2 A,B,C,D). Staff should be caring and well trained, and on-site management should be provided 24 hours a day. Life safety is a critical factor in these facilities.

Figure 3.2 A,B,C,D Interior visuals of a typical dwelling unit at an independent living facility at Riderwood Village, Silver Springs, Maryland. Shown are photos of the kitchenette, bathroom, bedroom and living/dining room.

The chief concern of most potential investors is the overall quality of management operations at the facility. Essential to preserving the security of the investment is the monitoring of staffing, maintenance procedures and funding.

Independent living facilities are comprised of residential units that function as a cross between an apartment and a full-service hotel. The tenants are senior citizens who are year-round residents. The dwelling units usually consist of one-bedroom apartments or in some cases a shared two-bedroom unit with living/dining area, bathrooms and kitchenettes. All units are to meet ADA standards including accessible doors and hardware, grab bars at toilets, and emergency call switches. A percentage of units are also provided for residents with specific disabilities.

Common areas include a central kitchen and dining facilities, seating/lounge areas, a library, activity areas (including craft and exercise rooms, TV screen), barber/beautician services and laundry facilities (Figure 3.3 A,B). It is very important that properties are attractively landscaped with mature trees, ample walking paths and grassed areas.

Assisted living facilities are generally smaller where the resident requires assistance with daily living tasks. Tenants are generally frail or functionally impaired but not ill. Tenant level of care falls into two general categories (both of which require 24-hour supervision): 1. Instrumental Activities of Daily Living (IADL) and 2. Activities of Daily Living (ADL)—this represents a higher level of care.

Nursing homes provide full-time resident care to the ill and infirm. Licensed medical staff provides all required ADL services and medical care. Semi-private or private furnished rooms are provided. Kitchenettes are not provided.

Continuing care retirement communities offer the whole range of senior living facilities and services. This includes care ranging from independent living to nursing homes. They often consist of a campus or group of related buildings sharing common services. They are regulated by the federal government and the state.

Figure 3.3 A,B Photos of common areas at the Riderwood Village facility for senior living, Silver Springs, Maryland.

The property survey should include observing property components, systems, and elements that are readily visible and accessible for the purposes of describing same, opining on their apparent physical condition, and identifying significant physical deficiencies. An emphasis should be placed on fire safety. The consultant is not required to prepare detailed calculations, to remove materials, operate equipment not typically operated by patients, or conduct any exploratory probing or testing. Although this is a non-intrusive survey, the consultant should make a reasonable attempt at discovery.

PCA survey procedures are to include:

- Walk-around visual survey
- Conduct random operation of equipment, fixtures and systems that are normally operated by senior tenants or patients. The survey is conducted on a sampling basis to determine system operability and characteristics.
- Noting any material building code violations of items, systems or faulty design that are readily apparent and discernible as a result of the "walk-through" survey.
- Taking measurements and system counts to adequately justify estimated costs to remedy physical deficiencies and to estimate replacement reserve expenditures. The bases for these costs are to be substantiated by the consultant within the report.

Representative sampling: Not every patient room or unit must be surveyed. However, all community areas, cafeteria, kitchen and other common elements should be surveyed. The consultant is required to survey a representative sampling of patient rooms and living units to opine with confidence as to the typical pattern of deficiencies to be encountered. Based upon his/her opinion of a representative sampling, the consultant will extrapolate results to those patient rooms and living units not surveyed for cost estimating purposes. As a guide, approximately 10 percent of the patient rooms and living units should be surveyed. It is the responsibility of the borrower or its representative to provide consultant with supervised, timely access to patient rooms and living quarters.

3.2 SURVEY PROCEDURES—METHODOLOGY

The primary objective of an assessment is to inspect the facility and note physical or operational deficiencies. Average life and costs of replacement of the property are estimated based on the date of construction or the last documented renovation of the system. The information generated by the life cycle cost model, and modified by the site assessment, is used to calculate the repair and replacement cost of the particular facility. Where the assessment is based on life cycle cost models and statistical inferences, the assessors do not need to identify detailed listings of deficiencies or corrections. The recognition of a "deficiency" involves not only the function of a component or system but also the relative cost for its repair, replacement or correction. In addition, non-functional consideration for the classification of deficiencies is the relative age of the component or system compared to its "expected useful life" or depreciable life. A "non-functional" classification shall be attributed to any deficiency whose relative age of the component or system exceeds its "expected useful life" or depreciable life. Each deficiency is classified by its respective physical or operational function in the facility—safety, site, external shell, internal shell, heating, cooling/vent, plumbing, electrical, etc. Based on these classifications, the pricing for each correction of a component or system deficiency is typically taken from the nationally recognized construction estimating resource, R.S. Means.

3.2.1 Property Survey

Observe property components, systems, and elements that are easily visible and readily accessible for the purposes of identifying significant physical deficiencies. The consultant is not required to prepare detailed calculations, remove materials, operate equipment not typically operated by tenants, or conduct any exploratory probing or testing. This is a non-intrusive visual survey. However, the consultant is to make a conscientious attempt at discovery. Property survey procedures are discussed in Chapter 4.

3.2.2 Research

The consultant is to provide the borrower with a Pre-survey Questionnaire and Disclosure Schedule (the questionnaire) and a Property Condition Assessment Document and Information Checklist (the checklist), which are to be completed by the borrower or its representative and forwarded to the consultant. The questionnaire and checklist shall be included as exhibits within the consultant's report, whether or not the borrower completes them and provided to the consultant.

The Pre-Survey Questionnaire: The Pre-survey Questionnaire (PSQ) is a multi-page document that can be customized to suit the building type. After selecting the building type and building use check boxes that apply to the subject property, the propriety software will generate an appropriate questionnaire. Alternatively, it can be done manually. If, for example, the subject property is a hotel, the questionnaire will have been formatted to ask about the average occupancy of the building. If the subject property is a retail shopping center, the questionnaire will ask the respondent to provide information on the center's clients in order of square footage of rented space.

It is important for the questionnaire to be sent out as soon as it is known who will be responsible for providing the information. The document asks for specific information that may take some time for the respondent to gather; therefore, advance time is required in order to ensure that a complete questionnaire is returned to the project manager. The information provided can then be reviewed and added to the body of the PCR, thus making it more complete, more accurate and more useful to the end user.

However, PSQs are often sent back incomplete, or with entire sections missing. A copy of the questionnaire as it was mailed/faxed is provided to the project manager/reviewer to verify that a good faith effort was made to find the required information. This copy of the original, unanswered PSQ can be included in the Red Rope folder and subsequent PCR, with notes being made to the appropriate parties that the information was not provided and under what circumstances.

Research shall be conducted using tenants, service providers, and those knowledgeable about the subject as sources. Standard & Poor's recommends that the following research be conducted as a minimum. Telephone interviews may be sufficient for most inquiries.

a. Interviewing building management, ownership and tenant(s).
b. Review of historical repair/improvement costs incurred by tenants/ownership along with the following documents:
    1. Certificates of Occupancy
    2. Maintenance reports and logs
    3. Passenger and freight elevator safety
    4. Inspection reports
    5. Warranty information

Freedom of Information Letters (FOILs): The FOIL request provides a means with which to check each subject property for building and code compliance, as well as locate its Certificate of Occupancy

(CO). The Research Log provides space in which to keep track of the numerous agencies and officials that are invariably contacted in an attempt to find which municipal departments record and maintain such information. It is also very important to submit these "FOIL" requests as soon as possible since most agencies, under the Freedom of Information Act, are allowed anywhere from seven to 10 business days to respond. Remember that the responses to these requests are to be used as exhibits in the PCR (see Chapter 4, Figure 4.3 A,B,C).

A Site Inspection Confirmation Letter (Figure 3.4) is issued as soon as the project manager knows the person with whom he/she will meet to perform the walk-through survey of the subject property. It confirms the date and time of the site visit.

The FOIL Payment Transmittal Letter is recorded to show costs of obtaining Freedom of Information disclosures. This happens most often with larger municipalities that require research time to locate the documents requested. Also copying fees are assessed in the event that open violations are discovered (the FOIL request asks for copies of outstanding violations). Since this requires mailing checks to the agency involved, response time is slowed. Therefore it is important to find out if such fees are assessed as soon as possible.

The Elevator Research Letter is submitted to the company that is contracted to service the conveyance systems of the subject property. This letter asks the company representative, preferably the individual who actually services the account, to respond to such queries as whether or not the elevators have fireman's returns and are compliant with the Americans with Disabilities Act (ADA). The project manager is almost always able to obtain the name of both the company and representative on their site visit.

The FOIL Follow-Up Letter is used to notify a client that a FOIL request has been received after the PCR has already been submitted to them. It is often the case that factors such as delays in sending the original FOIL request, slow response time from the agency involved, and report turn around time can play a role in a PCR going out to the client without an official response from a municipal entity. This adversely affects the quality of the report and should be avoided at all costs. This letter is a means of verifying that the response has arrived. It notes that the project manager has been notified and altered his/her report to reflect any salient information in the FOIL response. Finally, the original response has been added to the Red Rope folder either in the production office or the archive storage facility. A copy of the agency's response accompanies this letter.

3.2.3 Review of Documents

Review pertinent property records and studies as furnished by client and/or borrower. In general, document information will consist primarily of borrower-supplied leasing literature, historical receipts for repairs and/or improvements, schedule of component replacements or improvements complete with the costs incurred for same, pending proposal, schedule of landlord responsible operating expenses, etc. There may also be previously prepared property condition survey reports, appraisals, an ADA survey (if applicable), etc. that should be provided to the consultant as well.

3.2.4 Representative Sampling

Not every tenant space must be surveyed. However, the envelope of each building along with base building areas/systems shall be surveyed should more than one building exist. For multi-family buildings, as a guide, approximately 10 percent of the units should be surveyed. Should less than 10 percent of the units be surveyed, such percentage shall be sufficient for the consultant to opine with confidence as to the typical general condition of all units.

ABC **ABC International Corp.**

Architecture - Engineering - Due-Diligence

2431 Terracotta Avenue, Suite 110
Herndon, VA 20171
(200) 387-2000 (tel)
(200) 387-2007 (fax)
mikesmith@abcintl.com

To:	**Mr. John Doe, Owner**
Firm:	**ABC International Corporation**
Tel:	**200.387.2000**
Fax:	**200.387.2007**
Date:	**17 July 2007**
From:	**Michael Z. Smith**
Re:	**Property Condition Survey** **Anywhere Apartments** **300-Unit Multi-Family Complexes** **5075 Anywhere Drive** **Baton Rouge, Louisiana 70820** **ABC Project No.: A000000**

Dear Mr. Doe:

We are tentatively scheduled to conduct Property Condition Surveys of the above referenced properties on Tuesday 20 July 2007 at 11:00am. We will need access to the roof, all mechanical rooms, and a representative number of tenant spaces, both occupied and unoccupied. I am the Project manager and may be reached at 200.907.2222.

Furthermore, if it is possible for you to provide me with any or all of the following, it would be helpful:

- Plan set (complete set or just a site plan)
- Pre-written system descriptions (building shell, roof, HVAC, electrical service, fire protection, etc.)
- No. of parking spaces (total and handicapped accessible)
- Contractor list (paving, electrical, mechanical, roof, plumbing, etc.)
- Leasing literature/room layouts/rent roll
- Previous reports (property condition reports, appraisal, etc.)

Figure 3.4 Sample site inspection confirmation letter.

3.2.5 Photographs

The consultant will take as many representative photographs as is necessary to describe the subject property. These will typically consist of digital photographs with full captions to describe the photo. For most assignments, the number of photographs needed to adequately describe a property ranges from 20-40. Photo captions should identify the location, describe the system or component shown, and highlight any condition or physical deficiency depicted. Concentrate on horizontal photographs if possible. See also Chapter 4 for greater detail on the general requirements, elements and components to photograph, and sample template.

3.3 CONDUCTING PCA SURVEYS

The basic elements of a PCA survey include the following:

1. Identify significant defects, deficiencies, items of deferred maintenance and material building code violations (individually and collectively, physical deficiencies) as a result of a visual survey, review of documents, and research and interrogatories.
2. Prepare estimated costs to remedy physical deficiencies.
3. Prepare replacement schedule for the specified term.
4. Prepare a written report that opines on the subject's overall physical condition, including photos of representative systems and major physical deficiencies, and provide opinions of cost to remedy physical deficiencies and for annual replacement reserve expenditures.

The PCA Survey should conform to the following Scope of Work.

The consultant shall review available information to be provided by the client, make inquiries of the borrower, make observations sufficient to establish the type and approximate extent of physical deficiencies, and take representative measurements and quantity counts to estimate the cost to remedy physical deficiencies and to prepare the replacement reserve schedule.

The consultant should assume that the borrower will provide complete access to the property, staff, vendors, and documents. The borrower is to provide sufficient, safe and readily available access to all areas of the building(s) including roofs so as not to impede the consultant's procedures. The client will assist the consultant in securing access and information in the event that the borrower fails to cooperate. The consultant should not seek access to any property, staff, vendors, or documents if the borrower objects to this access or attempts to restrict the consultant from conducting its survey or research.

Should any document, vendor access, or information be requested by the consultant but knowingly withheld by borrower from consultant, the consultant shall contact the client. If this information is not provided before the preparation of the consultant's draft report, the consultant shall identify within the report, in the appropriate sections, any information or access requested but denied or not made readily available either at the time of the consultant's site visit or the report's writing.

3.4 THE PCA REPORT

Report format and content: This section should be read in conjunction with Chapter 4.

Content & context: The PCA protocol establishes the report content and structure. It is a dossier of statements of fact and subjective opinion based upon those facts, professional judgment and experience. The report should not be an assimilation of subjective opinions based upon conjecture. Likewise, it is not a representation or certification that all is "fine," sound, performing its function, in good working order or any other such conjecture. It essentially consists of:

- Binding and cover sheet
- Cover letter
- Table of contents

Executive summary: Provide a brief summary of the assignment and activities undertaken including information describing the property, its setting, size, construction type, configuration, principal systems and materials and opine on the subject's general condition and the apparent level of preventive maintenance exercised, significant deferred maintenance, and material physical deficiencies. Summarize the nature of the principal types of physical deficiencies, and the estimated cost to cure. If any significant improvements were recently implemented, this information should also be included. Include summary of assessments, conclusions, and recommendations and sufficient information provided so that the reader can visualize the subject.

Purpose and scope:

A. **Purpose:** Consultant is to provide a short paragraph specifically stating the purpose of this engagement and identifying the subject.

B. **Scope:** Consultant is to outline the scope and the methods used to conduct the survey (as outlined herein and in accordance with the consultant's Property Condition Assessment Agreement), and is to identify the individuals, firms, and/or governmental agencies interviewed for research purposes.

Property description—narrative body: Provide information in narrative, tabular, and outline form to describe the salient parameters and relationships in the planning, siting, servicing and zoning of the property.

1. **Overview:** Provide an introductory paragraph or two to generally orient the reader to the site, its location, buildings, adjacent properties, and development history of the property. Describe access, egress, siting, topography and major site features. Describe the general shape, orientation and character of the buildings.
2. **Site:** Compile the following information and include in report:
    - Property name address and location
    - Major access streets
    - Applicable zoning code jurisdiction, year-zone applicable to location
    - Site area—acres and square feet
    - Building coverage—percent of site or square feet
    - Hard surface area—percent of site or square feet
    - Approximate number of parking spaces
3. **Building:** Include applicable information in report:
    - Number of buildings

- Building area (by building) g.s.f., n.l.s.f., number of units
- Number of stories and height
- Typical floor bay size and clear height
- Construction classification
- Applicable building code (jurisdiction, code form, year)

4. **Services:** Name utility service providers and briefly indicate the source or connection location by which the site is hooked up to the utility network.
   - Electric power (total KW)
   - Gas (line size)
   - Water (line size) and hydrants
   - Storm drain
   - Sanitary drain (to main)
   - Phone, cable, other line services
5. **History:** Describe history of property including:
   - Year of development/age of each building
   - Major capital improvements (year and scope)
   - Evidence of compliance (certificates of occupancy, citations, ADA status and assessment report date, etc.). Include actual certificates as appendix exhibits, if available.

As previously mentioned, most major due diligence firms use proprietary software systems. These programs basically help prepare the initial draft report and serve to expedite the process of report preparation, while maintaining quality and consistency.

Corrections: Cost to correct deficiencies is discussed in Section 3.5.

Qualifications: Qualifications should be added to the PCA report to clarify the extent of the PCA services and the responsibility of the PCA service provider. It is important to identify what has not been included in the survey and why.

1. **Procedure, limitations, use and reliance restrictions:** In a paragraph or two, the consultant should describe techniques and methods used for observation and evaluation of the building. The consultant should use this section to establish the degree to which reliance upon third party sources underlies its conclusions. The consultant should indicate what reasonable or customary inquiry was not or could not be made and make statements or references as to the consequences of such limitations. The consultant should affirm that the work was done by qualified professional staff, using reasonable care and diligence. The consultant should use a standard paragraph to extend to lender and its related entities, rights of reliance upon the findings and conclusions contained in the report. The consultant should further state that work was done to standards normally adhered to in the profession for similar types of work under like circumstances.
2. **Resources and contacts:** The consultant should list (or refer to an appended list) sources from which information has been obtained. The consultant should identify the individual(s) who performed the work, qualifications and professional standing of the individual, and property, agency and contractor contacts. Documents which significantly contributed to findings of problems or deficiencies should be listed.

Limiting conditions, disclaimers and exclusions:

1. The consultant conducted this due-diligence Property Condition Assessment to opine on the subject's general physical condition on behalf of the client/owner in accordance with its agreement dated August 6, 2007. This report is not for the use and benefit of, nor may be relied upon, by any other person or entity without the advance written consent of the consultant.
2. The scope of this study was limited to a walk-through visual survey of areas that were readily observable and easily accessible at the time. Tests, exhaustive studies, removal or disassembly of any system, or dismantling or operating of electrical, mechanical, or conveyance equipment was not performed. This survey did not include an in-depth system/component problem analyses or studies, the preparation of engineering calculations of the structural, mechanical or electrical systems to determine compliance with any drawings that may have been submitted or with commonly accepted design or construction practice. Only a representative sampling of typical areas such as units, corridors, etc. was observed.
3. Neither a Phase I Environmental Assessment to determine the presence of hazardous wastes or toxic materials, nor a survey for asbestos, constituted part of the scope of this assignment. Furthermore, a survey for the presence of wood destroying insects/pests or damages caused by same were outside the scope of this study.
4. Excluded from the scope of this survey was an in-depth survey to determine compliance with the Americans with Disabilities Act (ADA); opinions regarding the ADA are only preliminary.
5. No responsibility is assumed for matters of a legal nature such as building encroachments, easements, zoning issues, or compliance with the requirements of governmental agencies having jurisdiction.
6. The consultant assumes no responsibility for the accuracy or completeness of information provided by management, service firms interviewed, or governmental agencies. Nor is the consultant responsible for any patent or latent defects that an owner or his agents may have withheld from the consultant whether by non-disclosure, passive concealment, or by fraud.
7. The consultant's observations, opinions, and this report are not intended, nor should they be construed, as a guarantee or warranty, express or implied, regarding the property's condition and building code compliance of same. The consultant's opinions are based solely upon those areas that were observed on the day of the site visit and information resulting from interviews and research.

Appendices & exhibits: Exhibits should be appended which illustrate or clarify information presented in the body of the report. Pertinent documents such as the Presurvey Questionnaire and Disclosure Schedule, professional reports (engineer, elevator, etc. complete and unedited), leasing literature, unit schedules, annotated site plans, unit or building plan excerpts, copies of pending proposals, certificates of occupancy and other relevant information should be provided where available and useful. Photographs of the property should be provided. Problems, conditions and deficiencies constituting significant cost to correct or replace should each be illustrated with a captioned photo.

Third party review*:* The PCA is often performed as a third party review. The third party review is intended to provide an unbiased opinion. Therefore, the reviewer should be objective and report the facts and offer professional opinions.

The Presurvey Questionnaire and Disclosure Schedule and the Property Condition Assessment Document and Information Checklist should be appended whether or not the borrower or its representative has completed them.

3.5 PCA COMMENTARY

3.5.1 Documentation & Photography

The PCA professional is relied upon to use judgment and care in reporting facts and opinions. Therefore, it is important that observations be clearly documented at the time they are made. This eliminates the potential for error that may result from forgetfulness or poor recollection. The use of standard forms and checklists provide a structured approach to the inspection and an effective means to record observations. Normally the inspector has limited time to complete the work and gets one pass through a property. Despite all best efforts to develop all encompassing forms and checklists, the unique nature of real estate dictates that the inspector exercise judgment in determining the information that needs recording. Photography is an extremely effective way of recording observations. Photographs can provide information detail that would be difficult to convey otherwise. Later, notes can be added to photographs to further explain the subject.

3.5.2 Condition & Age Assessments

The scope of this section should consist of a written, narrative report describing existing systems and their conditions. The subject is to be described by using a one to two page schedule that not only rates the overall condition of a system and its major components, but briefly describes it as well. In addition, the consultant is to provide representative color photographs showing typical elevations, site improvements, common or base building areas, and commonly encountered and/or major physical deficiencies.

The assessment of the condition and age of property components can involve many investigative techniques. The determination of age is often a challenge as information may not be reliable or available. In addition to examining the components first hand, the PCA professional should cross check the information gathered from various sources and determines if they agree and can be relied upon. The determination of condition also involves a combination of investigative means, including the review of operation and maintenance records, interviewing maintenance personnel and occupants, and comparison of technical data with industrial standards. Ultimately, the assessor/field observer must weigh the available information and, using experience and judgment, make a call.

3.5.3 Deficiencies & Remedies

A deficiency is a condition that adversely effects the function of the component for which it was designed. In the case of architectural components, this might be wear and tear and general appearance. In the case of building systems, this would be the performance of the system. Poor or inefficient design is not necessarily a deficiency. A remedy of a deficiency is the work to restore the building component to the condition for which it was designed. The upgrade or redesign of a building component to improve the function is beyond the scope of a remedy. The PCA professional should determine an appropriate remedy on the basis of value and use this as the basis of an opinion of cost.

3.5.4 Estimating Techniques

In order to establish an opinion on cost to remedy observed deficiencies it is necessary to establish a scope of work. The scope can be worked up from elements of work that can be quantified or classified by other means. Quantities or capacities do not have to be exact, but should reflect a reasonable approximation.

Using rough estimating techniques such as stepping off an area or industry or "rule of thumb" standard can make approximations.

3.5.5 Cost Schedules (estimates) to Remedy Deficiencies

The opinions of cost are supported by the breakdown provided in the cost schedule. The cost schedule should show the scope of work to remedy a particular deficiency. The work should be broken down to provide a reasonable explanation of the situation. The costs used in calculations should reflect the work and market rates at the time of the study.

Based upon (i) consultant's observations during the site visit, and (ii) information received from interview with building management, tenants, and service personnel, that for purposes of the report will be deemed to be reliable, prepare general scope, preliminary cost estimates for each physical deficiency. The consultant must describe the physical deficiency, provide its location, and offer and appropriate recommended remedy. The remedy must be commensurate with the subject and considered a prudent expenditure.

These estimates are for components or systems exhibiting either patent defects, significant deferred maintenance, or requiring major repairs or replacement. Repairs or improvements that could be classified as (i) a routine operating expense, (ii) part of parcel of a building renovation program, (iii) normal building preventive maintenance, or (iv) that are the responsibility of tenants, are not to be included.

Cost estimates for deficiencies shall be allowed into two categories. Terms used to describe these categories are defined below:

Immediate: Physical deficiencies that require immediate action as a result of: (i) existing or potentially unsafe conditions, (ii) significant negative conditions significantly impacting marketability or habitability, (iii) material building code violations, (iv) poor or deteriorated condition of critical element or system, or (v) a condition that if left "as is," with an extensive delay in addressing same, would result in or contribute to critical element or system failure within one year or a significant escalation in repair costs.

Short term (0-1 year): Physical deficiencies, which are inclusive of deferred maintenance, that may not warrant immediate attention, but requiring repairs or replacements that should be undertaken on a priority basis, taking precedence over routine preventive maintenance work within a zero to one-year time frame. Included are such deficiencies resulting from improper design, faulty installation and/or quality of original system or materials. Components or systems that have realized or exceeded their Expected Useful Life (EUL) and that may require replacement within a zero to one-year frame are also to be included.

The consultant's estimated costs are deemed to be preliminary. These costs are to be net of general conditions, construction management fees, and design fees. The consultant is to use market costs or costs incurred by the borrower that are documented and/or have been substantiated to consultant's satisfaction. However, these costs must be reasonable market costs. The borrower should document these costs by submitting paid invoices, executed or pending bona fide proposals, etc.

3.5.6 Reserves

The term "reserves" refers to accounts into which an organization or business regularly sets aside interest earning payments to ensure that there are funds available when required to pay for necessary replacements and capital improvements of a property during the loan term. Reserves usually represent a fixed amount that is deposited at periodic intervals into a dedicated bank account (typically an escrow) earmarked for future repairs or replacements of building systems or components that deteriorate with time.

OPERATING RESERVES (EXPENSES)	CAPITAL RESERVES (EXPENSES)
Repair and replace damaged roof tiles	Tear off and replace entire roof
Repair broken floor tiles in common areas	Replace all floor tiles throughout building
Replace leaking or defective valve	Replace galvanized piping in building damaged by oxidation or calcification
Paint and repair siding or trim	Remove and replace deteriorating building siding
Patch and seal coat driveways	Remove and replace driveway surface
Replace burnt-out bulbs and damaged light fittings	Rewire entire building with new electric fittings

Figure 3.5 Examples of operating reserves and capital reserves expenses.

The reserves schedule, and particularly reserve categories, should be established in conjunction with the user. The scope of work included in each reserve schedule category should be well defined, however general in nature. There are two categories of reserves: operating (current year) reserves and capital reserves.

1. **Operating (current year) reserves:** The operating reserves should include the current year component transferred from the capital reserve account and the contingency reserves. The contingency reserves are intended to provide a hedge for unforeseen events and budget estimate errors for any given year. There is no set rule for the amount of contingency to be set aside other than the use of common sense based on experience.
2. **The capital reserves:** These are intended to cover major repairs, overhauls and replacements at managed times in the future. The capital reserves should comprise of individual line time entries for each reserved common element category, engineering services, and contingency (say 10 percent). The total amount of the monthly reserve portion of the maintenance collected should be apportioned to each line item and accumulated over time (Figure 3.5)

Management of the capital reserves can be a relatively complex matter and it is not possible to determine exact reserve because of the many varying factors involved. For example, variations in inflation and interest rates, and fluctuations in useful life estimate resulting from changing conditions and use patterns. Should a major failure of a capital reserve item occur prematurely, that line item may not contain enough funds to cover the work that needs to be done. This would necessitate funds being transferred from the capital reserve account to the operating reserve and a special assessment must then be levied to make up the difference.

The purpose of a reserve study: The basic premise upon which all Common Interest Realty Associations (CIRA) are founded is that they bear the responsibility for maintaining common property as defined in their declaration and covenants. Maintaining and preserving the common property is the primary duty of the CIRA and its governing board of directors. The board of directors has a fiduciary responsibility to ensure that funds are adequately accumulated and held in a reserve fund for future expenditures. Without a reserve study, the association could either be overfunding or underfunding the reserve fund. In the case of overfunding, then the owners of today are paying more than their share of the common elements. If not enough money is being collected, the association may have to defer maintenance and/or require a special assessments or loan. To date, several states have passed legislation requiring that reserve studies be performed. The American Institute of Certified Public Accountants (AICPA) audit guidelines identify several advantages to accumulating funds in advance through periodic assessments:

- Funds are available to make repairs and replacements when needed, thus helping to avoid the dreaded special assessment.
- The current and future owners equally share in the repair and replacement costs. In other words, the owners are paying for the use of the common elements during their tenure.
- The market value of units or shares is preserved.

Conversely, the lack of reserves or inadequate funding for major future repairs or replacements has significant disadvantages including the following:

- It may adversely affect the ability of unit owners to sell because of concerns that a prospective buyer may have.
- It may adversely affect the unit owner's ability to refinance because of federal or quasi-federal lending restrictions.
- It may require the board to levy special assessments to fund needed repairs or replacements.

3.5.6.1 Reserve Study Procedures & Analysis

During a reserve study program, on site surveys of the common and limited common elements must be included in order to develop an estimate of their remaining useful lives. Specific problems and conditions which require corrective maintenance should be noted in the report. Inspection details need not be provided to the level of detail required for technical specifications. Another key consideration is the review and comparison of both capital repairs and operating maintenance. A clear distinction is required between capital repairs (reserve fund) and operating maintenance (maintenance budget).

Inspections: Elements normally surveyed for a reserve study include the common site areas, the building exteriors and interiors, and the mechanical (including HVAC and vertical transport systems), electrical and plumbing systems.

Minor maintenance items need not be included in a reserve analysis. However, the association's management should insure that they are included in the operating budget and maintenance system. These items should be incorporated in the consultant's report in a punch list. Where financing is involved, the lender may elect to exclude from the reserve study any item with a remaining useful life exceeding the life of the loan by some fixed amount.

Summary of data to be included in report:

1. A brief description of the common and limited common elements that are surveyed providing where possible, the name, manufacturer, model, serial number and ratings.
2. Extract the quantities to be used in the reserve study by analyzing the plans or by field estimates. The development of this information drives the cost of the reserve study.

3. The condition estimate should discuss the problems and defects noted and provide a qualitative estimate such as poor, fair, good or excellent. Specific deficiencies should be recorded with sufficient detail to estimate their impact on useful life and to provide a reasonable idea of the scope of the needed repairs. If possible, the age of the common element should be provided.
4. Important maintenance or repairs that need to be undertaken immediately or in the near term should be noted, and problems arising from deferred maintenance should be called to the owner's attention. Elements requiring minor repairs should also be recorded and presented in a punch list. If failure to take remedial action will negatively impact the useful life of any common element, this should be noted in the report.
5. Remaining useful life (EUL) should be estimated as a function of the conditions observed. Remaining life is impacted by several factors, particularly the quality of the maintenance program.

Reserve studies are most commonly performed on multi-family residential properties because it is the fiduciary responsibility of the governing board of directors to ensure that funds are adequately accumulated and held in a reserve fund for future expenditures. In several states there are legal requirements for providing "reasonable reserves."

3.5.6.2 The Scope of Work for a Reserve Study

A standard reserve study consists of two essential elements:

- Field Assessment—This involves a general, visual inspection to determine component inventory of the property's elements and to identify material specifications, assess their general current condition, and take measurements to determine quantities for repair or replacement.
- Reserve Analysis—Upon determining the current status of the fund, a funding plan needs to be set up based on a schedule of future repair or replacement costs for each of the elements included in the study.

Generated from the field assessment and reserve analysis is a narrative report documenting assumptions, general conditions, observed deficiencies, useful lifetimes, and remaining useful lifetimes for each element included in the study. Integrated in the narrative portion of the report are graphs, summaries, and photographs that make the report a useful and easy to comprehend tool for the client to utilize during the budgeting process.

Legal requirements: Not every state has a law pertaining to reserve funds. And of the states that do have laws, the law varies from state to state.

Reserve study standards: The Community Associations Institute publishes the National Reserve Study Standards that lists the following minimum content to be included in a reserve study:

- A summary of the association's number of units, physical description, and reserve fund financial condition.
- A projection of reserve fund starting balance, recommended reserve contributions, projected reserve expenses, and projected ending reserve fund balance for a minimum of 20 years.
- A tabular listing of the component inventory, component quantity or identifying descriptions, useful life, remaining useful life, and current replacement cost of each element.
- A description of the methods and objectives utilized in computation of the fund status and development of the funding plan.

- Source(s) utilized to obtain component repair or replacement cost estimates.
- A description of the level of service by which the reserve study is prepared.
- The fiscal year for which the reserve study is prepared.

How often should a reserve study be performed? As stated earlier, a reserve study is a financial planning tool for the future replacement of commonly owned property that wears out during the life of the development. The annual contributions made to the reserve fund are a means for an association to compensate for the difference between the ongoing deterioration of a property and its finances. Because elements deteriorate at varying rates and the finances of the association typically change yearly, the need to maintain balance between the two is an ongoing process. To maintain this balance, it is strongly recommended for the association to have the reserve study updated every two or three years. When considering an update to a study, the association should answer the following questions:

- Has there been a significant departure (i.e. 2 to 3 percent) from the anticipated rates for interest, inflation, and construction cost increases previously assumed?
- Have any major elements been added or replaced since the previous study?
- Have any elements sustained premature deterioration due to unseasonable weather or lack of maintenance since the previous study?
- Has the association accelerated or deferred any repairs or replacements from the estimated schedule previously generated?

If the answer is "yes" to one or more of the above questions, then the association should strongly consider having an update to their previous reserve study.

Generally, an association that is relatively new in age and is not performing any major repairs or replacements should have the reserve study updated approximately every three years to maintain the validity of the estimates. However, if the association is older and is experiencing major repairs or replacements, then the study should be updated on an annual basis. An update to a previous reserve study can typically be performed for a percentage of the original cost of the study. The re-evaluation can include an on-site inspection of the property, or simply an update to the tables.

3.5.6.3 Typical Estimated Useful Life Data

Repair needs may not simply reflect physical deficiencies but may be required due to age and maintenance costs. When the annualized cost to maintain a building system or component exceeds its annualized replacement cost, then it has exceeded its expected useful life (EUL). In these circumstances a suitable repair need should be identified, which will usually be replacement of the system or component.

Several organizations have published standard guides for use in calculating EUL data for various building systems and components. Assessors should use these guides when identifying EUL information. Assessors should make adjustments to the standard EUL data to reflect individual conditions, such as location, exposure, levels of maintenance, etc. (Figure 3.6).

A Reserve Data Analysis (RDA) study provides the client with an on-site survey in which the consultant completes a detailed inventory of all assets which the client is responsible. Using localized cost guides, economic and investments parameters and the consultant's detailed inventory of the client's assets, a complete reserve analysis study is produced which includes detail reports for each asset, a summary of assets by category, a distribution of accumulated reserves report, a required monthly contribution report and 30-

SYSTEM/COMPONENT (EUL in # Years)	BOMA	RS Means	BCIS	AVERAGE
EPDM roof	15	20	25	20
Asphalt built-up roof	25	28	35	29
Modified bitumen (2-ply)	20	25	20	22
Asphalt shingles (average)	22	20	N/A	21
Slate roof	75	70	75	73
Curtain wall-glass	30	N/A	45	38
Curtain wall-metal	40	35	45	40
Exterior windows (wood frame)	30	40	35	35
Exterior windows (aluminum frame)	30	50	45	42
Vinyl flooring	12	18	15	15
Exterior roll-up doors	N/A	35	25	30
Interior doors—hollow core	N/A	30	35	33
Carpet (broadloom)	5	8	15	9
Interior paint (walls)	5	5	N/A	5
Suspended ceiling	25	20	25	23
Fire alarm system	10	15	N/A	13
Sprinkler system	25	20	35	27
Air conditioners (package)	15	20	15	17
Air handling units (packaged)	25	15	N/A	20
Boilers (gas)	25	30	20	25
Furnaces	18	15	N/A	17
Unit heaters (electric)	10	15	N/A	13
Fans (axial)	20	20	15	18
Fan coil units	20	15	N/A	18
Ductwork	30	N/A	35	33
Package chillers (reciprocating)	20	20	15	18
Cooling towers (metal)	18	15	N/A	17
Condensers (air-cooled)	20	15	N/A	18
Pumps (base-mounted)	25	20	15	20
Electric transformers	30	30	N/A	30
Automatic transfer switch	25	18	N/A	22
Emergency generator	20	25	N/A	23
Interior light fixtures	20	20	15	18
Elevator (hydraulic)	15	N/A	30	23
Elevator (traction)	20	N/A	30	25
Domestic water heaters	10	15	N/A	13
Exterior pavement	30	25	25	27

Figure 3.6 Suggested approximate EUL data for different products and systems.

year projections. RDA reserve studies begin with a comprehensive analysis of the client's operating guidelines and other governing documents to determine the extent of the client's maintenance and reserve responsibilities.

The borrower shall provide the consultant with a schedule of all building expenses. Inasmuch as operating expenses may be expensed to tenants as additional rent, or assumed by tenant under a net lease structure, these costs are to be excluded from the consultant's replacement reserve schedule. However, any item that has a predictable Expected Useful Life and/or is not subject to routine preventive maintenance must be included.

3.5.6.4 Establishing Reserve Schedules

Calculating reserves: Community associations typically shoulder the responsibility for the repair, maintenance, and replacement of their common area facilities regardless of whether title is held in the association's name or if it is commonly owned by the members of the association. One of the duties of the association is to analyze its funding needs and set aside adequate funds from its annual budget to meet its long term obligations. This is a prudent step since common area facilities of any association deteriorate as they age. The association has the responsibility of maintaining the common area facilities that also includes providing a replacement funding program that considers the aging process, anticipates future costs, and provides a method of meeting those future costs.

The consultant shall prepare a Replacement Reserve Schedule that encompasses short-lived, mid-lived and long-lived recurring systems and components. Short-term recurring systems and components are typical of such items as exterior caulking, carpeting, pavement sealing and striping, domestic hot water heaters, etc. Mid-lived recurring systems are typically cooling towers, paving, roofing, appliances, kitchen cabinets, etc. Long-lived items are typically boilers, chillers, electrical systems, infrastructure components, supply and drainage piping, etc.

The following methodology should be employed when completing the Replacement Reserve Schedule. Submit these schedules typed in a spreadsheet format. An example of a typical Modified Capital Reserve Schedule is illustrated in Figure 3.7.

1. Do not double-dip: In other words, if the consultant identifies that the roof requires replacement as a short-term item under Section IV—"Cost Estimates to Remedy Deficiencies" do not require its replacement under year one in the Replacement Reserve Schedule. Treat the roof as if it were new with a Remaining Useful Life (RUL) equal to its commonly anticipated Expected Useful Life (EUL).

2. Opine on EUL and EFF age: The consultant is allowed to use his/her professional judgment in determining when a system or component will require replacement. Inclement weather, exposure to the elements, initial quality and installation, extent of use, and the degree of preventive maintenance exercised are all factors that could impact the RUL of a system or component. As a result of the aforementioned items, a system or component may have an Effective Age (EFF AGE) greater or less than its Actual Age (ACT AGE). For instance, a parking lot with an EUL of 18 years that has been religiously sealed with a squeegee applied asphalt emulsion slurry coat may have an EFF AGE equal to eight (8) years although its ACT AGE is 12 years. Therefore, its RUL will be 10 years (18 minus 8) instead of six years (18 minus 12). Should the borrower or client differ from the consultant as to a component or system's EUL, the borrower or client must substantiate this opinion by schedules, invoices, etc. The consultant is not to accept unsubstantiated EULs.

3. Phase replacements: Consultant may exercise professional judgment as to the rate or phasing of replacements. For instance, suppose that an office complex has an extensive quantity of paving that will realize its EUL in year eight. Instead of requiring the replacement of all paving in year eight, which may be a significant cost to be incurred in any single year, the consultant may phase the work over three years;

MODIFIED CAPITAL RESERVE SCHEDULE

Job Number:	A00292
Job Name:	Office Depot
Location:	33411
Description:	30,935 SFG Retail Building
Date:	August 2, 2007

Reserve Term:	12
Inflation Rate (%):	3.0
Building Age:	1
No. of Buildings:	1
Total Square Feet:	30,935

COMPONENT OR SYSTEM	Opinions Of Probable Cost	AVG EUL (Yr)	EFF AGE (Yr)	RUL (Yr)	QUANTITY	UNIT	UNIT COST ($)	CYCLE REPLMNT COST	PROBABLE REPLACEMENT DATES & ESTIMATED EXPENDITURES ($) 2000 1	2001 2	2002 3	2003 4	2004 5	2005 6	2006 7	2007 8	2008 9	2009 10	2010 11	2011 12	Total Reserve Items	Repair or Replace
Apply 1 1/2" Overlay to Asphalt Pavement		20	1	19	4,706	SY	2.75	12,942	0	0	0	0	0	0	0	0	0	0	0	0	0	Replace
Emulsion Sealcoat Asphalt Pavement		5	1	4	4,706	SY	0.65	3,059	0	0	0	3,059	0	0	0	0	3,059	0	0	0	6,118	Repair
Concrete Curb Replacement		25	1	24	1,300	LF	6.00	7,800	0	0	0	0	0	0	0	0	0	0	0	0	0	Replace
Lawn Irrigation System Repairs		12	0	12	1	EA	1,200.00	1,200	0	0	0	0	0	0	0	0	0	0	0	1,200	1,200	Repair
Replace Concrete Sidewalk Sections		30	1	29	1,750	SF	5.50	9,625	0	0	0	0	0	0	0	0	0	0	0	0	0	Replace
Replace Defective Site Lighting Luminaires		25	1	24	15	EA	1,500.00	22,500	0	0	0	0	0	0	0	0	0	0	0	0	0	Replace
Exteriors																						
Re-Paint Exterior Sidewall Surfaces		7	1	6	21,000	SF	0.45	9,450	0	0	0	0	0	9,450	0	0	0	0	0	0	9,450	Replace
Re-Caulking, Exterior Façades		7	1	6	1,050	LF	3.50	3,675	0	0	0	0	0	3,675	0	0	0	0	0	0	3,675	Repair
Replace Overhead Loading Doors		25	1	24	2	EA	1,000.00	2,000	0	0	0	0	0	0	0	0	0	0	0	0	0	Replace
Replace Aluminum Framed Storefronts		35	1	34	160	SF	65.00	10,400	0	0	0	0	0	0	0	0	0	0	0	0	0	Replace
Roofing																						
Re-Roof, Modified Bitumen Roof		15	1	14	30,935	SF	2.75	85,071	0	0	0	0	0	0	0	0	0	0	0	0	0	Replace
Seal Open Coping Panel Joints	$1,015																					Repair
Plumbing Systems																						
Replace Individual Water Heater, 10 Gallon		12	1	11	1	EA	375.00	375	0	0	0	0	0	0	0	0	0	0	375	0	375	Replace
Heating & Air Conditioning																						
Replace 13 Ton Rooftop Package Unit (RTU)		15	1	14	6	EA	14,300.00	85,800	0	0	0	0	0	0	0	0	0	0	0	0	0	Replace
Replace 4 Ton Rooftop Package Unit (RTU)		12	1	11	2	EA	4,400.00	8,800	0	0	0	0	0	0	0	0	0	0	8,800	0	8,800	Replace
Electrical System																						
Upgrade Electrical Switchgear		45	1	44	1	EA	3,000.00	3,000	0	0	0	0	0	0	0	0	0	0	0	0	0	Replace
Fire Protection																						
Replace Fire Alarm Panel		25	1	24	1	EA	10,000.00	10,000	0	0	0	0	0	0	0	0	0	0	0	0	0	Replace
ADA Modifications																						
Install Van Mounted Signage	$50																					Repair
	Please Note: Items listed below this row are provided for informational purposes only and are not part of the 'Modified Capital Reserve Schedule' calculations																					
Tenant Improvements																						
Upgrade Interior Spaces (Paint & Finishes)		15	1	14	30 395	SF	10.00	303,950	0	0	0	0	0	0	0	0	0	0	0	0	0	Repair
Toilet Rooms, Upgrade		30	1	29	2	EA	1,500.00	3,000	0	0	0	0	0	0	0	0	0	0	0	0	0	Replace
AVG EUL: Average Expected Useful Life	$1,065	ANNUAL REQUIREMENTS (UNINFLATED)							0	0	0	3,059	0	13,125	0	0	3,059	0	9,175	1,200	29,618	
EFF AGE: Effective Age		INFLATION RATE FACTOR @ 3%							1	1.0300	1.0609	1.0927	1.1255	1.1593	1.1941	1.2299	1.2668	1.3048	1.3439	1.3842		
RUL: Remaining Useful Life		ANNUAL REQUIREMENTS (INFLATED)							0	0	0	3,343	0	15,215	0	0	3,875	0	12,330	1,661	36,424	
*: Management Applied/Installed or Tenant Responsibility		UNINFLATED RESERVE/SFG/YEAR							.08													
***: Operating or CAM Expense		INFLATED RESERVE/SFG/YEAR							.10													

Figure 3.7 Example of modified capital reserve schedule.

i.e., the consultant may replace 40 percent in year eight, 40 percent in year nine and 20 percent in year 10. However, make sure that the other replacements recommended that complement it are also completed in this phase. For instance, if the paving overlay is to be completed in this phase. For instance, if the paving overlay is to be completed in phases, so must the striping. Phased replacement scheduling is also appropriate for allocating asbestos removal/abatement costs inasmuch as such work commonly coincides with lease terminations.

4. Component replacements: Certain mechanical equipment lends itself to be broken down into commonly replaced components so that funding to replace the entire piece of equipment at one time is not necessary. For example, the overall cost of a boiler may include pumps, a burner, etc., which may require replacement on a schedule different from that of replacing the entire boiler.

5. Replacement made thus far: Take into consideration if management has already begun a program of replacing multiple or single components that have realized their EUL. If, as a result of research, the consultant learns the extent of such replacements made to date, the consultant shall take this into consideration. The onus is on management to substantiate the replacements made and the reported costs incurred by submitting documentation to the consultant. Such documents should be included as an exhibit to the report.

6. Term: Complete a Replacement Reserve Schedule for the term of the loan plus two years. The length of the term or "window" may significantly impact reserve requirements. For instance, a 17-year reserve "window" would not include replacement of roofing (RUL—20 years) for a subject with a one-year-old roof, whereas a 22-year "window" would include such a cost. Generally, the smaller the window, the less the reserve monies required.

7. Replacement Costs: Replacement costs used shall be market or borrower's historical incurred costs, or substantiated third-party costs. Should the borrower or client differ from the consultant as to a component's or system's replacement cost, borrower or client must substantiate this opinion by submitting paid invoices, executed proposals, receipts, bona fide pending proposals, etc. The consultant is not to accept unsubstantiated replacement costs offered by the borrower or client. In addition projected future expenditures should incorporate an acceptable rate of inflation.

CHAPTER

4

Professional Standards & Methods

4.1 GENERAL

The consultant shall review available information and make inquiries and observations sufficient to establish the type and approximate extent of physical deficiencies, along with an estimated cost of correction. The focus of the investigation should be on acquiring information needed to prepare the *Property Condition Report* described below and in Chapter 3.

The consultant should assume that the property survey will be sufficient to accomplish property review objectives. If a consultant determines greater depth of investigation is required, he may request that additional work and fee be authorized. To the extent supplementary information is available from the lender and/or borrower, it may be provided to the consultant upon request.

The consultant should take note that the lender's interest in each property is subject to rights and restrictions established in the loan documents. The consultant should assume that the borrower will provide satisfactory access to the property, staff, and vendors. The Lender will assist the consultant in securing access and information within the Lender's rights in the event the borrower fails to cooperate. In no event should the consultant seek access to any property, staff, vendor, or documents if the borrower objects to such access or attempts to restrict the consultant from performing his investigative duties.

The investigative work described below should suffice to serve as a basis for the property report to be prepared by the consultant. Although the time required at a site and for other research varies with each project based on the property's size, configuration, type, and condition, Figure 4.1 may be used for rule of thumb estimates for a property survey by an architect or engineer knowledgeable in building construction, site development, and building systems.

	SMALL OR SIMPLE PROPERTY	MEDIUM OR AVERAGE PROPERTY	LARGE OR COMPLEX PROPERTY
Site Visit	1-3 hours	2-4 hours	4-8 hours
Investigative Work	2-3 hours	2-4 hours	4-6 hours
Verbal Report	1 hour	1 hour	1½ hours
Report Writing	2-4 hours	4-7 hours	8-12 hours
Totals	6-11 hours	9-15 hours	17½-27½ hours

Figure 4.1 Rule of thumb estimates for conducting a property survey.

4.2 QUALIFICATIONS OF THE CONSULTANT

4.2.1 General

The quality of a PCA depends to a very large degree on the qualifications and capabilities of the assessment team. An *assessor* or *field observer* (or assessor) is the person or team that performs the visual assessments and records the results. The PCR *reviewer* is a qualified individual or team that reviews and checks the accuracy of the assessor's results, and is designated to exercise responsible control over the assessor/field observer on behalf of the consultant and to review the PCR. The consultant is ultimately responsible for the PCA process.

PCA results are usually better when both assessors and reviewers are involved in the process, and ideally, they should be two functionally separate individuals or teams. They do not need to be organizationally independent of one another, and are often part of the same company, team, or organization.

The competency of the consultant is highly dependent on many factors that may include professional education, training, experience, certification, or professional licensing/registration of both the consultant's field observers and the PCR reviewer. It is important to identify factors that assessors or the user should consider when retaining a consultant to conduct a PCA, and that the consultant should use in selecting the appropriate field observer and PCR reviewer. No standard can be designed to eliminate the role of professional judgment, competence, and the value and need for experience during the walk-through survey and to conduct the PCA. Consequently, the qualifications of the assessor/field observer and the PCR reviewer are critical to the performance of the PCA and the resulting PCR. It should be recognized that the consultant has the responsibility to select, engage, or employ the assessor/field observer and the PCR reviewer; therefore, each PCR should include as an exhibit a statement of qualifications of both the assessor/field observer and the PCR reviewer.

4.2.2 Consultant Qualification Requirements

These guidelines are essentially based on guidelines developed by Standard and Poor's in conjunction with the due diligence firm, Inspection & Valuation International, Inc. (IVI). A response is requested to each of the sections below. The response may include promotional/marketing brochures and literature, letters of recommendation, etc.

Company Experience

1. How many years has your firm been in business? What year was it incorporated or the partnership formed? Since inception, has there been a corporate name change? Qualified consultants must be able to prove that they have been in operation for a minimum of three years.
2. How many, if any, branch offices do you have and where are they located? Provide addresses, number of personnel, manager's name and telephone number.
3. Provide a schedule of the last 12 building condition survey assignments completed by your firm, complete with scope of assignment(s), location, client and client telephone number.
4. Approximately how many property condition survey assignments were completed by your firm for each 12-month period going back three years?
5. Are there any pending claims or litigation against the firm? If so, please provide a brief overview as to the basis and status of same.

Personnel

1. The consultant is to provide resumes of each firm member who will be conducting property condition surveys and reviewing completed reports. All personnel conducting property condition surveys shall have all of the following qualifications:
   - A professional engineer's license or architectural registration; no exceptions will be permitted.
   - Four or more years of experience in specifically conducting property condition surveys on behalf of investors, lending institutions, or government agencies.
2. Provide the resume of the senior project manager who will be responsible for report review/quality control, final sign-off, and answering of rebuttal questions, if any. The individual signing off on the report must be a licensed professional engineer or a registered architect.

References

The consultant should provide the names, positions, companies and telephone numbers of four references who are able to opine on the firm's property condition survey reports.

Conflict of Interest

The consultant may not be affiliated with the borrower or its representative or engage in any business that might present a conflict of interest. The consultant is required to disclose whether he/she had been previously retained or employed by the borrower.

Insurance Requirements

Most clients require that consultants carry adequate insurance coverage to be considered for an assignment. Typically, a proposal submitted by a consultant will not be considered unless accompanied by the appropriate certificates of insurance. Typical insurance requirements are illustrated in Figure 4.2.

4.2.3 Staffing of the Assessor/Field Observer

It is recognized that for the majority of commercial real estate subject to a PCA, the assessor/field observer

Worker's Compensation

	Limit of Liability
Worker's Compensation	Statutory Benefits
Employer's Liability	$500,000

Comprehensive General Liability
(including coverage of contractual liability assumed by the contractor under indemnity agreement set forth below and completed operations coverage)

	Limit of Liability
Bodily Injury	$1,000,000 per occurrence
Property Damage	$1,000,000 per occurrence
Professional Liability	$1,000,000 per occurrence or claims made form (coverage shall be maintained for three years following expiration of the assignment)

Comprehensive Automobile Liability

	Limit of Liability
Bodily Injury	$1,000,000 per occurrence
Property Damage	$1,000,000 per occurrence

Of note, it is now common practice to limit liability to the consultant's fee or sum of say $50,000, whichever is greater.

Figure 4.2 Insurance requirements for due diligence firms.

assigned by the consultant to conduct the walk-through survey most likely will be a single individual having a general, well-rounded knowledge of pertinent building systems and components; however, a single individual will seldom have comprehensive knowledge, expertise or experience with all building codes, building systems and asset types that are applicable in all locales. Therefore, any decision to supplement the assessor/field observer with specialty consultants, building system mechanics, specialized service personnel, or any other specialized field observers should be a mutual decision made by the consultant and the client. This decision should be made in accordance with the requirements, risk tolerance level, and budgetary constraints of the client, the purpose the PCA is to serve, the expediency of report delivery, and the complexity of the subject property. The level of due diligence conducted during a PCA is often adjusted to the risk tolerance of the client.

4.2.4 Independence of the Consultant

The consultant is normally a person or entity acting as an independent contractor, who has been engaged by the user to conduct a PCA. In the event the consultant, assessor/field observer, PCR reviewer, or members of the consultant's staff are employees of, or of a subsidiary of, the user, such affiliation or relationship should be disclosed in the Executive Summary of the PCR.

4.2.5 The Assessor/Field Observer and PCR Reviewer

The PCR reviewer also may act as the assessor/field observer and conduct the walk-through survey. In such an event, the PCR reviewer should identify such dual responsibilities and sign the PCR, indicating that he or she has performed both functions.

It is recommended that the client consider a PCR reviewer who possesses either a professional designation in architecture or engineering, or appropriate experience and/or certifications in the construction fields, although many firms have dropped the use of professional designations due to potential liability concerns. The PCR reviewer should have experience commensurate with the subject property type and scope (size, complexity, etc.), as well as experience in the preparation of PCRs. Generally, professional architecture or engineering licensure/registration, and/or certifications, education, or appropriate construction experience related to these disciplines are recognized as acceptable qualifications for reviewing PCRs. However, the user and the consultant may mutually agree to define qualifications for the PCR reviewer, which may depend on the specific experience of the PCR reviewer and the scope of the subject property.

4.3 TYPICAL SEQUENCE OF EVENTS UPON BEING AWARDED A BUILDING INSPECTION ASSIGNMENT

4.3.1 Project Preliminaries

The following sequence is based on guidelines used by IVI. Upon initial client contact and expression of interest in the award of a project, a project file is created and a project number is assigned. This file will be maintained through the development and award of a contract. The sequence of activities is as follows:

1. The client typically calls or emails for a *quote* on an assignment.
2. A standard *proposal* is prepared with information for the proposal being saved in the appropriate file (IVI uses a proprietary computer program) for the individual client.
3. The information regarding the proposal is entered into a database.
4. Upon proposal being awarded, *mobilization* of the assignment begins.
5. The assignment is given a *project number* (anything related to this job is now filed via this number).
6. The database is updated to now show an "awarded" job, the project number, and any other current information with regard to the job. If the fees were negotiated, or any other special instructions may have been given, they should be noted here as well. If the assignment was not awarded, that information should be entered into the database also, and any debriefing as to why the assignment was not awarded is noted.

Documentary history: Review property records as furnished by the lender and/or borrower. In general, documentary information will consist primarily of borrower files containing descriptive information on construction materials and systems. Some files may have a prior engineering assessment report. If an ADA assessment has been performed, review its principal findings and note the major deficiencies identified. (If available, a copy of the ADA report summary should be incorporated into the report appendix.) Refer to drawings and specifications, if available on site, only for descriptive information on construction of the improvements. Plan review is not required.

4.3.2 Mobilization Documents

Upon notification by the client to proceed with the contract work, the division manager assigns the project to a project manager and informs the administrative staff. Following is a brief description of the various documents used to mobilize a Property Condition Assessment and subsequent Property Condition Report. It is important to remember that the information contained in these documents is used by different employees and at various stages in the completion of a project. Therefore, each document needs to be accurate and updated as promptly as possible. The documents will be listed in the order in which a typical job is mobilized, how many copies are produced, and to whom they are provided. Additional copies are easily provided since all documents mobilized for any given job are saved in that specific job number's folder.

Mobilization includes:

- A project manager is assigned to the Project.
- Preparation of an *Assignment Data Sheet* (the answers saved from the proposal should be used).
- A project file called *Redrope* is prepared and includes the following:
  - Contract with scope of work and terms
  - Site contact information
  - Property manager interview form
  - Parameter/Measurement schedules (for Residential Buildings)
  - Tenant survey forms (for retail buildings)
  - Condition assessment checklist (for building type: generic; multifamily, hotel, suburban office, high-rise office, shopping center/mall).
  - ADA checklist
- The Redrope exterior label should contain the project number, project name, city/state and client.
- The assignment data sheet goes into Redrope and the file is given to the project manager.
- The project manager calls the client for site contact information, if not provided.
- The project manager calls the site contact to arrange inspection date.
- Once an inspection date is scheduled, the client is faxed a *Client Site Inspection Confirmation Letter* (which includes the date and time of the site inspection and the name and contact information of the project manager).
- The project manager sends to the client contact (possibly superintendent, property manager, etc.) the *Pre-Survey Questionnaire and Documentation Checklist.*
- The project manager makes travel arrangements.
- Project research is initiated, which includes preparation and delivery of the following requests for municipal documentation:
  - *Flood Plain Map*
  - *Building Department FOIL* (Freedom Of Information Letter, Figure 4.3A)
  - *Fire Department FOIL* (Figure 4.3B)
  - *Zoning Department FOIL* (Figure 4.3C)
  - Other inquiries as necessary

Helpful Tips for Completing FOILs

1. Start by finding the area code of the property, and call information to get the numbers for the fire, planning, health, electrical, and water departments.

ABC International, Inc.

ABC Los Angeles
155 Anywhere Lane
Sherman Oaks, California 91403
(310) 925-2900

BUILDING DEPARTMENT INFORMATION REQUEST

Date:	______	**To:**	______
Subject:	______	**Dept.:**	______
	______	**Tel. No.:**	______
	______	**Fax No.:**	______
Sender:	______	**ABC Proj.No.:**	______

☐ **New York**	☐ **Washington, D.C.**	☐ **Los Angeles**	☐ **Miami**	☐ **Chicago**
(914) 694-0000 (tel)	(202) 907-0000 (tel)	(213) 896-0000 (tel)	(305) 358-0000 (tel)	(847).296-0000 (tel)
(914) 694-0001 (fax)	(202) 907-0001 (fax)	(213) 896-0001 (fax)	(305) 358-0001 (fax)	(847).296-0001 (fax)

ABC International has been commissioned to conduct a Property Condition Assessment Survey on the above referenced Subject. Please respond to the following documentation/information requests:

1. Does the Subject have any material outstanding building code violations within its file? If "Yes", please fax copies of same. **Yes ☐ No ☐**

2. Is there any existing or pending material building or fire/life safety code requirements that the Subject would not be grandfathered and therefore compliance would then be mandatory? If "Yes", please briefly explain. **Yes ☐ No ☐**

3. Do you have any general or specific knowledge of any physical conditions (site or building) that negatively impact the Subject such as localized flooding, sanitary sewer back-up problems, etc.? If "Yes", please briefly explain. **Yes ☐ No ☐**

4. Is the Subject within a 100 year frequency flood plain? If "Yes", please identify the Flood Hazard Zone as per FEMA's Flood Insurance Rate Maps. **Yes ☐ No ☐**

5. What Building Code is enforced, and what is the local Zoning Ordinance classification of the property?

6. Are there any municipal required procedures or mandated improvements that are triggered by a change of ownership/title such as: a re-inspection by the Building Department, the installation of sprinklers, installing water conservation devices, etc.? If so, what are they?

7. Please fax us a copy of the Subject's Certificate of Occupancy.

Thank you for your assistance. Should you have any questions or should there be any fees associated with providing the requested information, please call me.

Figure 4.3A Project research includes requests for municipal documentation: building department FOIL. *(continued on next page)*

ABC International, Inc.

ABC Los Angeles
155 Anywhere Lane
Sherman Oaks, California 91403
(310) 925-2900

FIRE DEPARTMENT INFORMATION REQUEST

Date:	______________	**To:**	______________
Subject:	______________	**Dept.:**	______________
	______________	**Tel. No.:**	______________
	______________	**Fax No.:**	______________
Sender:	______________	**ABC Proj.No.:**	______________

☐ **New York**	☐ **Washington, D.C.**	☐ **Los Angeles**	☐ **Miami**	☐ **Chicago**
(914) 694-0000 (tel)	(202) 907-0000 (tel)	(213) 896-0000 (tel)	(305) 358-0000 (tel)	(847).296-0000 (tel)
(914) 694-0001 (fax)	(202) 907-0001 (fax)	(213) 896-0001 (fax)	(305) 358-0001 (fax)	(847).296-0001 (fax)

ABC International has been commissioned to conduct a Property Condition Assessment Survey on the above referenced Subject on behalf of the mortgagee. Please respond to the following documentation/information requests:

1. Does the Subject have any significant outstanding fire code violations within its file? If "Yes", please fax copies of same. **Yes ☐ No ☐**

2. Is there any existing or pending significant fire/life safety code requirements that the Subject would not be grandfathered and therefore compliance would then be mandatory? If "Yes", please briefly explain. **Yes ☐ No ☐**

3. Do you have any general or specific knowledge of any physical conditions (site or building) that negatively impact the Subject such as lack of sprinklers that are required by code, inadequate alarm systems, back-up problems, etc.? If "Yes", please briefly explain. **Yes ☐ No ☐**

4. Any general comments or suggested life/safety improvements?

Submitted By: ______________________ **Date:** ______________

Thank you for your assistance. Should you have any questions or should there be any fees associated with providing the requested information, please call me.

Figure 4.3B Project research includes requests for municipal documentation: fire department FOIL.
(continued on next page)

ABC International, Inc.

ABC Los Angeles
155 Anywhere Lane
Sherman Oaks, California 91403
(310) 925-2900

ZONING DEPARTMENT INFORMATION REQUEST

Date:	______________	**To:**	______________
Subject:	______________	**Dept.:**	______________
	______________	**Tel. No.:**	______________
	______________	**Fax No.:**	______________
Sender:	______________	**Proj. No.:**	______________

ABC International has been commissioned to conduct a Property Condition Assessment Survey on the above referenced Subject. Please respond to the following documentation/information requests:

1. Does the Subject have any material outstanding zoning code violations within its file? If "Yes", please fax copies of same. **Yes** ☐ **No** ☐
2. Does the placement, quantity or area of signage comply with current zoning requirements? **Yes** ☐ **No** ☐
3. Is there any existing or pending material zoning code requirements/regulations that the Subject would be considered an existing non-conforming use? If "Yes", please briefly explain. **Yes** ☐ **No** ☐
4. Was the Subject built as of right? **Yes** ☐ **No** ☐
5. If yes to the above, was a variance necessary? **Yes** ☐ **No** ☐
6. In the event of a catastrophic loss, could the Subject be rebuilt to its current density? **Yes** ☐ **No** ☐
7. Is the Subject within a Zoning District? If "Yes", please identify the Zone/District and the requirements. **Yes** ☐ **No** ☐
8. What is the local Zoning Ordinance classification of the property?
9. When was the current Zoning Ordinance adopted?
10. Are there any municipal required procedures or mandated improvements that are triggered by a change of ownership/title such as: a re-issuance of Zoning Approval by the Zoning Department or Zoning Board of Appeals? If so, what are they?
11. Please fax us a copy of the Subject's Zoning Compliance Certificate, if any.

Thank you for your assistance. Should you have any questions or should there be any fees associated with providing the requested information, please call me.

Figure 4.3C Project research includes requests for municipal documentation: zoning department FOIL.

2. Before commencing, call the planning department to determine whether the property is located in the city or the county.
3. When calling the planning department, ask to fax the FOIL to a building inspector, city planner, or zoning administrator. In addition, ask if they know the names of the local water and electric companies that service the area. Finally, ask if they have aerial photographs available for the area, sometimes in a mapping department. If they do, ask for what years and get the department's address and hours of operation.
4. When calling the fire department, ask to fax the FOIL to a fire marshal, fire chief, or fire inspector.
5. When calling the health department, check whether it has an environmental division, and speak to someone there.
6. When calling the water department, ensure that this company services the property in question by giving them the address. Then find out where and whom you would need to send the fax to.
7. When calling the electrical service provider, ensure that it services the property in question by giving the address. Send the FOIL to someone who is familiar with PCBs and transformers.
8. Find the number for the Soil Conservation Service, listed by the county name. Call and find out whether it has aerial photographs for the area available. If it does, ask for what years and get the department's address and hours of operation.
9. Also find the number for the central library in the area. Call the library and find out if it has city directories available for the area. Often you will need to talk to the reference section. If it does, find out for what years and find out the library's location and hours of operation.
10. Finally, using one of the mapping programs, locate and map the planning department, soil conservation service, public library and site location.

Upon completion of the mobilization phase, the administrative staff shall create an electronic file and copy the following into it:

- **Report outline** (some firms generate this from a proprietary computer program and saves it in the answer files)
- Import the **reserve schedule** template, if applicable, into a subdirectory.
- The **cost schedule** template should be imported to a subdirectory.

4.3.3 Interviews

Prior to arriving on site, the project manager will have reviewed the information on the project returned by the client's representative. An interview with the representative will be conducted in accordance with the PCA interview form. If the owner/building manager has as-built drawings with him, these should be reviewed at this time. During the site inspection the opportunity may arise to interview tenants or maintenance personnel. These interviews are documented and the individual identified.

The importance of the assessor's research/interview skills and this phase of the PCA cannot be over stated as a means of gathering pertinent information about the property's condition. With the assessor acting as a technical investigative reporter, the most salient, yet obscure, information about the property will come to light as a result of the research and interviews.

Persons to interview: Who should be interviewed? Generally, the building's engineer or superintendent, the property manager, tenants, local building department/engineering department officials, past designers of record, service company personnel, manufacturer representatives, etc. It is prudent that prior to the site visit, the consultant ask the owner or user to identify a person or persons knowledgeable of the physical characteristics, maintenance, and repair of the property. If a property manager or agent of the owner is identified, the consultant should contact this individual to inquire about the subject property's historical repairs and replacements and their costs, level of preventive maintenance exercised, pending repairs and improvements, frequency of repairs and replacements, and whether there is any existing or pending litigation related to the property's physical condition. As a result of the consultant's research or walk-through survey, the consultant may also decide to question others who are knowledgeable about the property's physical condition and operation. It is within the discretion of the consultant to decide which questions to ask before, during, or after the site visit.

Incomplete answers: While the consultant makes inquiries in accordance with this section, the persons to whom the questions are addressed may have no obligation to cooperate. Should the owner or the property manager, building/facility engineer, or maintenance supervisor not be available for an interview, whether by intent or inconvenience, or not respond in full or in part to questions posed by the consultant, the consultant should disclose such within the Property Condition Report (PCR). Furthermore, should any party not grant authorization to interview, restrict such authorization, or should the person to whom the questions are addressed not be knowledgeable about the subject property, this should be disclosed within the PCR.

Coordination with facility representatives: During the physical inspection, daily communication with the facility representative should be conducted to address any misunderstandings or confusion that may arise with the staff or users of the facility. Regular meetings should be conducted and dialogue should be encouraged during the Pre-survey phase. Weekly progress reports should be produced during the Report Preparation phase.

Contact with facility staff and users: Professional interaction with all facility personnel ensures that normal facility operations will not be disturbed throughout the duration of the evaluation project. It is helpful if field investigators wear identification badges to assist the communication process. Professional and courteous communication and appropriate attire assure smooth interaction with the facility users.

Coordination during each phase is critical to the overall success of the PCA project. During the Pre-survey and Planning phase, the evaluation team should work closely with the facility representative and other designated personnel to ensure that all available documents are located and that the survey protocol, field investigation forms, computer format and report formats are responsive to the facility's needs and will provide accurate, concise data.

The Report Preparation phase will require close interaction with the facility representatives to ensure that the report is responsive to facility needs and that the recommendations provide workable solutions to the facility's concerns.

4.3.4 Site Visit/Inspection

Prior to travel the project manager shall review the project working file to understand the scope of work, including reporting requirements and the appropriate protocol. An Inspection Pack should be prepared, which should include basic needs for the survey, such as a moisture meter, combustible gas meter, digital camera, tape measure, electric current tester, flashlight, binoculars, screwdriver and pocket knife.

The PCA checklists are to be used during the site inspection to document observations. Other notes or field sketches should be made as well. The information on the forms and checklists should be completed as the site survey progresses. Information obtained should be attributed to the source by name and/or position.

Observe property components, systems and elements for evidence of significant physical deficiencies. Physical deficiencies should be deemed significant if either of the following can be concluded: the deficiency represents a cited or apparent code violation, an immediate life safety or health hazard to the occupants or users of the property, or a fire safety hazard to the property itself. Other physical deficiencies of lesser consequence should also be observed and individually noted for inclusion in an aggregated cost-to-cure estimate, which will be furnished by the consultant.

Field observations will consist of one or a combination of the following activities:

a. Walk-around exterior visual inspections:

- Building exteriors—all as visible from grade and accessed roofs and setbacks
- Principal hard surface areas
- Representative roofs and roof area
- Landscaped areas

b. Walk-around interior visual inspections:

Common area spaces

- Entries and entry lobbies (all)
- Toilet rooms (sample)
- Multi-tenant area corridors and elevator lobbies (sample)
- Egress stairs and exit ways (sample at various levels)
- Elevator interiors (typical of each bank)

Leased area spaces

- Vacant tenant areas (typical; if residential, 1 of each type)
- Occupied tenant areas (typical; up to 10 percent of space. No occupied residential units)

Service areas

- Typical service spaces and corridors
- Central service facilities (main equipment rooms and pad areas)

c. Equipment and system observations: Random operation of equipment, fixtures and systems on a sample basis to determine system operability, which may include:

Plumbing

- Sample operation of fixtures in toilet room
- Piping and insulation incidental to mechanical areas

Mechanical equipment (HVAC)

- Central equipment
- Typical residential, retail, or office unit installations (5 percent of total)
- Typical floor or zone installations and equipment (1 or 2 floors)
- Typical rooftop installations (on floors inspected)
- EMS system console

Electrical equipment

- Central equipment, including transformer vaults and pads
- Typical unit installations (residential, office, retail)
- Typical floor or zone installations
- Typical pattern of outlets, switches, jacks, lighting, (5 percent of area)

Elevator equipment—central equipment and control room

Life safety system equipment

- Central consoles and annunciator panels
- Fire pump and central valve stations
- Typical standpipes, sprinklers, smoke detectors, alarm stations, etc. (5 percent of area)
- Central security and surveillance consoles.

d. Nondestructive, noninvasive testing, sounding or detailed observation to determine representative conditions.

e. Recording of physical deficiencies.

Upon return to the office, the project manager shall send the client a *Debriefing Letter.* The project manager may call the client as appropriate to discuss the inspection and findings.

4.3.5 Organizing to Write the Report

The writing of a PCA report requires concentration and attention to detail. One method is to spread out the project materials on the desk and organize them to tell a story. This is especially important to do with the photographs, which can jog your memory. The assessor can then start developing his/her thoughts and mentally run through the report a few times to try and visualize it. Attempt to piece together all the information in a logical form.

The need for comprehensive documentation: Comprehensive documentation is two-fold. It consists of both the documentation available for review and analysis during the evaluation and the reported information at the culmination of the assessment process. The value of comprehensive documentation cannot be overstressed. The degree of confidence in a decision to acquire a facility is directly related to the thoroughness of the documentation review. If the document review is cursory, the chances are much greater that issues will be missed. A cursory review could mean that certain building systems or components of these systems are not reviewed or are not reviewed in a manner that will identify anything but the most superficial deficiencies.

A comprehensive review of the available documentation, from soils reports to structural drawings, is imperative for the evaluation to be of significant value, and is particularly appropriate for an in-depth inspection as opposed to a standard walk-through survey. The more vantage points from which a facility is viewed, the more likely the chance of noticing deficiencies or issues to be addressed. At times the structural system deficiencies will be discovered when the assessor crawls into the ceiling cavity. Other times, the issue will arise upon review of the construction drawings or specifications. The more documentation reviewed, the more valuable and accurate the survey report commentary and recommendations.

The other aspect of comprehensive documentation is the verification of evaluation findings and recommendations. The acquisition evaluation is the ideal time to begin what could be referred to as a working operations and maintenance manual. This may be the one time that the facility is reviewed comprehensively and the documentation of this effort can become a benchmark of the facility for the useful life of the facility.

4.3.6 Report Form and Content

The report form shall be determined by the intended use of the report, the client protocol, the type of property being surveyed, and the necessary level of diligence. Most firms have formulated standard report formats and language to ensure the quality and consistency of the final report product. This is discussed in greater detail in Chapter 3. Basically, for each property, a Property Condition Report (PCR) is provided, which generally addresses the issues outlined in Chapter 3 (where applicable). As mentioned earlier, most large due diligence firms like IVI use proprietary software systems to assist in generating the initial draft report and to expedite the process of report preparation, while maintaining quality and consistency.

4.3.7 Photographs

Prior to the advent of digital photography, the standard report photo size was 3 1/2 $\times$ 5 inches. However, digital cameras are almost exclusively used today. Consultants typically use one of two templates, one consisting of two photos per page and the other consisting of six (Figure 4.4). Captions explaining each photo are helpful to more clearly explain the subject. It is also sometimes helpful to add an arrow pointing to the particular item of interest in the photograph.

The consultant should document representative conditions with photographs and use reasonable efforts to document typical conditions present, including material physical deficiencies, if any. Photographs should include as a minimum: front and typical elevations and exteriors, site work, parking areas, roofing, structural systems, plumbing, mechanical and electrical systems, conveyance systems, life safety systems, representative interiors, and any special or unusual conditions present. For most assignments (depending on size, complexity and condition of facility), the number of photographs will range from 20–40. Each photograph should have an annotated description below it.

Photography is an extremely effective way of recording observations. As the saying goes, "a picture is worth a thousand words." Photographs can provide information detail that would be difficult to convey otherwise. Later, notes can be added to photographs to further explain the subject. Photographs are to be taken of the property and components.

Safety: Good safety practices are to be exercised at all times. Be aware of the nature of your surroundings at all times and avoid dangerous conditions. Do not enter confined or other hazardous spaces. Equipment should not be operated that is otherwise unavailable to the general public. Likewise, do not conduct exploratory probing or testing or expose yourself to hazardous materials or conditions, and report any and all accidents to the division manager immediately.

Before leaving the site: At the conclusion of the site inspection and before leaving the area, it is important to organize and review all relevant notes and to complete all field documentation. If information is missing, it can often be easily obtained before leaving the site.

4.3.8 Report Review

Upon completion of the report, check it for spelling, grammar, and conformance with the firm's report style for consistency. The style check should focus on both format and content. The writer is expected to submit a finished product. The finished report is submitted to the designated reviewer. The reviewer will examine the report to ensure that the scope of work and all other client and firm's criteria have been satisfied. The reviewer will consult with the assessor on substantive report issues, or if quality problems need to be addressed. The report will be returned to the assessor for rework and resubmission if the quality

000 Anywhere Drive
Manassas, Virginia

View of main entrance on the south elevation of Anywhere Drive Building.

View of loading dock. There are four dock height loading doors and one drive-in service with secured access.

View of data center located on the first floor and which is to be renovated.

View of four cell Marley/NC cooling tower.

View of Amtrak 450 KW generator on the first floor.

Ingersoll-Rand 400 CFM air compressors at 112 PSI-100 HP @ 480 volt, to operate air handlers, etc. located in power plant.

ABC International Corporation **ABC Project No. 1234567**

Figure 4.4 Typical template using six photographs per page. For this PCA project in Manassas, Virginia, 36 digital colored photographs were required for the report.

standards are not met. Once the reviewer passes the report, the report is finalized, set for production and issued.

4.3.9 Production & Distribution

Depending on the size of the firm, the project manager or the Administration/Production staff accomplishes production of the report. The report is prepared, copied, collated, and assembled into a final product. The production staff supervisor will give the report copies a final quality check before sending to the client. A project billing report will be sent to accounting upon the release of the report product and accounting will send a billing invoice to the client.

4.3.10 Client Follow-up and Closeout

The project manager or the administrative staff will call the client within three business days of sending the report to confirm its receipt. The project manager will field any questions or comments from the client, and revise and resubmit the report to the client as appropriate. Upon direction from the client the report will be issued as final.

4.4 QUALITY CONTROL/QUALITY ASSURANCE

The quality of the survey and report product is vital to a consultant's continued success.

4.4.1 Roles & Responsibility

The consultant is normally responsible for quality assurance oversight. Management should establish quality standards that are conveyed to the staff. Management should also establish training programs (when possible) to ensure that employees comprehend the necessity of attaining quality goals. However, the overall responsibility for each PCA project, including the quality of the survey and report, resides with the project manager from receiving the assignment to acceptance of the final report by the client.

4.4.2 Quality Review

Management review of the final report product is a quality assurance measure and does not relieve the individual project manager of responsibility for the report product. The review process serves to ensure that the final report product meets quality standards. It also gives management an understanding of the weaknesses in the PCA process that requires attention.

4.4.3 Feedback and Methods Improvement

The goal of a consultant is to maintain the quality of the PCA service and the report product while improving the PCA work process. Each member of the consultant's team is encouraged to provide feedback on established methods and systems, and to offer suggestions for improving the way the work is carried out.

CHAPTER

5

Developing a Condition Evaluation Program & Strategy

5.1 GENERAL

While no property condition assessment (PCA) can possibly eliminate or prevent all risks related to one's real estate (RE) purchase, a PCA properly performed can go a long way in helping the prospective buyer or RE investor make an informed purchase decision. And should the buyer decide to purchase the property, a PCA as outlined herein provides an added benefit in helping to reduce, anticipate, and plan ahead for repairs down the road. Moreover, in cases where the PCA discloses major deficiencies prior to the actual purchase of the property, this information can prove to be a useful negotiating tool, saving the buyer or RE investor considerable time, money, and needless aggravation in attempts to reduce the purchase price or to back out of the deal. Indeed, a PCA properly performed serves to protect and limit the liability of bank and mortgage companies with a vested interest in the property, and can facilitate a loan that takes into account major deficiencies identified/disclosed beforehand. These arrangements make it easier for the borrower to pay back the loan and thus less likely to default.

Today, PCAs are typically performed according to the ASTM "Standard Guide for Property Condition Assessments," and do little more than provide an overall cursory inspection of the property in question. Because of the general nature of the standard, many firms have developed their own guidelines and protocols that allow them to provide a more exacting and detailed inspection of both residential and commercial property, thereby improving the service they are able to deliver to their clients.

5.2 PROPERTY CONDITION EVALUATION CRITERIA OVERVIEW

The role of the Property Condition Assessment consultant has changed significantly over the last decade, due largely to liability issues. Today, roughly 80 percent of liability claims are related to the building envelope (roofs, EIFS, windows, masonry, etc.), followed by code-related issues. For this reason, many of the larger firms now explicitly delete code compliance from their work scope.

Similarly, due diligence terminology has changed. For example, the term "inspection" has become "survey" to reduce liability risk. Moreover, because of incessant liability concerns and the industry's exorbitant insurance rates and deductibles, many firms have also dropped using the words "engineering," "architecture," and others from their marketing brochures, correspondence and reports. These omissions are mainly because the words connote a higher standard of care to be exercised than simply conducting a walk-through survey in accordance with the ASTM E2018-01 "Standard Guide for Property Condition Assessments: Baseline Property Condition Assessment Process," the industry's most commonly used standard for real estate transactions. Professional designations (RA, PE, AIA, etc.) have also been dropped by many due diligence consultants for the same reason. Nevertheless, some providers continue to sign their reports as PEs or RAs, inviting a plaintiff to breach the corporate veil and sue the field observer personally. This is all very unfortunate and does not bode well for the future of the industry, building owners, or investors.

The establishment of pertinent assessment criteria is paramount to a successful assessment survey moving forward. Many institutions today face an urgent need to address existing facilities for deferred maintenance, capital budgeting, operating cost, energy use and optimization, and facility upgrades. However, institutions are faced with increasing needs to prioritize renewal and replacement dollars today. Communicating and selling these financial needs to the institution's business officers requires that needs assessments, condition analyses, and presentation of material be done in a consistent, defendable, and repeatable manner that establishes the credibility and accuracy of the requests.

To do this, the institution must develop and execute a protocol that logically and competently reflects its condition and needs assessments in a methodical and efficient manner. A basic process consists of a number of steps, including the following:

- Statement of survey objectives
- Establishment of assessment criteria
- Establishment of assessment standards
- Development of standard assessment templates
- Actual facility survey and assessment
- Compilation of data
- Analysis of the data
- Financial planning, programming, and feedback mechanisms
- Maintenance and renewal program development
- Execution of the recommendations

Statement of survey objectives: Establish a clear project statement that defines the general objectives and expectations for the assessment survey. A project survey statement at this level helps align expectations from the beginning of the project and minimizes any concern for scope adjustments downstream. It also aligns the needs and expectations of the building owner and lender with those of the facilities manager before the task is undertaken, making communication of the results and cooperative goal setting in the future easier to attain.

Establishment of assessment criteria: This has been an area of considerable debate over the years, where various industry associations have established baselines for capturing relevant survey data. Surveys now incorporate more data than several years ago, including photos, CAD drawing updates, enhanced field descriptions, nameplate data for Computerized Maintenance Management System (CMMS) and Computer Aided Facilities Management (CAFM) systems, in-field cost estimating, compliance with regulations, location information, related conditions, and potential solutions.

More organizations are requesting the survey information be provided to the client in a format that can be managed, not in a fixed-report format that is static and just gets filed. The criteria allow for an organization to establish its own "specification" of sorts, defining the expectations, knowledge, and experience to the Property Condition Assessment (PCA) survey team for field-level data collection.

The assessment criteria also allow for the selection of additional information that either has not been gathered in the past, or was not measured effectively. Areas of concern that require an increase in the gathering of detailed asset information are generally high-value assets, such as mechanical HVAC and electrical systems, and risk assessments.

By defining the survey requirements for the various elements that compose a thorough assessment, the survey can be developed on specific "system" requirements, or for a more comprehensive assessment, which may be oriented toward the building. Building-oriented assessments tend to require a survey team with more broad-based facilities knowledge with expertise in many areas, rather than only in mechanical or electrical systems professionals.

Surveys can also involve everything from code compliance (often omitted from standard PCA scopes), safety/risk audits, environmental surveys, sustainability, site assessment, equipment system surveys, and actual preventive maintenance work efforts, all of which require specific criteria to provide the most effective return on the survey investment.

Establishment of assessment standards: The assessment standards must be established from the beginning due to the importance of the evaluation, the depth of the system components and their gathered data, and the expected reporting process and accuracy of the final document. The standards for a baseline assessment must coincide with the assessment criteria so that the survey component of the process is well defined and the data gathered is properly completed.

Many of today's due diligence firms provide survey teams that can develop the criteria and establish the standards for collating the data and preparing the report. Standards may include naming conventions, maintenance hours and scheduling, facilities and components replacement values, assigned codes, and a costing database, all of which will provide an opportunity to query and pull information and valuation criteria from the reports once the survey has been completed.

The data standards allow flexibility in assessing the data for future reporting, along with the ability to assign effective costs to the survey data. Many of today's industry standard unit cost models (RS Means, etc.) apply standards for specific data elements and units of measure, allowing conformity in aligning cost structures to data elements. The Construction Specifications Institute (CSI) provides either a Uniformat or Master Format for defining the various detailed elements of building design systems and construction.

Spending planning time up front, prior to the survey, to define expectations from a reporting standpoint will assist in the proper definition of standards going into the survey, and result in a more efficient survey execution.

Application of standard assessment templates: Many firms have developed their own survey templates based on their own experience and industry standards which allows for an expedited and competent survey. This process is addressed more fully in Chapters 3 and 4. These forms may be in either electronic or paper form, depending on the program and process established for the survey team. The purpose of the templates is to maintain general consistency in data gathered and presented, specifying condition and maintenance needs and costs being established, and future reporting tools for assessment of the effectiveness of the program. Overall, such tools and processes result in greater overall efficiency and effectiveness for survey teams.

Templates need to be clear and concise, with minimal areas for extensive field notations. The format of the template can be established and stored electronically and preferably resides on a PDA, laptop, or an electronic storage medium.

Actual facility survey and assessment: As we have seen, numerous types of surveys can be performed to support a facility or organization. The type of survey and depth of information being developed is a direct result of the mission and objectives established for the assessment. While areas of specialty have arisen from the demand for various types of surveys, the predominant types of surveys performed for facilities involve either property sites, broad building models, combined assets of either the site or building, or the actual specific systems and subsystems within the buildings and property sites. A comprehensive system analysis can be conducted either through use of internal resources, an independent survey team or consultant (preferable), or through the primary non-proprietary PCA software firm engaging a specialist as a subcontractor.

Compilation and analysis of survey data: Upon completion of the survey and subsequent reports, one can then commence to rationally interpret and evaluate the results. Many of these reports can be overwhelming to the inexperienced user, and the benefits of a reporting, standard becomes evident. An effective plan can be extremely helpful at this stage and an analysis of the results falls on the survey team. Areas of priority are established and the results can be compiled and then interpreted for decision-based analysis and implementation.

5.3 THE BENEFITS OF EVALUATING BUILDING SYSTEMS

Regardless of the role of the facilities professional, whether he is a property owner, facilities manager, real estate seller or real estate buyer, the evaluation of existing building systems can be advantageous. Each group of professionals utilizes evaluations for specific reasons, and the surveys themselves must be designed and coordinated accordingly. Property evaluations minimize the surprises and headaches normally associated with facilities acquisition and management (Figure 5.1).

Facility operations and maintenance: The role of the facilities professional is one of diversity, complexity and typically, crisis management. One may suddenly find that the conference room has an air conditioning problem and the Board of Directors is scheduled to meet in a couple of hours, or the roof of a storage depot starts leaking just before the weekend break. Building users never seem to be satisfied; and when they are, they never seem to be satisfied for long.

Building owners utilize building systems evaluations for numerous reasons. For the most part, these reasons revolve around improving the financial viability, operational efficiency, quality, and safety of the facility. Evaluations ensure that the building owner knows what to do to take the most effective care of the property as an operational facility and as an investment. For example, one of the results of a typical evaluation may be recommendations for energy-saving measures. Owners who have a concern that their building users are comfortable and safe also have a lot to gain from building evaluations. Building systems evaluations typically highlight issues and conditions of safety which, in the day-to-day management of the facility, may not be apparent to the on-site staff.

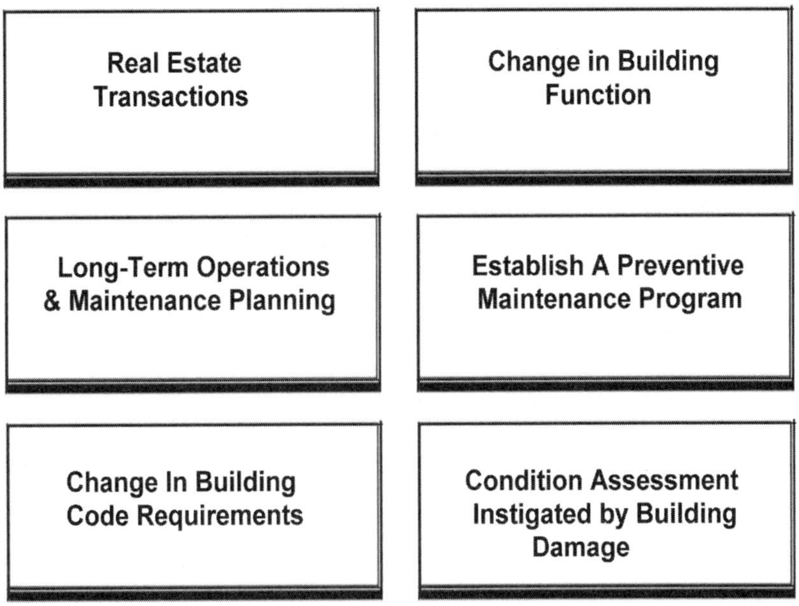

Figure 5.1 Reasons for performing a PCA survey.

Evaluations enable the building owners and managers to better plan and manage a facility and to prioritize and perform any required repair work in a competent manner. Facility evaluations also often bring to light potential money-saving measures. Based on the survey report findings and recommendations, implementation of the repair and replacement of building components can be effectively managed. In a comprehensive survey, existing unsafe conditions, such as deficient structural members or overloaded electrical equipment, are discovered and action is taken to remedy them, thus reducing the potential for accidents and liability. An evaluation is thus a planning tool that provides owners and managers an opportunity to assess the status of the systems in a facility and to recommend a course of action to address any identified deficiencies.

Furthermore, evaluations ensure that the maintenance and management of the facility does not become uncontrollable, they help operational managers spend money more efficiently, and they show how crises can be averted through proper remedial measures. PCA surveys will provide information and recommendations on what to do with each deficient building system and why the work needs to be performed. As a result of the building systems survey, decisions can be based on objective data and reason, and not simply on subjective interpretation. The PCA survey can be designed in a manner that moves everyday decisions regarding maintenance and repairs from the realm of crisis management into the realm of objective efficiency. These sound decisions enable future planning and forward thinking, which will minimize the pitfalls and mistakes encountered during the operational performance of the facility.

The survey and recommendations will allow building owners to operate the facility in a manner that increases the life of the facility and its component parts. As a result of a PCA survey, roofing membranes are repaired periodically, thus avoiding years of possible moisture penetration that would have accelerated the deterioration of the system. The periodic evaluation of the HVAC and electrical components enables minor repairs to be performed as needed, rather than waiting for the system to fail.

Real estate transactions: It is to the advantage of the real estate investor to perform a detailed evaluation of the property during the real estate transaction period. This will ensure that the property is a good investment and will assuage fears of any hidden costs associated with the facility operations or maintenance after purchase. A PCA evaluation will provide the buyer with an understanding of the property operations before actual ownership.

Acquisition surveys typically include a facility review for building deficiencies that will significantly affect the value or operation of the property. A limited acquisition survey may include a general review of specific systems, such as roofing and air conditioning, which tend to require more frequent repair or replacement. Comprehensive acquisition evaluations include a review of each building system and recommendations addressing any remedial work that will be required at the facility within the foreseeable future. The PCA report will provide the buyer with specific cost estimates on deficient systems or components requiring remediation immediately or in the upcoming years.

Using the evaluation report as a negotiation tool in the transaction can result in most of the deficiencies and concerns identified and work recommended in the evaluation either being performed by the seller or in the purchase price being decreased by the cost of correcting these deficiencies. If the seller agrees to perform the work, it is important to take precautions to ensure that the work is done to acceptable standards. Often, the buyer and seller simply agree that certain work needs to be done, and then the buyer finds that the work does not meet his or her qualitative or aesthetic standards. It is important to be very specific about negotiated work to be performed by the seller.

Often, the cost of the recommended repairs will simply be subtracted from the purchase price. This may be to the advantage of the buyer, since in many cases the work might be performed for less than the recommended amount, depending upon the accuracy of the cost estimates and upon who performs the work. In most cases, the estimate will be based on industry standards and the assumption that outside contractors will perform the work. If the buyer has in-house staff with the needed capabilities and qualifications, or if they have a good relationship with good licensed contractors, it is likely that the actual cost of the work will be less than estimated in the PCA report, saving the buyer money.

Real estate sellers are increasingly performing evaluations during the preparation for the real estate transaction. These disposition studies can show the potential buyer the quality of the property and alleviate some of the usual fears associated with the transaction. The disposition study can result in third-party verification of the worth and quality of the building systems. For this reason, it is important that the report be written objectively by an outside source. Care must be taken, though, to design and present the scope and focus of a disposition study in such a way as to honestly, but complimentarily, identify the key issues of the property. An evaluation carelessly designed will become more of a liability than an asset. Naturally, if the property is in good condition and there are no significant deficiencies, this can be presented and highlighted with ease.

5.4 THE ROLE OF A PCA IN ACQUISITION

5.4.1 Overview of the Acquisition Process

The acquisition process is one with many complexities and idiosyncrasies, and while the process is unique to each real estate transaction, several aspects occur during most property acquisitions.

Once the decision has been made to make an acquisition and the financing and funds have been arranged, the site selection process goes into effect. During the site selection phase, it is not uncommon for a buyer to review many different properties for every one that is actually acquired. Of these properties, a good percentage of them are physically reviewed in some type of cursory evaluation.

Eventually a property is selected and the negotiation and due diligence processes begin. This period, which lasts anywhere from seven to sixty days, allows the prospective buyer to verify the quality, condition, and worth of the property. It is during this phase that an evaluation is performed. This evaluation typically includes both standard PCA surveys, sometimes referred to as facilitity evaluations, as well as environmental assessments.

The PCA survey, report preparation, and the performance of any follow-up evaluation or testing work that may be needed must be completed within the time period allotted. Finally, when the buyer is convinced that they possess a good understanding of the property, and the negotiations are fruitful, the transaction can be finalized and executed.

5.4.2 When a PCA Should Occur

As indicated above, the initial series of limited surveys produce a list of acceptable properties for acquisition. These limited surveys are sometimes referred to as "windshield surveys," denoting the relative depth of this type of evaluation, which might require nothing more than a drive-by review to observe the facility while remaining behind the windshield. In reality, most investors do perform a cursory review of the property at this stage, but in-depth evaluation is not conducted until later.

Once the acquisition process has moved into the negotiation and due diligence phase, it is time for the typical building assessment. Ideally, this phase allows enough time to thoroughly evaluate the property. As a rule of thumb, the field observer requires approximately one day per 50,000 square feet reviewed. Adequate access to the facility should then be arranged. If there is a need for further evaluation, it is also performed within the original due diligence period. The majority of the deficiencies identified in acquisition surveys relate to the roofing, HVAC, building envelope, site, and interior systems.

As with many facility-related issues, it often seems that the time allocated to conduct a thorough and comprehensive survey is less than adequate. This needs to be taken into account when designing and agreeing to a time schedule, as well as in selecting the survey assessor(s).

In the current state of the real estate market, the need for comprehensive acquisition evaluations and improved communication in the evaluation process have increased. During the due diligence period, it is becoming commonplace for daily communication to occur between the investor's representative and the assessor. Significant issues identified by the field observer are then discussed immediately with the buyer instead of simply waiting to present the issues in the report. This ensures that any additional testing and analysis will be performed within the agreed time schedule.

5.4.3 The Limitations of Acquisition Studies

In nearly all evaluations, no matter how comprehensive, some minor issues are missed. Due to the intricacy and interrelationship of the systems, there may be issues which could never be addressed in an evaluation performed by an individual or a team of engineers over a time period of just a few weeks. Some issues will only be noticed during ongoing observation in everyday situations.

A competent building survey, performed by a professional, should identify all significant building system deficiencies. In some facilities, minor issues, such as a non-working electrical receptacle or light fixture may be missed, but because of their relatively insignificant nature, this will not impact the value or benefits of the evaluation.

5.4.4 Effects of Current Real Estate Climate on Assessments

It has become obvious that the consistently healthy real estate market and funding availability of the 1980s has changed dramatically. With this change, building assessments have shifted in methodology and emphasis for the real estate investor. While many investors have diversified by region, property type and investment structure, the returns realized in the late 1970s through the 1980s have not continued. The majority of experts argue that while development in many markets has exceeded demand, the most significant factor impacting the real estate market of the 1990s is the decreased availability of capital.

Given the condition of the real estate market and financing availability, PCA evaluations have become even more useful for owners and investors. Owners are looking toward utilizing the facilities they already have as efficiently as possible in order to postpone purchasing or constructing a new facility.

The changes in the real estate field have brought about shifts in real estate transaction assessments. Transactions are more closely scrutinized, with increased depth and caution required in evaluations. During the early 1980s acquisition evaluations were performed only on significant transactions, and the scope often consisted of a general review of the existing conditions at the property. In the 1990s, comprehensive assessments in real estate transaction became commonplace, with the emphasis placed on engineering and environmental issues, operating and tenant improvement costs, and on future capital improvement costs. Assessments concentrated more on how the property would perform during the entire investment cycle.

The current trend of pension fund investors moving away from traditional office, retail, and industrial property investment and toward apartment and other specialty properties is expected to continue. With that trend, evaluations will adjust from standard "boilerplate" reviews to property-specific studies. More interaction and communication between the investor and the PCA assessor will be required. More conservative evaluation techniques, including destructive testing and analysis, will be performed to ensure increased security in the investment.

5.5 TYPES OF ASSESSMENTS

Building systems evaluations identify and quantify existing conditions and provide a framework for future facilities management. The type of assessment, whether for acquisition or for establishing a preventive maintenance program, impacts the time required to conduct it. The more in-depth and comprehensive the evaluation, the more time needs to be allocated. In Figure 5.1, we see the many reasons why real estate owners and investors find it advantageous to perform systems evaluations. Depending on the reasons, building assessments can range dramatically in scope and depth from single system reviews of the electrical or roofing system for example, to comprehensive evaluations of each building system. The level of depth in the evaluation of each system may range from a simple cursory survey performed during a brief visit to the property, to extensive documentation review, field investigation, testing, and laboratory analysis. Evaluations can consist of destructive or non-destructive testing of system components and equipment, which is discussed in Chapter 6. In an adequately planned evaluation, the reasons for the evaluation, as well as its scope and depth, are identified and implemented in such a way as to provide the maximum results to the owner, manager, or investor.

Of note, visual inspections are not really suitable to detect and quantify deterioration at an early stage, as visual symptoms are usually not yet observable. More advanced techniques, preferably non-destructive ones, must be applied. Assessors and field observers are usually expected to be able to predict the future development of the facility's condition using their expert knowledge and personal experience.

The level of effort expended in a survey is usually correlated to the monetary or public relations investment in a property. If the public works department is acquiring a storage shed on the outskirts of town, an extensive review of the property is not necessary. But if the property is a downtown high-rise housing corporate offices, or will cost in excess of say, $50 million to acquire, an in-depth evaluation is warranted.

CHAPTER

6

Elements of Property Condition Evaluations

6.1 TYPES OF EVALUATIONS

Evaluations can be designed in a great variety of ways. They can involve all major building systems or simply one or two. Evaluations can be limited, cursory reviews or comprehensive examinations based on test documentation and laboratory analysis. They may include nondestructive testing, hazardous material review, or a building code compliance review.

The scope is determined by several factors. The intended result of the evaluation needs to be identified, and the evaluation designed accordingly. If the evaluation is to be used in a real estate transaction, the scope and emphasis will be different from an annual resurvey evaluation for a property manager. An evaluation of a specific property deficiency, such as damaged paving, will be designed differently than a review of existing conditions to establish a Preventive Maintenance program.

6.1.1 Variations of Scope in Evaluations

Facilities can generally be reviewed in three accepted levels of detail, as illustrated in Figure 6.1A. Of these, the single system and comprehensive evaluations are the most common.

Single system evaluations typically consist of a review of a single system. Such surveys are predominantly performed for the roofing, HVAC, or structural systems. These surveys are cost-effective and very useful if there is only one issue of concern or deficiencies involving only one system at a facility. For example, a single system evaluation would be performed in a building that is experiencing cracks, waterproofing problems or is having difficulty providing adequate ventilation. However, because building systems are typically interactive in nature, a deficiency in one system can at some point impact the other systems.

Multiple system surveys include more than one system and normally three or four. This type of evaluation is cost effective, with only the systems with known deficiencies being surveyed. While this type of evaluation is more focused and specifically directed to the systems with known deficiencies, an obvious limitation is that systems that may contain deficiencies which are not apparent from a walk-through survey may be missed.

Comprehensive evaluations include a review of the total facility and all its systems from the site to the floor slab to the roofing system. The cost is typically more expensive than the two previous types of evaluation due to the extra expertise and time necessary to adequately evaluate the systems. The higher cost is balanced by the value of determining the existing condition of the facility in its entirety. The advantage of an adequately performed comprehensive evaluation is that the owner or potential purchaser is not faced with any operational or budgetary surprises later on.

6.1.2 Levels of Effort in Evaluations

The type of survey will determine the level of effort involved, which can range anywhere from cursory standard walk-through survey to a very detailed comprehensive one. For most real estate transactions, a standard survey of a property is adequate to ascertain its overall condition and quality. In other cases, a client may request a comprehensive inspection of a particular system or of the complete facility. Figure 6.1B illustrates the three levels of depth in an evaluation survey process.

The main element of a standard survey is the scoping, which constitutes the minimal level of effort performed in an evaluation. When a facility has severe deficiencies, these will most likely be identified during this limited survey. This type of limited review is typically employed in the case of a real estate transaction of small and medium-sized properties. Also, with a building owner operating a large number of facilities, it is useful to do a series of scopings to determine the overall status of the building portfolio. In this way, the buildings requiring additional evaluation or more comprehensive investigation can be addressed specifically, saving both time and money.

The depth of an evaluation can vary to meet the needs of the client. Time can be taken to survey and evaluate each and every piece of equipment and machinery. Tests and analytical readings can be performed to gather detailed information, from material chemical composition to precise moisture content or capacity determinations.

The client and consultant should consider several factors before deciding which level of effort may be appropriate for a given evaluation. The scope and level of effort directly impacts the cost of the evaluation. The schedule and required capabilities of the assessor or evaluation team must also be considered. Lastly, it is very important to know and identify the purpose of the collected information, i.e., how the information is to be used.

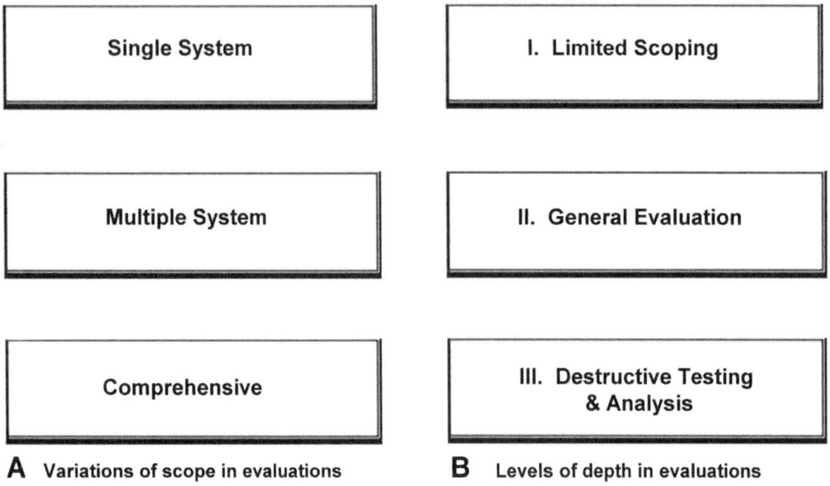

Figure 6.1 A. Scope variations in Property Condition Assessments. B. Levels of depth in Property Condition Assessments.

6.2 TYPES OF TESTING: DESTRUCTIVE VS. NONDESTRUCTIVE

Building evaluations can utilize either destructive or nondestructive testing, or both. In destructive testing, the building material or construction conditions are modified and/or damaged during the investigative process. Concrete core sampling or removing portions of walls that conceal building components to be evaluated are examples of destructive testing. This method is typically more costly than nondestructive testing, but the cost brings with it additional assurance that the building is being comprehensively investigated. Destructive testing is not normally necessary unless an initial evaluation has identified a deficiency requiring further investigation, confirmation, and analysis.

6.2.1 Nondestructive Testing (NDT)

Testing that does not destroy the test object is also sometimes called *nondestructive evaluation* (NDE) or *nondestructive inspection* (NDI). NDE is vital for constructing and maintaining all types of a facility's components and structures. To detect different defects, such as cracking and corrosion, there are numerous methods of testing available, such as X-ray scanning (where cracks show up on the film) and ultrasound (where cracks show up as an echo blip on the screen). Other techniques are also available to measure surface displacements, crack propagation or simply to detect the presence of defects or deficiencies, such as moisture penetration. These techniques include acoustic emission, electrical strain gauging and optical techniques.

The majority of evaluations consist primarily of nondestructive testing in which the building and its components are not damaged during the evaluation. In this type of evaluation, building components concealed or rendered inaccessible by the building construction are not typically evaluated. While it may seem as though the building and its systems would not be sufficiently investigated unless destructive testing is employed, experience has shown that in most cases the condition of a building can be ascertained accurately by careful, nondestructive testing and/or visual observation. Some of the conventional techniques employed include the following:

Ultrasound is one of the most commonly used techniques for NDT. A transducer coupled to a test object emits ultrasonic pulses in a frequency range of 1 MHz to 20 MHz. The pulses travel though the object and are either reflected, diffracted or refracted by defects or discontinuities in the material. A receiver detects the pulses on the other side of the material or, more typically, the returning echo signal. The loss in signal amplitude is then used to determine the existence of a defect and its size. The advantages of this technique include its ability to detect deep sub-surface defects, which cannot be detected by other NDT techniques. However, its disadvantages include complex image analysis and the fact that the ultrasound transducer generally needs to be in direct contact with the test object or must have a suitable coupling medium, such as water, between it and the object's surface.

Infrared building envelope and electrical-mechanical analysis is another well-proven nondestructive method for troubleshooting building heat loss and moisture problems. Heat losses from buildings are accelerated by structural problems, poor construction practices, missing or inadequate insulation, moisture infiltration, and air leakage. Escaping heat creates a thermal signature that can be detected with infrared thermography. Building envelope analysis uses thermography to pinpoint underlying problems in a building. From the collected data, the field observer produces a report detailing location, causes, and extent of the problems within the building envelope.

Because thermography consists of a non-contact, nondestructive testing method, production need not be interrupted, nor is there a need for a costly shutdown. Moreover, infrared detection technology allows accurate detection of thermal anomalies that can threaten the safety and reliability of a facility's electrical and mechanical systems, in which excessive heat is a sign of impending problems and potential failures. These failures often elude visual and manual inspections in addition to being costly and time-consuming.

Acoustic Emission Testing (AT) is a nondestructive testing method capable of detecting and locating faults in mechanically loaded structures, components, and specimens. AT provides comprehensive information on the origin of faults in a loaded object and the development of the fault as a function of load. Loading can be mechanical, thermal, or chemical. When subjected to stress, many materials will emit acoustic waves arising from energy released as the material undergoes plastic deformation and fracture. These acoustic waves propagate through the material to the surface where they are detected using high sensitivity piezoelectric materials. The technique is commonly applied in the study of fatigue and crack propagation.

Acoustic Emission (AE) occurs when defects in metals, plastics and other materials cause them to rapidly release energy when subjected to mechanical loading. The energy propagates in the form of high-frequency stress waves. AE sensors on the surface of the specimen detect these types of oscillations and convert them to electrical signals, called bursts. The AE analysis is the characterization of the bursts according to intensity and frequency content. Analyzing bursts from several sensors at well-placed positions on the test object allows inspectors to determine the location of the AE source(s) on the test object.

Acoustic Emission (AE) analysis is an extremely powerful technology that can be deployed within a wide range of usable applications of nondestructive testing such as metal pressure vessels, piping systems, reactors, and similar systems. AE differs from ultrasonic testing, which actively probes the structure; it listens for emissions from active defects and is very sensitive to defect activity when a structure is loaded beyond its service load in a proof test. One of the advantages compared to other NDE techniques is the opportunity to observe damage processes during the entire load history without any disturbance to the specimen.

The disadvantage of AE analysis is that commercial AE systems can only estimate qualitatively how much damage is in the material and approximately how long the components will last. Other NDE methods are still needed to do more thorough examinations and to provide quantitative results. Nevertheless, because the physical process of acoustic emission occurs in a wide variety of materials and under a large range of loading conditions, the technique offers great potential for use as a continuous monitoring technique.

X-Ray scanning has until recently been better known for biological applications than as an NDT technique for materials testing. However, because X-Rays have a high penetrating power, they are useful for examining the majority of structural types. The rays pass through the specimen and are detected at the other side, usually by photographic film. As in biological applications, the developed film shows areas where attenuation is lowest as darker regions. The differences in intensity will be caused by differences in thickness and density of the object. In this way subsurface defects are easily recognizable. The obvious disadvantage of this technique is the dangerous effects the radiation can have on biological tissue. The interpretation of the developed film also demands both experience and skill.

Electrical transducers: Measurement of the deformations under loading conditions is usually obtained in mechanical tests by means of strain gauges applied directly to the object, or by displacement transducers connected at points of interest. Variations in length cause changes in resistance of the strain gauge material, which can be measured using a suitable circuitry to give accurate measurements of strain. However, both of these methods provide values averaged over the evaluated area only, and it is often not possible to assume with certainty that the presence of a gauge does not affect the measurements.

Optical NDT methods have high sensitivity and they allow a full-field analysis of the inspected area without any need for physical contact with the surface. They can sometimes provide additional information where the other techniques fail or cannot be applied. For example, in the analysis of building materials it is possible to obtain information about the displacement distribution over the whole surface. Therefore, the strain distribution and crack formation and propagation in structures can be easily observed. The main *op-*

tical interferometric techniques for measuring deformations are *photoelasticity, moir methods, holographic interferometry* and *speckle techniques.*

Visual testing is extremely important and is often the only form of nondestructive testing (NDT) used on some specimens. Moreover, in some areas it can account for a significant percentage of the testing conducted. The main point of visual testing is that the field observer must be able to view the surface being tested.

Sometimes, a visual review of the specimen is insufficient. A number of physical or mechanical aids may be required to determine if the specimen is correct. Tape measures or rules, calipers, microthickness gauges, squares or angle measurement devices, levels and plumb lines, thread gauges and a variety of weld gauges may be needed to assist the field observer in determining the "fitness for use" of a specimen. Without some of these simple mechanical aids, the test might prove to be inadequate or incorrect.

6.2.2 Nondestructive Testing Equipment

Break-off tester: This measures the in-situ strength of concrete. The test involves casting cylindrical plastic forms into the fresh concrete. The break-off tester can also be used for other purposes, including control of concrete strength, checking strength against specification, measurement of strength development in prestressed concrete, assessment of concrete strength in existing structures, and control of curing (Figure 6.2A).

Pipe and cable fault locator: This device is designed for detecting and accurately locating buried metal pipes and cables. It detects and traces metallic objects using the receiver to sense the transmitter signal which is coupled to the object to be traced. It is used in various applications, including locating discrete metallic objects, tracing of pipes and cables, determining depth of pipes and cables, and tracing wires in a building.

Concrete test hammer: This tool which is also called a *rebound hammer,* is often used for quick measurement of the quality and compressive strength of concrete. It meets the testing standard ASTMC805 and BS1881 (Figure 6.2B).

Rebar locator, profometer and covermeter: These tools consist of electromagnetic cover devices used to determine the position and direction of reinforcement bars. These instruments give precise measurements of the concrete cover and estimation of rebar diameter.

Crack measuring microscope, digital X-Ray microscope: These microscopes are specially designed to measure crack width in concrete; they are high definition microscopes that operate via an adjustable light source provided by high-power batteries (Figure 6.2C).

Pull-off test and limpet: This test is used to determine the bond strength of a wide variety of materials, including concrete, screeds, repair mortar, and epoxy resin coating. It is also used sometimes to measure the strength of the adhesive applied.

Borescope with cold light supply and camera: These are precision instruments that come in a variety of models and are used to inspect cracks in narrow and dark places. Flexible borescopes are ideal for inspecting complex parts and castings where the view is not straight ahead. Operators can expand the benefits of borescope video inspection through specialized software on the market (Figure 6.2D).

Ultrasonic pulse velocity tester: An ultrasonic device commonly used for crack and void detection, measurement of layer thickness and elastic modulus, uniformity, and deterioration of concrete. The unit, which may be operated from the main electrical supply or via an internal battery, generates low frequency pulses and measures the time required for the pulses to pass between the two transducers placed at the ends of the specimen being tested. It meets the testing standards ASTMC597 and BS1881: Part 203 (Figure 6.2E).

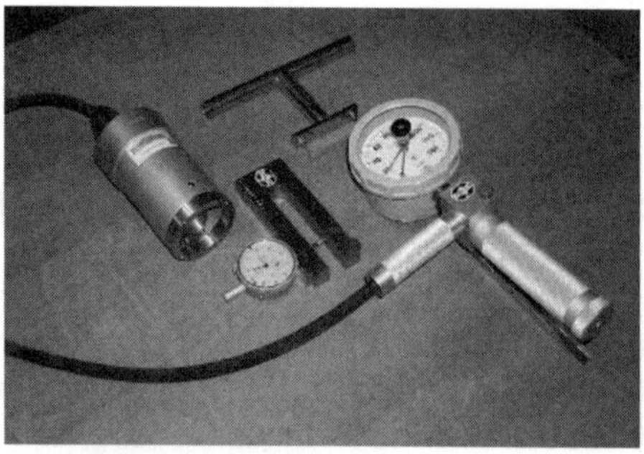

a. Break-Off Tester

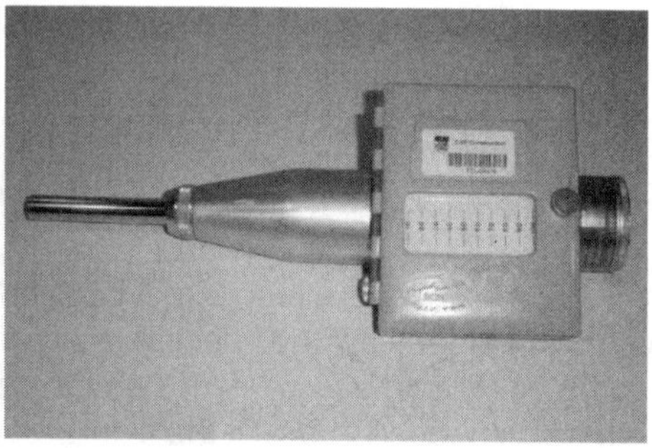

b. Concrete Test Hammer

c. Crackwidth Microscope

d. Borescope

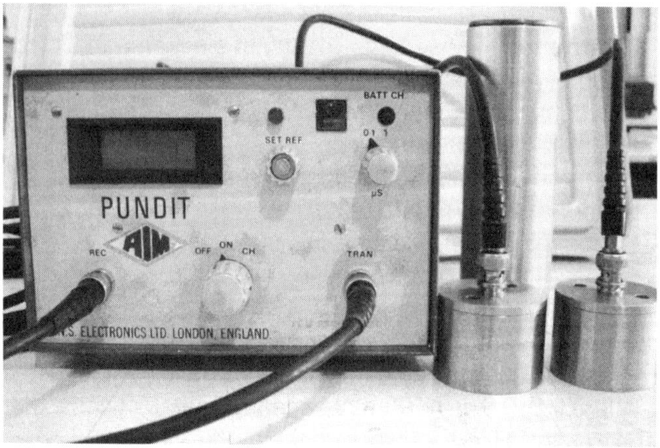

Ultrasonic Pulse Velocity Tester

Figure 6.2 Various types of NDT instruments: A. Break-off tester. B. Concrete test hammer. C. Crack measuring microscope—digital X-Ray microscope. D. Borescope with cold light supply and camera. E. Ultrasonic pulse velocity tester.

6.2.3 Destructive Testing

Figure 6.3 A Universal Testing System (UTS) for destructive testing.

From time to time, based on observations during the walk-through survey, the field observer may find it necessary to recommend a more detailed examination of an element or component by actually changing its condition in some manner. When the examination goes beyond mere observation and risks or entails changing the condition or appearance of the element, special considerations arise and the testing is referred to as *destructive testing.*

Destructive testing can cover a spectrum of activities ranging from merely changing a product's position to actually cutting or extracting a sample or component in order to subject it to analysis beyond the visual. While the spectrum of activity is broad, the words "destructive testing" often connote some analysis that subjects a portion of the element or component to stresses, forces, or chemical influences to better reveal the condition or cause of failure.

Destructive testing usually provides a more reliable assessment of the state of the test object, but destruction of the test object usually makes this type of test more costly to the test object's owner than nondestructive testing. Destructive testing is also inappropriate in many circumstances, such as in forensic investigation. That there is a tradeoff between the cost of the test and its reliability favors a strategy in which most test objects are inspected nondestructively. In destructive testing, characteristics of a given part, such as tensile strength, impact strength, or burst pressure of a vessel are measured as the part is destroyed, and once a measurement is taken for a particular part, that part ceases to be available for additional measurements (Figure 6.3).

6.3 FORMULATING A PREVENTIVE MAINTENANCE PROGRAM

For standard facility surveys that include buildings and assets, planned maintenance is a mandatory process for the longevity of the asset. In some assessments, a Preventive Maintenance (PM) program is established, the goal of which is to control and reduce repair and replacement costs by providing a scheduled program of inspections, repairs, and maintenance. The PM program should take advantage of the facility owner's maintenance operations, whether centralized or decentralized. By working with facility maintenance representatives, the evaluation team should establish short-term and long-term goals and priorities that will enable the facility to avoid costly breakdowns and emergency repairs. Historical policies and preferences should be researched and organized. Existing and projected staffing levels should be reviewed periodically to develop long-range staffing and efficiency goals.

Applying industry standard processes for maintenance can improve the financial and operational performance of an asset. Effective budgeting for maintenance is mandatory these days to ensure the safety and usability of buildings.

By definition, *deferred maintenance* is maintenance, system upgrades, or repairs that are deferred to a future budget cycle or postponed until funding becomes available. In order to address a deferred maintenance backlog, the building owner, facility manager or housing association must do the following:

1. Identify why projects, maintenance, and repairs have been deferred: The primary reason that maintenance is deferred is because there simply isn't the money to pay for it. If budget planning does not allocate adequate funding, or the budget is cut mid-year, an increase in deferred maintenance is inevitable. Additionally, if maintenance would interrupt or interfere with business operations, or if allocated funding is diverted to pay for emergencies and more visible projects, the risk of equipment failure and building deterioration increases. Maintenance is also sometimes postponed due to lack of available labor, lack of personnel with the expertise to perform necessary maintenance, lack of necessary parts to conduct maintenance, or because major renovations that can address the necessary repairs and upgrades are planned for the near future.

2. Recognize and comprehend the scale of the problem: Understanding the extent of the backlog is crucial to minimizing the volume of deferred maintenance and substantiating the need for funding. A facility assessment (also called a facility audit) can help eliminate any unknowns and provide a clearer picture of the extent of the deferred maintenance problem. The survey should evaluate the building's condition, its code compliance, and the performance and age of all finishes, systems, and equipment. The result is a building inventory and list of necessary projects, repairs, and system upgrades for each facility. When conducting an assessment, consult with the facilities professionals that are most familiar with each building and its particular systems.

3. Quantify and communicate the financial impact of deferred maintenance: Unless you can calculate the consequences of deferred maintenance, your rationale for funding isn't likely to be very persuasive. The most convincing argument against deferring maintenance is one that includes the following:

- **Estimated risk potential:** As a result of deferred maintenance, will liability and safety hazards increase, tenant satisfaction and employee productivity decrease, or business operations be affected?
- **Subsequent escalation of costs:** Estimate escalation of costs for future expenses as a result of postponed maintenance.
- **Historical data:** To add credibility to your financial predictions, provide examples from the past that prove the significance of the long-term costs of deferred maintenance.

4. Prioritize projects and develop a strategy to secure adequate funding: Prioritize deferred maintenance projects if it is unlikely that sufficient funding will be provided immediately to address entire backlog in a one-year period. A set of criteria should be developed to facilitate prioritizing projects. One simple prioritization method may be:

- *Currently critical*—Projects that require immediate action to return facility to normal operation, to stop accelerated deterioration, or to correct a cited safety hazard
- *Potentially critical*—Projects that will become critical within 1 year if not corrected
- *Necessary, not yet critical*—Projects that require reasonably prompt attention to preclude predictable deterioration and higher costs if deferred further

Elements or projects with immediate health- and safety-related ramifications or business-continuity implications should be in the "currently critical" category. The ability to maintain the reliability of the building and its systems to support business needs must remain a priority.

Even the best preparation and presentation skills may not garner the required financing to complete all of the deferred maintenance projects classified as "potentially critical." Additional economic motivation can often be found. For instance, a project that reduces peak demand or increases energy efficiency may qualify for rebates offered by utility companies. There may also be grants to upgrade the efficiency of lighting or heating and cooling systems through local power authorities. Utilities may provide partial funding to have certain systems upgraded to improve energy efficiency and lower energy costs.

5. Conduct preventive maintenance and complete repairs promptly to avoid backlog redevelopment: Deferred maintenance tends to accumulate, even under the best circumstances. To prevent accumulation, an effective preventive maintenance program needs to be in place to minimize a facility's rate of decay and dysfunction. When the building owner understands the potential escalation of costs, obtaining adequate funds may be less difficult to obtain. By making the business case for funding and proactively managing maintenance every day, the owner is less likely to develop a deferred maintenance backlog that seems too overwhelming to overcome.

The PM program should include recommendations for capital improvements, identification of items for deferred maintenance and step-by-step implementation guidelines for establishment of the program. More specifically, the PM program should specify the location of each maintenance item, its type, tasks to be performed and frequency of maintenance, the cost for maintenance of each item, and the number of personnel hours required to conduct each maintenance item.

Preventive maintenance ensures that building equipment is appropriately installed and managed for the long term. For residential high-rise buildings, as well as other commercial and institutional facilities, predictive maintenance plays a key role in maintaining property value and reducing risk for the building owner. Whereas higher property value is often perceived as a result of attractive building appearance or amenities, the building systems behind the facade have the greatest impact on value.

Poor maintenance practices often result in equipment failure and expenses for the building owner, as well as inconvenience, discomfort, and unexpected costs to residents. Unless building equipment is maintained in accordance with manufacturers' specifications, warranties can become null and void, and a property's value can plummet. Moreover, because predictive maintenance keeps building systems in good condition, the equipment operates more efficiently and unnecessarily high utility costs are reduced. The life expectancy of the equipment also is extended, and expensive replacement costs can be deferred for longer periods of time.

The following are some general guidelines for developing an effective preventive maintenance program:

1. Install appropriate building equipment: The first step in preventing unnecessary breakdowns and maximizing a property's value is to specify the appropriate equipment to suit the building's needs.

2. Develop a predictive maintenance schedule: Developing a maintenance schedule that systematically checks a building's vital systems is a crucial step in reducing breakdowns and unnecessary repair costs.

Systems such as air-conditioning, water treatment, fire and life safety, plumbing, and electricity should all be regularly maintained in accordance with the manufacturers' guidelines. A typical checklist might include symptomatic conditions to look for, how often these items must be checked, and a location for an inspector's signature. Creating checklists for each piece of equipment is the simplest method of tracking maintenance and guarantees that the appropriate work is being performed in order to meet warranty requirements.

3. Document all maintenance: Record-keeping plays the most significant role in predictive maintenance and warranty management. Once inspection schedules have been created, it is imperative that the maintenance engineer document all work that is completed. Signed and dated reports specifying the exact work performed will be required by the manufacturer to validate a warranty.

4. Follow up: The maintenance records not only serve as recommendations for necessary repairs; they provide a reference for building owners to track maintenance and repair history, and also serve as evidence to the manufacturer that all necessary maintenance has been performed. Maintaining or increasing the value of a high-rise property depends on the operational capacity of its vital mechanical, electrical, and plumbing systems.

6.4 COMPLIANCE WITH BUILDING CODES

A building code is a set of rules that specifies the minimum acceptable level of safety for constructed objects, such as buildings and non-building structures, and is discussed in greater detail in Chapter 16. The main purpose of building codes is to protect public health, safety, and general welfare as they relate to the construction and occupancy of buildings.

Building codes are generally intended to be applied by architects and engineers, but are also used for various purposes by safety inspectors, real estate developers, contractors and subcontractors, manufacturers of building products and materials, insurance companies, facility managers, tenants, and other categories of users.

The inclusion of building code compliance issues is nearly always a source of debate when considering the scope of an evaluation. As the depth of code compliance review increases, the cost of the evaluation will increase accordingly. The jury is still out on the degree to which building code issues should be included in an evaluation. There are times when including building code review within the scope of an evaluation will simply hinder the process with too much unnecessary detail. Other times, the review of code issues can identify several facility construction areas that could drastically improve the facility operations and safety if corrected. However, as seen in the next section, code compliance issues represent the second largest category of lawsuits against due diligence firms in the US, which is why some major consultant firms have decided to omit this category from their PCA surveys.

Inclusion of code-related issues can vary in depth from a cursory review of the base code aspects for each system to a comprehensive review of detailed issues, such as structural nailing or plumbing fitting information. It is usually sufficient to include a cursory review of code-related issues, with the scope limited to significant safety violations or issues for which fines may be involved if discovered by regulatory officials. With no real increase in the cost or effort involved in the evaluation, these issues can usually be addressed by any competent evaluator.

6.5 CONSTRUCTION CLAIMS AND LITIGATION

Building projects are generally required to adhere to zoning and building code requirements. Projects that fail to do so can expose the design consultant to multimillion dollar litigation. Recently, the construction industry has had to deal with higher premiums for all types of insurance, but since September 11, those costs have skyrocketed beyond all expectations. Legal claims for building envelope failures continue to rise and are typically made against developers, contractors, property management corporations, architects, engineers, building trades, and government authorities (Figure 6.4).

According to Carl de Stefanis, President of Inspection & Valuation International, Inc. (IVI), a prominent construction consulting and due diligence firm, claims against firms providing property condition assess-

Resolution Process	Advantages	Disadvantages
Negotiation/ Assisted Negotiation	• Parties have control • Confidential	• No structure • Entrenched bargaining positions likely
Mediation	• Structured • Skilled mediator helps avoid entrenched positions • Control and resolution lies with parties • Helps maintain future commercial relationship for parties • Costs less than litigation • Quick result • Confidential	• No decision if parties do not agree • A resolution may not be reached
Arbitration	• Structured • Can be quick, timetable controlled by parties • Costs may be less than litigation • Confidential	• Parties do not have control • Imposed decision • May jeopardize future relationship of parties
Litigation (Court Action)	• Structured	• Timetable controlled by Court • Costs may be significant • Parties do not have control • Imposed decision • May jeopardize future relationship of parties • Long waiting times • Goes on public record (no confidentiality

Figure 6.4 The various types of dispute processes applied in litigation.

ments (PCA) is an increasing problem, and many of the plaintiffs are those claiming to be third-party beneficiaries of the work product. About 80 percent of the claims are building envelope related (roofs, EIFS, windows, masonry, etc.). The next largest category of claims against due diligence firms is building code related. Moreover, because of incessant liability concerns and the industry's skyrocketing insurance rates and deductibles, it is critical to establish the PCA's procedures, the standard of care to be exercised, and a limit of liability commensurate with the fee for services. The extent of due diligence exercised is a client decision, and is commensurate with the client's risk tolerance position. This is influenced by such factors as the intended period of hold, the client's position with respect to financial responsibility of physical deficiencies discovered after the transaction has closed, the equity investment, if any, and time and access constraints in conducting the PCA.

Many building surveying firms have also stopped using the words *engineering* and *architecture* in marketing or describing the services they offer, so that clients do not infer that they are receiving such professional services. Mainly, this measure is because the terms connote a higher standard of care to be exercised than simply conducting a walk-through survey in accordance with the ASTM E2018-01 "Standard Guide for Property Condition Assessments: Baseline Property Condition Assessment Process," the industry's most commonly used standard for real estate transactions. Furthermore, such firms cannot legally provide such services in most states under an S-corp or C-corp structure. Avoidance of the terms *engineering* or *architectural services* also extends to the use of professional designations by the service provider's proposal signer, the Property Condition Report's (PCR) preparer or field observer, and the PCR's reviewer.

Mold-related claims have become a primary concern for the insurance industry. Mold litigation has increased dramatically as have the number and size of water-related property claims. Many insurance companies are now grappling with how to address mold claims and many are excluding mold from their coverage entirely. The insurance industry is further responding by changing policy language, claims-handling procedures, and loss reserving, while trying to keep the regulators at bay.

Unfortunately, phrases and acronyms such as Indoor Air Quality (IAQ), Sick Building Syndrome (SBS) and Building Related Illness (BRI) are tossed around to the degree that building owners and managers just shrug them off. They do so even though recent studies indicate that the instances of commercial buildings with poor IAQ and the frequency of litigation over the effects of poor IAQ are increasing substantially. These increases have ramifications for insurance carriers, which pay for many of the costs of health care and general commercial liability.

The dramatic rise in building litigation has given an increased urgency for specialist lawyers, consultants, and experts. Experts are persons that have acquired special knowledge, skill, experience, training, and/or education beyond that of ordinary members of the public. Experts and consultants often play critically important roles in litigation and can significantly impact the outcome. The more important or complex the matter, the more likely it is that one or more experts will be involved for each side.

The role that experts play will vary depending on the case. Sometimes an expert will serve solely as a consultant to the lawyer, remaining in the background without his or her name ever being known to the other side. At other times an expert may be used in the pre-trial stages, perhaps to give an affidavit supporting issues pertinent to the case. In other cases the expert may serve solely as an expert witness at trial. Sometimes an expert will play a combination of these roles (Figure 6.5).

While there are no specific requirements to be an expert—this depends on the type of case and issues involved—there are certain criteria that most lawyers look for when choosing an expert or consultant. These criteria include:

- Previous experience as an expert witness or consultant to lawyers
- Specific knowledge of the subject
- Education, degrees, training and field experience
- Licensing and certification
- General compatibility
- Presentation skills

Experts are usually paid for their time and not their expertise. This involves not only their time on the witness stand, but the time they spend in evaluating matters, studying files or reviewing evidence, meeting with lawyers, coming to conclusions, and sitting around waiting to testify, and sometimes clearing their schedule to be available to testify. Some experts also charge for travel time. The expert's time on the witness stand is typically a small percentage of the expert's total fee. Many experts impose a minimum fee to prevent their taking on minor matters that generate more mental anguish than income. Most experts who testify are paid at rates comparable to the normal fees they earn from other assignments. If the amount is out of line, the judge or jury may conclude that the expert is being paid more than usual in an effort to "sway" his or her testimony.

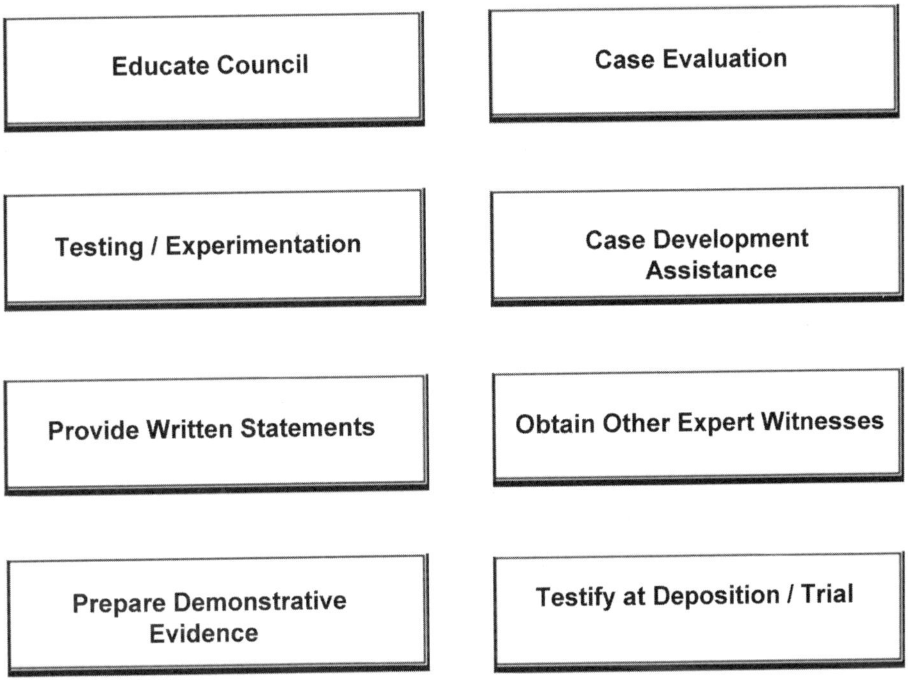

Figure 6.5 Examples of the type of work experts and consultants are sometimes required to perform in litigation cases.

Typical mistakes that experts sometimes make include:

- Failing to master the facts of the case in which they are employed
- Offering opinions that are outside their area of expertise
- Disregarding the opposing lawyers' and experts' view of the case
- Billing for work not previously authorized by the attorney or client
- Relying on a review of attorneys' deposition summaries instead of personally reading the whole deposition
- Allowing "ego" to impact a deposition or trial testimony
- Neglecting to tell their attorney about related prior testimony, affidavits, speeches or publications, job assignments or lawsuits, even if only remotely relevant

All claims have a statute of limitations. That means that if a plaintiff does not file suit within the appropriate period of time, that person loses his or her right to file. Generally, a civil action relating to building work cannot be brought against anyone after 10 years from the date of the work that caused the problem. This time limit is stipulated in the Building Act of 2004, section 393, and is called the statute of limitations for filing suit on latent defects. Latent defects are generally defined as those that are not discoverable by normal inspection.

CHAPTER

7

The Building Site

7.1 GENERAL

The site on which the facility is located includes some of the most important and diverse evaluation components. Several site issues, including paving, landscaping, and drainage, can be significant budget issues and should be reviewed carefully. The diversity of the site components is illustrated in Figure 7.1. The site system can be divided into three general divisions: the natural environment, site structures, and site infrastructure.

The natural environment, including soil, topography, and landscaping, is the most obvious site issue. The trees, groundcover and lawns of a facility site directly impact both the value and aesthetics of a property. Common deficiencies in the natural environment of the site include irrigation and drainage problems and dead or missing vegetation.

Site structures should also be evaluated when considering site issues. These structures include retaining and dividing walls, shacks, fountains and other building structures. Common deficiencies include general damage, deterioration and poor maintenance.

Identify the extent of the site systems and visually observe each system. Site assets that are not reportable as *constructed assets* are considered to be land elements. Adjoining assets should also be included in the report if part of a building or within the property boundary.

When walking the site the field observer should indicate condition of landscaping, lighting, parking surfaces, curbs, walks, drainage, retaining walls, and so on. Note any unusual site features such as wells, retention ponds, etc.

Lastly, the site infrastructure, which includes the irrigation system, lighting system, and traffic circulation patterns, should be considered when evaluating the quality and performance of the site. Infrastructure deficiencies include insufficient coverage, deterioration, and inconsistent usage.

7.2 COMPONENTS TO BE EVALUATED

Site Elements: Identify and observe the condition of site elements, such as sidewalks, plazas, patios, decks, retaining walls, irrigation systems, fountains, lighting, signage, ponds, and recreational facilities, and note any physical deficiencies.

7.2.1 Topography

The topography of the site should be observed and any unusual or problematic features or conditions noted.

7.2.2 Storm Water Drainage

Storm drains collect the site water and deliver it to the sewer system. The system includes a series of field drains built into paving or landscaping to remove water from the site surface. Identify and observe the condition of the storm water collection and drainage systems and note the presence of retention or detention basins, on-site surface waters, and retention or detention basins, and any other problems with the removal of storm water, such as evidence of ponding or clogging. Also note any evidence of poor or buried curbing and gutter systems. The system typically includes the following:

- **Trench drains:** Designed to remove surface water, usually constructed using a metal grated cover.
- **Culverts:** Used for storm water runoff, typically under roads or walkways. They are usually constructed of reinforced concrete pipe, corrugated metal, or plastic. Culverts should be in good condition and well-maintained. They should also be evaluated for sealant or joint deterioration.

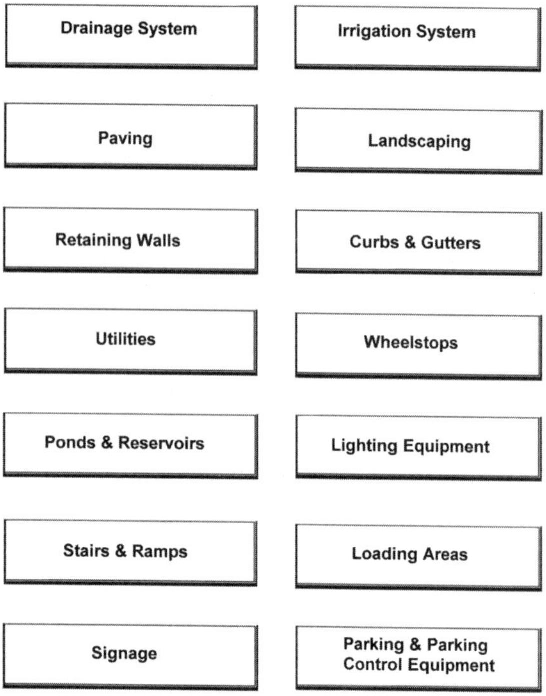

Figure 7.1 Typical components to be surveyed during a site evaluation.

7.2.3 Access and Egress

The site's main means of ingress and egress should be observed. Building codes require that exit passageways be provided for a building from every section of every floor to a public street or alley. When the rated number of occupants exceeds a certain number, additional exits are required.

7.2.4 Paving, Curbing, and Gutters

One of the most significant issues to review in a property is the condition of the paving systems. Paving is important for several reasons. Potential liability conditions can be created if the paving is damaged or deteriorated. Also, due to the large quantities of paving on most properties, the paving quality directly impacts the perceived quality of the entire property.

Paving systems include both vehicular surfaces and pedestrian surfaces. Vehicular surfaces include driveways, parking, and loading areas. Pedestrian surfaces include patios, sidewalks, and other walkways. The paving at a site most often comprises a variety of materials. The most common of these are concrete, asphaltic concrete, and precast pavers.

The paving system may range in condition from very deteriorated to excellent (Figure 7.2). When deteriorated, the paving exhibits several defects, as shown in Figure 7.3. One issue to keep in mind during the survey of paving systems is whether there has been extensive patching and repair work. Such work could indicate a likelihood of substantial problems in the future. If slurry seal work has been performed, inspection should determine whether the work has addressed and handled system deficiencies or simply consists of a cosmetic improvement.

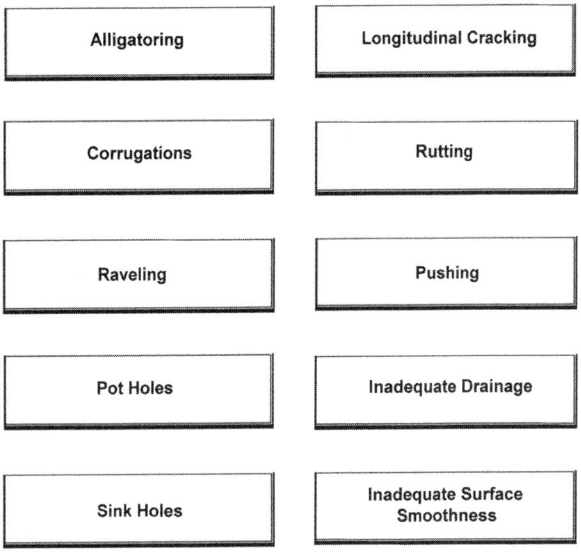

Figure 7.2 Typical paving system defects.

The make-up of the paving section includes the condition and type of the subsoil, base layer, interim layer and top layer. In properties where significant paving deficiencies are found, the paving section can be identified and analyzed by performing a core test (which is not in the normal scope of a standard PCA). A core of two to four inches in diameter is taken at various locations around the site. The depth of the test may range from six to sixty inches, depending on the paving section and the intended test result.

Paving evaluation should assess type, location and general condition, evidence of cracking, sink holes, or other areas of settlement. The field observer will also look for evidence of ponding, extensive remedial patching, spalling, etc. The joint seals should be in good condition. There should also be adequate control joints and drainage.

Figure 7.3 Example of paving defects found in a small shopping center, showing a lack of proper maintenance.

Curbing: Curbs adjacent to pedestrian or vehicular areas include poured-in-place or extruded concrete or asphalt. Curbs should be checked for their general condition, and for cracking or other damage.

Gutters: Similar to curbs, gutters are typically poured-in-place or extruded concrete or asphalt. Gutters should be in good condition, well maintained and not clogged or buried.

7.2.5 Parking

On-site parking should be provided to meet current design standards. The number of spaces provided for disabled drivers should meet ADA requirements (Figures 7.4A, B, 7.5).

Parking space count and parking zoning requirement review: Using a combination of re-

Figure 7.4 A. General parking lot behind typical shopping strip in Bethesda, Maryland. B. Typical handicap parking in front of office building.

viewing site surveys and field counting, the field observer should identify and record the existing number of available parking spaces (including ADA parking). Review zoning requirements and compare to actual number of spaces.

Parking Space Count:

a. Compact spaces
b. Regular spaces
c. Spaces for disabled Americans
d. Van-accessible spaces for disabled Americans

Parking Zoning Requirements:

a. Estimate the various square footages (from rent rolls or floor plans) of each occupancy type currently built out; calculate the required parking spaces; compare with actual number of spaces.
b. Consider vacant and occupied space and indicate whether parking limitations may impact amount and type of occupancy in the remaining space to be leased.

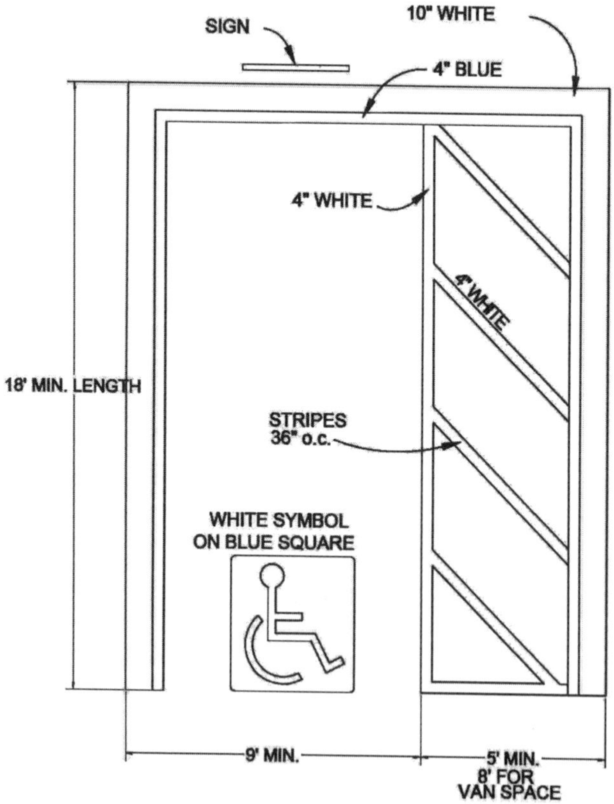

Figure 7.5 Drawing of ADA-compliant parking space.

c. In non-office type zones, check for zoning regulations that might set a maximum percentage of office use vs. warehouse or manufacturing use.

Parking control equipment: This equipment includes the control gate and arms, ticket dispensers, and attendant booths. The equipment should be evaluated for its type and general condition and whether it is operating satisfactorily. It is also important to ensure that the equipment is well maintained and that adequate and visible signage is in place.

7.2.6 Utilities

Because site utilities are often not directly accessible, field observers must rely on the questionnaire and interview to indicate potential issues. Assessors should therefore seek to gather information about hidden utilities by performing interviews with site personnel and reviewing relevant available records. Visual observations are generally limited to directly observable components. Examples may include water systems, wastewater treatment systems, power generation systems, gas supply pipelines, telecommunications lines, etc. Utilities and components that are the responsibility of utility companies should be excluded. Review and note operating costs against age and use of the systems. Assessors should not access concealed spaces, such as underground services, manholes, or utility pits.

Note visual signs of distress, and document deficiencies or deterioration of utilities. Deficiencies may include visible physical deterioration, leakage, obvious non-compliance with codes, or other visible evidence that may indicate a hidden condition. Update equipment inventories and estimate take-off quantities using either estimates taken on site or review of available drawings to determine the costs of replacement or repairs necessary to correct deficiencies. Identify issues that may require more detailed evaluations or testing.

Identify and document the type and provider of the utilities provided to each property (water, electricity, natural gas, oil, telephones, steam, and storm and sanitary drainage). Identify the presence of any on-site utility systems, such as water or wastewater treatment systems and special power generation systems. Where applicable and available through document research, identify system type, manufacturer, system size/capacity, age, and maintenance history to determine remaining useful life. Assessors shall not perform demolition, nondestructive or destructive testing or uncovering of any existing finishes, systems, or components to gain access to hidden conditions. Operating any systems or accessing manholes or utility pits, either in person or using remote-controlled equipment, is not required.

7.2.7 Irrigation Systems

The irrigation system includes the components necessary to deliver water to the landscaping. Sprinklers include both automatic and manually controlled systems. Attention should be paid to the condition of the landscaping during the review of the irrigation system. The field observer should check for the presence of a backflow preventer and for evidence of leaks or exposed lines.

7.2.8 Landscaping

The landscaping system includes planting and soil conditions. The planting on a site usually consists of a combination of turf, trees and shrubs. The field observer should note for evidence of overwatering, underwatering, and poor drainage. Likewise, the Assessor should check whether the site is well-maintained (or if there are dead, dry, or vacant areas), or whether the land slopes towards the building.

7.2.9 Stairs and Ramps

If a site has a change of topography, or if the building is at a different elevation than the surrounding property, stairs and ramps are typically employed. These stairs and ramps should be evaluated for safety, operational efficiency and handicap accessibility. In addition to the general condition of stairs and ramps, the field observer should check for evidence of tread wear or unsafe conditions, railing damage, cracking, or other damage (Figure 7.6).

7.2.10 Loading Areas

Truck docks and other loading areas should be assessed during the site review. In addition to their general condition, loading areas should be checked for damaged walls, platforms, or doors and for missing bumpers and guards (Figure 7.7).

7.2.11 Signage and Light Bases

Exterior signage, lighting, and the accompanying equipment should be reviewed during the site evaluation. The review of signage is especially important in acquisition studies, because of its effect on the marketability of a property. Signage should be consistent, well-designed and have good visibility. The sign and light bases are typically of wood, metal or concrete. Equipment should be well maintained and evaluated for signs of vandalism, damage, rusting, etc.

Figure 7.6 Photo of stairs built into retaining walls inset between sidewalls.

7.2.12 Ponds and Reservoirs

Evaluations should include a review of any ponds, reservoirs, or other bodies of water that exist on the site. Location, depth, and approximate surface area square footage should be recorded. Indication should also be made as to the primary function of the water. The pond or reservoir may be in place for cosmetic purposes or for water retention or overflow containment. The field observer should take notes on whether the system is natural or manmade and whether there is a PVC or other type of waterproofing or filtering system in place. Railings or other types of pedestrian protection should be in place. Ponds and reservoirs should be checked for evidence of flooding or soil saturation surrounding the area (Figure 7.8).

Figure 7.7 Photo of typical loading bay behind shop.

Figure 7.8 Artificial lake adjoining Trinity Center Office Complex in Centreville, Virginia.

7.3 SYSTEM DIAGNOSTICS

System diagnostics for the building site are very diverse. Unlike some other building systems, the site is comprised of several very different types of subsystems. The site evaluation, including planting, irrigation, paving and structural amenities, requires a wide range of expertise. In some facilities, the site evaluation will take as long as the building evaluation.

The evaluation of the site should be started at one location and thoroughly and systematically conducted. Depending on the size or complexity of the site, it is often more effective to assess the subsystems or components one at a time. For example, it may be more efficient to assess all areas of asphalt vehicular paving and curb areas, than all the concrete walkways and the paved areas. The measurements of damaged areas should be taken using one of any commercially available rolling measuring wheels. After the paving assessment, it may be useful to review the landscaping in conjunction with the irrigation. This approach typically makes the complexity of the site more understandable and the issues for review more digestible. In this way, there is less chance that an issue in any subsystem will be omitted.

With this methodology, the paperwork for each subsystem can be completed and any system deficiencies diagnosed fully prior to moving to the next component. This is the preferred method for complex sites or groups of site subsystems, but is unnecessarily time consuming in sites that are simple and/or in very good condition.

With simpler building sites, the components of the property should be evaluated simultaneously during the field investigation walk through. In less complex sites and sites in good condition with relatively few deficiencies to be addressed, this method will save time. General notes and specific condition and equipment identification can be produced during the walk through.

CHAPTER

8

Structural Systems

8.1 GENERAL

The structural system is intended to enable the building to resist any and all forces placed upon it. These loads include those of the building's equipment, materials and users, as well as earthquake and wind forces. There are a multitude of types of different structural systems used today in new buildings and they are made of countless materials, including concrete, steel, and wood predominant among them.

Most tall buildings constructed today extend one or several floors below grade level. These below-grade areas provide functional space for uses such as storage, parking, office space, mechanical/electrical rooms, etc. While below-grade areas in buildings provide important critical functions for the building, the subject of below-grade building enclosure systems is seldom understood or analyzed. Acceptance of poor performance of the below-grade building enclosure is typical and historically not questioned. Leaking into basement areas is a common problem for building operators and managers. Air quality, radon presence, and air conditioning in terms of humidity levels are typical areas of concern.

Durability of design and materials is mandatory with below-grade enclosure systems. Unlike some other building components that might be designed to be replaced several times within the overall building service life, below-grade systems need to be built to approximate overall service life. Below-grade systems are often inaccessible for repairs and extremely costly if repairs or modifications are necessary. For the design and materials of below-grade enclosure systems, property owners/investors must not focus on the first initial cost, but should consider the life cycle costs of various design options.

8.2 BUILDING STRUCTURAL TYPES

A structural or engineering survey is above all an opinion as to the structural condition and integrity of the building. The survey establishes the opinion of the engineer in terms of the following:

1. Were the structural elements (foundation, framing roofing, interior and exterior wall, special conditions, etc.) designed and built to accept the anticipated loads to be placed upon them?

2. Are these elements continuing to perform their intended function?

The ability to render such an opinion is fundamental to the success of the structural survey. In many states, such as New Jersey, only a registered Professional Engineer is permitted to render an opinion as to the structural integrity of a building.

Steel frame system: In resisting lateral forces, steel frame systems can be rigid, non rigid or ductile. They are designed to predictably address, resist, and evenly distribute all forces. Used extensively in high-rise construction, steel frame systems can be erected more quickly than concrete. The beams and columns in steel frame construction are fastened together by rivets, bolts or welds. Decking materials used with steel frame systems typically include either steel or concrete, or a combination of the two. In many buildings, steel members are typically fireproofed through the use of spray-applied material, gypsum materials, or concrete. Steel frame systems should be evaluated for their general condition, including corrosion, bowing, deformation and any alignment inconsistencies. The system's ability to resist lateral loads should also be checked as well as the design strength of the rigid frame.

Concrete frame system: Concrete frame systems are fairly common in buildings. The system can comprise both precast and cast-in-place members. Less expensive than steel frame systems and stronger than wood frame construction, concrete is fireproof. The system should be observed for deformation, bowing, alignment inconsistencies, and the condition of expansion joints, as well as areas of exposed rebar, spalling, delamination, or discoloration. The assessor should ensure that the members have been designed to adequately resist lateral loads.

Wood frame system: Wood framing is used mostly in low-rise construction and can be constructed more easily than either steel or concrete systems. These framing systems include light wood, heavy timber and glue-laminated members. Plywood is typically used for the horizontal and vertical diaphragms. The assessor should look for dry rot and termite damage as well as possible delamination of members and evidence of cracking or splitting.

Steel joists and truss floor construction: Open web steel joists are typically welded to the steel beams and attached to bearing walls using masonry anchors or preset embedded plates. Metal deck systems are then connected to the joists and trusses. Concrete decks are also utilized. The Field Observer should check for evidence of buckling, cracking or deteriorated welds, and signs of corrosion. Also the assessor should look for possible loose, damaged, or missing bolt connections.

Concrete slab floor construction: This system includes poured-in-place waffle and flat slabs of steel-reinforced concrete as well as precast, pre-stressed members, planking and single and double "T" beams. The main deficiencies to look for include cracks, spalling, or discoloration, and whether the expansion joints are in satisfactory condition. In typical office environments, the concrete floor slab itself is composed of 4 to 6 inch thick concrete reinforced with one layer of welded wire fabric at mid depth.

Wood joists and truss floor construction: Wood joists and trusses are used in smaller buildings and many old buildings, and often are used in conjunction with wood decking systems. Such systems are used extensively in warehouses, hangars and supermarkets. The main issues to look for are dry rot and termite damage, evidence of cracking or splitting, evidence of water damage, and evidence of delamination of members.

8.3 STRUCTURAL ELEMENTS

This section should be read in conjunction with the relevant sections of Chapter 14 and Chapter 15.

8.3.1 Below-grade Elements

Below grade enclosures typically comprise three main elements (Figure 8.1):

1. Foundations and foundation walls
2. Floor slabs
3. Plazas/tunnels/vaults

1. Foundations and foundation walls: Foundations are designed to support several different types of loads, including the dead and live load of the building, wind loads, earthquake loads, and horizontal forces of soil and water below grade. They are designed to resist the overturning moment forces on the

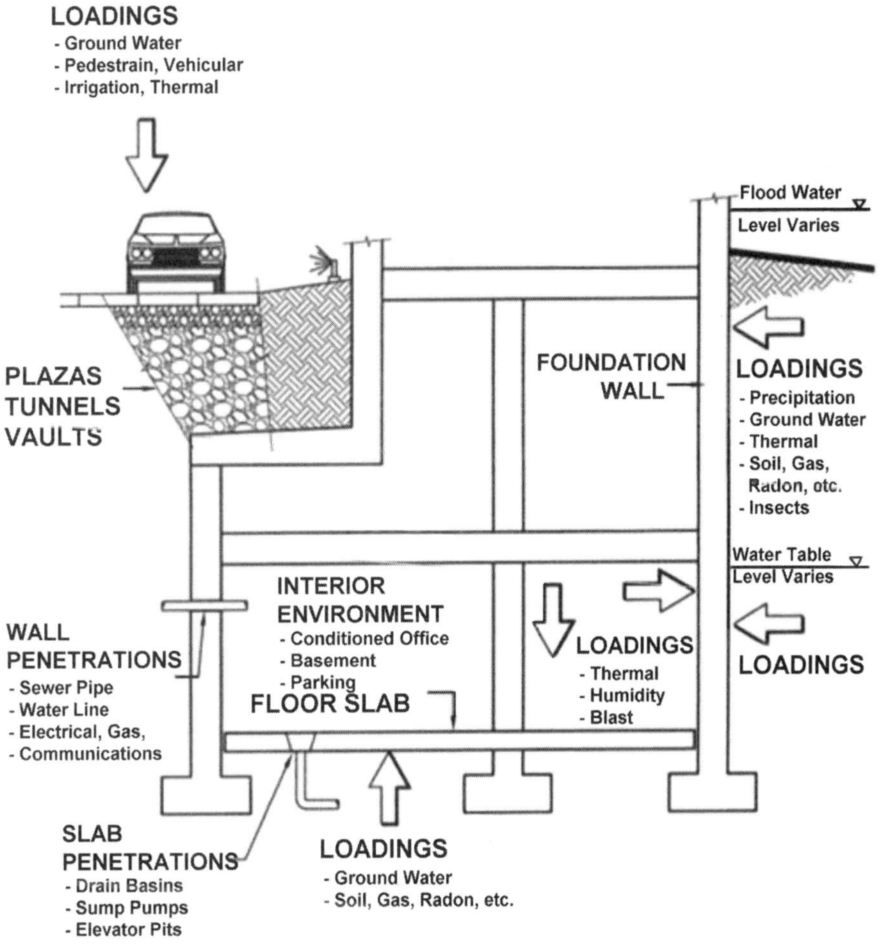

Figure 8.1 Below-grade building systems schematic graphically illustrating the three main elements and the typical loadings for below grade building enclosure systems (*Courtesy Tom Smith AIA*).

structure. The design and configuration of a foundation are directly related to the load-bearing capacities of the soil. All foundations experience at least minor settlement, but damage to foundations occurs most often when differential settlement is experienced.

The foundation wall of a building may be a cast-in-place concrete retaining or basement wall or a structural wall complete with load-bearing pilasters. Materials used may be concrete or reinforced masonry (Figure 8.2). The foundation wall system may include an earth retention system of soldier piles and wood lagging or shotcreted rock, requiring consideration of waterproofing applied to the earth retention system. For most portions of the foundation wall, water removal and control is of prime importance. In the upper areas of the foundation wall, thermal loading considerations must be addressed.

2. Floor slabs: The base floor within a building may simply be a cast-in-place concrete slab-on-grade with limited design considerations for structural support or environmental control functions. The base floor may also be composed of a mud or structural foundation slab complete with waterproofing and wearing slab with the overall system designed to carry structural hydrostatic pressure loads and maintain a con-

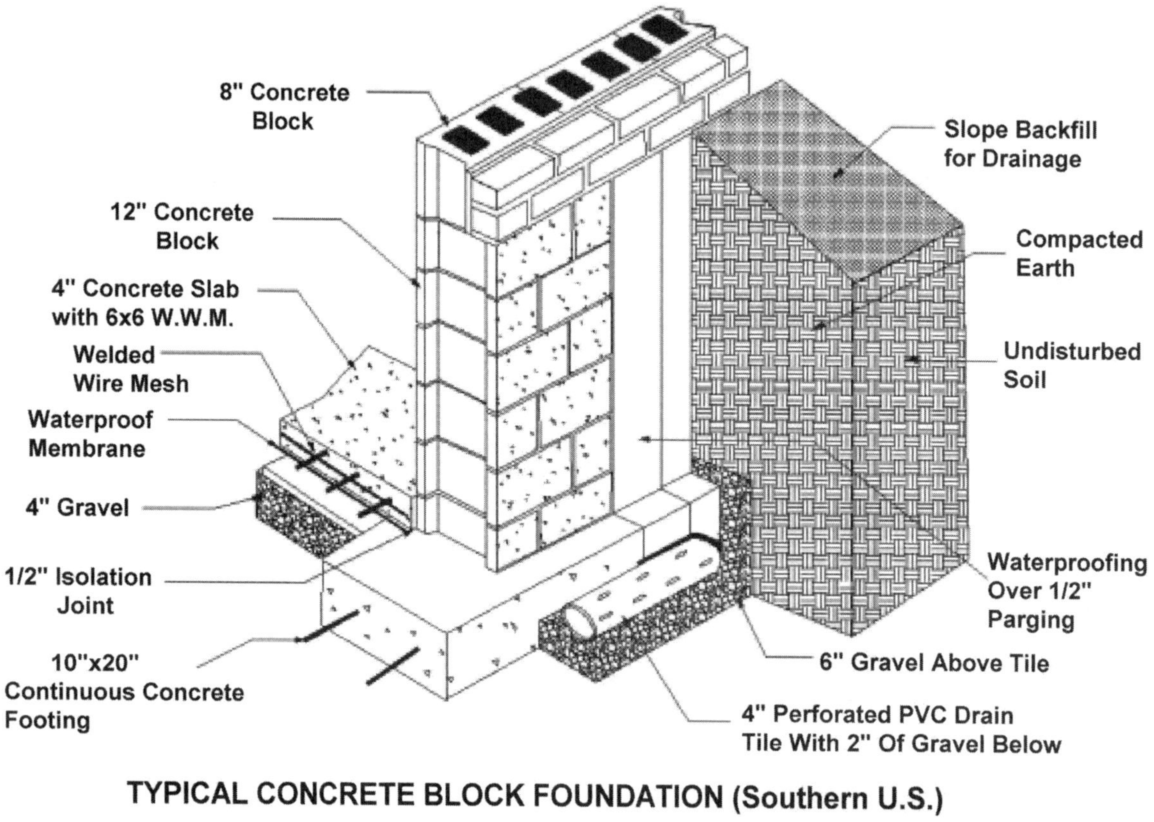

Figure 8.2 Typical concrete block foundation.

trolled environment. Floor slabs are often the source of leakage into the building, with slab cracking of common concrete materials being a primary cause. Controlling soil gas emissions, such as radon, may also be of importance.

Floor slabs of below-grade building enclosures must be capable of carrying downward vertical gravity loadings as well as any upward soil or hydrostatic pressure loadings. Downward vertical gravity loadings are the result of the floor slab's dead weight plus the presence of occupancy live loads. Floor slabs may also resist upward soil or hydrostatic pressure loadings. Upward soil pressures may be applied to the floor slab in situations where it acts as a matt foundation and the building point loads on the foundation result in an upward pressure on the floor slab.

A typical base floor slab where the design criteria include controlling moisture migration and water vapor transmission into the interior space can be referred to as a waterproof system. The components of the system include a compacted yet well-draining granular drainage system placed directly on unexcavated, undisturbed ground. The granular drainage system provides a collection area for moisture to accumulate and dissipate as well as a firm support for slab loadings. To provide a solid base material on which to apply the waterproofing membrane, a mud slab or compacted earth layer is provided (Figure 8.3). In some instances with significant hydrostatic pressure, or to accommodate building loadings, a matt foundation slab is used in lieu of the mud slab. The waterproofing is then applied directly to the matt foundation slab and protected with protection board. In this case a wearing floor slab is poured on top of the protected waterproofing system.

3. Plazas, tunnels, and/or vaults: Buildings frequently have plazas, vaults, tunnels or extensions below grade. The planning, development, detailing and construction of waterproofing for such features are

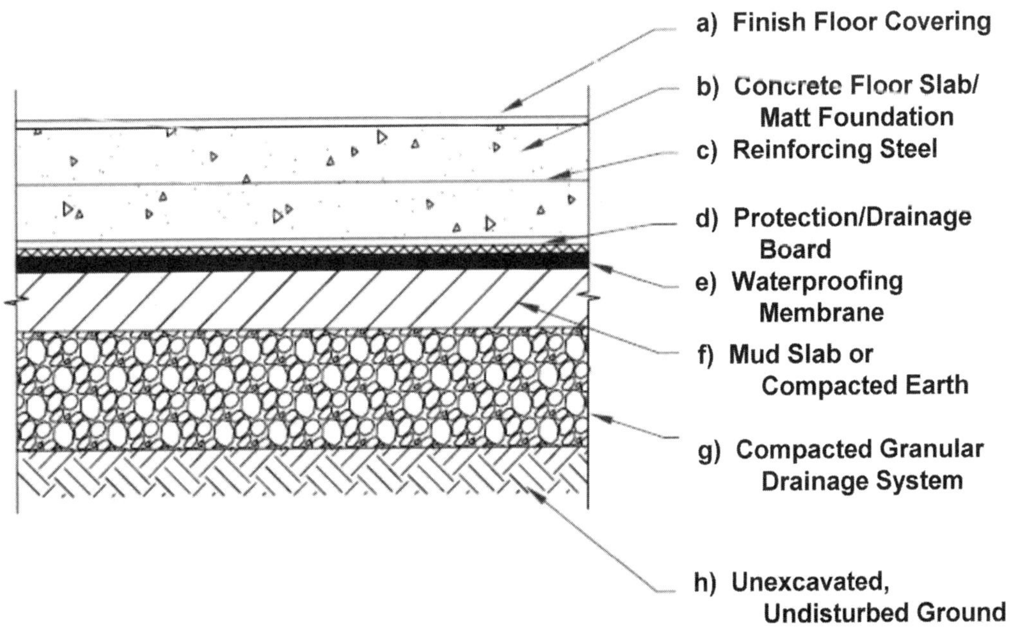

Figure 8.3 Below-grade slab floor detail showing waterproofing membrane.

significant. Although much more complex and far more maintenance intensive, these features are generally not treated with the same detailing attention that roof assemblies receive. In all such areas, regardless of membrane detailing, protection, drainage and isolation along with thermal considerations must be incorporated into the design.

Plaza decks, tunnels, and vaults are often subject to deterioration and distress more rapidly than other structural systems due mainly to poor design, poor construction and abnormal or excessive loading. Other common causes of plaza deterioration or failure are severe exposure, including freeze thaw, moisture, thermal effects, chemical applications, overload, and improper materials selection and application.

Structural systems for tunnels, vaults, and plazas are typically cast-in-place concrete, either conventionally reinforced or post-tensioned. The use of precast concrete elements for these areas should be avoided due to difficulties in obtaining effective joint and surface waterproofing.

8.3.2 Wall Systems

Structural masonry walls: Structural masonry load-bearing walls can be single or double-staggered with or without reinforcing. They are essentially self supporting and transfer roof and other loads directly to foundation systems. The simplest form of this construction consists of a single thickness of hollow core, concrete block. When reinforced, the reinforcement consists of vertical steel reinforcing bars inserted into the cores for the full height of the wall and the block cores are then filled with mortar. Horizontal steel joint reinforcement is imbedded within the horizontal mortar joints of every other course of block. Masonry buildings require verification as to whether they are unreinforced. Unreinforced masonry buildings are susceptible to severe damage in areas of seismic activity and are required to be upgraded in California.

Concrete walls: Reinforced concrete walls are employed not only for both bearing and non-structural walls, but also for shear walls for lateral resistance. They can be precast or poured-in-place. Concrete tilt-up buildings constructed prior to 1972 were often constructed with inadequate anchorage between the tilt-up wall and the roof. These buildings should be investigated thoroughly and in most cases, additional ties should be installed.

In tilt-up buildings, concrete walls can be used as shear walls, designed to resist lateral forces. This type of construction involves precasting horizontally, erecting (tilting up) and joining of exterior concrete walls at the building site. Wall panels are custom made (in a wide variety of finishes) using the floor slab as the form for the exterior panel face. Panels range in thickness from 6 to 8 inches and are formed as close to their final position as possible.

Wooden stud-framed load-bearing walls: This system is a form of sandwich construction used extensively in residential construction. The cross-sectional configuration typically consists of a number of elements, including an exterior facing component known as cladding, a water-resistant sheet membrane (vapor barrier), a layer of sheathing, vertically aligned lumber framing members (called studs), wall insulation between the studs (e.g. fiberglass batting), and a gypsum panel of wallboard constituting the interior wall. The vertical stud bottom sits on a horizontal wooden member (sole plate) and the tops are capped by another horizontal wooden member (top plate). Figure 8.4 is a typical example of wooden-stud load-bearing walls.

Retaining walls: Retaining walls are designed and constructed to contain soil at extreme change of slopes. The walls are constructed of various materials, including concrete, stone, metal, and treated wood. Retaining wall failure consists typically of cracking or other fracturing, overturning, sliding, or undermining by ground water. Common deficiencies in concrete retaining walls include cracking, poor alignment, and bowing. Common deficiencies in timber retaining walls include rotted wood, deterioration, and poor alignment and bowing due to insufficient tie-back members.

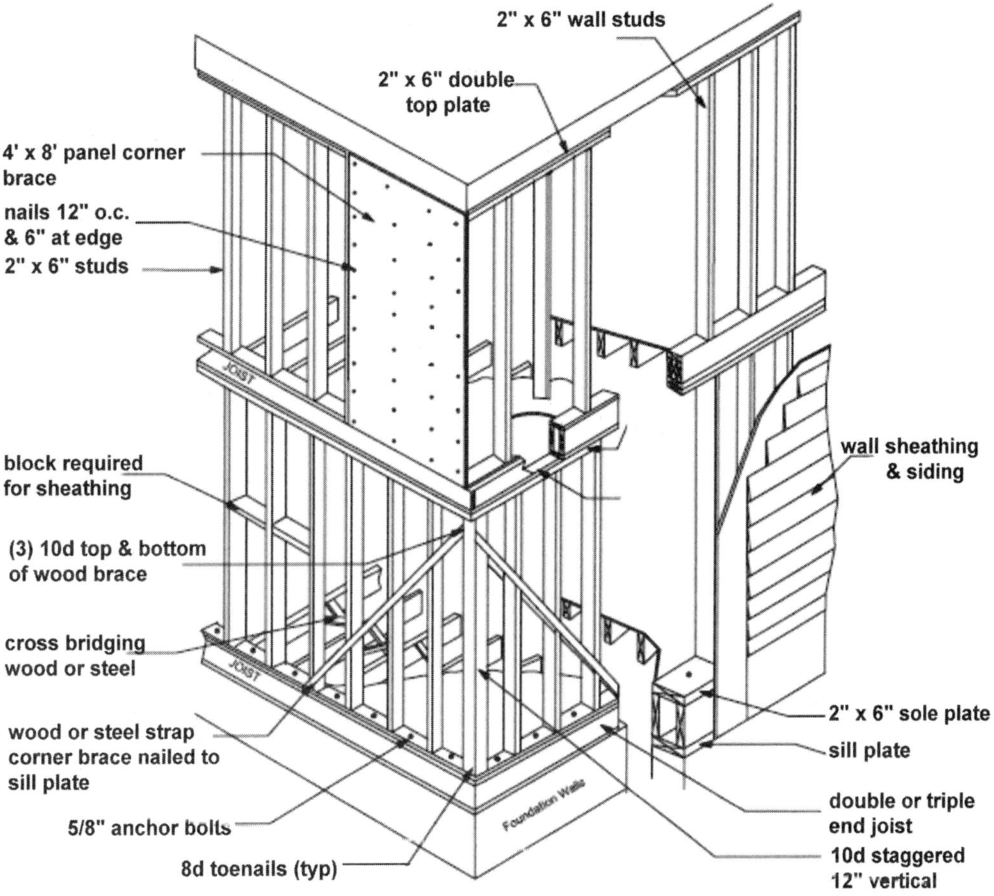

Figure 8.4 Example of a two-story exterior timber load-bearing wall system.

8.4 SEISMIC CONSIDERATIONS

About half of the states and territories in the United States are at risk from seismic hazards (Figure 8.5). In the U.S. it is estimated that the average direct cost of earthquake damage is $1 billion a year while indirect business losses are estimated in excess of $2 billion a year. This is because damage to the structure by earthquake forces is the highest risk to most buildings, although newer buildings, particularly mid- and high-rise buildings, are generally constructed to a higher level of earthquake resistance than older buildings. In areas of high potential seismic activity, building evaluations should include a seismic analysis of the building. The issues of concern to assessors range from analyzing the degree to which objects and furnishings are fastened down to evaluating the evidence of deterioration in structural members. As a general rule, buildings designed to resist earthquakes should also resist blast (terrorism) or wind, suffering less damage than they might if they were not designed to resist earthquakes.

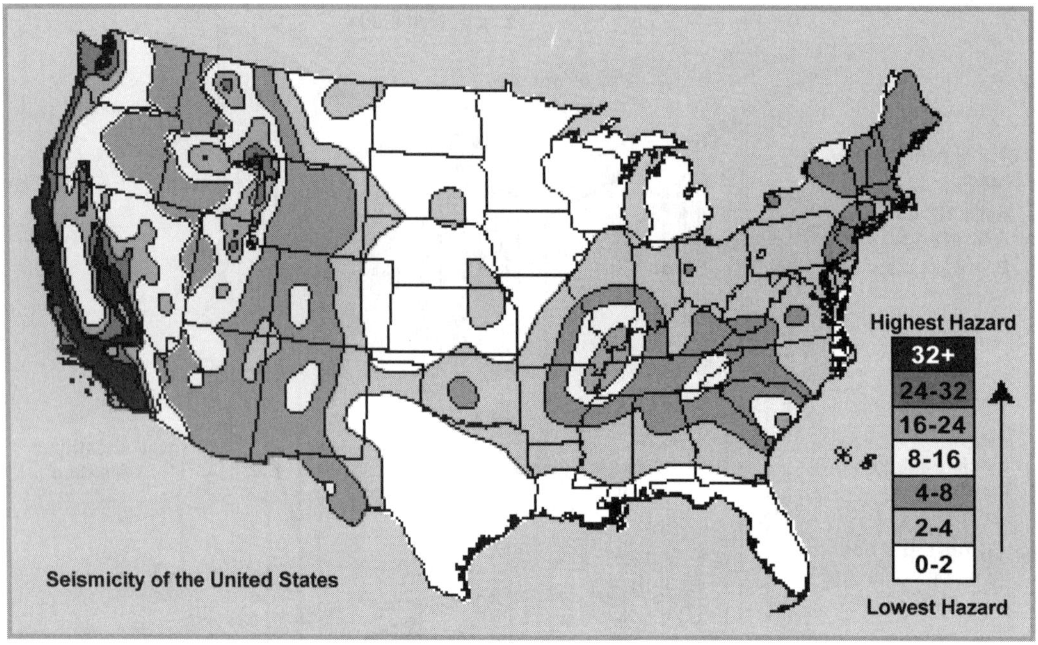

Figure 8.5 Seismicity map of the United States.

For mortgage loan reports, a single loss estimate is typically required, whereas acquisition reports normally require two loss estimates. The loss estimate shall be stated as a percentage of the property's current replacement cost. This number reflects the consultant's best judgment of potential repair costs of this particular structure(s) based on analysis, observations and past experiences. A brief description is to be provided in the report of the methodology used to generate the loss estimate. Where loss estimates are generated via mathematical algorithms, the values for all variables used as input should be indicated.

8.4.1 General Considerations

A variety of issues are included in a typical seismic study. And, as with building evaluation in general, seismic studies may be performed in a variety of depths. The study may be as simple as a general field survey and a cursory review of the structural drawings. In a standard seismic study, the drawings are reviewed and calculations are performed on a representative number of structural members in the building. The building is also reviewed for potential seismic hazards, both structural and non-structural.

Existing buildings can be seismically retrofitted to reduce earthquake risk based upon vulnerabilities identified in an evaluation report. Besides structural considerations, the evaluation report can include architectural, mechanical, and electrical components, which typically incur far more earthquake damage. Recommendations should include retrofit items, their costs, and a schedule prepared to improve a building's expected earthquake performance. Although tall buildings will undergo several modes of vibration during seismic activity, for seismic purposes (except for very tall buildings) the fundamental period, or first mode, is usually the most significant (Figure 8.6).

Seismic studies should be performed by licensed structural engineers or qualified geotechnical engineers. The evaluation should take into account the probability of seismic activity in the region, as well as the type and configurations of materials and structural members in the facility. Present building codes, as well as those in effect at the time of construction, are referenced and any retroactive code changes are evaluated.

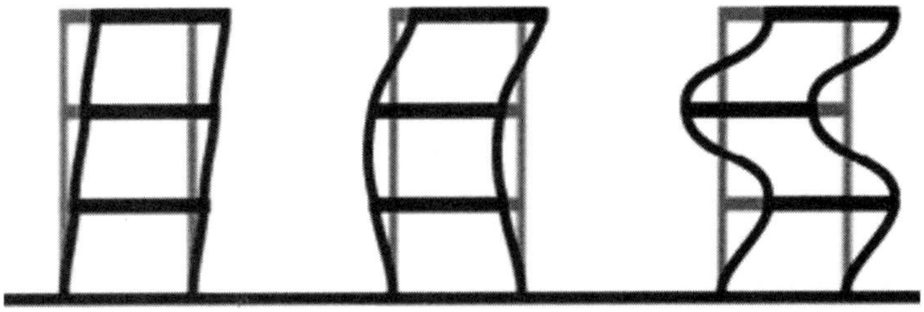

Figure 8.6 Diagram showing various modes of vibration of tall buildings during an earthquake.

For detailed seismic studies, full structural analysis is expected. This may consist of a new set of calculations or a review of the existing calculations. The analysis should consider both vertical and lateral loads, and overstressed members are located, identified, and recorded. A seismic analysis will often consider the following structural issues:

- Primary and secondary structural resistance system
- Shear walls and lateral load-resisting frame systems
- Foundations and retaining walls
- Columns and support details
- All walls and their connections, except non-structural interior partitions
- Diaphragm chord and collector system
- Shear transfer connections
- Horizontal framing members and their connections
- Horizontal diaphragms and sub-diaphragms

All items that are not part of the structural system are considered "nonstructural," and include such building elements as:

- Exterior cladding and curtain walls
- Parapet walls
- Elevators
- Partitions, doors, windows
- Suspended ceilings
- Furniture and equipment
- Mechanical, plumbing, electrical and communications equipment
- Stacks and chimneys
- Canopies and marquees

These items must be stabilized with bracing to prevent their damage or total destruction. Building machinery and equipment can be outfitted with seismic isolating devices, which are modified versions of the standard vibration isolators.

8.4.2 Seismic Analysis (Probable Maximum Loss)

The Probable Maximum Loss (PML) can be defined as the estimated cost to rectify the damage from seismic action of a defined intensity, expressed in dollars or as a percentage of a building's insured value or total structural reproduction cost. It thus reflects the monetary loss potential of a building, taking into account the location of the property and the maximum probable earthquake magnitude of the area.

Numerous firms specialize in conducting probabilistic studies of the expected loss to buildings from damage associated with earthquakes. The reports assess the probable and scenario loss potential. They are intended to allow the user to satisfy a critical part of the transactional due diligence requirements with respect to assessing a property's potential for building losses associated with earthquake potential. In addition, there are now also a number of specialized software packages on the market to assist investors in Probable Maximum Loss (PML) evaluation.

The building's history: A seismic inspector should find out how old the building is, its type of construction, and what if any changes or alterations have occurred to the facility. The building's age may be an indicator of potential vulnerabilities. The region around the building within a 100-mile radius should be investigated for large earthquake faults.

Estimating seismic risk: Estimates of seismic risk should always be calculated from the building's structural reproduction cost. In areas with a high probability of damage from earthquakes, an understanding of the seismic vulnerability of a new investment property should always be included as part of the real estate investment underwriting process. Buildings designed in accordance with codes will still sustain direct physical damage to the building structure and to major non-structural elements. Non-structural damage to all but the most earthquake resistant structures can equate to losses of 20 to 30 percent of a building's reproduction cost from a modestly significant event. Because many lenders do not understand seismic risk, there is no universal requirement to insure against seismic risk as a condition of a mortgage loan, as is now required for other potential casualty losses.

In processing loans, there should be a simplified analytical method to rapidly assess the degree of expected risk. There are many sophisticated computer-based rapid risk analysis methodologies available on the market. The best of these are based on a method developed by the Applied Technology Council and is based upon the opinion and experience of seismic experts regarding the expected response of building types to a range of seismic events. The method provides estimates for expected losses for various building structural types at various earthquake intensities. These expected losses are expressed as probable maximum loss (PML).

Unless a lender has estimated the structural reproduction cost, he or she will not know the PML represented in terms of dollars (PML$ = PML% × structural reproduction cost in dollars). The PML of a building is often determined during an evaluation of the structural system, even though it is not an exact science. For older properties whose market values are lower than their original construction costs, a PML of 20 percent when converted to dollars can represent 50 percent (and more) of the market value.

8.4.3 Seismic Code Compliance

Many building codes and governmental standards exist pertaining to design and construction for seismic hazard mitigation. Building code requirements are primarily prescriptive and define seismic zones and minimum safety factors for design purposes. Codes pertaining to seismic requirements may be local, state, or regional building codes or amendments and should be researched thoroughly by the design professional. Many governmental agencies at the federal level also have seismic standards, criteria, and program specialists who are involved in major building programs and can give further guidance on special requirements.

Building codes typically do not mandate seismic retrofit, but state and local jurisdictions may adopt/issue mandatory ordinances to retrofit existing higher-risk buildings. For example, some building departments have enacted ordinances that require strengthening of Un-reinforced Masonry Buildings (URMs) located in areas with high seismic activity.

Structural resistance to the potentially destructive forces of an earthquake has long been a design criterion for buildings. The new International Building Code (IBC) adds a key dimension: maintaining the use of designated life safety systems in certain building types immediately after a seismic event.

8.5 TYPICAL DEFICIENCIES

Stress-related deficiencies are most common in structural components. Thus, the evaluation of the structural system should concentrate on the areas where the stress level is the highest in the structural members. In beams, the mid-span portion of the component is where the flexural stress is the highest. Connections and fasteners for both beams and columns should be investigated to determine any areas of questionable integrity.

Figure 8.7 illustrates some of the forms of damage and deterioration that structural members can experience. Evidence of deterioration in concrete can take several forms, including cracking, spalling, and discoloration. Steel systems deficiencies can include rotation and deformation from inadequate sizing or connection details. Wood structural systems experience problems such as dry rot, insect infestation, moisture deterioration and overstress, resulting in cracking or shearing.

During the evaluation of the structural system, special attention should be paid to the susceptibility of the roof to water ponding. Flat or nearly flat roofs, in combination with long structural spans and clogged drains, can provide an opportunity for extensive ponding, which greatly increases the loading of the structural members and the potential for failure (Figure 8.8).

Slab moisture: Many moisture related problems can be traced to floor slabs which have been finished when floors were not dry. The moisture content of any floor slab should be measured before any floor finish is applied. Again, this requires experience and the proper testing equipment.

The field observer should consider the age of the building during the review of the structural system. While older buildings are typically found to have been built in conformance with the building codes at the time of their deconstruction, they usually provide less seismic resistance than newer buildings. Recent building codes require more reinforcing to resist lateral leads. While these codes are not retroactive, the structural evaluation of older buildings, especially in areas with a high potential for seismic activity, should concentrate on the need for additional lateral bracing.

8.6 SYSTEM DIAGNOSTICS

The scope and depth of inspection in diagnosing the structural system can vary widely, but it generally consists of a visual survey subject to limitations of or affecting accessibility and safety. The system's components can be reviewed superficially during a general walk through of the interior and exterior of a building. This level of review will typically identify the most obvious deficiencies. For example, the deflecting of a cracked structural member will be discovered during this level of review.

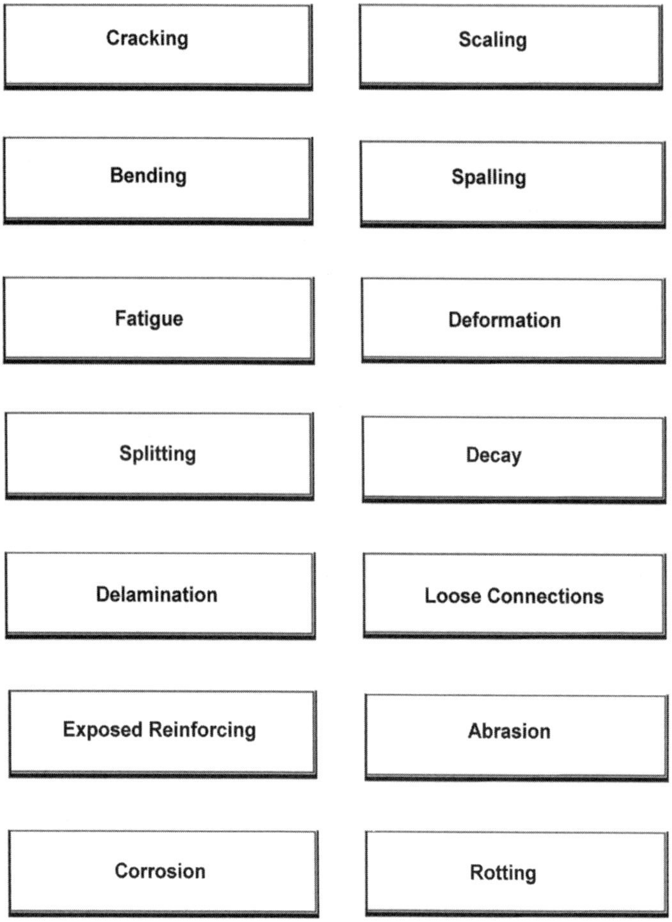

Figure 8.7 Types of damage and deterioration that structural systems can experience.

Observations of the building's structure generally are to be limited to vantage points that are on-grade or from readily accessible balconies or rooftops. In order to adequately understand the structure, where drawings are available, assessments should include a detailed drawing review. The assessment should not include a review of original design assumptions or calculations or structural design analyses. The assessor should not enter crawl or confined space areas, but should observe conditions to the extent easily visible from the point of access to the crawl or confined space areas. Structural assessment does not include determination of previous substructure flooding or water penetration, unless easily visible, or if such information is provided.

Identify and observe the condition of the structure for each constructed asset. Observe the substructure, including the foundation system, superstructure or structural frame (floor and roof framing systems). Observe the structural elements for visible signs of distress (wall cracking, displacement, etc.). Perform seismic evaluations (Probable Maximum Loss (PML) Studies) in high earthquake risk areas that have been identified according to NEHRP guidelines.

The structural system can also be reviewed in greater depth than almost any other building system. Complete structural calculations and 3D modeling can determine design and actual load capacities for any given member in a building. This type of detailed analysis is most easily done if the original construction drawings are available.

The structural system's components will have been designed with an adequate factor of safety and, with the exception of lateral design, significant deficiencies are unusual. Also, the majority of the system's components are concealed behind building finishes, both exterior and interior, so in-depth observation is often cost-prohibitive. The system's horizontal components and connections can usually be investigated by accessing a ceiling or floor cavity. Often, a representative number of members and connections are accessible for review to provide a sufficient indication of the system's condition. In some instances, destructive testing is warranted to verify structural connections.

During an evaluation of walls, attention should be paid to the joints and grouting between units or panels. If a wall is leaning to the extent that a plumb line, if hung down the center of the wall, falls outside the middle one-third of the base of the wall, it is generally considered unsafe.

Basement water problems are often diagnosed during surveys for the prospective buyer. These are usually diagnosed using some form of moisture detection equipment by a building inspector. The use of electronic moisture detection equipment is valuable for detecting moisture problems, but should not be used as the sole source of information in making decisions about the problem. Amongst other limitations, a moisture meter will not identify the source of the problem. When relying on moisture meters to make a diagnosis, using the wrong meter could lead to false positive or negative readings. It is important that the inspector know how to correctly diagnose building pressures, condensation issues, dew-points, humidity, construction materials and practices, etc.

Figure 8.8 Photo showing clear evidence of ponding on a flat roof. Ponding increases potential for water penetration and system failure.

It is important for the building owner to select a structural engineer that is experienced with the type of construction under inspection. The structural engineer should be able to identify any building gravity and seismic deficiencies based upon his/her review, and to summarize these in a verbal or written report. At the owner's request, the engineer can develop drawings outlining the repairs and retrofit measures required or recommended. These construction documents should be submitted to the local building department for review and approval.

While the most direct and common investigation of the structural system is through visual observation, various building diagnostic instruments have been developed to assist in the investigation. Pachometers, fiber-optic borescopes and other instruments are available to enable investigators to test material capabilities and view concealed spaces during an evaluation. The most common of these include the following:

Cover meters and pachometers: These are hand-held, battery-operated tools designed to assist the evaluation and inspection of as-built conditions. Cover meters are used to determine the depth of reinforcement cover in concrete. Pachometers also measure the size of the reinforcement bars.

Borescopes and fiberscopes: The advent of fiber-optic technology has provided two very valuable tools for diagnosing building systems. Borescopes and fiberscopes enable the evaluator to visually access concealed and enclosed areas of the structure. These instruments are excellent for inspecting the conditions inside a duct shaft, ceiling cavity, or wall space. They are also used extensively to inspect machinery. The main distinction between the two instruments is that the borescope wand is rigid and the fiberscope wand is flexible. Being rigid, a borescope has higher resolution and is less expensive than a fiberscope.

Moisture meter: This type of meter is generally used to determine the moisture content of timber structural members. If the content is above 20 percent, further investigation for rot or infestation is warranted.

Stereoscope: A stereoscope is used to determine the depth of flaws found in building materials. It is a portable magnifier containing a built-in scale for measuring the dimensions of a flaw. It can be used to identify whether a crack is shallow or deep.

In addition to the above instruments, there are a number of other simple non-destructive tests that field observers use in their surveys. The reliability of these tests however is sometimes questioned.

Masonry hammer test: This test evaluates the structural soundness of masonry units and the bond of the adjacent mortar. The masonry unit is lightly tapped with the hammer and the resulting resonance sound is evaluated.

Acoustic impact test: This test indicates the soundness and relative density of the test materials. It is performed by producing consistent audible vibrations by tapping the materials. It is the method that most people use to locate a wood stud behind a wall to hang a picture. The test can be performed with a hammer or any other solid object, and in fact can even be performed by knocking the surface with fingers or a fist.

This test can be used to locate voids, cracks and delaminations within both composite and homogeneous materials. It is also useful to detect areas of wood rot.

Schmidt rebound hammer test: This test is a widely used non-destructive test of the relative strength and quality of existing concrete components. It is also used to determine when formwork should be removed from newly poured concrete. While it is imprecise and experts disagree on the value of the test, it has gained wide acceptance in the building material inspection field.

By determining the rebound distance of a steel weight dropped on concrete, the relative strength of the material is measured. The tool consists of a tubular frame that houses the steel weight, a plunger, and a tension spring. It is easy to operate, and calibration charts are used to interpret the correlation between the test results and the compressive strength of the concrete.

There are other tests from the American Society of Testing and Materials (ASTM) and the American Concrete Institute (ACI) for the structural system components, including the following:

- ASTM C803, "standard test for penetration resistance of hardened concrete"
- ASTM C805, "test for rebound number of hardened concrete"
- ASTM E447, "test method for compressive strength of masonry prisms"
- ASTM E518, "test method for flexural bond strength in masonry"
- ASTM E519, "test method for diagonal tension in masonry assemblages"
- ACI 201.R, "guide for making a condition survey of concrete in service"

Limitations and exclusions: The field observer is not required to survey and report on building systems and components other than provided in the scope of works in the protocol agreement with the client. Also excluded from the PCA survey would be systems and components that are not readily accessible to view or that may present a potential safety hazard.

CHAPTER

9

Roofing Systems

9.1 GENERAL

A roofing system protects the building and its contents from the elements. It also provides drainage of storm water to the various drainage systems (roof drains, scuppers and gutters) and directs it to the ground, retention ponds or to a storm sewer. In addition, the roof structure is designed to transfer the combined weight of live and dead loads to the support members. Live load considerations include snow, rain, wind, moving installation equipment, etc. Dead loads include HVAC units, roof drains, roofing system and the deck itself.

There are varying opinions regarding roof areas that can be effectively drained by one drain, but as a very general rule of thumb for minimized ponding with adequate drainage, two roof drains are required for roof areas of 10,000 square feet or less, and at least one drain is required per 10,000 square feet of area for larger roofs. Individual judgment is needed when considering quantity and placement of drains on roofs where shape and size of sections may dictate departure from the 10,000 square feet per drain recommendation. In the replacement of drains, uniform distribution is generally desirable to achieve proper roof drainage. Likewise, careful consideration of roof structural members, dividers, expansion joints, and other projections, including rooftop equipment, is essential in planning for adequate drainage of each area of the roof (Figure 9.1).

System longevity is one of the most critical aspects of smart building management. Moreover, due to the common occurrence of deficiencies in roofing design, construction, materials, and maintenance, and the importance of system integrity to the building and its contents, the roofing system is one of the most frequently evaluated. More money is spent on roofing repair, maintenance, and replacement than on any other building system. The roofing system, in coordination with the exterior closure system, is the first line of defense against the intrusion of water into a building.

The roofing system consists of two basic components: the waterproofing members and the structural members. The waterproofing members, which typically include rolled or liquid-applied membranes as well as shingles, are intended to prohibit moisture from entering the structure. The structural members typically are constructed of concrete, wood, or steel, and include elements such as beams, rafters, and decking surfaces. The role of the structural members is to hold the membrane in place and support any additional rooftop loads that may exist, such as equipment or pedestrian traffic.

Future developments: It is likely that as the industry moves through the early part of the twenty-first century, there will be relatively minor-but-important changes to products due to environmental, health, or labor-saving concerns. The introduction of significantly different types of roofing materials is unlikely. The trend toward more sustainable roof design and construction will likely continue.

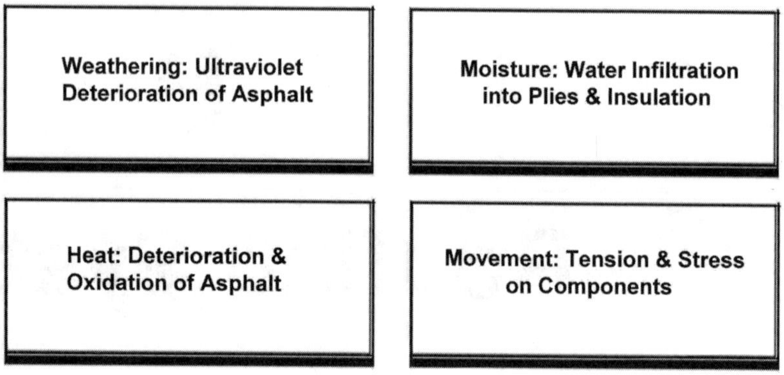

Figure 9.1 Considerations when evaluating a built-up roofing system.

The use of advanced roof design technologies, such as expert systems, may develop, but this is not likely to occur in the near future. However, we may see an increased use of computer programs to evaluate performance issues, such as moisture gain within roof systems. The design of very robust roof systems may also become more commonplace on some buildings.

The past has shown that the introduction of new materials and system designs has not been easy. After commercializing a new material or system design, it has typically taken several years for unexpected problems to be identified and successfully solved. Minor changes to materials and system designs have also often resulted in problems, but these have generally been less difficult and more quickly resolved. It is therefore prudent for designers and contractors to be cautious when specifying and installing new products and system designs.

9.2 SYSTEM TYPES AND SPECIFICATIONS

The majority of roofing systems types consist of built-up or single-ply roofing, shingles, tiles or panelized systems.

9.2.1 Built-up (Multi-ply) Roofing

A built-up roof (BUR) is the most common flat roofing type and consists essentially of three elements: felts, bitumen, and surfacing. In construction of a BUR, the felts, usually in two to four plies, and which are made of vegetable, glass, or asbestos fibers (no longer used), act as reinforcement for the thin layers of bitumen. The felts are necessary as tensile reinforcement to resist the extreme pulling force in the roofing material. Built-up roofs thus offer additional layers of protection against moisture penetration. This feature, together with the bitumen's ability to seal itself during warm weather, makes BUR a good waterproofing system. The bitumen, whether asphalt or coal-tar-pitch, "glues" and holds the felts together (Figure 9.2).

The surfacing typically consists of gravel or slag, mineral granules, or a mineral-coated cap sheet. The gravel, slag, and mineral granules may be embedded into the still-fluid flood coat. The surfacing material acts as ballast and protects the felts from direct sunlight, severe weather, fire, and impacts. Surfacing materials also provide reflectivity, thereby lowering surface temperatures and insuring longer membrane life. The BUR is attached to a structural roof deck either by mechanical means, such as nails, or non-mechanical means, such as hot-mopping bitumen. BURs are usually applied to roofs with slopes of up to one-half inch per foot. When assessing a BUR system, the field observer should take into account the following:

1. Weathering: ultraviolet deterioration of asphalt
2. Heat: deterioration and oxidation of asphalt
3. Moisture: water penetration into plies and insulation
4. Movement: tension and stress on components

Figure 9.2 Example of conventional built-up (multi-ply) roofing with asphalt bitumen surfacing being installed.

BUR roofs can perform well for 20 years or more when correctly constructed and maintained.

9.2.2 Single-ply Roofing

Single-ply membranes or elastomeric roofing systems are factory-fabricated and installed in a single thickness (Figure 9.3). The system is relatively easy to install on steep or complex roof slopes. In comparison to BUR or Modified Bitumen (MB) membranes, they are also very light weight (except for ballasted systems). However, they do not offer the same resistance to abuse as do BUR and MB membranes. Primary methods for securing the membrane to the roof deck or other substrate include the following:

1. The *fully adhered* method, which uses a continuous layer of adhesive. This method is particularly suitable for high-rise buildings.
2. The *partially adhered* method, which uses a series of strips or plate fasteners and no ballast to attach the membrane to the supporting structure.
3. *Loose laid* over the substrate and ballasted to resist wind uplift (with fused or glued end laps to form a continuous sheet and covered with 1/4 to 1/2 inch of stone). Ballasted systems are limited to a maximum slope of 2:12.
4. It can be *mechanically* attached, where the membrane is loose-laid except for discrete rows of fasteners. There are a variety of fastening and seam fabrication techniques used with this method.
5. The *thermoplastic single-plies* method, in which field-fabricated seams are welded by robotic hot-air welders. Hand-held hot-air welders are used to weld seams at flashings and penetrations.

There are four categories of single-ply systems:

1. *Thermosetting* (vulcanized or "cured" elastomers) types include EPDM (Ethylene, propylene), neoprene (synthetic rubber), and PIB (polyisobutylene).

2. *Thermoplastic* (non-vulcanized or "uncured" elastomers) types include PVC (Polyvinyl chloride) and CPE (Chlorinated polyethylene).
3. *Chlorosulfonated polyethylene* (CSPE). CSPE is neither a thermosetting nor thermoplastic material.
4. *Composite types* include glass-reinforced EPDM and neoprene, various modified bitumen and polyethylene combinations, and nylon or polyester-reinforced PVC.

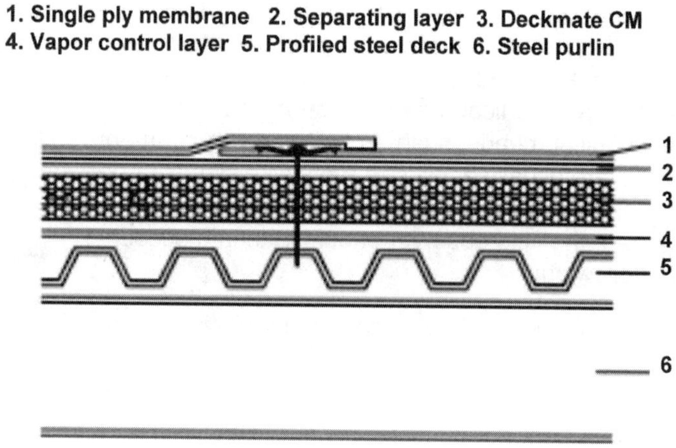

Figure 9.3 Example of mechanically fixed single-ply roofing (SPR) system.

EPDM is a lightweight, synthetic elastomer material that currently enjoys the largest market share of single-ply roofing in America (Figure 9.4). Reasons for its success include EPDM's properties of resilience, tensile strength, elongation, greater flexibility to accommodate wide ranges of movement, moisture resistance (provided it is not torn or punctured), ease of repair, and generally a cleaner installation process. It also offers superior resistance to heat, ozone, ultraviolet light, ponding water and weathering in general. However, EPDM punctures easily, and should not be used on high traffic roofs unless adequate precautions are taken (e.g. use of extensive walk pads). EPDM is also susceptible to swelling when exposed to aromatic, halogenated and aliphatic solvents, and animal and vegetable oils such as those exhausted from kitchens.

Polyvinyl chloride (PVC) membranes are among the oldest single-plies currently on the market. If in contact with polystyrene insulation, the polystyrene will cause the plasticizers in the membrane to leach out. When used with polystyrene, a separator sheet needs to be installed between the membrane and the polystyrene to avoid membrane embrittlement.

Thermoplastic polyolefin (TPO) is the latest thermoplastic membrane introduced into the marketplace. It is made from polypropylene, polyethylene or other olefinic materials. TPO membranes do not rely upon plasticizers for flexibility (unlike PVC and PVC blends), and therefore embrittlement due to plasticizer loss is of no concern.

9.2.3 Shingles and Tiles Roofing

Constructed of wood, asphalt, slate, or clay, shingles and tiles are typically used on roofs with slopes greater than 3 1/2 inches per foot. Usually one or more layers of felt are placed between the structure and the shingles or tiles.

Asphalt shingles consist of a fiberglass mat impregnated with asphalt and covered with mineral surface granules. They are formed into 1 $\times$ 3 foot sheets and nailed in a checkerboard pattern, overlapping to provide double coverage (two layers of thickness). Asphalt shingles are classified by weight. Their life expectancy is between 15 years for standard weight to 25 years for heavy weight. The organic core felt in the shingles was gradually replaced with glass fiber felt. Glass fiber shingles do not absorb moisture and are more resistant to wear. Likewise, they are incombustible and do not rot, mold or mildew.

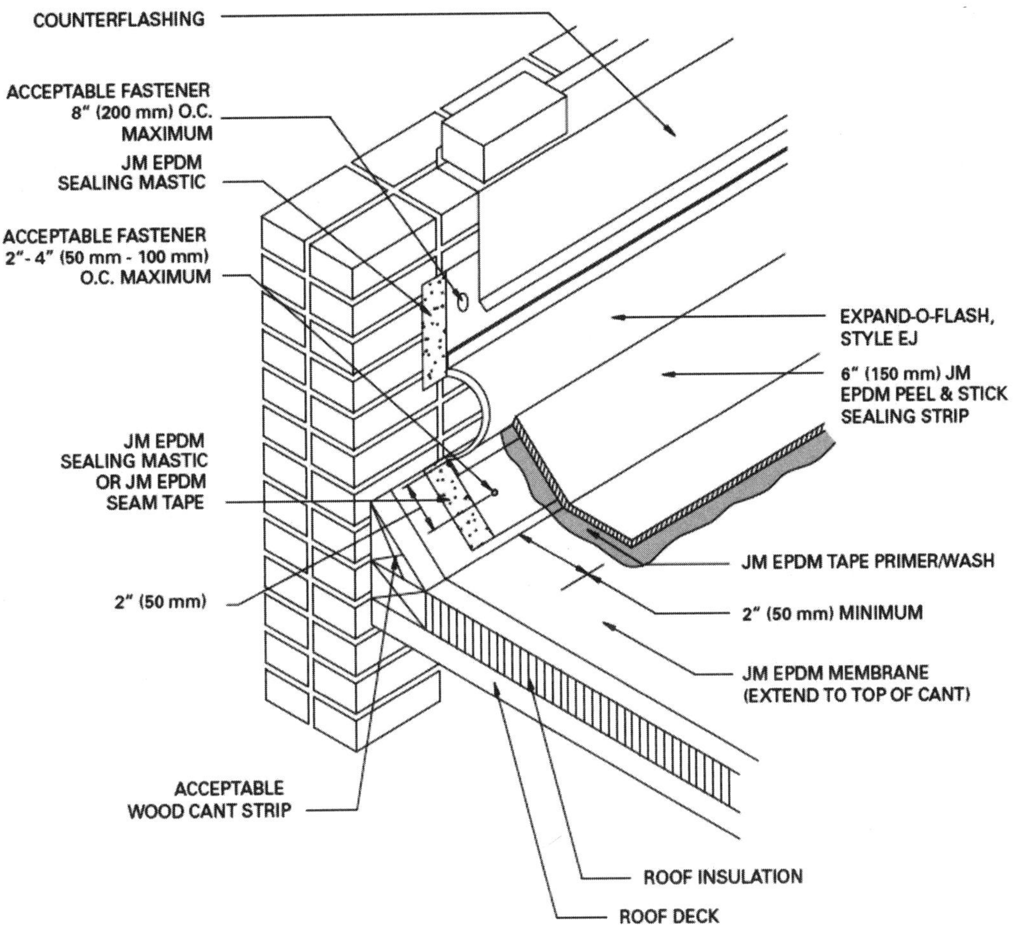

Figure 9.4 Drawing of an EPDM single-ply membrane roofing system with expansion joint *(Courtesy Johns Manville)*.

Asphalt roll roofing products are made in the same manner as asphalt shingles but are formed into rolls of material three feet wide. Roll roofing has a useful life expectancy of about 10 years. It is not suitable for applications where slopes are less than one inch per foot.

Wood shingle and shake roofing share the disadvantages of other wood products, namely, insufficient fire resistance and vulnerability to drying, curing, splitting, mold, and mildew. Many codes in many jurisdictions prohibit the use of shakes and shingles due to the risk of fire. Both wood shingles and wood shakes are available in pressure-treated wood to meet U.L.790 fire-rated standards for Class A roofs. When properly installed and with the correct slopes, wood shingle roofs can last up to 20 years.

Slate tile roofing is rarely used today due largely to its exorbitant cost. Slates should only be used where the slope exceeds 6 inches per foot. Copper nails are the only suitable nails to be used with slate. Properly installed, slate roofs can last up to 100 years.

Tile roofing consists largely of molded clay and precast concrete products and is a very versatile and durable roofing material. Tiles come in a variety of shapes, patterns, and colors. Today clay tile roofing can be seen throughout much of the United States, particularly in commercial and retail facilities, garden offices, restaurants and residences. This type of roofing system should have a minimum slope of three inches to the foot, and because clay tile is a heavy material, clay tile roofing requires appropriate structural allowances if used.

In locations that have winter temperatures below 30 degrees Fahrenheit, an ice shield should be installed consisting of #43 felt mopped in steep asphalt. Moreover, special attention must be paid to the manner in which open valleys are installed in tile roofs. The requirements include an extra ply of dry-in felt installed before the metal valleys are fitted. Metal valleys and flashing should always be fabricated out of copper, stainless steel, or other non-corrosive metal.

Critical to tile roofs are the attachment nails and wires. Galvanized or copper products should be used or corrosion will cause tile loosening and damage. Tiles will often shift and crack underfoot and are also vulnerable to significant breakage in transit. It has a high useful life expectancy but its high cost limits its widespread application.

9.2.4 Metal Panels Roofing

Metal roofing is relatively lightweight, has strong architectural appeal and durability, and is relatively easy and quick to install. Prefabricated metal panels may be made of copper, terneplate, galvanized steel, or aluminum. Various seam configurations allow for metal roofing on both flat and pitched roofs. Various custom panel sizes, profiles, colors and finished coatings are available for commercial applications. Metal roofing's attributes are impressive, offering long-term weatherability, low maintenance, and aesthetic value (Figure 9.5).

The popular standing seam metal roof is constructed of interlocking panels that run vertically from the roof's ridge (the top of the roof) to the eave. The interlocking seam, where two panels join together, is raised above the roof's flat surface, allowing water to run off without seeping between panels.

Two methods are commonly used to secure the panels to the roof sheathing. The first (and better) system consists of concealed fastener clips that are secured to the raised portion of each interlocking panel, and subsequently covered by the next adjoining panel during installation. The second (simpler and less costly) method utilizes exposed fasteners that are driven through each metal panel into the roof sheathing.

One of the chief concerns presented by metal roofing is movement caused by thermal expansion. This continuous movement resulting from expansion and contraction sometimes causes the fasteners to loosen, thereby affecting the system's integrity of water tightness.

Figure 9.5 Example of metal panel roofing, Knightsbridge Financial Center, New Jersey *(Courtesy Englert, Inc.)*.

9.2.5 Other Roofing Systems

A **Modified Bitumen (MB)** roof system is a hybrid built-up roof initially developed in Europe. The term modified refers to the addition of plastic or rubber-based polymeric binders to asphalt to improve its performance. It has the benefits of the built-in redundancy of the BUR, along with the added strength, flexibility and UV resistance of a modified membrane. The membrane consists of an asphalt and polymer blend, which allows the asphalt to take on characteristics of the polymer. There are several surfacing options for this system, including a factory-applied mineral surface, a gravel surface laid in bitumen, or a liquid applied coating that is typically reflective. Modified bitumen membranes are typically applied like a traditional BUR, but because there is only one "ply," the labor cost is reduced.

The idea behind modified bitumen roofing is a simple one: by pre-manufacturing the cap sheet component of BUR systems in controlled factory environments, material suppliers could add polymer modifiers that improve the performance of multi-ply roofs, which had traditionally been fabricated in the field. Today's high-performance polymer modifier technology is selectively targeted at enhancing increasingly specific performance attributes, such as low-temperature flexibility or ultraviolet-radiation resistance. Similarly, yesterday's cotton felts have given way to high-strength alternatives such as fiber glass and polyester.

Durability is the most significant performance advantage of modified bitumen roofing. Not only do the modifiers improve the roof's ability to withstand foot traffic and other abuses, but they also help roofs age more gracefully. Unlike other less resilient commercial roofing options, modified bitumen roofs lend themselves to restorative alternatives as they age, delaying the need for tear-off and re-roofing. With consistent monitoring and proactive maintenance, modified bitumen roofs remain watertight for decades. MB membranes are typically composed of pre-fabricated polymer-modified asphalt sheets. Polymers are added to bitumen to enhance various properties of the bitumen.

The three most popular primary types of MB sheets, as well as field-applied modified mopping asphalt are: Atactic polypropylene (APP), styrene butadiene styrene copolymer (SBS) and styrene butadiene rubber (SBR).

To minimize potential surface cracking, a field-applied coating (such as aluminum-pigmented asphalt, asphalt emulsion, or acrylic), factory-applied surfacing (granules or metal foil), or a sheet with protective reinforcement near the top should be used.

The **Styrene-isoprene-styrene (SIS)** roofing system consists of self-adhering sheets blended with SIS polymer, asphalt and fillers. The mixture is then factory fabricated into either 3 feet or 1 meter wide rolls. The top of the prefabricated sheet is available with embedded mineral granules or a factory-laminated UV-protective surfacing, such as aluminum foil.

Styrene-ethylene-butylene-styrene (SEBS) polymer is generally blended with asphalt in the factory. The SEBS modified asphalt is then reheated at the job site in specially-designed tankers or kettles. The hot modified asphalt is applied similarly to BUR systems. The membrane is typically surfaced with aggregate.

Sprayed Polyurethane Foam (SPF) is a very unusual type of roof system in that the membrane is constructed by spraying a two-part liquid onto a substrate. The mixture expands and solidifies to form closed-cell polyurethane foam. The substrate can either be the roof deck, an existing roof membrane (provided the existing roof is suitable for re-covering), gypsum board, or rigid insulation. The foam is applied with hand-held sprayers or by robotic sprayers. Each pass of foam is typically between 1/2 to 1 1/2 inches (13 to 38 mm) thick. If a greater total thickness is desired, two or more passes would normally be required. The total thickness of the foam can easily be adjusted to provide adequate slope for drainage (Figure 9.6). If the foam is exposed to UV radiation, it will break down and fail. Prevention is normally achieved by using one of the coatings outlined below, and which should be applied on the same day as the SPF whenever possible or at least within 24 hours.

Figure 9.6 Photo showing worker applying sprayed Polyurethane Foam (SPF) on existing single-ply membrane roof *(Courtesy Servcor International, Inc.)*.

Coating Classifications: Elastomeric coatings are capable of 100 percent elongation under load, and can recover to their original dimensions. There are several types of coatings, the most popular of which are:

Acrylic Latex coating: This is the least expensive of the coatings, but normally offers the shortest service life (re-coating is required about every 10 to 15 years, although the best acrylics can last longer than some of the polyurethane coatings).

Polyurethane coating: When properly formulated, this coating offers long service life. This can be the toughest coating available in terms of impact and tear resistance, although a wide range of physical properties is available in this product category.

Silicone coating: Silicone coatings offer exceptionally good weather resistance and long service life. More than other coatings, silicone coatings are prone to being pecked by birds. To avoid the pecking, granules are commonly set into the coating while it is wet.

Mineral granules: Mineral granules (similar to those used to surface asphalt shingles) can increase the durability of a coating and provide greater slip-resistance. Course sand can also be used for this purpose. Granules or sand are placed into the coating while it is wet.

Aggregate surfacing: Properly formulated and installed, SPF is quite resistant to liquid water. Therefore, aggregate of the size used on BUR systems can be applied directly over the foam. As with aggregate-surfaced BUR, consideration should be given to aggregate blow off.

Other types of coating include neoprene (Hypalon), butyl rubber, epoxies and modified asphalts. Whichever coating is applied, it is important that the coating used be compatible with the SPF product and approved by the SPF manufacturer. Some coatings, such as acrylic latex, asphalts, and vinyls, require that the SPF be sprayed first with a primer for good adhesion.

SPF systems have several important attributes. Besides readily lending themselves to complex roof shapes, SPF systems are exceptionally thermally efficient, since they do not have mechanical fasteners or insulation board joints, which create thermal bridges. And notably, an SPF roof is not in imminent danger of leaking if the coating is weathered away or ruptured or the aggregate surface is displaced, provided that the penetration does not extend all of the way through the foam.

9.3 COMPONENTS TO BE EVALUATED

The Roof Deck (or Field): The roof deck supports the waterproofing membrane of the roof. It can be made of various materials, including steel, concrete, wood, and formboard. In many roofs the deck is constructed of plywood. In some cases this can be inspected from below to identify any splits or damage to the deck. A corrugated deck is typically covered by rigid insulating boards or insulated with vermiculite, perlite, or cellular types of roof fill, on top of which is the roofing material. A concrete deck can be a waffle slab or pan joist and can be pre-cast or poured in place. A formboard deck is a dense composite board, usually made from wood fibers, cement, and occasionally, urethane foam. When evaluating existing roof decks, the field observer should note and address the following issues:

- The type and general condition of the roof
- Adequacy of drainage (no ponding) and whether roof drains are clean
- Whether the slope of the roof is adequate for the roofing system used
- That there are no exposed areas of felt or areas missing aggregate
- Have the materials been sampled and analyzed for asbestos?
- Whether the adhesion of the felt membranes is adequate
- Is there any debris and discarded equipment evident?
- Whether there is evidence of punctures or openings at the edge wrinkle of a felt lap (in BURs)
- Check for evidence of alligatoring, ridging, splitting, or raised blisters

Base Flashing: Each type of roofing material requires a flashing material with similar characteristics to achieve a good seal. Base flashing is used to seal the roof field membrane at upturned edges and is typically found at parapets, penthouse walls, and equipment penetrations (Figures 9.7). Flashing materials typically include asbestos, organic, or glass fibers in combination with bitumen, various types of rubber and PVC, and metals including aluminum, copper, lead, and steel. The Environmental Protection Agency (EPA) has now effectively eliminated the use of asphalt-saturated asbestos felts, which were used extensively as base flashing or as support for base flashing in BURs.

Upon noting the base flashing locations, the field observer should note its type and general condition, and whether there is evidence of punctures, blistering, or general deterioration. Often flashings will tear from thermal movement that has not been sufficiently considered. In addition, an assessment can confirm that the caulking is in good condition, that the flashing is properly attached, and that there is no evidence of open laps or areas of ridging.

Counter Flashing: Covering the exposed edges or joints of the base flashing, counter flashing is made of materials similar to base flashing. Counter flashing should be evaluated for issues similar to those of base flashing.

Parapet: The parapet is the wall around the roof, typically 2 1/2 to 5 feet high, which usually is an extension of the exterior wall of the building (Figure 9.8). The field observer should check that the parapet's general condition is satisfactory, the mortar joints are in good condition, the scuppers adequately sealed and that there is no evidence of cracking or spalling.

Coping: Coping is a flashing, typically of metal, masonry, or wood, located at the top of a wall, pier, or chimney (Figure 9.9). The basic function of coping is to act as a protective cap and should be waterproof, weather resistant, and sloped to shed water. The assessor should also note whether the joints and caulking are in satisfactory condition and that there are no signs of corrosion or discoloration of adjacent surfaces due to water runoff.

Gravel Stops: Gravel stops are installed to prevent gravel from washing off the roof, as a counterflashing, or to provide a decorative edge finish detail to roofs not using parapets. Gravel stops are typically constructed of aluminum, copper, lead-coated copper, PVC, galvanized or stainless steel. Gravel stops should be examined for their type and general condition and for evidence of deterioration of material, joints, or caulking in addition to evidence of corrosion or discoloration of adjacent surfaces due to water runoff. Likewise, attachment and fastening to the building should be examined for adequacy.

Gutters, Downspouts, and Drains: This equipment is installed to collect, distribute and convey rainwater from the roof area. Gutters are constructed of various materials, including metals, plastic and vinyl.

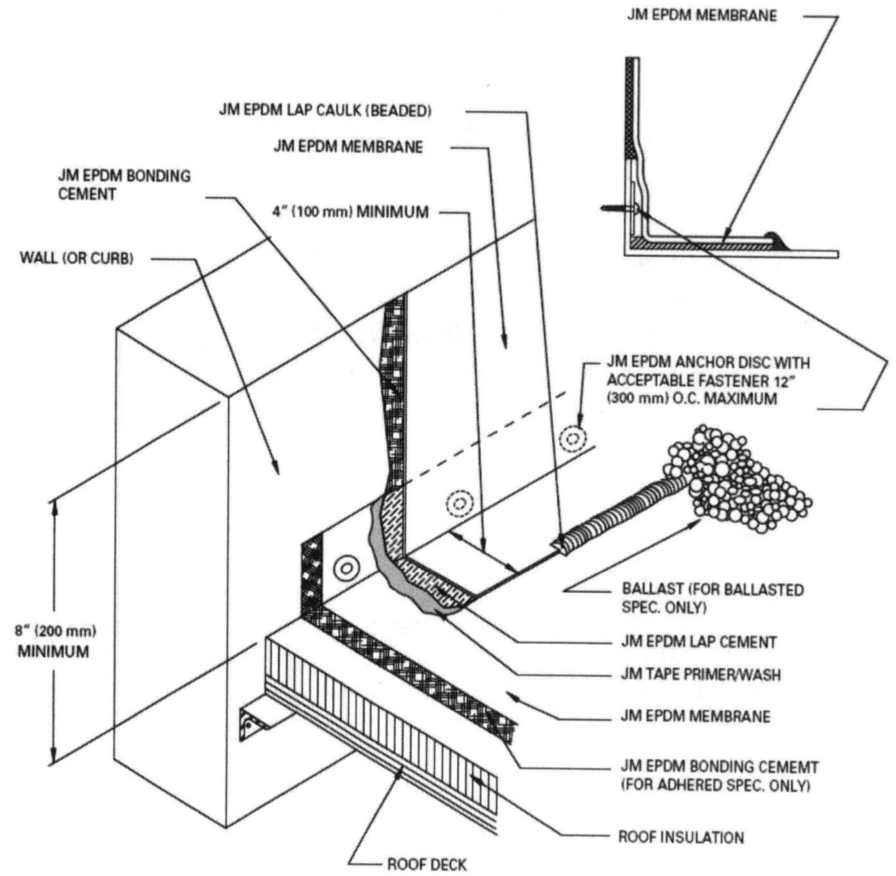

Figure 9.7 EPDM base flashing detail *(Courtesy Johns Manville)*.

Downspout materials also include black steel or cast iron. Roof drains are typically constructed of cast iron, brass, galvanized steel, copper, lead, or PVC, and usually discharge water into a drainage system (Figure 9.10A,B). PVC drains are compatible with elastoplastic systems, but are not suitable for torching or hot-mop applications because they melt under high temperatures. Gutters should not have leaks and should contain basket strainers at downspouts to capture any debris. Downspouts should be plumb and should be installed away from wood products to prevent moisture accumulation and rot. In addition, an adequate overflow back-up system should be in place.

Equipment Penetrations and Supports: Every penetration in a roof membrane threatens the roof's integrity. Ducts, pipe vents, and other mechanical components, equipment penetrations, and supports, are common avenues for water infiltration and should be given special examination. Included in this category are *pitch pans,* which are metal containers surrounding equipment supports, structural columns, or any other roof penetration. Some of the issues to check when surveying equipment penetrations and supports include: general condition, adequacy of flashing methods, evidence of thermal movement of penetrations

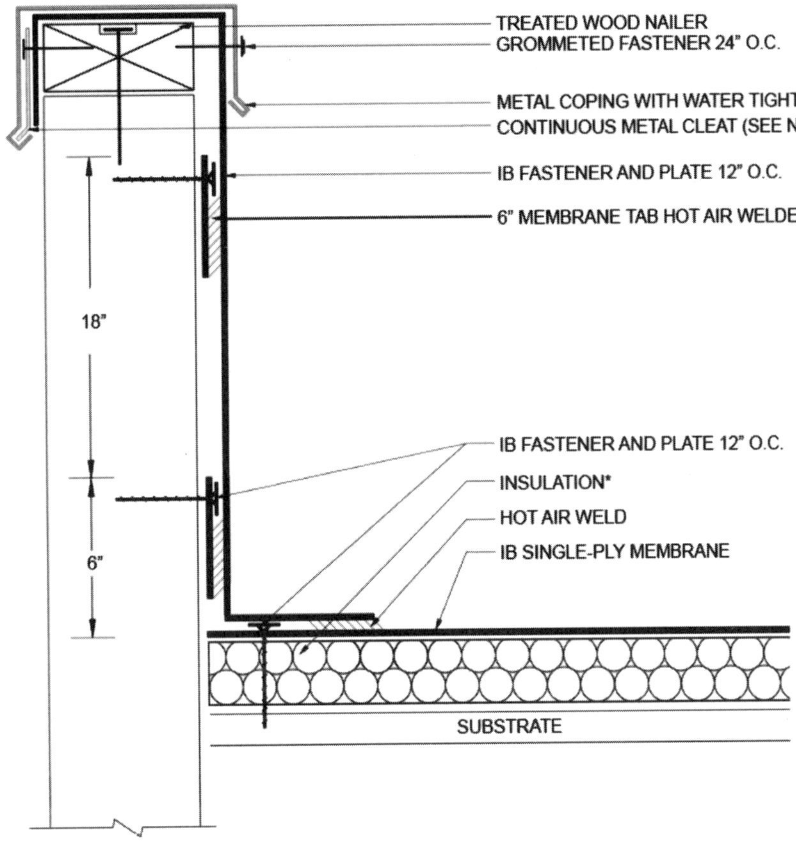

Notes: 1. If winds exceed 75 mph notify the IB Technical Department.

2. Continuous metal cleat is required to be fastened according to FM Loss Prevention Data Sheet 1-49.

Figure 9.8 Mechanically attached parapet wall–Single-ply roof *(Courtesy IB Roof Systems).*

or supports, signs of excessive field wear from maintenance operations around equipment, pitch pan fill material shrinkage evidence and whether element is sufficiently attached.

Expansion Joints: Expansion joints are installed to allow full-depth separation of roofing materials to allow relative thermal or structural movement to take place without causing damage to the roofing system (Figure 9.11). Expansion joint construction at the roof typically consists of a blocking material to raise the joint above the roof, a prefabricated protective covering of rubber, neoprene, or metal to prevent water penetration, and a compressible filler of felt, rubber or neoprene to keep the joint clean. Expansion joints for built-up applications are required at intervals of 150 feet.

A PCA survey should verify that expansion joints are in good condition and check for signs of deterioration, rusting, or other signs of corrosion. The assessor should also look for evidence of punctures or splits in the joint or cover material, or for any open joints where covers have been removed or omitted and that the attachment and fasteners are in good condition.

Rooftop Projections and Fixtures: Flagpoles, antennas, satellite dishes, access hatches, skylights, rooftop projections, and fixtures should be included in an evaluation of the roofing system. Skylights in particular can be problematic due to leaking seals between the lens and the frame. Basically, their general condition should be evaluated and whether they are adequately fastened or braced. They should also be monitored for evidence of damaged or deteriorated flashing or waterproofing.

Insulation: Roof insulation is used to reduce heat transfer through the roof. It can be installed above or below the roofing membrane. The insulation is made of various materials, including mineral fiberboard, fiberglass boards, perlite sheets, polystyrene, urethane, various composite sheets, and poured-in-place lightweight concrete.

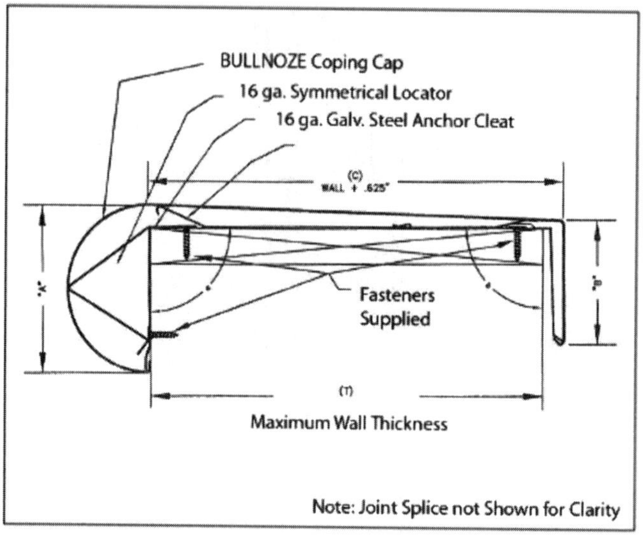

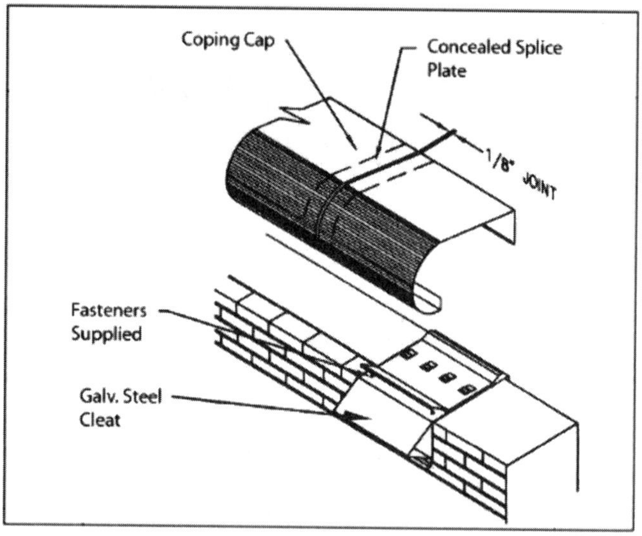

Figure 9.9 Example of bullnose parapet wall coping *(Courtesy W.P. Hickman Co.)*.

9.4 TYPICAL DEFICIENCIES

In general, the performance deficiencies in the roofing system fall into two categories: initial application and maintenance-related. Deficiencies in the roofing system consist of breaches in the system's waterproofing capabilities. Most deficiencies can be detected from visual observation. Water stains on walls for example, may indicate fascia problems. Wet spots on the walls, or wall cracks, can indicate a separation of the building, probably at a structural beam. Bare spots on bituminous roofs may be due to wind sweeping, flow of floodcoat, blistering, etc. Unlike some building systems, where there may be graduating levels of effective and adequate performance, the roofing system is performing adequately only if the integrity of the waterproofing barrier is intact. Roofing failures can be due to a number of causes including:

1. Moisture penetration
2. Improper flashing

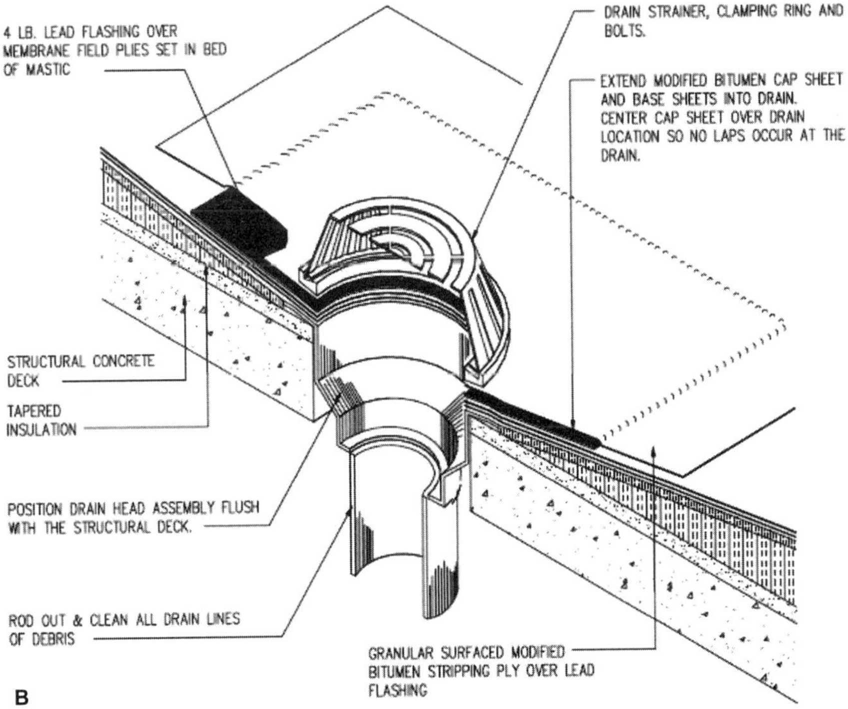

Figure 9.10 A. Examples of different drain types *(Courtesy, Smith Drainage Systems)*. B. Drawing of roof drain detail.

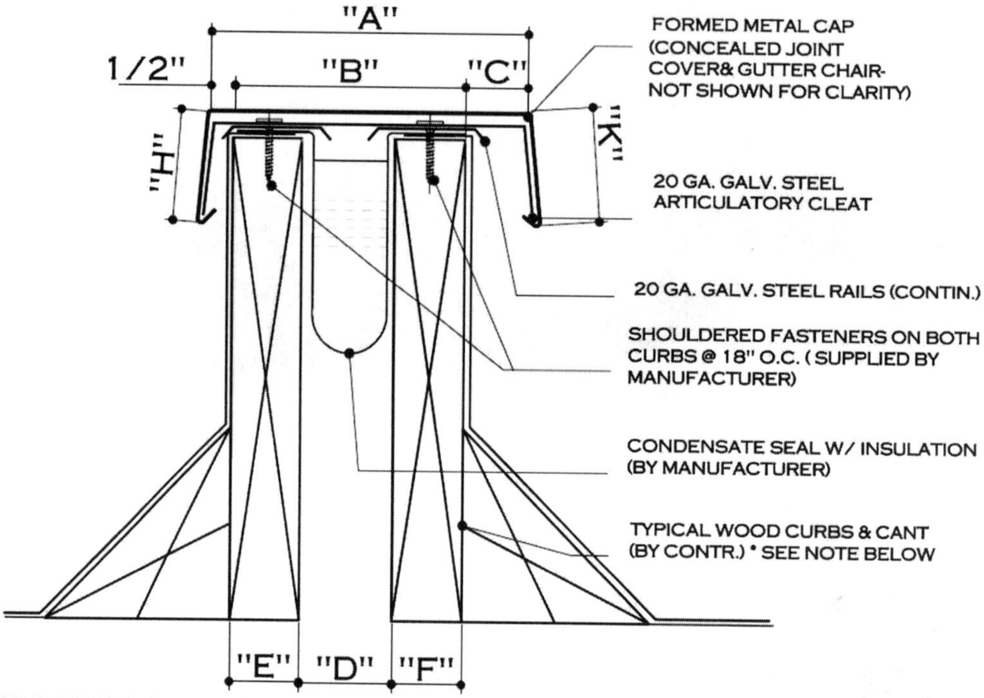

Figure 9.11 Typical roof-to-roof expansion joint detail *(Courtesy W.P.Hickman Co.)*.

3. Improper patching
4. Poor maintenance
5. Thermal movement
6. High roof drains
7. Inadequate inspection
8. Improper flashing
9. Improper material selection
10. EPDM membrane shrinkage
11. Inadequate surfacing
12. Improper equipment supports and penetrations

Application: The majority of roofing deficiencies are caused by application-related problems. Numerous problems can arise due to errors in application methodology or judgment. The most common error in BUR systems is installing the materials at an improper temperature, thereby causing inadequate or defective adherence and waterproofing integrity.

Maintenance: The most important reason for establishing a program of regular roof maintenance inspection is to protect the owner's investment. A well executed maintenance program not only adds years to the life of the roof, but it also allows detection of roofing problems before damage becomes widespread, so that the internal functions of the building are not interrupted. Often taking corrective measures in time, such as basic repairs, can pay substantial dividends to the owner. Roof penetrations are typically the single most common source of roof leakage, which is why surveys should carefully include individual rooftop equipment, including the metal work, to see if there is evidence of moisture entry into the roofing system.

9.5 SYSTEM DIAGNOSTICS

In most roofing systems, it is not unusual to find at least some level of material deterioration and signs of insufficient maintenance, such as leaves and other debris clogging the drains. It is therefore wise to conduct periodic roof maintenance surveys as part of a facility's preventive maintenance program. This alone will lengthen the service life of a roofing system. Standard PCA surveys are basically confined to a visual examination of the roof.

Before performing the physical maintenance inspection, the roof's historical and repair records should be examined, (e.g. to determine whether the roof is still under warranty). Upon completing the initial research, it is useful to inspect the ceiling of the upper floor of the building for any signs of water penetration or damage indicative of a deficient roofing system. Indicative signs of water entry include stained ceiling tiles, dry rot in a wood deck, rust in a steel deck, or efflorescence in a concrete deck. All deteriorated areas and their locations should be noted.

The next step would include a walk around the perimeter of the building checking for cracks and/or other signs of structural movement. The field observer should look for evidence of water entry into walls, such as efflorescence of masonry buildings rusting fasteners, lintels, shelf angles, and other metal components. The field observer should also look for evidence of open expansion joints and sealant joints at wall penetrations. Drainage accessories (downspouts, scupper heads and gutters) should be examined for signs of leakage, rusting, or loose attachments.

These steps should be followed by a review of the parapets and flashing around the perimeter of the roof, followed by an evaluation of the roof deck (field). Drains and the flashing surrounding the drains should be checked for the presence of upward movement caused by pipe expansion. Downspouts should be inspected to ensure that the straps securing them are in place. Evidence of ponding should be noted, and in the absence of standing water, check for other symptoms, such as discoloration of the roof membrane, growth areas of algae or other vegetation, and accumulations of dirt. Areas of heavy foot traffic should also be checked for punctures, deterioration, and bare spots in the surfacing.

Unlike for some of the other building systems, various diagnostic tools are readily available to evaluate the roofing system. Although these diagnostic tools go beyond the scope of a standard PCA, the field observer should still be familiar with them. These tools and methods can monitor the extent to which moisture has entered the system and include:

Roof Cut: One of the standard tests of a roofing system is the roof cut. The purpose of this test is to determine the existing construction and conditions of the roof. Once the cut is removed, the sample can be evaluated to determine the condition and the moisture content of the materials. This test should not be conducted where a warranty exists as this may be jeopardized.

Moisture Meters: Moisture detection in a roofing system is greatly aided by the use of instrumentation. The presence of moisture in roofing and structural members can be detected by several portable diagnostic tools, with moisture meters being the most common.

Infrared Thermography: Infrared thermography identifies radiation wavelengths within building materials and components. By using infrared thermography to spot thermal anomalies in the roof, many leaks can be tracked, verified, and repaired. Since the moisture is usually of a lower or higher temperature than the surrounding materials, the scanner registers the areas of differential temperature. Infrared can quickly let you see the true condition of the roof's insulation, and by applying infrared thermography, it is possible to save money by replacing only the moist areas of insulation. Moreover, when the roof develops a leak, infrared surveys can locate the trapped water. Because the leak is typically found to be within the boundary of the wet insulation, the wet area is marked for removal and repair. That keeps the roof in a dry condition, minimizing roof degradation and extending the life of the roof.

Nuclear Moisture Detector: Another type of moisture detection instrument is the nuclear moisture detector. It works by emitting a cone of high-velocity neutrons into the roof. As the neutrons are reflected back, a reading is taken to determine the speed of their return. Neutrons that have come in contact with the hydrogen in water return more slowly, allowing areas of moisture to be identified. Unlike the infrared meter, the nuclear meter can be used during the day. A license to operate the equipment is required by the U.S. Nuclear Regulatory Commission.

The Troxler Roof Reader™ is an example of a commercial roof nuclear moisture detector (Figure 9.12A). It essentially maps the hydrogen concentrations within the roofing structure, permitting repair or replacement of only saturated areas (Figure 9.12B). As part of a preventative maintenance program, the RoofReader can quickly pinpoint problem areas, saving time and minimizing capital outlay.

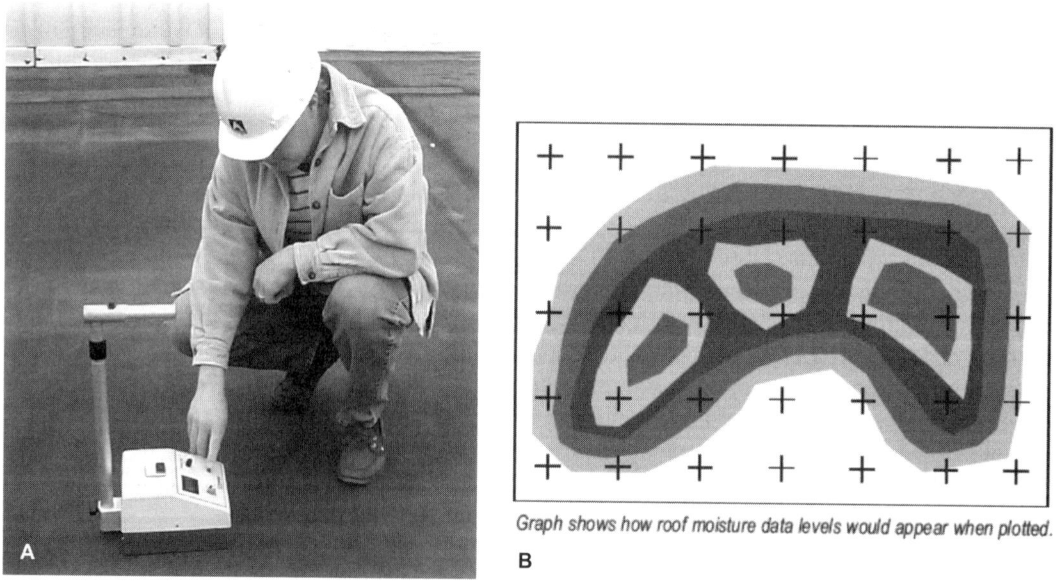

Figure 9.12 A. Applying a nuclear roof moisture detector *(Courtesy Troxler Labs)*. B. Mapping of moisture data levels on nuclear moisture gauge *(Courtesy Troxler Labs)*.

CHAPTER

10

Heating, Ventilating, and Air Conditioning (HVAC) Systems

10.1 GENERAL

HVAC systems have changed the way buildings are designed, built, and occupied. The development of air conditioning in particular brought about the biggest changes because it allowed investors and companies to build larger, higher, and more efficient buildings than was previously the case. However, it took many years and a long educational and empirical process to get building owners and architects to recognize the significance and impact of long-term operating costs in their planning and not just the initial cost of equipment. Statistics indicate that HVAC systems account for approximately 40 percent of the energy used in commercial buildings in the United States. Consequently, building owners have the potential to realize significant savings by improving their control of HVAC operations and improving the efficiency of the systems used.

The mechanical aspects of air conditioning developed at an extraordinary pace during the first half of the 20th century and have taken center stage since then. Computers continue to play a pivotal role in this development and have given electronics manufacturers much-needed help in designing equipment more intelligently. Moreover, electronics in equipment have made HVAC systems smarter, smaller, and more efficient. They have reshaped how the systems are installed, how they are maintained, and how they operate.

Another important recent development in HVAC equipment design is the introduction of Variable Air Volume (VAV). In such systems, anyone who has conditioned air circulating in, on, or around them can control the temperature in their own personal space. For example, if two persons are on the same system and one wants to increase the temperature, the system can heat that person's space and cool the other. It can also change the volume of air delivered to the space. In addition, with variable air volume systems, it is possible to damper off a space that is unused or unoccupied, increasing efficiency.

Psychologists and scientists have known for many years that physical comfort is critical to work effectiveness, satisfaction, and physical and mental well-being. Empirical evidence shows that uncomfortable conditions in the workplace invariably restrict the ability of workers to function to their full capacity, leading in many cases to lower job satisfaction and increases in illness symptoms. And since humans generally spend about 90 percent of their time indoors, health and comfort in buildings are crucial issues. And while there are many system configurations, as we can see in Figure 10.1, the main components of a system consist of a fairly standard boilerplate design on which an assessment can be based.

The energy source that provides power to an HVAC system is usually gas, solid fuels, oil, or electricity. The conducting medium is typically water, steam or gas. The heating and cooling source equipment

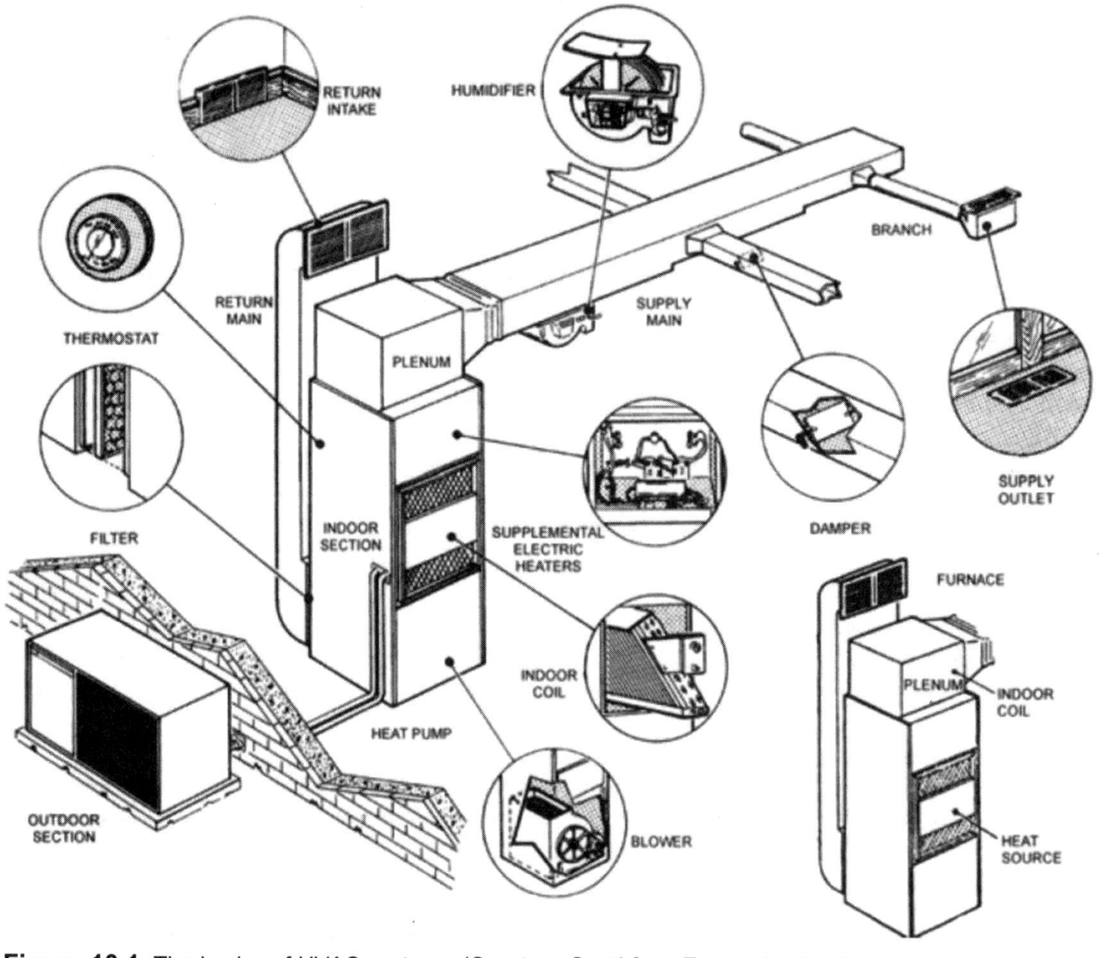

Figure 10.1 The basics of HVAC systems *(Courtesy Southface Energy Institute)*.

consists of components that use the energy source to heat or cool the conducting medium. The heating and cooling units (such as air conditioners and air handling units) are the components of the system that modify the air temperatures for the interior environment.

The assessment of the HVAC system is one of the main components of a PCA survey. This is in large part due to the cost of operations and maintenance typically associated with HVAC systems.

10.2 REFRIGERANTS: HYDROCHLOROFLUOROCARBONS (HCFCS) AND CHLOROFLUOROCARBONS (CFCS)

Refrigerants are fluids that produce a refrigerating effect while expanding or vaporizing and make the mechanical cooling cycle possible. The two refrigerant families most often used in air conditioning systems are Hydrochlorofluorocarbons (HCFCs) and Chlorofluorocarbons (CFCs). The Environmental Protection Agency, in accordance with the Montreal Protocol, is now obligated to phase out over a period of years hydrochloroflourocarbon (HCFC) refrigerants used in heat pump and air conditioning systems because of their impact on ozone depletion. To date, the main alternatives are HFCs and HFC blends, although there are several potential non-HFC alternatives as well. But while Hydroflourocarbons (HFCs) may be suitable as short to medium-term replacements, they may not be suitable for long term use due to their high global warming potential (GWP).

Chlorofluorocarbon (CFC) refrigerants manufacture has been banned in the United States since 1995, largely because its release into the atmosphere has been linked with the depletion of the Earth's protective ozone layer producing the "greenhouse effect." This refrigerant phase out of CFCs and HCFCs will have a significant impact on proposed real estate purchases that still utilize this equipment. This means that owners and administrators need to take the long view when making decisions about their capital investments. This should all be documented in the PCA report, which would also include a review of capitalization requirements associated with the phase-out of CFC/HCFC-containing refrigerants. Any decision to replace such equipment needs to be based upon a thorough engineering and cost analysis.

10.3 TYPES OF HVAC SYSTEMS

Occupied buildings all require a supply of fresh air, and depending on outdoor conditions, the air may need to be cooled or heated before it is distributed into the occupied space. This is typically where HVAC systems come into play. While there are a wide variety of HVAC systems in use in today's real estate, no system is right for every application. HVAC systems range in complexity from stand-alone units that serve individual rooms or zones to large, centrally controlled systems serving multiple zones in a building.

10.3.1 Heating Systems

Electric heating: The practice of using electricity for heating is increasing in both residences and public buildings. Electric heating generally costs more than energy obtained from combustion of a fuel, but the convenience, cleanliness, and reduced space needs of electric heat can often justify its use. The heat can be provided from electric coils or strips used in varying patterns, such as convectors in or on the walls, under windows, or as baseboard radiation in part or all of a room. The overall cost of electric heating can be substantially reduced through the incorporation of a heat-pump system.

Electric baseboard heaters: Sometimes called electric strip heaters, baseboard radiation is a fairly common heat source and heating system. Electric baseboard heaters are typically installed along the lower part of outside walls to provide perimeter heating. Room air heated by the resistance element rises and is replaced by cooler room air, establishing a continuous convective flow of warm air while in operation. Baseboard heaters are typically controlled by an electric thermostat, which may be in an adjacent or remote location.

Central heating is often used in cold climates to heat a single building or group of buildings. Present-day systems contain a central boiler or furnace to heat water, pipes to distribute the heated water, and heat exchangers or radiators to conduct this heat to the air. In large systems, steam or hot water is usually employed to distribute the heat. The vast majority of modern commercial buildings including office buildings, high-rise residential, hotels and shopping malls are today provided with central heat.

All but the simplest systems have a pump to circulate the water and ensure an equal supply of heat to all the radiators. The heated water is often fed through another heat exchanger inside a storage cylinder to provide hot running water. Forced air systems send air through ductwork, which can be reused for air conditioning, and the air can be filtered or put through air cleaners. The heating elements (radiators or vents) should be located in the coldest part of the room, typically next to the windows.

Furnace: A furnace is a heating system component designed to heat air for distribution to various building spaces. Small-capacity furnaces that rely on natural convection for heat distribution would be classified as local systems and usually effectively condition only one space. Furnaces equipped with fans to circulate air over greater distances or to several rooms would be found in central systems. All four heat source categories are used with furnaces, including on-site combustion (solid fuels, oil, natural gas, propane), electric resistance, on-site energy collection (solar energy), and heat transfer (heat pumps). A furnace is a packaged assembly of components that normally includes a heat-source element (burner or coil), a fan (for central units), and an air filter. A burner consists of an arrangement of nozzles that permits the efficient combustion of liquid or gaseous fuels by providing good mixing between the fuel and the oxygen necessary for combustion. A coil consists of a series of heat exchange surfaces that are either the heat source itself (electric resistance coils) or that provide close thermal contact with a heat distribution medium (hot water or steam coils in air handling units or fan-coils). Most furnaces are controlled by remote thermostats placed at strategic locations.

One of the main methods of direct heating is by radiation, and the term *radiant heating* is usually applied to systems in which walls, floors, or ceilings become the radiating units. Steam or hot water pipes are built into the walls or floors during the construction process. When electricity is used as the heating medium, the panels containing heating elements are placed on a wall, baseboard, or the ceiling. Radiant heating provides uniform heat that is both efficient and relatively inexpensive to operate.

Warm air systems: A basic warm air heating system consists of a firebox and waste-gas passage set within a sheet-metal casing, with ducts leading to the different spaces to be heated. Placing the furnace below the first floor of the facility ensures natural circulation of the warm air, because warm air has a tendency to rise. Cold air, whether from within the building or from outside, enters between the firebox and the casing and becomes heated through contact with the hot surfaces of the furnace. The furnace is often arranged so that the warm air is made to pass over a water pan in the furnace for humidification before being circulated through the building. Once the air is heated, it passes through various ducts to individual grills or registers in each space of the upper floors. The grills or registers can be opened or closed to control the temperature of the rooms.

In a forced-circulation system a fan or blower is installed in the furnace casing to ensure adequate circulation of air even under unfavorable conditions. In addition, if combined with cooling, humidifying, and dehumidifying units, forced-circulation systems can also be used for heating and cooling.

Hot water systems: This type of system typically employs a central boiler, in which water is heated to a temperature of from 140 to 180 degrees F (60 to 83 degrees C). The water is then distributed by means of pipes to some type of coil units, such as radiators, located in the various rooms. Although distribution of the hot water can be achieved by pressure and gravity, forced circulation using a pump is preferable because it provides greater flexibility and control. In the rooms, the emitters give out the heat from their surfaces by radiation and convection. The cooled water is then returned to the boiler. In addition, there are combination systems that use ducts for supplying air from the central air handling unit, and water to heat the air before it is transferred into the conditioned space.

Either a one-pipe or a two-pipe system is used to circulate the heated water. In a one-pipe system, water enters each radiator from the supply side of the main pipe, circulates through the radiator, and flows back into the same pipe. In the two-pipe system, radiators are all supplied with hot water at the same temperature from a single supply pipe, and the water from these radiators flows back to the furnace through a common return pipe. The two-pipe system provides a more efficient system that is easier to control than the one-pipe system. In both systems an expansion tank is necessary to compensate for variations in the volume of water in the system.

Steam systems: Steam heating systems are very similar to hot water systems except that steam rather than hot water is distributed by a pipe system to the radiators. In the radiators, the steam condenses and gives up its latent heat. Both the one-pipe and two-pipe arrangements are used to circulate the steam and then returning to the boiler the water formed by condensation. The three most popular types of steam systems currently in use are: air-vent systems, vapor systems, and vacuum, or mechanical-pump systems.

Heat pumps: A heat pump extracts available heat from one location and transfers it to another, unlike a furnace, which creates heat. Even cold air contains some heat, and heat pumps can extract heat from the outside air on a cold day and transfer it inside to maintain a comfortable temperature. During the heating season, a liquid refrigerant is pumped through a coil that is outside the area to be heated. As the refrigerant is cold, it absorbs heat from the outside air, the ground, or some other source. It then flows to a compressor, which raises its temperature and pressure and transforms to vapor, after which it flows to an indoor coil. There the warmth is radiated or blown into the room or space to be heated. Upon giving up much of its heat, the refrigerant then flows through a valve where its pressure and temperature are lowered further. Before being liquefied, the refrigerent is pumped into the outdoor coil to continue its cycle. To air condition a space, valves are used to reverse the flow thus allowing the refrigerant to pick up heat from the interior and discharges it outside. As with furnaces, heat pumps are usually controlled by thermostats.

Heating is achieved by reversing the cooling cycle. Heat pumps are actually air conditioners that run in reverse to bring heat from outdoors into the interior. In certain weather conditions they are extremely efficient, especially when the outside temperature is around 50 degrees Fahrenheit. However, as the outdoor temperature begins to drop, the heat loss of a space becomes greater, requiring the heat pump to operate for longer stretches of time for it to be able to maintain a constant indoor temperature.

The majority of heat pumps use atmospheric air as their heat source. This presents a problem in regions where winter temperatures often drop below freezing, making it difficult to raise the temperature and pressure of the refrigerant. Should the outdoor temperature continue to drop, the heat pump will require assistance from traditional electric resistance heat coils. The thermostat will most probably have a light that comes on when this happens. It is usually labeled as emergency or auxiliary heat.

Geothermal heat pumps, also known as ground source heat pumps, are a highly efficient renewable energy technology that is gaining wide acceptance for both residential and commercial buildings. Indeed, business owners around the United States are now installing geothermal heat pumps to heat and cool their buildings. In addition to providing increased comfort for employees, customers and tenants, this technology offers significant dollar savings in energy and operation and maintenance costs.

Its great advantage is that it works by concentrating naturally existing heat, rather than by producing heat through combustion of fossil fuels. For heating, a geothermal heat pump removes the heat from the fluid in the Earth connection, concentrates it, and then transfers it to the building. For cooling, the process is reversed. Conventional ductwork is generally used to distribute heated or cooled air from the geothermal heat pump throughout the building. If the thermostat light is on while the heat pump is working, the system requires the attention of a professional. Figures 10.2 and 10.3 illustrate two typical applications of geothermal pump systems.

The more heat a system can produce or remove using a given amount of electricity, the more efficient it is. A common measurement of this performance is the Seasonal Energy Efficiency Ratio (SEER). The highest SEER heat pumps currently manufactured are a little over SEER 16. It should be noted that the new Federal Appliance Standards, which took effect on January 23, 2006, will require the new standards for central air conditioners be a minimum of 13 SEER.

A number of relatively new innovations are improving the performance of heat pumps. Unlike standard compressors that can only operate at full capacity, two-speed compressors allow heat pumps to operate close to the heating or cooling capacity that is needed at any particular moment. This saves large amounts of electrical energy and reduces compressor wear. Two-speed heat pumps also work well with zone control systems.

Some models of heat pumps are equipped with *variable-speed* or *dual-speed motors* on their indoor fans, outdoor fans, or both. The variable-speed controls for these fans attempt to keep the air moving at a

Figure 10.2 A typical commercial-size geothermal heat pump, used to circulate water through ground-source heat exchangers to provide space heating/cooling and hot water on the Georgia Tech campus *(Courtesy Craig Miller, U.S. Department of Energy)*.

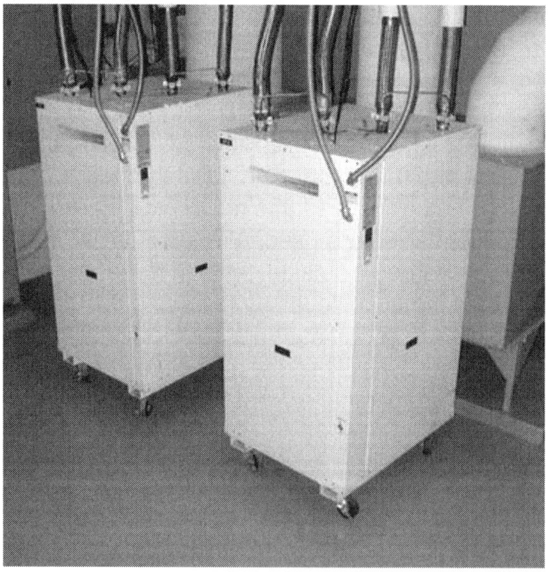

Figure 10.3 Two 36-ton geothermal heat pumps used for space heating at the College of Southern Idaho *(Courtesy Bruce Green)*.

comfortable velocity, minimizing cool drafts and maximizing electrical savings. Another advance in heat pump technology is the *scroll compressor,* which consists of two spiral-shaped scrolls. One remains stationary, while the other orbits around it, compressing the refrigerant by forcing it into increasingly smaller areas.

Although most heat pumps use electric resistance heaters as a backup for cold weather, heat pumps can also be equipped with burners to supplement the heat pump. The use of back-up burners helps to solve the problem of the heat pump by delivering relatively cool air during cold weather while simultaneously reducing its use of electricity.

Vapor compression refrigeration unit: The most commonly used active cooling approach involves the operation of a vapor compression refrigeration cycle to induce heat to move in a direction contrary to gross environmental temperature differences. During the overheated period, the outside air temperature is usually not just above the balance point temperature, but also above the indoor air temperature. Under such conditions, heat flow will be from higher to lower temperature (from outside to inside). Maintaining thermal comfort during the overheated period requires that heat be removed from a building, not added to it. Through a series of artificially maintained temperature and pressure conditions in a heat transfer fluid (refrigerant), a refrigeration system can induce heat to flow from inside a cooler building to a warmer outside environment.

A vapor compression unit establishes a heat sink through the flow of a refrigerant in a fixed loop between a compressor, a condenser, an expansion valve, and an evaporator. The compressor adds energy to the refrigerant that increases its pressure. From the compressor, high-pressure, high-temperature refrigerant is circulated to a condenser. The condenser indirectly exposes the refrigerant to air or water of lower temperature. The exchange of heat from the refrigerant to air or water permits the refrigerant to condense from the vapor state to the liquid state. This change of state releases a substantial amount of heat that is also absorbed by the air or water flowing through the condenser. Liquid refrigerant with lower energy content is then circulated to an expansion valve. The expansion valve produces a pressure drop large enough to cause part of the liquid refrigerant to evaporate. The change from the liquid to vapor state requires energy input. As a small percentage of the refrigerant evaporates after passing through the expansion valve, the temperature of the refrigerant is reduced as heat is removed to drive the evaporation process. The cooler refrigerant mixture is then circulated to the evaporator.

Room air or chilled water brought into indirect contact with the refrigerant provides heat for the complete evaporation of all remaining liquid refrigerant. The transfer of this heat from the air or water to the refrigerant reduces the temperature of the air or water. The cooled air or water may then be used as a heat sink for the building. In an absorption refrigeration unit the water acts as a refrigerant, circulating between a generator, a condenser, an evaporator, and an absorber. Heat is added to the generator, which causes the refrigerant to evaporate. The vapor-state refrigerant is conveyed to the condenser where heat is removed by transfer to condenser water or air and the refrigerant is condensed to liquid. The refrigerant is then transferred to the evaporator where it accepts heat from room air or chilled water. The fully evaporated (gaseous) refrigerant then travels to the absorber and from the absorber to the generator where the cycle continues.

Solar thermal collector: Solar collectors may be used to heat air or water for building heating purposes. Water-heating collectors may replace or supplement a boiler in a water-based heating system. Air-heating collectors may replace or supplement a furnace. As solar energy in an active solar system is typically collected at a location remote from the spaces requiring heat, solar collectors are normally associated with central systems. Solar water-heating collectors may also provide heated water that can be used for space cooling in conjunction with an absorption refrigeration system.

10.3.2 Ventilation

Buildings in which people live and work must be ventilated to replenish oxygen, dilute the concentration of carbon dioxide and water vapor, minimize unpleasant odors, and remove contaminants from the air of the occupied space. Ventilation includes both exchange of air to the outside as well as circulation of air within the building. Ventilation can be accomplished passively through natural ventilation, or forced ventilation through mechanical distribution systems powered by fans.

In cold climates *natural ventilation* is often just a matter of opening a window, but in hot climates it is an important consideration in the design of buildings. *Forced ventilation* may be used to control humidity or odors. Kitchens and bathrooms typically have mechanical ventilation to control both. Heat recovery ventilation systems, on the other hand, employ heat exchangers to bring the fresh air temperature to room temperature.

Factory ventilation systems must remove hazardous airborne contaminants from the workplace. Nearly all chemical processes generate hazardous waste gases and vapors, and these must be removed from the workplace environment in a cost-effective manner.

Engineers estimate that for adequate ventilation, the air in a room should be changed completely from one and a half to three times each hour, or that about 10 to 30 cubic feet (about 280 to 850 liters) of outside air per minute should be supplied for each occupant. To provide this amount of ventilation will typically require the use of mechanical devices to augment the natural air flow. Ventilating systems may be combined with heaters, filters, humidity controls, or cooling devices and often include heat exchangers.

10.3.3 Air Conditioning

An air-conditioning system, according to the ASHRAE definition, is a system that must accomplish four objectives simultaneously. These objectives are to: 1. control air temperature, 2. control air humidity, 3. control air circulation, 4. control air quality. In fact, an air-conditioning system will typically provide heating, cooling, ventilation and humidity control for a building or facility. Systems are usually installed in modern offices and public buildings, but it is difficult to retrofit because of the bulky air ducts required. Moreover, systems must be carefully maintained to prevent the growth of pathogenic bacteria in the ducts and to ensure efficient operation.

Exterior wall or window air-conditioning units: Wall or window electric air-conditioning units are often used in small buildings and trailers. They are also used in retrofit situations in conjunction with an existing system. Basically, they are small ductless units with casings extending through the wall. The units are generally noisy, and being ductless, are only practical for cooling small areas. If you take the cover off of an unplugged window unit, you will find that it contains a compressor, an expansion

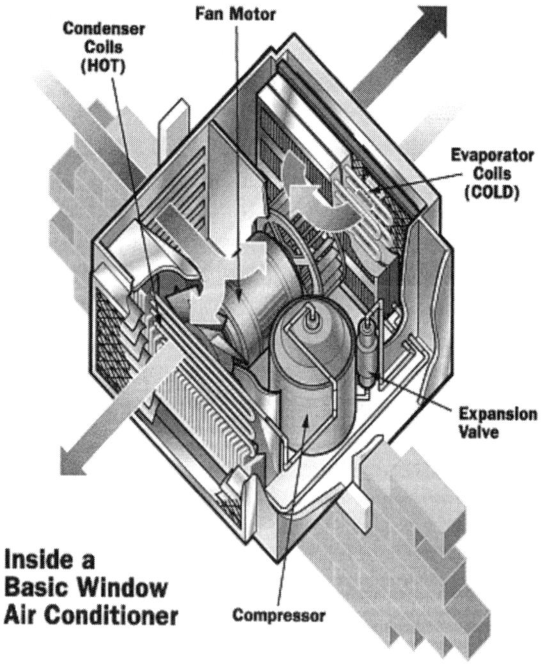

Figure 10.4 Components of a basic window AC unit *(Courtesy HowStuffWorks.com)*.

valve, a hot coil (on the outside), a chilled coil (on the inside), two fans, and a control unit (Figure 10.4). The fans blow air over the coils to improve their ability to dissipate heat (to the outside air) and cold (to the room being cooled).

Central air-conditioning systems: Today, centralized air-conditioning systems provide fully controlled heating, cooling, and ventilation, and are employed extensively in modern offices, theaters, stores, restaurants, and other building types. Because of the complexity of such systems, they are generally incorporated into the design and are installed during the building's construction. Computer technology is increasingly being used to automate these systems for purposes of energy conservation and improved efficiency. Older buildings may be equipped with a refrigerating unit, blowers, air ducts, and a plenum chamber in which indoor air is mixed with air from the exterior. These installations help cool and dehumidify during the summer months, while allowing the use of the regular heating system during the winter.

The design of any air-conditioning system depends mainly on the type of structure in which the system is to be used, the size of space to be cooled, the function of that space, and the number of occupants using it. A building having large windows facing the sun, or an indoor office space with many heat-producing lights, requires a system with a larger cooling capacity than a windowless space in which cool fluorescent lighting is used. Similarly, the circulation of air must be greater in a space in which the occupants are permitted to smoke than in a space of equal capacity in which smoking is prohibited.

Split system: The term *split system* generally implies that the condenser and compressor are located in an outdoor package and the refrigerant metering device and the evaporator are in an internal package. For reverse cycle applications, the heat exchangers can swap roles, with the heat exchanger exposed to outside air becoming the evaporator and the inside heat exchanger becoming the condenser (Figure 10.5).

Split systems may have a variety of configurations. The four basic components of the vapor compression refrigeration cycle—compressor, condenser, refrigerant metering device, and evaporator—can be grouped in several ways. The grouping of components is based on practical considerations, such as available space, ease of installation, keeping noise outside occupied spaces, etc. The inside equipment may include heating coils, which are usually electric resistance elements.

In warehouses, businesses, malls, large department stores, etc., the condensing unit is normally located on the roof and can be quite massive. Alternatively, there may be many smaller units on the roof, each attached inside to a small air handler that cools a specific zone in the building. In larger buildings and particularly in multi-story buildings, the split-system approach begins to run into problems. Either the distance between the condenser and the air handler exceeds pipe distance limitations, or the amount of duct work and the length of ducts becomes unmanageable.

Packaged systems: With a packaged system, all components are located in a single outdoor unit that may be located on the ground or roof. A packaged rooftop unit is a self-contained air handling unit, which is typically used in low-rise buildings. These are mounted directly onto roof curbs and discharge conditioned air into the building's air duct distribution system (Figure 10.6). They come in many capacities, from a unit of just over one ton to systems of several hundred tons that contain multiple compressors.

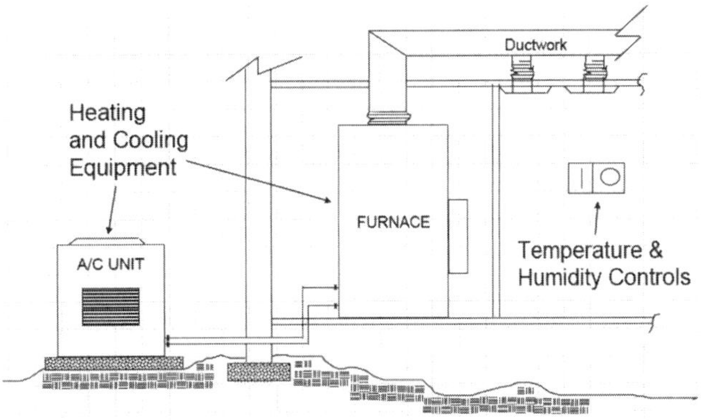

Figure 10.5 A drawing illustrating how a split system works *(Courtesy Southface Energy Institute)*.

Packaged units commonly use electricity to cool and gas to heat. The system may be for single or multiple-zone application. In the process of assessing packaged rooftop units the inspector should essentially confirm the type, location, and condition of the unit and whether it is operating satisfactorily. Also to be checked is whether the condensate line and pan are watertight and free of leaks and whether there is evidence of rust or corrosion. Filters should also be checked to see if they require replacement.

Figure 10.6 Example of packaged rooftop units.

All-air systems cool or heat spaces through the utilization of conditioned air. Heat is ducted to the space with supply and return air ducts.

Larger buildings in the United States generally incorporate one of several variations of primary system types, including central chilled water plant with floor-by-floor air handling units and variable air volume distribution, central condenser water with floor-by-floor self contained air units, variable air volume distribution systems, and central condenser water systems with console heat pumps and constant volume on the interior zones. High-velocity dual duct and multizone systems are also used for small buildings and outside the U.S.

Constant air volume systems utilize single-duct, single-zone systems, whereas single-duct, dual-duct, and multizone systems can be either constant air volume or variable air volume systems. A multizone system is typically used in large multistory buildings where it is not practical or efficient to use many AHUs, each serving a single zone. Instead, several zones are served, each with its own thermostat control.

10.4 HVAC SYSTEM REQUIREMENTS

Commercial construction usually takes advantage of ceiling plenums to run horizontal ducts while vertical ducts are typically contained within their own chases. Depending on the type of structure and depth of the plenum, large ducts may occupy much of this depth, leaving little or no space for recessed light fixtures. Occasionally, commercial construction uses access flooring (typically in computer room applications), which consists of a false floor of individual panels raised by pedestals above the structural floor. This is designed to provide sufficient space to run electrical and communication wiring as well as HVAC ductwork. Sometimes small pipes are designed to run within a wall system, whereas larger pipes may need deeper walls or even chase walls to accommodate the pipes.

Where the plenum is used as a return air space, most local and national building codes prohibit the use of combustible materials such as wood or exposed wire within the space in commercial construction. Building codes stipulate that access be provided to certain components of mechanical and electrical systems, basically to allow for maintenance and repair, and includes such elements as valves, fire dampers, heating coils, mechanical equipment, and electrical junction boxes.

10.5 TYPES OF DEFICIENCIES

In the majority of cases, the chief cause of HVAC deficiencies is maintenance related. As the maintenance of the equipment is deferred or performed by unqualified personnel, the system will increasingly experience problems. When properly maintained, a building's HVAC system can enjoy a life span of up to 60 years.

In general, HVAC deficiencies fall into two main categories: issues that are fairly simple to address, such as the replacement of filters or belts, and issues that require the attention of specialized personnel, such as the replacement of a pump or boiler. Another common deficiency is that the system is not adequate for the size of the facility. A rule of thumb in an assessment is to compare the actual tonnage of the unit to the standard design tonnage using the formulas below:

$$\text{BTU of Unit} \div 12{,}000 = \text{actual tonnage of the unit}$$

$$\text{Square footage of the building} + 350 = \text{design tonnage}$$

From these two formulas, the inspector should be able to ascertain whether the unit is of adequate size or not. Note that most designers of mechanical systems now utilize computer analysis software to determine heating and cooling loads.

In assessing a facility's heating systems, the inspector should observe the heating and distribution equipment in place with regard to its installation and working condition. The report should likewise include any readily accessible component found to be in need of immediate or major repair.

The method of survey will largely be visual, as noted in the building survey report. Readily accessible service doors or access panels will be removed as provided by the equipment manufacturer for routine servicing and maintenance. Upon getting permission from the client, the inspector may then operate the equipment using normal operating controls.

The following are typically excluded from an HVAC PCA survey:

1. Heating equipment not otherwise known or able to be determined from information as normally provided by the client, an authorized agent, or real estate listing received prior to the inspection, unless mutually agreed upon at the time thereof.
2. Heating equipment excluded from or not otherwise stated in a building inspection proposal as submitted and agreed to before conducting a commercial property inspection.
3. Observation of or reporting on any heating system components not readily accessible to view.
4. Evaluation of the working condition of heating equipment that has been shut down, abandoned, or disused for any length of time.
5. Major tear down or disassembly of any HVAC equipment in order to observe system components or parts thereof not otherwise readily accessible to view upon removal of service access panels.
6. Operation or testing of safety controls and devices installed by the equipment manufacturer.
7. Observation or operation of equipment that does not comply with building codes or when doing so would compromise the safety of the inspector or the building occupants.
8. Determination or evaluation of the efficiency of the heating system.

In evaluating the cooling and air handling equipment of a building or facility, the inspector would basically address the same issues and use the same assessment methods as in surveying heating systems. This also applies to items and issues normally excluded from a standard PCA survey.

Defect recognition is a major part of any commercial survey. A field observer would be required to observe and report on the following during an HVAC systems survey:

1. Type of equipment: chiller, water cooled, air cooled, single or multizone
2. Size of the equipment: tons, horsepower, or BTUs
3. Location of equipment: roof, basement, attic, or on grade
4. Types of thermostat controls: low voltage, hi-voltage, pneumatic or interior duct controls
5. Installation concerns: roof curbs, vibration eliminators, air distribution, free returns or ducted returns, etc.
6. Water temperature for cooling towers
7. Ventilation and fresh air requirements
8. Circulating water temperature required for each chiller convector
9. Refrigeration circuit: leaks, piping, and arrangements, condensate discharge

Common deficiencies and other conditions to look for when carrying out an HVAC inspection include:

1. Evidence of excessive component vibrations
2. Insufficient air movement to reach all parts of the room or space being cooled
3. Return air at the return registers is not at least 10 to 15 degrees Fahrenheit warmer than the supply air
4. The presence of drafts in the room or space being cooled
5. Identify the location of the thermostats
6. Any evidence of any fan alignment deficiencies
7. Any evidence of excessive noise
8. Evidence of leaking caused by inadequate seals
9. Evidence of deterioration, corrosion, or scaling
10. Evidence of unsafe equipment conditions, including instability or absence of safety equipment (guards, grills, or signage)
11. Does the building have an exhaust system?
12. Is there a fresh air make up system in the building?
13. Are the toilets vented independently or mixed with the common area venting system?
14. Is the duct work used in the building metal or fiber glass?

Many of the comfort problems that plague buildings are often caused by missing insulation or excessive air leakage. Often, tenants "solve" these comfort problems by turning up the thermostat and adding extra heat. While some air exchange is essential for a healthy building, too much can prove costly, indeed.

10.6 HVAC EQUIPMENT COMPONENTS AND SYSTEMS

Numerous systems and components are used in combination to provide fresh air and temperature and humidity control in commercial real estate.

10.6.1 Basic Components of an HVAC System

The basic components of an HVAC system (Figure 10.7) that delivers conditioned air to maintain thermal comfort and indoor air quality are:

- Outdoor air intake
- Mixed-air plenum and outdoor air control
- Air filters located at return registers or possibly at or in the air handler
- Heating and cooling coils
- Humidification and/or de-humidification
- Equipment
- Supply fan
- Ducts
- Terminal device
- Return air system
- Exhaust or relief fans and air outlet
- Self-contained heating or cooling unit
- Controls
- Boiler
- Cooling tower
- Water chiller

It should be noted that for each commercial property type, some systems will perform better than others. From a lender's perspective, performance is judged by how well the needs of tenants and owners are met regarding comfort, operating costs, reliability, flexibility, and aesthetics.

Ductwork: The air handling duct system is an important component of the HVAC system, providing a distribution network of conditioned air to the various building spaces. Fiber glass insulation products are currently used in the majority of duct systems installed in the United States, and serve as key components of a well-designed, well-operated, and well-maintained HVAC system that will provide both thermal and acoustical benefits for the life of the building.

The different materials used for duct systems can substantially affect the overall performance of the systems. Examples of materials used for duct construction include fibrous glass, galvanized steel, black carbon steel, aluminum, stainless steel, copper, fiberglass reinforced plastic, polyvinyl steel, and concrete.

Periodic maintenance inspection will reveal any system breaches, which are typically more prevalent at duct intersections and flexible connections between the ductwork and the unit. Both supply air and return air may utilize ductwork, which may be located in the ceiling cavity or below the floor slab, depending on the configuration of the system. There are single-duct systems, with both cool air and hot air utilizing the same ducts, or double-duct systems, with separate ducts for cooling and heating. Fire dampers are required where ducts penetrate a fire wall. Modern fire dampers contain a fusible link that melts and separates when a particular temperature is reached, causing it to slam shut in the event of a fire.

Acoustic consideration is one of the major factors impacting the fabrication and design of duct systems, and unless properly designed and constructed, ducts can act as large speaker tubes transmitting noise throughout the building.

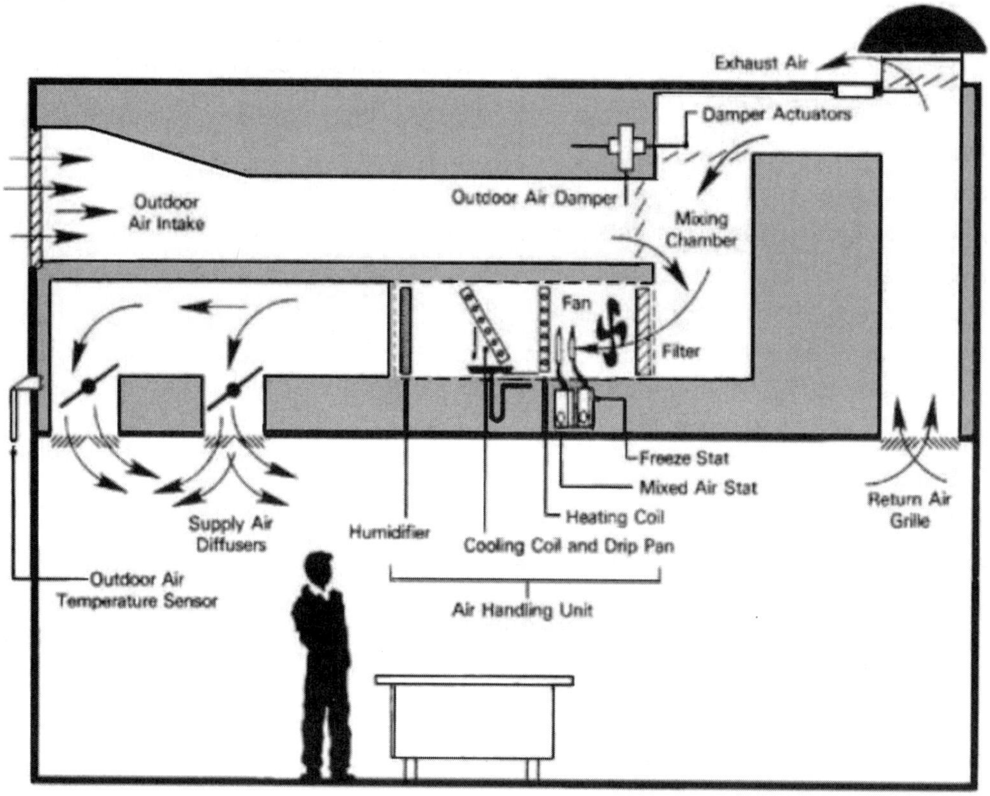

Figure 10.7 Typical HVAC system components that deliver conditioned air to a building or space to maintain thermal comfort and indoor air quality *(Courtesy Terry Brennan, Camroden Associates)*.

Grills, registers, and diffusers: Used in conjunction with ductwork, registers, diffusers, and grills assist in the return, collection and supply of conditioned air. Grills, registers, and diffusers are some of the major systems components used in residential and commercial buildings for producing clean and purified air.

The location of supply air diffusers and return air grills should be integrated with other ceiling elements, including lights, sprinkler heads, smoke detectors, speakers, and the like, so that the ceiling is aesthetically pleasing and well planned. To assist in this integration, these components are usually connected to the main ductwork with flexible ducting to allow some adjustability in their placement.

Registers are adjustable grill-like devices that cover the opening of a duct in a heating or cooling system, providing an outlet for heated or cooled air to be released into a room. Supply air registers are in essence grills equipped with double deflection adjustable vanes at the face and a damper behind the face for balance and to control the direction of flow and/or flow rate. A diffuser performs the task of diffusing the gas. The grills, registers, and diffusers introduce and blend the fresh air with the air of another environment or location. When fitted together, the grills take in fresh air, the registers blow the air out, and the diffusers scatter the air in the surroundings.

Thermostats: These are devices that control the operation of HVAC systems, turning on heating or cooling to bring the building to the set temperature. Modern programmable thermostats provide the basic function of maintaining comfortable indoor temperatures, but they include other valuable features as well. For example, they are capable of being programmed to automatically raise or lower the temperature of a facility according to predefined schedules. Most programmable thermostats allow input of weekday and weekend schedules. More sophisticated thermostats will allow humidity control, outdoor air ventilation, and can signal when the system filters need changing. Some modern thermostats can also include a communications link and demand management features that can be used to reduce air conditioning system energy use during periods of peak electrical demand or high electricity costs. Manufacturers claim that when combined with programmable thermostats, zoning systems can save up to 30 percent on heating and cooling costs while providing superior comfort.

Thermostats are typically placed 48–60 inches above the floor and away from exterior walls and heat sources. Their location should be coordinated with light switches, dimmers and other visible control devices.

Zoning: Control of an HVAC system is critical to its successful operation. The issue of system control leads to the concept of HVAC zoning. An HVAC system can have single-zone or multizone capabilities. Most of today's newest HVAC systems are being designed to incorporate many individually controlled temperature zones to improve occupant comfort. Thus in a single-zone system, the entire building is considered one area, whereas in a multizone system, the building is divided into various zones, allowing specific control of each area. For example, if an office manager prefers to have the conference room at a cooler temperature than the rest of the office, he can accomplish this. Zoning allows you therefore to eliminate the wasted energy of over conditioning areas in your office or home that have reduced exposures or that may be unused or unoccupied.

Boilers: A boiler is a heating system component designed to heat water for distribution to various building spaces. As water can not be used to directly heat a space, boilers are only used in central systems where hot water is circulated to delivery devices (such as baseboard radiators, unit heaters, convectors, or air-handling units). Once the delivery device is heated with the hot water, the water is returned back to the boiler to be re-heated and the water circulation loop continues. Depending upon design intent, a boiler may produce either hot water or steam. An on-site solar energy collection system may serve in lieu of a boiler. Heat transfer systems (heat pumps) likewise may serve as a substitute for a boiler. Constructed of cast iron or steel, and occasionally copper, there are several types of boilers including:

- Gas-fired, steam or hot water, cast iron or steel construction (Figure 10.8)
- Electric, steam or hot water, steel construction
- Oil-fired, steam or hot water, cast iron or steel construction
- Gas/Oil combination, steam or hot water, cast iron or steel construction

Chillers: Chillers can be air cooled or water cooled, with small systems utilizing a built-in air-cooled condenser. The difference between the two types has to do with how the chillers refrigeration system gets rid of the heat it removed from the water process loop.

Air-cooled chillers: Many small to medium chiller plants use air-cooled chillers with air-cooled screw chillers in the 150 to 400-ton range being the most common. Air-cooled screw chillers offer very good performance particularly at part load (Figure 10.9). The compressors are modulating rather than stepped, which provides more accurate control. Air-cooled chillers avoid the need for cooling towers, condenser pumps, and condenser piping which can offer substantial capital savings. Moreover, they do not require mechanical room space, which offers additional savings. Another advantage of air-cooled chillers is that they do not consume water like water-cooled chillers.

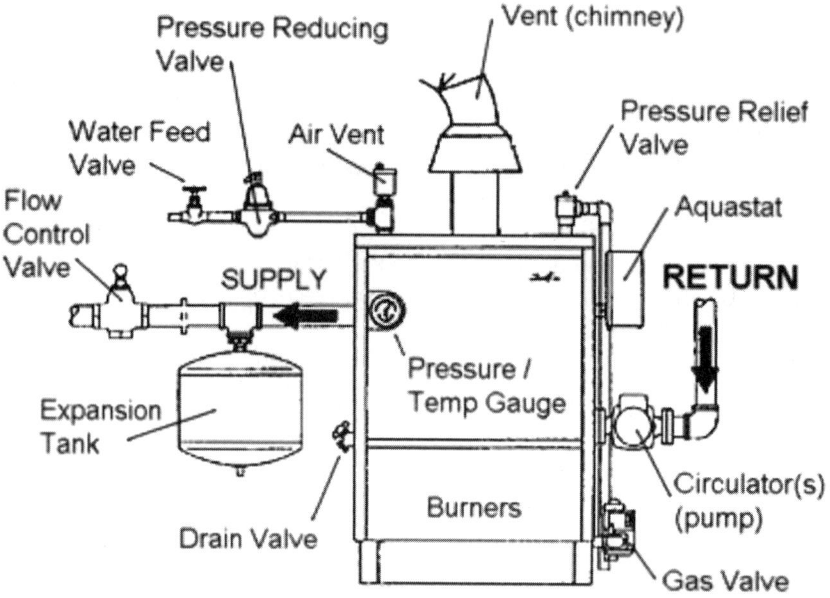

Figure 10.8 Diagram showing main components of a gas-fired hot water boiler *(Courtesy Home-Cost.com)*.

Since an air-cooled chiller transfers the heat from the process to its surroundings in the form of air, the environment in which the chiller will be used must be suitable. For example, to avoid overheating, air-cooled chillers must be located in an open, well-ventilated space. Larger air-cooled systems use a remote condenser connected to the chiller by refrigerant piping. Often an air-cooled chiller is the only solution in the absence of an existing cooling tower or the absence of 85-degree F plant water to use for the condenser.

Water-cooled chillers: In the case of a water-cooled chiller, heat is rejected to another water source, such as a cooling tower plant chilled water system. Water-cooled systems pipe water to a remote condenser source, such as a cooling tower or a pond.

Water-cooled chillers are typically designed to cool both the process as well as the process machine. In a typical plant layout, the evaporator and condenser are located inside the chiller unit, while the cooling tower is located on the outside. For chilled water-cooling systems, water chillers come in three basic designs. The *reciprocating compressor,* direct-expansion type is usually powered by an electric motor. The *centrifugal compressor,* direct-expansion type is typically powered by an electric motor or sometimes a steam-turbine drive. The *absorption type* uses approximately 10 percent of the electrical power of the other two types, and uses water as a refrigerant and lithium bromide or other salts as an absorbent.

The choice between a water-cooled chiller and an air-cooled unit partly depends on whether there is a cooling tower. The water chiller option is often preferred over the air-cooled unit because it costs less, has a higher cooling capacity per horsepower, and consumes less energy per horsepower. Compared to water, air is a poor conductor of heat, making the air-cooled chiller much larger and less efficient.

Evaporatively-cooled chillers: These are essentially water-cooled chillers in a box. The hot gaseous refrigerant is condensed by water flowing over the condenser tubes and evaporating. This ties the condensing temperature to ambient wet bulb, like a water-cooled chiller. The condenser, water sump and pump, etc., are all integral to the chiller. Whereas a water-cooled chiller will require a cooling tower, condenser pump, and field erected piping, the evaporatively-cooled chiller comes as a complete package from the factory. Evaporatively-cooled chillers offer the ease and savings of air cooled chiller installation while providing performance comparable to water-cooled chillers. Evaporatively-cooled chillers will require makeup water, water treatment, and drains, and have similar limitations as air-cooled chillers.

Figure 10.9 Air-cooled chillers: They must be located in an open, well-ventilated space to avoid overheating. In a typical plant layout, the evaporator and condenser are located inside the chiller unit. *(Courtesy 1st Choice Portable Chillers Inc).*

Dual-compressor chillers: Modern dual-compressor centrifugal chillers offer many advantages over conventional chillers. From a performance point of view, the chiller is most efficient at 50 percent capacity. At this point, only one compressor is operating and the evaporator and condenser are twice the size normally used for a compressor of that size (Figure 10.10A).

Variable frequency drive chillers (VFD): VFD chillers use a combination of VFDs and inlet guide vanes to modulate the capacity of the chiller. Performance savings are obtained when the VFD is used rather than the inlet guide vanes. The VFD can only be used when the lift on the compressor is reduced. The lift is reduced when the chiller load is decreased or when the condenser water temperature is lowered and/or the chilled water temperature is raised (Figure 10.10B).

A B

Figure 10.10 A. Dual-compressor centrifugal chillers have many advantages over conventional chillers. B. The VFD is used to change the speed of the compressor. They use a combination of VFDs and inlet guide vanes to modulate the capacity of the chiller *(Courtesy McQuay International).*

The best way to take advantage of a VFD chiller is to reduce the condenser water temperature as much as possible. Climates with reasonable annual changes in wet bulb are prime candidates for VFD chillers. Both dual compressor and VFD chillers operate much more efficiently at part load, whereas conventional chillers operate most efficiently at or near full load.

Heat recovery chillers: There are two types of heat recovery chillers. Both can produce condenser water from 105 to 115 degrees F rather than the normal 95 degrees F. Typically a heat exchanger is used to transfer the heat from the condenser loop into the hot water loop. This is done to avoid contamination from the open tower condenser loop entering the hot water loop. The second type has an additional condenser shell that allows the rejected heat to be rejected to a separate heat recovery water loop.

Chillers continue to evolve, both from sustainability and maintenance standpoints. Consider frictionless chillers that operate with oil-free magnetic bearing technology as the system does not have an oil cooler, oil pump, or oil heater.

Cooling towers: The basic function of cooling towers is to remove heat from the water discharged from the condenser so that the water can be discharged to the environment or recirculated and reused. Cooling towers are used in conjunction only with water-cooled chillers. Most buildings use mechanical draft cooling towers, located outside the building and typically on the roof. There are currently two common types of mechanical draft towers used in the HVAC industry: induced draft and forced draft. Induced draft towers have a large propeller fan at the top of the tower (discharge end) to draw air upward through the tower while warm condenser water spills down. They require much smaller fan motors for the same capacity than forced draft towers (Figures 10.11A, B).

Figure 10.11 A. Forced draft towers with fans on the air inlet to push air either counterflow or cross-flow to the movement of the water. Forward curved fans are often employed which use more fan power than induced draft. B. Induced draft towers have a large propeller fan at the top of the tower to draw air counterflow to the water. Induced draft towers are considered to be less susceptible to recirculation, which can result in reduced performance *(Courtesy McQuay International)*.

Forced draft towers utilize a fan at the bottom or side of the structure. Air is forced through the water spill area and discharged out the top of the structure. After the water has been cooled in the cooling tower, it is pumped to a heat exchanger or condenser in the refrigeration unit where it picks up heat again and is returned to the tower. The piping system is called the condenser water system.

Cooling tower process: Cooling towers expose the condenser water directly to the ambient air in a process that resembles a waterfall. The process can cool condenser water to below ambient dry bulb. The water is cooled by a combination of sensible and latent cooling. A portion of the water evaporates to provide the latent cooling. As the wet bulb temperature drops, cooling towers rely more on sensible cooling and less on latent cooling. Ambient air below freezing can hold very little moisture which leads to large plumes; and in some cases winter conditions may require a larger tower than summer conditions.

Winter operation: Cooling towers required to work in freezing winter environments require additional care. The condenser water must not be allowed to freeze, particularly when the tower is idle. Common solutions include the placement of electric or steam injection heaters or a remote sump within the building envelope.

Cooling tower controls: Cooling tower controls provide condenser water at the correct temperature to the chillers. Defining correct water temperature is very important. Lowering the condenser supply water temperature (to the chiller) increases the effort by the cooling tower and more fan work can be expected. It also improves the chiller's performance.

Cooling towers and energy efficiency: Cooling towers consume power to operate the fans. Induced draft towers should be selected since they typically use half the fan horsepower that forced draft towers use. Some form of fan speed control is also recommended, such as piggyback motors, multi-speed motors or Variable Speed Drives (VSDs).

Control valve basics: Control valves are used to maintain space temperature conditions by altering chilled water flow. Valves can be broken down into groups in several ways. Valves can be two-position or modulating. Two-position valves are either on or off. Control comes from time weighting. The percentage that the valve is open over a certain time period dictates the amount of cooling that the cooling coil actually does. Modulating valves vary the flow in response to the actual load at any given time. Valves can also be classified as two-way or three-way types. Two-way valves throttle flow while three divert flow. There are several different physical types of valves such as globe valves, ball valves and butterfly valves which are commonly used in the HVAC industry.

Condensers: Condensers are used in air conditioning systems to cool and condense the refrigerant gas that has become hot during the evaporation phase of the cooling process. The cooling process is accomplished using air, water, or both. Condenser types include air-cooled and cooling tower. Air-cooled condensers are the most basic and the most common way to condense the refrigerant in a refrigeration system.

In air-cooled condensers, the installation of variable-speed drives (VSDs) to control pumps and fans will deliver significant energy reductions in many commercial and industrial applications. The primary reason is that there is a cube relationship between power and speed (Figure 10.12). In an air-cooled system, this will normally consist of a multifan condenser with the fans sequenced individually from a step control to maintain the required pressure. When a single inverter is applied to control all of the fans in parallel, we can maintain a set pressure of 16 bars by modulating all the fans together.

On many condensers that have been operating for some time, the motors fitted to the first fans in sequence need constant attention due to the mechanical shock caused by constant cycling to maintain the correct pressure. The bearings on the last fans in sequence become seized, often because they have been idle during the winter. The application of inverter control means that all fans are kept rotating and do not need to cycle to maintain conditions.

Figure 10.12 Liebert Quiet-Line air-cooled condensers *(Courtesy Liebert Corp).*

Often, a visual inspection will show the first section of the condenser is blocked as a result of the lead fans pulling air through this section at high velocity. The use of an inverter means that low-velocity air passes through the entire condenser face, resulting in less debris blocking the heat exchanger while simultaneously solving the problem of excessive noise generated by the condensers.

Water-cooled condensers: Water-cooled evaporative air conditioning has numerous advantages over air-cooled units. Except for small air-conditioning installations, heat rejection via cooling towers is more efficient, takes up less space, and has an overall lower life-cycle cost than dry coolers. Energy savings of up to 30 percent are consistently possible. Not only are evaporative systems smaller and quieter than air-cooled condensers, but they also offer much lower life-cycle costs.

Large chilled-water air-conditioning systems have traditionally utilized large constant-speed pumps to circulate the chilled water, with throttle valves to control the flow. Variable-speed pump development makes possible new approaches to circulating water in the various parts of such an air-conditioning system—enhancing performance while reducing running costs.

One of the drawbacks of water-cooled systems, however, is that the condenser tubes sometimes develop mineral and bio-fouling problems, which significantly reduce overall performance and increase the energy cost for operation. It is therefore important to prevent or control such fouling at the condenser tubes of these systems. This can be done by the use of scale-inhibiting chemicals that are added to circulating cooling water and discharged to the sewer. The use of such chemicals is expensive and increasingly being discouraged due to concerns regarding fresh water pollution.

Pumps: A pump is used to convey, raise or otherwise change the pressure of fluids. Pumps are utilized in many applications, including increasing water pressure in the fire sprinkler systems and conveying hot and chilled water throughout the building. The pumps most commonly used are centrifugal, driven by an electrical motor and constructed of cast iron or bronze. Types of pumps include in-line centrifugal, close-coupled centrifugal, base mounted centrifugal and submersible sump.

In addition to noting their type, capacity, general condition, and location, pumps should be checked to see if the motor is operating satisfactorily. The field observer should also check that the valves are all operable and free of damage and that the strainer is in satisfactory condition. Sometimes a field observer might discover that the pump is not working. This may be due to it being seized or frozen, or due to a faulty pressure switch, worn bearings, or the motor simply being burned out. If the pump short-cycles or runs continuously, this may be an indication that the foot valve is leaking, the pressure tank is waterlogged, there is a leak in the piping system, or it may be due to a pressure switch. Where there is evidence of excessive noise or vibration, this may be caused by poor alignment or worn bearings.

Fans: Fans typically consist of an electric motor and a belt or direct motor drive, blades, and a wheel or propeller. Fans are best served by routine maintenance to calibrate and make ongoing adjustments. There are several types of fans, including centrifugal and belt drive models.

Roof ventilators: Roof ventilators are designed to provide ventilation in a building without the use of a fan (Figure 10.13). Ventilators remove air from or deliver air to a building through natural convection or wind force. They are normally constructed of galvanized steel or aluminum and should be adequately secured to the roof.

Figure 10.13 Daltec's Upblast and Hooded Roof Ventilators are designed to provide an efficient and economical means of exhausting large volumes of air.

Air filters: Filters are primarily used to remove particles from the air. The filter's type and design determine the efficiency at removing particles of a given size and the amount of energy needed to pull or push air through the filter. Filters are rated by different standards and test methods, such as dust spot and arrestance, which measure different aspects of performance. In order to maintain clean air in occupied spaces, filters must also remove bacteria, pollens, insects, soot, dust, and dirt with an efficiency suited to the use of the building.

Filters should be selected for their ability to protect both the HVAC system components and general indoor air quality. The main issues to look for when inspecting the filters in addition to their general condition, is whether they are sized properly and are correctly installed.

Tanks: Constructed typically of steel or fiberglass, tanks are used in many applications, including hot water or oil storage, expansion tanks for forced hot water heating systems, and water storage for fire extinguishing systems.

10.7 SYSTEM DIAGNOSTICS

The best method of determining whether the HVAC system is doing its job is the degree to which the building users are healthy and comfortable. When a building's HVAC system performs poorly, managers can find themselves faced with a significant loss of building efficiency. Indoor air quality can suffer, bacteria can grow in cooling towers, and occupant health can deteriorate, leaving companies at risk for low productivity, excessive sick time, degraded system performance, and possible liability claims. Having the capability to quickly diagnose operational problems in HVAC equipment means that equipment will operate as intended for a higher percentage of the total run time.

Ongoing changes to standards and evolutions in equipment are shaping the future of HVAC systems. As a result, two of ASHRAE's standards affecting HVAC systems in commercial facilities underwent recent changes. *ASHRAE 90.1* was updated as of 2004. The standard now offers more stringent energy-efficiency requirements for controls and equipment, as well as for building construction and operation. The equivalent *International Energy Conservation Code (IECC)* also underwent similar updates in its most recent release published in 2001. The *ASHRAE 62.1* standard for ventilation has also been updated and includes new requirements for ventilation. Some of the changes include the need to base ventilation rates in multiroom buildings on the ventilation requirements of each room and on requirements of spaces and the recirculation of air. This standard also specifies requirements for exhaust separation and inlet air locations.

Ideally, the evaluation of the HVAC system should begin with a review of all construction documents to determine the layout, components, and design of the system. During the PCA, the consultant should identify potential problem areas where possible, and present reasoned recommendations for correction.

Interviews with building staff and maintenance personnel usually provide important information regarding the condition, operation, and capabilities of the HVAC system. If the building superintendent or maintenance manager is attentive to the trends and conditions of the system, the deficiencies will be much easier to pinpoint and correct.

The physical inspection should begin at the main equipment area. This could be a mechanical room or at the rooftop package units. After reviewing the energy source equipment, the distribution system should be reviewed. This may be the ductwork, a ceiling plenum, or a combination of the two. The registers and outlets should be observed and reviewed during the physical survey of the interiors of the facility.

When reviewing the building interior, the adequacy of service and general performance of the system should be reviewed. Verification should be made as to whether the heat source for each room is functioning. Restroom exhaust fan operation should be evaluated. In kitchen areas, vented range hoods should be operated and surveyed. Buildings are insulated to control conductive losses or gains of thermal energy. When the proper levels of insulation are installed correctly, heat transfer by conduction is minimized and the building's users are comfortable.

Any assessment by the field observer of the appropriateness and adequacy of the HVAC systems requires:

1. An understanding of the principals of HVAC equipment selection
2. Specific knowledge to visually recognize equipment observed
3. Adequate understanding of equipment components regarding operation, uses, control parameters, and maintenance issues
4. An understanding of the equipment/system combinations that provide effective comfort, control, and flexibility to meet tenants' needs

Critical defects in air-conditioning equipment: During a PCA assessment, the field observer should look for critical defects in the HVAC system. Critical defects are those defects which form an immediate, significant safety hazard as well as defects that are quite likely to involve significant repair or replacement cost, and/or which involve components or systems that are necessary to occupy and use the building. Such defects would include:

- Air-conditioning compressor needs replacement
- Cooling is delivered to only a section of the building, e.g., only to one floor
- Unsafe return air intake that may draw in carbon monoxide at heating equipment
- Unsafe electrical wiring: Aluminum branch circuits are often used to power the compressor. Look for evidence of overheating or over fusing at the service cutoff and in the electrical panel.
- Uneven air supply resulting in uneven temperatures, especially on the first floor of a two story house with ductwork between the first and second floor
- Inadequate cooling capacity for the building
- Low temperature split (indicating inadequate cooling due to refrigerant leak)
- Refrigerant leaks at condenser or evaporator coils (usually requires coil replacement)

- Dirty air handler (This is a major expense to clean properly.)
- Leaking return ducts in crawl space (Note: Field observers do not enter crawl spaces.)

Methods for detection and diagnosis of these defects are discussed below. While several diagnostic tools and instruments can be used in the diagnosis of specific conditions in the HVAC system, the interviews with building personnel and observation during the physical survey will be the method most typically employed. This methodology will discover most of the significant issues at a given facility. Infrared sensors, thermometers and humidity testing equipment, while typically outside the scope of a standard PCA survey, can be used in a follow-up investigation to quantify and analyze the existing conditions of the system.

The location of return grills may mean the difference between an efficient system and an inefficient one. If the returns are positioned too close to the supplies, the result will be very little air circulation into the space. Hot spots will appear in the space because the air cannot reach the specified area due to short cycling between the supply and return air. Return air is usually 15 to 20 degrees warmer than the supply air.

The presence of drafts in a room or space often indicates poor duct design; however, one must also check for registers or diffusers that have been blocked off. In office environments, women are frequently colder than their male counterparts, and therefore, may prefer to close off the register in their areas. This can create problems in other areas because the balance will have been altered, creating drafts in these areas.

Even when registers and diffusers are closed, they will still allow about 10 percent of the air in the system to escape. Moreover, closed registers are usually noisy. This is due to duct systems that have no volume dampers. Volume dampers are designed to close off the air supply at the trunk line and reduce the noise at the register, and are also better for balancing the system. However, when too many registers or diffusers are closed, the cooling system cycles on and off; it then freezes up, delivering no cooling at all.

Thermostat location is also of prime importance because in order to maintain a balanced system of heating or cooling, the thermostat must be able to adequately regulate the temperature in all parts of the space. The blower fans should be run continuously to ensure total circulation within the space to achieve a well balanced system.

Where there is excessive noise, the reason may be due to the closing off of supply registers. High noise levels from equipment, water towers and outdoor condensing units may be due to worn bearings, failed vibration eliminators, or failed pads or curbs. Chillers, too, are noisy by nature and should be located in an area removed from the general working area. Whenever possible, chillers and compressors should incorporate sophisticated vibration eliminators to help reduce noise levels. Rooftop equipment, towers, condensers, fans, and other HVAC equipment should all be located to allow easy access and servicing.

Relative humidity testing devices: Relative humidity is the percentage of saturation of air by moisture. The higher the relative humidity, the more likely deterioration of components and building material will occur. A number of testing instruments and methods are available for use by inspectors.

With humidity indicator cards like the *Cobaltous Chloride Humidity Indicator,* the chemical is applied to a blotting paper attached to a portable wand. As the paper is exposed to the atmosphere, the color begins to change.

A *hygrometer* is another tool with which to determine relative humidity. It consists of both a wet and dry bulb thermometer. After the reading of the temperatures, calibration charts are referenced to determine the percentage of relative humidity which corresponds to the difference between wet and dry bulb temperatures.

A *sling psychrometer* (also called a whirling psychrometer) is a sling that allows the evaluator to spin the two thermometers of a hygrometer in the air. This provides a more accurate relative humidity reading than a stationary hygrometer. A sling psychrometer is used to determine relative humidity, dew point, and vapor pressure.

Figure 10.14 Infrared thermal image showing evidence of moisture.

A *draft gauge* measures air velocity and can gauge whether there is an adequate supply of air flow in a given location. Draft gauges can be used to monitor the performance of air-conditioning systems.

Infrared thermography is a technology that actually allows us to see thermal energy or heat. Thermography can be used in any circumstance where the identification of thermal patterns can be used to find something or diagnose a condition. An infrared scanner is often used on steam trap to locate areas of leakage without destructive testing (Figure 10.14).

Thermal imaging is a type of infrared imaging. Thermographic cameras detect radiation in the infrared range of the electromagnetic spectrum (roughly 900–14,000 nanometers or 0.9–14 micrometers) and produce images of that radiation. Since infrared radiation is emitted by all objects based on their temperatures, thermography makes it possible to "see" one's environment with or without visible illumination. The amount of radiation emitted by an object increases with temperature, so thermography allows one to see variations in temperature. When viewed by a thermographic camera, warm objects stand out well against cooler backgrounds.

Thermal imaging photography finds many uses in property condition assessments. For example, where thermal insulation becomes faulty, building maintenance technicians can see heat leaks to improve the efficiencies of cooling or heating. Moreover, thermography allows you to find deteriorating components prior to failure and measurement can be taken in areas inaccessible or hazardous for other methods.

Velometers are used for HVAC balancing, static pressure measurements, energy audits, and more. Since these instruments use a swinging vane measuring technique, they do not require a power source or batteries.

CHAPTER

11

Electrical & Lighting Systems

11.1 GENERAL

The electrical system provides a facility with accessible energy for heating, cooling, lighting, and equipment and appliance operation. In many facilities, the electrical system provides the power with which most of the other building systems operate. The system controls the energy required in the building and distributes it to the location utilizing it. Most frequently, distribution line voltage carried at utility poles is 2400/4160 volts. Transformers step down this voltage for use within buildings. The most common form of electric service is delivered into buildings through overhead wires. The site of delivery is known as the "service drop."

Commercial electrical inspections differ considerably from residential inspections. The equipment and wiring methods can vary a great deal from one survey to the next. The electrical needs of a commercial building can be simple, with only a few lights, or complex, with transformers and heavy industrial equipment. Some of these differences include:

- Voltage and number of phases
- Inspection protocol
- Services
- Materials and equipment
- Applicable rules and codes
- Special equipment and environments
- Special problems, such as harmonics

Before operating a switch or device, perform a visual inspection for damage, looseness, burning or arcing, or heat. Devices missing cover plates are unsafe and risk both shock and fire. Metal cover plates also present shock risks.

Care should be taken when turning on switches found off in the service panel. A circuit found in the off position may be that way due to an unsafe condition or a repair in progress. It is prudent to leave it off and document the finding. The property owner should be consulted for permission before turning on any electrical device that has been found shut down. Care should also be taken when turning off switches found on. You may damage a computer data base, reset an alarm system, or turn off a marginal switch for the heat that leaves the property with no heat in freezing weather.

Integral with the electrical system is the lighting system in the facility. Designed to ensure adequate visibility for both the interior and exterior of a facility, the lighting system comprises an energy source, distribution elements typically consisting of wiring, and the light-emitting equipment.

Deficiencies are often subtle, but measurable, within the electrical and lighting systems. Power surges, tripped circuit breakers, noisy ballasts and other more obvious conditions, such as inoperative electrical receptacles or lighting fixtures are frequently discovered or observed during a system review. As illustrated in Figures 11.1 and 11.2, a number of typical deficiencies are found in both the electrical and the lighting systems.

Several different electrical codes exist and are enforced in various areas throughout the U.S. Many larger cities, including New York and Los Angeles, have created and adopted their own electrical codes. The National Electrical Code (NEC) and the National Fire Protection Code (NFPC), published by the National Fire Protection Association (NFPA), cover almost all electrical system components. Municipalities commonly adopt the NEC in whole or in part.

The major load placed on a given electrical system comes from the lighting requirements; therefore, the distribution and management of electrical and lighting loads must also be considered in a comprehensive evaluation.

If in your opinion unsafe conditions exist at a property you are inspecting, you should notify all parties concerned, including building occupants/management/owners, realtors involved, and other appropriate authorities. *Where a code compliance inspection of the electrical and lighting system is required by the client, it should be conducted by an electrical engineer specialist as it is outside the scope of a typical PCA survey.* The depth of the electrical inspection is affected by the use and occupancy of the building. Very large facilities with complex electrical equipment may be operated under engineering supervision or facilities manager.

11.2 SOME DEFINITIONS: AMPS, VOLTS & WATTS

In most places around the world, electrical service is brought into a building at either 240V or 120V. These numbers are "nominal," meaning that the actual voltage may vary. Most modern buildings receive 240V service, a total achieved by the provision of two individual 120V incoming power lines. Older buildings and electrical services are often delivered only 120V. Knowing which voltage level is available is important, but knowing the voltage alone does not indicate the amount of electrical power available inside a building. For that we need to know both the service voltage at a building, and the service amperage.

Amperage: Amperage, or *Amps* provided by an electrical service is the flow rate of electrical current that is available, and the voltage level provided by an electrical service, combined with the ampacity rating of the service panel determines the electrical load or capacity. Branch circuit wire sizes and fusing or circuit breakers used set the limit on the total electrical load or the number of electrical devices that can be run at once on a given circuit. If you have a 100A current flow rate available, you could, speaking roughly, run ten 10-amp electric heaters simultaneously. If you have only 60A available, you won't be able to run

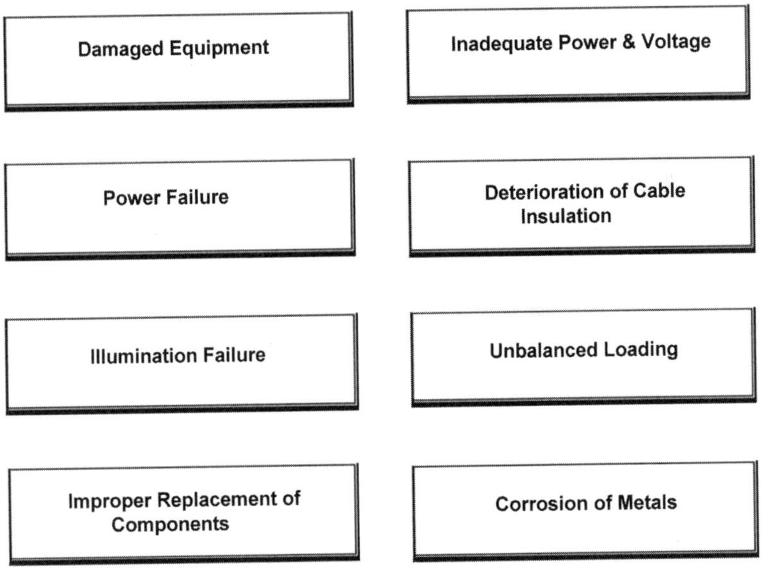

Figure 11.1 Typical deficiencies found in electrical systems.

more than six such heaters without risk of overheating wiring, causing a fire, tripping a circuit breaker, or blowing a fuse.

To determine the amount of electrical service provided to a facility, the service ampacity and voltage is required. In the US and Canada service voltages are commonly 240 volts (nominally) at the electrical panel, a system which supports both 120V and 240V circuits in the building. Typically, two 120V hot wires entering the building provide 120V for circuits connected from an individual entering wire and the neutral bus, and 240V for circuits connected between the two incoming individual 120V circuits.

The safe and proper service amperage available at a property is set by the smallest of: the service conductors, the main disconnect fuse or switch, or the rated capacity of the electric panel itself. The Field Observer should consider all three of these and report any inconsistencies among them. The main fuse/ circuit breaker (CB) is the only component that actively limits amperage at a property by shutting off loads drawing more than the main fuse rating.

Volts: Volts can be defined as the potential difference across a conductor when a current of one ampere dissipates one watt of power. If we bring 100A into a building at 240V, we have twice as much power available as if we bring in 100A at 120V. Volts are thus a measurement of the strength of an electrical source at a given current or amperage level. If we exceed the current rating of a wire it will get hot, risking a fire, which is why we use fuse devices to limit the current flow on electrical conductors to a safe level to avoid risks of overheating and fires.

As mentioned earlier, a 240V circuit is a nominal rating that im-

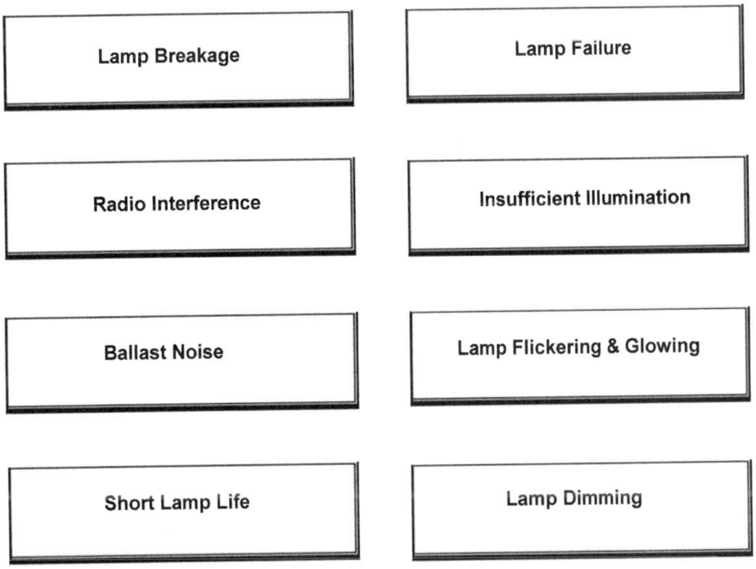

Figure 11.2 Typical deficiencies found in lighting systems.

plies that the actual voltage level will vary. In a three phase circuit, even if you are using only two phases, the voltage between the phases is $1.732 \times 120 = 207.6$, or approximately 207 Volts, and not 240 Volts. In various countries the actual voltage level varies around both the nominal and actual delivered voltage rating. Most modern electrical equipment is designed to handle small voltage variations and differences. Sensitive electronic equipment may require that a voltage stabilizer be installed.

You can determine electrical service voltage by visual examination of overhead electrical wires at the service entry at the point of connection between the service drop and the service conductors, not including underground conduit. The service conductors are also called the service entry cable or SEC, and underground wiring up to the building is called a service lateral. A 240V electrical service will include three wires connected to the building—the two 120V "hot" legs, which together provide 240V, and a third grounded conductor. A 120V service will have only two wires, a 120V power line and a grounded line or neutral.

Services provided through underground conduit do not allow visual inspection of the service conductor prior to the electric meter, and actual conductors are visible only in the service panel.

Watts: In electricity, a watt is equal to current (in amperes) multiplied by voltage (in volts). The formula, Watts = Volts × Amps, basically describes this relationship. In buildings the unit of electricity consumption measure is the watt hour, which is usually in thousands, called kilowatt hours (kWh). In larger buildings, not only is the total consumption rate measured, but the peak demand is as well.

11.3 COMPONENTS TO BE EVALUATED

11.3.1 Service Connection

The service connection equipment provides a connection between the power company service and the facility. The connection can be located either overhead or underground. The service connection should be checked for type (i.e., voltage, amperage) and general condition and whether the total power adequately serves the facility's requirements. The equipment should be clean and free from overgrown planting or debris.

11.3.2 Switchgear and Switchboards

The switching equipment controls the power supply in the facility and all the services arriving on the site are called the service drop. This drop consists of the wires from the main line, a transformer, a meter, and a disconnect switch. The main service switch is the system disconnect for the entire electrical service. To avoid excessive voltage drop and flicker, the distance from the transformer to the meter should not exceed 150 feet. In commercial construction the panel and disconnect is preferably located outside the building but may be located inside if it is directly accessible from an exterior door. Switchboard covers should not normally be removed.

The main switchboard controls and protects the main feeder lines of the system. The equipment includes:

- Low voltage switchgear (600 volts or less)
- High voltage metal-clad switchgear (600 volts or more)
- Metering switchboards
- Multisection service/distribution switchboards

Meters: In residential applications, only the total electric consumption is measured (using "feed-through" type metering). In larger buildings, both the total consumption and peak rate demand are measured. This is because large peaks require the utility company to build more power generating capacity to meet the peak. In a multiple occupancy building, there may be separate meters for each tenant or common metering. If tenants are billed a share of the common bill a determination should be made as to the presence of any post-service metering equipment.

Switchgear and switchboards should be readily accessible, in good condition, and have protective panels and doors. They should also be checked for signs of overloading or burn marks.

11.3.3 Panelboards

Panelboards and their cabinets house an assembly of circuit breakers. The panelboards control and protect the branch circuits, providing a central distribution point for branch circuits for a building, a floor, or part of a floor. Each breaker serves a single circuit, and the overload protection is based on the size and current-carrying capacity of the wiring in that circuit. A building may have a number of panelboards and a main panel, with a disconnect switch for the entire building (Figure 11.3). Lighting panel types include bolt-on circuit breakers (1-pole, 2-pole, 3-pole), plug-in circuit breakers (1-pole), and fusible switch.

To find the electric service panel ampacity, look for a tag (normally paper) or embossed rating on fuse pull outs on the panel itself; these tags often include the amperage rating of the panel. This information is usually present in newer panels on a panel side, or on the panel cover. Actual dimensions of an electric panel are not a reliable indicator of ampacity. For example, many larger panels can be fitted with a variety of bus-bar and main switch assemblies of varying ampacity.

Panelboards should be checked for their general condition and for evidence of wear or disrepair. The equipment should be accessible and protective covers and doors should be in place. The field observer should also check for evidence of blown or replaced circuits.

11.3.4 Aluminum Components

Aluminum wiring has a tendency to loosen from connections, increasing the potential for arcing. Where aluminum contacts or wiring are present, a program should be established for inspecting and tightening connections at the source of electrical system and at utilization units.

Introduction of the aluminum wire "alloys" in the early 1970s did not successfully resolve the majority of connection failure problems. Aluminum wiring is still permitted and used for certain applications, including residential service entrance wiring and single-purpose higher amperage circuits such as 240V air conditioning or electric range circuits. Although the fire

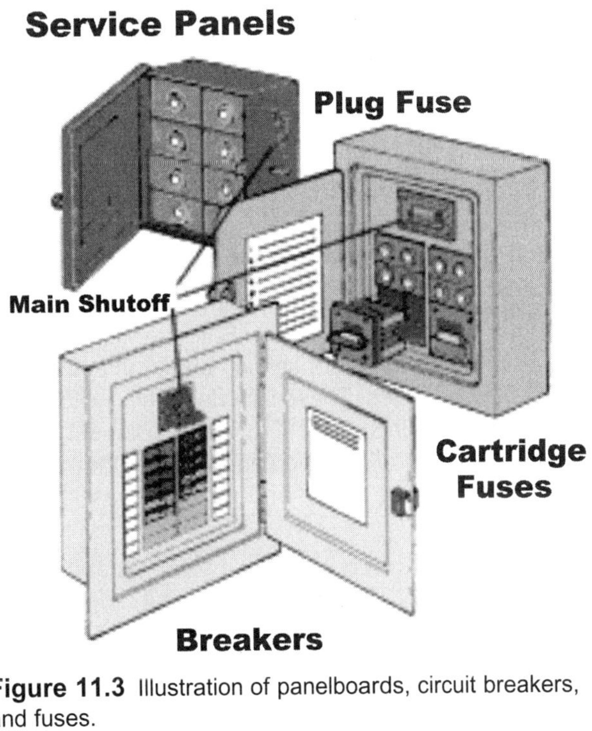

Figure 11.3 Illustration of panelboards, circuit breakers, and fuses.

risk from single purpose circuits is much less than for branch circuits, they nevertheless remain a potential fire hazard.

How to identify aluminum wiring: Look for the word "Aluminum" on the wiring. Without opening any electrical panels or other devices, a building inspector can still look for printed or embossed letters on the plastic wire jacket where wiring is visible at the electric panel. Some aluminum wire has the word "Aluminum" or a specific brand name such as "Kaiser," "Alcan," "Aluminum," or "AL/2" plainly marked on the plastic wire jacket.

11.3.5 Service Outlets

Service outlets include convenience receptacles, motors, lights and appliances. They should be checked for general condition as well as satisfactory operation and whether any outlets display evidence of power surges or shorts.

Receptacles: These are commonly known as outlets or sometimes erroneously as wall plugs (a plug is what actually goes into the outlet). It is preferable for outlets to be three-prong, where the third prong is grounded. Outlets in a large space should not all be on the same circuit so that when a fuse or circuit breaker trips due to an overload, the space will not be plunged into complete darkness.

Grounding: Grounding of services to earth is a basic safety precaution and is necessary mainly to protect against lightning strikes and other high-voltage line strikes. Earth grounding in a commercial building may be to a grounding rod inside a switchboard, to a plumbing system's steel cold water pipe, or to a building's steel frame, depending on the equipment or system to be grounded.

Motors: Basically, there are four types of motors in general use. The DC motor is used for small scale applications and for elevators, where continuous and smooth acceleration to a high speed is important. Single-phase AC motors are used in various sizes and shapes, typically 3/4 horsepower or less. Larger motors are typically three-phase induction motors and are characterized by extreme reliability, remaining constant in RPM unless heavily overloaded. The fourth type of motor in general use is the universal motor, which runs on either DC or AC current, and which varies in speed based on the load. Motors should always be protected against overload by thermal relays, which shut off the power when any part of the motor or housing overheats.

11.3.6 Switches and Controls

The switches and controls direct the flow of power service to the electrical equipment. Safety switches are installed in locations where service cut-off is available in case of emergencies. These include toggle switches, dials, and levers. Switches and controls should be checked for general condition and whether they operate satisfactory and are safely and readily accessible (Figure 11.4).

Figure 11.4 A typical electrical room in a Chicago hotel.

11.3.7 Emergency Power and Emergency Lighting

Many facilities have standby power with which to ensure continued electrical service in case the standard power service shuts down. Emergency power is required for life support systems, fire and life safety circuits, elevators, and exit and emergency lighting. Facilities that require full operation during emergencies or disasters, such as hospitals and shelters, always have back up power. Computer facilities, to ensure continued storage and survival of the data, also commonly have emergency power. For major equipment, a diesel engine generator with an automatic starting switch and an automatic transfer switch is often provided for emergency power (Figure 11.5), while battery units are installed for lighting. The typical AC power frequency in the United States is 60 cycles per second or 60 Hertz, whereas in Europe, 50 Hertz is the common frequency for power.

Figure 11.5 Photo of Amtrak generator for emergency back-up power inside a building.

Emergency lighting in a facility is needed in the event of a power failure, thus enabling the occupants to exit safely. Emergency lighting can consist of individual battery units located in all corridors and areas that would require sufficient lighting for building users exiting, such as in interior and some exterior exitways. Alternatively, the lighting can be powered by a central battery unit. Since batteries are typically 12 volt, fluorescent lamps will require some method of power conversion.

11.3.8 Transformers

A transformer changes the voltage of an alternating current (AC) circuit to a higher or lower value. While a transformer changes the voltage in a circuit, it has practically no effect on the total power in the circuit. Transformers are used to step up voltage (called step up transformers) in order to transmit power over long distances without excessive losses, and to subsequently step down voltage (called step down transformers) to more useable levels.

Transformers are either dry or wet type. Lower voltage types are dry, and typically noise generating, with minimal requirements for insulation and ventilation of heat generated by voltage changes. In wet type high voltage transformers, fluids that are often toxic serve as part of the insulation system and also as a medium to carry away the heat generated in the transformer due to the change in current. Wet type transformers typically contain a type of fire-resistant fluid or mineral oil, such as PCBs.

There should be clear access to exterior transformers and adequate ventilation and access for interior transformers, which should be inside a fireproof vault. On-site transformers in parking lots may require bollards or other protection (Figure 11.6). Transformers should be analyzed for PCBs and their registration numbers noted.

Figure 11.6 Illustration of a transformer outside a building protected by bollards.

11.4 BUILDING AUTOMATION

Building controls or automation continues to increase in complexity. Wikipedia describes building controls (a.k.a. building automation) as a "programmed, computerized, 'intelligent' network of electronic devices that monitors and controls the mechanical and lighting systems in a building. The intent is to create an intelligent building and reduce energy and maintenance costs." According to Thomas Hartman, P.E., a building automation expert, there are three cardinal elements of an intelligent building. These are:

1. **The occupants:** Harman states, "This is what buildings are really all about. An intelligent building is one that provides easy access, keeps people comfortable, environmentally satisfied, secure, and provides services to keep the occupants productive for their purpose in the building."
2. **Structure and systems:** An intelligent building is one that, at a bare minimum, significantly reduces environmental disruption, degradation or depletion associated with the building while ensuring a long-term useful functional capacity for the building.
3. **Advanced technologies:** An intelligent building is one that, because of its climate and/or use, is challenged to meet items 1 and 2 above, and succeeds in meeting those challenges through the use of appropriate advanced technologies.

Most engineers today understand an intelligent building to be a building that incorporates computer programs to coordinate many building subsystems to regulate the interior temperatures, HVAC, and power consumption. The goal is usually to reduce the operating cost of the building while maintaining the desired environment for the occupants (Figure 11.7).

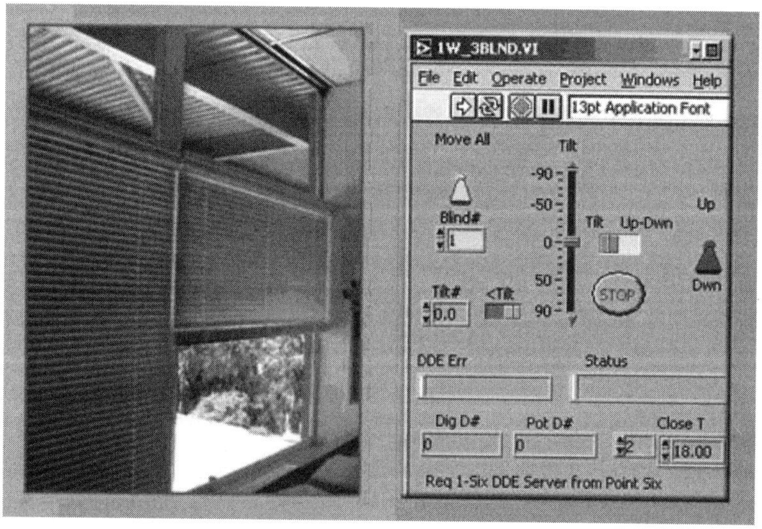

Figure 11.7 A Venetian-blind system at a Berkeley Lab office building is equipped with a "virtual instrument" panel for IBECS control of blinds settings (Courtesy HPCBS).

Most facility and building managers recognize the potential value of building automation systems (BASs) as a powerful energy saving tool, but the initial costs sometimes makes managers hesitate. Commercial-off-the-shelf building automation systems (BAS) are now readily available. A basic BAS saves energy by widening temperature ranges and reducing lighting in unoccupied spaces. A BAS also reduces costs for electricity by shedding loads when electricity is higher priced.

Because many subsystems contribute to the costs of operating a building, customized building automation can be complex depending on the needs of the client. Some intelligent buildings have the ability to:

- Manage thermal transmissions through windows or walls
- Anticipate forecasted weather, utility costs, or electrical demand
- Learn and adapt to building occupants
- Track individual occupants to adapt building systems to the individual's wants and needs (e.g., setting a room's temperature and lighting levels automatically when a homeowner enters)
- Detect and report faults in mechanical and electrical systems, especially critical systems

There are other, non-energy uses for automation in a building that include security, rent, or consumables charges based on actual usage, giving directions within the building, scheduling preventive maintenance, and customized lighting to meet different needs, or to create ambience. Some of the more common elements and components of building automation include:

Controller: The controller is normally one or more application-specific controllers, often with less complex programming. These controllers come in a wide range of sizes and capabilities to control devices that are common in buildings.

Occupancy sensors: Occupancy is usually based on time-of-day schedules, with override possible through different means. Some buildings can sense occupancy in their internal spaces by an override switch or sensor.

Lighting: Lighting can be turned on and off with a building automation system based on time of day or by the occupancy sensors and timers. One typical example is to keep the lights in a space on for a half hour since the last motion was sensed. A photocell placed outside a building can sense darkness and the time of day and modulate lights in outer offices and the parking lot.

Air handlers: Most air handlers mix return and outside air so less temperature change is needed. This can save money by using less chilled or heated water (not all AHUs use chilled/hot water circuits). Some external air is necessary to keep the building's air healthy.

Analog or digital temperature sensors may be placed in the space or room, the return and supply air ducts, and sometimes the external air. Actuators are placed on the hot and chilled water valves, the outside air and return air dampers. The supply fan is started and stopped based on either time of day, temperatures, building pressures or a combination of these factors.

Constant Volume Air-handling units: The less efficient type of air-handler is a Constant Volume Air Handling Unit, or CAV. The fans in CAVs do not have variable-speed controls. Instead, CAVs open and close dampers and water-supply valves to maintain temperatures in the building's spaces. They heat or cool the spaces by opening or closing chilled or hot water valves that feed their internal heat exchangers.

Variable Volume Air-handling units: A more efficient unit is a Variable air volume (VAV) Air handling unit. VAVs supply pressurized air to VAV boxes, usually one box per room or area. A VAV air handler can change the pressure to the VAV boxes by changing the speed of a fan or blower with a variable frequency drive or by moving inlet guide vanes to a fixed-speed fan. The amount of air is determined by the needs of the spaces served by the VAV boxes.

Each VAV box supplies air to a small space, like an office. Each box has a damper that is opened or closed based on how much heating or cooling is required in its space. The more boxes are open, the more air is required, and a greater amount of air is supplied by the VAV air-handling unit. Some VAV boxes also have hot water valves and an internal heat exchanger. The valves for hot and cold water are opened or closed based on the heat demand for the spaces it is supplying. A minimum and maximum CFM must be set on VAV boxes to assure adequate ventilation and proper air balance.

VAV Hybrid Systems: Another variation is a hybrid between VAV and CAV systems. In this system, the interior zones operate as in a VAV system. The outer zones differ in that the heating is supplied by a heating fan in a central location, usually with a heating coil fed by the building boiler. The heated air is ducted to the exterior dual duct mixing boxes and dampers controlled by the zone thermostat calling for either cooled or heated air as needed.

Central plant: A central plant is needed to supply the air-handling units with water. It may supply a chilled water system, hot water system and a condenser water system, as well as transformers and auxiliary power unit for emergency power.

Chilled water system: Chilled water is often used to cool a building's air and equipment. The chilled water system will have chiller(s) and pumps. Analog temperature sensors measure the chilled water supply and return lines. The chiller(s) are sequenced on and off to chill the water supply.

Condenser water system: Cooling tower(s) and pumps are used to supply cool condenser water to the chillers. The condenser water supply to the chillers has to be constant, so speed drives are commonly used on the cooling tower fans to control temperature. Proper cooling tower temperature assures the proper refrigerant head pressure in the chiller. Analog sensors measure the temperature of the condenser water supply and return lines.

Hot water system: The hot water system supplies heat to the building's air-handling units or VAV boxes. The hot water system will have a boiler(s) and pumps. Analog temperature sensors are placed in the hot water supply and return lines. The boiler(s) and pumps are sequenced on and off to maintain supply.

Alarms and security: Many building automation systems have alarm capabilities. If an alarm is detected, it can be programmed to notify someone. Notification can be through a computer, pager, cellular phone, or audible alarm. If occupancy sensors are present, they can also be used as burglar alarms.

There are numerous propriety protocols and industry standards on the market, including: ASHRAE, BACnet, DALI, DSI, Dynet, Energy Star, KNX standard, LonTalk, and ZigBee. Details of these systems are outside our scope.

11.5 LIGHTING & OTHER SYSTEMS

Different artificial sources produce different kinds of light and vary significantly in their efficiency, which is the calculated lumen output per watt input.

11.5.1 Interior Lighting

There are many types of interior lighting systems, which enable the full use of a facility around the clock. The most common types include fluorescent, incandescent, and high intensity discharge. Interior lighting should meet minimum illumination levels (Figure 11.8). Typically, the light needed for visibility and perception increases as the size of details decreases, as contrast between details and their backgrounds is reduced, and as task reflectance is reduced. Illumination levels are outside the scope of a PCA survey and should be determined by a lighting consultant.

Interior lighting is not to exceed allowed power limits. Interior lighting includes all permanently installed general and task lighting shown on the plans but does not include specialized lighting for medical, dental, or research purposes or display lighting for exhibits in galleries, museums, and monuments.

During the useful life of a lighting installation, its efficiency progressively decreases due to dirt accumulation on the surface and aging of the equipment. In lighting scheme design we must take account of this fall by the use of a maintenance factor and plan suitable maintenance schedules to limit the decay.

AREA	FOOTCANDLES
Building Surrounds	1
Parking Area	5
Exterior Entrance	5
Exterior Shipping Area	20
Exterior Loading Platforms	20
Office Corridors & Stairways	20
Elevators & Escalators	20
Reception Rooms	30
Reading or Writing Areas	70
General Office Work Areas	100
Accounting/Bookkeeping Areas	150
Detailed Drafting Areas	200

Figure 11.8 Table of recommended illumination levels.

11.5.2 Exterior Light Types

Facility surveys often identify inadequate exterior lighting conditions. Incandescent and high intensity discharge are the most common types. The exterior lighting illumination levels should be adequate and in good condition. Full cut-off lighting fixtures are required for all outdoor walkway, parking lot, canopy and building/wall mounted lighting, and all lighting fixtures located within those portions of open-sided parking structures that are above ground.

Automatic controls are required for all exterior lights. The control may be a directional photocell, an astronomical time switch, or a building automation system with astronomical time switch capabilities. The control should automatically turn off exterior lighting when daylight is available. Lights in parking garages, tunnels, and other large covered areas that are required to be on during daylight hours are exempt from this requirement.

11.5.3 Additional Components

Other systems may be assessed for operations and existing conditions during the review of the electrical and lighting systems. These include:

- Telephone system: Telephone and communication systems are low-voltage systems, which makes the requirements for conduit and other protection less stringent than for high-voltage power. As with all telecommunications wiring, good insulation and separation from the main electrical wiring is necessary.
- Security system (see Chapter 19)
- Conduit and wiring of central computer system: Wiring in commercial buildings differs from that in residential buildings. Commercial wiring methods normally utilize rigid or intermediate metal conduit, EMT, PVC and MC cable. Wires must be physically protected in addition to being insulated. In commercial applications this is accomplished by housing them in a conduit such as rigid conduit, intermediate metallic conduit (IMC), electrical metallic tubing (EMT), flexible metal conduit, or interlocked armored cable. Industrial buildings may also have other wiring methods, such as busways and cable trays.
- Fire alarm system (see Chapter 18)

11.6 HARMONICS DISTORTION

11.6.1 Overview

State-of-the-art electrical building control devices along with the implementation of a comprehensive lighting retrofit can generate significant savings on a typical electric bill. In today's competitive marketplace, understanding the issues and embracing winning power management strategies has become a necessity. While the topic of harmonic distortion is outside the scope of PCA surveys, it remains vitally important for field observers to understand it.

Loads connected to electricity supply systems may be broadly categorized as either linear or nonlinear. Until quite recently, the vast majority of loads have been linear. Examples include induction motors and incandescent lamps. Linear loads may exhibit high or low power factor, but in either case, they draw current only at the powerline fundamental frequency. In contrast, nonlinear loads, such as rectifiers or switchmode power converters, also draw significant current at harmonic frequencies. Harmonic currents flowing through electric power supply systems cause voltage distortion. To date, voltage distortion caused by growing penetration of nonlinear loads has in many cases been accommodated without serious consequences.

Utility companies are clearly concerned about emerging problems caused by increasing concentrations of nonlinear loads resulting from the growing proliferation of electronic equipment. The higher concentrations of nonlinear loads tend to increase the number and severity of supply problems. The National Electrical Code guidelines address building wiring requirements for nonlinear loads.

11.6.2 Elements & Equipment that Create Harmonic Distortion

As previously mentioned, the majority of loads connected to the electricity supply system draw power which is a linear (or near linear) function of the voltage and current supplied to it. These linear loads do not usually cause disturbance to other users of the supply system. Examples include lighting, heating, directly driven motors, pumps etc.

Certain types of loads cause a distortion of the supply voltage/current waveform due to their nonlinear impedance. The largest contributors of reflective harmonic currents for commercial buildings are personal computers and their AC to DC power supply converters, and electronic controllers. Problems occur when such activity causes interference or permanent damage to equipment that is connected adjacent to the disturbing load.

However, there are many other contributors, too, including battery chargers, copiers, computer power units, telecommunication equipment, variable speed drives (VSD), discharge lighting (fluorescent, mercury, sodium, etc.), electronic ballasts, elevators, fax machines, rectifiers, uninterrupted power supplies (UPS), and welders. Repeated power quality problems will negatively impact the tenant's environment, ability to conduct business, and overall satisfaction.

11.6.3 Cause of Harmonic Distortion

The actual problems that any building will encounter from harmonic distortion will vary depending on the types and number of installed harmonic producing loads. Most buildings can withstand nonlinear loads of up to 15 percent of the total electrical system capacity without major concern. However, when the nonlinear loads exceed 15 percent, some non-apparent negative consequences can be expected. Power quality site surveys are performed to identify current or anticipated power quality problems and to determine suitable solutions.

The heating impact of harmonic currents can cause equipment failure, demise of conductors, and fires. The results can be unpredictable with legal and financial ramifications. Harmonic currents and voltage distortion is rapidly becoming one of the most severe and complex electrical challenges facing the electrical industry.

11.6.4 Reduction of Harmonics

If it appears that there is excessive harmonic distortion, it is advisable to bring in a specialized consultant. However, some of the options available include:

1. Request a design of lower harmonic current from the equipment supplier or seek a different supplier who can provide this.
2. Consider installing supplementary equipment, such as a harmonic filter, which can absorb most of the harmonic current and prevent it from propagating into the supply system.
3. In the case of a very large installation, the supplier may consider modification of the supply system to reduce the system impedance.

11.7 SYSTEM DIAGNOSTICS

Diagnosis of the electrical and lighting systems can be more complicated than for other systems, and electrical inspections can pose some danger to the inspector and to the users of the system. Electrical surveys should only be performed by qualified persons, and should a field observer encounter situations or equipment that is not familiar, it would then be advisable to recommend follow-up inspections by specialists. In addition, much of the equipment is inaccessible, and the system may be on the brink of failure with no immediate visual indications. Oftentimes, the system deficiencies are experienced by building users while not necessarily being observable at the equipment.

Thus, more than for other systems, the evaluators should emphasize discussion with the building users and maintenance staff. Because of the very nature and configuration of the electrical system, determining ongoing performance trends is as important as one-time field investigation observation. Several conditions may occur in the electrical system components that may indicate significant deficiencies or insufficient capacity such as frequent overheating problems or the tripping of protective relays in the equipment.

As with other systems, the field survey should be conducted after a review of the components and configuration delineated in the construction drawings and specifications. The physical survey should begin at the main electrical vault containing the main connection and transformer. Each electrical equipment room should be reviewed as well as all circuit breaker panels in the building. The inspector shall observe amperage and voltage ratings of the service.

The lighting and electrical components, such as receptacles and switches, should be systematically reviewed during the physical survey of the interiors. Switches should be operated during the survey to identify any dimmed or flickering lighting, which may indicate electrical deficiencies within the circuit. All electrical equipment in a given area should be operated simultaneously to determine that the circuit capacity is adequate. In an occupied building the field observer should never pull a fuse or shut off any component. A review of the exterior lighting should be performed, both after dark to determine actual nighttime illumination, and during the daylight to review the condition of the fixtures.

Limitations and exclusions: Assessments should exclude the removal of electrical panel and device covers, electrical testing, EMF issues, or operating of any electrical devices. Process-related equipment is also excluded from the assessment scope. The following processes should also be excluded:

1. Testing or operation of any overcurrent electrical device other than Ground Fault Circuit Interrupters (GFCI) and Arc Fault Circuit (AFCI) Interrupters when present
2. Removal or dismantling of any electrical device or component other than to remove dead front covers of the electrical equipment
3. Power shutdown, major dismantling or disassembly in order to permit opening of larger service or high voltage electrical equipment for inspection thereof
4. Inspection and evaluation of indoor/outdoor power transformers other than to observe the compatibility of rated ampacities and voltages with regard to the supply thereto
5. Observation of and reporting on electrical equipment according to these parameters when: a) equipment is not readily accessible, b) the inspection thereof serves to compromise the safety of the inspector, c) the equipment is owned and maintained by the utility company or some other designated or authorized personnel, d) the inspection thereof is objected to by the building's owner or authorized representative, e) the equipment is excluded from or not otherwise stated in the building inspection proposal as submitted and agreed to prior to inspection of a commercial property
6. Testing or evaluation of the resistance of the electrical wiring and grounding systems
7. Observation of and reporting on sound, security, and alarm systems
8. Observation of and reporting on low voltage or ancillary wiring, systems, and components that are not part of the primary electrical power and distribution system

There are various measuring instruments being deployed in electrical inspections. An ammeter measures current, a voltmeter measures the potential difference (voltage) between two points, and an ohmmeter measures resistance. A multimeter combines these functions into one piece of equipment, and a light meter measures the amount of light. Infrared thermography is often employed to inspect electrical and lighting systems.

CHAPTER

12

Plumbing Systems

12.1 GENERAL

Plumbing systems consist of pipes and fittings. Metal or plastic pipes are joined by a variety of fittings designed to couple lengths in a straight line, turn corners, reduce or enlarge pipe size, or connect to some type of fixture. Plumbing systems generally refer to indoor piping systems—which do not include piping associated with the operation of an HVAC system. Plumbing is further distinguished from water and sewage systems in that a plumbing system serves one building, while water and sewage systems serve a group of buildings or a city.

Plumbing systems constitute long-term investments and should be designed so that they do not become outdated and require replacement while their major components are still serviceable. This requires a careful analysis of present and future needs so that the correct capacity can be specified. The capacity and dimensions of component parts in a plumbing installation should be capable of meeting both immediate needs and anticipated future use.

The complexity and number of subsystems within the plumbing system vary greatly with the size, type, and function of a building. There are several possible subsystems and components that may need to be evaluated in a review of the plumbing system. In simple buildings, the plumbing may consist of hot and cold water systems, a storm drain system and a natural gas distribution system. More complex buildings, such as hospitals, may have several unique plumbing systems, including a variety of temperatures of hot water as well as oxygen, nitrogen, nitrous oxide and other gas systems. Sometimes a building is constructed below sewer lines and sewage ejectors need to be installed to pump the sewage up into the sewer system. Industrial facilities, for example, might contain cryogenic or other low temperature systems in the process piping, which could be included in the plumbing evaluation. All of these components may vary according to the type of facility, so the evaluation of the plumbing system in each facility is unique.

The plumbing system basically consists of water being provided by a public system (or sometimes a private well for houses or small structures), and enters the building through the floor slab. The water company uses a meter to measure the amount of water consumed. The water service delivers water to the meter through a large pipe called a main, which is often parallel to the street. Once the water passes through the main and meter, it goes into distribution piping, which runs throughout the building and is controlled at different locations in the building by various types of valves.

The plumbing system also includes a waste collection subsystem. At each lavatory, sink, tub, shower and toilet, there will be a connection to waste collection piping. Waste water is channeled down and out of the building. If there is a public waste treatment, a pipe from the building will join a major public sewer line. If there is on-site treatment, the pipe will lead to a septic treatment system.

Waste collection piping also has vents to let sewer gas into the atmosphere, and to let air into the system to help it work. Those vents should go through the attic and out the roof so that sewer gases are vented into the atmosphere. Between the water supply and the waste collection systems, there are fixtures. A fixture may be an appliance, such as a water heater, washing machine, or dishwasher. Or it may be a lavatory, shower, tub or toilet. The fixture is where the water distribution and the waste collection systems join.

As mentioned above, the main distribution element of the plumbing system is the piping. In many facilities the piping consists of several different materials and is often concealed in walls and ceiling cavities. In other facilities, the piping is exposed and readily accessible. The deficiencies in the piping system are frequently associated with the fittings that connect sections of piping. Typical piping materials include steel, copper, plastic, flexible tubing, cast iron, wrought iron, and brass.

As with many systems, the final assessment of the condition of the plumbing system is the adequacy of service it provides to the users of the building. While the system may include a few or several components, the evaluation of the plumbing components of a building is fairly straightforward. Since the design of the system is such that many of the components are concealed and inaccessible for review, an evaluation will typically concentrate on the adequacy of service and condition of accessible equipment.

12.2 COLD WATER DISTRIBUTION

Most modern western water systems are directly fed from a municipal water system by a high-pressure pipe, usually located under the road or street. A water meter is installed to allow the supplier to charge appropriately for the water usage. Many houses in rural areas still use a cistern or a well where convenient water supply is not available; a pump and pressure tanks are used to create and maintain system pressure needed for operating the plumbing fixtures.

The typical cold water system distributes water to the plumbing fixtures that require cold water. The largest users of cold water are water closets (toilets), outdoor hose bibbs, and the irrigation system, but cold potable water is needed at lavatories, sinks, bathtubs, showers, water fountains, humidifiers, and ice-makers, too, for example. Cold water is also supplied to water heaters if a building is so equipped. The cold water supply system may include filter or water softener appliances. It basically comprises the piping and accessories that connect the building to the water main of the water supply utility, and includes the underground piping and shutoff valves between the building and the water main in the street. Buildings with fire standpipes (vertical piping usually located in stairwells that connect to the fire hose and fire sprinkler systems) may require one or more additional, independent water services to serve the fire protection system.

12.3 HOT WATER DISTRIBUTION

Most buildings have a central hot water system. In larger buildings as well as apartment buildings, a circulating pump is also installed. Commercial buildings with kitchen facilities are designed with an additional hot water system for the dishwashers, which require much higher temperatures than restrooms. The temperature and pressure relief valve on the hot water heater should be checked to ensure the lever is functioning. Basically, the same issues that apply to the cold water systems would apply here.

Hot water systems should be carefully designed to avoid health hazards. Equipment for heating and storing heated water should be designed and installed in ventilated areas to guard against dangers from explosion or overheating. Pipes used for the conveyance of hot water should be made of materials suitable to withstand the temperature of their contents, and water temperatures should be maintained at the specified levels.

12.4 PLUMBING FIXTURES

Plumbing fixtures are an integral component of any plumbing system and should be adequately surveyed during a review. They include a wide variety of fixtures, such as lavatories (sinks), water closets (toilets), urinals, showers, spas, bathtubs, dishwashers, water heaters, and drinking fountains. The minimum number of each type of fixture required in commercial buildings is regulated by the locally adopted plumbing code. The most widely applied plumbing code is the Uniform Plumbing Code, which states that the number of occupants served determines the quantity of fixtures. Fixtures should be evaluated for adequacy of operation, ADA compliance, and general condition.

The main water supply shutoff valve should be periodically closed and opened to ensure that it has not stuck in the open position. Fixture shutoff valves should also be periodically checked. Both the main valve and fixture valves need to be operable so that water can be turned off in an emergency or when plumbing repairs are necessary.

Buildings and properties of public accommodation are required by law to comply with the Title III provisions of the Americans with Disabilities Act: Accommodations and Commercial Facilities (ADA). The Act stipulates that new construction and new areas of public accommodation within commercial buildings must include accessible accommodations for persons with disabilities, such as accessible toilets and toilet fixtures (see Chapter 17).

In commercial structures, designers try to concentrate most plumbing in a single area near the core where it serves the toilet rooms, drinking fountains, and similar facilities. To provide service to sinks, private toilets, and the like, wet columns are sometimes included in the building. These are usually positioned at structural columns, where hot and cold supply and drainage and vent risers are located. They are designed to allow individual tenants to easily tap into them without having to connect to more remote plumbing at the core of the building.

12.4.1 Tank Water Heaters

Heating water by gas, oil, or electricity, tank water heaters are found in most buildings. Water heaters supply hot water for bathing, cooking and cleaning. They are classified by fuel, size and recovery rate. The recovery rate is how fast the water heater can bring cold water up to the desired temperature. Oil-fired water heaters are the fastest to recover and usually have the smallest tanks. Gas-fired water heaters rank second in recovery rate, and electric water heaters have a much slower recovery rate. Electric heaters may be located anywhere in the building, while gas and oil heaters must be in a well-ventilated area and require an exhaust flue. Water heaters will normally experience one or more of several different deficiencies. Typically, water heaters fail because of rusting. To delay this process, manufacturers insert anode rods, usually made of magnesium. This element attracts the rust and corrosion that might otherwise affect the tank itself. The

GENERAL LAVATORY ALLOWANCES

Type of Space	Number of Occupants	Minimum Number of Lavatories
Non-industrial office buildings, public buildings, and similar establishments	1 to 15	1
	16 to 35	2
	36 to 60	3
	61 to 90	4
	91 to 125	5
	126 and over	1 additional fixture for each additional 45 occupants

Figure 12.1 Generally recommended lavatory allowances for offices and public buildings. Actual code requirements will depend on the jurisdiction in which the property is located.

useful life and condition of the equipment can be ascertained by the speed with which the water heats.

During a survey of tank heaters the general condition of the heater should be checked, as well as whether there is evidence of leakage around the tank, and whether its valves, dials, and controls operate satisfactorily. The piping, connections, and bracing should be checked for evidence of rust or corrosion.

12.4.2 Lavatories & Sinks

Lavatories will be made available in all places of employment according to the requirements for lavatories as specified in Figure 12.1. In a multiple-use lavatory, 24 linear inches (610 mm) of wash sink or 20 inches (60 mm) of a circular basin, when provided with water outlets for each space, will be considered equivalent to one lavatory.

Aerators on faucets should be periodically cleaned (every three or four months), depending upon water hardness. Leaking faucets should be noted and recommendations to repair as needed. If the faucet is the washer type, the washer should be replaced in case of leaks, and if is the washerless type, the entire faucet needs to be replaced.

For other types of employment, at least one lavatory for three required water closets will be provided. For "High hazard" occupancies involving exposure to skin contamination with poisonous, infectious, or irritating materials, 1 lavatory per 5 persons is recommended. For drinking fountains, one fountain is recommended for each 75 building occupants or fraction, and at least one fountain per floor will be provided.

12.4.3 Toilets (Water Closets)

Toilets sometimes continue to run water in the tank after they are filled. If water still runs, the situation can usually be corrected by adjusting the ball float or flapper valve inside the tank. Alternatively, the inner mechanisms of the tank need to be replaced. Where the toilet itself rocks, the bolts may have loosened and/or the seal beneath the toilet has dried and broken and requires replacing. The seal is there to prevent water leaks under the toilet and to prevent leakage of sewer gas. Additionally, each plumbing fixture drain pipe should incorporate a "P" trap to provide a water filled seal that keeps sewer gases from rising into the building interior. Within buildings, short horizontal runs of drain piping are typically connected to vertical stacks,

WATER CLOSET ALLOWANCE RECOMMENDATIONS

Number of Occupants	Minimum Number of Water Closets
1 to 15	1
16 to 35	2
36 to 55	3
56 to 80	4
81 to 110	5
111 to 150	6
151 and over	6 for the first 150, plus 1 additional fixture for each additional 40-45 occupants

Figure 12.2 Recommended water closet allowance. Note that these are "rules of thumb" recommendations. Actual code compliance depends on the jurisdiction of the property in question.

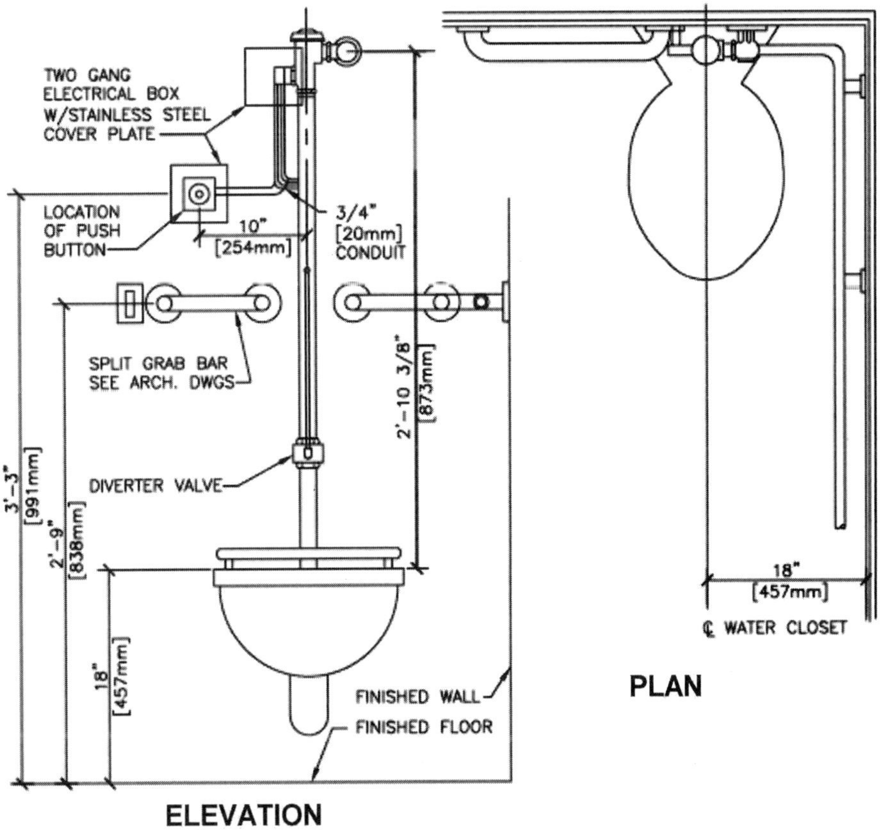

Figure 12.3 ADA-compliant water closet details.

which in turn are vented up through the roof to provide a suitable escape for the gases. Figure 12.2 indicates general recommendations for water closet allowances in commercial and public buildings.

Toilet fixtures and fittings include levers and other parts that control the flush and water inlet valves. The ballcock assembly is the primary mechanism that controls water supply in the tank and toilet (Figure 12.3). Where toilet rooms will not be used by women, urinals may be substituted for some water closets, except that the number of water closets in such cases will not be reduced to less than one-half to two-thirds of the minimum specified.

12.4.4 Tubs and Showers: Grout and Caulk

Tubs and showers are typically surrounded by special water resistant material to keep the water from penetrating the walls and floor. Joints between ceramic tiles are filled with grout, which is designed to seal the joint. However, like all masonry products, it is still porous and water can still penetrate it, albeit in minute amounts. The inspector should check the caulking around the rim of the tub where it joins the wall, and at the joint between the tub and the floor. Unlike grout, caulk seals stay pliable.

12.4.5 Clothes Washers and Dishwashers

Washing machines and dishwashers have hoses that connect the washer to the hot and cold water supply, and these can rupture or leak. Look for evidence of leaking as a constant leak can cause rotting of the sub-floor underneath.

12.5 NATURAL GAS & FUEL OIL DISTRIBUTION SYSTEMS

Gas and oil heating systems use combustion to produce heat. The heat can then be transferred to air, as is the case with a furnace, and the heated air is then circulated through the building in a system of box-like enclosures called ducts. Alternatively, the heat can be transferred to water; in this case, the system is referred to as a boiler. The heated water is then circulated through the building in pipes, which feed into a device in each heated room that spreads the heat, typically radiators or baseboard convectors, or circulates beneath the floor or ceiling as a radiant heat system.

Exhaust gases from combustion can contain carbon monoxide, an odorless, colorless, and poisonous gas. When inhaled, it depletes the oxygen in your blood and is lethal with enough exposure. The threat of carbon monoxide is increased when the system is not operating efficiently. The service record should be checked to ensure maintenance schedules have been adhered to.

Combustion heating appliances and exhaust flues deteriorate with age. If the gas or oil heating system is 15 years or older, it may contain cracks or pinhole leaks that could allow exhaust gases to escape. If this happens, it is possible for the gases to mix with the air stream going throughout the building, which is why it is essential to have regular periodic maintenance. A gas regulator shall be provided to maintain the correct inlet pressure to each gas appliance. Likewise, gas piping in plenums should not contain valves or unions. Natural gas piping to island sinks shall be in an accessible trench in the floor with a removable cover.

Fuel oil distribution systems are installed mainly in the eastern U.S. as a source of energy in HVAC systems. In some applications, including in many Navy installations, both natural gas and fuel oil systems are installed. Basically these subsystems should be evaluated for the general condition of the piping and connections, evidence of leakage, evidence of rust or corrosion and whether the piping is accessible for necessary repair. Exposed pipes should not be susceptible to impact or damage and supports and braces should be secure.

12.6 SANITARY SEWER SYSTEM

A building's waste-disposal system has two basic elements: the drainage system and the venting system. The drainage system (also called *traps and drains*), is designed to collect waste water from the indoor plumbing fixtures. The waste water from the various appliances, fixtures, and taps is transferred to the waste and sewage removal system via the sewage drain system, which is outdoors. The building sewer is then connected to a municipal sanitary sewage disposal system. Where connection to a municipal sewage system is not possible, a local, private, code-approved septic system is required. This system consists of larger diameter piping, water traps, and is well vented to prevent toxic gases from entering the living/working space of a building. Cesspools and outhouses do not normally meet health codes.

The venting system consists of pipes leading from fixtures to the outdoors, usually via the roof. Vents provide for relief of sewer gases, admission of oxygen for aerobic sewage digestion, and maintenance of the trap water seals that prevent sewer gases from entering the building. All fixtures are required to have an internal or external trap; double trapping is prohibited by plumbing codes. With exceptions, all plumbing fixtures must have an attached vent. The top of stacks must be vented too, via a stack vent.

Plumbing drainage and venting systems maintain neutral air pressure in the drains, allowing flow of water and sewage down drains and through waste pipes by gravity. As such, it is critical that a downward slope be maintained throughout. In relatively rare situations, where a downward slope out of a building to the sewer cannot be created, a special collection pit and grinding lift sewage ejector pump are needed. By comparison, potable water supply systems operate under pressure to distribute water up through buildings.

The piping is sloped to permit the wastewater to flow by gravity through the building and out to the underground public sewer system. The piping material used for sanitary sewer systems is usually cast iron or plastic (copper is rarely used because of its prohibitive cost). Cast iron piping consists of either hub and spigot systems, or is hubless. Joints for hub and spigot fittings usually consist of lead and oakum caulked joints or neoprene push-on compression gaskets. For hubless piping joints, a neoprene tube gasket is usually used. This is banded tight around the piping by incorporating stainless steel multi-band couplings.

Plastic piping consists mainly of either PVC (polyvinyl chloride) or ABS (acrylonitrile-butadiene-styrene). For underground piping, asbestos-cement (AC), vitrified clay, and concrete types may be employed. Plastic piping types utilize push-on, bell and spigot ends (joints). AC and clay piping ends use rubber gasket seals while concrete ends are plastered with mortar.

12.7 STORM DRAIN SYSTEM (RAINWATER SEWER)

Installed in a building to drain water off the roof, the storm drain system is typically evaluated within the plumbing system. Rainwater falling on the roof can be managed in two ways:

1. It can be collected and channeled directly into the public stormwater drainage system (codes prohibit stormwater from being channeled into sanitary sewer).

2. It is directed to the ground surface and sheet flow along with all other site runoff to on-site drainage systems. Systems are normally installed with an overflow backup system of drainage, and the drain pipes may be located adjacent to columns or in furred wall construction.

Sewage ejector system: Installed in buildings with plumbing-equipped areas below street level, sewage ejectors transport sewage up to the sewage system.

12.8 FITTINGS & VALVES

In addition to the straight pipe or tubing, many fittings and valves are required in a plumbing system, such as elbows, tees, and unions. While there are hundreds of specialized fittings manufactured, some fittings are used extensively in piping and plumbing systems. Some of the more common components are discussed below.

Elbow: A pipe fitting installed between two lengths of pipe or tube allowing a change of direction, usually 90 or 45 degrees. The ends may be machined for butt welding, threaded or socketed, etc. When the two ends differ in size, it is called a reducing or reducer elbow.

Tee: A tee is used to either combine or split a fluid flow. Most common are tees with the same inlet and outlet sizes, but “reducing” tees are available as well.

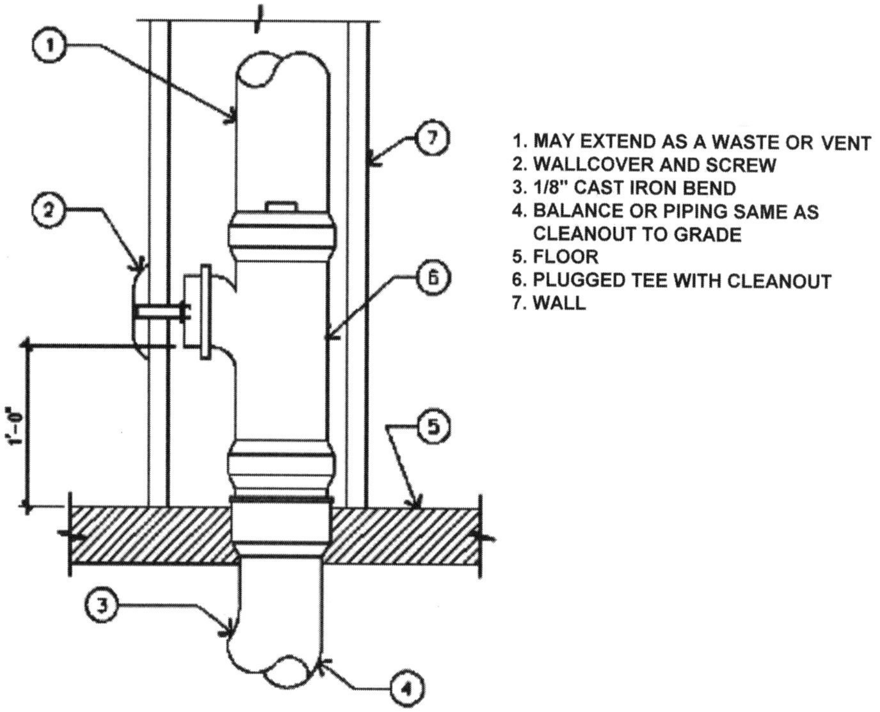

Figure 12.4 Drawing of typical wall cleanout detail.

Cross: A cross has one inlet and three outlets, or vice versa. Crosses are common in fire sprinkler systems, but not in plumbing due to their extra cost as compared to using two tees.

Coupling: A coupling connects two pipes to each other. If the material and size of the pipe are not the same, it may be called a "reducing coupling," or reducer, or an adapter.

Cap: A type of pipe fitting, often liquid or gas tight, which covers the end of a pipe.

Union: A union is similar to a coupling, except that it is designed to allow quick and convenient disconnection of pipes for maintenance or fixture replacement. While a coupling would require either solvent welding or being able to rotate all the adjacent pipes, as with a threaded coupling, a union provides a simple nut transition, allowing easy release at any time.

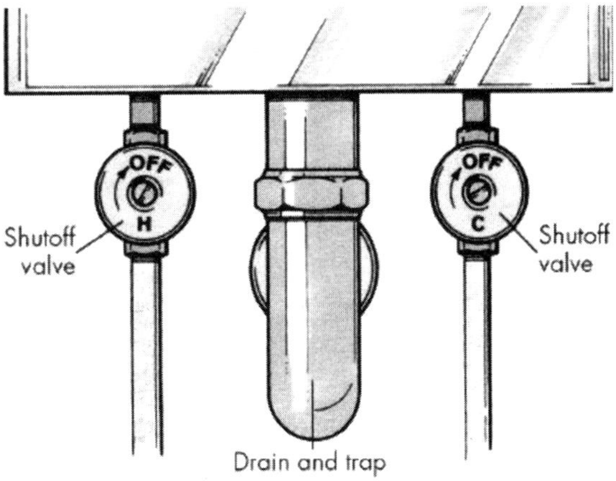

Figure 12.5 Example of valves (hot water and cold water) below lavatory basin.

Nipple: A nipple is a short stub of pipe that has two male ends. A nipple can usually be replaced by use of a street elbow.

Closet flange: The closet flange is the drain pipe flange to which a toilet is attached.

Clean-outs: Clean-outs are fittings that access drains without removing plumbing fixtures. They are used to allow an auger or "plumber's snake" to clean out a plugged drain. Clean-outs should be placed in accessible locations throughout a drainage system outside the building because these augers have limited length. Clean-outs normally come with screwed-on caps (Figure 12.4).

Trap primers: Trap primers regularly inject water into traps so that water seals are maintained. This seal is necessary to keep sewer gases out of buildings.

Valves are devices that regulate the flow of substances (gases, fluidized solids, slurries, or liquids) by opening, closing, or partially obstructing various passageways (Figure 12.5).

A large variety of valves is available on the market. Valves have many applications, with sizes ranging from tiny to huge; the more common valves used in plumbing include:

- Angle valve—has metering or flow restriction capability
- Ball cock—often used as a water level controller (cistern)
- Ball valve—used for on/off control
- Bibcock—provides a connection to a flexible hosepipe
- Butterfly valve—particularly in large pipes
- Check valve or non-return valve—allows the fluid to pass in one direction only. It is essentially a backflow preventer and is critical in avoiding contamination of the community supply.
- Faucet (American English), Tap (British English), is the name for a valve used to regulate water flow.
- Foot valve—a check valve on the foot of a suction line to prevent backflow
- Gate valve—mainly used for on/off control
- Globe valve—used for on/off control and for regulating flow
- Needle valve—used for gently releasing high pressures

- Plug valve—for on/off control
- A pressure reducing valve (PRV), also called a pressure regulator, reduces pressure to a preset level downstream of the valve.
- A pressure sustaining valve, also called a back-pressure regulator, maintains pressure at a preset level upstream of the valve.
- A safety valve or relief valve operates automatically at a set differential pressure to correct a potentially dangerous situation, typically over-pressure.
- Stopcocks restrict or isolate the flow through a pipe of a liquid or gas.
- A three-way valve routes fluid from one direction to another.
- Vacuum breaker valves prevent the back-siphonage of contaminated water into pressurized drinkable water supplies.

12.9 BACKFLOW ISSUES

Where water or water-using appliances are used with fluids or materials which could contaminate the water, there must be adequate protection to prevent backflow of potentially contaminated water into other parts of the system, especially drinking water. The regulations introduced a new specification of five fluid risk categories describing types of contaminant and detailing the appropriate type of prevention device that must be fitted to guard against backflow of contaminated water. A backflow preventer should be included on all incoming systems.

12.10 SYSTEM DIAGNOSTICS

Much like with the electrical system, the evaluation of the plumbing system is typically carried out at selected access points. Much of the plumbing equipment and piping is typically out of sight and inaccessible (e.g., behind walls), so when leaks occur, they are not normally immediately visible.

Precautions should be taken against damage to the property or danger to the health of its occupants in the event of system malfunction. Fixtures should be provided with adequate overflow capacity. Roof tanks and other hidden elements of the system should be similarly provided with overflows that discharge in such a way as to act as a warning before causing damage. Pressure vessels that are part of the system should be equipped with a temperature and pressure relief valve. Food preparation and storage rooms within the building should be located so that any leakage or backflow in the drainage system cannot contaminate their area or contents. In the case of industrial or commercial premises where food is processed or prepared, or where sterile goods or similarly susceptible materials are stored or handled, additional precautions should be taken by indirect connections of the internal fixtures to the plumbing system.

The evaluation of the system should typically commence with a review of the construction drawings to determine the location and design of the system's main components and equipment. Piping and other equipment concealed in wall or ceiling cavities can be located and kept in mind during the field survey. It is not uncommon to discover that drains, vents, or clean-outs that were originally designed or installed have been omitted, removed, or plugged. Regular users of the system should be interviewed to get more information on the typical ongoing conditions.

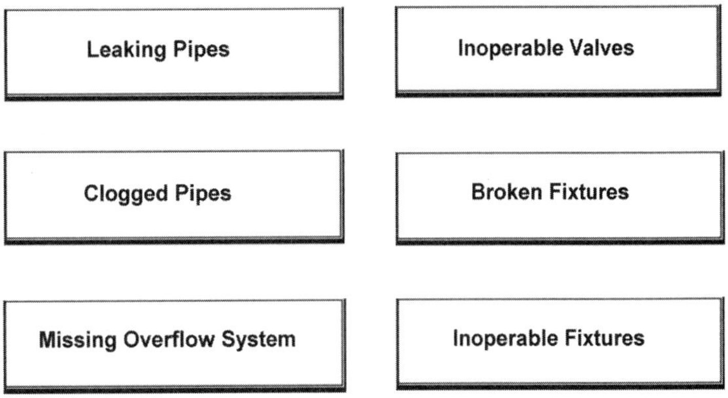

Figure 12.6 Typical deficiencies in plumbing systems.

After reviewing the construction drawings, the physical survey should start at the connection to the water main. This is followed by a review of the system's components from the water heating and storage source to the fixtures and outlet areas. During the physical survey of the interior spaces of the building, wall and ceiling finishes should be investigated for any evidence of damage or stains caused by defects in concealed plumbing system components, such as leaking or broken piping. Identify the apparent or reported ages of plumbing systems where available and, combined with visual observations, identify their remaining useful life (RUL). Assessment should exclude determining adequate pressure and flow rate, fixture quantities, or pipe size verification.

Some of the typical deficiencies found in a review of the plumbing systems are illustrated in Figure 12.6. More often than not, when problems occur with the plumbing system, they usually relate to leaks and should be dealt with promptly. The water system is under pressure, and a rupture in the system—even a minor leak—will cause water to continue spilling into the building. In some cases, a source of carbon dioxide may be present in the water and is attacking the copper piping. If the piping in the building being evaluated is the only one in the area experiencing leaking, it is likely that the piping has been undersized.

Faucets should be turned on and off several times while evaluating the supply and drain lines for any leakage. Each sink should be filled and allowed to drain to determine whether drainage is adequate. All fixtures in a given area, a kitchen or restroom for example, should be operated simultaneously to confirm the adequacy of water flow. A small amount of water should be drained from the water heater tank and inspected for sediment and rust. The inspector should be conversant with the location of all major shut-off valves, from where the water service pipe enters the building to the various fixtures. Most plumbing fixtures have shut-off valves mounted on them that can be used to isolate the fixture from the water system in case of leaking or pipe breaks. Typically they are below the fixture, except those on clothes washers.

Loud vibrating noises (water hammer) are common in plumbing supply lines. The condition occurs when faucets are rapidly opened and closed and can often be corrected by anchoring or fastening pipes more securely. Air chambers can be added at the end of long pipe runs to solve this problem.

Water pressure gauge: This is a device used to measure water pressure at each fixture by attachment to the fixture outlet. As a rule of thumb, most fixtures should have a minimum flow pressure of eight psi.

CHAPTER

13

Vertical Transportation Systems

13.1 GENERAL

Without elevators tall commercial buildings would not be possible, and the contemporary city as we know it would not exist. Buildings would be limited to four or five stories and office towers, hotels and high-rise apartment buildings would remain a figment of one's imagination.

Fortunately, the arrival of elevators and escalators has resolved the problem of efficient travel to and from the various levels in a building. The advent of the elevator and escalator into standard construction design vocabulary at the turn of the century brought about an efficient, convenient and safe form of transportation between building floors. Today, there are a wide variety of vertical transportation system types available for use in buildings, and with space at a premium, facilities professionals find themselves challenged to make buildings safer, more intelligent, reliable, and efficient—all while maximizing the amount of useable space.

Elevators, escalators, and moving walks have thus become an integral part of daily life as populations continue to increase, along with the number of people living and working in high-rise buildings. Fueling this growth are new elevator and escalator system installations, as well as the resurgence of modernization programs to upgrade buildings that were built during the construction boom of the 1970s and 1980s. Although elevators continue to develop, they have not changed dramatically in recent years and are unlikely to do so in the near future. Control systems are being developed that will learn from past traffic patterns and use this information to predict future needs in order to reduce waiting times. Laser controls are coming into use, both to gauge car speed and distance, as well as to scan building floors for potential passengers.

The cost of an elevator system is a significant part of a building's total cost, and taking care of it is a means of protecting one's investment. The way these elevators look, how smoothly they run, how fast they answer calls, and how often they're out of service are all factors that impact a building's reputation and marketability potential. This means that elevators require regular inspection, adjustment, and lubrication. Preventive maintenance keeps elevators operating at their best, helps prevent major replacements, and prolongs their useful life.

Assessment of transport systems in buildings should include both the equipment components and the associated service areas such as machine rooms and elevator pits where applicable. Safety, convenience, and quality of maintenance and testing are the main issues to be reviewed in vertical transportation systems. Each mode of transportation includes several safety features such as emergency devices, alarm bells, and miscellaneous safety equipment.

13.2 ELEVATOR SYSTEMS

An elevator is a transport device used to move goods or people vertically. Elevators are usually installed in a building during construction. Modernizations and renovations may consist of replacements for hoistway (floor landing) doors, car doors, interior cab finishes, controls, all hoistway wiring and cab wiring, hoist machines, governors, hydraulic pistons, hall fixtures, and even replacement of the entire cab. Often an upgrade may require additional code compliance.

While the modern passenger lift reflects a simple means of transport within a building, this apparent simplicity belies a complex and sophisticated mechanical, electrical and microelectronic system. For example, continuous developments in electronics and technology have made it possible for elevator relay control systems to go to solid state. Other recent developments are destination-oriented elevators (also called "destination-based" elevators), which eliminate control buttons in elevator cars; instead, passengers enter the elevator-lobby area and select a floor. Based upon the floor they're visiting, they're assigned an elevator car. We now also have the express elevator, which does not serve all floors. For example, it moves from the ground floor or a skylobby to a range of floors, skipping floors in between.

There are basically two types of elevators used in new commercial construction: hydraulic and electric. A general rule-of-thumb requires that one elevator is provided per 35,000 square feet of rentable space minimum above the first floor. This rule does not apply to buildings over 20 stories or whose floor area is less than 10,000 square feet. Another applicable rule is that one elevator at minimum is needed for every 225 to 250 occupants.

During the last decade we also saw the introduction of the machine-room-less elevators (MRL) into the United States. This revolutionary elevator system is based on the first major breakthrough in lifting technology for many years and was initially designed for buildings of up to 20 stories. The MRL system employs a smaller sheave than conventional geared and gearless elevators. The reduced sheave size, together with a redesigned motor, allows the machine to be mounted within the hoistway itself, eliminating the need for a bulky standalone machine and equipment room on the roof (Figure 13.1).

Not only does an MRL save space, but the motor uses substantially less horsepower than a traditional hydraulic elevator. "[When] using the smaller motor [of an MRL], you're not only using less energy, you're generating much less heat; hence, you're using less power to cool the building or to cool the machinery area. All those kinds of things snowball into significant reductions in energy," says Ken Segel, vice president of marketing for Morristown, NJ-based Schindler Elevator Corp.

Elevator technology advances have also resulted in quicker floor-to-floor operations, improved reliability, and reduced waiting times, The majority of gains have come in the form of microprocessor-based control systems that supersede the electromechanical relay-based controllers, and in silicon control (SCR) drives that replace the motor generator sets. The computerized control systems monitor cars and calls to determine which car can answer the call most effectively. The SCR drives also provide better speed control. "With microprocessor control, you can pick up (at least) 15 percent efficiency in response to a call," says Van Deusen of Van Deusen & Associates in Livingston, New Jersey. "On a six-car group, that's like adding another car."

Other benefits of the microprocessor and solid-state controls are smoother and faster acceleration and deceleration, as well as improved leveling so passengers will not trip as they enter and exit the elevator cars. The controllers also ensure that the elevators operate at their optimum speed, which saves on wear and tear as the equipment gets older.

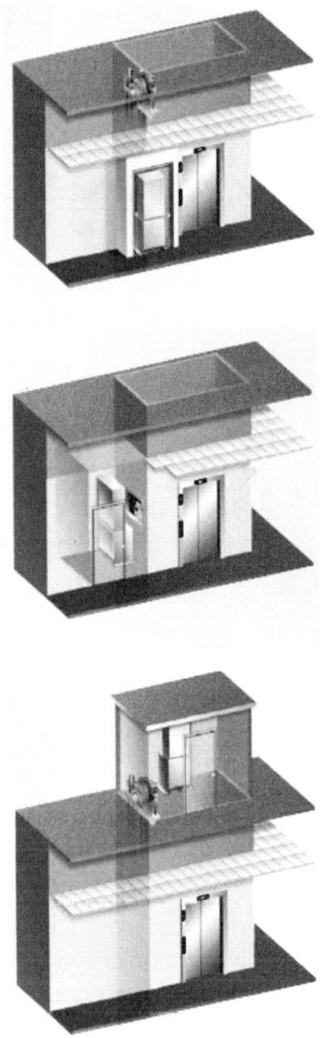

Figure 13.1 Space saving machine room configuration options *(Source Shindler Elevator Corp).*

13.2.1 Drum Elevators

The Winding Drum Machine is the oldest type of elevator system used, and is no longer permitted in the United States for new elevators except for residential applications and freight cars with a maximum speed of 50 fpm and maximum rise of 40 feet.

Cable winding drum elevators use steel cables that wind and unwind on an electric motor and are essentially used in residential applications. This type of elevator travels about 30 fpm and has a weight capacity of 500 to 750 pounds (Figure 13.2). While they are slightly less expensive than hydraulic elevators, the hydraulic elevator has a smoother ride with softer starts and stops. The standard size for a home elevator cab is 3 × 4 feet and is available up to 3 × 6 feet. Should major repairs to the drum be needed, the entire machine must be replaced with a traction type system.

13.2.2 Hydraulic Elevators

There are two major types of power elevators used in new installations—hydraulic-drive elevators and electric-drive elevators. Hydraulic elevators are power elevators in which the energy is applied by means of a liquid under pressure in a cylinder that is equipped with a plunger or piston. Hydraulic elevators are used extensively in low-rise installations—typically in buildings averaging five or six stories in height, where moderate car speed (between 50 and 200 feet per minute) is acceptable.

Hydraulic elevators do not use large overhead hoisting machinery like geared and gearless systems do. The car is connected to the top of a long fluid-driven piston that travels up and down inside a cylinder. The car moves up when an electric motor pumps hydraulic fluid into the cylinder from a reservoir, raising the piston. The car is lowered when the hydraulic fluid returns to the reservoir. Electrical valves control the release of the oil for a gentle descent.

Because of their relative simplicity of operation, hydraulic elevators cost less than electric elevators. Also, because they have no wire cables or overhead machinery, they do not need a penthouse. Hydraulic elevators move by means of extension and contraction of a hydraulic piston located below the elevator cab. Because of their short travel distance at relatively low speeds, hydraulic elevators are normally used for freight in industrial and low-rise commercial buildings, and for passengers in garden apartments, motels, and malls.

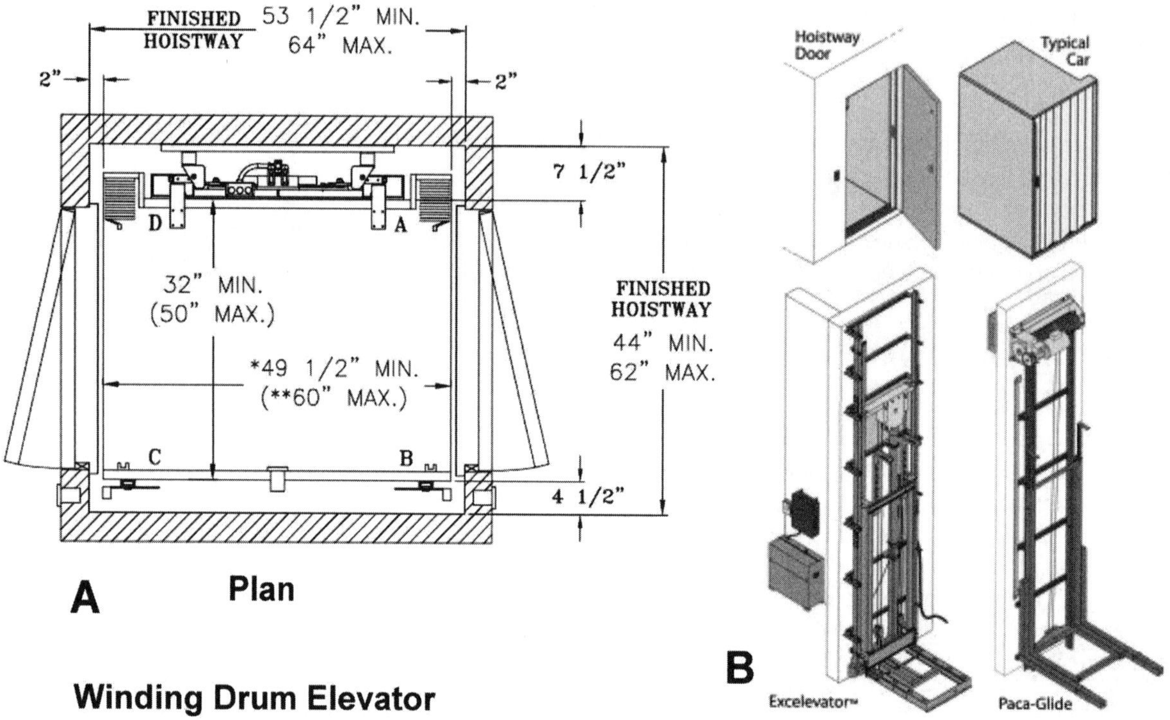

Figure 13.2 A. Plan of a drum elevator. B. Typical design of drum home elevator.

New elevators are usually of the electrohydraulic type. In these elevators, the problems associated with older hydraulic elevators (generally lower efficiency, the difficulty of keeping the valves and stuffing boxes tight, etc.) have been eliminated by using modern technology and materials and by following proper maintenance programs. The Elevator Code requires that new elevators be equipped with (1) anticreep-leveling devices, (2) hoistway door locking devices, (3) electric car-door or car-gate contacts, (4) hoistway access, and (5) parking devices. This equipment is the same as that required for electric-drive elevators.

Because most electrohydraulic elevators do not have a counterweight, the motor must supply the required pressure to lift the entire weight of the car and the load. In addition, it must be more powerful than the motor of the traction drive of an electric-drive elevator, on which the weight of the car and part of the load is compensated for by the counterweight, to maintain the same speed. Electrohydraulic elevators contain all the electrical protective devices (interlocks, car-gate contacts, limit switches, etc.) found on electric elevators.

The main advantages of hydraulic elevators over traction type elevators are essentially that they are easier to install and maintain, use simpler technology, and cost less to install. The main disadvantages include slower operating speed, which precludes their use in high-rise buildings, and inferior operation and performance.

Types of Hydraulic Elevators

Conventional hydraulic elevators are quite popular for low and medium rise buildings (2–6 floors) and use a hydraulically powered plunger to push the elevator upwards. On some, the hydraulic piston (plunger) consists of telescoping concentric tubes, allowing a shallow tube to contain the mechanism below the lowest floor. On others, the piston requires a deeper hole below the bottom landing, usually with a PVC casing (also known as a caisson) for protection. The inspector should check older systems for leaks because they are "single" bottom design and do not have secondary containment.

Holeless hydraulic elevators utilize an above-ground cylinder and piston design and do not require holes for the hydraulic cylinder (Figure 13.3). All piping and hydraulic fluid is contained above-ground, and the cab is usually lifted by a pair of hydraulic jacks, located on each side of the elevator. Holeless hydraulic configurations include the following:

1. Roped hydraulic elevators use a combination of ropes and hydraulic power for greater travel
2. Duel piston holeless
3. Single piston design (Cantilevered Design)

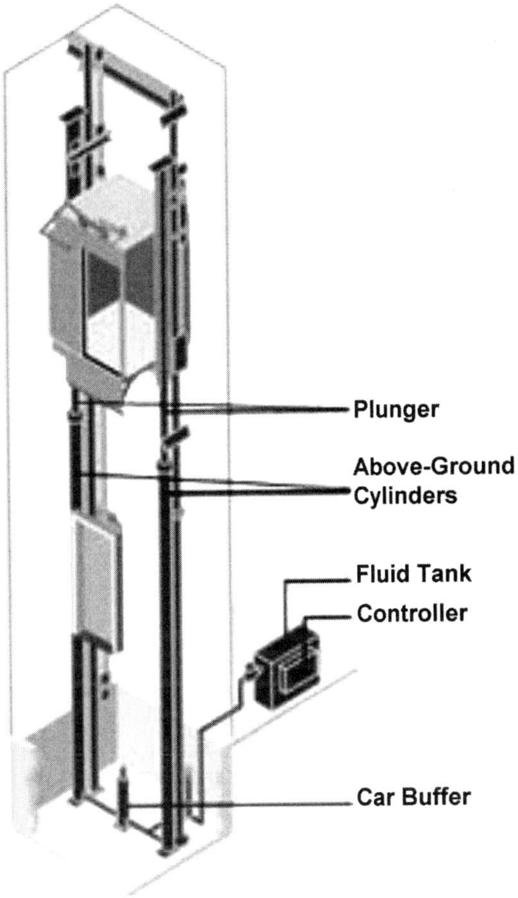

Figure 13.3 Example of holeless hydraulic elevator *(Source Otis)*.

The advantages of holeless versus the conventional system (in-ground design) are:

1. No drilling is required.
2. Environmentally friendly, using less hydraulic fluid, which is contained above-ground.
3. Holeless systems are easier to install in the majority of cases where drilling is a concern.
4. Newer technology.

The main disadvantages are greater complexity and higher cost.

13.2.3 Traction Elevators

Traction geared elevators: These systems are found mainly in low and mid-rise buildings. Geared machines use worm gears to mechanically control movement of elevator cars by "rolling" steel hoist ropes over a drive sheave that is attached to a gearbox driven by a high speed motor. Geared traction machines are driven by AC or DC electric motors located with the gearbox in an elevator machine room above the elevator shaft and the cab. While the lift rates are slower than in a typical gearless elevator, the gear reduction offers the advantage of requiring a less powerful motor to turn the sheave. An electrically controlled brake between the motor and the reduction unit stops the elevator, holding the car at the desired floor level.

These elevators typically operate at speeds from 125–500 fpm (38 to 152 meters per minute) and carry loads of up to 30,000 pounds (13,600 kilograms). Geared machines are generally the best option for basement or overhead traction use, and although they cost less than gearless systems, they generally give a poorer performance in mid- and high-rise buildings.

Traction gearless elevators: These systems are typically found in mid to high-rise buildings. For these, a cab is hung on a counterweighted cable and is driven by a DC motor directly connected to the cable sheave that winds the cable up and down. The motor is in an elevator machine room located above the elevator shaft and the cab. These are capable of attaining the greatest travel speeds and can travel up to about 1,200 fpm. Speeds of at least 700 fpm are often preferred for high-rises and some mid-rises.

The most popular of these is the roped elevator (or cable system), in which the car is raised and lowered by traction steel ropes rather than pushed from below. The cable system is used in high-rise elevator installations that typically use gearless traction systems, as well as in mid-rise installations that generally use geared traction systems. The elevator has a counterweight that balances the weight of the car and ensures that the hoist-rope's friction grips the driving sheaves (pulleys) so that when you rotate the sheave, the ropes move, too. The sheave is connected to an electric motor, and when the motor turns in one direction, the sheave raises the elevator, and when it turns in the opposite direction, the elevator is lowered (Figure 13.4).

Figure 13.4 Shindler traction gearless elevator system with side counterweight for buildings up to twenty floors *(Courtesy Shindler)*.

The machinery to drive the elevator is housed in a machine room usually directly above the elevator hoistway. To feed electricity to the car and receive electrical signals from it, a multi-wire electrical cable connects the machine room to the car. The end is attached to the car and moves with it. Most modern traction elevators now have microprocessor controls that require air conditioning (Figure 13.5).

13.2.4 Freight Elevators and Lifts

A freight elevator (or goods lift) is an elevator designed to carry goods rather than passengers and is typically hydraulic type. Freight elevators are usually exempt from some code and fire service requirements, although new installations are not. Freight elevators are often required to be larger and capable of carrying heavier loads than passenger elevators.

The assessment of elevators usually focuses on safety. In light of the fact that the majority of lawsuits involving elevators are door-related, the quality of door operations and cab leveling should be emphasized in an assessment.

General elevator controls: Modern elevator controls provide more convenient, efficient operation for mid- to high-rise buildings. Old, outdated controls consist of electromechanical relays. All new elevator controls are microprocessor-based; elevators are controlled by software that may incorporate algorithms to save energy. This software allows the elevator system to place cars where they are most needed in the interest of smooth operation with minimal waiting times and to shut down extra elevators when they are not needed. The algorithms used in such software are based on analyses of elevator usage patterns called "traffic studies."

Figure 13.5 Example of elevator control system for high rise buildings *(Courtesy Total Elevators)*.

Destination selection control systems: Destination elevators are computer controlled for maximum efficiency of the system. At each floor there is a touch screen keypad where the rider selects which floor they wish to go to. Passengers are grouped according to their destinations; in certain applications, there aren't even any buttons inside the elevator cabs. The system then directs the passenger to an elevator that will be stopping at their floor. This avoids time-consuming stops and helps passengers reach their destinations more quickly. Destination dispatching systems calculate the shortest possible time to the distance instead of the shortest waiting time in front of the elevator, realizing an average time savings of up to 25 to 30 percent.

Modern passenger elevators will typically contain:

- Call buttons to choose a floor and which are designed to meet ADA requirements Some of these may be key switches (to control access). In some elevators, certain floors are inaccessible unless one swipes a security card, enters a pass code, or uses a key.
- Door open and door close buttons to instruct the elevator to close or remain open longer, but holding the door open for too long may trigger an audible alarm.
- A stop switch (this is not allowed under British regulations) to halt the elevator (often used to hold an elevator open while freight is loaded)
- An alarm button or switch, which passengers can use to signal entrapment

Elevators may also incorporate one or more of the following:

- An elevator telephone, which trapped passenger can use to call for help
- A hold button to delay the door closing timer
- A fireman's key switch, which places the elevator in a special operating mode designed to aid firefighters
- A medical emergency key switch, which places the elevator in a special operating mode designed to aid medical personnel
- Security controls to control/prevent unauthorized floor access

Other controls that may be in place but which are generally inaccessible to the public, include:

- Switches to control the lights and ventilation fans in the elevator cab
- Inspector's switch, which places the elevator in inspection mode
- PASS button: When used by elevator attendants that have access to the operator panel, this button causes the car to not answer hall calls while button is depressed. Feature may also be automatically activated if elevator computer detects that the car is near its full capacity.
- GO button: Useful for attendant serviced elevators, this button is used to close doors and start the elevator, where it would be waiting with the doors open.

13.3 ESCALATORS

An escalator is a power-driven, continuously moving, inclined stairway. Varying by design and planned usage, an escalator can rise from 4 feet to over 100 feet and may go floor-to-floor or skip floors. Escalators and moving walks have become indispensable parts of our society. Whether in department stores, train stations, modern stadiums, luxury casinos, hotels, office complexes, or airports, escalators and moving walks keep people moving safely and effectively (Figures 13.6A, B; 13.7).

Less frequently encountered than elevators, escalators are designed to transport large numbers of people in a continuous flow from floor to floor, particularly in department stores, airline terminals and public concourses, with a relatively low

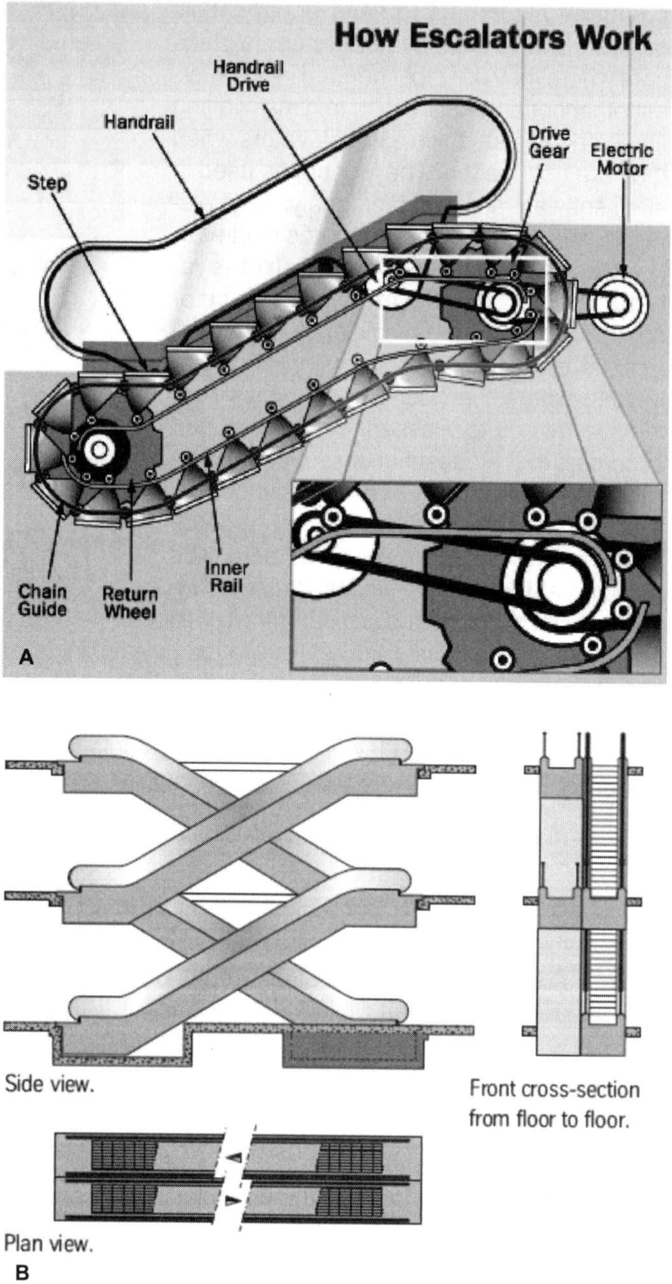

Figure 13.6 A. Diagram of how an escalator works *(Courtesy Tom Harris, HowStuffWorks, Inc)*. B. Diagram of criss-cross escalators *(Courtesy ThyssenKrupp Elevator)*.

cost of operation. Typically there are two escalators installed, with one ascending and the other descending.

The core of an escalator is a pair of chains that is looped around two pairs of gears driven by an electric motor (the motor also moves the handrails). The steps are designed to always stay level, at both top and bottom of the escalator, collapsing on each other to create a flat platform, to allow persons to get on and off.

Many of today's escalators have more intelligent capabilities than in the past. For example, escalators can now sense how much power is needed and adjust the energy consumption accordingly.

Figure 13.7 Velino commercial duty escalator *(Courtesy ThyssenKrupp Elevator).*

13.4 MOVING WALKS AND RAMPS (INCLINED MOVING WALKS)

For decades, experts have been discussing the possibility of moving walks for distances of 150 to 1,000 meters that allow passengers to enter and exit at normal speed and accelerate much faster in the central section, allowing greater distances to be covered more quickly and in greater comfort. The latest moving walks feature entry and exit sections that move at 2 feet per second, while the central section accelerates to up to 6 feet per second—twice the normal walking speed.

The mechanics of moving walks are similar to escalators except that the passenger-carrying surface remains parallel to its direction of motion and is uninterrupted. Inclined moving walks or ramps serve a similar function to that of escalators. They are especially developed for shopping malls and provide quiet, comfortable transportation from floor to floor, even with a fully loaded shopping cart. In contrast to escalators, moving ramps have a continuous tread and incline up to 15 degrees. They are also frequently installed in airport terminals, train stations and major department stores, being used in locations requiring the expedient transportation of large numbers of people. They are ideal for use wherever the elimination of long walks is desired (Figure 13.8).

Figure 13.8 Shindler 9500 Moving Walk, Munich Fair, Germany *(Courtesy Shindler).*

13.5 BUILDING CODES AND ADA COMPLIANCE

Several building codes regulate the installation and use of vertical transportation. The National

Electrical Manufacturers' Association (NEMA) Code regulates electrical motors and generators. The National Electrical Code, sponsored by the National Fire Protection Association, regulates electrical controls. A third code is the American National Standards Safety Code for Elevators, Dumbwaiters, Escalators, and Moving Walks, which is sponsored jointly by the American Society of Mechanical Engineers (ASME), the American National Standards Institute (ANSI), and the American Institute of Architects (AIA). The Safety Code includes requirements for new installations, existing installations, modernization/upgrading, periodic inspections and tests, and proper maintenance.

Passenger elevators may also be required to conform to the requirements of the Safety Code A17.3 for existing elevators where referenced by the local jurisdiction. Passenger elevators are tested using the ASME A17.2 Standard. The frequency of these tests is mandated by the local jurisdiction, which may be a town, city, state or provincial agency.

In addition, passenger elevators must conform to various ancillary building codes, including the local or state building code, National Fire Protection Association standards for electrical, fire sprinklers and fire alarms, plumbing codes, and HVAC codes. Passenger elevators are also required to conform to the Americans with Disabilities Act and other State and Federal civil rights legislation regarding accessibility (see Chapters 16–18). These should be referenced as needed during an assessment.

Residential elevators are required to conform to ASME A17.1. Platform and wheelchair lifts are required to comply with ASME A18.1 in most U.S. jurisdictions.

Most elevators have a location in which the permit for the building owner to operate the elevator is displayed. While some jurisdictions require the permit to be displayed in the elevator cab, other jurisdictions allow for the operating permit to be kept on file elsewhere—such as the maintenance office—and to be made available for inspection on demand.

Because of liability concerns, PCA consultants do not typically survey for code compliance unless such evaluation is specifically agreed upon in the protocol with the client and additional fees are agreed upon.

13.6 BASIC COMPONENT GROUPS TO BE EVALUATED

1. Machine room and equipment
2. Hoistway
3. Pit
4. Cab and equipment
5. Floor landings and equipment

13.6.1 Machine Room

The machine room is typically located in the overhead or in the basement, although some designs also incorporate it at the side of the hoistway. When located in the basement area, there will be an overhead space for traction or roped hydraulic elevators. This overhead space will contain the overhead sheaves, the overspeed governor assembly, and other needed equipment (Figures 13.9, 13.10).

Safe and convenient access should be provided to machine rooms. At least 7 feet (2.1 meters) of headroom should be provided between the machinery platform and the machine room's roof to allow sufficient headroom for persons repairing or inspecting elevator hoisting machinery.

As with pits, elevator machine rooms should not be used as thoroughfares. The one exception would be if the elevator's equipment were in a separate locked enclosure. Rooms should be well ventilated and

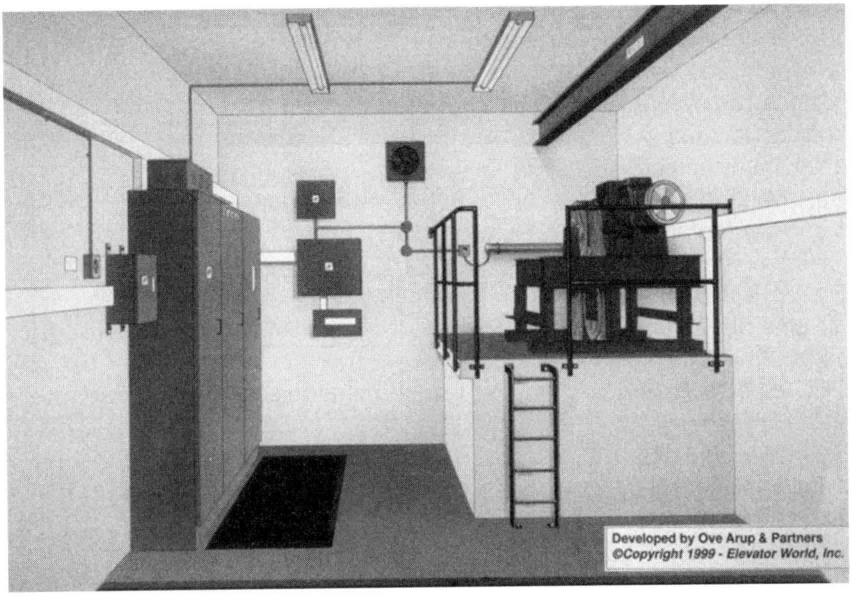

Figure 13.9 Drawing of conventional machine room and controller developed by Ove Arup & Partners *(Courtesy Elevator-World.com)*.

Figure 13.10 Drawing of typical elevator cab from above developed by Ove Arup & Partners *(Courtesy Elevator-World.com)*.

lighted with not less than 10 foot-candles (108 lux) at floor level. Doors are to be kept locked with affixed warning signs to prevent entry by unauthorized persons.

Depending on the machine room's location, traction and drum machines can be located in the overhead or basement. Hydraulic Drive Systems are typically located in the basement (Figure 13.11).

The typical life expectancy is between 50 and 75 years depending on maintenance and use patterns. When conducting a survey, the consultant should check for excessive oil leakage or unusual noise. Where a team approach is used for the survey, it is common to include an elevator consultant.

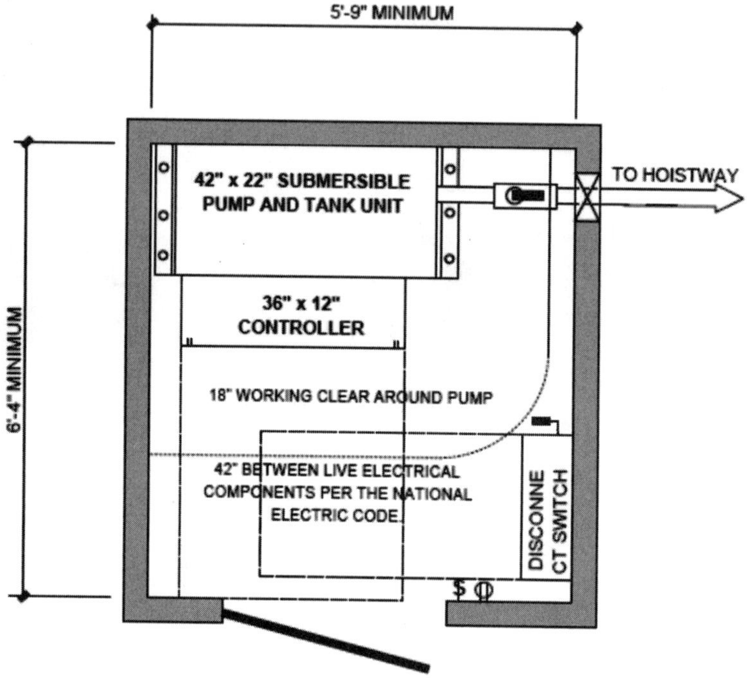

Figure 13.11 Drawing of a typical hydraulic machine room layout *(Courtesy Mitsubishi Electric).*

Drive motor(s): Running on either Direct Current (DC) or Alternating Current (AC), the motor transmits power to the machine through the motor armature shaft. The typical life expectancy of the motors is between 25 and 40 years.

Motor generator or power drive: Older elevator systems usually employ a motor generator, whereas newer systems may employ a "solid state" or frequency drive unit. Essentially these machines convert the incoming power supply from AC (Alternating Current) to DC (Direct Current) for use by the drive motor. They also provide proper electrical current for control of elevator starting, acceleration, and operation. The life expectancy is usually 25 to 35 years.

Controller: This is the main panel and "brains" of the elevator system. It controls the operation of the elevator in response to a signal from an operating device (car or hall push button). Older systems have large panels with large mechanical relays and limited features. Newer systems, on the other hand, employ microprocessor controls with solid state technology and fewer moving parts. When inspecting the controller, look for worn components and dust accumulation. Typical life expectancy is 20 to 30 years.

13.6.2 Hoistway (Elevator Shaft)

The hoistway or elevator shaft is the space that the elevator travels in and extends from the pit to the underside of the overhead machinery space floor. The hoistway typically consists of:

Guard rails: These should be kept clean and properly aligned. Their life expectancy is about 75 years and roped systems contain car and counterweight.

Wire rope cables: These serve as hoist, compensation, and governor cables. In traction and roped systems, the cables provide the connection between the car, machine, and counterweight assembly, and have a life expectancy of roughly 10 to 15 years depending on use, maintenance, etc. Multiple cables are often used to increase safety. They should be routinely inspected for wear and/or breaks and should be replaced on a timely basis.

Mechanical safety equipment and counterweights: The counterweights provide system balance and are connected to the elevator cab by wire rope cables. Additional counterweights may be required if larger loads are added to the cab (e.g., heavy wall panels, stone floor, etc.). The mechanical car safety is located below the car platform. In emergency cases, safety features may activate and stop the elevator by "clamping" onto the rails. The life expectancy is normally 50–75 years.

Hoistway door equipment: Includes hoist door panels, support tracks and hangers, interlocks and closers. Tracks, hangers, interlocks and closers must be routinely inspected and kept clean and free of debris. Interlocks serve 2 main functions: 1. to prevent the opening of the hoistway door from the landing side when the car is out of the landing zone, and 2. to prevent the operation of the driving machine unless the hoistway door is in the closed position. Life expectancy is usually between 25 and 40 years.

Most codes for building elevators require that new elevators be installed in two-hour, fire-resistant hoistways. These hoistways should have 1 1/2 hour fire doors that fill the entire opening to prevent the rapid spread of fire from floor to floor.

Pipes shall not be installed under any elevator or counterweight hoistway that convey gas or liquids that could endanger lives if discharged into the hoistway. Low-pressure steam or hot water pipes used only for heating the hoistway and the machine room (or penthouse) are permitted if certain conditions are met. Only electrical wiring and equipment used directly in connection with the elevator may be installed in the hoistway.

13.6.3 Pit Area

The pit is the area located at the bottom of the hoistway, and extends from the threshold level of the lowest landing to the hoistway floor. The main components in the pit include the governor tension sheave (or pit sheave), car and counterweight buffer assemblies, pit light and stop switch, and pit sump pump. With hydraulic systems, the cylinder and piston will also be found in the pit. A light switch and emergency stop switch must be reachable from the pit's access door. Adequate lighting should be provided at the pit's floor level (Figure 13.12).

A minimum clearance should be maintained of 2 feet (60 cm) between the lowest projection on the underside of the cab's platform and any obstruction in the pit (excluding compensating devices, buffers, buffer supports, and similar devices). Measurements should be taken when the cab is resting on fully compressed buffers.

Figure 13.12 Illustration drawing of an elevator pit developed by Ove Arup & Partners *(Courtesy ElevatorWorld.com)*.

Figure 13.13 Example of elevator cab interior by Shindler.

Counterweight runways should be enclosed from a point not more than 1 foot (30 cm) above the pit floor to a point at least 7 feet (2 m) above the pit floor and adjacent pit floors, except where compensating chains or cables are used. Screen partitions, at least 7 feet (2 m) high between adjacent pits, will protect persons in one pit from cabs and counterweights in adjacent pits and will also protect employees from hazards when adjacent pits are at different levels.

13.6.4 Cab and Equipment

The main components include the cab enclosure, the door operating equipment, and the top of car equipment (Figure 13.13).

The cab enclosure includes the interior panels and flooring, the cab panels, and the car operating panel (including push buttons, position indicators and signals, intercom/phone system, etc.). Life expectancy is usually about 20 years, depending on maintenance.

Door operating equipment has a life expectancy of about 20–30 years. It includes the cab door operator, which automatically opens and closes the cab doors and the door safety edge, which provides protection for passengers entering and exiting the cab.

Top-of-car equipment includes an emergency exit hatch and a work light and convenience outlet to provide a station for manual operation of the elevator for inspection purposes.

13.6.5 Floor Landings and Equipment

Floor landings will contain elevator system components typically found in the lobby and at the other floor landings. The life expectancy of equipment in this section will vary, but 20–30 years can be expected. The main components include:

- Hall push button fixtures.
- Position indicators that display the position of the elevator in the hoistway.
- Hall lanterns or direction indicators indicate the direction of elevator travel.
- Lobby intercom station for communications with elevator cab.

13.7 TYPICAL SYSTEM DEFICIENCIES

Elevators should be assessed for the following issues:

1. The system's type, capacity, location and general condition
2. Whether the maintenance contract is adequate and equipment well maintained.

3. Whether previous inspection reports identify any recurring trends or deficiencies.
4. If the guide rails and accessories in good condition.
5. If the electric motors and accompanying components in good condition.
6. If the hydraulic reservoir piping and pressure relief valve is in good condition.
7. Do the floor-to-floor travel times meet standards?
8. Are the safety devices installed and operating properly?
9. Do the door interlocks, buffers, and closers operate adequately?
10. Do the limit, landing, and slowdown switches operate adequately?
11. Do the alarm bells and phone operate adequately?
12. Do the door opening and closing times meet standards?
13. Are the acceleration and deceleration adequate?
14. Is the pit maintained adequately?
15. When were buffers last tested and are hoist and safety ropes in good condition?
16. Is the equipment obsolete or in need of replacement?
17. Are the controllers properly maintained?
18. What is the type of supervisory control?
19. Is there adequate standby power in place?
20. Is the signage visible and legible?
21. Have seismic requirements been assessed and modifications made to suit?
22. Are the fire control requirements met?

13.8 SYSTEM DIAGNOSTICS

Unlike many building systems, the vertical transportation system is localized and not situated throughout the building. It is common to find a bank of elevators or an escalator area centrally located in a building. It is also common to find the system in generally good working order, since the operation of most buildings is severely hampered when the system is down.

Prior to a physical PCA the consultant should review all documents pertaining to the design, construction, operation, and maintenance of the elevator system. During the physical assessment, the consultant should interview in-house or third-party maintenance staff who currently operate the system. The consultant should seek out information on problem areas and areas that need attention. Based on visual observation, the consultant should report on the status of overall car control and monitoring and of individual door controls, with the necessary recommendations. Review the elevator maintenance contract, and compare its specifications to the actual system. Note all deficiencies and areas for improved enforcement.

Infrared scanning of electrical equipment, vibration testing on motor and hoistway equipment, and other tests on door closures and safety devices may be required. The scope of work will be provided in a separate guidance document or shall be submitted by the consultant and pre-approved by the client.

Most building owners contract a service and maintenance firm to provide regular preventive maintenance, which typically includes monthly inspections and repairs. The evaluation of the system should therefore include a review of both the maintenance agreement and inspection reports. The agreement should be evaluated to ascertain whether it includes all necessary items and whether it meets the requirements of the system. The inspection reports should be reviewed to identify any recurring trends or deficiencies. It is useful to interview the maintenance representatives who have been servicing the system. It is likely that they can provide information on the past, present conditions, and future capabilities of the system, information not otherwise available in a one-time evaluation, no matter how thorough. The past and present conditions and quality of maintenance will determine the remaining life of the equipment. Figure 13.14 details the average useful life of some types of vertical transportation.

TYPE	USEFUL LIFE
Electric Passenger Elevator	25
Hydraulic Passenger Elevator	20
Hydraulic Freight Elevator	20
Single-width Escalator	30
Moving Walk	30

Figure 13.14 The average useful life of typical vertical transportation types.

A significant aspect of a vertical transportation evaluation is a determination of the degree of obsolescence of the equipment. It can be difficult to find equipment and replacement parts for older systems. The potential benefits of modernization should also be reviewed. In some cases, the increased safety, efficiency, and equipment availability provided by new systems warrants replacement or modernization.

During an evaluation of an elevator, several areas are accessed. These include the machine room, the top of the elevator cab, the elevator pit, and the cab itself. The machine room should be reviewed for general maintenance and housekeeping. Rotating equipment and the controllers should be evaluated for signs of wear or deterioration. The top of the cab should be surveyed and also reviewed for adequacy of maintenance. The top of the cab should be ridden to determine operational characteristics, the degree of hoist and safety rope wear, and the adequacy of seismic safety precautions. The elevator pit should then be inspected for general cleanliness and the condition of the buffers.

The cab inspection is the final aspect of the elevator inspection. Signage, fire safety, handicap accessibility and code requirements are evaluated. A tachometer and a stopwatch are used to aid in determining various operational information, including acceleration, deceleration, floor-to-floor speeds and door open and closing speeds.

Evaluation of vertical transportation systems relies mostly on visual observation. In facilities that historically have experienced problems, more in-depth evaluation may be warranted. For example, pressure and load tests may be required in hydraulic elevators that have experienced hydraulic-related deficiencies in the past.

A limited review of the vertical transportation system can be performed by anyone with some knowledge of the system and its operations. An in-depth evaluation of the system should be performed by a knowledgeable professional, such as an elevator or vertical transportation consultant.

When to modernize: Elevators generally become candidates for modernization as they approach the 20- to 25-year-old range when they approach the end of their efficient life span. Naturally, this life span can vary depending on how well the elevators are maintained and whether they are heavily used, such as in hospitals or hotels. The level of modernization can be determined after a complete survey and analysis is performed and an initial budget is decided upon. The considerations should include "building related" items such as machine room air conditioning/ventilation, incorporation of fire safety systems, main electrical system upgrade, etc.

If an elevator upgrade is needed, the owner should have a modernization program based on the needs of the specific building. Those needs should be determined before the owner requests proposals.

One of the prime reasons to modernize elevators is to allow older buildings to compete with newer buildings and with existing ones that have been renovated. This goal is advanced by improving reliability—e.g., by reducing system failures due to normal aging or wear, reducing the number of shut-downs and entrapments and by replacing obsolescent components. Older, less-efficient elevators suffer from more frequent reliability problems. Modernization will improve performance and efficiency in addition to reliability. Passengers prefer to ride in elevators that start and stop smoothly and provide a quiet ride. Speed is important in mid- to high-rise buildings. In low-rise buildings, acceleration and deceleration are more important than maximum travel speed. Higher performance can be achieved by reducing passenger waiting times and traffic handling capability caused by inefficient operation. Ride and operation quality can improve by reducing excessive cab vibration, door noise, and harsh stopping. Finally, modernization can improve the aesthetics by replacing outdated or worn cab finishes and aged or outdated fixtures. It also gives an opportunity to upgrade communications.

Entrapment: Due to entrapment concerns, all elevators are required to have communication connection to an outside 24-hour emergency service, automatic recall capability in a fire emergency, and special access for fire fighter use in a fire. Elevators should not be used by the public if there is a fire in or around the building. Numerous building codes require signs near the elevator to state "USE STAIRS IN CASE OF FIRE". Some countries allow the use of elevators in emergency evacuations.

CHAPTER

14

Interior Systems

14.1 GENERAL

The interior system of a facility comprises several different aspects including floors, walls, ceilings, finishes, fixtures, and special systems. Interior components are installed in a facility for various reasons, including appearance, acoustics, utility, and safety.

The design of interior space, particularly office space, has been getting a lot of attention lately. After staffing, office space is typically an organization's second largest expense. Moreover, because office space can impact the ability to recruit employees, as well as their satisfaction and productivity, many organizations have started to look carefully at how their space is working for them and are revisiting their space standards and the quality of their environments. Investors have come to realize that interior environments, from both aesthetic and health standpoints, are playing an increasingly important role in influencing major tenant decisions on leasing. Some of the factors that impact the evaluation of an interior systems survey are shown in Figure 14.1.

According to Lawrence Berkeley National Laboratory (LBNL) researchers WJ Fisk and AH Rosenfeld, U.S. companies could save as much as $58 billion annually by preventing sick-building illnesses and an additional $200 billion in worker performance improvements by creating offices with better indoor air. The researchers also found that the financial benefits of improving office climates can be eight to 17 times larger than the costs of making those improvements.

14.2 FLOORS

Floors are generally designed to provide a wearing surface on top of a flat support structure. Their form and materials are selected for architectural, structural, functional, and cost reasons. A ground-supported floor may be of almost any firm material, ranging from compacted soil to reinforced concrete. It is supported directly by the subsoil underneath it.

Wooden floors are generally used in light residential construction. Such flooring generally consists of a finish floor installed on a subfloor of tongue-and-groove planking or plywood, spanning between wooden

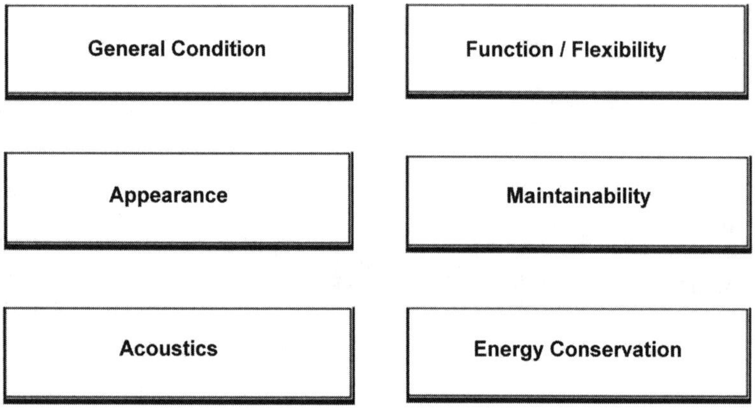

Figure 14.1 Some of the factors that impact the evaluation of an interior systems survey.

beams called joists (Figure 14.2). Slabs of reinforced concrete are a common type of floor for heavier loading. The concrete is cast on forms, and reinforced with properly placed and shaped steel bars (re-bars), so as to span between steel or reinforced concrete beams or between bearing walls. Composite floors are commonly used in modern office building construction. Concrete is cast on, and made structurally integral with corrugated metal deck, which spans between steel joists of either solid-beam or open-web types, generally spaced between about 16–48 inches (40–120 cm) on center. Prestressed concrete is used for long span slabs. Highly prestressed high-tension steel wires within the high-strength concrete slab produce a thin, stiff, and strong floor deck. A lift slab is used for economy and efficiency. A concrete slab is first formed at ground level, reinforced and cured to adequate strength, and then carefully jacked up into its final position on supporting columns.

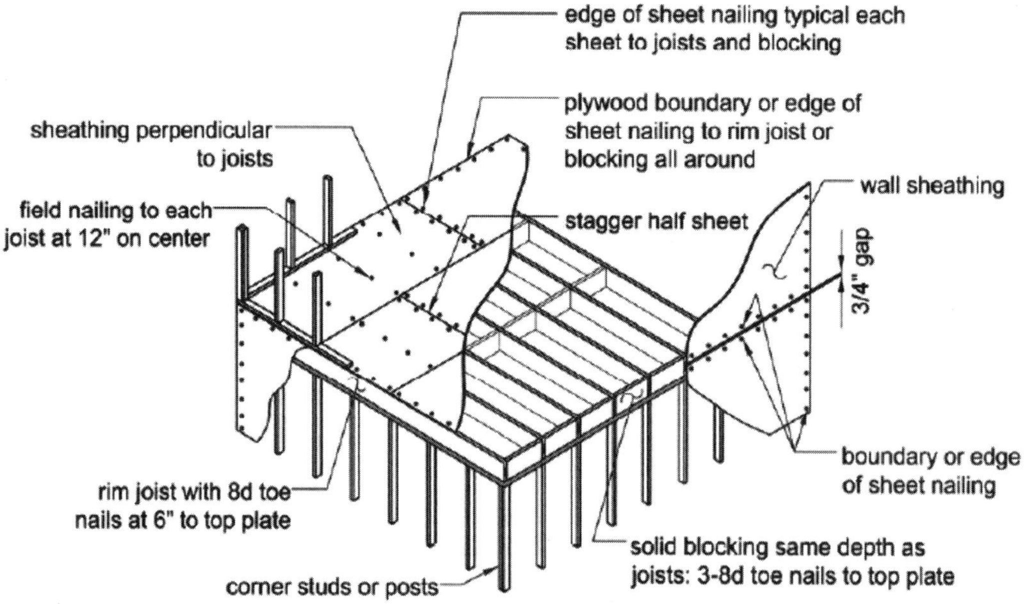

Figure 14.2 Wooden floor joist system construction.

Wood-framed floors normally consist of repetitive joists or trusses at predetermined spacing, sheathed with either boards or wood structural panels attached to the top surface. Finish materials such as gypsum board are typically applied to the bottom surface where it serves as the ceiling for the space below. Blocking between joists or trusses is usually employed at the ends of the floor joists or trusses and where walls occur above or below. Floor systems also incorporate beams, girders, or headers as needed to support the joists.

Joists can be sawn lumber, end jointed lumber, or a variety of prefabricated (engineered) members. Examples of engineered lumber include wood I-joists, trusses, or solid rectangular structural composite members, such as parallel strand lumber (PSL), laminated veneer lumber (LVL), and laminated strand lumber (LSL). Beams, girders, or headers and blocking can also be either sawn lumber or engineered lumber.

Elevated floors span between, and are supported by, beams, columns, and bearing walls. A floor is designed to be strong and stiff enough to support its design loading without excessive deflection; to provide for an appropriate degree of fire resistance; and to supply diaphragm strength to maintain the shape of the building as a whole, if necessary.

Concrete has a proven record for strength, durability, and cost effectiveness for a variety of applications, including floors, walkways, patios and driveways. Concrete floors are found in a variety of residential settings, from high-rise condominiums to basements remodeled for extra living space, and to below grade and slab-on-grade construction (Figure 14.3). Interior concrete is commonly covered with carpet, vinyl, or other flooring materials. For exterior surfaces, materials like slate, granite, or brick are preferred to standard concrete when budgets allow.

The life expectancy of concrete slabs far exceed that of flooring materials often used to cover them. Carpeting and vinyl are subject to tears, staining, damage from flooding, and general wear. Persons with allergies may also have concerns about dust or molds that may be harbored in carpet fibers. In addition, many floor coverings need to be replaced every few years.

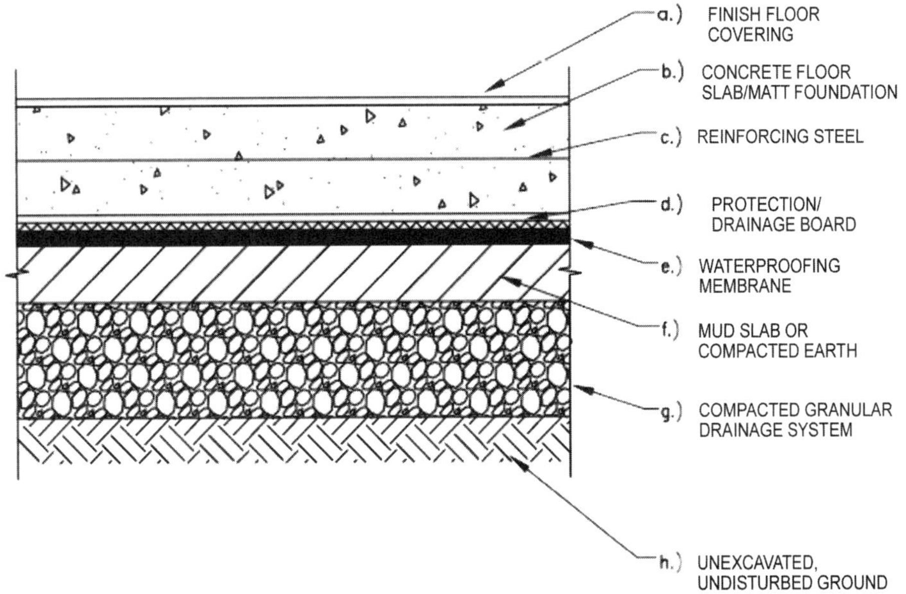

Figure 14.3 Below-grade slab concrete floor and waterproofing detail.

Decorative finishes can be applied to existing or new concrete slabs. The finishes can last the lifetime of the concrete, and are durable, sanitary, and easy to maintain. The treatment may be as simple as coloring walkways to match architectural features or to blend them into the landscape. If the look of natural materials is preferred, a slab might be stamped to create the appearance of slate or granite, complete with subtle color shifts, surface texture, and real grout placed in the formed joints between pavers.

Thin layers of cementitious material can also be applied to existing concrete floors. The material may be self-leveling, to flatten an irregular surface, or trowelable where pattern stamping is desired. Colored materials can likewise be applied to seal and waterproof concrete surfaces. Manufacturers offer a broad range of products for various applications, ranging from buffing waxes for interior floors to industrial sealers for high traffic exterior settings.

Concrete is relatively inexpensive and the costs for decorative concrete may still be less costly than installing a floor of different material. It lasts longer than most other floors and can withstand much abuse without damaging its look.

All concrete flatwork must comply with applicable building code requirements for thickness, composition, and strength. There may be requirements for slip resistance on exterior walkways that preclude very smooth or glossy finishes. Moreover, some contractors will warrant their work against cracking for a period of several years, generally about 5 to 10.

Radiant floor heating is another energy-efficient technology that can easily be incorporated into slab floors. A decorative finish on the concrete will allow the system to provide maximum heat transfer with no thermal barriers from added floor coverings. Besides conditioning the space, the floor will also feel comfortably warm underfoot.

Prestressed concrete is concrete with stresses induced in it before use to counteract stresses that will be produced by loads. Prestress is most effective with concrete, which is weak in tension, when the stresses induced are compressive. One way to produce compressive prestress is to place the concrete member between two abutments with jacks between its ends and the abutments, and to apply pressure with the jacks. The most common way is to stretch steel bars or wires, called tendons, and to anchor them to the concrete; when they try to regain their initial length, the concrete resists and is prestressed.

14.3 WALLS

Interior walls today are typically constructed of gypsum board, often referred to as drywall or wallboard. Gypsum board is generally nailed or screwed to vertical support pieces called studs, which are usually made of wood. Where drywall sections join, the joints are covered with a strip of special tape, and with metal pieces at corners. Joints are then finished with a joint compound, sometimes referred to as spackle.

The term *plaster,* when it comes to wall systems, focuses on gypsum-based plasters. This robust material resists abuse and gives designers a bit of artistic leverage. The best levels of plaster walls are conventional, full-thickness systems. These abuse-resistant walls boast a highly desirable monolithic surface—a look revived by modern designers' specs. Traditional plaster walls can be finished smooth or textured, and provide long-term beauty and performance.

Traditional plaster is expensive, however. Depending upon the application, plaster systems can cost up to four-times more than drywall. In many cases, it can be at least double the cost. However, many older structures have plaster walls. Plaster was typically installed over a support structure called lath, often thin strips of wood, with the plaster squeezing between, curling around and locking on. Sometimes plaster was installed over a gypsum board with holes in it which allowed the plaster to enter and grip the board. When light stresses are put on the plaster walls, the plaster cracks, especially at the corners of windows and doors. If the crack is hairline, you can easily patch it and restore it to its original condition.

The biggest problem for plaster walls is water. Water leaks from plumbing fixtures not only create problems for the plaster, but can rot wood lath beneath or cause gypsum lath to crumble. Should this occur, a major repair job lies ahead because the damaged plaster and the rotted wood must both be cut out. Plaster work is an art. For homes with plaster walls, it is recommended that someone who is experienced and adept at working with plaster be found to complete repairs.

Veneer plasters: If a high-quality, conventional plaster look fits the bill, but not the budget, another option is a veneer plaster system. Two-coat veneer plasters—which are composed of a gypsum plaster baseboard, a 1/16- to 1/32-inch basecoat, and a veneer finishing material—provide monolithic finishes and good-to-excellent wear resistance.

High-strength, one-coat veneer plaster finishes rank a step above drywall and a step down from two-coat veneer systems. These finishes offer up to 100 times the abrasion resistance of drywall and at least four-times more indentation resistance than drywall.

Given favorable drying conditions, one-coat plaster systems are ready for finishing in as little as 48 hours. Drywall joint treatments normally require multiple drying cycles, spanning four or five days. With plaster, work can be completed several days sooner, depending upon the application. Today's drywall systems provide a smooth, serviceable finish at the lowest possible initial installed cost.

Gypsum fiber panels have been used as interior walls, as a high-strength flooring underlayment, and as an exterior sheathing worldwide, especially in Europe, since the early 1970s. The most popular commercial construction application for these panels is in wall systems, where they typically are specified as an abuse-resistant alternative to drywall and plaster systems.

Extensive research efforts resulted in the development of innovative panels made from a unique manufacturing process that combines cellulose fibers and gypsum, the primary ingredient in traditional drywall products. Many of these products now also incorporate water-resistant technology, which provides increased resistance to indentation and penetration without the need for a paper face that can tear or scratch.

Gypsum fiber panels are now routinely specified in hospitals, schools, prisons, and other facilities that are subjected to occasional moist conditions and are likely to experience abrasions, indentations, and other forms of abuse caused by supply carts, gurneys, machinery, or equipment being moved routinely throughout the premises.

Since the advent of the first gypsum wood fiber products, the manufacturing technology and science have improved continually. Today, the manufacturing process actually grows gypsum crystals in and around the pores of wood fiber, more fully integrating the two materials. This contributes to many of the products' superior performance features, including greater strength-to-weight ratio, better fire and weather resistance, improved fastener holding, consistent dimensional stability, uniform surface smoothness, and full recyclability.

Because gypsum fiber panels have an intrinsic strength, there's no need to include additional layers to bolster their strength. Drywall panels, for example, require paper facings to provide strength. By comparison, a 1/2-inch thick gypsum wood fiber panel is approximately 20 percent stronger than a 1/2-inch paper-faced gypsum panel and provides superior fire resistance.

Gypsum wood fiber panels provide a smooth, flat surface for finished walls that can be painted. They also require less cutting, fewer joints, and no transitions between different types of substrates. In addition, gypsum wood fiber panels are, by their composition and design, extremely environmentally friendly. Many are made from 95-percent recycled materials. Several of these products have been awarded the "Green Cross" certificate for their high recycled content from Scientific Certification Systems, a leading independent testing organization.

Drywall manufacturers have in recent years become concerned with the mold issue in the building industry. Mold in new construction is an issue for builders due to the additional cost of remediation, not to mention visibility with owners and investors. For solid materials, such as framing members, mold remediation involves cleaning and treating, but for drywall, cleaning may not suffice, leaving a more expensive effort of removal and replacement.

Mold growth requires moisture and a food source. Therefore, some gypsum board manufacturers have developed products with gypsum cores that will not absorb moisture as easily as typical gypsum board. The current standard for mold-resistant characteristics of drywall is ASTM D3273, "Standard Test Method for Resistance to Growth of Mold on the Surface of Interior Coatings in an Environmental Chamber." This standard measures the ability of the drywall product to resist mold and mildew growth under certain prescribed moisture conditions, and a number of manufacturers quote the performance of their products when tested to this standard.

Mold-resistant does not mean that mold cannot grow. Under the right conditions, mold can grow on almost any surface. These products limit the conditions that encourage and facilitate organism growth, reducing the chances for mold to establish itself.

14.4 INTERIOR DOORS

The design, specification, and detailing of a door can significantly impact the function and performance of a structure. Doors come in a variety of standard heights, widths, and thicknesses, yet they may also be custom designed, assume a variety of shapes and forms, and be constructed with a variety of materials. The design, specification, and detailing of a door is, in fact, a rather complex task.

A door is typically set within a frame or jamb (Figure 14.4), but may also be installed within a wall without a frame or jamb. The frame/jamb interface between door and wall partition is another area requiring special attention by the designer. The design of a door includes hardware, hinges, locksets, closers, stops, and thresholds—just a few of the hardware elements that a designer must consider.

There are basically two types of door panel construction: steel stiffened and laminated core. Hollow metal swing door construction types include: full flush with continuously welded edge seams, full flush with unfilled edge seams, flush stile and rail, and recessed panels.

It is important in a review of the interior systems to operate and evaluate as many of the doors as possible. When a door is found to be severely sticking, and there are other doors or windows in the same area that are sticking as well, they could be out of rack, which may indicate a serious problem involving the building's

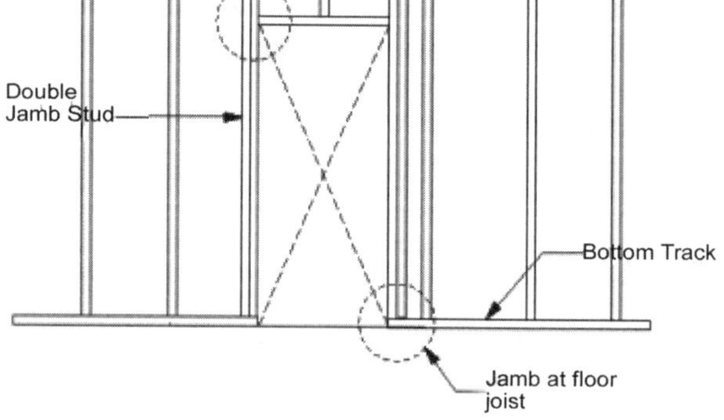

Figure 14.4 Typical door frame opening less than 4 feet wide, non-load bearing.

Hour Rating	Class	Door Type	Frame Type	Use
20-minute	none	wood or hollow metal	wood or hollow metal	corridor doors in 1-hr partitions
3/4-hr	C	wood or hollow metal	hollow metal	1-hr corridor doors and exitway doors
1-hr	B	hollow metal	hollow metal	stairways in low-rise buildings and discharge corridors
1 1/2-hr	B	hollow metal	hollow metal	2-hr vertical shafts for stairways
3-hr	A	hollow metal	hollow metal	3- or 4-hr walls

Figure 14.5 Table showing typical fire-rated door classifications.

structural system. There are several different interior door types, including hollow core, solid core, fiberglass, bi-folding, accordion, operable partitions, de-mountable partitions and fire doors. Figure 14.5 shows the various fire-rated door classifications.

Reinforced fiberglass doors and frames systems are tough and lightweight and are preferred over metal doors where corrosive or humid conditions exist. They last longer, are easy to install, and the colors are molded in and therefore require no painting or maintenance. Many industries, such as food processing, water/waste management, pulp and paper, and pharmaceutical, are well aware of the potential cost savings and have started to take advantage of this.

14.5 STAIRS

Odd dimensions of stair tread width, height, depth, or nose, low or flimsy stair railings, loose stair components, and a host of other stair and railing defects are the sources of more injuries and more lost time from work in the United States (and probably other countries) than any other source of injuries after automobile accidents.

Treads are the one stair component that gets the most wear, which can result in uneven wear, cracks, splitting, or even extensive scratching to the extent that replacement is the best option. Conversely, risers are probably the least likely to become worn; however, over time they may be subjected to cracks or dents and need replacement as well. Stock treads are available with integral factory-milled nosings. Whether the staircase is open on one or both sides, or located between walls, replacing treads and risers is a relatively simple procedure. Circular stairs pose special problems regarding tread shape, potential walking area, and railing design.

The field observer should review construction details, structural connections, loose connections, modifications, support, posts, weather exposure/covering, weathering, rot, tread damage, tread nose wear/damage, moss, algae, cupping, splitting, stairway obstructions, tread connection and support, rail obstructions, rail grip, and permits. Structural conditions to observe include connections, proper number and type of fasteners, spans, and condition of materials.

Prefabricated stair construction consists of a pair of spaced, parallel stair stringers, either one or both being a free-span member between support beams. They achieve the strength of a rigid truss by the join-

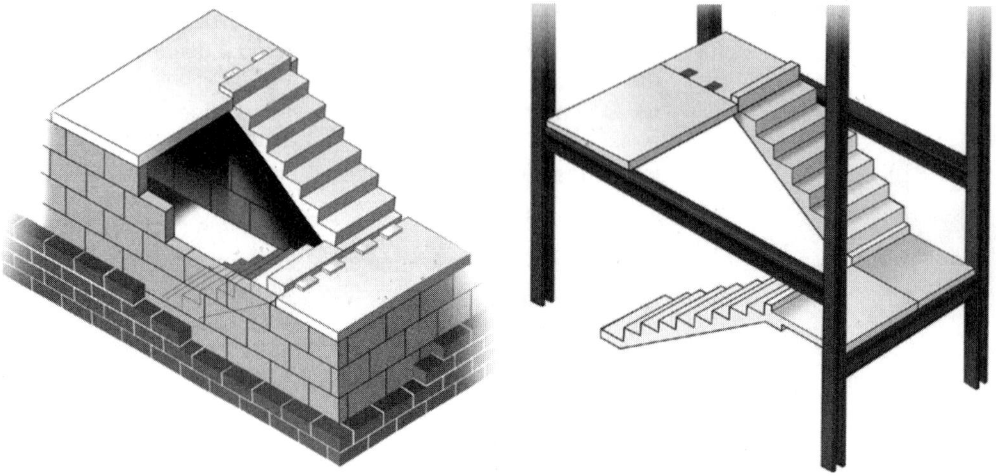

Figure 14.6 Stairs-flights with integral top and or bottom landings.

ing of stair rails, balusters and stringer into a single unit. The stringers are joined together by a number of precast treads secured at each end to the stringer by two welded flanges, the treads having a reinforced nose portion and riser to decrease the bending moment of the tread (Figure 14.6, 14.7). When replacing an existing stair with a prefabricated stair, caution must be taken with the demolition work. Older stairs are sometimes part of the building's structure and may be difficult to remove.

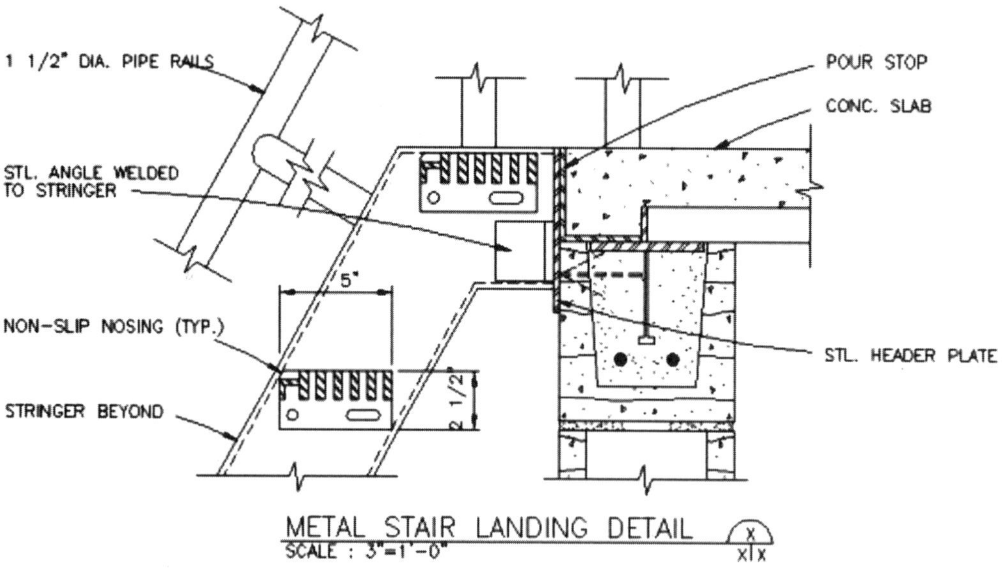

Figure 14.7 Example of metal stair landing detail.

Fiberglass molded stair tread covers are used to cover existing stairs to provide a convenient non-slip surface. Fiberglass stair tread covers can be placed over any type of stair: concrete, metal, fiberglass, etc. Stair tread covers are typically used for environments where corrosive or slippery conditions exist. The high resin composition of 65 percent and lower glass composition of 35 percent provides for optimum corrosion resistance. The covers are low maintenance and will never rust or need to be painted. In addition, they can cover up existing stairs that have holes in them to allow for high-heeled traffic.

14.6 FINISHES: FLOOR, WALL & CEILING

14.6.1 Floor Finishes

Several types of floor finishes are typically encountered during a facility evaluation. Floor finishes include carpet, resilient tile, ceramic tile, concrete, wood, brick, and stone. Floor finishes are especially susceptible to damage, wear, and deterioration, especially at heavily trafficked areas. Corridors, entrances, and office areas typically exhibit more pronounced deterioration than low traffic areas. The durability of the existing materials should be considered as the evaluation is being performed. Pronounced deterioration often results from a material installation in which the type, grade, or weight of material installed is inappropriate for its intended use.

Flooring tends to set the tone of the interior, whether in the home, the office, or the mall. Although aesthetics plays an important role in any design solution, flooring must be practical in today's environment. Flooring can pull a design together or visually fragment it. The use of one continuous material increases the flow and homogeneity and suggests that areas share equal importance and are equally accessible, whereas the introduction of accent flooring suggests that special areas exist. The material itself often gives a clue to the activity of the space, since it is the one material that is always in contact with the users. Thus, rubber flooring and vinyl tile suggest a high traffic area that is expected to take punishment and get dirty, and therefore should not require high maintenance.

Wood is a widely used floor material that has maintained its popularity over the centuries. It is practical, both functionally and aesthetically, and works in most environments. Its warm mellow tone, soft touch, and easy maintenance make it a favorite in residential applications. It lasts well, comes in a variety of formats and makes an excellent base for decorative rugs.

Wood usually comes in hardwood strip, block, parquet, or board form. The most common species used are beech, maple, ash, birch, pine, or oak. Most types of strip flooring are tongue-and-groove so that the planks fit together without leaving any gaps. Parquet flooring is composed of small blocks of hardwood fitted together in certain patterns. In older homes, wood floorboards are typical and usually found laid horizontally across the room, resting on the joists that run from the front of the house to the back.

Carpet denotes a more relaxed, contemplative, and higher status area because it is softer underfoot and therefore quieter. Carpet also has low maintenance costs compared with other commercial floor coverings. Corporations can also incorporate product colors and company logos in their flooring designs. Likewise, for many rehab applications, carpeting presents a low-cost, easily installed solution to flooring problems (Figure 14.8A).

The inherent cushioning and non-slip characteristics of carpet contribute to a comfortable and safe work environment by reducing the likelihood of falls and minimizing potential injuries. Additionally, the insulating properties of carpet keep floors warm in winter and cool in summer, which helps reduce heating and cooling costs. Carpet's acoustical benefits include absorbing airborne sound, reducing surface noise, and helping to block sound transmission to floors below.

Vinyl and linoleum: Vinyl comes in an infinite variety of colors and patterns, often with designs that simulate other more expensive types of flooring such as wood, tile and marble. It is a wholly synthetic material and contains a varying percentage of PVC, which adds to its flexibility. It is also inexpensive, and comes in sheet or tile form.

Linoleum is likewise available in sheet or tile form and comes in a comprehensive range of colors and patterns. Its recent rediscovery is largely due to its improved performance and because it is made up of entirely natural ingredients.

Hard tiles and mosaic: Hard tiles, including ceramic, terracotta, and quarry tiles, are generally machine-made, which gives them a precise size, and are particularly suited to areas where water is often present, like kitchens and bathrooms. Tiles of baked clay, such as the popular quarry tile, are similar to masonry materials and require a sturdy subfloor.

Because it is impervious to water, ceramic tile has traditionally been used as a floor and wall finish in damp areas such as bathrooms, kitchens, basements, and entryways. Because of its relative durability, low maintenance, and decorative qualities, ceramic tile is increasingly used in other spaces as well. Typical installation methods include thick-set (the traditional method, sometimes called mud-set), set in 3/4 inch to 1 1/4 inches of Portland cement paste/mortar laid over a previously set mortar bed or concrete slab; and thin-set that is set in an organic or epoxy adhesive.

Ceramic tile is divided into glazed and unglazed varieties. Most historic floor tiles were unglazed and were the color of the clay and added oxides or pigments from which they were made (current examples are quarry tiles). Glazed tile is colored with a variety of glossy or mat glazes applied to the tile surface. It is subject to scratching and abrasion from extended use and is usually installed in low-traffic areas or covered with rugs.

Tile failures are caused by a number of factors, including improper maintenance, such as the use of inappropriate cleaning agents, degenerative effects of standing water on the grout, the erosion of grout over time from traffic cleaning, and structural problems. The latter include cracking and loosening of tile from overloading, sudden impacts, or frequent vibrations; defective or deteriorated substrates, such as concrete floors that have cracked, heaved, or settled; wood floor substrates that deflect excessively (too springy), have buckled, swelled or deteriorated; and concrete or wood floors that have improperly mixed or applied tile bonding materials.

The small scale of **Mosaic tiles** gives them an almost soft appearance. They consist of small cubes of terracotta, marble, ceramic, or stone and are bedded in mortar. Mosaic works best when restricted to small areas like bathrooms.

Marble and granite are more widely used in countries of the Middle East, Greece and Italy than in the United States. Both materials have prestigious connotations and are primarily used in banks and foyers of commercial buildings and in some custom dwellings.

Terrazzo is a relative newcomer to the American scene. It has been popular in Mediterranean countries for many years. Terrazzo is an aggregate of marble or granite chips mixed into a cement mortar and either laid in place or as slabs or tiles. The mix is then ground and polished to a smooth surface after it has set. Both formats are expensive in the United States and require professional installation.

Other materials—stone, brick, concrete, rubber, cork, etc.: Stone is a traditional material having been used for thousands of years in many countries around the world. It can bring an unmatched depth of richness and character to the interior or exterior. Natural stone comes in a variety of formats, colors, patterns and textures. Moreover, the thicker, larger flags or tiles are heavy and need a solid subfloor to bear their weight. Slate and limestone are the varieties most often used by designers.

Several types of hardwearing brick are available for indoor use. These should be laid on concrete, and should be sealed for a stronger finish and to prevent dust. These bricks are also used for exterior paving and in restaurants and residential patios. Sometimes it is used as an accent or divider in conjunction with other materials.

Concrete is basically a structural material and can provoke strong reactions when used in commercial or domestic settings. It can be troweled to a smooth surface and treated in a number of ways to alter its texture and color. It should either be sealed and polished or painted with special floor paint. Although generally regarded as acceptable only in utility areas, the material has considerable machismo when properly used.

Studded rubber flooring was introduced to residential applications with the arrival of high tech, and enjoyed a brief spurt of popularity. It has now reemerged and is available in a variety of colors, and in sheet or tile, with either a smooth finish or in relief.

Cork is a warm material and soft to the touch. It is produced in tile or sheet form and is sealed with polyurethane. It is used more in Europe than in the United States.

14.6.2 Wall Finishes

Wall finishes are another area of important review during a survey of the interior. Typical wall finishes include plaster, drywall, paints and coatings, ceramic tile, masonry, concrete, wood, and wall covering of vinyl, paper, or fabric. Wall finishes are frequently damaged by impact from equipment and goods. Common deficiencies include wear, warping, bulging, stretching, insufficient fastening, and normal deterioration and damage. Signs of exterior water penetration should be investigated and appropriately remedied.

Walls are important elements of any design scheme because they define spaces, segregate activities, and mark out personal domains within the home or office. Their importance is highlighted by the enormous variety of treatments available that draw attention to the walls themselves.

Paint: Paint and wallpaper are the two most common protective and attractive finishes applied to walls. Color is a key element in most contemporary interiors, and paint is one of the simplest and least expensive ways of providing an acceptable finish to the office, home, or store, which perhaps explains why it is the most widely used finish. Paint is either oil- (alkyd) or water-based (latex, vinyl, or acrylic). Oil-based paint is less permeable, shows streaks less, is more durable, and usually takes longer to dry than water-based. Because it does not take abrasion as well as oil-based paint, water-based paint was historically less commonly used. Today's waterbased formulations however, especially the all-acrylic paints, have improved significantly, and are now the most common type of paint used because it is easy to maintain, quick drying, and does not require thinning agents for clean-up.

Wallpaper: Wallpapers are used to provide a quick and easy finish. Historically, they were made of colored paper and applied to walls with adhesives. Today, these coverings commonly contain vinyl and are pre-pasted, applied with water and a sponge. Vinyl coverings are easy to maintain and are more durable than papers.

Wallpaper offers a large variety of textures, patterns, and imagery, often making it a viable alternative to paint. Wallpapers are traditionally made of paper, cloth, or paper-backed PVC. Vinyl papers are water and steam-proof, washable and tougher than normal paper, which makes them suitable for use in kitchens, bathrooms and utility areas. Wallpaper also remains popular because it is a practical way of hiding surface imperfections. The vinyl type is frequently used in both commercial and residential applications.

Marble, stone and brick: Marble is widely used in monumental spaces and prestige locations, such as banks. Marbles are available in varied colors and veining patterns.

Cladding: Wall cladding makes practical sense in many situations, and allows the character of raw materials to be explored in the context of contemporary wall decoration.

Wood is the classic cladding material and often reflects a feeling of luxury.

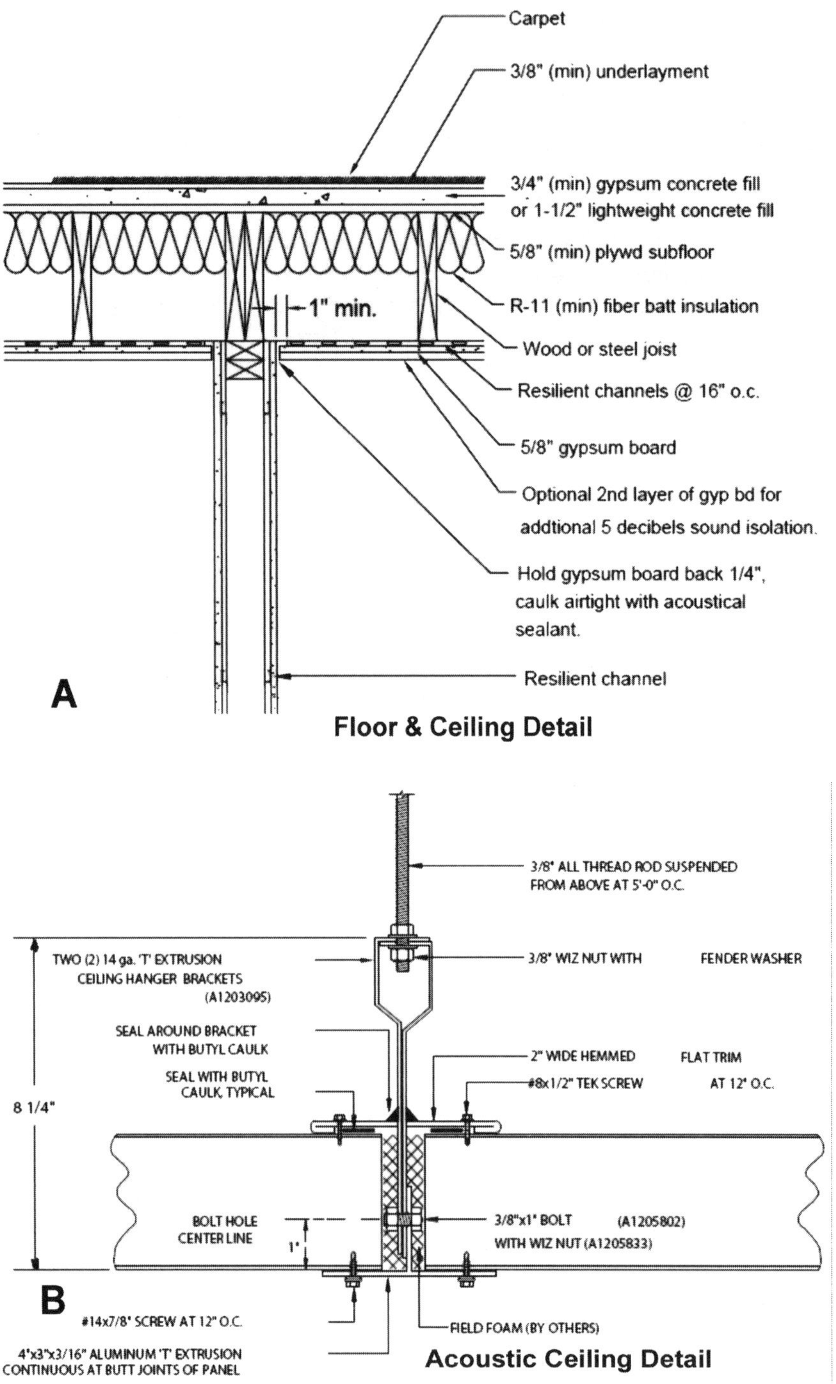

Figure 14.8 A. Typical floor/ceiling detail. B. Ceiling suspension system detail with aluminum 't' extrusion.

Tiling is a tried and tested formula for areas of heavy wear or maximum exposure to water and heat, typically kitchens, bathrooms, and areas around pools. The material comes in a multitude of colors, shapes, textures, patterns, and sizes, from the tiny mosaic to the large squares and rectangles of ceramic tile (see floor finishes).

Mirror is a material often used in confined areas where an illusion of increased space is desired.

Although **fabric** is traditionally popular as a material for wall covering, and is available in a variety of colors and textures, vinyl and other plastic sheet materials have increased in popularity and are now often preferred as wall covering.

14.6.3 Ceiling Finishes

Ceiling finishes receive some of the same impact and deterioration as wall finishes, although not as frequently. Ceiling finishes are typically designed for both aesthetics and acoustics (Figure 14.8A, B). Typical ceiling finishes include acoustical tiles and panels, plaster, wood gypsum board, or exposed structure. Common deficiencies of ceiling finishes are damage from impact of equipment and improper use. For example, if a building user decides to attach a plant or some sort of hanging equipment on a plaster or acoustical ceiling panel system, this may result in deformation. Attention should be paid to stains or water damage on the upper level, which are often caused by roof leaks.

Ceilings somewhat resemble walls. The newer ones are constructed of gypsum board placed over wood supports, while the older ones are plaster over either wood lath or gypsum lath. The same principles apply to them as apply to walls. Maintenance usually is minimal. You may see a hairline crack where the ceiling joins the wall where joint compound has dried out, or because there has been some movement. If the crack is small, resealing with caulk and repainting ought to do the trick. On the other hand, if the separation is larger, it will be difficult to completely hide it. You may want to think about installing crown molding to cover the separation and add beauty in the room.

On occasion, ceilings may sag due to the gypsum drywall panels loosening, or if you have plaster, the plaster coats may be pulling away from the lath underneath. It may also be structural, such as an overloading of a ceiling joist or truss above. Or it could be water—a leak that is working its way behind and under the ceiling material and causing deterioration. If this condition develops, it is time to call for professional help (Figure 14.9).

Figure 14.9 Upper floor suspended ceiling tiles showing clear evidence of water penetration.

14.7 SYSTEM DIAGNOSTICS

The interiors of a facility require a diagnostic methodology of a more in-depth systematic nature than most other building systems. The interior materials and conditions often vary a great deal within a given facility. The lobby may have marble and carpeting, the corridors may have wood and resilient sheet flooring, and individual offices may have any of a variety of different materials.

During walk-through surveys, the field observer should identify and observe the condition of floors, walls, ceilings and door finishes of typical internal areas, including, but not limited to, lobbies, corridors, assembly areas, and restrooms. Lack of adequate maintenance is one of the main deficiencies noticed in surveys. The condition of building amenities or other special features that are secured to the building fabric should be noted as well as major components (such as pools, spas, fountains, major kitchen appliances, etc.). Portable items (such as furniture or portable kitchen appliances) are beyond the scope of the condition assessment process. Assessors are not required to activate or operate appliances or fixtures. Assessments should exclude determining or reporting STC (Sound Transmission Class) ratings, and flammability issues/regulations.

The paperwork of the evaluation team should be designed to facilitate the notation of conditions and deficiencies in several aspects of the interiors as the walk-through occurs. For example, the forms should be designed in such a way that the evaluator can conveniently make notes pertaining to the flooring, walls, and ceilings within the space being evaluated. These records should be maintained throughout the survey with both unusual and typical conditions being noted.

When floor moisture problems are encountered, it is most often associated with concrete slabs-on-grade (floors supported by soil). Problems most often occur with non-breathable floor coverings such as vinyl, resin terrazzo, plastic-backed carpet, or vinyl composition tile. The primary cause of the problem is moisture vapor that emits from the concrete—it can result in debonding, bubbling, or warping of the floor covering from moisture vapor condensing beneath the floor covering. If a good-quality vapor barrier is used under the slab during construction, floor vapor levels normally remain at acceptable levels after initial drying.

Several diagnostic methods and tools are employed during the evaluation of the interiors. The majority of the techniques consist of straightforward sensory evaluation. System components should be visually reviewed for deterioration or inability to perform the intended tasks. Cosmetics and function should both be reviewed to make recommendations towards a more pleasing and usable facility.

During the evaluation, it is useful to probe as much as possible behind installed finish materials, in case more serious defects have been concealed. This includes damage and defects existing behind wallpaper, paneling, ceiling tiles, and other finishes.

To summarize, the field observer during a walk-through PCA survey should:

1. Observe interior floors, walls, and ceilings, including a representative number of primary doors and windows inside the building with regard to their integrity and working condition
2. Report signs of water penetration into the building, including any signs of abnormal or harmful condensation on building system components observed inside the building
3. Report signs of abnormal settlement, damage, or deterioration—excepting normal wear and tear—observed in floors, walls, and ceilings inside the building
4. Observe the operation of a representative number of receptacles and permanently installed switch controlled lighting fixtures inside the building
5. Observe the polarity and grounding of a representative number of receptacle wall outlets inside the building, including all receptacles located within six feet of interior plumbing fixtures, and all receptacles located just above the finish grade on the exterior of the building
6. Report any receptacle type wall outlets found to exhibit reverse polarity or open ground

The following **are not** to be included in a walk-through survey unless specifically agreed to with the client:

1. Movement of furniture, appliances, personal storage, and the like in order to observe interior floors, walls, or ceilings blocked or concealed from view
2. Determination of the exact cause or origin of water penetration or stains as observed at the time of inspection
3. Removal of ceiling tile, other than at random locations, in order to observe the entire space or structure above
4. Observation of or reporting on the condition of finish treatments such as paint, wallpaper, or carpeting on interior floors, walls, or ceilings with the exception of buildings built before 1979 and characterized by loose or flaking paint

CHAPTER

15

The Building Envelope

15.1 GENERAL

The building envelope consists of all the exterior components of a building (roof, walls, windows, below-grade waterproofing, etc.) that separate the exterior environment from the interior environment. There are many envelope systems in use, each consisting of multiple components and complex technologies. These components need to be properly detailed and maintained for an envelope to be effective. The condition of the building envelope is vitally important since failures can result in safety and health problems, as well as structural damage. Proper evaluation of the building envelope is often a first step toward stabilization and rehabilitation of the building.

The envelope is a complicated and integral entity of a building and yet, it is often the most neglected. The building envelope must be properly designed, constructed, and maintained to prevent water and air infiltration through the envelope, and to prevent moisture condensation from developing within the envelope system(s).

It is essential to understand the condition of a structure, as well as its major building systems and components in order to determine the structure's economic viability. The building envelope can represent a considerable percentage of a building's cost (Figure 15.1) and is paramount in the determination of the overall performance of the building, with an emphasis on the thermal environment, lighting, and acoustical characteristics. It is also the main determinant of the exterior aesthetic quality of the building.

Building envelope systems can be categorized into two types: dual stage and single stage. A dual-stage system includes a primary barrier with a secondary waterproofing system. An example of a dual-stage system is a brick masonry veneer wall. The brick veneer is the primary barrier, but because water readily migrates through masonry, a secondary waterproofing membrane and flashing system are provided to capture and divert water back to the exterior. If weep holes (openings in the masonry to allow water to drain) are covered with sealant, water can back up in the cavity behind the brick, potentially causing severe problems.

A single-stage system relies on the exterior "skin" to prevent leakage without the need for a secondary system. Examples of single-stage systems are roof membranes and insulated metal panels. In single-

Building Type	Floor Slab	Exterior Wall	Roofing	Total
Hospital 4-8 floors	0.6	9.5	0.6	10.7
Manufacturing Plant 1 Floor	6.4	9.5	6.7	21.6
Office 12-20 Floors	0.3	19.9	0.4	20.6
Jr. High School	2.3	14.5	2.5	19.3

Figure 15.1 Typical building envelope costs as a percentage of whole building cost *(Source RS Means Square Foot Costs).*

stage systems, any water leakage (or condensation) behind the exterior skin typically becomes trapped and prematurely deteriorates the system. Regardless of the type of system, flashing must be reliably integrated to prevent or capture leakage.

Though it can be an expensive process to construct and/or maintain a comprehensive and reliable building envelope, the consequences of not doing so are even higher. For new buildings, unreliable building envelopes can permit water leakage from the beginning, requiring significant effort to correct deficient components. For existing buildings, as maintenance is deferred, water infiltration into the wall system can go unnoticed for extended periods of time, with building components continuing to deteriorate. With construction costs increasing annually and the amount and extent of deterioration multiplying, the cost of a comprehensive building envelope restoration project significantly increases. By implementing a periodic maintenance program, the service life of the building envelope can be increased and the cost of deferred maintenance can be decreased.

15.2 EXTERIOR WALL SYSTEMS

15.2.1 Masonry Wall Systems

Masonry has been used in building construction for thousands of years. It can be used to form a durable cladding system with various aesthetic effects. In addition to forming the exterior cladding, masonry walls can serve as a portion of the structural framing for the building. Masonry walls also typically increase the fire resistance of the wall system or structural elements.

Masonry is typically site constructed where the units are laid in mortar to various heights, with the strength of the assembly being achieved during curing of the mortar. Masonry can also form structural elements (typically bearing walls, columns, or pilasters) and/or the finished cladding system.

Masonry units: Common masonry unit types include clay and concrete units. These may be solid or hollow, and glazed or unglazed. Other masonry unit types include cast stone and calcium silicate units. Masonry walls can be single or multi-wythe. A wythe (also called a tier) of masonry refers to a thickness of wall equal to the thickness of the individual units.

Clay brick units are normally used in brick masonry construction, and depending on the clay used and the manufacturing technique, they can have various colors, sizes and textures. Clay masonry units are typically formed of soft clay extruded into the required shape in the manufacturing plant. These brick units come in different finishes, such as wire cut or sand finished. The units can be hollow or solid. Units categorized as solid typically contain cores for handling and to allow more uniform firing. For most exterior walls, units categorized as solid are used. Figure 15.2 illustrates the different positions that a brick can take within a wall.

Brick types: The standard for clay masonry units is ASTM C216 ("Standard Specification for Facing Brick"). In this standard and in building specifications, clay units are categorized by grade in accordance with the use and exposure to which it will be subjected (Grade SW—Severe weathering, MW—Moderate weathering, and NW—No weathering).

Facing brick is brick that will be exposed to view and is manufactured by a controlled mixture of clay or shale to produce high quality units in specific sizes, colors and textures. It is typically manufactured to SW and MW grades. Facing is classified according to criteria affecting its appearance.

Hollow brick is available in SW and MW grades, and is also classified by factors affecting its appearance. Modular bricks have dimensions such that one or more brick courses plus the mortar joints produce courses with an exact dimension, usually a multiple of 4 inches.

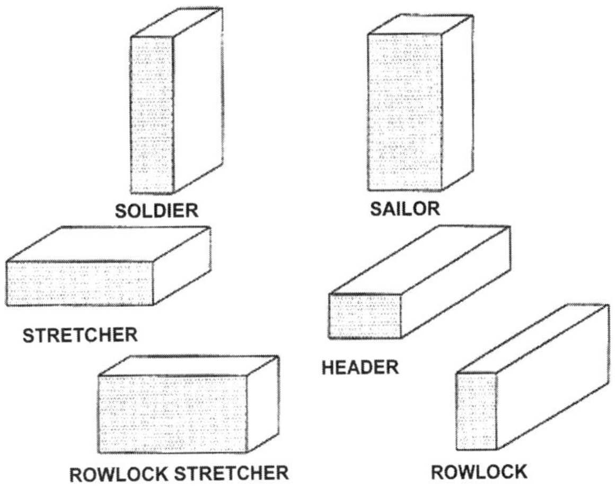

Figure 15.2 The various positions that a brick unit can take within wall construction.

Glazed clay masonry units should be manufactured to ASTM C126 standard ("Standard Specification for Ceramic Glazed Structural Clay Facing Tile, Facing Brick, and Solid Masonry Units").

Concrete masonry units (CMUs) are typically made from a mixture of Portland cement and aggregates under controlled conditions. Standard unit dimensions (nominal) are 8 inches high by 16 inches wide, although the units can be manufactured to custom sizes and face textures. The units are often used when masonry is to form a load-bearing wall or an interior partition between spaces within a building.

Concrete masonry units should meet the requirements of ASTM C90. The unit's categorization is based on its weight (lightweight, normal weight and heavyweight). Structural masonry units are either normal weight or heavyweight. Lightweight units are used for non-load-bearing conditions or as veneers.

Since these units are typically larger than brick units, the construction time required for laying the units is usually less than that for brick. The units can be solid or hollow (two or three cores) and can have solid or flanged ends. The cores provide continuous vertical voids where reinforcement is often placed. Steel bars are placed in the cores with grout installed surrounding the bars. This allows the wall to function similar to a reinforced concrete element.

Proper tooling of mortar joints is important because it assists in sealing the wall surface against moisture penetration. Mortar joints are typically tooled when they are "thumbprint" hard, (pressing the thumb into the mortar leaves an indentation, but no mortar is transferred to the thumb) with a jointer slightly larger than the joint. It is important that joints are tooled at the appropriate time to optimize their effectiveness and appearance. Joints that are tooled prematurely often smear and result in rough joints. If too much time elapses before tooling the surface of the joint cannot be properly compressed and sealed to the adjacent brick.

Concave, "V," and grapevine joints best resist water penetration in exterior brickwork. These joints produce a denser and more weathertight surface, as the mortar is pressed against the brick. For interior masonry work, other joints such as the weathered, beaded, struck, flush, raked or extruded joints can also be used (Figure 15.3).

Installation: Masonry must be installed on a solid, rigid base such as a concrete foundation or structural steel or concrete beam system. Most building codes do not allow the weight of the masonry to be supported by wood framing, due to the strength loss of the wood member when exposed to moisture. Support systems must be designed for small deflections (typically 1/600th of the span) to avoid cracking of the masonry.

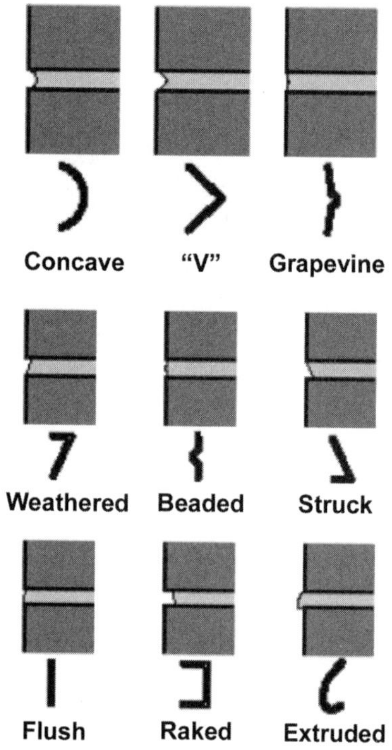

Figure 15.3 Typical brick mortar joint details used in masonry construction *(Courtesy The Brick Industry Association).*

The masonry units are laid in a bed of mortar. The horizontal joints between units are called bed joints while the vertical joints are called head joints. Clay brick masonry should include solid (full) head and bed joints. In concrete masonry it is common to lay the units with mortar only on the face shells. Full bedding of CMUs is typically only performed where a portion of the cells will be filled with grout. Where grouting is performed, mortar should be kept from falling into the cells to avoid the formation of a weak plane in the grout.

Expansion and shrinkage of units: Following manufacture, clay masonry units expand when exposed to moisture. This volumetric change in the unit results in an accumulated growth of the wall system that is irreversible. Concrete masonry units typically shrink following manufacturing. These movements, if not accommodated in the design of the masonry elements, can cause cracking, spalling, and displacements in the masonry. In clay masonry construction this issue is addressed by the incorporation of expansion joints, particularly in areas exposed to the exterior where the units will encounter moisture. Expansion joints are typically needed at corners, offsets, and other changes in wall plane as well as changes in wall construction. They are normally incorporated at regular intervals (typically 20 to 30 feet on center maximum, depending on the units).

Concrete masonry walls are typically reinforced with joint reinforcement for shrinkage control. The spacing of control joints varies, being determined by the size and spacing of the reinforcement. However, control joints are required in all concrete masonry walls. Guidelines for control joint placement are provided in National Concrete Masonry Association Tech Note 10-A.

Both clay and concrete masonry also undergo cyclic thermal movements, expanding in warm temperatures and contracting in cold temperatures. The movement joints must also accommodate these movements.

Wall systems: Masonry walls can be either 1. a veneer system, or 2. a structural/load-bearing wall system.

Water penetration through exterior masonry elements exposed to rain should be anticipated. Water typically flows through separations between the mortar and the units. This can be due to bond separations, voids, and cracks. Water penetration can also occur, although typically to a lesser degree, due to absorption through the units and mortar. Measures must be taken in exterior masonry construction to prevent water penetration into the wall system.

Masonry veneer consists of an exterior wythe (or tier) of masonry that forms a cladding material only, and thus lateral support for the masonry veneer is required. This is typically provided by an interior wall. Common interior walls (backup walls) are typically cold-formed steel framed walls with water-resistant sheathing and concrete masonry.

Veneer walls are designed as drainage walls due to their resistance to water penetration. An air space/drainage cavity should be installed behind the masonry veneer to allow water that penetrates the masonry to flow down to the base of the wall, where it can be directed to the exterior. This drainage cavity should remain open to allow water to freely drain. Where restrictions in the cavity exist, flashings are recommended to collect water and drain it to the exterior. This is required at openings in the masonry, such as at windows, supports, etc. At the base of the drainage cavity, a flashing system should be installed that consists of a three-sided pan, typically formed by metal and/or membrane materials, to collect water that penetrates into the drainage cavity and direct it to the exterior via drains or weeps. These flashings must be designed to be watertight, particularly at corners, laps, and terminations of the masonry. End dams are required at terminations to prevent water from flowing laterally off the flashing and into the adjacent construction. Common flashing materials are stainless steel, copper, and lead-coated copper. These metal flashings are durable, can be sealed, and include soldered corners and end dams. Membrane materials, such as rubberized asphalt and EPDM, can also be used in conjunction with metal flashings to seal the top of the metal flashing to the backup construction.

It is critical that a moisture barrier be present on the interior face of the drainage cavity (on the surface of the backup) to prevent the passage of water into the backup construction. The recommended cavity width behind the masonry veneer is 2 inches minimum. In addition, cavity seals are typically recommended at windows, doors, and other openings to prevent the passage of cavity air (and moisture) to the door/window frames.

Vertical support for the masonry veneer is typically provided at each floor line. For a brick masonry veneer, provisions must be made at each of the vertical supports to accommodate the masonry's vertical expansion. This is accomplished by omitting the mortar between the top course of masonry and the underside of the support. This joint should be designed to accommodate the vertical expansion of the masonry, as well as structural deflections of the support. In concrete structures, creep of the concrete frame should also be accommodated.

Metal ties are required to provide the lateral attachment of the veneer to the backup wall. These are typically spaced at 16 inches on center in each direction.

Structural masonry walls are typically constructed using concrete masonry. The concrete masonry can be reinforced both vertically and horizontally to achieve the required flexural resistance. Vertical reinforcement that is installed within the cells of the concrete masonry is generally grouted solid. Horizontal reinforcement is typically installed using prefabricated welded wires that are embedded in the bed joints. The horizontal reinforcement improves the strength of the masonry, particularly for horizontal spans, and also helps control shrinkage cracking.

If structural masonry walls are to serve as exterior walls, a second tier of masonry is typically recommended. In this construction, the masonry can be built as a composite wall (both tiers act as one unit to resist loads) or as a non-composite wall (individual tiers act independently to support loads). If single-wythe exterior walls are to be used, a barrier should be provided on the exterior surface, such as a fluid-applied, breathable masonry coating or over-cladding (EIFS, metal panels, stucco, or similar material) to prevent water penetration into the masonry. Admixtures can be incorporated in the fabrication of concrete masonry units to reduce water penetration through absorption. While these systems can be effective in reducing the amount of water penetration into the masonry, they should not be relied upon to eliminate water penetration.

Thermal performance: The thermal performance characteristics of the masonry are primarily based on the insulation placed within the wall cavity or within the backup wall. It is normally assumed that the masonry itself provides little insulating value. When exposed to sunlight, masonry temperatures can rise to well in excess of 100 degrees Fahrenheit. The masonry absorbs the heat and radiates it to the surrounding components of the wall system. During cold temperatures, masonry will be cool, particularly in shaded exposures.

Fire safety: Masonry provides a significant improvement in fire safety characteristics for building walls. Concrete masonry is typically used for firewall construction. The fire resistive characteristics are based on the thickness of the masonry.

Acoustics: Because of its mass, masonry wall systems offer better sound insulation properties than lighter wall systems. To further improve acoustical performance, concrete masonry is typically filled with insulation to eliminate the voids in the cores.

Maintenance: When properly constructed, masonry wall systems require relatively little maintenance compared to other wall systems. The service life of masonry walls can be 100 years or more, depending on the detailing and maintenance. The most frequent elements or components that require maintenance is the regular replacement of sealants in expansion joints, perimeter of openings (windows, doors, etc.), and at through-wall flashings. The time frame for sealant replacement varies but usually ranges from 7 to 20 years. Repointing of the mortar joints in exterior masonry is typically required every 20 to 30 years after installation.

Types of wall construction: Brick exterior walls can be classified as either barrier walls, which are constructed of solid masonry without drainage cavities, or drainage walls, which are constructed of single or multiple wythes, entirely of brick, or with concrete masonry unit or terra cotta back-up. Multiple wythe brick barrier walls are designed to prevent water infiltration to interior spaces through mass. Ideally, the amount of water absorbed by a wall over a given period of time is less than can be dissipated in the same time period. In a barrier wall constructed with two wythes of brick, or in composite walls, a collar joint joins face brick with a masonry back-up. Water that penetrates the face brick follows the collar joint down to flashing where it is either expelled through the bed joint and/or at weeps, or it dissipates through the face of the wall.

When brick exteriors fail: Symptoms of deterioration in brick exterior walls are generally attributable to water infiltration and include staining and efflorescence (Figure 15.4), cracking/spalling/displacement, and deterioration in mortar joints, among other things. These issues are discussed in the deficiencies section of this chapter.

Wall System Selection as Recommended by the Brick Industry Association:

- Drainage walls provide maximum protection against water penetration.
- Barrier walls are designed to provide a solid barrier to water penetration and provide good water penetration resistance.
- Single-wythe masonry walls require careful detailing and construction practices to provide adequate water penetration resistance.

Through-Wall Flashing Locations:

- Install at wall bases, window sills, heads of openings, shelf angles, tops of walls and roofs, parapets, above projections, such as bay windows, and at other discontinuities in the cavity

Through-Wall Flashing Installation:

- Lap continuous flashing pieces at least 6 inches (152 mm) and seal laps
- Turn up the ends of discontinuous flashing to form end dams
- Extend flashing beyond the exterior wall face
- Terminate UV-sensitive flashings with a drip edge

Figure 15.4 A masonry brick wall showing signs of efflorescence.

Weeps:

- Open head joint weeps spaced at no more than 24 inches (610 mm) o.c. recommended
- Most building codes permit weeps no less than 3/16 inch (4.8 mm) in diameter and spaced no more than 33 inches (838 mm) o.c.
- Wick and tube weep spacing recommended at no more than 16 inches (406 mm) o.c.

New developments in masonry wall design include the use of pre-stressed masonry. This consists of building a concrete masonry wall with cables within the cells, similar to a pre-stressed concrete element. After the wall is constructed, the cables are tensioned and anchored to the masonry. This can greatly increase the resistance of the masonry wall to flexural loads and bending.

15.2.2 Stone Wall Systems

Thin stone wall systems used for exterior building envelopes typically consist of stone panels ranging in thickness from 3/4 inch to 2 inches. Most panels are fabricated from granite, while marble, limestone, travertine, and sandstone are also used to a lesser extent. A common panel thickness is 1 3/16 inch (3 cm). Overall panel dimensions can vary significantly for different buildings, depending on the strength of the stone used and architectural effect desired (Figure 15.5).

However, maximum panel dimensions are usually approximately 3 to 4 feet and usually not more than approximately 6 feet. Typically each panel is independently supported to the building structure or back up system using an assemblage of metal components and anchors. Joints at the perimeter of each panel are usually 3/8 inch in width and are filled with sealant. A drainage cavity is typically located behind the stone panels to collect and divert to the exterior water that penetrates through the joints.

For certain applications, such as at building entrances and near grade-level installations of limited extent, the stone system may not incorporate a drainage cavity but instead be a barrier system. In this type of system, the stone is applied directly against and attached to solid masonry backup such as concrete masonry units (CMU) or concrete. In these localized applications, several panels may be stacked.

Stone types: Granite is the most commonly used stone type in thin stone wall systems. The commercial classification of granite usually refers to a stone that includes any visibly granular igneous rock, consisting of mostly feldspar and quartz minerals. This commercial term encompasses a wide variety of geologic stone types rather than only the limited number that fall under the geologic classification of granite. Geologically, marble is a metamorphic rock resulting from the recrystallization of limestone. While less commonly used in this type of application today, marble is also sometimes used in thin stone wall systems. Sedimentary rocks such as limestone and sandstone can also be used in thin stone wall systems. However, panels fabricated from these stone types are usually not less than 2 inches in thickness because of the lesser strengths of these stones relative to granite and marble.

Support and anchorage systems: There are two primary types of stone installation. The first is the hand-set method, in which each stone is individually attached to the building's primary structural frame or onto a secondary wall framing system. The second is the panelized installation method, in which the stone panel or multiple panels are preinstalled onto a frame or attached to a precast concrete panel. The frames or panels are transported to the building, where the entire assembly is attached to the building's structural frame or secondary structural members or framing system. In either installation system, anchors must be used to attach and support the stone panels to the building's primary or secondary framing system, or to the panelized system frame or element.

Structural aspects of design: Stone wall systems are traditionally constructed as a curtain wall or veneer, in which no building loads are transferred to the stone panels. Most typically, the stone wall sys-

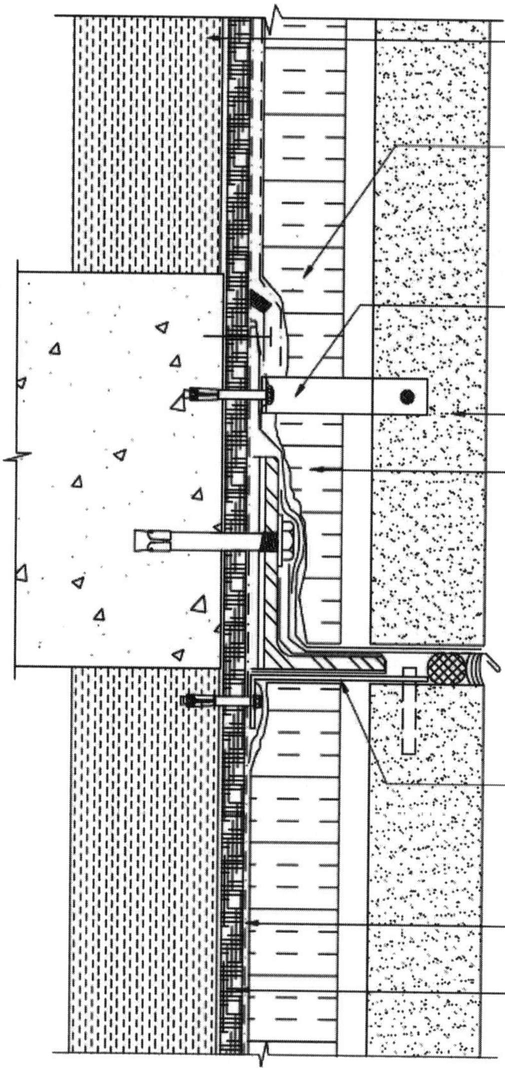

Figure 15.5 Detail of stone veneer with through-wall flashing *(Courtesy WBDG)*.

tem must resist lateral loads directly imparted on it, such as from wind and earthquake, as well as vertical loads resulting from the weight of the stone wall system. These loads must be transmitted through the stone wall system and secondary structural elements to the building's structure. Other loads related to impact, construction, and transportation must also be taken into account in the design.

Joints between panels must be wide enough to accommodate thermal expansion and differential movements between panels; 3/8 inch wide joints are typically used. Joints between panels are most commonly sealed with sealant and are the primary line of protection against water penetration into the wall cavity. The wall cavity space and the back up wall, which is usually covered with a water resistant membrane, provide a secondary line of protection against water penetration into the building. Through-wall flashing is usually located throughout the height of the wall at regular intervals to divert water that enters the cavity back to the exterior.

Thermal performance: Thin stone wall systems derive their thermal performance characteristics primarily from the amount of insulation placed in the wall cavity or within the backup wall. The stone and supporting elements of the wall provide little insulating value.

Moisture protection: The most common moisture protection system used with stone wall systems is the wall cavity drainage system described above. Rain screen systems are also used with thin stone wall systems. In these systems, the primary water resistant barrier is located on the surface of the backup wall, joints are left unsealed, and the stone panels provide a rain screen that minimizes the amount of water that can reach the back up wall. Barrier systems are sometimes employed on certain stone wall systems where the stone panels are in direct contact with the backup wall.

Fire safety: Stone wall systems are not considered to provide any improvement in fire safety for the building exterior wall. In fact, for high-rise buildings, stone wall systems can pose a serious safety hazard when a fire occurs that breeches the exterior envelope. Because stone exposed to intense heat from fire can crack and the cracked portions of stone can fall from the building, fire safety personnel may be in danger from falling stone.

Acoustics: Because of their mass, stone wall systems may provide better sound insulation than lighter wall systems, such as metal panels.

Material/Finish durability: Stone used in wall systems can have several finishes: for granites and marbles, a polished, highly reflective finish is common. Thermal finish is a rough textured finish that is often employed with granite. Also, smooth honed finishes are commonly used on all stone types used in stone wall systems. Granites have had a long history of durable service as have certain marbles.

Most distress observed in stone wall systems can be attributed to anchors used to attach stone panels to the structure. Panel cracking, displacements, or other distress conditions can occur at locations where anchors are inadequately or improperly connected to the stone. Poor construction is often the result of poor quality control and out-of-tolerance fabrication or erection of the panels. Also, damage from handling during construction can result in pancl cracking, some of which may not become evident for several years.

Maintainability: When properly constructed, stone wall systems require relatively little maintenance as compared to other wall systems. Typically the only maintenance required is replacement of sealant in joints between panels; the time frame for this activity depends on the sealant used but usually ranges from 7 to 20 years. However, it should also be noted that periodic review and evaluation of thin stone veneers may be desirable in order to determine if any evidence of structural distress exists in the panels due to strength loss and/or accumulated stresses at anchor points. Similarly, periodic review and evaluation of exposed stone surfaces may also be desirable, depending upon the location and exposure of the building.

Applications: Stone wall systems have been employed to achieve a wide range of architectural styles, aesthetic affects, and appearances. Generally, thin stone wall systems are used in all environments. However, certain stone types, such as certain marbles, may not be appropriate for environments with significant thermal cycling.

Several proprietary anchoring systems have been developed in recent years to facilitate the uniform, systematic installation of more traditional thin stone veneers. One of the more interesting recent developments in this industry has been the emergence of "ultra-thin" stone panels in commercial construction. These systems have become increasingly popular in recent years for facade applications on larger, more complex multi-story commercial office and retail projects. These products, which were initially developed to provide a light-weight alternative to traditional thin stone veneers, typically include a natural stone facing fully adhered to a fiber-reinforced epoxy "skin," over an aluminum honeycomb-reinforced back-up. The fiber-reinforced epoxy skin is intended to provide a waterproof barrier, improved flexural strength and impact resistance. Use of "ultra-thin" applications should be carefully evaluated where longevity is an important performance factor.

15.2.3 Concrete

In today's lexicon, the word concrete has come to symbolize strength and the image of being set in stone. Yet, for all its seeming permanence, concrete has come under attack from both natural and manmade forces since the time it was first formed and poured. The relative rate of degradation resulting from these assaults depends on a wide variety of factors, only some of which are controllable. Fundamental understanding of these factors provides the foundation for recognizing when a facility is in need of repair.

Architectural precast concrete came into wide use in the 1960s. The exterior surface of precast concrete can vary from an exposed aggregate finish that is highly ornamental to a form-face finish that is similar to cast-in-place. Some precast panels act as column covers while others extend over several floors in height and incorporate window openings.

Normally, the architect selects the cladding material for appearance, provides details for weatherproofing, and specifies performance criteria. The structural engineer designs the structure to hold the cladding, designates connection points, and evaluates the effects of structural movement on the cladding. The precast concrete manufacturer designs the cladding for the specified loads, erection loads, connection details, and provides for the weatherproofing, performance, and durability of the cladding itself (Figure 15.6).

Precast concrete wall systems offer a wide variety of shapes, colors, textures, and finishes to the designer. As a result, the assessment of samples is a key component when using precast concrete. The majority of the review and approval process is conducted at the precast plant prior to precast panel production. This assessment is in addition to the quality control and field testing that takes place during the production phase.

There are generally four types of precast panels used as part of building envelopes:

- Cladding or curtain walls
- Load-bearing wall units
- Shear walls
- Formwork for cast-in-place concrete

Precast cladding or curtain walls are the most common use of precast concrete for building envelopes. These types of precast concrete panels do not transfer vertical loads but simply enclose the space. They are only designed to resist wind, seismic forces generated by their own weight, and forces required to transfer the weight of the panel to the support. Common cladding units include wall panels, window wall units, spandrels, mullions, and column covers. These units can usually be removed individually if necessary.

Load-bearing wall units resist and transfer loads from other elements and cannot be removed without affecting the strength or stability of the building. Typical load-bearing wall units include solid wall panels, and window wall and spandrel panels.

Precast concrete shear wall panels are used to provide a lateral load resisting system when combined with diaphragm action of the floor construction. The effectiveness of precast shear walls is largely dependent upon the panel-to-panel connections.

Structural aspects of design: Precast concrete wall systems are most often constructed as a curtain wall or veneer, in which no building loads are transferred to the concrete panels. Most typically the precast concrete wall system must resist lateral loads directly impacted on it, such as from wind and earthquakes, as well as vertical loads resulting from the weight of the precast wall system itself. These loads must be transmitted through the wall system and secondary structural elements to the building's structure.

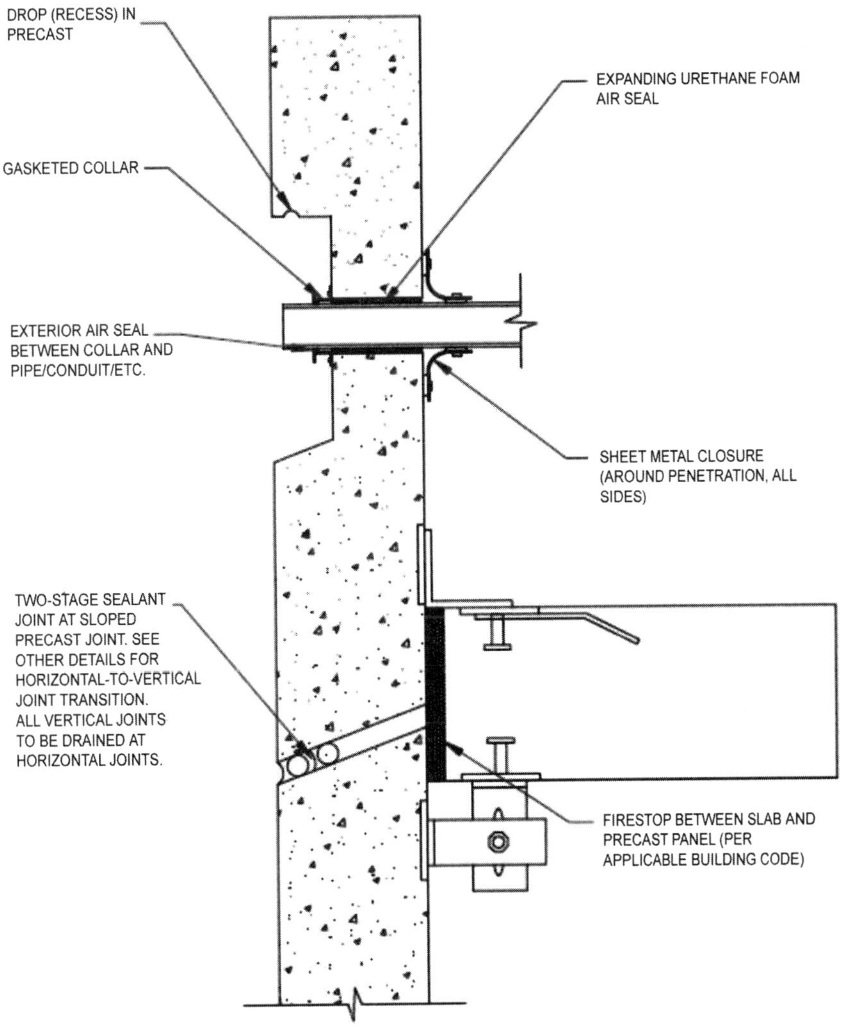

Figure 15.6 Architectural precast round penetration flashing detail *(Courtesy WBDG).*

Joints between panels must be wide enough to accommodate thermal expansion and differential movements between panels. Joints between panels are most commonly sealed with sealant to prevent water penetration into the wall cavity. The wall cavity space and back up wall, which is usually covered with a water resistant membrane, provide a secondary line of protection against water penetration into the building.

Most distress and deterioration encountered with precast concrete wall systems can be attributed to problems during erection, anchors used to attach panels to the structure, or corrosion of the embedded reinforcing steel. Panel cracking, displacements, or other distress conditions can occur at locations where anchors are inadequately or improperly connected.

Foremost among all causes of concrete degradation is the internal damage caused by the corrosion of the embedded reinforcing steel. In addition to deterioration of the steel itself, the corrosion affects the concrete surrounding it, which results in cracking, delamination, and spalling. Since virtually all of the concrete found in structures is steel-reinforced, this is a widespread problem.

Creating a successful repair program depends on the incorporation of a number of solutions. Basic understanding of these options—surface repair, protection, stabilization, strengthening, and waterproofing—will allow selection of the best program for a facility. Evidence of cracking or spalling may be visually apparent and an engineer should be consulted to diagnose the problem. A concrete repair specialist can also help determine both the underlying cause of the problem and the optimal solution.

15.2.4 Exterior Insulation and Finish System (EIFS)

Exterior Insulation Finish System, or simply EIFS, is an exterior wall covering made to look like traditional Portland cement stucco. It is an exterior wall cladding that utilizes rigid insulation boards on the exterior of the wall sheathing with a plaster type exterior skin. EIFS in its current basic form was developed in West Germany in the 1960s by Dryvit and later introduced into the United States. EIFS is generally composed of fiber glass mesh on top of insulation board that is secured to the exterior wall, over which a water-resistant base coat is applied, with a durable finish coat as the outermost layer. Over the years, variations of the system have been developed, and according to the EIFS Industry Member Association (EIMA), EIFS currently comprises about 17 percent of the U.S. commercial exterior wall market.

The most common type of EIFS is the polymer based (PB) system. This system has a nominally 1/16 inch thick reinforced base coat applied to the insulation prior to application of the finish coat. The insulation typically consists of closed expanded polystyrene (EPS) and can be either adhesively or mechanically attached to the sheathing. The second and less common type of EIFS is the polymer modified (PM) system. This system has a nominally 3/16 inch to 1/2 inch thick reinforced base coat applied to the insulation prior to application of the finish coat. The insulation typically consists of extruded expanded polystyrene (XPS) and is mechanically attached to the sheathing and or wall structure.

EIFS is available in two basic types—a barrier wall system or a wall drainage system. Barrier EIFS wall systems rely primarily on the base coat portion of the exterior skin to resist water penetration. Therefore, all other components of the exterior wall must either be barrier type systems or be properly sealed and flashed to prevent water from migrating behind the EIFS and into the underlying walls or interiors. Wall drainage EIFS systems are similar to cavity walls; they are installed over a weather barrier behind the insulation that acts as a secondary drainage plane. The weather barrier must be properly flashed and coordinated with all other portions of the exterior wall to prevent water from migrating into the underlying walls or interiors.

In general, construction conditions of the EIFS should be detailed if they exist on the building, including terminations, openings, joints, objects mounted onto the surface, and special treatments to the surface.

The concern that has arisen with EIFS is that, if not properly installed or maintained, moisture can penetrate through openings in the cladding and become trapped. In the case of a wood framed structure, the trapped water is absorbed by the wood and wood rot, decay, fungus, and insect infestations become problems, none of which are externally visible.

Because of the insidious nature of the problem, detailed visual inspections and moisture analyses by experienced and certified EIFS inspectors are recommended on buildings with this type of cladding system. Field observers often use electronic moisture scanning instruments with visual inspection to look for problematic areas. The inspectors should render opinions as to the acceptability of the moisture levels and should make remedial recommendations.

For new installations of EIFS, the review of drawings and detailed inspections during various application phases can ensure that the system is installed according to the manufacturer's specifications (Figures 15.7, 15.8A,B).

Thermal performance: The popularity of EIFS comes from its superior insulating qualities, which reduce thermal loads on the exterior building wall and the light weight, low cost, and the ability of the system to be sculpted into shapes and patterns to achieve different aesthetic effects. The thermal performance of

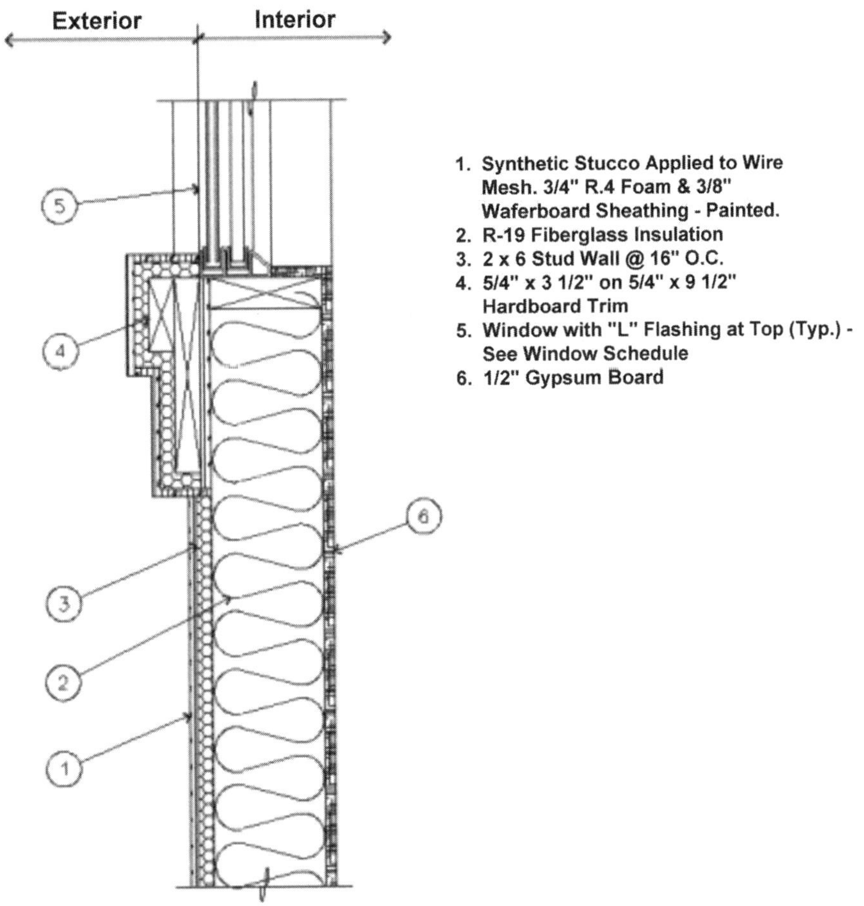

Figure 15.7 Typical stucco ledge detail.

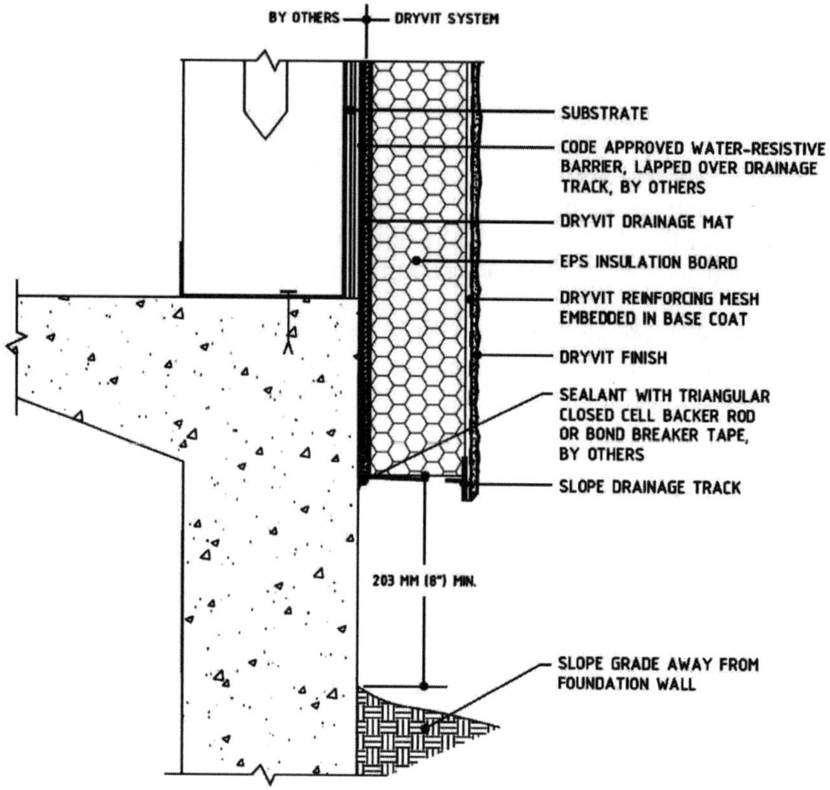

Figure 15.8A EFIS application-foundation with starter track *(Courtesy Dryvit)*.

the exterior insulation is based on the thickness of the insulation selected. The insulation should never be installed or modified to less than 3/4 inch in thickness.

Moisture protection: As mentioned earlier, problems observed with in-service EIFS installations are primarily related to moisture intrusion. EIFS provides protection against moisture infiltration at the base coat; however, moisture migration through window openings (Figure 15.9), flashings, and other items, or holes and cracks in the EIFS itself, have allowed leakage to occur on EIFS clad buildings. With barrier EIFS installations, or where weather barriers and flashing are improperly installed in conjunction with wall drainage EIFS installations, moisture can enter the wall system at these locations and cause damage to the wall sheathing and framing. The extent of these occurrences on wood frame structures has led to class action lawsuits.

Common EIFS-related problems include:

- Failure to install or to properly install sealant joints around windows, doors, pipes, conduits, and other penetrations of the field of the EIFS
- Failure to flash window and door openings in the field of the EIFS to divert leakage through the window or door to the exterior

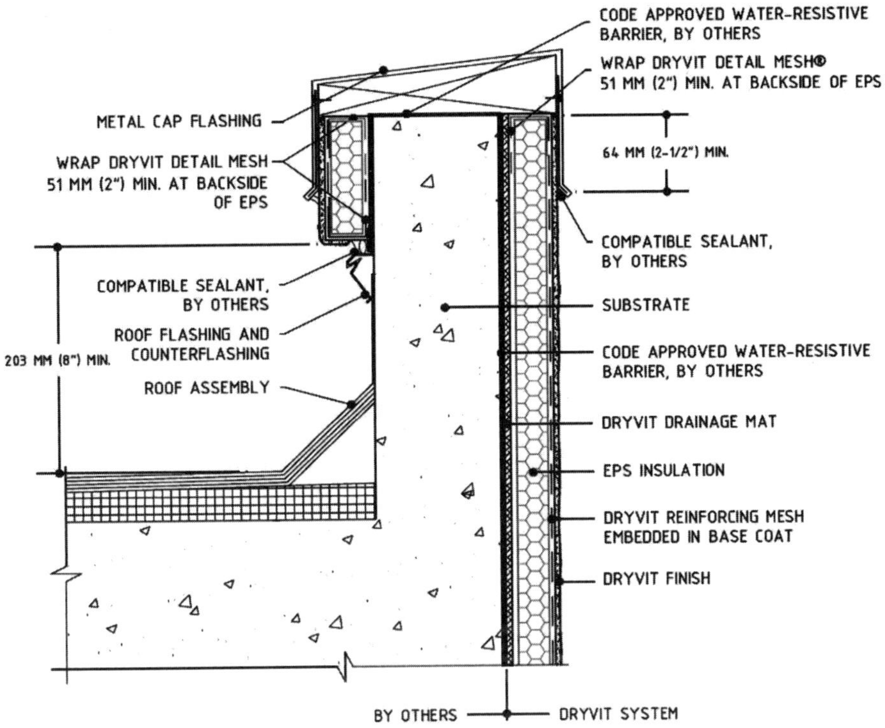

Figure 15.8B EFIS application-light parapet with solid substrate and cap flashing *(Courtesy Dryvit)*.

- Failure to install diverters (kick-out flashing) at ends of roof flashing terminating in the EIFS wall
- Failure to install expansion joints at floor lines in EIFS applied over wood frame construction
- Failure to notch insulation boards at corners of openings for windows and doors to avoid insulation board joint at the corner of the opening
- Failure to install diagonal mesh in lamina at corners of openings for windows and doors
- Failure to terminate EIFS above grade, especially in termite-prone regions
- Inadequate base and finish coat application in reveals and at corners
- Installation of reveals at board joints
- Lack of adequate slope on sky-facing surfaces

Maintainability: Maintenance of the EIFS lamina and sealants at penetrations or terminations is critical to the performance of the water resistive characteristics of the EIFS. Holes and cracks should be repaired as soon as possible. Maintenance of joints sealants is the same as that for other types of wall claddings, except that care must be taken to prevent damaging the EIFS when removing existing sealants.

15.2.5 Curtain Walls

Figure 15.9 An example of damage caused by water penetration through window opening of EIFS installation.

A curtain wall is any exterior wall that is attached to the building structure and that does not carry the floor or roof loads of the building. This includes heavy wall types such as brick veneer and precast concrete panels. In common usage, curtain walls are often defined as thin, usually aluminum-framed walls containing infills of glass, metal panels, or thin stone.

Curtain walls can be classified by their method of fabrication and installation into two general categories: stick systems and unitized or modular systems. In the stick system, the curtain wall frame (mullions) and glazing panels are installed and connected together piece by piece. In the unitized system, the curtain wall is composed of large units that are assembled and glazed in the factory, shipped to the site, and erected on the building. Vertical and horizontal mullions of the modules mate together. Modules are generally constructed one or two stories tall and may incorporate numerous panels and glazing units.

Both the unitized (Figure 15.10A,B) and stick-built systems (Figure 15.11A,B) are designed as either interior or exterior glazed systems. Interior and exterior glazed systems offer different advantages and disadvantages. Interior glazed systems allow for glass or infill installation in the curtain wall openings from the interior of the building. They are typically specified for applications with limited interior obstructions so as to allow access to the interior of the curtain wall. In exterior glazed systems, glass and infill are installed from the exterior and are secured with glazing stops or pressure bar retainers. These systems are typically specified for systems that have obstructions on the interior of the curtain wall or are monolithic systems that cover large structural elements or entire elevations of the building. Exterior glazed systems require swing stage or scaffolding access to the exterior of the curtain wall for glass and infill repair or replacement. Some curtain wall systems allow glazing from either the interior or exterior.

Typical infill panels include vision glass, spandrel glass, metal panels, thin stone, and other opaque panel materials, such as FRP (fiber-reinforced plastic).

The curtain wall often consists of only one part of a building's wall system. Careful integration with adjacent elements, such as other wall claddings, roofs, and base of wall details is required for a successful installation.

Thermal performance: Overall curtain wall thermal performance is a function of the glazing infill panel, the frame, construction behind opaque (spandrel and column cover) areas, and the perimeter details. Some curtain wall systems utilize pressure bars that are fastened to the outside of the mullions to retain the glass. These systems frequently include gaskets that are placed between the pressure bar and mullions and function as thermal breaks as well as waterproofing barriers.

Opaque curtain wall areas are subject to wide swings in temperature and humidity, and require careful detailing of insulation and air/vapor barriers to minimize condensation. Many curtain wall systems include condensation drainage provisions, such as condensate gutters, that collect and weep condensate from spandrel areas to the exterior. At the curtain wall perimeter, maintaining continuity of the air barrier reduces airflows around the curtain wall. Integration of perimeter flashings helps ensure watertight performance of the curtain wall and its connection to adjacent wall elements. Proper placement of insulation at the

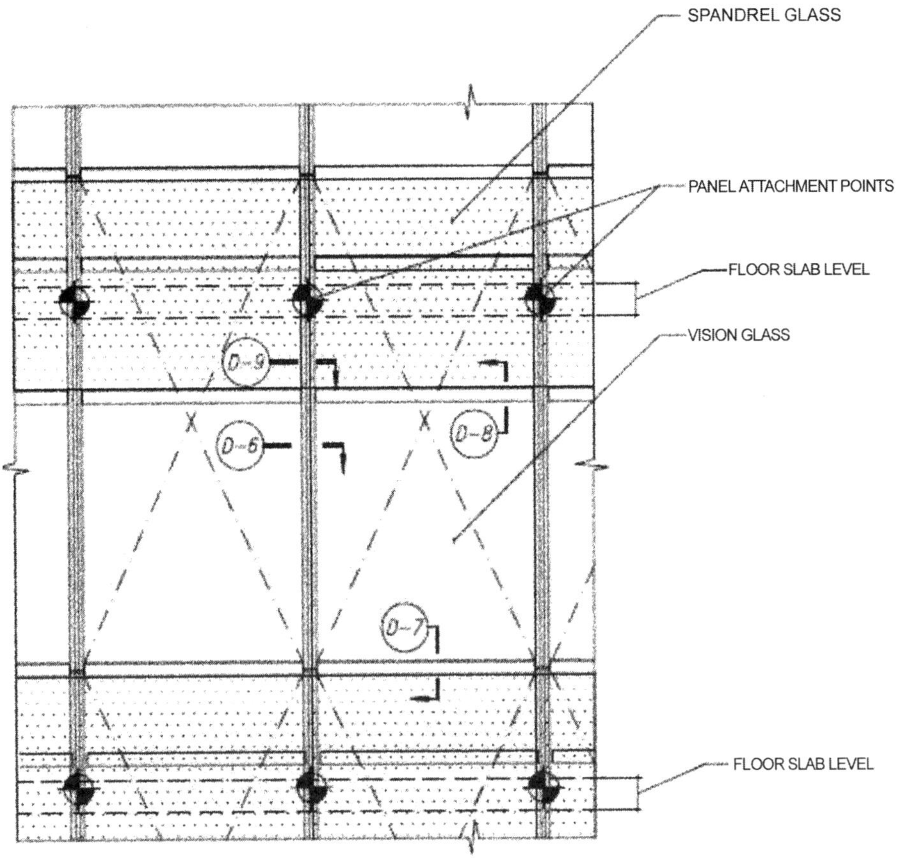

Figure 15.10A Typical elevation unitized curtain wall system *(Courtesy WBDG)*.

curtain wall perimeter reduces energy loss. Furthermore, curtain wall systems should be designed with swing stage tiebacks to stabilize swing stage rigs used by maintenance and cleaning crews.

Common curtain wall durability problems include:

- **Glazing failures:** Spandrel glazing problems specific to curtain wall construction include visual obstruction from condensation or dirt, damage to opacifier films from material degradation, condensation and/or heat build-up, and insulating glass unit (IGU) issues/laminated glass issues.
- **Failure of internal gaskets and sealants** from curtain wall movements (thermal or structural), prolonged exposure to water (good drainage features reduce this risk), heat/sun/UV degradation. Repairs (if feasible) require significant disassembly of curtain wall. If restoration of internal seals is not possible, installation of exterior surface seals at all glazing and frame joints is often performed.
- **Failure of exposed gaskets and sealants,** including perimeter sealants, from curtain wall movements (thermal or structural), and environmental degradation. Repairs require exterior access.

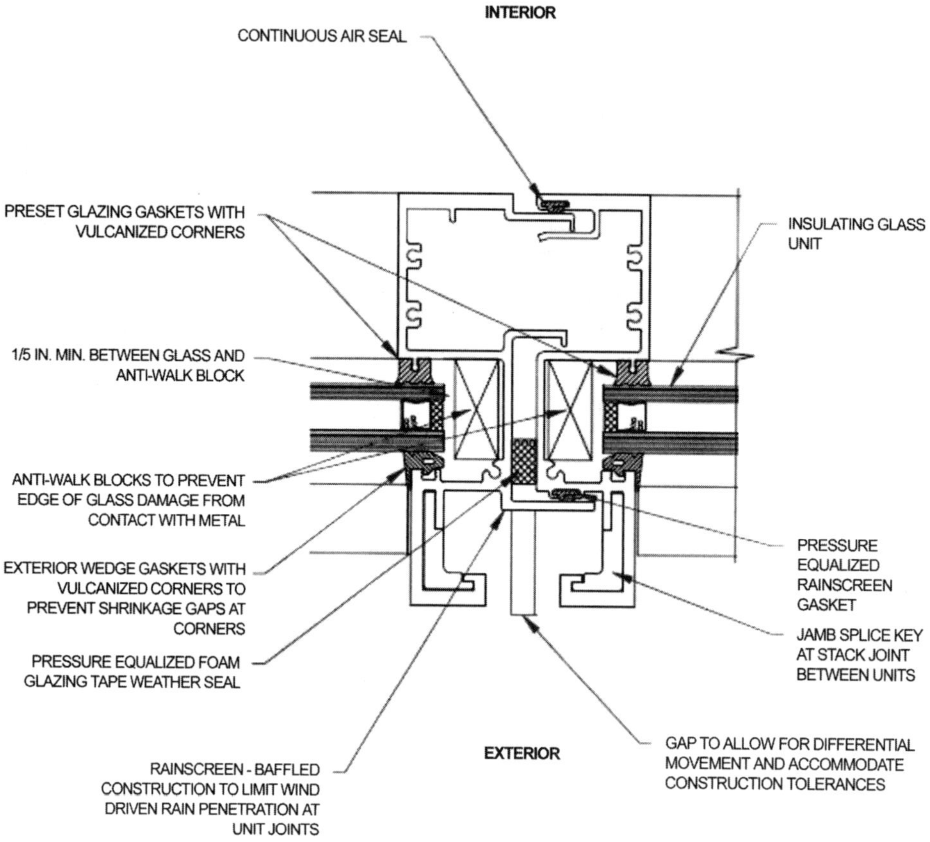

Figure 15.10B Vision glass jamb detail, unitized curtain wall system *(Courtesy WBDG)*.

Maintainability and reparability: Curtain walls and perimeter sealants require maintenance to maximize their service life. Perimeter sealants, properly designed and installed, typically have a service life of 10 to 15 years, although breaches are likely from day one. Removal and replacement of perimeter sealants requires meticulous surface preparation and detailing.

Aluminum frames are generally painted or anodized. Factory applied fluoropolymer thermoset coatings have good resistance to environmental degradation and require only periodic cleaning. Recoating with an air-dry fluoropolymer coating is possible but requires special surface preparation and is not as durable as the original baked-on coating.

Emerging trends and technology: "Smart" curtain walls, like smart windows, control visible light transmittance by employing electrochromic or photochromic glass coatings. Double-skin systems, which employ a ventilated space between the inner and outer walls are rare in the U.S., but have been used in Europe and Asia where energy costs are much higher. Similar in concept to air-flow windows, the ventilated space is intended to conserve energy by modulating the temperature conditions inboard of the curtain wall. During the heating season, the space acts as a buffer between the exterior and interior, and can be used to temper outdoor supply air. During the cooling season, warm interior air is exhausted into the space.

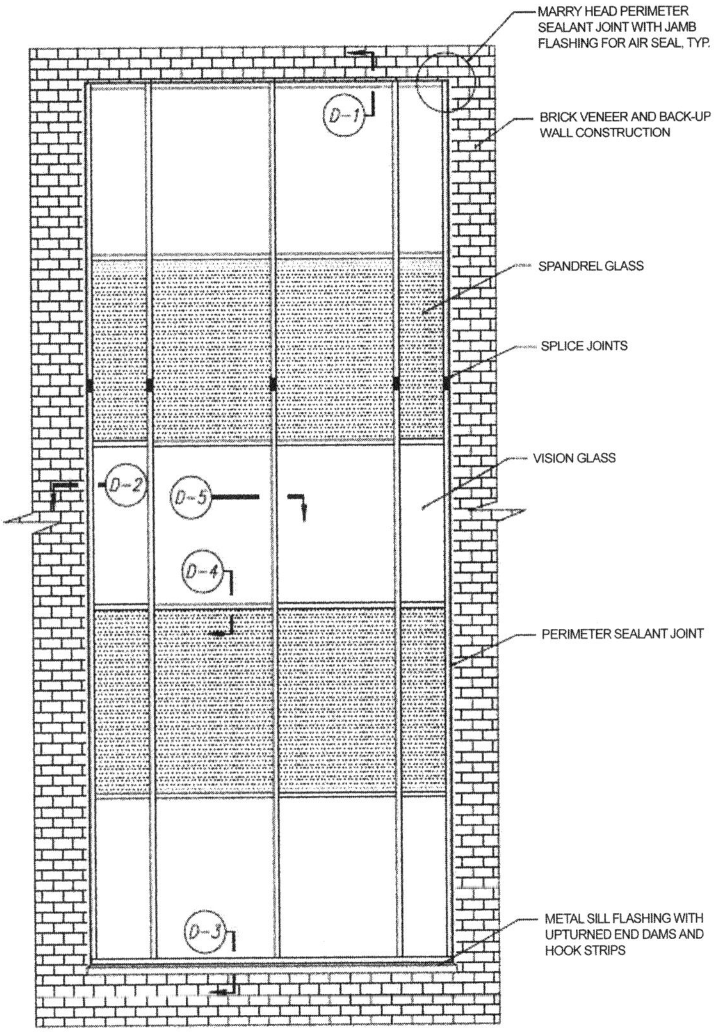

Figure 15.11A Typical elevation stick-built curtain wall system *(Courtesy WBDG)*.

Evaluation and maintenance of curtain wall: Routine inspections and evaluations will help identify issues that can compromise curtain wall integrity and efficiency. A thorough curtain wall check would include (but not be limited to):

- Examination of gaskets or sealants for splits, breaks, or openings, and the replacement of any that have failed
- Inspection of system joints to ascertain whether the framing components are admitting water into the curtain wall system
- Evaluation of thermal insulation capabilities of the system's vision and insulating panels

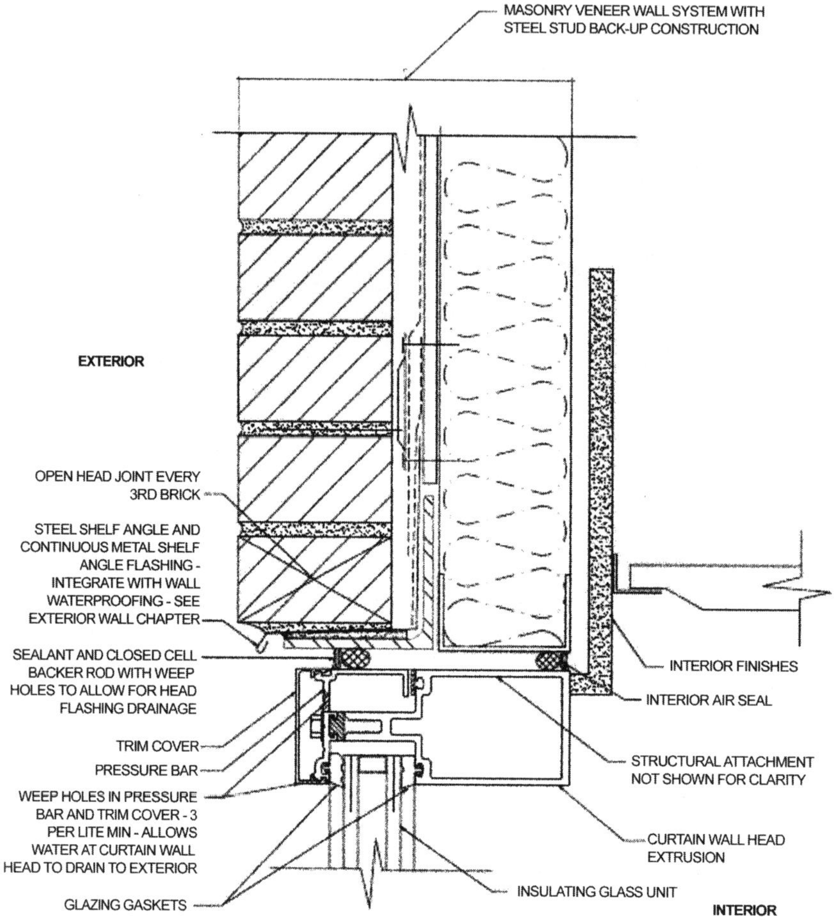

Figure 15.11B Curtain wall head detail, stick-built system *(Courtesy WBDG)*.

An effective curtain wall maintenance program would include:

- Following a preventive-maintenance program as suggested by manufacturer
- Scheduling periodic inspections, cleaning, and prompt repair of minor problems. Inspection reports should be passed on to management for necessary action. Hardware repairs and replacements should be carried out by professionals.
- Update maintenance records to document problems and solutions (This assists maintenance personnel to make effective and informed decisions.)
- Many factors affect the performance of curtain wall systems. These factors can lead to deterioration and failure if not appropriately addressed. Weather (wind and rain) is one of the main sources of deterioration of the exterior components of a building. Gasket and sealant material selections are critical in preventing air and water infiltration; inferior quality can lead to early disintegration and failure. Proper panel installation is key.

- Check for air and water leaks in curtain wall, as they can contribute to indoor air-quality problems by supplying liquid water and condensation moisture for mold growth. Water or condensation can often remain unnoticeable within the wall system until the concealed wall components experience significant deterioration and mold growth, thus requiring costly repairs or replacement.
- Building-code requirements govern many aspects of curtain wall design, such as type and thickness of glass, maximum permitted glass area, design wind loads, and firestopping of wall cavities. However, checking building code compliance is not normally part of the standard PCA.
- Routine inspections and evaluations help identify issues that can arise and compromise the curtain wall's efficiency. Thoroughly check the system's gaskets, seals, system joints, and thermal insulation capabilities of the vision and insulating panels.

There are a variety of assessments to measure how well your curtainwall system is performing. These tests include measuring air leakage, water resistance, water drainage, wind resistance, ability of the curtain wall to support its own weight, safety, and thermal performance.

Panelized metal wall systems: A wide variety of panelized metal wall systems are available for installation as a building's exterior wall cladding. Each system must be specially adapted to its intended building use. Metal wall panels are usually fabricated of aluminum but can also be manufactured from steel, stainless steel, copper, or composite materials.

The following types of metal panel systems are available:

1. Lap-seam metal panels
2. Composite metal wall panels
3. Foamed-insulation core metal wall panels
4. Laminated-insulation core metal wall panels
5. Honeycomb core metal wall panels
6. Flat plate metal wall panels
7. Metal-faced composite panels

The size of flat plate and metal-faced composite panels is generally less than 10 feet by 10 feet. These panels are generally fastened by proprietary installation systems. The thickness of the system depends on the structural support system for the panels. The greater the size and span of the panel, the deeper the thickness of the system. The thickness of the metal panel system can range from 2 inches deep for small panels to over 6 inches deep if the panels are large and need to span end to end between supports. The panels can be either directly fastened to the structural system or to a secondary structural system of metal studs, hat tracks, and supporting channels.

A wide variety of solutions are implemented to prevent water leakage for metal panel systems, including face sealed barrier systems, weeped drainage systems, and rainscreens. Rainscreen metal panel designs can be pressure equalized and back-ventilated. In general, simpler metal panel systems tend to be barrier systems while larger, more complex buildings feature drainage systems with back-up membranes or rainscreen design principles.

Support and anchorage systems: Metal panel systems are engineered to support gravity, seismic forces, and wind loading. The fastening of the panels also needs to accommodate interstory drift requirements in seismic zones. The support system of the panels needs to be able to accommodate tolerance from existing construction and fabrication. The metal panels are typically screwed or bolted on a structural frame, which usually consists of metal studs.

Joints and joint detailing: Since metal is impervious to water, panel joint design is critical to the water tightness of the system. A metal panel building typically has an extensive number of joints. How the joints perform is a factor of the panel design and construction. If the metal panel system is designed based on a barrier system design, the joints between the metal panels are typically face sealed. If the system is a rainscreen or drainage design, the joints between the panels are typically left unsealed. Some designers select a rainscreen or drainage system for both performance characteristics and the aesthetic criteria of unsealed joints.

Compared to concrete or masonry cladding elements, metal panel systems have higher coefficients of expansion for thermal movement. Designers of metal panel systems need to calculate the expected movement of metal panels due to changes of temperature. For example, a 20 feet long aluminum extrusion may expand or contract 0.30 inches when subjected to a 100-degree temperature change.

Joints between panels must be wide enough to accommodate thermal expansion and differential movements between panels. Joint sizes can vary from 1/4 inch wide for small panels to 1 inch wide for larger panels. Factors that influence joint size include panel size, panel location on the building, and tolerance issues. Generally, larger panels require larger joints than smaller panels.

Common backup wall elements: The following elements are often present in a metal panel cladding system:

1. **Insulation:** With the exception of insulated metal panels, metal panels do not typically provide any insulation value to wall systems. When non-insulated metal panels are used, the insulation is typically provided by batt insulation set within the stud wall behind the metal panel cladding.
2. **Air and moisture barrier:** While face sealed systems do not require an air and moisture barrier, drainage and rainscreen metal panels typically require a secondary air and moisture barrier system. The selection of the air and moisture barrier is an important decision that needs to be customized to the specific nature of the metal panel system, the exterior sheathing, geometry, and HVAC requirements of the building. The air and moisture barrier may include building papers, house wraps, elastomeric coatings, or peel-and-stick waterproofing membranes.
3. **Metal stud framing:** The design of the metal stud framing needs to be integrated with the panel design and fastening system.

Potential Problems

Pitting: Over time, as metal panels are exposed to weather and pollution, their protective coating can be attacked, resulting in a pitted appearance. While the pitting is not a structural concern, the pitting detracts from the appearance of the panel and the building.

Oil canning: Oil canning is characterized by pillowing or waviness of the metal panel. The oil canning can be caused by problems in fabrication, design, or installation. Oil canning detracts from the appearance of the panel, since part of the selection criteria for metal panels is often flatness. Flat plate metal wall panels are least vulnerable to oil canning compared to other types of panels, which are fabricated out of thin sheets of metal.

Shadowing: Installing welds or stiffeners on the backsides of metal panels can result in shadowing, a condition in which the weld or stiffener is visible on the panel face.

Dissimilar metals: The use of dissimilar metals can result in two types of problems: water runoff staining and galvanic corrosion. When water runs off one type of metal onto another, it can stain and corrode the other metal. Runoff from metal surfaces can also stain some types of stones and other materials.

Galvanic corrosion occurs when one type of metal is in physical contact with another type of metal. The less noble metal will corrode, and this corrosion can affect the panel's structural strength. When dissimilar metals are in close proximity, they should either be physically separated or reviewed for galvanic action potential.

Maintainability: When properly designed and constructed, metal panel systems require little maintenance. However, over the life of the structure cleaning and sealant replacement are required. If the system includes sealant, the time frame for sealant replacement usually ranges from seven to over 20 years, depending on the sealant used and the joint design.

15.2.6 Siding

Fiber-cement siding is composed of cement, sand, and cellulose fiber that has been cured with pressurized steam to increase its strength and dimensional stability. The fiber is added as reinforcement to prevent cracking. The planks come in 5 1/4 to 12-inch widths and 5/16 inch and 7/16 inch thickness. Fiber-cement siding should be more durable than wood and is termite-resistant, water-resistant, non-combustible, and warranted to last 50 years.

Like wood siding, fiber-cement siding is installed over studs or exterior wall sheathing with an appropriate weather-resistant barrier (WRB), using galvanized nails or screws that penetrate into wall studs. Although fiber-cement products come either primed or unprimed, priming and painting in the factory are recommended.

Vinyl siding: Two new products give vinyl siding a competitive edge by increasing its energy efficiency and enhancing its impact resistance. One product is an insulative foam underlayment, custom contoured to fit snugly behind hundreds of different brands and styles of vinyl siding. The other is a line of vinyl siding products fused to a foam backing material, to create an all-in-one siding and insulation system (Figure 15.12).

Progressive Foam Technologies, Inc. makes contoured foam underlayment under the brand name "Thermowall." The material is shaped to precisely fit behind nearly any manufacturer's siding profile sold in the United States. Installed over exterior walls just before placement of the siding, the underlayment provides a continuous solid backing that helps vinyl siding resist impacts that might otherwise cause cracks or dents. By adding an additional foam insulation layer, the R-values of exterior walls are increased by R-2.8 to 3.3, depending on the profile, not including the vinyl siding. The manufacturer states that the foam is made from environmentally benign expanded polystyrene (EPS), which has thermal expansion properties nearly identical to vinyl siding, and moderate vapor permeability to allow the siding to breathe.

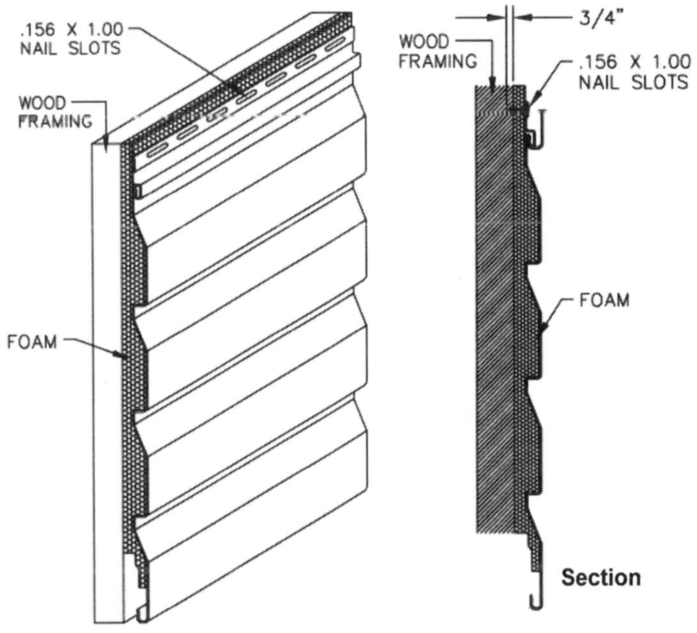

Figure 15.12 Example of insulated vinyl siding cladding.

Crane Performance Siding uses a similar concept to create lines of solid-core siding products, including Craneboard and Techwall Plus. These products fuse a contoured polystyrene backing material to a vinyl exterior facing for a solid insulated wall system with an overall R-rating of 4 to 4.5, depending on the product selected. The manufacturer states that the product also helps to bridge wall irregularities, and interlocks tightly at seams to create a straight, solid finished wall appearance without the waviness sometimes associated with vinyl siding. The panel sections are up to 18 inches high, covering nearly twice as much area as most vinyl panels, allowing installation to proceed more quickly.

Mortarless brick veneer siding: Mortarless brick veneer is an exterior siding system which uses interlocking-shaped concrete bricks that require no mortar for installation. The product is supported by the wall, not the foundation of a building. Installation does not require a skilled mason and can be accomplished by someone with basic carpentry skills (Figure 15.13). In most applications, the existing wall framing structure supports the weight of the bricks, so foundation ledges are not required, and the system is suitable for retrofitting existing walls.

15.2.7 Exterior Doors, Windows and Glazing

This section includes entrance and exit doors, as well as industrial loading dock doors, and addresses waterproofing and durability requirements, primarily. Doors and windows are an important element of the exterior closure system because they provide visual and physical access between the exterior and interior environments. These components are the areas of most frequent water and air infiltration into buildings. For this reason, special weatherproofing precautions are often installed around the perimeter of doors and windows (Figure 15.14A).

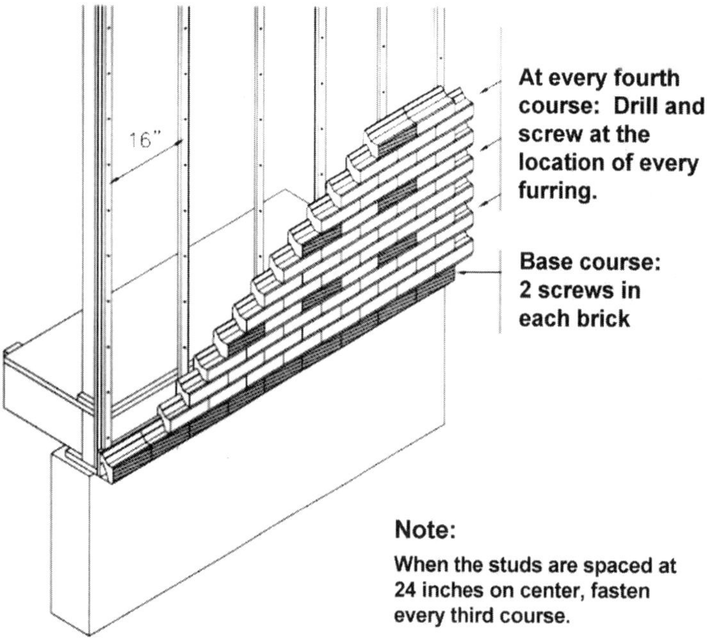

Figure 15.13 Example of a mortarless brick veneer siding system—Novabrik *(Courtesy WBDG)*.

Entrance and exit doors generally serve as building entrances for the general public or as service entrances for building operations personnel. They typically serve double-duty as emergency egress (Figure 15.14B). The International Building Code (IBC), government regulations, including the Americans with Disabilities Act (ADA), and local codes govern many entrance/exit door requirements pertaining to life safety and accessibility, which are discussed in Chapter 18 (Life Safety Systems).

Industrial doors provide access for material handling in buildings. Although functionally "doors," they are typically rolling or coiled gates, or sliding security grills, that can open large apertures in a building wall to allow unloading and loading trucks that back up to an elevated dock, or to allow building access for vehicles.

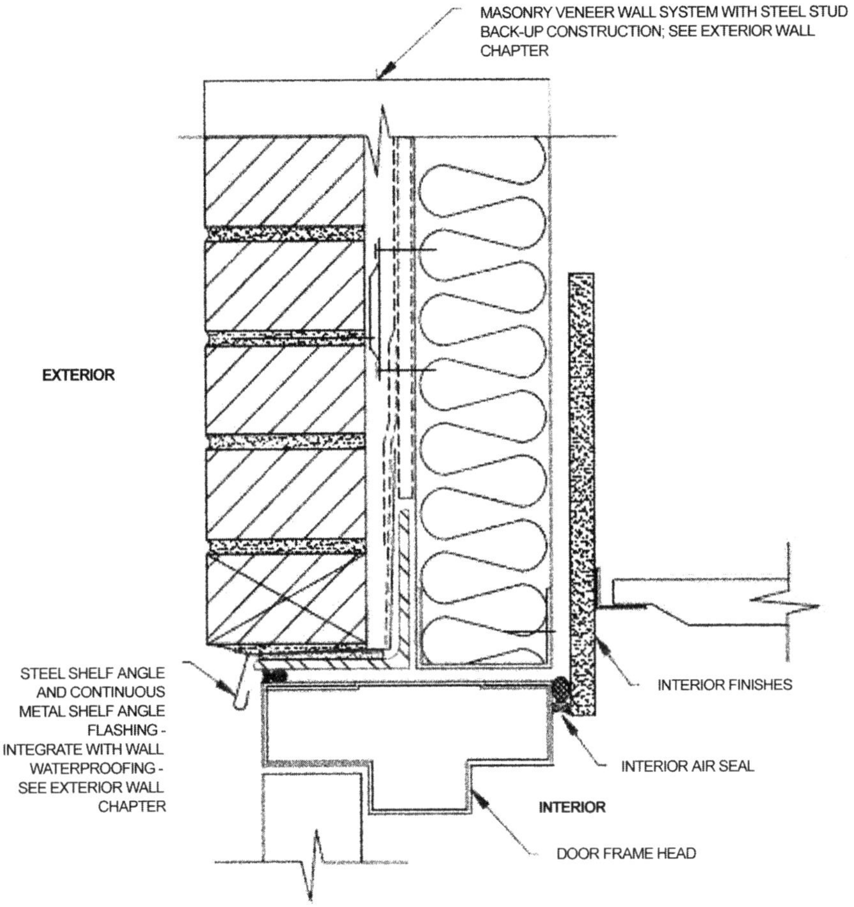

Figure 15.14A Section at door head detail.

Commonly used door materials include aluminum, steel, wood and glass. Doors that are integrated with commercial storefronts are typically aluminum frames with glass in-fills, or all glass. Steel-clad doors are generally utilized for service entrance/exit functions. Wood doors are most commonly employed in low density residential construction. Monumental wood or wood-and-glass doors are sometimes used in commercial or institutional buildings. Wood doors are beyond the scope of this chapter.

Industrial doors are used for material handling, not for pedestrian access. Their main function is to provide security. They are, therefore, frequently not designed for building envelope performance. Rolling doors typically consist of a steel frame that is anchored to the perimeter construction to resist wind and operating loads, structural guides for the door edges, and a hood that contains the rolled up "curtain" when the door is in the open position. Larger industrial doors are motorized; smaller units can be operated by manual push-up, chain hoists, or cranks. Motorized doors are often opened and closed with automatic gate operators.

Egress requirements for doors are governed by the applicable building code based on building use, occupancy load, and door type (swing, sliding or revolving). Chapter 10 of the International Building Code

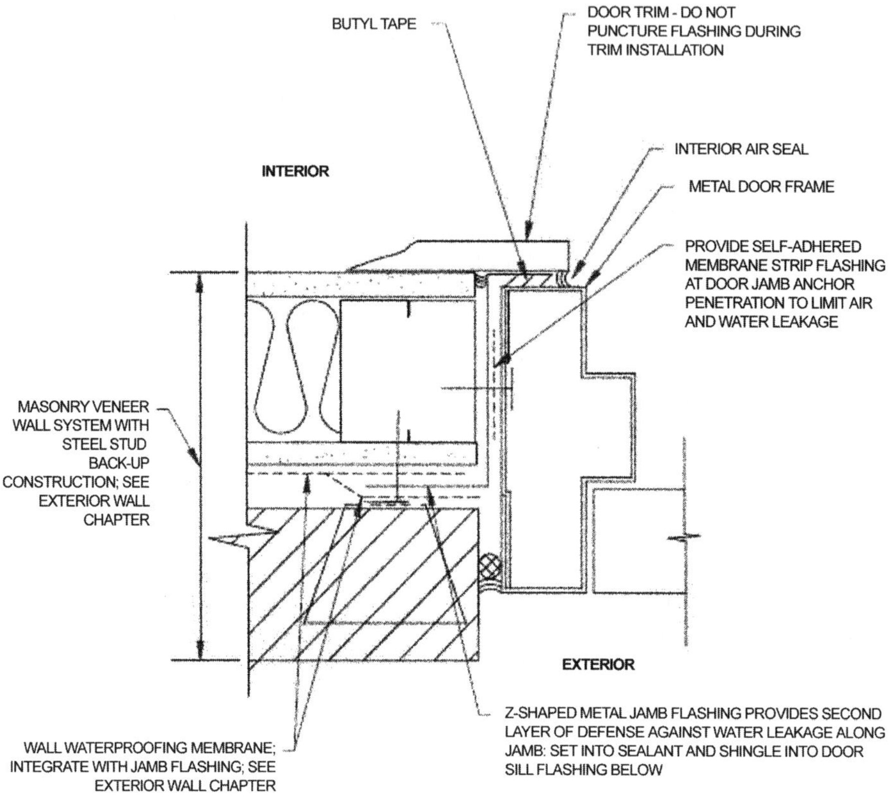

Figure 15.14B Plan showing section through door jamb.

(IBC)—Means of Egress—contains egress requirements, including minimum door height and width, maximum door leaf width, panic hardware, step down dimensions to the exterior, requirements for threshold geometry, door swing direction, illumination, operating force, signage, etc. Revolving doors must fold flat in the direction of egress and must have outswinging doors nearby.

Accessibility: The intent of accessibility regulations is to allow persons with physical disabilities to independently enter and use a building. Because non-compliant doors can present obstacles to wheelchair-bound individuals, door design must account for accessibility. This is discussed in Chapter 17 (Barrier Free Design—ADA Requirements).

Thermal performance: Doors are frequently problematic components of a building's thermal envelope. Typical issues include heat loss from air movement during operation, heat loss from air movement through the perimeter detail, and radiant heat loss through the door materials themselves. Door frames that do not incorporate adequate thermal isolation form thermal bridges that tend to lead to wintertime condensation. Overall door thermal performance is a function of the type of operation (e.g. swing, sliding, and revolving), the glazing (if applicable), the frame and perimeter details, the sash and sash weatherstripping, and the door materials.

Aluminum-framed doors that are part of curtain wall or storefront assemblies sometimes have thermally broken frames and insulating glass units, which provide improved thermal performance. See the discussions in Glazing and Curtain walls. Opaque entrance doors or loading dock doors often have foamed-in-place insulation between their exterior and interior metal skins, which typically provides better thermal performance than insulating glass. These insulated doors must have internal stiffeners to stiffen the face skins and provide adequate structural performance.

Heat loss from air leakage is the most significant challenge to thermal performance for heavily used entrance and exit doors.

Revolving doors minimize heating and cooling losses from air movement and minimize wind effects on door operability. Since they cannot be left open, they also make mechanical loads on the building more predictable, and are therefore preferable for the building's HVAC design. In colder climates, air curtains provide a barrier of fast-moving warm air that limits penetration of cold exterior air while the door is open and are frequently used with sliding doors. The warm air may also be used to raise the surface temperature of the doors, which limits condensation.

Entrance vestibules with separate inner and outer doors provide improved energy performance over a single entrance door, mainly by limiting loss of conditioned air during door operation. When they are closed, all doors rely on weatherstripping between the operable sash and the door frame to limit air movement (Figure 15.15).

Windows: There are many configurations of operable window, broadly classified as sliding seal windows or compression seal windows. Compression seal windows generally provide better long-term air infiltration and water penetration resistance than sliding seal windows because they reduce friction and wear on the weatherstripping. Window units can be fixed, operable, or a combination of the two. Fixed windows generally offer better air infiltration and water penetration resistance, and require less maintenance than operable windows.

Commonly used window frame materials include aluminum, steel and wood. Aluminum frames are the most widely used window frame material; they provide design flexibility because of the wide range of available stock systems and the relative economy of creating custom extrusions. Steel frames are less common than aluminum; there are relatively few manufacturers who produce high quality steel windows. Design flexibility is generally limited by the available stock rolled shapes. The cost premium for custom shapes is larger for steel frames than for aluminum frames. Wood frames are widely used in the residential market, often with aluminum or vinyl cladding to reduce maintenance.

Window perimeters should have flashings (sill, jambs and head) that are integrated with the waterproofing at adjacent walls and the head, and sill flashings should be sloped to the exterior for proper drainage. Many windows tend to leak at sill-to-jamb corners. To collect this leakage and drain it to the exterior, sill flashings with a panned up interior leg and end dams are required. Do not penetrate the horizontal portion of the sill flashing with window fasteners. Instead, where attachment of the sill frame is required, provide an attachment angle inboard of the window sill and fasten through the upturned leg of the sill flashing into the back side of the sill frame.

Aluminum frames are painted or anodized. Factory applied fluoropolymer thermoset coatings have good resistance to environmental degradation and require only periodic cleaning. Recoating with an air-dry fluoropolymer coating is possible but requires special surface preparation and is not as durable as the original baked-on coating.

The main complaint expressed by building owners and managers relating to building facades is water leakage. Much of this leakage can be attributed to window systems and their interface with other facade components. Understanding the basic waterproofing principles of window systems, common failure modes, and typical repair strategies can help resolve this issue.

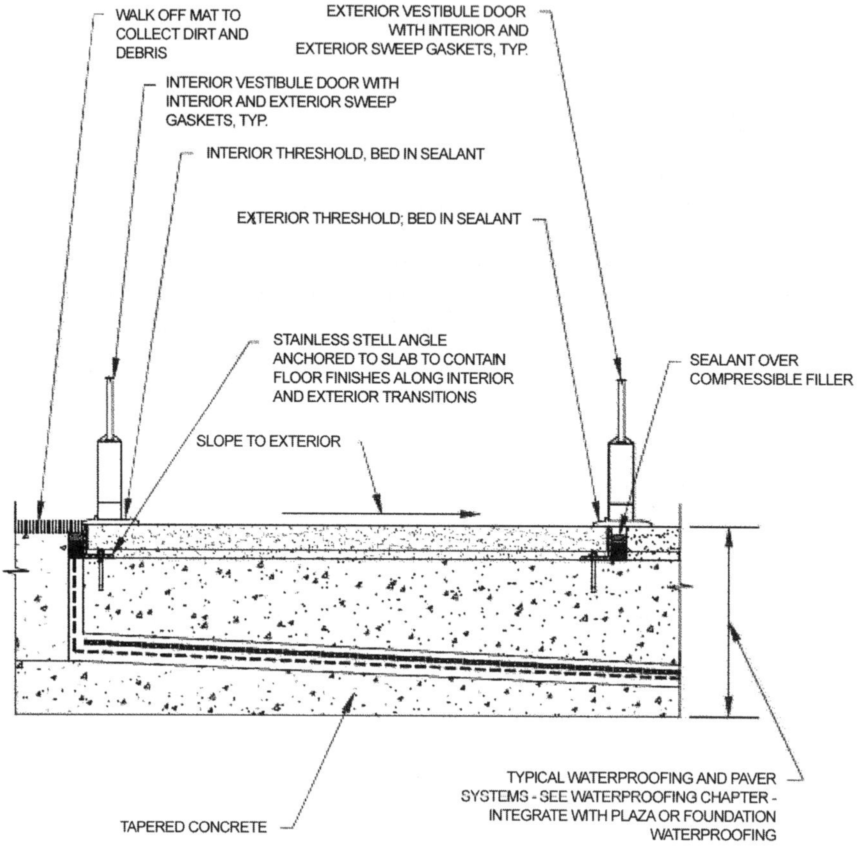

Figure 15.15 Section detail at exterior vestibule with double doors *(Courtesy WBDG)*.

Types of window systems: The most common type of modern, non-residential (inoperable) window system is known as a drainage system, also referred to as a rain screen or skin-barrier system. This system has essentially two lines of defense against water leakage: the outer seals and an internal drainage system. The outer seals generally consist of rubber gaskets, preformed pliable tape, or sealants. The internal drainage system utilizes a network of window framing components, internal flashings, and sealant to capture any water that penetrates the outer seals and channel it back to the exterior. A less common type of window system is a barrier system, which relies on the outer seals as the only line of defense against water leakage.

Emerging trends and technologies: Smart windows control visible light transmittance by using photochromic or electrochromic coatings. Some high R-value glazing includes the use of evacuated insulating glass units, which limit conductive and convective heat loss compared to conventional interior glass units. Air-flow windows incorporate a separate interior lite of glass and uses either supply or exhaust air to modulate the surface temperature of the interior glass unit.

Among the most promising switchable window technologies today is the electrochromic (EC) window, which has the ability to change from clear to a colored transparent state without compromising views and consists of an electrochromic coating (typically five layers, totaling about 1 micron in thickness) deposited on a glass substrate. The electrochromic stack consists of thin metallic coatings of nickel or tungsten oxide sandwiched between two transparent electrical conductors. When a voltage is applied between the transparent electrical conductors, a distributed electrical field is established. This field moves various coloration ions reversibly between the ion storage film through the ion conductor (electrolyte) and into the electrochromic film. The effect is that the glazing switches between a clear and a transparent, Prussian-blue-tinted state with no degradation in view, similar in appearance to photochromic sunglasses.

The main advantage of EC windows is that they typically only require low-voltage power (0 to 10 volts DC), remain transparent across their switching range, and can be modulated to any intermediate state between clear and fully colored. Switching occurs through absorption (similar to tinted glass), although some switchable reflective devices are now in research and development. Low-emittance coatings and an insulating glass unit configuration can be used to reduce heat transfer from this absorptive glazing layer to the interior. A low transmission is desirable for privacy and for control of direct sun and glare, potentially eliminating the need for interior shading. A high transmission is desirable for admitting daylight during overcast periods. Therefore, the greater the range in transmission, the more able the window is to satisfy a wide range of environmental requirements.

Glazing: Architectural glass comes in three different strength categories. Annealed glass is the most commonly used architectural glass. Because it is not heat treated and therefore not subject to distortion typically produced during glass tempering, it has good surface flatness. Heat-strengthened and fully-tempered glass is a heat-treated glass product. Heat-strengthened glass has at least twice the strength and resistance to breakage from wind loads or thermal stresses as annealed glass. The necessary heat treatment generally results in some distortion compared to annealed glass. Like annealed glass, heat-strengthened glass can break into large shards. Fully-tempered glass provides at least four times the strength of annealed glass, which gives it superior resistance to breakage. Similar to heat-strengthened glass, the heat treatment generally results in some distortion. If it breaks, fully-tempered glass breaks into many small fragments, which makes it suitable as safety glazing under certain conditions.

Laminated glass consists of two or more lites of glass adhered together with a plastic interlayer. Because it can prevent the fall-out of dangerous glass shards following fracture, it is often used as safety glazing and as overhead glazing in skylights. The plastic interlayer also provides protection from ultraviolet rays and attenuates vibration, which gives laminated glass good acoustical characteristics. Because laminated glass has good energy absorption characteristics, it is also a critical component of protective glazing, such as blast and bullet-resistant glazing assemblies.

Coated glass is covered with reflective or low-emissivity (low-E) coatings. In addition to providing aesthetic appeal, the coatings improve the thermal performance of the glass by reflecting visible light and infrared radiation.

Tinted glass contains minerals that color the glass uniformly through its thickness and promote absorption of visible light and infrared radiation.

Insulating glass units consist of two or more lites of glass with a continuous spacer that encloses a sealed air space. The spacer typically contains a desiccant that dehydrates the sealed air space. The air space reduces heat gain and loss, as well as sound transmission, which gives the indoor glass unit superior thermal performance and acoustical characteristics compared to single glazing. The service life of an indoor glass unit is typically determined by the quality of the hermetic sealants installed between the glass and the spacers and the quality of the desiccant.

Self-cleaning or easy-to-clean glass was recently developed and uses titanium dioxide coatings as a catalyst to break up organic deposits. It requires direct sunlight to sustain the chemical reaction and rain-water to wash off the residue. Inorganic deposits are not affected by the coatings.

Photochromic coatings incorporate organic photochromic dyes to produce self-shading glass. Originally developed for sunglasses, these coatings are self-adjusting to ambient light and reduce visible light transmission through the glass.

Glass with **electrochromic coatings** utilizes a small electrical voltage, adjusted with dimmable ballasts, to adjust the shading coefficient and visible light transmission. Like photochromic coatings, they are intended to attain lighting energy savings.

Point-supported glazing is sometimes used in wall systems that are all glass. These systems utilize mechanical anchors at discrete locations near the glass edge, rather than continuous edge supports.

15.3 WEATHERPROOFING

In today's competitive construction and renovation markets, building owners and investors desire a structure that remains aesthetically pleasing and leak free for as many years as possible. Every year moisture intrusion into buildings causes billions of dollars in property damage. In addition, moisture in buildings is the number one cause of mold and mildew growth. Moisture enters buildings in a number of ways. Rain-water penetrates through leaks in walls, floors, roofs, windows, and doors due to improper design, construction and maintenance.

Moisture also enters the building from improperly designed and/or constructed vapor barriers in walls, roofs and floors. This condition is normally aggravated by the use of air conditioning and construction in hot and humid climates. Moisture in buildings is the number one contributor to mold and mildew growth. Mold and mildew should be removed before it contaminates the entire building and its occupants (Figure 15.16).

Figure 15.16 Photo showing effects of water penetration contributing to mold growth.

The envelope is a complicated and integral entity of a building. When looking at these components from a weatherproofing perspective, it is important that each component be taken into consideration to prevent moisture or air from migrating into the building. The building envelope must be properly designed, constructed, and maintained to prevent water and air infiltration through the envelope, and to prevent moisture condensation forming within the envelope.

15.3.1 Air Barriers

Air permeability is one of several means of transporting moisture. As hot, humid air contacts colder surfaces and temperatures, condensation occurs and moisture gathers, creating a potentially ideal breeding ground for numerous airborne organisms. The control of air leakage improves the indoor air quality of a facility, ensuring extended building durability and energy efficiency. It is estimated that air leakage can account for as much as 40 percent of a structure's heat loss and/or gain.

15.3.2 Control/Expansion Joints, Sealants and Caulking

Control/Expansion joints allow relative movement of adjacent building components while keeping a seal between the components. Vertical expansion joints are often employed to prevent cracking by accommodating movement of the wall or of structural elements adjacent to the wall. These joints are vertical separations built into the wall at locations where cracking is likely to occur due to excessive horizontal stress. Control joints relieve horizontal tensile stresses due to shrinkage by reducing restraint and permitting movement to take place, but they should have sufficient shear and flexural strength to resist lateral loads and should be weather tight when located in exterior walls. Their size and spacing along the wall length will vary from one project to another and depend upon: 1. estimated magnitude and direction of potential wall movement(s) or other elements, 2. resistance of wall to horizontal tensile stress, and 3. extent and location in the wall of windows, door recesses, chases, and other areas of stress concentration.

Sealants are separated into three basic classifications reflecting their movement capability. Low performance sealants are capable of 2–5 percent movement, will last from 1–5 years, and include oil base (vegetable, linseed, soya, etc.), bituminous (asphalt, pitch), synthetic resins and polybutenes. Medium performance sealants are capable of 5–10 percent movement and will last 5–10 years. These include butyl rubber, latexes (Vinyl and acrylic), neoprene and similar rubbers. High performance sealants are capable of 25–50 percent movement and will last 15–20 years or more and include polysulfides, polyurethanes, silicones, acrylics, and modified urethanes.

Caulking and sealants are used to seal the spaces between intersecting building elements to provide a watertight seal and are integral elements in a building's design and construction. Caulking compounds are made up of a combination of oils, resins, plastics, and synthetic rubbers and usually applied with a caulking gun, which emits a consistent quantity of material. The chief function of a sealant is to prevent the infiltration of air, water, and other environmental elements from entering or exiting a structure while allowing limited movement of the substrates. Specialty sealants are used in special applications, such as for fire stops and for electrical and thermal insulation.

Selection of sealants: The proper application of sealants involves not only choosing the material with the correct physical and chemical properties, but also ensuring a good understanding of the joint design, substrates to be sealed, performance required, and the costs involved in the installation of the joint sealant. Typical considerations in selecting a sealant type for construction/building applications include the following:

Joint design: The specifics of the joint design and configuration must match up with the sealant's movement capabilities in installed conditions. The practicality of placement and aesthetics also need consideration.

Physical and chemical properties: Mechanical properties of the sealant like modulus of elasticity, its stress/strain recovery characteristics, tear strength, and fatigue resistance are all factors that influence a sealant's performance in a joint.

Durability properties: The adhesion properties of the sealant to the specific substrates, and the aging properties of the cured sealant as they relate to its resistance to ultra-violet radiation, moisture, temperature, cyclic joint movement, and bio-degradation can significantly impact the useful life of the installed sealant.

Application/Installation properties: The consistency of the sealant, tack free time, application temperature range, and low temperature ability to be dispensed by sealant gun are all important considerations. Sealants used for interior applications, including high-rise or light commercial structures, will have properties and needs different from those used in other applications, such as structural glazing or exterior building facades.

Joint sealants come in many different types, and include:

1. **Liquid applied in the field**
   - Latex (water-based, including EVA, acrylic)
   - Acrylic (solvent-based)
   - Butyls (solvent-based)
   - Polysulfides
   - Silicones
   - Polyurethanes
2. **Factory molded**
   - Gaskets and seals
   - Strip seals
   - Compression systems

Relevant codes and standards: ASTM has developed various standards and guide specifications used in the design, manufacture, testing, and installation of joint sealants. Additional information can be attained from the ASTM website: www.astm.org.

15.4 TYPICAL DEFICIENCIES

Many wall systems unrealistically base performance on a perfect barrier to the weather by sealing every surface, joint, and penetration. Hands-on, close-up inspection is critical to the correct diagnosis of facade problems.

Once a problem is detected, it needs to be appropriately addressed. An investigation should be conducted to look at the entire building envelope (roofs, walls, and basements), the building structural system, and mechanical systems to identify the real cause of the problem. Hands-on, close-up inspection (not just binocular inspection) can be pivotal to the correct diagnosis. It's important to keep in mind that what works for one building may not work for another.

Cracks often reflect the need of a material to expand or contract. Some materials, like concrete and stucco, develop fine shrinkage cracks (similar to cracks in dried-out mud); these are normal and nothing to worry about. Signs that may indicate more serious problems include wide cracks, vertical cracks running up concrete or masonry columns, and cracks near a building's corners. After an earthquake, x-shaped cracks often appear in piers between windows, as well as where towers and lower portions of buildings come together and pound against each other. All cracking should be evaluated by a trained engineer who can recognize which cracks are normal and which represent serious underlying problems.

Building materials move in response to temperature fluctuations. Many also move in response to moisture changes. However, obvious displacement of one material vs. another often indicates a lack of necessary control joints to accommodate such expected movements. Continued displacement can result in serious damage to the materials and possibly pose a danger to the public. Look up at your building and assess cracks and pieces of the cladding that are out of plane with the rest of the facade.

Windows can leak through the window parts themselves (less likely) or around the windows (more likely). Through-the-window leaks generally result from frame corners that were once sealed in the factory but have become unsealed, or from external gaskets that have lost their ability to seal between frames and glass. Window-perimeter leaks generally result from inadequate design and/or construction of the joint between the window and the facade. It is critical to determine the cause of the leak before undertaking a repair.

Building materials need periodic maintenance. Look for hardened or cracked sealant joints, shrinkage of window gaskets, cracks and erosion in mortar joints, and blistered or peeling paint. Particular attention should be paid to window sills, ledges, and tops of parapets.

Steel in buildings is usually hidden beneath the surface as reinforcement in concrete buildings and as anchors and ties in brick, stone, and terra cotta-clad buildings. When this steel rusts, the rust product expands with enough force to crack and cause the surrounding concrete or masonry to fall off. Early indications are orange rust stains and cracks in locations where steel is likely to be found (over windows and at steel columns in masonry-clad buildings, and in a regular grid in concrete buildings). The sooner the water supply is cut off and the corrosion repaired, the less damage will be encountered later.

Efflorescence occurs when water washes soluble salts out of mortar and onto the surface of brick. It is apparent in the form of white crystalline particles that develop on brick surfaces as water evaporates.

Conditions required for efflorescence:

- Soluble salts must be present.
- There must be a source of water.
- A path of migration of salt solution must exist so that evaporation can take place.

Source of soluble salts and their potential for efflorescence:

- Brick (masonry) units: low
- Mortars: moderate
- Lime: low or none
- Cement: high
- Sand and mix water: low
- Rainwater/Groundwater: high

Cracks and spalls in brick can result when water absorbed/retained by brick freezes. The expansion of steel (embedded reinforcing or lintels) from rust in brick wall systems can also cause cracking and displacement.

15.5 SYSTEM DIAGNOSTICS

Diagnosis of the exterior closure system varies greatly depending on the size, orientation and construction materials of a facility. Some exteriors are simply constructed using only a few different materials. Other exteriors consist of several different materials that interface in complex connections and details. The evaluation of a one-story concrete tilt-up warehouse building will differ greatly in time, effort and level of expertise required compared to a high-rise curtain wall building.

Generally, the exterior closure system should be evaluated systematically in three parts. The system review should begin by reviewing the construction documentation. The system should then be reviewed from the exterior of the building followed by a survey of the interior surface of the exterior walls.

Especially important in curtain wall buildings, the review of drawings, specifications and change orders should be performed prior to field investigation. This review may uncover inadequate or insufficient flashing details or other waterproofing deficiencies that may not be apparent during the physical review. Areas of concern should then be noted and inspected in the field.

Identify and observe the condition of the building envelope including facades and/or curtain wall system, glazing system, exterior sealants, exterior balconies, windows, doors, stairways, parapets, canopies, etc., and record physical deficiencies, including masonry pointing and sealant repair requirements. Identify the apparent or reported ages of building exterior elements and, combined with visual observations, identify the remaining useful life (RUL).

The easiest way to conduct the exterior review is to begin at the main entrance. Verify the conditions and operation of the entrance door. The facade should be reviewed for existing conditions. The evaluation should progress from the main entrance around the building and end upon return to the main entrance. High level access either by ladders, lifting machines or exterior suspended platforms or slings is excluded. Observations of the building's exterior generally are to be limited to vantage points that are on-grade or from readily accessible balconies or rooftops.

During the review the exterior walls should be evaluated from the ground level to the roof line. In smaller buildings this does not pose a difficult problem from a standpoint of access or visibility. In most instances, the wall surfaces of buildings one to three stories in height can be reviewed easily with the naked eye by standing twenty to thirty feet away from the building.

In the case of buildings above three stories, visibility is improved by several methods. It may be possible to gain access to an adjacent building from which to view the building to be evaluated. Otherwise, view magnifying devices such as binoculars or a telescopic viewer can be useful to inspect the exteriors. Powered lifts or platforms in some cases can be used. Most high-rise and several mid-rise buildings are equipped with powered scaffolding or swing stages used by window cleaning crews. For those trained to use the equipment, these devices are excellent in providing access to the system during evaluation.

The interior side of the exterior closure system should also be accessed and inspected. This is perhaps most conveniently done during the physical inspections of the interior system. Signs of any breach of the closure system should be investigated. These signs are most typically damage related to water infiltration at material intersections and penetrations, such as soffits, windows, and doors.

Infrared thermography: In addition to the uses of infrared thermography as outlined in previous chapters, this diagnostic process can also be used for the identification of the avenues of air leakage and excessive heat and energy loss through the building envelope. Since thermography can locate and identify changes in heat patterns, areas of heat leakage can be determined. Areas of missing insulation within the building envelope can be observed and located and areas of heat loss due to insufficient sealant or caulking can be identified around doors and windows.

CHAPTER

16

Building Codes

16.1 GENERAL

Building codes are an essential part of the design and construction process and are the law of the land. Building codes govern the construction of public buildings, commercial buildings and places of residence. In the United States, codes are enforced by local governments, whereas in Canada enforcement responsibility lies with the provincial and territorial governments. The purpose of building codes is to regulate construction and thereby to protect the people's health, safety, and welfare and provide occupants with a safe and healthy environment. To do this, building codes define minimum standards for safety and comfort that must be met in new construction and major renovations. Prior to having obtained a building permit to construct a commercial property, the developer was required to produce design plans that conformed to the building codes in effect at the time.

Typically, existing properties are not required to conform to newer code requirements unless major renovations are performed. When older properties are to be updated, local regulations dictate the conditions when compliance with newer codes is required. Typically, when interior renovation includes reconstruction of 25–50 percent of a floor, local regulations require compliance with existing life-safety code requirements. It is therefore important to determine all major life-safety items of functional obsolescence. This is particularly relevant to office buildings and hotels, where interior renovations and reconfigurations are periodically performed.

Building codes are essentially local laws and each municipality (county or district in sparsely populated areas) enforces a set of regulations (Figure 16.1). A strong and sustained movement has been underway for over a decade to unify the various local codes around the nation in response to the building industry's repeated requests for the setting up of a single unified building regulatory system. The majority of states have already moved in that direction. With this in mind, the three main model code organizations came together and formed the International Code Counsel (ICC), whose cardinal mission is to unify the code system into a single set of comprehensive building codes that can be used anywhere in the United States.

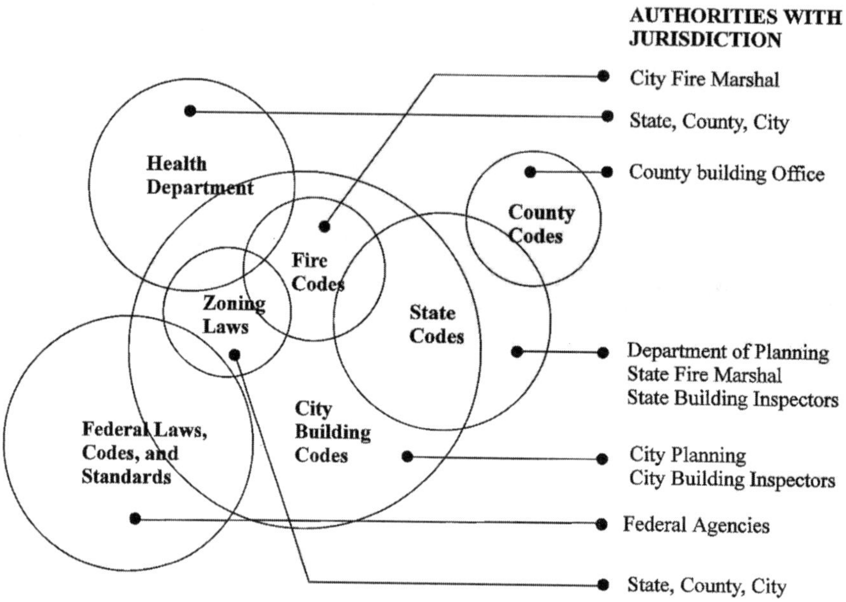

Figure 16.1 Illustration showing overlapping code structure and complexity of current regulations *(Source Specifications for Commercial Interiors by S.C. Reznikoff)*.

16.2 BUILDING CODES TODAY

One of the most confusing aspects of American codes and standards is that unlike Europe, Canada and many other parts of the world, there is a complete absence of uniformity between federal agencies, states, counties, and municipalities, although in recent years there have been major efforts to unify codes on the national level.

When dealing with counties and municipalities we are confronted with other issues. For example, cities like Houston have large oil refineries that create certain hazards, and cities like Chicago and New York require special codes and standards that relate to high-rise buildings and population density. The state of California has also decided against using the IBC codes and elected to continue using the 1997 Uniform Building Code T as the basis for the 2001 edition of the California Standards Code. On the other hand, a town that lies in the path of hurricanes may require special storm protection standards. It is no surprise therefore that some codes have evolved through modifications necessitated by particular geographic and population needs.

The terrorist attacks of September 11 and Oklahoma City continue to impact code development, and a change to the International Building Code (IBC) related to the World Trade Center collapse was recently approved. The IBC now requires that buildings 420 feet and higher have a minimum three-hour structural fire-resistance rating. The previous requirement was limited to two hours. This change provides increased fire resistance for the structural system leading to enhanced tenability of the structure and gives firefighters additional protection while fighting a fire.

The International Code Council updates its codes every three years through a governmental consensus process. Proposed code changes and comments on the proposals are accepted from anyone and everyone in public hearings. However, the final decision on code changes rests in the hands of the International Code Council's governmental members, building, and fire officials, who have no vested interest other than public safety.

The International Code Council also participates in an American Society of Mechanical Engineers task force to investigate the use of elevators in fires and other emergencies. This group began meeting following the World Trade Center attacks to examine the use of elevators for occupant exit and firefighter entry into burning buildings.

The IBC establishes minimum standards for the design and construction of building systems. It addresses issues such as use and occupancy, entry and exit during emergencies, engineering practices and construction technology. Figure 16.2 is a general checklist to indicate whether a project is code compliant or not.

CODE COMPLIANCE CHECKLIST

1. DETERMINE WHICH CODES ARE REQUIRED
   - Building Code and Other Code Publications
   - Standards and Tests
   - Government Regulations
   - Local Codes and Ordinances
2. OCCUPANCY REQUIREMENTS
   - Determine Types of Occupancy Classification(s)
   - Calculate Occupancy Load(s)
   - Review Specific Occupancy Requirements
   - Compare Code and Accessibility Requirements
3. MINIMUM TYPE OF CONSTRUCTION
   - Determine Construction Type
   - Determine Ratings of Structural Elements
   - Calculate Maximum Floor Area (as required)
   - Calculate Building Height (as required)
   - Check All Enforced Standards
4. MEANS OF EGRESS REQUIREMENTS
   - Determine Quantity and Type of Each Means of Egress
   - Calculate Travel Distance
   - Calculate Minimum Widths
   - Determine Required Signage
   - Compare Code and Accessibility Requirements
   - Check All Enforce Standards
5. FIRE RESISTANT REQUIREMENTS
   - Determine Fire and Smoke Barriers
   - Determine Through Penetration Opening Protective
   - Review Type of Fire Tests and Ratings Required
   - Compare Code and Accessibility Requirements
   - Check All Enforced Standards
6. FIRE PROTECTION REQUIREMENTS
   - Determine Fire and Smoke Detection Systems
   - Determine Fire Suppression Systems
   - Review Possible Sprinkler Tradeoffs (as required)
7. REVIEW PLUMBING REQUIREMENTS
   - Determine Types of Fixtures Required
   - Calculate Number of Each Fixture Required
   - Compare Code and Accessibility Requirements
   - Coordinate with Engineer (as required)
8. REVIEW MECHANICAL REQUIREMENTS
   - Determine Access and Clearance Requirements
   - Figure Zoning and Thermostat Locations
   - Determine Type of Air Distribution System
   - Check for Accessibility Compliance
   - Coordinate with Engineer (as required)
9. REVIEW ELECTRICAL REQUIREMENTS
   - Determine Location of Outlets, Switches, and Fixtures
   - Determine Emergency Power & Lighting Requirements
   - Determine Types of Communication Requirements
   - Check for Accessibility Compliance
   - Coordinate with Engineer (as required)
10. FINISH AND FURNITURE REQUIREMENTS
    - Review Tests and Types of Ratings Required
    - Determine Special Finish Requirements
    - Determine Special Furniture Requirements
    - Compare Code and Accessibility Requirements
    - Check All Enforced Standards

NOTE: Consult the jurisdiction having authority at any step in question.

Figure 16.2 A checklist used to determine general code compliance *(from The Codes Guidebook for Interiors by S.K. Harmon and K.G. Kennon).*

16.3 MODEL CODES ORGANIZATIONS

16.3.1 ICC (International Code Council)

For years, the building industry has been clamoring for a single, unified building regulatory system to be used throughout the United States. In 1994 The International Code Council (ICC) was established as a nonprofit organization dedicated to developing a single set of comprehensive and coordinated national model construction codes.

The founders of the ICC are Building Officials and Code Administrators International, Inc. (BOCA), International Conference of Building Officials (ICBO), and Southern Building Code Congress International, Inc. (SBCCI). The Council of American Building Officials (CABO) was also incorporated into the ICC in 1998. Since the early part of the last century, these nonprofit organizations developed the three separate sets of model codes used throughout the United States. Although regional code development has been effective and responsive to our country's needs, the time came for a single set of codes. The nation's three model code groups responded by creating the International Code Council, which combines the strengths of the regional codes without regional limitations in its *International Codes* (I-Codes). I-Codes respond to the needs of the construction industry and public safety. A single set of codes has strong support from government, code enforcement officials, fire officials, architects, engineers, builders, developers, and building owners and managers (Figure 16.3).

For decades, the three chief nonprofit model code organizations that founded the ICC, have provided separate sets of model codes for use throughout the United States. Although these regional code developments have been effective and responsive to our country's needs, the time was seen to be ripe for a single set of codes. Today, an overwhelming majority (97 percent) of cities, counties and states that adopt building and safety codes are using documents published by the International Code Council and its members. Like its predecessors, The IBC will be updated every three years and will gradually replace the existing model codes. BOCA, ICBO and SBCCI have agreed to merge their respective organizations into one model code group. This will allow a single approach to the proper interpretation, training and other services for the International Codes.

ICC objectives: There are substantial advantages in combining the efforts of the existing code organizations to produce a single set of codes. Code enforcement officials, architects, engineers, designers, and contractors can now work with a consistent set of requirements throughout the United States. Manufacturers can put their efforts into research and development rather than designing to three different sets of standards, and can focus on being more competitive in worldwide markets. Uniform education and certification programs can be used internationally. A single set of codes may encourage states and localities that currently write their own codes or amend the model codes to begin adopting the International Codes without technical amendments. This uniform adoption would lead to consistent code enforcement and higher quality construction. The code organizations can now direct their collective energies toward wider code adoption, better code enforcement and enhanced membership services. All issues and concerns of a regulatory nature now have a single forum for discussion, consideration and resolution. Whether the concern is disaster mitigation, energy conservation, accessibility, innovative technology or fire protection, the ICC provides a single forum for national and international attention and focus to address these concerns.

According to ICC's mission statement, the organization was formed to "promulgate a comprehensive and compatible regulatory system for the built environment, through consistent performance-based regulations that are effective, efficient, and meet government, industry and public needs." One of ICC's primary goals is to safeguard public health, safety, and welfare, while enhancing economic development through

- 47 states plus Washington, D.C. use the *International Building Code*
- 45 states plus Washington, D.C. use the *International Residential Code*
- 42 states plus Washington, D.C. use the *International Fire Code*

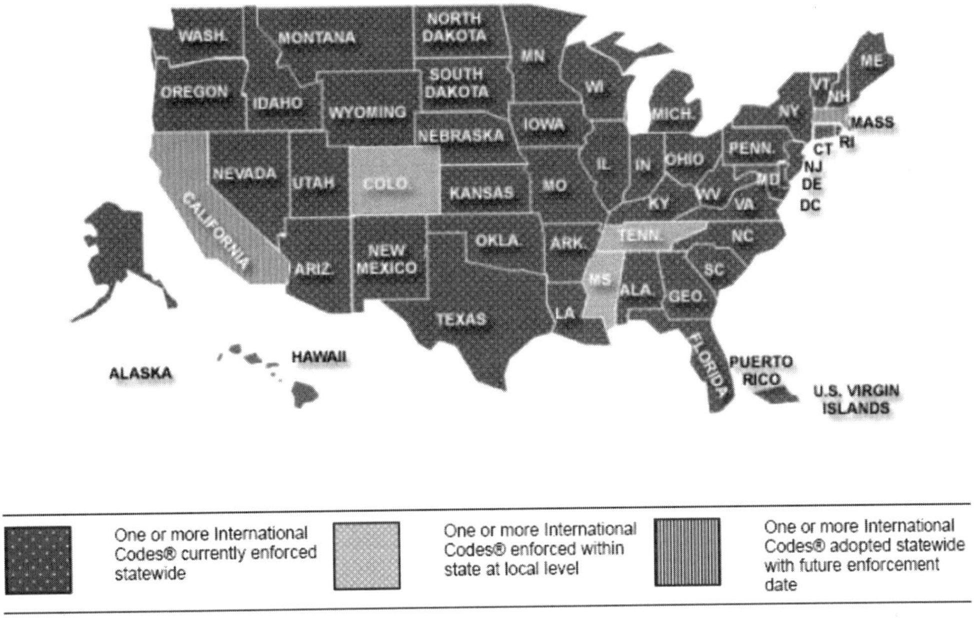

Figure 16.3 A general map of the United States showing the states that have adopted the I-Codes *(Source International Code Council)*.

the use of state-of-the-art technology in materials research, design, and construction practices, and risks/hazards to the public in buildings and structures. ICC also seeks to simplify the existing building regulatory system by adopting a single family of codes that brings with it consistency and compatibility while continuing to meet the many requirements at the international, federal, state, and local levels.

ICC made great strides when in 2000 it published its first codes called the International Building Code (IBC)—a single family of codes that is being adopted across the nation. It is hoped that as the IBC codes gain popularity, the existing regional and local model codes will be phased out.

The ICC's International Codes continues to widen its appeal, and its first complete set of International Codes (I-Codes) was published in 2000, followed by the 2003 and 2006 editions. In 2007, one or more of the I-Codes were in use within 47 states as well as the District of Columbia, Puerto Rico, and the United States Department of the Navy, and were either enforced statewide or at the local level. ICC has developed and made available numerous international code publications pertaining to construction, energy conservation, fire, fuel gas, mechanical and plumbing systems, residential standards, property maintenance, private sewage disposal, and zoning, as well as the ICC electrical code administrative provisions and the ICC *Performance Code for Buildings and Facilities.* All of the above codes are comprehensive and coordinated with each other.

16.3.2 BOCA (Building Officials & Code Administrators International, Inc)

The Building Officials & Code Administrators (BOCA) was incorporated in 1938, and is the oldest professional association of construction code officials in America. BOCA was specifically set up as a forum for the interchange of information and expertise concerning building safety and construction regulation. BOCA now fully supports the ICC codes.

BOCA is one of the major publishers of model codes and maintains international resources for a comprehensive collection of printed materials related to codes and code enforcement, including the ICC International Codes and the BOCA National Codes. The BOCA National Building Code provides minimum standards to ensure the public safety and health, and the welfare of buildings, structures, or premises.

Building Officials and Code Administrators (published the BOCA National Building Code and other national codes) is now incorporated in the International Code Council (ICC).

16.3.3 ICBO (International Conference of Building Officials)

The Uniform Building Code is published by the International Conference of Building Officials (ICBO), which is headquartered in Whittier, California; it was formed in 1922 and published its first edition of the UBC (Uniform Building Code) in 1927. ICBO's main purpose was the publication, maintenance, and promotion of the Uniform Building Code and its related documents. The Uniform Building Code is used mainly on the west coast. However, these codes have been translated into many languages, and serve as the bases for the national codes of numerous nations around the world. In addition, they have become the design basis for the Tri-services Manual of the Army, Navy, and Air Force of the United States. The code is updated and published every three years.

16.3.4 SBCCI (The Southern Building Code Congress International)

The Standard Building Code is published by the Southern Building Code Congress International, in Birmingham, Alabama. The code is updated and published every three years.

The (SBCCI), was founded by local government officials in 1940 as a nonprofit organization, with the purpose of developing and maintaining a set of model building codes for use by local jurisdictions. SBCCI provides technical, educational, and administrative support to governmental departments and agencies engaged in building codes administration and enforcement. SBCCI also provides similar support to others in the building design and construction industry. Its publication, the Standard Building Code (SBC), formerly the Southern Standard Building Code, is performance based and was first published in 1945. The SBC is used in much of the southeastern United States. SBCCI joined with BOCA and ICBO in 1994 to set up the International Code Council. Its codes are expected to be increasingly adopted as reference by local and state agencies governing construction.

16.3.5 CABO (Council of American Building Officials)

CABO was created in 1972 by the three nationally recognized model code organizations, BOCA, ICBO, and SBCCI. Its express purpose was to establish a communications channel in Washington, D.C., between building officials and congressional, federal, and industry organizations. CABO's *One and Two Family Dwelling Code* is a compilation of BOCA, SBCCI and NFPA. The latest edition (2000) of the code has been renamed the International Residential Code (IRC).

National uniformity in code requirements has always been a major objective of CABO, and in 1998, it became part of the ICC. CABO established the BCMC (Board for the Coordination of the Model Codes) and later developed the National Evaluation Service (NES) as a national program for the evaluation of innovative building materials, products, and systems. CABO also established the Building Officials Certification Program to enhance professionalism in the field of building code enforcement.

16.4 INSTITUTES & STANDARDS ORGANIZATIONS

There are hundreds of organizations writing and maintaining standards. The vast majority are developed by trade associations, government agencies or standards writing organizations. Likewise, there is a long-standing relationship between construction codes and standards that address design, installation, testing, and materials related to the building industry. The pivotal role standards play in the building regulatory process is that they represent an extension of the code requirements and are therefore equally enforceable.

However, standards only have legal standing when stipulated by a particular code that is accepted by a jurisdiction. Building standards function as a valuable design guideline to architects while establishing a framework of acceptable practices from which many codes are later taken. When a standard is stipulated, the acronym of the standard organization and a standard number is called out. The most important and relevant of these organizations for building owners and consultants are the following:

- The American National Standards Institute (ANSI)—It approves standards as American National Standards, and provides information and access to the world's standards. It is also the official U.S. representative to the world's leading standards bodies, including, the International Organization for Standardization (ISO). It provides and administers the only recognized system in the United States for establishing standards.
- The American Society of Heating, Refrigerating and Air-Conditioning Engineers (ASHRAE)—It is an international organization whose purpose is to advance the arts and sciences of heating, ventilation, air conditioning and refrigeration for the public's benefit.

  ASHRAE's stated purpose is to write "standards and guidelines in its fields of expertise to guide industry in the delivery of goods and services to the public."
- The ASTM International (previously known as American Society of Testing and Materials)—It is one of the largest voluntary standards development organizations in the world and provides a global forum for the development and publication of voluntary consensus standards for materials, products, systems, and services having internationally recognized quality and applicability.
- The National Standards Systems Network (NSSN)—Its primary mission is promulgating standards information to a broad constituency, and serves as a one-stop information repository. NSSN's "National Resource for Global Standards" is becoming the Internet's most comprehensive data network on developing and approving national, foreign, regional, and international standards and regulatory documents.
- The National Fire Protection Association (NFPA)—It is a worldwide leader in providing fire, electrical, and life safety to the public since 1896. Their testing requirement coverage is comprehensive, ranging from doors to fire fighting equipment and means of egress design. NFPA already publishes over 300 codes and standards through a full, open-consensus process, and the new NFPA 5000 set of codes, which incidentally does not use the standard group designations, competes with the International Codes so each jurisdiction will have to choose the set of codes it wants to enforce.

- The Underwriters Laboratory (UL)—It was founded in 1894 and is essentially a testing agency that approves products. UL maintains and operates laboratories around the world for the testing and examination of devices, systems, and materials to determine their properties and their relation to life, fire, casualty hazards, and crime prevention.

Regulations: Various federal agencies and departments collaborate with trade associations, private corporations, and the general public to develop federal laws for building construction. Federal agencies also use rules and regulations to implement laws passed by Congress. These regulations are often national laws that supersede or supplement local building codes. Each federal agency has its own set of rules and regulations that are published in the Code of Federal Regulations (CFR). Consultants should be familiar with the following governmental agencies that produce building regulations that may impact the project under review:

- Access Board (previously named the Architectural and Transportation Barriers Compliance Board). This Board is an independent federal regulatory agency charged with ensuring that certain facilities designed, constructed, leased, or altered with federal funds since September 1969 are in compliance with standards developed under the Architectural Barriers Act (ABA).
- The Department of Energy's (DOE) primary goal is to provide a framework for a comprehensive and balanced national energy plan through the coordination and administration of the energy functions of the federal government.
- The U.S. Environmental Protection Agency (EPA) was created to protect human health and to safeguard the natural environment—the nation's land, air, and water. It sets national standards for a variety of environmental programs and delegates to states and tribes responsibility for issuing permits and monitoring and enforcing compliance.
- The Federal Emergency Management Agency (FEMA) was formed to help cope with the full spectrum of emergencies, from natural disasters to nuclear war. The agency coordinates its activities with the Office of Homeland Security.
- The General Services Administration (GSA) was established in 1949 and its stated purpose is to "help federal agencies better serve the public by offering, at best value, superior workplaces, expert solutions, acquisition services, and management policies."
- The U.S. Department of Housing and Urban Development (HUD) is the main federal agency responsible for programs concerned with housing and community development, fair housing opportunities, and improving and evolving the nation's communities.
- The National Institute of Standards and Technology (NIST) was founded to assist industry in the development of technology and procedures to enhance product quality, productivity, and reliability, as well as to facilitate rapid commercialization of products based on new scientific discoveries.
- Occupational Safety and Health Administration (OSHA) is a branch of the Department of Labor and was enacted to ensure safe and healthful workplaces in America by regulating the design of buildings and interior projects where people are employed.

National organizations: Many national organizations support other organizations that produce codes and standards, and are essential to their development, while they are not themselves directly responsible for their production. Two such organizations are the National Conference of States on Building Codes and Standards (NCSBCS), and the National Institute of Building Sciences.

16.5 CODE ELEMENTS & APPLICATIONS

Occupancy requirements, classifications and loads: The majority of code requirements for fire and smoke protection are based on occupancy classifications. Occupancy refers to the type of use for which a building or interior space is intended, such as a residence, an office, a school, a restaurant. The occupant load is a term used to specify the number of people that a building code assumes will occupy a given building structure or portion of it. Occupant load calculations are based on the assumption that certain categories of occupancy have greater densities of people than others and that exiting provisions should adequately reflect this. It should be noted that load factors are depicted in either gross square feet or net square feet.

The formula used to determine the occupancy load is: Occupancy Load = Floor Area (sq. ft.) ÷ Occupant Factor. Thus, the square footage of the interior space that is assigned to a particular use is divided by the occupant load factor for the occupancy use as given in the code. Occupant load factors help determine the required occupant loads of a space or building, and range from a low of 3 square feet per person for a waiting space to a high of 500 square feet per person for storage areas. In ascertaining the occupant load, it is presumed that all parts of the building will be occupied at the same time. Where a building or building area provides more than one use, i.e., it has mixed occupancies, the occupant load is determined by the use that reflects the highest concentration of people.

Types of occupancy: Occupancy refers to the type of use of the building or interior space, such as a residence, office, store or school. An occupancy classification must be assigned to any building or space, and determining the occupancy classification is an essential part of the code process. The concept behind occupancy classification is that certain building uses are more hazardous than others. For example, a large theatre with hundreds of people is more dangerous than a single-family residence.

Code publications divide their occupancies into different categories based on the activities occurring in the space, the associated level of hazards present, and the anticipated number of people occupying the space at any given time. Ten of the most common occupancy classifications used by model codes are:

- Assembly
- Business
- Educational
- Factory and Industrial
- Hazardous
- Institutional
- Mercantile
- Residential
- Storage
- Utility and Miscellaneous

Classification by construction type: Construction type indicates the fire resistance of certain building elements, such as fire and party walls, stair and elevator enclosures, exterior and interior bearing and non-bearing walls, columns, shaft enclosures, smoke barriers, floors, ceilings and roofs. Fire ratings are based on the number of hours a building element will resist fire before it is adversely affected by the flame, heat, or hot gases.

All buildings are classified into one of five or six types of construction. Type I buildings are the most fire resistive and typically contain structural members that are noncombustible. Type I buildings also have the highest fire rating, usually 2–4 hours. Type V buildings (Type VI in the SBCCI codes), have the lowest fire rating and are typically of wood frame construction.

Adjuncts to building codes: Building codes typically have additional companion codes and standards that govern other aspects of construction, which, with the exception of the electrical code, are usually published by the same group that publishes the model building codes. For example, the International Code Council also publishes the International Mechanical Code (IMC) and the International Plumbing Code (IPC). The National Electrical Code (NEC) published by the National Fire Protection Association (NFPA) is the main electrical code used in the United States. The ICC published the ICC Electrical Code-Administrative Provisions (IEC) in 2000.

Model codes frequently use industry standards developed by trade associations, government agencies, and standards-writing agencies such as the American Society for Testing and Materials (ASTM), the American National Standards Institute (ANSI), and the National Fire Protection Association (NFPA). Building codes reference these standards by name, number and date of latest revision, and become law when a code is accepted by a jurisdiction. In addition, local jurisdictions may maintain energy conservation codes, health and hospital codes, fabric flammability regulations, and codes that regulate construction and finishes.

Test ratings and fire resistant materials and finishes: It is estimated that roughly 75 percent of all codes deal with fire and life safety issues, and the primary aim of fire codes is to confine a fire to its area of origin, thus limiting its spread and preventing flashover. To facilitate this end, all approved materials and construction assemblies referred to in building codes are assigned ratings based on standardized testing procedures. The rating of an assembly is ascertained by evaluating its performance during testing and by examining its fire resistive properties. There are hundreds of standardized tests for building materials and construction assemblies.

Any approved testing laboratory can undertake the testing of building materials, provided that standardized procedures are followed. The American Society for Testing and Materials (ASTM), the National Fire Protection Association (NFPA), and Underwriters Laboratories (UL), in collaboration with the American National Standards Institute (ANSI), are amongst the best-known organizations, having developed a large variety of standardized tests and testing procedures.

Types of tests: There are basically two categories of fire testing of materials for interior design components. These are: 1. Tests that rate the ability of a construction assembly to prevent the passage of fire and smoke from one space to another, and 2. Tests that rate the flammability of a finish material.

Ratings and fire resistive standards of materials and finishes: Upon being subjected to one of the standard tests, a material is given a rating based on its performance during the test. The ASTM E-84 test classifies materials into one of three basic groups based on their tested flame spread characteristics. These groups and their flame spread indexes are listed below. Class I is the most fire resistant.

Class	Flame Spread Index
I (A)	0–25
II (B)	26–75
III (C)	76–100

Class A, B, and C designations for wall and ceiling finishes used by the Life Safety Code (LSC) and the Standard Building Code (SBC) correlate directly with the Class I, II, and III designations used by the National Building Code (NBC) and the Uniform Building Code (UBC). Sometimes, when an approved sprinkler system is used, the building code will allow you to reduce the required class of the finish materials by one.

For construction assemblies tested according to ASTM E-119, the rating given is according to time—how long an assembly will contain a fire, retain its structural integrity, or both. The test evaluates a construction assembly's performance regarding the temperature rise on the protected side of the assembly, the amount of smoke, gas, or flame that penetrates the assembly, and the assembly's structural performance during exposure to fire. The ratings are 1-hour, 2-hour, 3-hour, and 4-hour; 20, 30, and 45-minute ratings are also used for doors and other opening assemblies. Assemblies that consultants and field observers must be concerned with include fire walls, fire separation walls, shaft enclosures (like stairways exits, and elevators), and floor/ceiling constructions as well as doors and rated glazing. Because of liability issues, a number of major due diligence firms have now removed code compliance from their standard scope of works.

Building codes typically have tables that stipulate the type of construction that meets the different hourly ratings. Thus when a building code states that a 1-hour rated partition assembly is required between an exit corridor and an adjoining tenant space, the designer must select and detail a design that incorporate the requirements for 1-hour construction.

Means of egress: Exiting is one of the most critical requirements of building codes. It comprises essentially three main categories: 1. Exit access, 2. Exit, and 3. Exit discharge (Figure 16.4).

Arrangement of exits: Arrangement of exits is specified by code. They should be located as far apart from each other as possible so that if one is blocked in an emergency, the other(s) can still be reached. The code states that when two or more exits are required, they must be placed a distance apart equal to not less than one-half the length of the longest diagonal dimension within the building or area to be served, as measured in a straight line between the exits. This is known as the half-diagonal rule and is shown in Figure 16.5.

Maximum travel distances: The codes limit the length of travel distance from within a single space to an exit access corridor. This is defined as the maximum distance and cannot exceed 200 feet (61 m) in an unsprinklered building and 250 feet (76.25 m) in a sprinklered building (Figure 16.6). There are exceptions to the rule, such as when the last portion of the travel distance is entirely within a 1-hour-rated exit corridor. Basically, codes classify travel distances into two types. The first relates to the length of travel distance from within a single space to the exit access corridor (also known as the common path of

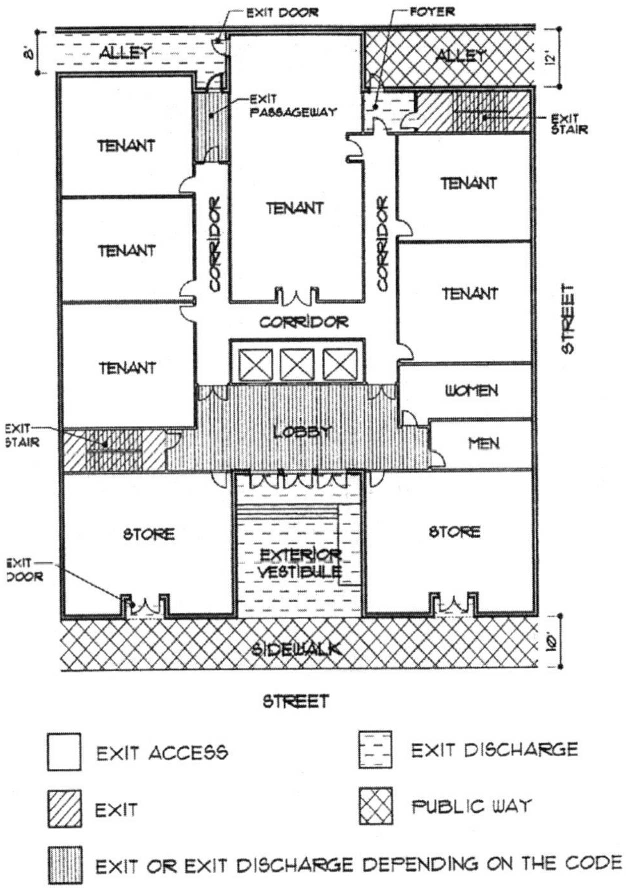

Figure 16.4 Typical building example of means of egress *(from The Codes Guidebook for Interiors by S.K. Harmon and K.G. Kennon).*

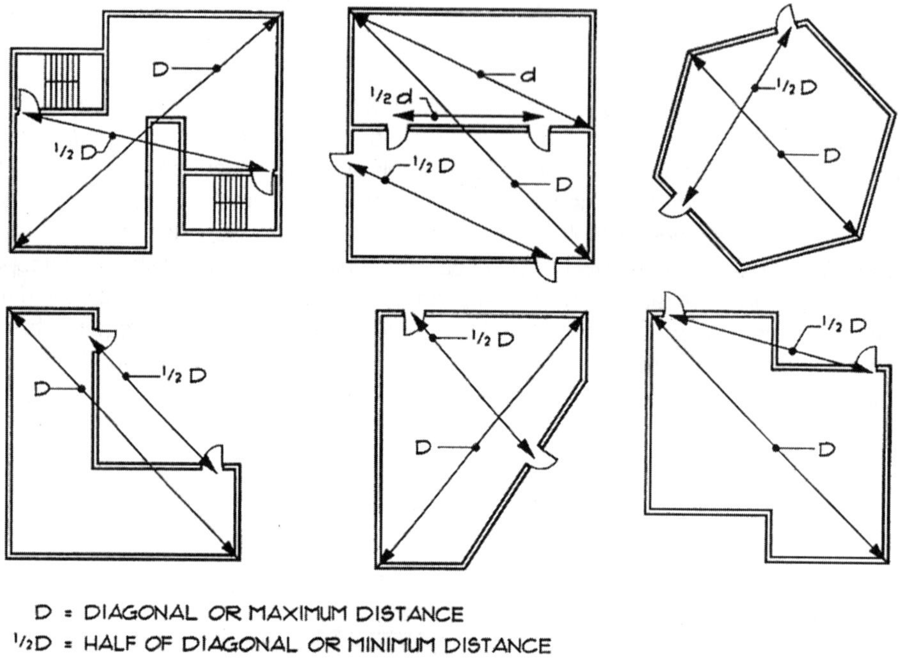

Figure 16.5 Illustrating the one half-diagonal rule to determine egress distances states that two exits shall not be located closer than one half the length of the maximum diagonal dimension of the area served *(from The Codes Guidebook for Interiors by S.K. Harmon and K.G. Kennon).*

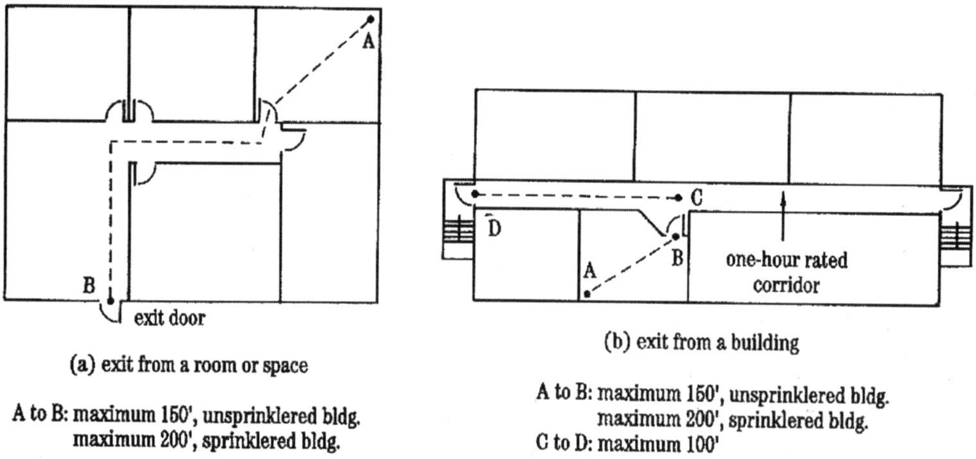

Figure 16.6 Maximum acceptable distances required to exits *(from Interior Design Reference Manual by D.K. Ballast).*

travel), and the second regulates the length of travel distance from anywhere in a building to the floor or building's exit. Typically however, if the travel distance within a tenant space exceeds 75 feet (22.9 m), then an additional exit is required, even if it is not required by the occupant load.

Exits through adjoining rooms: Codes usually allow a room to have a single exit through an adjoining or intervening room, provided it affords direct and unobstructed means of travel to an exit corridor or other exit, as long as the total stipulated maximum travel distances are not exceeded. However, exiting is not permitted through kitchens, storerooms, rest rooms, closets, or spaces used for similar purposes. Codes normally categorize foyers, lobbies, and reception rooms constructed as required for corridors (with a one-hour-rated wall) as intervening rooms, thereby allowing them to be used for exit purposes.

Widths of exits: A capacity-factor or specific width variable furnished by the codes specifies the minimum width for stairways and horizontal exits based on the use of the space. Most indoor activities require stairwells to have 0.3 in. of width for each person on the floor with the greatest number of occupants, but areas with hazardous contents require 0.7 in. per person, a much greater capacity. The width variable for other exits is 0.2. This total width must be divided approximately equally among the separate exits.

Corridors are intended to provide a safe means of egress from a room or space to a building exit or to another approved exitway, such as a stairway. Where two exits are required, corridors should be designed to simultaneously allow travel in two directions to an exit. Lengths of dead-end corridors with only one means of exit are limited to a maximum of 20 feet in the model codes. Minimum corridor width (in feet) of a corridor is determined by multiplying the occupant load it serves by 0.2. Where the corridor serves an occupant load of 50 or more, the minimum width must not be less than 44 inches (1.12 m). For occupant loads less than 50, the minimum width is 36 inches (0.91 m). The width of a corridor must be unobstructed, but handrails and fully opened doors can protrude a maximum of 7 inches (17.8 cm) total. In certain occupancies, codes may require wider corridors.

Typically, corridor construction must be of 1-hour fire-resistive construction when serving an occupant load of 10 or more in R-1 and I occupancies and when serving an occupant load of 30 or more in other occupancies. The 1-hour-rated corridors must extend through the ceiling to the rated floor or roof above unless the ceiling of the entire story is 1-hour rated. Where a duct penetrates a fire rated corridor, a fire damper must be provided that closes automatically upon detection of heat or smoke so as to restrict the passage of flame.

Doors and their components (door, frame, hardware, and doorway or wall opening) are regulated by code and depend on the fire rating of the wall where they are to be located. Other door assemblies may comprise more than the four main components listed above. Below are some of the more common types of door and window assemblies used:

Regulated Fire-Rated Doors
- access doors
- bi-parting doors
- conveying system doors
- chute doors
- Dutch doors
- folding doors
- hoistway doors
- horizontal doors
- revolving doors
- rolling steel doors
- service counter doors
- swinging doors

Regulated Fire-Rated Windows
- borrowed lights
- casement windows
- double-hung windows
- fixed windows
- glass block
- hinged windows
- pivot windows
- side lights
- sky lights
- tilting windows
- transom lights
- vision panels

Stairs are of various types, including the straight run, curved, winder, spiral, scissor, etc. Exit stairs should be wide enough to allow two people to descend side by side with no sudden decrease in width along the path of travel. Stairs must also adhere to specific code and accessibility requirements and must be constructed in a manner and using materials consistent with the construction type of the building. Model codes usually require that a run of stairs not rise in excess of twelve feet without an intermediate landing and that they have a landing at the top and bottom. Typically, new stairs are required to have a minimum width of 44 inches, an 11 inch tread depth, and a maximum riser height of 7 inches (Figure 16.7). Handrails and guardrails are likewise regulated.

Escalators and moving walks, like elevators, are not usually allowed as a means of egress, and should not be taken into account as such in egress calculations. Exceptions are allowed, but must be provided with standby power and must comply with emergency operation and signaling device requirements.

Fire protection systems: Interior fire codes are designed to protect a building's occupants, allowing them time to evacuate during a fire, and affording access for fire fighters and equipment. Statistics show that smoke and toxic gases are the main cause of death in a building fire. Unhampered, fire and smoke travel quickly both horizontally and vertically, which is why action needs to be taken to prevent this from happening. Because the control of fire and smoke is such a life safety issue, the prevention of fire and smoke spread is addressed in the codes in several ways. The codes and standards place strict require-

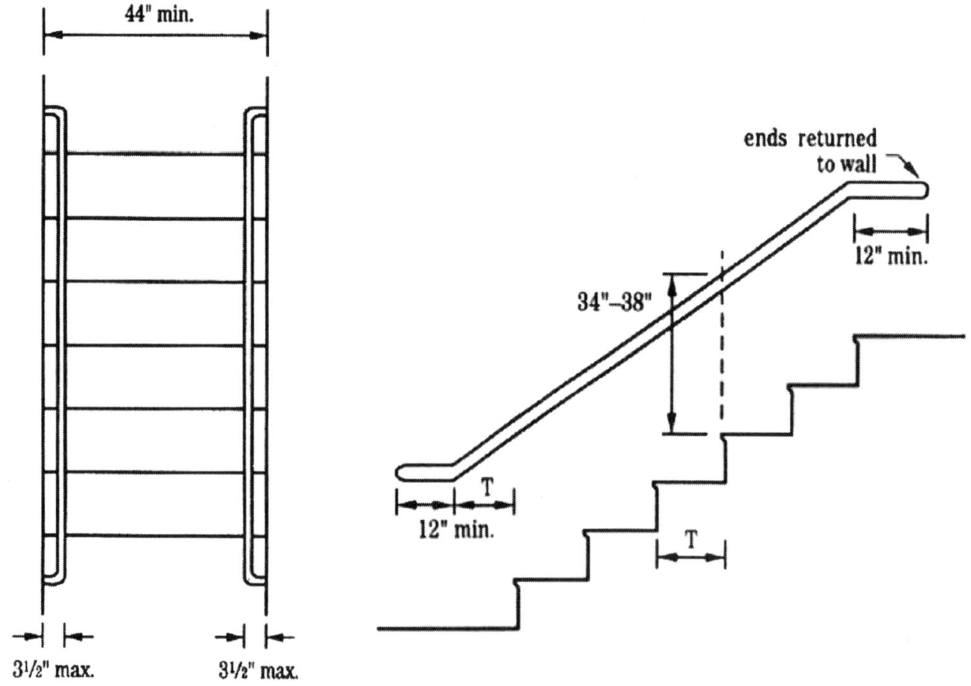

Figure 16.7 Code requirements for stair and handrails *(from Interior Design Reference Manual by D.K. Ballast).*

ments on the materials used to construct a building. Depending on a building's classification, an hourly fire rating is typical of structural elements in a building, including walls and floor assemblies. This is discussed in more detail in Chapter 18 (Life Safety Systems).

Note that the American with Disabilities Act Accessibility Guidelines (ADAAG) and other accessibility standards do not play an essential role in fire prevention calculations, although many of the fire resistant elements (e.g. fire doors) are still required to meet the accessibility requirements.

16.5.1 Miscellaneous Issues

Exit lighting: Because each jurisdiction has slightly different requirements, one must review the local codes in force. In the event of a power failure, adequate lighting must be available for the evacuation of a building's occupants. Where there are two or more exits, exit lighting (sometimes called emergency lighting) is required. Generally, artificial lighting is required in the path of exit discharge where a building is in use, with some exceptions for residential occupancies. Exit lighting and exit signs are required at all exits and corridors, aisles, ramps, passageways, and lobbies leading to an exit. They must be located and illuminated so as to facilitate the exit of occupants safely out of a building. In fire-rated ceilings and wall assemblies, only certain types of light fixtures are permitted.

Glazing: The codes regulate the use of glass in hazardous locations, such as doorways, vision panels, and places where people are likely to accidentally trip through a piece of glass. In such locations, the use of safety glazing (tempered, wired or laminated glass) is required. Common interior applications of approved rated glazing material are in corridor walls, room partitions, and smoke barriers. When glass products are used in a rated wall, they must meet NFPA 257 requirements, provided the total area does not exceed 25 percent of the area of the wall of the room that it is separating.

Plumbing systems: Plumbing and mechanical codes address issues relating to health and welfare concerns rather than life safety issues. Previously, major code organizations published separate plumbing and mechanical codes. Then the International Code Council (ICC) published the first International Plumbing Code (IPC) in 1997 and the International Mechanical Codes in 1998. Model codes specify in great detail how a plumbing or mechanical system should be designed. Plumbing codes specify the number of sanitary fixtures required based on the type of occupancy.

Sound ratings: Model building codes sometimes require the use of insulation to control sound transmission in wall and floor assemblies separating dwelling units or guest rooms in residential occupancies from each other and from public spaces. Acoustics design can dramatically influence the transmission of sound and noise. The transmission of sound between spaces can be prevented or minimized by the materials used, their mass, and to a lesser degree, their stiffness. Codes usually specify the minimum sound transmission class (STC) for walls or impact insulation class (IIC) for floors. Construction details can then be designed to satisfy these requirements.

Residential exiting: Requirements for residential exiting (individual dwelling units and single-family houses) are not as strict as for commercial occupancies. Codes typically have a sub-classification specifically for dwelling units; the one best covered is the International Residential Code (IRC), which is specifically designed for one and two family houses. The designer must verify which code is applicable to a particular project.

The IRC requires at least one regulated exterior door per residence with minimum dimensions of 3 feet 6 inches × 6 feed 8 inches. Bedrooms located on upper floors typically require an emergency means of egress for these areas—usually an operable window as long as it is not more than 44 inches from the floor. Stair and ramp dimensions are also regulated, but are not as strict as those for commercial use. One handrail is normally required in residential stairs and ramps.

CHAPTER

17

Barrier Free Design—ADA Requirements

17.1 GENERAL

When it comes to providing built environments that are accessible to people with disabilities, the United States is undoubtedly a world leader. The two most cardinal pieces of legislation dealing with accessible design are the *Americans with Disabilities Act* (ADA) and the *Fair Housing Amendments Act.* The latter extends the nondiscrimination protections of the Fair Housing Act to persons with disabilities as well as persons with families. Signed into law on July 26, 1990, the ADA is a federal civil law that prohibits discrimination against people with disabilities. Britain has the Disability Discrimination Act (DDA), which is modeled on the ADA, and which came into law in November of 1995. The Dutch have the *Geboden Toegang* ('Access demanded!'), and the European Union has issued the *European Manual for Accessibility.*

The ADA legislation is designed to make American society more accessible to persons with disabilities, and with certain exceptions that will be discussed later, all buildings, existing as well as new construction, must comply with the Americans with Disabilities Act. Moreover, ADA requirements are liable to change as regulations are modified to improve access or to make it easier for entities to comply with ADA guidelines. When new requirements are proposed, a formal procedure is in place that calls for public comment followed by an agency review before the proposal is finalized. Modifications to existing requirements or to new requirements are initially issued as a proposed rule and published in the Federal Register.

While the employment provisions of the ADA apply to employers of fifteen employees or more, its public accommodations provisions apply to all sizes of business, regardless of number of employees. State and local governments are covered regardless of size.

The ADA comprises the following five titles:

1. **(Title I) Employment:** Business must provide reasonable accommodations to protect the rights of individuals with disabilities in all aspects of employment. Possible changes may include restructuring jobs, altering the layout of workstations, or modifying equipment. Regulated aspects of em-

ployment may include the application process, hiring, wages, benefits, and all other aspects of employment. Medical examinations are highly regulated.

2. **(Title II) Public Services:** The regulations of Title II apply to public services provided by state and local governments, and include public school districts, the National Railroad Passenger Corporation, port authorities, and other government units, whether or not they receive federal funds. In order to make the services offered accessible to people with disabilities, new construction and alterations are required to incorporate barrier-free design. Additionally, program accessibility in existing buildings may necessitate alterations in order to enhance the existing degree of accessibility.
3. **(Title III) Public Accommodations:** This segment of the law applies mainly to commercial facilities, and prohibits privately owned and operated businesses from denying goods, programs or services to persons with disabilities. All new and altered commercial facilities are subject to the accessibility requirements of Title III. Furthermore, it has been incorporated into the Americans with Disabilities Act Accessibility Guidelines (ADAAG) as developed by the Architectural and Transportation Barriers Compliance Board (ATBCB or Access Board). ADA compliance may not be required for certain entities, such as facilities owned and operated by religious entities, one- and two-family dwellings, private clubs, and certain government facilities.

   A place of public accommodation as defined by the ADA is any facility that is owned and operated by a private entity whose operation affects commerce and falls within at least one of 12 specified categories:

   - Places of lodging, such as hotels, motels, and inns (does not include establishments in which the owner resides and rents out no more than five rooms)
   - Establishments serving food or drink, such as restaurants, cafeterias and bars
   - Places of exhibition or entertainment, such as theaters, stadiums, and concert halls
   - Places of public gathering, such as auditoriums, convention centers, and lecture halls
   - Sales or rental establishments, such as stores, bakeries, and shopping centers
   - Service establishments, such as banks, dry cleaners, travel agents, gas stations, attorney premises, hospitals, and clinics
   - Stations used for specified public transportation, such as private company bus terminals and depots
   - Places of public display or collection, such as museums, libraries, and galleries
   - Places of recreation, such as parks, zoos, and amusement parks
   - Places of education, such as private sector educational establishments
   - Social service center establishments, such as daycare centers, facilities for the elderly, and homeless shelters
   - Places of exercise or recreation, such as health spas, gymnasiums, and golf courses

   New construction as well as modifications to existing buildings must typically be accessible to individuals with disabilities. Where full accessibility is not technically feasible due to structural, physical, or site constraints, accessibility is to be provided to the maximum extent possible. For existing facilities, barriers to services must be removed if readily achievable, and when an existing place of public accommodation is structurally altered, the ADA stipulates that the facility must then comply with its guidelines.

4. **(Title IV) Telecommunications:** This section is aimed at federally regulated telecommunications companies and federally funded public service television offering services to the general public. Telephone companies offering general service to the public must offer telephone relay service to individuals who use telecommunication devices for the deaf (TTYs) or equivalent. Additionally, close-captioned messages for hearing impaired viewers must be available for public service messages.
5. **(Title V) Miscellaneous:** This section includes a provision prohibiting coercion, threats or retaliation against the disabled or those attempting to aid people with disabilities in the assertion of their rights under the ADA.

   Gerald Morgan AIA, an ADA expert, believes that the most significant changes between the current ADAAG and the New ADAAG are portrayed in the following lists. These lists have been grouped to reflect the anticipated economic impact they will have on facility owners and managers and are examples of revisions that reduce economic impact:

   - Restaurants and cafeterias: A new exemption requires that only 25 percent of the tiered dining areas in sports facilities be connected to an accessible route.
   - Press boxes: Exemptions were added for accessible routes to certain types of elevated press boxes that have areas not exceeding 500 square feet.
   - Limited use/limited application (LULA) elevators and private-residence elevators: A new exception was added that allows a facility that is exempt from elevator scoping requirements (less than 3 stories or less than 3,000 square feet) to install a LULA elevator, which is typically less expensive than a passenger elevator. Private-residence elevators are also allowed for use in multi-story dwelling units.
   - Urinals: If a toilet room has only one urinal, an accessible urinal is not required.
   - Visible alarms: In alterations to existing facilities, visible alarms are required only when an existing fire-alarm system is upgraded or replaced, or when a new fire-alarm system is installed.
   - Wheelchair spaces in assembly areas: The number of wheelchair spaces in assembly areas with more than 500 seats has been significantly reduced. Scoping requirements are also clarified with regard to seating areas, luxury and club boxes, and stadium and arena suites.
   - Handrails: New guidelines provide more flexibility than the current guidelines for handrail gripping surface shape and size; a round gripping surface is no longer the only acceptable shape. New guidelines also reduce the required extension of the handrail at the bottom of a stair run—the horizontal extension will no longer be required. This change will eliminate the hazard created when the horizontal extension of the handrails protrude into the circulation path.
   - Water closet location: It will now be acceptable to install the accessible toilet fixture between 16 and 18 inches from the side wall.
   - Alternate roll-in showers: These are now permitted to be used in any facility, not just hotel guestrooms. Also, new guidelines are more flexible regarding required seat and control locations within the shower compartment.
   - Accessible showers: A fixed showerhead located at a maximum of 48 inches above the shower finish floor shall be permitted in lieu of a handheld spray unit in facilities that are not medical care facilities, long-term care facilities, transient lodging guestrooms, or residential dwelling units. Shower spray units shall deliver water that is 120 degrees F. maximum temperature.

- Shower thresholds: One-half-inch high thresholds are now allowed in roll-in showers, and 2-inch maximum thresholds are allowed in transfer showers in existing facilities where provision of a 0.5-inch-high threshold would disturb the structural reinforcement of the floor slab.
- Detectable warnings: The revised guidelines only require detectable warnings (truncated domes) at transit platform edges. Detectable warnings for curb ramps, hazardous vehicular areas, and reflecting pools are not covered in the New ADAAG. The Access Board plans to add the detectable warning requirements (new truncated dome design) to future "right-of-way" guidelines currently being developed. The current ADAAG requires the installation of detectable warnings in various locations such as curb ramps.

17.2 AMERICANS WITH DISABILITIES ACT REVIEW

Of particular importance to architects and engineers are Titles III and IV of the ADA. The Department of Justice (DOJ) and the Department of Transportation (DOT) enforce Titles III and IV of the Act throughout the United States with the intention to jump start American Society to being more accessible to people with disabilities. The information provided here is an overview of the types of issues to be reviewed and standard handicap compliance modifications required at a typical facility. Also, prior to conducting an actual survey, it is important to determine and review the handicap building codes currently in effect for the facility. Figure 17.1 shows the typical components that are evaluated for ADA compliance.

1. Accessibility guidelines: The site surrounding the facility should be surveyed during the review for handicap accessibility, and pedestrian and vehicular circulation and layout should be reviewed for unimpeded access to the entrance of the facility. Likewise, the handicap accessibility of the parking area, including the adequacy of location, dimensions, and identification of parking stalls, should be reviewed and recorded. Walkways should provide adequate access between various site areas and the building. These walkways should not be less than 48 inches wide and should not have a slope in excess of 5 percent (a 1-foot rise in 20 feet).

Accessibility is achieved by addressing the requirements of the ADA and other applicable codes as well as state and local regulations. There are essentially three accessibility documents that designers and consultants most frequently use and should be familiar with. These are:

- The ANSI A117.1 was developed by the American National Standards Institute (ANSI), and is one of the first accessibility guidelines to be used in the United States. The latest edition of the ANSI A117.1/ICC is the 1998 edition, which was developed jointly with the International Code Council and the Access Board. This edition has been modified to be more in step with the ADAAG.
- The Americans with Disabilities Act Accessibility Guidelines (ADAAG) was developed by the Architectural and Transportation Barriers Compliance Board (ATBCB or Access Board) as guidelines for ADA legislation. It was based on the 1986 ANSI A117.1, but after the incorporation of additional requirements it became stricter than ANSI. The Access Board is responsible for making revisions to the ADAAG and is currently working with the DOJ on updating the ADAAG.
- The Uniform Federal Accessibility Standards (UFAS) is based on the 1980 ANSI standard and applies mostly to government buildings and organizations that accept federal funding. These buildings are not currently required to conform to ADA regulations.

Although there is not a great deal of difference between them, it is important to know which document applies to the facility being surveyed. It is outside the scope of this book to elaborate on all the requirements of the above accessibility documents. Nevertheless, relevant issues are discussed with illustrations to give the reader a broad understanding and overview of these requirements.

The ADA stipulates that new construction and alterations to existing facilities comply with the ADAAG. For example, a new tenant space within an existing building is now considered by the ADA to be new construction and must comply with the ADAAG. Rules of compliance for alterations and renovations to existing buildings are sometimes complex, and under Title III of the ADA, altered buildings must be made accessible if that is readily achievable. When prevailing conditions prevent barrier removal, a public accommodation has to make its services available through alternative means, such as relocating activities to accessible locations.

Figure 17.1 Typical components to be evaluated for Americans with Disabilities Act (ADA) compliance.

2. Accessible routes: The ADAAG defines an *accessible route* as, "a continuous, unobstructed path connecting all accessible elements and spaces in a building or facility." This includes pathways, corridors, doorways, floors, ramps, elevators, and clear floor space at fixtures. Designing safe and barrier-free accessible routes is essential for people with disabilities, and enhancing their movement is critical to their well being. Likewise, well designed and well placed signage is important in giving direction to people with vision, hearing and mobility limitations. Travel distances should also be taken into consideration, particularly when designing for persons with low stamina capabilities or who use mobility devices.

Adequate corridor width is essential to passage for someone with mobility or vision impairment. The ADAAG puts great emphasis on the provisions for access and egress and clearly delineates the requirements for length, space, lighting signage, and safety measures. Corridors for example, should ideally be a minimum of 42 inches (1065 mm) wide and not more than 75 feet (22.9 m) long. They should be well lit with indirect lighting to prevent glare. Wall finishes should incorporate blends of contrasted colors to increase visual acuity. Figure 17.2A shows minimum width and length requirements stipulated by the Code of Federal Regulations (CFR) for straight hallways. Openings that form part of an accessible route should not be less than 32 inches (815 mm) wide; the minimum passage width for two wheelchairs is 60 inches (1525 mm) as shown in (Figure 17.2B). If an accessible route is less than 60 inches (1525 mm) wide, then passing spaces at least 60 inches by 60 inches must be provided at intervals not to exceed 200 feet (61 m).

The ADAAG stipulates that the minimum clear floor space required to accommodate one stationary wheelchair is 30 inches (762 mm) by 48 inches (1220 mm). For maneuverability, a minimum 60-inch (1525 mm) diameter circle is required for a wheelchair to make one 180-degree turn. In place of this, a T-shaped space may be provided.

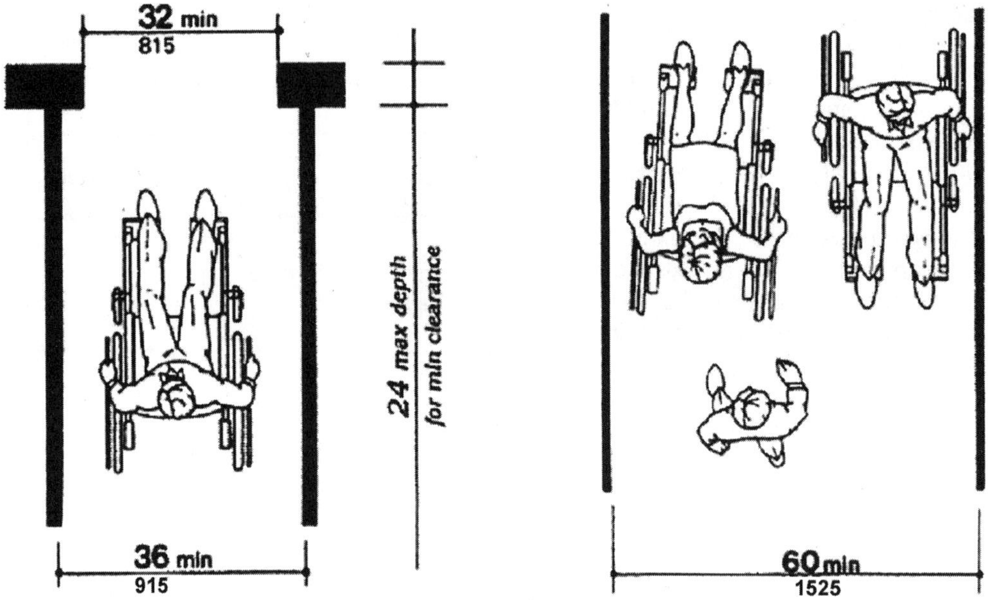

Minimum Clear Width for Single Wheelchair

A

Minimum Clear Width for Two Wheelchairs

B

Figure 17.2 A. Openings in straight hallways should not be less than 32 inches (815 mm) wide *(from 28 CFR Ch.1, Pt. 36, App. A, Fig.1, 7-1-94 Edition)*. B. When an accessible route is less than 60 inches (1525 mm) wide, passing spaces not less than 60 inches × 60 inches must be provided at intervals not exceeding 200 feet or 61 meters *(from 28 CFR Ch.1, Pt. 36, App. A, Fig.2, 7-1-94 Edition)*.

3. Doors and doorways: Doors should have a clear opening width of between 32 (815 mm) and 36 inches (915 mm) when the door is opened at 90 degrees. The maximum depth of a 32 inches wide (815 mm) doorway is 24 inches (610 mm) as shown in Figure 17.3. If the depth exceeds this, then the width must be increased to 36 inches (915 mm). Threshold heights should not exceed 1/2 inch (12.7 mm), and should not contain any sharp slopes or abrupt changes but should be beveled so no slope of the threshold is greater than 1:2. Door closers should not hamper a door's use by the handicapped.

No part of an accessible route may have a slope more than 1:20 (1 inch rise for every 20 inches/508 mm distance). If a slope is greater than this it is classified as a ramp and must meet different requirements, including the handrails provision (Figure 17.4).

Minimum maneuvering clearances are required for wheelchairs at standard swinging doors (that are not automatic or power assisted) to allow easy operation of the latch and to provide for a clear swing. The floor or ground area within the required clearances shall be level and clear for a minimum distance of five feet in the direction of the door swing. When inadequate maneuvering clearance at doors is provided, impaired persons and persons using wheelchairs find opening the door very awkward (Figure 17.5A). Ideally, the opening of an inward opening single door can be facilitated by the provision of a clear wall space to the side of the door handle of about 30 inches (762 mm) as shown in Figure 17.5D. For two hinged or pivoted

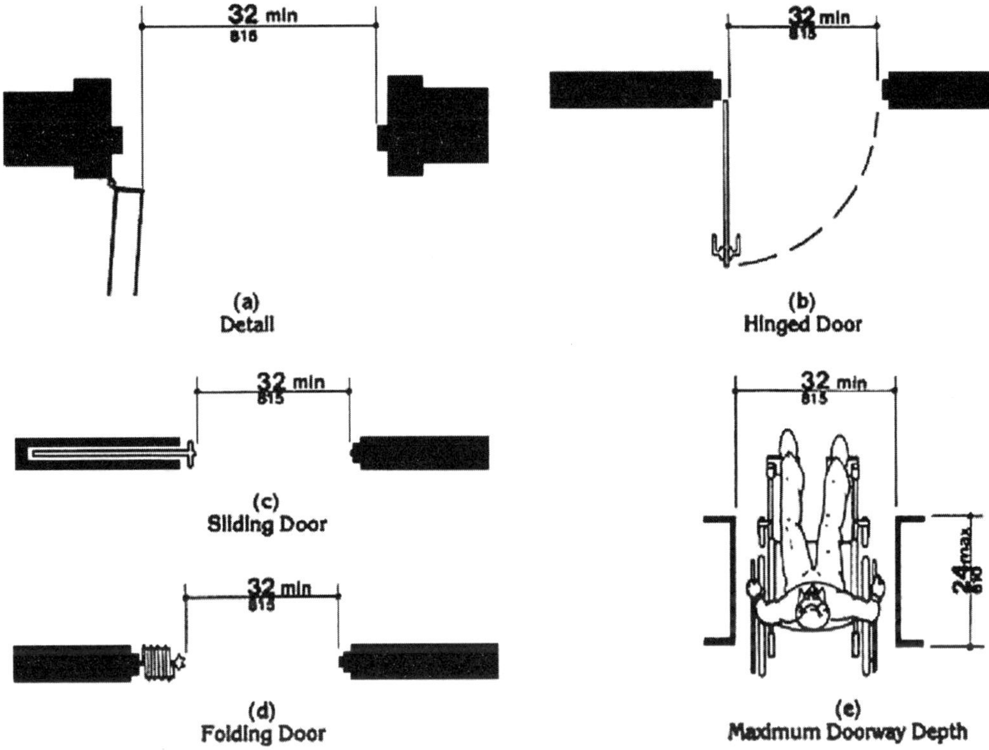

Figure 17.3 Clear doorway width and depth *(from 28 CFR Ch.1, Pt. 36, App. A, Fig.24, 7-1-94 Edition).*

doors in a series, the minimum space is 48 inches (1220 mm) plus the width of any door swinging into the space. Doors in series shall swing either in the same direction or away from the space between the doors.

Where provided, door closers should be adjusted to slow the closing time. The pressure or opening force required to push or pull open interior doors should not exceed 5 lbs (2.27 kg). Pocket doors with push plates are preferable because their swing is not in the direction of a wheelchair user. Automatic openers are useful for making doors accessible when the door opening pressure is excessive or there is insufficient maneuvering clearance on one or both sides of the door. Such automatic or power-assisted doors should comply with relevant codes.

Barrier-free codes also require that door hardware meet certain specifications. Lever handles on doors for disabled people are usually cost effective. All hardware on doors, cabinets and windows should be easy to grasp and operate with one hand, and should not need a tight grip for turning. This includes lever operated and push type mechanisms, and U-shaped handles (Figure 17.6). Standard door knobs do not meet ADA requirements.

Controls should be clearly visible and accessible. Switches and controls for lights, heat, fire alarms, windows, etc., which are often of essential use, should be located no higher than 48 inches (1220 mm) above the floor nor lower than 15 inches (381 mm), as shown in Figure 17.7.

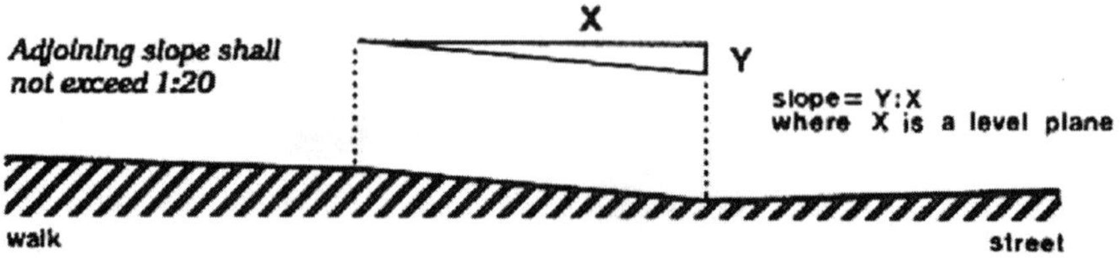

Figure 17.4 The maximum slope of any part of an accessible route is 1:20. If the slope is greater, it is classified as a ramp *(from 28 CFR Ch.1, Pt. 36, App. A, Fig.11, 7-1-94 Edition).*

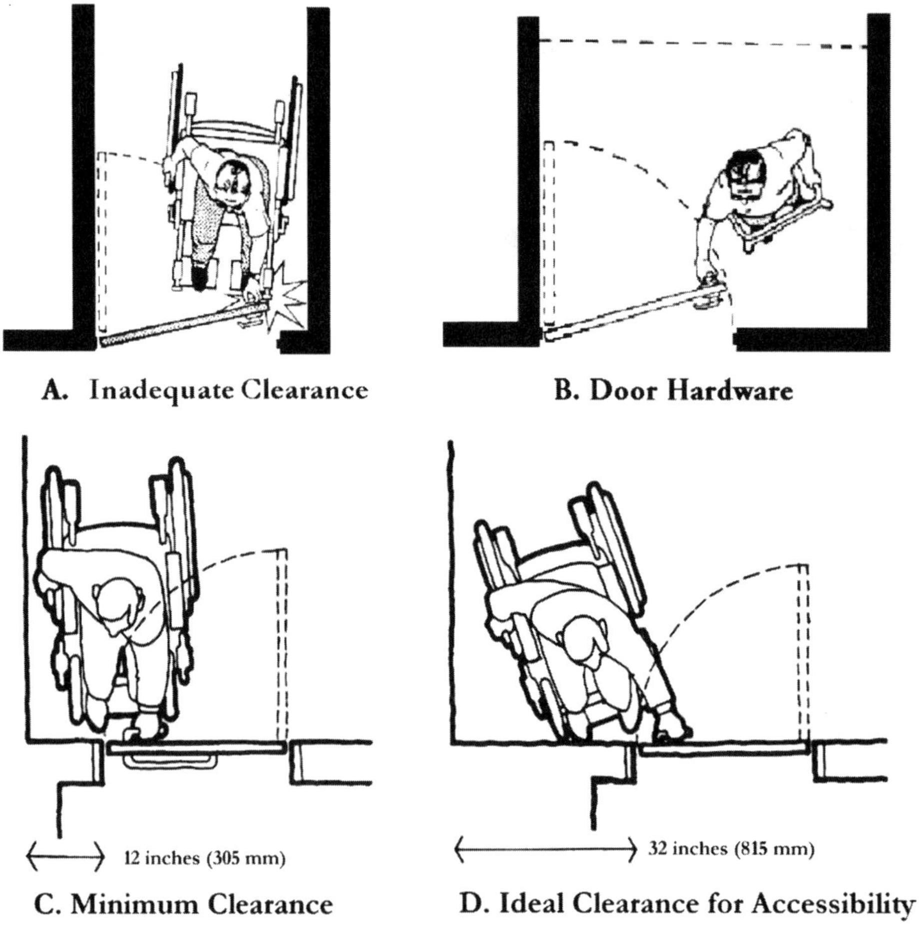

Figure 17.5 A,B,C,D Inadequate clearances can hamper accessibility *(Figure 17.5C and D, courtesy Selwyn Goldsmith, Designing for the Disabled: The New Paradigm, Architectural Press).*

4. Plumbing Fixtures and Public Lavatories

A. Toilet stalls: If toilet stall approach is from the latch side of the stall door, clearance between the door side of the stall and any obstruction may be reduced to a minimum of 42 inches (1065 mm). Many toilet stalls are positioned at the end of a path of travel between the row of stalls and the wall (Figure 17.8). The advantage of using an end toilet for the accessible stall is that the grab bars can be fixed to the wall rather than to a partition, which allows sturdier anchoring to meet minimum strength requirements. In existing buildings that have a multiple-stall toilet room with typical inaccessible stalls, it is usually possible to create an accessible stall by removing one toilet and combining the space of two stalls, providing it continues to meet the local plumbing codes requiring a certain number of fixtures for a given building density.

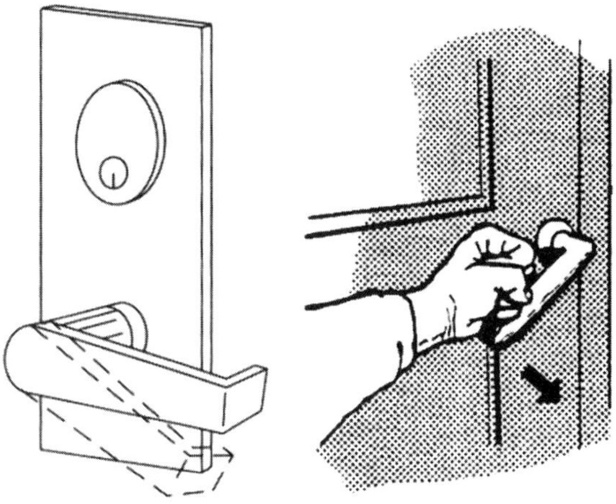

Figure 17.6 Example of Lever-type handle. Door hardware must also comply with ADA codes *(Courtesy Deborah S. Kearney, The ADA in Practice, R.S. Means Company, Inc.).*

Several toilet stall layouts meet ADA requirements. Minimum clearances for standard stall layouts are shown in Figures 17.9A and 17.9B. Toilet rooms as well as toilet stalls must have at minimum a 60-inch (1525 mm) clear internal turning space. However, the clear floor space at fixtures and controls may extend up to 19 inches (483 mm) under a wall-mounted sink. The clearance depth varies depending on whether a wall-hung or floor-mounted water closet (60 inch by 56 inch minimum clear inside dimensions) is used. In most cases, the door must provide at minimum a clear opening of 32 inches (815 mm) and must swing out, away from the stall enclosure. If a stall is less than 60 inches (1525 mm) deep, a 9-inch (225 mm) toe clearance is required under partitions. In planning toilet rooms, a five foot diameter (1525 mm) clear space should be allowed for.

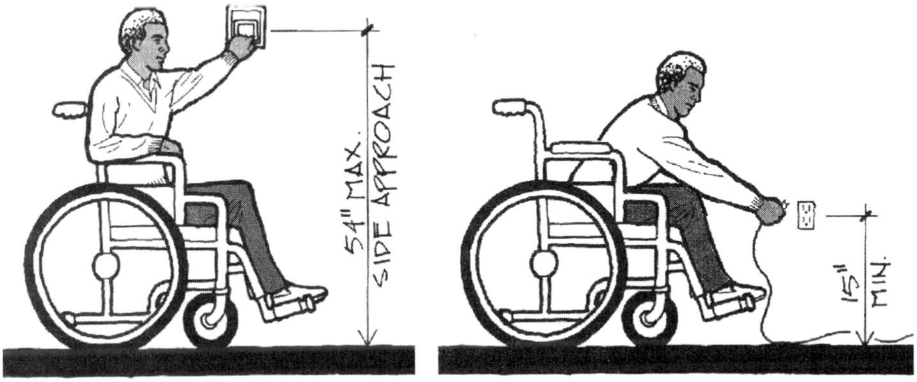

Figure 17.7 Positioning controls to be accessible *(Courtesy Means ADA Compliance Pricing Guide, R.S. Means Company, Inc.).*

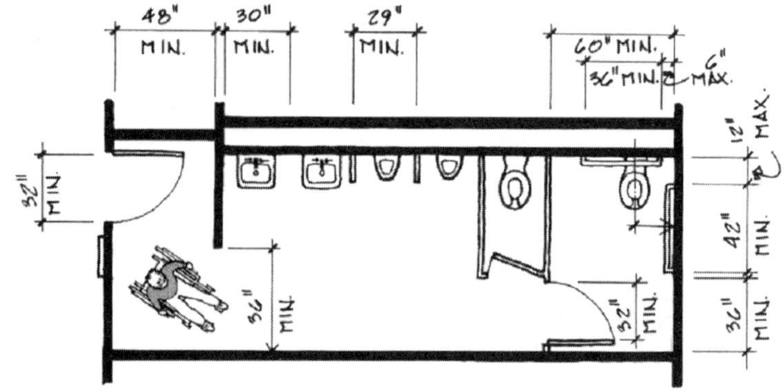

Figure 17.8 An example of a typical end toilet stall *(Courtesy of Means ADA Compliance Pricing Guide, R.S. Means Company, Inc.)*.

Grab bars must also be provided as shown in Figure 17.9A,B, and must be mounted from 33 inches (838 mm) to 36 inches (915 mm) above the finished floor. Grab bars should be a minimum of 42 inches (1065 mm) long at a side wall and 36 inches (915 mm) long minimum at a rear wall. It should have a diameter of 1.5 inches (38 mm), and be not more than 1.5 inches (38 mm) from the wall. In many toilets there is a lateral space to the side of the water closet, which only allows provision of a side horizontal rail. Toilet paper dispensers are to be located below the grab bar, a minimum of 19 inches (483) above the finished floor.

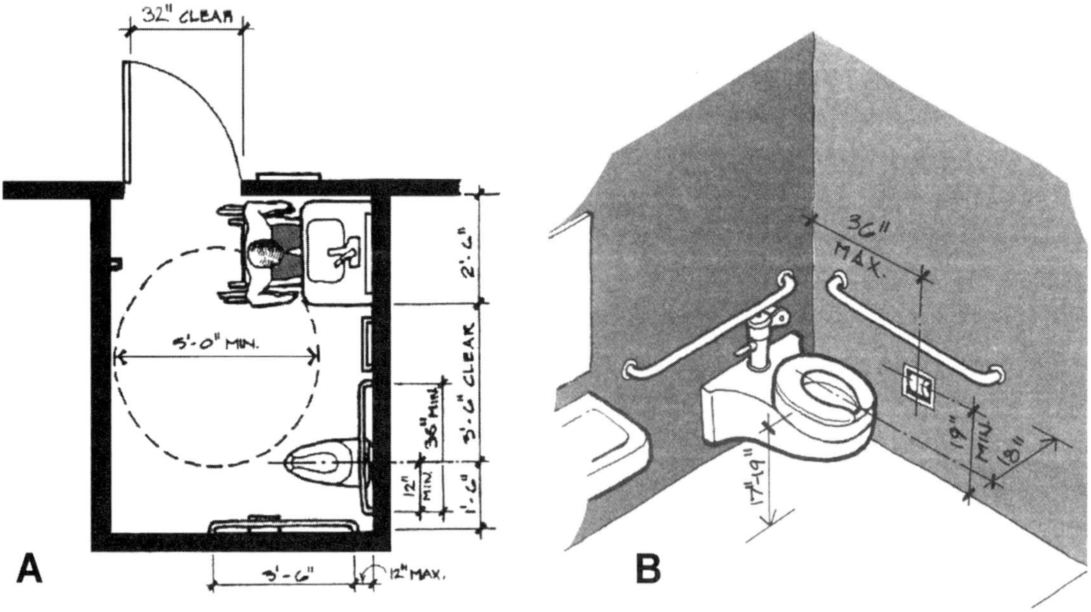

Figure 17.9 A, B Minimum ADA toilet and stall configurations *(Courtesy of Means ADA Compliance Pricing Guide, R.S. Means Company, Inc.)*.

In the absence of toilet stalls, the centerline of the toilet must still be 18 inches (455 mm) from a wall with back and side grab bars. A clear space should be provided in front of and to the side of open water closets.

B. Urinals: Where urinals are installed, the stall type or wall-mounted urinals must be used with an elongated rim no more than 17 inches (430 mm) above the floor. A clear floor space of 30 inches (762 mm) by 48 inches (1220 mm) must be provided in front of the urinal. This space may adjoin or overlap an accessible route.

C. Lavatories: The Code of Federal Regulations (CFR) stipulates that public lavatories must allow wheelchair users to move under the sink and easily use the basin and water controls (Figure 17.10). Notice that because of these clearances wall-mounted lavatories are the best type to use when accessibility is a concern. Any exposed piping below the lavatory must be insulated or otherwise protected. ADAAG makes a distinction between lavatories, which are basins for hand washing, and sinks, which are other types of basins. Faucets must be easy to operate with one hand without tight grasping, or twisting of the wrist. Lever-operated, push-type, and automatically controlled mechanisms are acceptable.

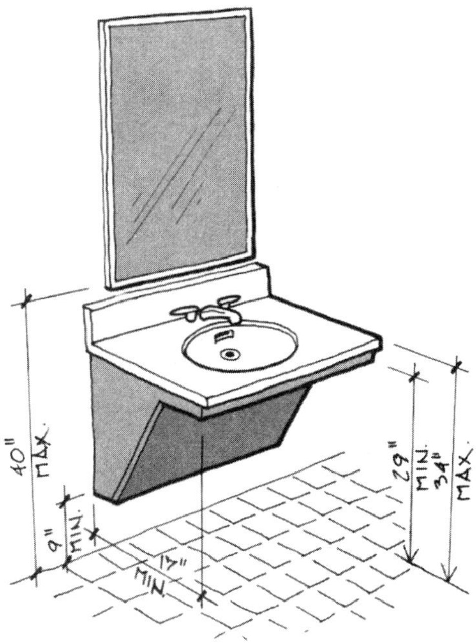

Figure 17.10 Typical accessible lavatory dimensions *(from 28 CFR Ch.1, Pt. 36, App. A, Fig.31/Fig.32, 7-1-94 Edition).*

At least one mirror must be accessible with the bottom edge of the reflecting surface mounted no higher than 40 inches (1015 mm) above the floor, and should preferably be tilted for reflectance.

D. Residential bathrooms: Private residences are not typically subject to Title III of the ADA requirements; nevertheless, consultants should familiarize themselves with such requirements so as to be able to serve their clients better. In Figure 17.11A we see a typical ADA compliant residential bathroom in a senior living complex. Figure 17.11B illustrates a prefabricated shower unit with strong grab bars in the shower, installed at different heights, along with a hand-held showerhead. These reflect some of the essentials of the accessible bathroom in the home.

E. Water fountains and coolers: Drinking water should be accessible with up-front spouts and controls that can be either hand or floor-operated. Accessible height should not exceed 36 inches (915 mm), and an alcove recess should not be less than 30 inches (762 mm) wide. Drinking fountains that are free-standing or built in without a clear space below must maintain a clear floor space in front not less than 30 inches (762 mm) by 48 inches (1220 mm), to allow a parallel approach to the unit by a person in a wheelchair.

Where only one drinking fountain is provided per floor, it should be accessible to people using wheelchairs, as well as persons who have difficulty bending or stooping. This can be resolved by the use of a "hi-lo" type fountain, whereby one fountain is at a low level and accessible to those using wheelchairs, and another is at the standard height for those who have difficulty bending.

5. Stairs and ramps: Ramps should be installed as needed in areas of pedestrian access level changes. They are required to provide a smooth transition between changes in elevation for both wheelchair-bound persons as well as those whose mobility is otherwise restricted. In general, designers should

Figure 17.11 A. Typical accessible bathroom in a senior living complex in Maryland, U.S.A. B. Prefabricated shower unit with strong grab bars *(Courtesy Charles A. Riley II)*.

use the least possible slope, but in no case should a ramp have a slope greater than 1:12 (1 inch in rise for every 12 inches in run). The maximum rise for any ramp is typically limited to 30 inches (762 mm) after which a level landing is required. A slope of up to 1:8 is permitted if the maximum rise does not exceed 3 inches (76 mm). In all cases a non-skid surface should be in place to enable traction in inclement weather.

A ramp's clear width must not be less than 36 inches, with landings that are at least as wide as the widest segment of the ramp leading to them. Landing lengths must not be less than 60 inches (1525 mm), and if ramps change direction at a landing, the landing must be at least 60 inches square (Figure 17.12).

Handrails on both sides of ramps are to be incorporated where the ramps have a rise greater than 6 inches (152 mm) or lengths exceeding 72 inches (1825 mm). The top of the handrail should be from 34 (864 mm) to 38 inches (965 mm) above the ramp surface. Handrails must extend at least 12 inches (305 mm) beyond the top and bottom of the ramp segment, and a diameter or width of gripping surface from 1 1/4 inches (32 mm) to 1 1/2 inches (38 mm) is required for both ramps and stairs. Notice that the New ADAAG handrail guidelines are more flexible than the current guidelines (Figure 17.13A,B).

The stairways should provide accessibility between building floors, and when these stairs are not connected by an elevator, they must be designed according to certain standards specifying the configuration of treads, risers, nosings, and handrails. The maximum riser height is 7 inches (178 mm), and the treads must be a minimum of 11 inches (280 mm) as measured from riser to riser. Open risers are not permitted. The undersides of the nosings must not be abrupt and must conform to one of the styles shown in Figure 17.14. Stairway users are more likely to stumble or fall while going down stairs than when going up. Tread depth is pivotal in stair design. Typically when climbing stairs, users place only part of their foot on the tread, whereas when descending, the whole foot or most of the foot is placed on the tread.

Stairway handrails must be continuous on both sides of the stairs. The inside handrail on switchback or dogleg stairs must always be continuous as it changes direction. Other handrails must extend beyond the top and bottom riser. A handrail's top gripping surface must be between 34 (864 mm) and 38 inches

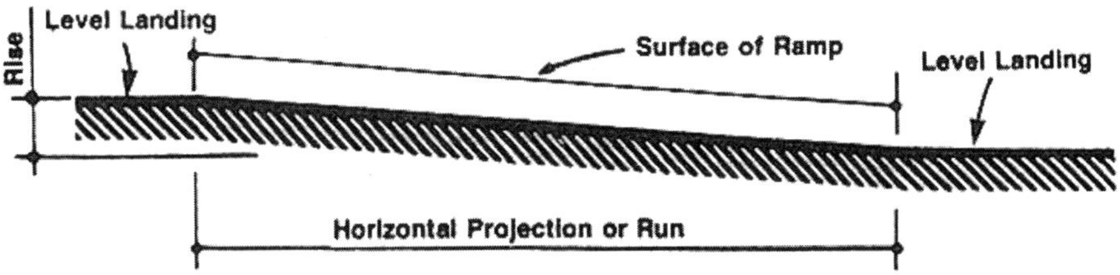

	Maximum Rise		Maximum Horizontal Projection	
Slope	in	mm	ft	m
1:12 to < 1:16	30	760	30	9
1:16 to < 1:20	30	760	40	12

Components of a Single Ramp Run and Sample Ramp Dimensions

Figure 17.12 Ramp dimensions *(from 28 CFR Ch.1, Pt. 36, App. A, Fig.16, 7-1-94 Edition).*

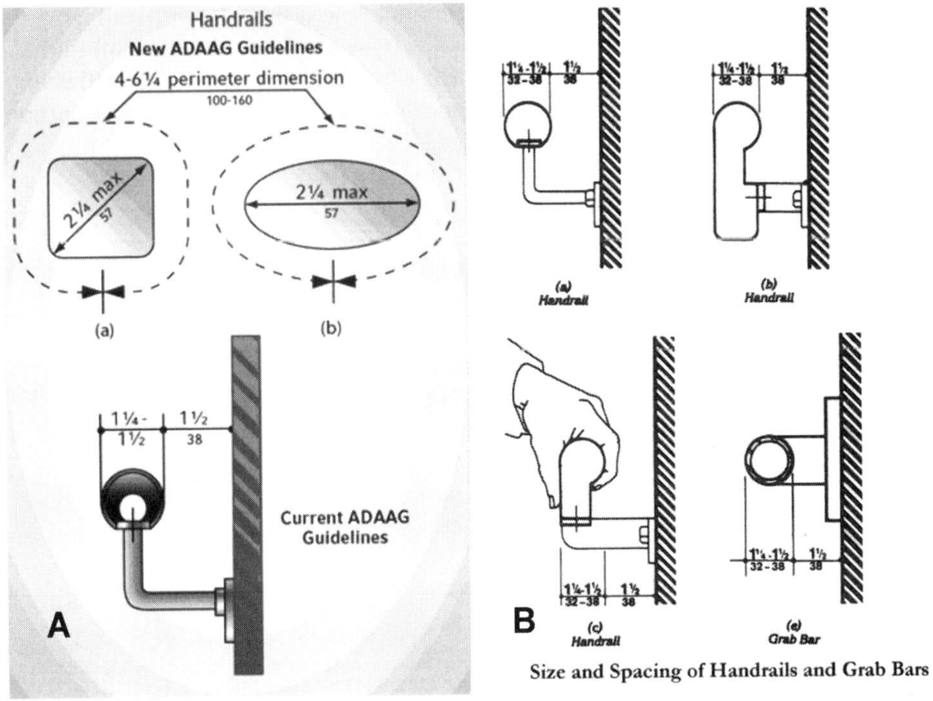

Figure 17.13 A,B New and current handrail requirements for ramps and stairs *(New ADAAG, courtesy Gerald J. Morgan; current ADA guidelines from 28 CFR Ch.1, Pt. 36, App. A, Fig.39, 7-1-94 Edition).*

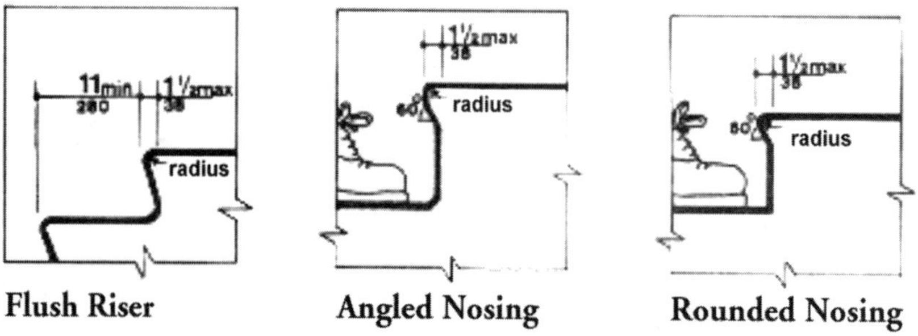

Figure 17.14 Tread and Nosing requirements *(from 28 CFR Ch.1, Pt. 36, App. A, Fig.18, 7-1-94 Edition).*

(965 mm) above stair nosings. In addition, handrails must have a diameter or width of gripping surface of between 1 1/4 inches (32 mm) and 1 1/2 inches (38 mm). There must also be a clear space between the handrail and the wall of at least 1 1/2 inches (38 mm) as shown in Figure 17.13A,B.

6. Floor surfaces and tactile pavings (detectable warnings): Floor finishes in a facility must be firm and slip-resistant and should provide easy access throughout the building. If there is a change in level, the transition must meet the following requirements. If the change is less than 1/4 inch (6.4 mm), it may be vertical and without edge treatment. If the change in level is between 1/4 inch (6.4 mm) and 1/2 inch (12.7 mm), it must be beveled and its slope no greater than 1:2. Changes greater than 1/2 inch changes the classification to a ramp, which must then meet the requirements outlined in the previous section. Bathroom floors should have a non-slip finish.

Carpet must have a firm cushion or backing or no cushion and have a level loop, textured loop, level-cut pile, or level-cut/uncut pile texture, and its pile must not exceed 1/2 inch (12.7 mm) in height. Carpet must be securely attached to the floor and all exposed edges concealed with a trim along its length.

Detectable warning surfaces are required for areas in front of stairs, hazardous vehicular areas, and other places where a hazard may exist in the absence of a guardrail or other method of warning someone. The surface must be a textured surface that contrasts with its surrounds, like exposed aggregate concrete, cushioned surfaces of rubber or plastic, raised strips, or grooves.

Door handles are also required to have a textured surface if they are part of a door that leads to an area that might prove dangerous to a blind person, including doors to loading platforms, boiler rooms, and stages.

7. Public telephones: Telephones are one of the easiest building elements to make accessible. They should be positioned so that they can be reached by person(s) in a wheelchair. Accessible telephones may be de-

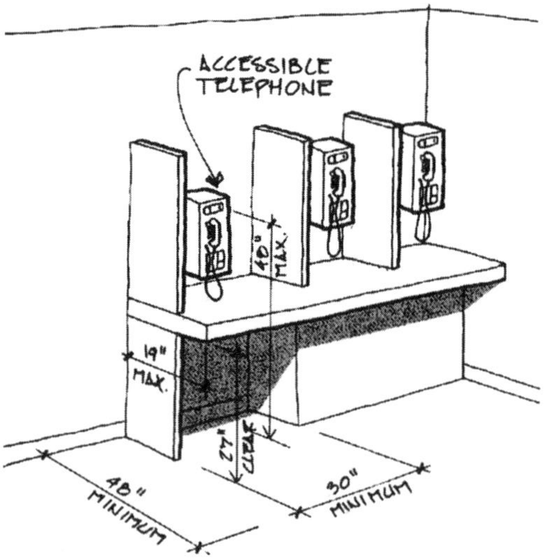

Figure 17.15 Accessible public telephone *(Courtesy Means ADA Compliance Pricing Guide, R.S. Means Company, Inc.).*

signed for either front or side access. In either case a clear floor space of not less than 30 inches (762 mm) by 48 inches (1220 mm) is to be provided. Telephones should have pushbutton controls and telephone directories that are accessible by a person in a wheelchair (Figures 17.15).

Title III stipulates that in new construction at least one TTY is to be provided inside any building that has four or more public pay telephones (counting both interior and exterior phones). A TTY must also be provided whenever there is an interior public pay phone in a stadium, convention center, hotel with a convention center, covered shopping mall, or hospital emergency, recovery, or waiting room. Title III also stipulates that one accessible public phone must be provided for each floor of new construction, unless the floor has two or more banks of phones, in which case one accessible phone should be provided for each bank.

8. Protruding objects: There are restrictions on objects and building elements that project into corridors and other walkways because protruding objects present a hazard for visually impaired people. These restrictions are shown in Figure 17.16, and are based on the needs of people with severe vision impairments walking with a cane. There are no restrictions on protruding objects where their lower edge is less than 27 inches (686 mm) above the floor because these can be detected by a person using a cane. However, protruding objects cannot reduce the clear width required for an accessible route or maneuvering space, and a guardrail or other barrier must be provided in areas adjacent to accessible routes where the vertical clearance is reduced to less than 80 inches (2 m).

9. Signage and alarms: Signage with emergency information and general circulation directions should give clear guidance for visually impaired people. Of importance in evaluating signage criteria is the ability to be viewed by people with low vision (i.e. 20 percent of normal) from a distance of 30 feet (9.14 m). Signage is also required for elevators and handicap accessible entrances/exits, handicap accessible toilets, and other handicap accessible provisions. For optimum clarity, adequate luminescence should be provided. Contrasted colors can also enhance legibility (70 percent or more contrast between letters and background is recommended).

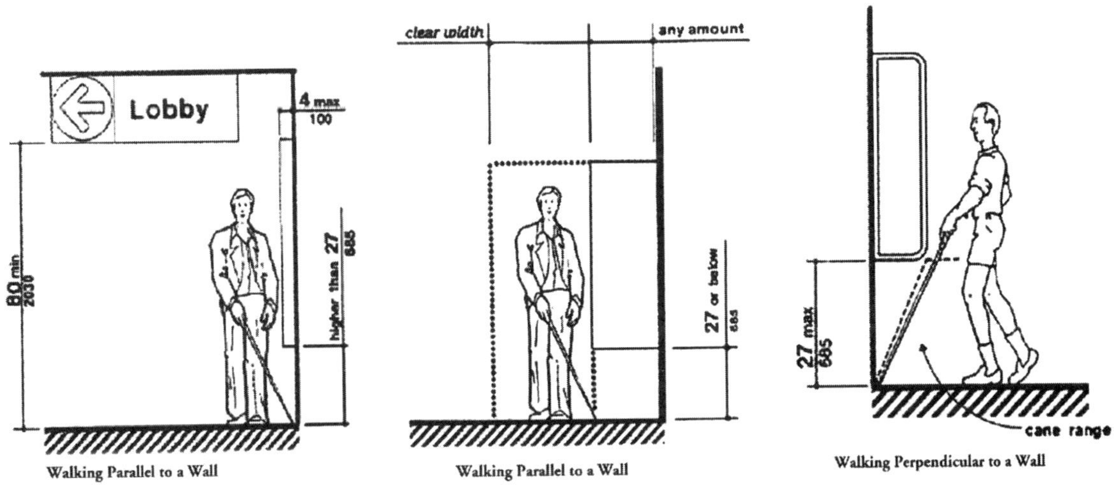

Figure 17.16 Objects should not protrude more than 4 inches (100 mm) into walks, corridors, or passageways *(from 28 CFR Ch.1, Pt. 36, App. A, Fig.8, 7-1-94 Edition).*

The ANSI standards specify the width-to-height ratio of letters and how thick the individual letter strokes must be. They also require that characters, symbols, or pictographs on tactile signs be raised 1/32 inch (0.79 mm). If accessible facilities are identified, the international symbol of accessibility must be used (Figure 17.17). Braille characters must be Grade 2.

The ADA Accessibility Guidelines 4.1.3(14) state that,

> *"If emergency warning systems are provided, then they shall include both audible alarms and visual alarms complying with 4.28. Audible alarms must produce a sound that exceeds the prevailing sound level in the room or space by at least 15 decibels. Visual alarms must be flashing lights that have a flashing frequency of about one cycle per second. Sleeping accommodations required to comply with 9.3 shall have an alarm system complying with 4.28. Emergency warning systems in medical care facilities may be modified to suit standard health care alarm design practice."*

10. Elevators and elevator cars: All elevators shall be accessible from the entry route and all public floors, and shall comply with the applicable codes for elevators and escalators. Elevators must be provided with handrails fixed 32 inches above the floor, on all three sides of the cab. Minimum cab size should be 67 inches (1.7 m) to allow a wheelchair to maneuver (Figure 17.18A,B). Both visual and audible hall signals are important to inform elevator passengers where an elevator is and in which direction it is going. This is particularly important at elevator banks with more than one car. Elevator controls should comply with ANSI A117.1 standards regarding visual, tactile and audible controls (Figure 17.19).

11. Miscellaneous issues: Theater seating: Theater design takes into account many factors, including sight lines, acoustics, maximizing seating, and fire considerations. Traditionally, however, accessibility has not been a major element in the design process, and integrating accessible seating into existing theaters has often been overlooked. Yet it is of paramount importance to make these public facilities accessible and compliant (Figure 17.20A,B).

Dining and seating: In new construction, dining areas, loggias, and outdoor seating areas are required to be accessible. Dining areas are often designed to maximize seating capacity, and access may not be a prime consideration. Where dining areas are on an accessible route, it is usually possible to create accessible seating and accessible services without major alter-

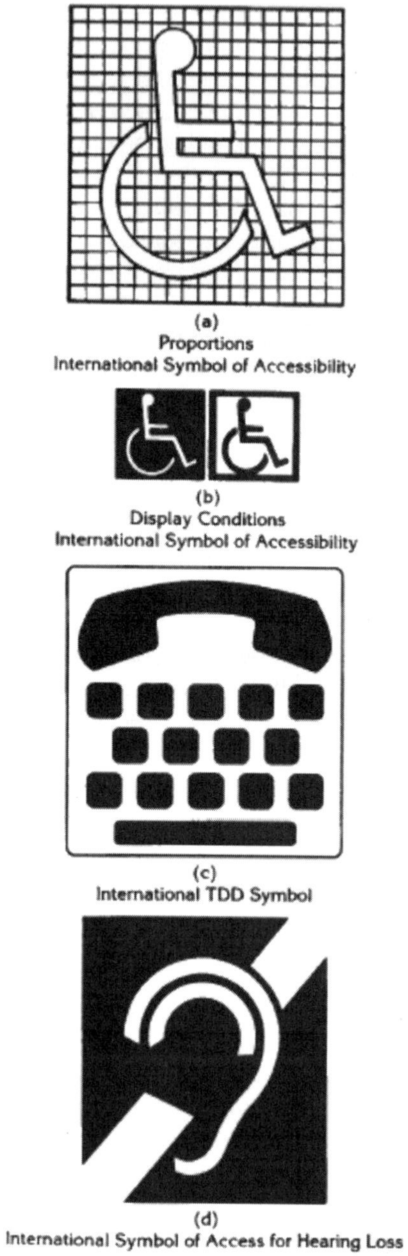

International Symbols

Figure 17.17 International symbols for accessibility *(from 28 CFR Ch.1, Pt. 36, App. A, Fig.43, 7-1-94 Edition).*

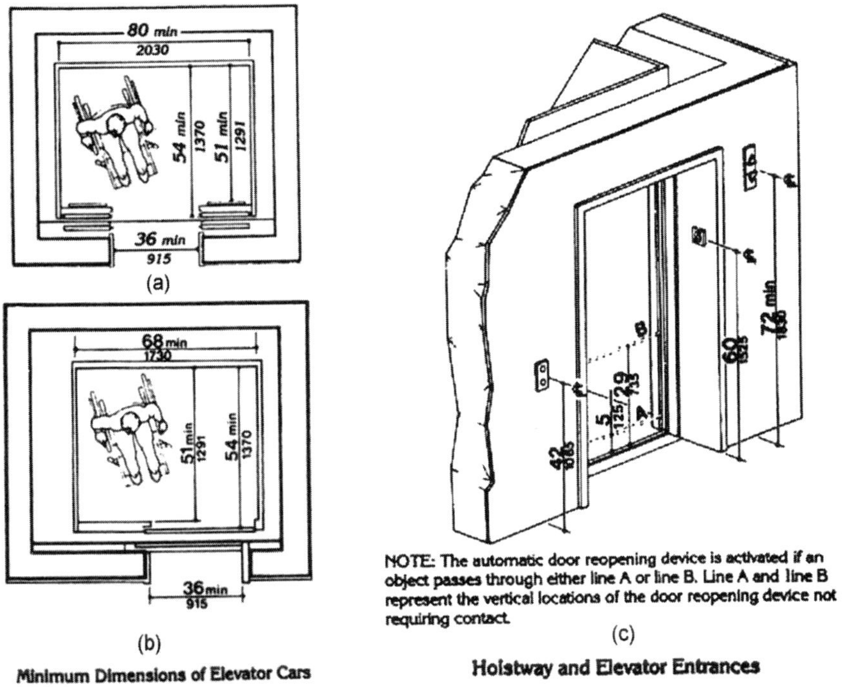

Figure 17.18 A,B,C Minimum dimensions for elevator cabs *(from 28 CFR Ch.1, Pt. 36, App. A, Fig.22, 20, 7-1-94 Edition).*

Figure 17.19 Elevator hall signals *(Courtesy Means ADA Compliance Pricing Guide, R.S. Means Company, Inc.).*

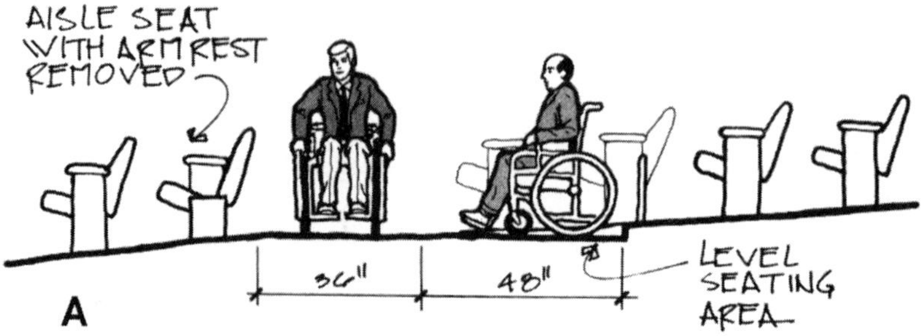

Figure 17.20 A Accessible theater seating dimensions *(Courtesy Means ADA Compliance Pricing Guide, R.S. Means Company, Inc.).*

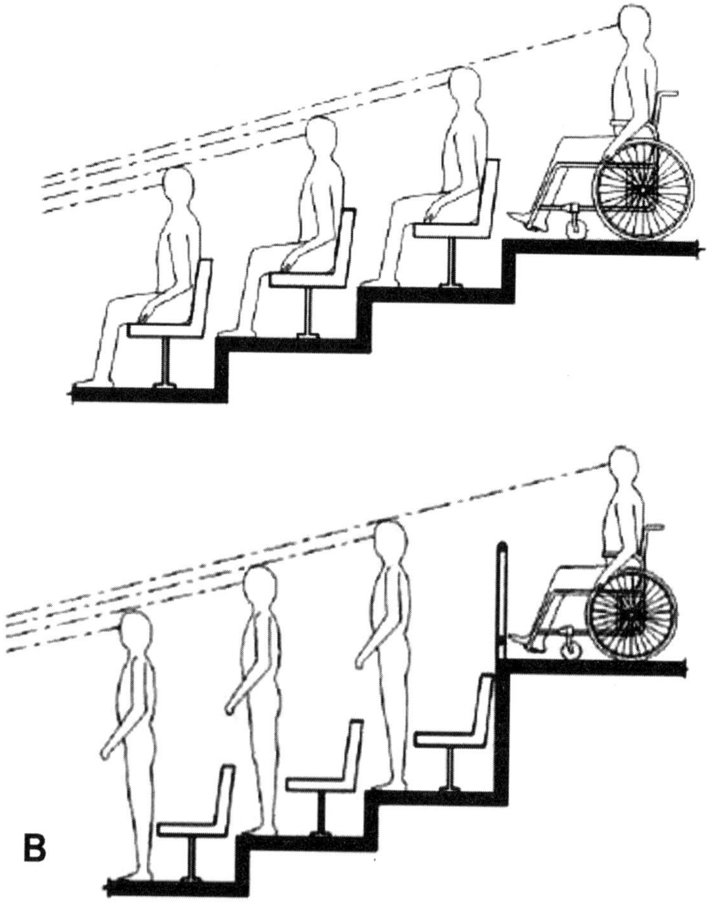

Figure 17.20 B New ADAAG guidelines—lines of sight over seated and standing spectators *(Courtesy Gerald J. Morgan).*

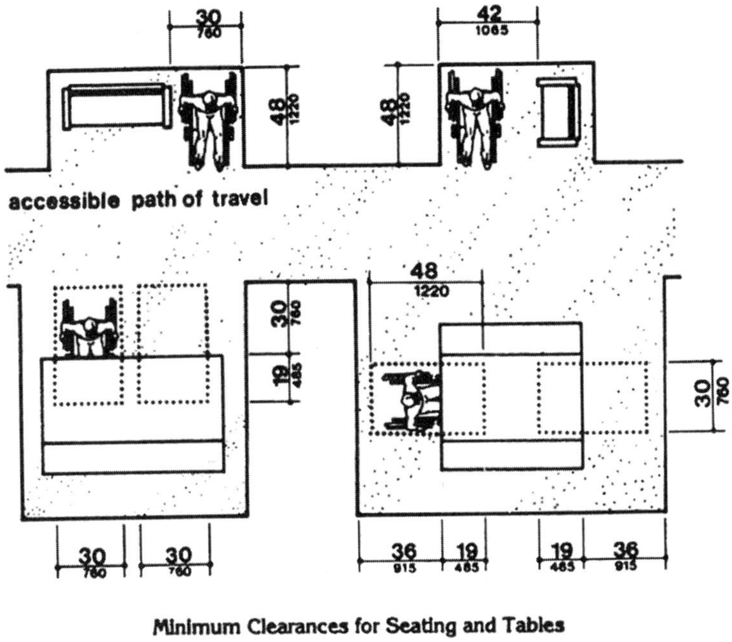

Figure 17.21 Accessible seating in dining areas and restaurants *(from 28 CFR Ch.1, Pt. 36, App. A, Fig.45, 7-1-94 Edition).*

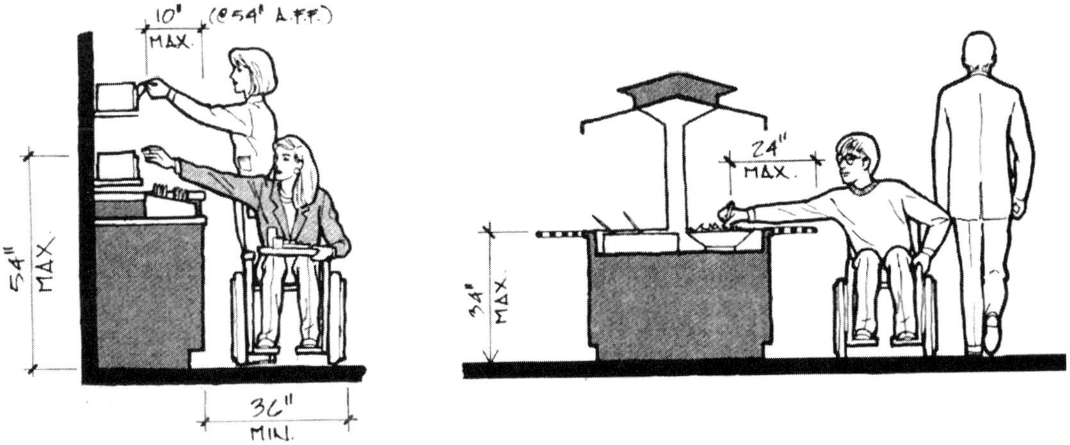

Figure 17.22 Accessible food counters and salad bars *(Courtesy Means ADA Compliance Pricing Guide, R.S. Means Company, Inc.).*

ations to the space. A clear 36-inch (915 mm) path of travel is required with slip-resistant floor surfaces.

Fixed or built-in seating or tables are required to comply with 4.32.2 through 4.32.4 of ADAAG (Figure 17.21). Tops of accessible tables and counters shall be from 28 inches to 34 inches (710 mm to 865 mm) above the finish floor level. Adequate clear floor space below the tables is also required (30 inches/762 mm × 48 inches/1220 mm), with 19 inches (485 mm) under table space. Figure 17.22 shows accessible food counters and salad bar requirements.

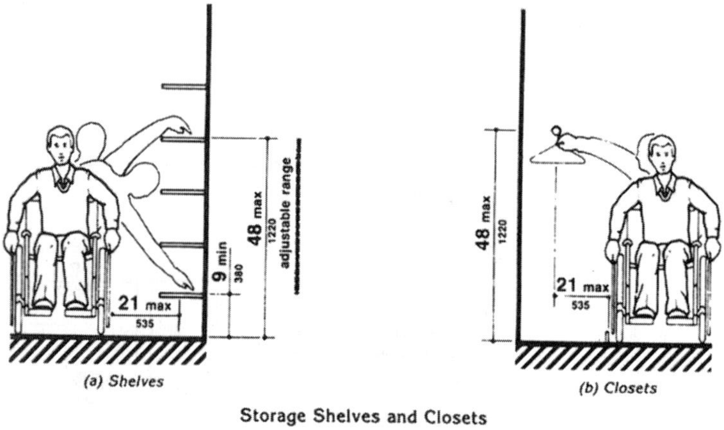

Figure 17.23 Storage shelves and closets *(from 28 CFR Ch.1, Pt. 36, App. A, Fig.38, 7-1-94 Edition).*

Space allowances and reach ranges: Various interior fixtures and equipment should be handicap accessible. The ADA mandates rights for people with disabilities, and a very significant portion of the provisions prescribed in its accessibility guidelines (ADAAG) are geared to facilitate accessibility by wheelchair users. This is why it is imperative to understand and familiarize oneself with the dimensions and characteristics of a typical adult wheelchair.

According to the ADA Standards for Accessible Design, "fixed storage facilities such as cabinets, shelves, closets, and drawers are required to be accessible" as shown in Figure 17.23. It is further stipulated that storage facilities provide a clear floor space of not less than 30 inches by 48 inches (762 mm by 1200 mm), to permit either a forward or parallel approach by a person using a wheelchair.

The maximum height for fixtures and fittings is generally 54 inches (1370 mm) prior to 1996 for unobstructed situations, and 46 inches (1170 mm) for side reach over an obstruction. In 1996 the 54 inches was reduced to 48 inches (1200 mm) in response to representations from national organizations for people of short stature. The eye level of disabled persons (including chair-bound persons) is another factor that must be taken into consideration, particularly when designing or positioning signage, displaying goods, positioning lift controls, etc. (Figure 17.24).

Transient lodging facilities: The ADA Guidelines stipulate that transient lodging facilities must comply with applicable requirements, and such facilities are to provide accessible sleeping rooms in the ratios stipulated in ADAAG; this depends on the size and nature of the facility. Factors to keep in mind when surveying such a facility include the following:

- The entrance into the facility should be clearly demarcated by appearance, signage, and access, and should be located on an accessible route.
- Adequate lighting should illuminate the entrance into the facility.
- Flush transitions from driveways to pavements are essential to facilitate transfer from the street to the pavement and to assist in unloading of luggage.
- Outdoor walkways should consist of smooth but non-slip surfaces.
- Elevators should have a 20 second time delay on door closing to facilitate access.
- Public spaces should provide a variety of seating options.

- Spaces should be flexible to allow reconfiguration or to add or remove furnishings or equipment.
- Controls should be easy to operate with limited hand function.
- Circulation routes should be well organized with clear signage to exits and functions.
- Guestrooms and guest bathrooms should have adequate widths for maneuverability (Figure 17.25). Critical to guest bathrooms is the ability to maneuver between the toilet, lavatory, and bathing areas.
- Emergency signal systems (visual and auditory) with visual alarms that flash in conjunction with other building emergency systems must meet ADA requirements.
- At least one of each type of storage (i.e., shelves, drawers, closets) should be accessible to ADA standards).

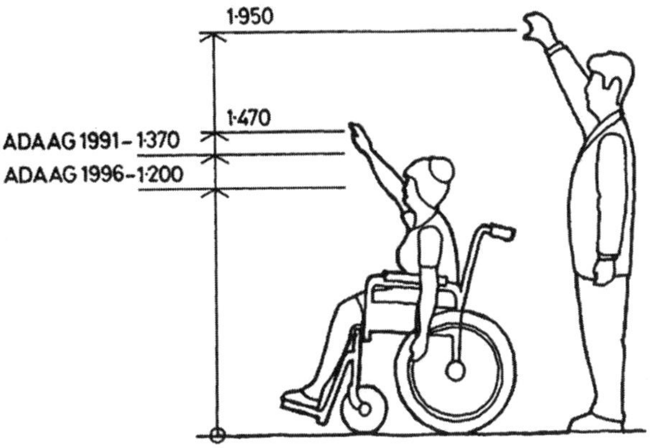

Figure 17.24 Height considerations when designing for the disabled *(Courtesy Selwyn Goldsmith, Designing for the Disabled, The New Paradigm, Architectural Press)*.

Finally, consultants are advised to keep abreast of the new ADAAG requirements as they are issued. Compliance requirements with ADAAG are usually clearly stated. However, when additional information or clarification is needed, help can be received from the Access Board's web site at: www.access-board.gov.

17.3 TYPICAL DEFICIENCIES

Since accessibility regulations have only been in effect for two or three decades, many older buildings lack adequate provisions for the handicapped. Furthermore, in many facilities the handicap retrofit work is done in a piecemeal fashion, with incomplete provisions. Therefore, during a survey for handicap accessibility, two general issues need to be addressed. The first is whether handicap provisions exist at all, and the second is whether the provisions that do exist are in compliance with ADA requirements.

Whether provisions exist will be evident upon general review of the property, and the recommendations borne out of such review are fairly straightforward. The facility will either have signage at the parking stalls or not. The restrooms will either be ADA compliant or not. If no signage exists, some should be installed. If fixtures are not handicap accessible, they should simply be replaced by handicap modified ones.

A detailed evaluation of a facility will help determine whether the handicap accessibility provisions at the facility are adequate. Features such as ramps, railings, or equipment should be measured against standard recommended heights and features, based on the building codes in effect at the property. Sometimes a ramp has been installed but has excessive slope or the retrofit of a restroom lacks sufficient handrails or door widths. In many cases, full compliance is cost-prohibitive or would require significant modification to the building. Thus, variances are often granted to building owners who remodel older facilities but cannot reasonably comply with the handicap regulations in force. The field observer should review this issue with the facility representative to see if this is the case prior to issuing a report with extensive handicap recommendations.

17.4 SYSTEM DIAGNOSTICS

Evaluation for handicap accessibility can be considered an adjunct to both the review of the building codes and building systems. It is not uncommon to discover that within the same facility, some building details and components are accessible to the handicapped while others are not. A thorough review of the facility will identify areas and components that, if modified or replaced, would provide consistent and adequate handicap accessibility.

While the review can be performed at the same time as the review of either the interior or the site, an evaluation for handicap accessibility is best performed as a single walk-through. Each of the ADA-related site components, including the parking, signage, ramps, and building entry, should be reviewed and evaluated. Then, each of the interior components should be addressed. In this way, all components of accessibility will be addressed thoroughly and consistently.

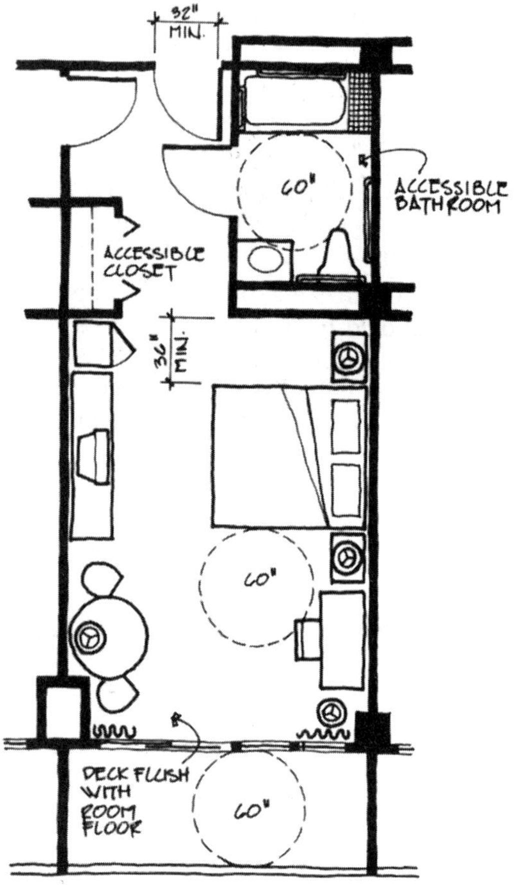

Figure 17.25 Requirements for an accessible sleeping room *(Courtesy Means ADA Compliance Pricing Guide, R.S. Means Company, Inc.).*

Compared to many systems evaluated at a facility, evaluation for handicap accessibility uses relatively simple tools. Even so, the state of handicap accessibility at a facility is one of the more time-consuming issues to review, depending upon the depth of the evaluation performed. Complete verification of the accessibility of construction conditions requires measurement of each ramp, stairway, entrance door and designated fixture.

The tools utilized in a handicap accessibility survey would include a level, a force meter and a tape measure. An ordinary level is valuable in reviewing handicap accessibility to quickly determine adequacy of slope on pedestrian surfaces and wheelchair ramps. Levels 12 inches in length work quite well and should be used in at least two locations on each ramp to verify the consistency of slope. A tape measure is another important tool used to determine adequacy of handicap provisions. This can be used in place of a level with the slope being calculated by measuring distance and length. A force meter will determine the degree of force required to open and close doors.

CHAPTER

18

Life Safety Systems

18.1 GENERAL

Planning for fire protection involves an integrated approach in which system designers need to analyze building components as a total package. To achieve the most beneficial symbiosis between these components, an experienced system designer, such as a fire-protection engineer, should be involved in the early stages of the planning and design process.

It is often argued that the life safety system is the most important system to be evaluated in a facility. Since the purpose of the system is to safeguard the building and its occupants, the condition assessment of this system is important to an accurate overall evaluation of a facility. The various components of modern fire-protection systems should work together to effectively detect, contain, control, and/or extinguish a fire in its early stages—and should be able to survive during the fire.

The complexity of the life safety system varies with the type, size, and use of a facility. In some smaller structures, smoke detectors and fire extinguishers compose the system. In others, a complete fire suppression system, such as the fire sprinklers, is installed throughout the facility. An important aspect of the evaluation of any life safety system includes verification of periodic maintenance, inspection and testing of the main components of the system.

As indicated in Figure 18.1, there are several types of life safety systems employed to address fire safety requirements. Each of these gives rise to its own set of issues that must be considered in facility surveys. The extent of a life safety system survey and the expertise required to perform such an evaluation vary greatly from facility to facility.

Code compliance is the first objective in any design. Codes are legal minimum requirements; you have to meet the minimum with any design, and fire codes can vary substantially from one jurisdiction to another.

According to Frank Monikowski and Terry Victor of SimplexGrinnell, some of the advances and emerging technologies that can be found in today's life safety systems include:

- Control mode sprinklers—These are standard manufactured sprinklers that limit fire spread and stunt high heat release rather than extinguish a fire; they also "pre-wet" adjacent combustibles.

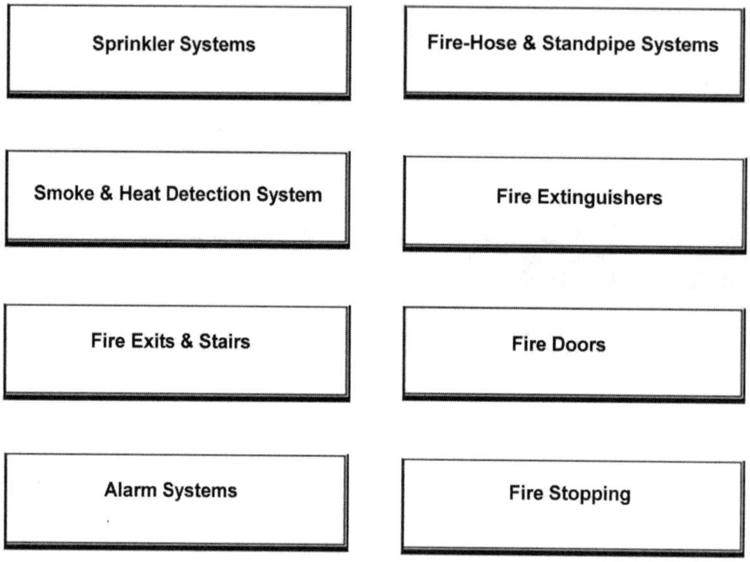

Figure 18.1 Typical life safety systems components.

- Suppression sprinklers—These sprinklers operate quickly for high-challenge fires, and are expected to extinguish a fire by releasing a high density of water directly to the base of the fire.
- Fast-response sprinklers—These provide quicker response than standard systems and are now required for all light-hazard installations.
- Residential sprinklers—Sprinklers designed specifically to increase the survivability of an individual who is in the room where a fire originates.
- Extended coverage sprinklers—Sprinklers designed to reduce the number of sprinklers needed to protect a given area. These come in quick-response, residential, and standard-response types, and are also available for both light- and ordinary-hazard occupancies.
- Special sprinklers, such as Early Suppression Fast Response (ESFR)—These systems are designed for high-challenge rack storage and high-pile storage fires. In most cases, these sprinklers can eliminate the expense and resources needed to install in-rack sprinkler heads.
- Low-pressure sprinklers—These provide needed water coverage in multi-story buildings where pressure may be reduced. These low-pressure sprinklers bring a number of benefits: reduced pipe size, reduction or elimination of a fire pump, and overall cost savings.
- Low-profile, decorator, and concealed sprinklers—These sprinklers are designed to be more aesthetically pleasing.
- Sprinkler system valves that are smaller, lighter, and easier to install and maintain and, therefore, less costly
- A fluid delivery time computer program that simulates water flowing through a dry system in order to accurately predict critical "water-to-fire" delivery time for dry-pipe systems

- The use of cost-efficient CPVC piping for light-hazard and residential sprinkler systems
- Advanced coatings on steel pipes, designed to resist or reduce Microbiologically Influenced Corrosion (MIC) and to enhance sprinkler system life
- Corrosion monitoring devices to alert users of potential problems
- More efficient coordination in evaluating building sprinkler system need, including site surveys, accurate measurements, and the use of CAD and hydraulics software to ensure that fire sprinkler system designs respond to the specific risks and the physical layout of the premises.

A new *Emergency Evacuation Planning Guide for People with Disabilities* was developed and recently issued by the National Fire Protection Association (NFPA). The document provides general information to assist in identifying the needs of people with disabilities related to emergency evacuation planning. The guide covers five general categories of disabilities: mobility impairments, visual impairments, hearing impairments, speech impairments, and cognitive impairments. The four elements of evacuation information needed by occupants are notification, way finding, use of way, and assistance.

18.2 COMPONENTS TO BE EVALUATED

18.2.1 Sprinkler Systems Types

Sprinklers are the most common, widely specified and most effective fire suppression system in commercial facilities—particularly in occupied spaces. There are several types of sprinkler systems, including wet- and dry-pipe, pre-action, deluge, and fire cycle. Of these, wet-pipe and dry-pipe are the most common. In a wet-pipe system, the sprinklers are attached to a water supply, enabling immediate discharge of water at sprinkler heads opened by the heat of the fire. In a dry-pipe system, the sprinklers are under air pressure and, when the pressure is eased by the opening of the sprinkler heads, the system fills with water.

In situations where sprinklers are not feasible because of special considerations (e.g., water from sprinklers would damage sensitive equipment or inventory), alternative fire-suppression systems might be used, such as gaseous/chemical suppression. In the final analysis, the type of sprinkler system used depends on a building's function. Of note, most of today's fire sprinklers incorporate the latest in design and engineering technologies to provide an extremely high level of life-safety and property protection. The features and benefits now available are making fire sprinkler systems more efficient, reliable, and cost effective.

As sprinkler systems become more affordable and the benefits become more obvious, sprinkler systems in residential structures are becoming more common. These systems usually fall under a residential classification and not a commercial one. A commercial sprinkler system is designed to protect the structure and the occupants from a fire. Most residential systems are primarily designed to suppress a fire to allow for the safe escape of the building occupants. While these systems will often also protect the structure from major fire damage, this remains a secondary consideration. In residential structures sprinklers are typically omitted from closets, bathrooms, balconies, and attics since a fire in these areas would not normally impact an occupant's escape route. When sprinkler systems operate as designed, they are highly reliable. However, like any other mechanical system, sprinkler systems need periodic maintenance and inspection in order to sustain proper operation. In the rare event a sprinkler system fails to control a fire, the root cause of failure is often the lack of proper maintenance. Figure 18.2 is an example of a fire sprinkler control valve assembly, including pressure switches and valve monitors.

Wet-pipe systems: Wet-pipe sprinkler systems are by far the most common and have the highest reliability. The systems are simple, with the only operating component being the automatic sprinkler. A water supply provides pressure to the piping, and all of the piping is filled with water adjacent to the sprinklers. The water is held back by the automatic sprinklers (Figure 18.3) until activated. When one or more of the automatic sprinklers is exposed to sufficient heat, it operates, allowing water to flow from that sprinkler. Each sprinkler operates individually. Figure 18.4 shows a drawing of a typical wet pipe sprinkler system.

Figure 18.2 Typical fire sprinkler control valve assembly *(Courtesy Wikipedia).*

Dry-pipe systems: These are the second most common sprinkler system type in use. Regulations typically stipulate that these systems can only be used in spaces in which the ambient temperature may be cold enough to freeze the water in a wet-pipe system, thus rendering it inoperable. We often find dry pipe systems used in unheated buildings and in refrigerated coolers.

Water does not enter the piping until the system operates. The piping is pressurized with air, at a "maintenance" pressure that is relatively low in comparison with the water supply pressure. To prevent the larger water supply pressure from forcing water into the piping, the design of the dry pipe valve intentionally includes a larger valve clapper area exposed to the maintenance air pressure, as compared to the water pressure.

The system operates when one or more of the automatic sprinklers are exposed to sufficient heat, allowing the maintenance air to vent from that sprinkler. Each sprinkler operates individually. As the air pressure in the piping drops, the pressure differential across the dry- pipe valve changes, allowing water to enter the piping system. Water flow from sprinklers needed to control the fire is delayed until the air is vented from the sprinklers. Dry-pipe systems are therefore not as effective as wet-pipe systems in fire control during the initial stages of the fire.

Figure 18.3 Drawing of typical ceiling-mounted sprinkler head *(Courtesy Scott Easton).*

Deluge systems: In a deluge system the sprinklers are open—the heat sensing operating element is removed during installation so that all sprinklers connected to the water piping system remain open. These systems provide a simultaneous application of water over the entire hazard and are typically used for special hazards where rapid fire spread is a major concern. Water is not present in the piping until the system operates. Because the sprinkler orifices are open, the piping is at ambient air pressure. To prevent the water supply pressure from forcing water into the piping, a *deluge valve* is used in the water supply connection, which is a mechanically latched non-resetting valve that stays open once tripped.

Because the heat sensing elements present in the automatic sprinklers have been removed (resulting in open sprinklers), the deluge valve must be opened as signaled by a specialized fire alarm system. The type of fire alarm initiating device used is based mainly on the hazard (e.g., smoke detectors or heat detectors). The initiation device signals the fire alarm panel, which in turn signals the deluge valve to open. Activation can also be manual, depending on the system goals. Manual activation is usually via an electric or pneumatic fire alarm pull station, which signals the fire alarm panel, which in turn signals the deluge valve to open, allowing water to enter the piping system. Water flows from all sprinklers simultaneously.

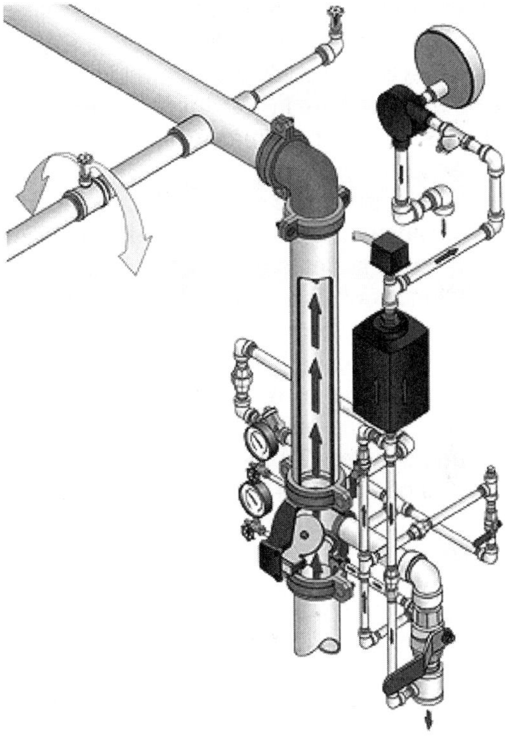

Figure 18.4 Diagram of typical wet-pipe sprinkler system.

Pre-action Systems: Pre-action sprinkler systems are specialized for use in locations where accidental activation is undesired, such as in museums with rare art works, manuscripts, or books. There are two sub-types of pre-action systems: single interlock, and double interlock. The operation of single interlock systems are similar to dry systems except that they require that a "preceding" and supervised event (typically the activation of a heat or smoke detector) takes place prior to the "action" of water introduction into the system's piping due to opening of the pre-action valve (a mechanically latched valve). Once the fire is detected by the fire alarm system, it basically converts from a dry system into a wet system.

The operation of double interlock systems is similar to a deluge system except that automatic sprinklers are used. These systems require that both a "preceding" and supervised event (typically the activation of a heat or smoke detector), and an automatic sprinkler activation take place prior to the entrance of water into the system's piping. There is also a little used variation known as non-interlock.

Foam water sprinkler systems: A foam water fire sprinkler system is a special application system discharging a mixture of water and low expansion foam concentrate, resulting in a foam spray from the sprinkler. These systems are typically used with special hazards occupancies associated with high-challenge fires, such as flammable liquids and airport hangars.

18.2.2 Fire Hose and Standpipe Systems

Connected by manual valves in locations throughout the building, a fire hose system is found in many facilities. The main pipe of the system, the standpipe, can be wet or dry, and additional water can be supplied to the system by the fire department using the Siamese inlet connections located on the exterior of the building at street level. Types of hose systems on the market include the semi-automatic swing rack, the hump back swing rack, and the swing reel.

A standpipe system can be a wet or dry system and consists of piping, valves, outlets, and related equipment designed to provide water at specified pressures and installed exclusively for the fighting of fires. The system is used in conjunction with sprinklers or hoses and basically consists of a water pipe riser running vertically through the building. Dry systems are normally empty and are not connected to a water source. A Siamese fitting is located at the bottom end of the pipe, allowing the fire department to pump water into the system. In a wet-type system, the pipe is filled with water and attached to a tank or pump. This type also contains Siamese fittings for the fire department's use. There are three common classifications of standpipe systems:

Class I standpipe systems are equipped with two and one-half (2 1/2)-inch hose connection for use by fire departments and those trained in handling heavy fire streams.

Class II systems are directly connected to a water supply and are equipped with one and one-half (1 1/2)-inch outlets and hose for the control or extinguishment of incipient stage fires.

Class III systems are combined standpipe systems directly connected to a water supply; they are for the use of in-house personnel capable of furnishing effective water discharge during the more advanced stages of fire in the interior of workplaces. Hose outlets are available for both one and one-half (1 1/2)-inch and two and one-half (2 1/2)-inch hose. Hose connections for class III systems may also be made through two and one-half (2 1/2)-inch hose valves with easily removable reducers two and one-half (2 1/2)-inch by one and one-half (1 1/2)-inch in size.

Standpipe systems having the control valve located within a stairwell should ensure that the maximum length of hose does not exceed 100 feet. If the control valve is located in areas other than the stairwell, the length of hose should not exceed 75 feet. Code requires that fire hose on Class II and Class III standpipe systems be equipped with a shut-off type nozzle.

18.2.3 Hand-held Fire Extinguishers

There are basically four different classifications of fire extinguishers, each of which extinguishes specific types of fire (Figure 18.5). Newer fire extinguishers use a picture/labeling system to designate which types of fires they are to be used on. Older fire extinguishers are labeled with colored geometrical shapes with letter designations (Figure 18.6).

Classification of hand-held fire extinguisher ratings:

Class A extinguishers will put out fires in ordinary combustibles, such as wood, textiles and paper. The numerical rating for this class refers to the amount of water the extinguisher holds and the amount of fire it will extinguish.

Class B extinguishers should be used on fires where the smothering effect of extinguishing is important, such as fires involving gasoline, oil, grease, and fat. The numerical rating for this class states the approximate number of square feet of a flammable liquid fire that a non-expert person can expect to extinguish.

Class C extinguishers are suitable for use in electrical equipment where a non-conducting material is required. This class does not have a numerical rating. The letter "C" indicates that the extinguishing agent is non-conductive.

Class D extinguishers are special types approved for specific combustible materials. There is no picture designator for this class. These extinguishers generally have no rating, nor are they given a multi-purpose rating for use on other types of fires.

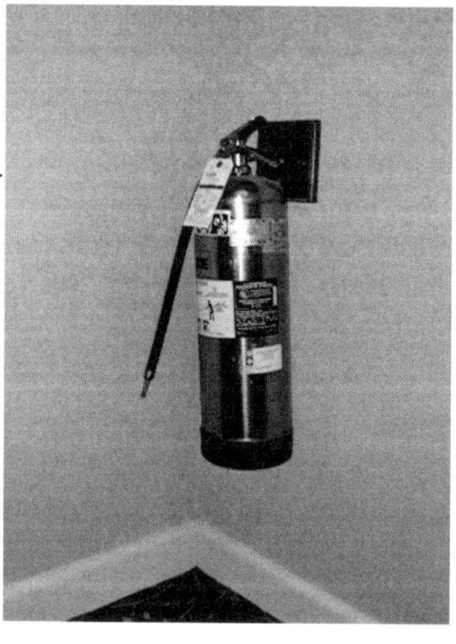

Figure 18.5 Typical wall mounted hand-held fire extinguisher.

Many extinguishers available today can be used on different types of fires and will be labeled with more than one designator, e.g., A-B, B-C, or A-B-C. If a multi-purpose extinguisher is being used it should be properly labeled.

Types of fire extinguishers:

Dry chemical extinguishers are usually rated for multi purpose use. They contain an extinguishing agent and use a compressed, nonflammable gas as a propellant.

Halon extinguishers contain a gas that interrupts the chemical reaction that takes place when fuels burn. These types of extinguishers are often used to protect valuable electrical equipment since they leave no residue to clean up. Halon extinguishers have a limited range, usually 4 to 6 feet.

Water extinguishers contain water and compressed gas and should only be used on Class A (ordinary combustibles) fires.

Carbon dioxide (CO_2) extinguishers are most effective on Class B and C (liquids and electrical) fires. Since the gas disperses quickly, these extinguishers are only effective from 3 to 8 feet. The carbon dioxide is stored as a compressed liquid in the extinguisher; as it expands, it cools the surrounding air. The cooling will often cause ice to form around the "horn" where the gas is expelled from the extinguisher. However, because the fire could re-ignite, continue to apply the agent even after the fire appears to be out.

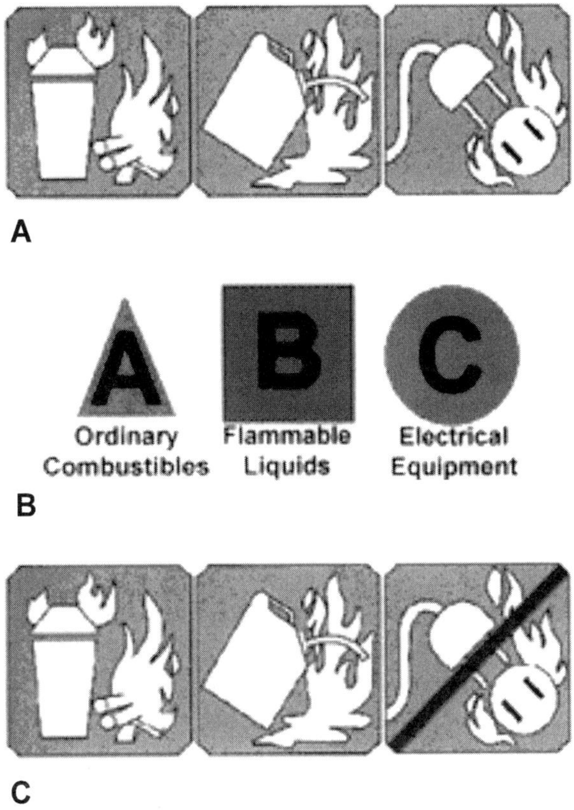

Figure 18.6 New and old style of labeling indicating suitability for use on Class A, B, and C fire extinguishers.

NFPA Code 10 addresses all the issues pertaining to portable fire extinguishers. Recognized as a first line of defense against fires, portable extinguishers can prevent a fire from spreading beyond its point of origin when maintained and operated properly on a small containable fire.

NFPA Code 10 requires owners of extinguishers to have monthly inspections performed and to maintain records of the inspections. These records should be inspected during a PCA survey. The inspection must determine that the extinguisher is at its designated location and that it is mounted properly, that signage showing its location is visible and readable, and that access to the extinguisher is not blocked. Additionally, annual maintenance requires a thorough evaluation of the extinguisher's ability to function properly in the application for which it's designed.

18.2.4 Smoke and Heat Detection Systems

A smoke detector or smoke alarm is a device that detects smoke and issues an alarm to alert nearby people that there is a potential fire. A household smoke detector will typically be mounted in a disk-shaped plastic enclosure about 150 mm in diameter and 25 mm thick, but the shape can vary by manufacturer

(Figure 18.7). Laws governing the installation of smoke detectors vary depending on the jurisdiction.

Because smoke rises, most detectors are mounted on the ceiling or on a wall near the ceiling. To avoid the nuisance of false alarms, most smoke detectors are mounted away from kitchens. To increase the chances of waking sleeping occupants, most homes have at least one smoke detector near any bedrooms, and ideally in a hallway as well as in the bedroom itself.

Figure 18.7 Drawing of a ceiling-mounted smoke detector *(Courtesy Scott Easton)*.

Smoke detectors are usually powered by one or more batteries, but some can be connected directly to household wiring. Often the smoke detectors that are directly connected to the main wiring system also have a battery as a power supply backup in case the facility's electricity goes out. Batteries should be checked and replaced periodically to ensure appropriate protection.

Most smoke detectors work either by optical detection or by ionization, and some use both detection methods to increase sensitivity to smoke. Smoke detectors may operate alone, can be interconnected to cause all detectors in an area to sound an alarm if one is triggered, or can be integrated into a fire alarm or security system. Smoke detectors with flashing lights are available for the deaf or hearing impaired. Smoke detectors cannot detect carbon monoxide to prevent carbon monoxide poisoning unless they come with integrated carbon monoxide detectors.

An optical detector is a light sensor. When used as a smoke detector it includes a light source (infrared LED), a lens to collimate the light into a beam like a laser, and a photodiode or other photoelectric sensor at right-angles to the beam as a light detector. In the absence of smoke, the light passes in front of the detector in a straight line. When smoke enters the optical chamber into the path of the light beam, some light is scattered by the smoke particles, and some of the scattered light is detected by the sensor. An increased input of light into the sensor sets off the alarm.

Projected beam detectors are also utilized in large interior spaces, such as gymnasia and auditoria. A unit on the wall sends out a beam, which is either received by a receiver, or reflected back via a mirror. When the beam is less visible to the "eye" of the sensor, it sends an alarm signal to the fire alarm control panel. Optical smoke detectors are generally quick in detecting slow burning, smoky fires.

Ionization detectors, although cheaper than optical detectors, are sometimes rejected for environmental reasons. An ionization detector can detect particles of smoke that are too small to be visible. It includes a tiny mass of radioactive americium-241, which is a source of alpha radiation. The radiation passes through an ionization chamber, which is an air-filled space between two electrodes, and permits a small, constant current to flow between the electrodes. Any smoke that enters the chamber absorbs the alpha particles, thus reducing the ionization and interrupts the flow of current, which sets off the alarm.

Modern smoke-detection systems go beyond the small device that senses smoke and triggers the alarm system. Intelligent smoke detectors can differentiate between different alarm thresholds. These systems typically have remote detectors located throughout the facility that are connected to a central alarm station. Heat detectors are another option. They can trigger alarms and notification systems before smoke even becomes a factor.

A heat detector can be either electrical or mechanical in operation. The most common types are the thermocouple and the electro-pneumatic, both of which respond to changes in ambient temperature. Typically, if the ambient temperature rises above a predetermined threshold, an alarm signal is triggered.

The main benefit of good detection (beyond triggering the alarm system) is that, in many cases, there is a chance to extinguish a small, early blaze with a fire extinguisher.

18.2.5 Fire Doors

A fire door is a door made of fire-resistant material that can be closed to prevent the spread of fire; it is designed to provide extra fire-spread protection for certain areas of a building (Figure 18.8). Fire doors are commonly installed at:

- Staircases from corridors or rooms, cross corridor partition, entrances to laboratories, plant rooms, workshops, storerooms, machine rooms, service ducts, kitchens and to defined fire compartments
- Certain circulation areas that extend the escape route from the stair to a final exit or to a place of safety, entrances and lobbies
- At routes leading onto external fire escapes
- Corridors that are protected from adjoining accommodation by fire resisting construction—mainly corridors in dead-end conditions and routes leading off the corridor, including offices.

The National Fire Protection Association (NFPA) rates doors according to the number of hours they can be expected to withstand fire before burning through. There are 20, 30, 45, 60, 90-minute rated fire doors as well as 2HR and 4HR rated fire doors that are certified by an approved laboratory such as Underwriters Laboratories. The certification only applies if all parts of the installation are correctly specified and installed. For example, the wrong kind of glazing may severely reduce the door's fire resistance rating.

Because fire doors are rated physical fire barriers that protect wall openings from the spread of fire, they should close automatically in the event of fire detection with governed speed control. Fire doors are also designed for daily use to provide security and access control, but are for use in openings that are not part of a required means of egress.

Fire doors should usually be kept closed at all times, although some are designed to stay open under normal circumstances, and to close automatically or manually in the event of a fire. Whichever method is used, the door's movement should never be impaired by a doorstop or other obstacle. Proper bounding of fire doors should be routinely checked and ensured. They are used in commercial and industrial applications where a fire barrier is required. Fire door closing devices must be UL listed and labeled, and are required to be tested every 6 months. Release devices are electro-mechanical devices that enable automatic closing fire doors to respond to alarm signals from detection devices such as smoke detectors, heat detectors, and central alarm systems. This permits closing the door before high temperatures melt the fusible link. Fusible links should always be used as back up to the releasing device. The closing system can be weight close, spring reel close, or motorized. Descriptions of each type are below:

Weight close system: A weight box mounts next to the door and pulls the door closed when the fuse link separates, or through an electromagnetic release device, which can be tied to the building's life safety system.

Reel close system: The door is closed by a spring-loaded cable reel mounted at track height when the fuse link separates, or by an electromagnetic release device, which can be tied to the building's life safety system.

Motorized: The operator system includes heat detectors and a battery backup system that closes the door when heat is detected. The battery backup ensures that the door operates, even during a power failure. Motorized systems may also be tied to the building's life safety system.

CLASS	FIRE RATING	LOCATION AND USE	GLASS LITE SIZE ALLOWED AREA	HEIGHT	WIDTH
A	3 hour	Fire walls separating buildings or various fire areas within a building 3 to 4 hour walls	None Allowed	None Allowed	None Allowed
B	1½ hour (H.M.) 1 hour (other)	Vertical shafts and enclosures such as stairwells, elevators, and garbage chutes 2 hour walls	100 inches	33 inches	10-12* inches
B	1 hour	Vertical shafts in low-rise buildings and discharge corridors 1 to 1½ hour walls	100 inches	33 inches	10-12* inches
C	¾ hour	Exit access corridors and exitway enclosures 1 hour walls	1296 inches	54 inches	54 inches
N/A	20-minute	Exit access corridors and room partitions	No Limit	No Limit	No Limit

Figure 18.8 Table showing interior fire-rated doors and glass lites.

Conventional fire door automatic closing systems release spring tension and require mechanical resetting by a trained door systems technician. Although these old fire door systems are available and frequently specified, the industry has evolved to address today's issues of annual door testing requirements, more frequent alarm testing, recessed installation, and power outages.

All fire products should be provided with a multiple fuselink setup to close the door automatically when any link melts. Standard fuselinks are designed to melt at 165 degrees F and are to be located at the ceiling level above the fire door. For units with an automatic closing system or those tied into an alarm system or local detectors, a fuselink set-up should still be provided as a back up mechanical closing system.

Hinges: The National Fire Protection Association Standard specifies that two hinges must be used for doors up to 60 inches in height. An additional hinge is required for each additional 30 inches in height or fraction thereof.

Fire-rated door assemblies: Assemblies complying with NFPA 80 are listed and labeled by UL for fire ratings indicated, based on testing according to NFPA 252. Assemblies must be factory-welded or come complete with factory-installed mechanical joints and must not require job site fabrication.

Figure 18.9 Example of EXIT signage.

18.2.6 Fire Exits and Stairs

Exit routes: An exit route is a continuous and unobstructed path of exit travel from any point within a workplace to a place of safety. Every building has fire exits, which enable users to exit safely in the event of an emergency. Well-designed emergency exit signs are necessary for emergency exits to be effective. In the United States fire escape signs often display the word "EXIT" in large, well-lit, green or red letters (Figure 18.9).

Basic requirements: Each exit route must be a permanent part of the workplace and must be separated by fire resistant materials. Construction materials used to separate an exit from other parts of the workplace must have a one-hour fire resistance rating if the exit connects three or fewer stories and a two-hour fire resistance rating if the exit connects four or more stories (Figure 18.10).

Openings into an exit must be limited. An exit is permitted to have only those openings necessary to allow access to the exit from occupied areas of the workplace, or to the exit discharge. An opening into an exit must be protected by a self-closing fire door that remains closed or automatically closes in an emergency upon the sounding of a fire alarm or employee alarm system. Each fire door, including its frame and hardware, must be listed or approved by a nationally recognized testing laboratory.

Exit routes: At least two exit routes must be available in a workplace to permit prompt evacuation of employees and other building occupants during an emergency, unless otherwise stipulated by code. The exit routes must be located as far away as practical from each other so that if one exit route is blocked by fire or smoke, employees can evacuate using the second exit route. More than two exit routes must be available in a workplace if the number of employees, the size of the building, its occupancy, or the arrangement of the workplace is such that all employees would not be able to evacuate safely during an emergency.

Figure 18.10 Principles of exit safety. Egress design should be based upon an evaluation of a building's total fire protection system *(Courtesy Yngve Anderberge)*.

A single exit route is permitted where the number of employees, the size of the building, its occupancy, or the arrangement of the workplace is such that all employees would be able to evacuate safely during an emergency.

The NFPA 101-2000 *Life Safety Code* can be consulted to help determine the number of exit routes necessary for a particular facility or building.

Exit discharge: Each exit discharge must lead directly outside or to a street, walkway, refuge area, public way, or open space with access to the outside. The street, walkway, refuge area, public way, or open space to which an exit discharge leads must be large enough to accommodate the building occupants likely to use the exit route.

Exit stairs that continue beyond the level on which the exit discharge is located must be interrupted at that level by doors, partitions, or other effective means that clearly indicate the direction of travel leading to the exit discharge.

Exit door access: An exit door must be unlocked from the inside. Furthermore, employees must be able to open an exit route door from the inside at all times without keys, tools, or special knowledge. A device such as a panic bar that locks only from the outside is permitted on exit discharge doors. Exit route doors may be locked from the inside only in mental, penal, or correctional facilities and then only if supervisory personnel are continuously on duty and the employer has a plan to remove occupants from the facility during an emergency.

Outdoor exit routes: An outdoor exit route is permitted if it has guardrails to protect unenclosed sides if a fall hazard exists. The outdoor exit route must be covered if snow or ice is likely to accumulate along the route, unless it can be demonstrated that any snow or ice accumulation will be removed before it presents a slipping hazard. The outdoor exit route must be reasonably straight and have smooth, solid, substantially level walkways, and the outdoor exit route must not have a dead-end that is longer than 20 feet (6.2 m).

18.2.7 Fire Stopping

Compartmentation: A fire compartment is a space within a building extending over one or several floors that is enclosed by separating members such that the fire spread beyond the compartment is prevented during the relevant fire exposure. Fire compartments are sometimes referred to as fire zones. Compartmentation is important in preventing fire spread into large spaces or into the whole building. The division of the building into discrete fire zones offers perhaps the most effective means of limiting fire damage (Figure 18.11). Designed to contain the fire to within the zone of origin, this approach provides at least some protection for the rest of the building and its occupants, even if first aid fire fighting measures are used and fail. It also delays the spread of fire prior to the arrival of fire fighters.

Halls and landings should typically be separated from staircases to prevent a fire from traveling vertically up or down the stairwell to the other floors. To be effective, compartmentation needs to be planned and implemented properly. There is no point in upgrading the fire resistance of a door and then not adequately protecting the plywood duct next to it which runs through to the floor above, or to the adjacent space.

The fire resistance required by a compartment depends upon its intended purpose and on the expected fire. The separating members enclosing the compartment should either resist the maximum expected fire or contain the fire until occupants are evacuated. The load-bearing elements in the compartment must always resist the complete fire process or be classified to a certain resistance measured in terms of periods of time, which is equal or longer than the requirement of the separating members. The most important elements to be upgraded are the doors, floors, and walls, penetrations through floors and walls, and cavity barriers in the roof spaces.

Fire stopping should be designed to stop the spread of fire between floors of a building. The flame retardant material is installed around floor openings designed to contain conduit and piping. Firestop is a product that, when installed properly, impedes the passage of fire, smoke, and toxic gases from one side of a fire-rated wall or floor assembly to another. Typical firestop products include sealants, sprays, mechanical devices (firestop collar), foam blocks, or pillows. These products are installed primarily in two applications: 1) around penetrations in fire-resistive construction for the passage of pipes (Figure 18.12), cables, or HVAC systems, and 2) where two assemblies meet, forming an expansion joint such as the top of a wall, curtain wall (edge of slab), or floor-to-floor joints. Typical opening types include electrical, mechanical, and structural through-penetrations, non-penetrated openings (e.g., openings for future use), re-entries of existing firestops, control or sway joints within fire-resistance rated wall or floor assemblies, junctions between fire-resistance rated wall or floor assemblies, and "Head-of-wall" (HOW) joints, where non-load bearing wall assemblies meet floor assemblies.

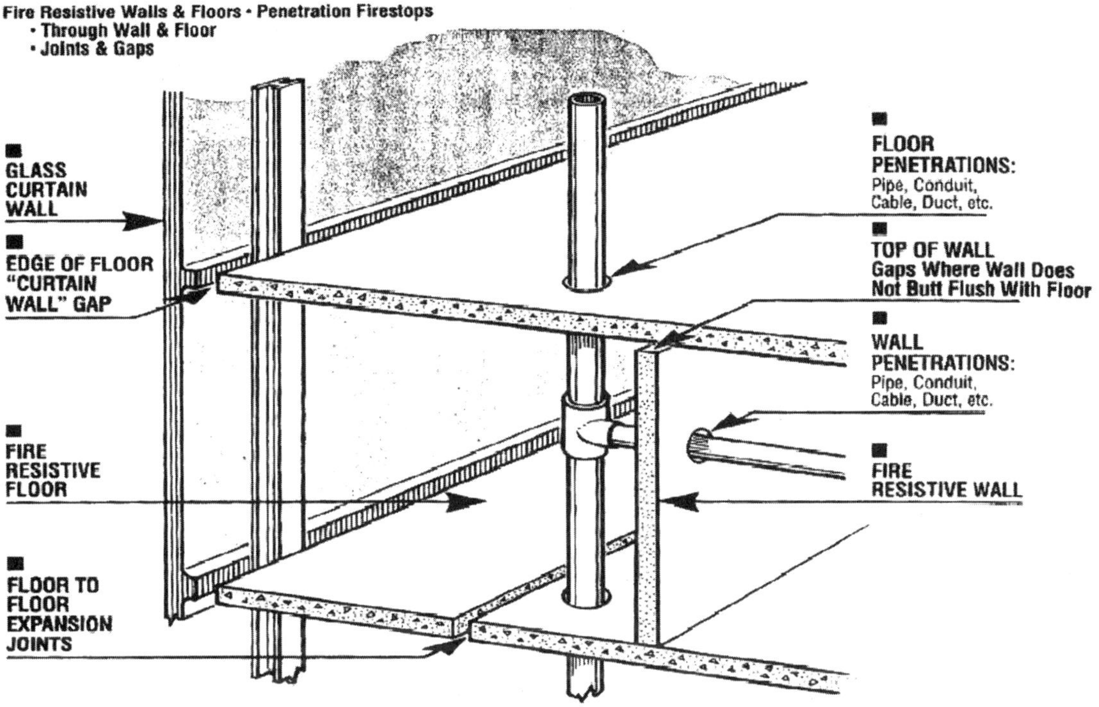

Figure 18.11 Unprotected horizontal and vertical openings are primary causes of fire and smoke spread.

Figure 18.12 Example of firestop system.

A building owner's responsibility is to comply with all applicable laws and regulations relating to the property. One of these is the adopted and enforced fire code within a specific jurisdiction. Fire codes govern the construction, protection, and occupancy details that affect the fire safety of buildings throughout their lifespan. Numerous different fire codes have been adopted throughout the United States, the vast majority of which are similar and based on one of the model codes available today or in the past. One requirement in all of these model codes is that fire-safety features incorporated into a building at the time of its construction must be maintained throughout a building's life. Therefore, this would require any fire resistance-rated construction to be maintained (Figure 18.13).

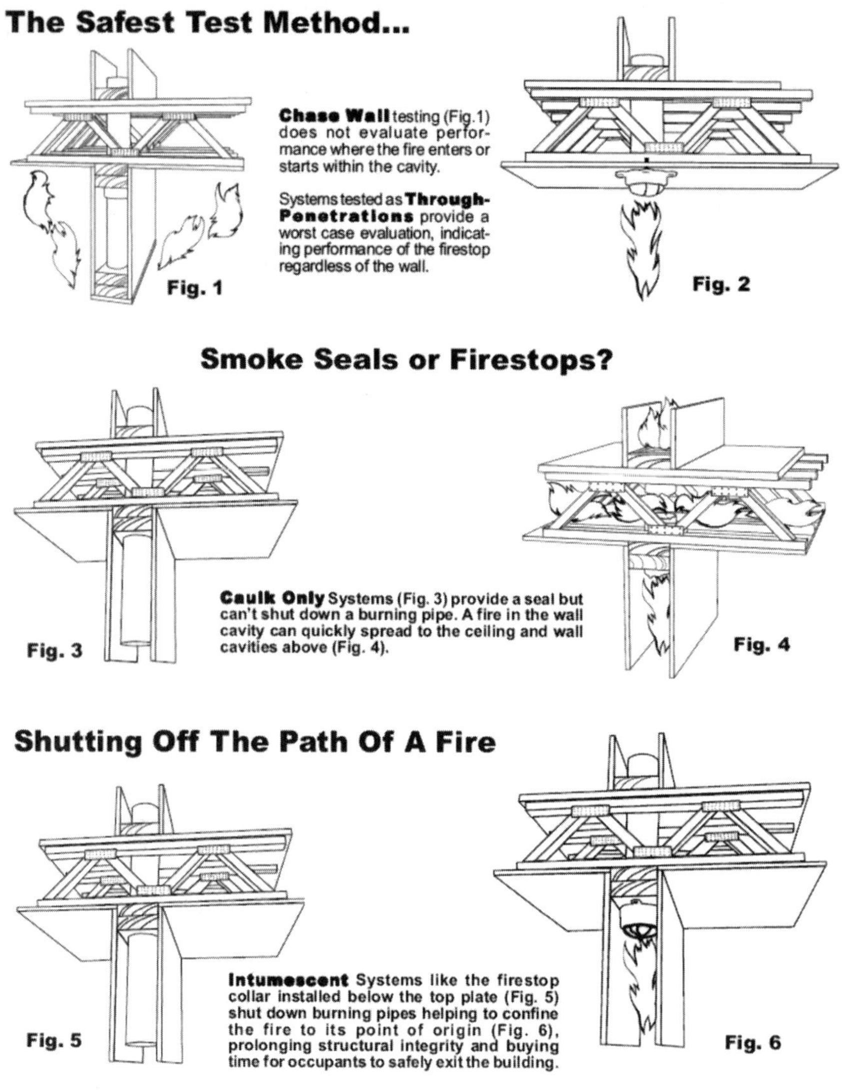

Figure 18.13 Drawing showing various firestopping methods.

18.2.8 Alarm Systems and Notification Systems

Early warning is vital for saving lives, particularly in large buildings where there may be visitors or personnel who are unfamiliar with their surroundings. Alarm systems are therefore essential to any facility—alarms that alert building occupants of a fire and alarms that alert emergency public responders (police and fire) through a central station link to initiate an appropriate response. Fire detection and notification system requirements, at a minimum, will address the following elements:

- Detection
- Notification
- Survivability of systems

Today's systems have the ability to provide more information to the fire department and first responders. In some cases, they can do more than just tell them that there has been an alarm in the building; they can be directed by the kind of alarm and where the alarm is. Moreover, many modern systems now include speakers that provide alerts in place of (or in addition to) traditional bell-type alarms. These speakers also can be used in emergencies other than fires to instruct and inform occupants of the situation.

These voice-actuated systems can include pre-recorded or live messages that play in the event of fire or another emergency. Typical pre-recorded messages tell occupants that an alarm has been sounded and that they should remain in their designated area for further instruction. Building management can then manually use the system to deliver additional information and prepare occupants for an evacuation, if necessary. Alert systems can also close fire doors, recall elevators, and interface and monitor the installed suppression systems, such as sprinklers.

The systems can also connect with a building's ventilation, smoke management, and stairwell pressurization systems, all of which are critical to life safety. Again, these features are dependent on the building in which the system is installed.

Annunciator panels are sometimes installed in large buildings. The annunciator panel is used to monitor the fire alarm devices in a designated fire zone. There may be several fire zones in a building. Each fire zone is clearly marked on the panel. Should a fire occur, an indicator light flashes on the panel. The indicator light identifies the fire's location. For example the light on the panel might indicate that a fire has occurred in Fire Zone 4. This information allows the Fire Department to quickly locate the fire. An example of a typical annunciator panel is shown in Figure 18.14.

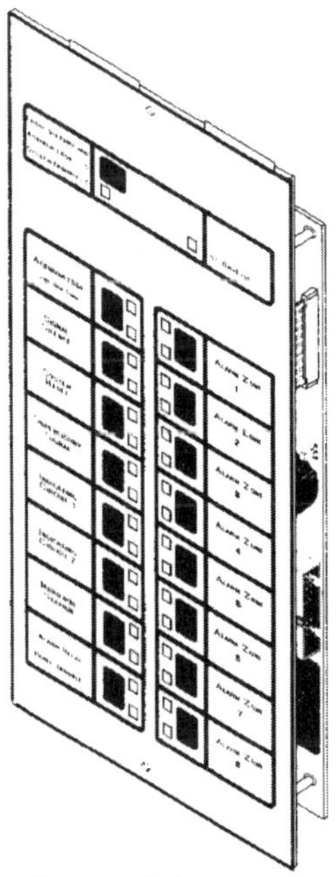

Annunciator

Figure 18.14
Example of a typical annunciator panel.

18.3 SYSTEM DIAGNOSTICS

The survey of the life safety system consists of several aspects. The evaluation should include both a review of existing conditions as well as an inspection of previous certifications for the system. In most facilities, the life safety system is one of the best maintained systems. This is mainly due to the importance of the system and the diligence and frequency of inspections for life safety equipment by the fire department. In fact it is uncommon, upon review of a facility, to find fire sprinkler inspection paperwork outdated and hand-held fire extinguishers in disrepair. The periodic inspection of a life safety system can significantly increase the useful life of the system. Indeed, beyond the components that actually make up an integrated fire-protection system, maintenance is a vital factor that affects the system.

An improperly maintained system lacks reliability and, therefore, true protection. If a system is not maintained properly, its reliability degrades rapidly. A system should not be installed that cannot be routinely maintained and easily and effectively tested. Periodic inspection of field-installed sprinklers is an important element of a comprehensive maintenance program for sprinkler systems and is required by code. As specified in *NFPA 25,* sprinklers showing signs of leakage, field painting, corrosion, damage, or loading are to be replaced. All of these conditions can lead to the degradation of sprinkler performance during a fire.

The most serious sprinkler system failures revolve around the water supply. Without the appropriate water supply, a sprinkler system is of little use. The importance of a consistent water supply cannot be overstressed. Where a water failure occurs, it is more often due to the water control devices than the water supply itself. For example, sprinkler system control valves can be closed inadvertently by authorized personnel, intentionally closed by an arsonist, or due to a physical deficiency in the valve. Public water system valves that are closed for maintenance purposes can also significantly impact the sprinkler system water supply.

Mechanical failure or sediment accumulation in backflow preventers can cause excessive pressure loss, and dry-pipe sprinkler systems are susceptible to internal corrosion and scale, which can clog sprinkler orifices during a fire. The water supply in some locations can cause microbiological influenced corrosion (MIC), leading to pinhole leaks or deposits that can obstruct piping. Obstructions of physical objects in the water supply main can also be a cause for failure.

Construction documents should be reviewed to determine the life safety system components designed to be installed in the building. In some cases, last minute changes in construction result in omission of certain components. It is especially important to verify in the field the building areas shown to be protected by fire sprinklers on the documents. It should not be taken for granted that simply because the system is designed one way, the construction completely follows that design.

During the physical survey of a facility's interior systems, the life safety system should be reviewed. The condition and coverage of smoke and fire detection and suppression systems should be noted and evaluated. All system components should be checked, beginning with verifying that the main fire valve is open. All smoke detectors and emergency lighting should be tested.

Identify and observe the condition and capabilities of structural fire protection, means of egress, fire suppression systems, and fire detection and alarm systems. Risks to general health and safety should also be observed and recorded. Identify and observe the condition of life safety and fire protection systems, including sprinklers and standpipes (wet or dry, or both), fire hydrants, fire alarm systems, water storage, smoke detectors, fire extinguishers, emergency lighting, stairwell pressurization, smoke evacuation, etc. Identify the apparent or reported ages of life safety/fire protection systems and, combined with visual observations, identify the RUL. Assessments should exclude determining NFPA hazard classifications, classifying, or testing fire rating of assemblies.

The certifications are usually filed with the maintenance staff and should be reviewed for completeness, original compliance, and current compliance. Special life safety system forms should be utilized that provide a checklist and information on the various components of the system.

CHAPTER

19

Property Security

19.1 GENERAL

The design and construction of safe and secure buildings continues to be the primary goal for owners, consultants, and project managers. Terrorism in particular is now a recognized international phenomenon against which governments need to institute protective measures. 168 people were killed in the destruction of the nine-storey Alfred P. Murrah Federal Building in Oklahoma City, and in the World Trade Center attacks of 9/11, nearly 3,000 people were killed (Figure 19.1A,B). These disasters highlight the lack of adequate security in public facilities as well as in the workplace. But today's disasters come in different shapes and forms, from inside and outside the building. Even disgruntled employees can become potential time bombs. Planners must therefore study all aspects of security, including the new challenges they face today, whether it concerns employees, the building's structure, or the business activities within it.

Today, in recognizing concern for natural disasters, acts of terrorism, indoor air quality, materials hazards, and fires, the design team must take a multi-hazard approach towards building design that accounts for the potential hazards and vulnerabilities. Applicable multi-hazard events include bomb threats, terrorist acts, nuclear, radiological, chemical, or biological threats, fires, medical emergencies, demonstrations and civil disorders, power failures, spills or leaks of hazardous substances, and natural disasters such as hurricanes, tornados, floods, and earthquakes.

Designing buildings for security and safety requires a proactive approach that anticipates—and then protects—the building occupants, resources, structure, and continuity of operations from multiple hazards. The first step in this process is to understand the various threats and the risks they pose. Based on an assessment and analysis of these risks and threats, building owners and other invested parties select the appropriate safety measures to implement. Such selection will depend on the security requirements, acceptable levels of risk, the cost-effectiveness of the measures proposed, and the impact these measures have on the design, construction, and use of the building.

The majority of security system guidelines typically utilize multiple layers or "rings" of protection that provide the greatest potential for detecting, evaluating, and responding to a threat. This multiple-layer design, which originates protection at the building's perimeter, increases its level of security with each subsequent ring. The rings provide deterrence, detection, and delay, while the area between the rings provides an incident response zone.

Protection—One Ring at a Time

The first ring of security for a typical facility could include:

- A combination of fences to stake out property boundaries
- Microwave and/or infrared sensors to detect movement
- Electronic barriers that restrict vehicle access
- Intercom systems that provide communication when requesting entry
- Card readers that authenticate and allow entry
- CCTV cameras that record activities occurring along the perimeter

The second ring could include:

- A combination of perimeter doors and locks
- Card readers
- CCTV cameras
- Revolving doors
- Optical turnstiles

The third and final ring could include:

- CCTV cameras
- Electronic locking devices
- Dual authentication readers (card and fingerprint) for entry to the facility's core assets, such as data centers and vaults

Even with revised design and engineering measures, the threat of terrorism against property will not be completely resolved, and no building can be made 100 percent terrorist-proof. Surveying such systems is rarely within the scope of the field observer's assignment.

19.2 TYPES OF SECURITY THREATS

Just as the nature and source of threats are continuously changing, buildings professionals must also adapt to provide the best defense for their facilities. Many types of threats to an organization can impact the safety and welfare of its employees, its profitability, and its very existence. The most important include:

19.2.1 Loss from Natural Disasters (Fire, Floods and Earthquakes)

Each year tens of billions of dollars and many lives are lost due to natural hazards. Recovery efforts include repairing damaged buildings and infrastructure from the impacts of hurricanes, floods, earthquakes, tornados, blizzards, and other natural disasters. Loss of life and property would be significantly less if buildings properly anticipated the risk associated with major natural hazards.

Hurricanes, typhoons, and tornados: The key strategy in protecting a building from high winds caused by tornados, hurricanes, and gust fronts is to maintain the integrity of the building envelope, including roofs and windows, and to design the structure to withstand the expected lateral and uplift forces. Roof trusses and gables should be braced; hurricane straps should be used to strengthen the connection between the roof and walls; and doors and windows should be protected by covering and/or bracing. When planning renovation projects, designers should consider opportunities to upgrade the roof structure and covering and to enhance the protection of fenestration.

Flooding: Flood mitigation is best achieved by hazard avoidance—proper site selection away from floodplains. Should buildings be sited in flood-prone locations, they should be elevated above expected flood levels to reduce the chances of flooding and to limit the potential damage to the building and its contents when it is flooded. Flood mitigation techniques include elevating the building so that the lowest floor is above the flood level; dry flood-proofing, or making the building watertight to prevent water entry; wet flood-proofing, or making uninhabited or non-critical parts of the building resistant to water damage; relocation of the building; and the incorporation of levees and floodwalls into site design to keep water away from the building.

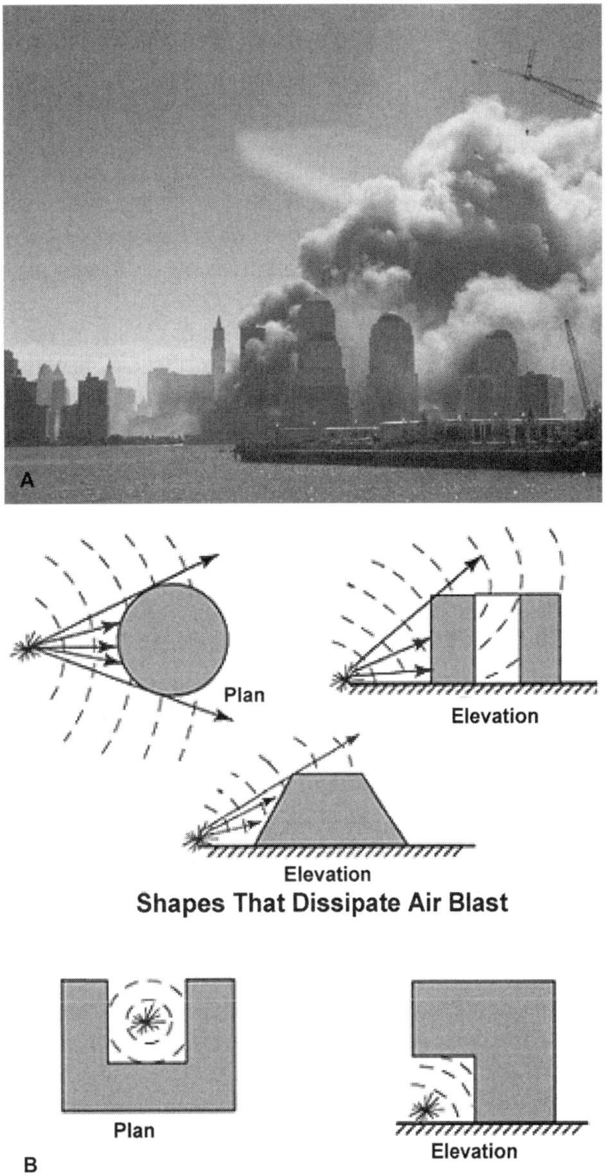

Figure 19.1 A. The September 11, 2001 terrorist attacks on the World Trade Center in New York created new urgency for the issues of building security. B. Effect of building shape on air-blast loading.

Earthquakes: The security threat that is posed by earthquakes is influenced by the level of seismic resistance incorporated in the building design. This can range from prevention of nonstructural damage in frequent minor ground shaking to prevention of structural damage and minimization of nonstructural damage in occasional moderate ground shaking, and even avoidance of collapse or serious damage in rare major ground shaking. These performance objectives can be accomplished through a variety of measures, such as structural components like shear walls, braced frames, moment resisting frames, diaphragms, base isolation, energy dissipating devices such as visco-elastic dampers, elastomeric dampers, and hysteretic-loop dampers, and bracing of nonstructural components.

Forest fires: As residential developments expand into wild land areas, people and property are increasingly at risk from wildfire. A cleared safety zone of at least 30 feet (100 feet in pine forests) should be maintained between structures and combustible vegetation, and fire-resistant ground cover, shrubs, and trees should be used for landscaping (for example, hardwood trees are less flammable than pines, evergreens, eucalyptus, or firs). Only fire-resistant or non-combustible materials should be used on roofs and exterior surfaces. Roofs and gutters should be regularly cleaned, and chimneys should be equipped with spark arrestors. Vents, louvers, and other openings should be covered with wire mesh to prevent embers and flaming debris from entering. Overhangs, eaves, porches, and balconies can trap heat and burning embers and should also be avoided or minimized and protected with wire mesh. Windows allow radiated heat to pass through and ignite combustible materials inside, but dual- or triple-pane thermal glass, fire-resistant shutters or drapes, and noncombustible awnings can help reduce this risk.

Tsunami: A tsunami is a series of ocean waves generated by sudden displacements in the sea floor, landslides, or volcanic activity. In the deep ocean, the tsunami wave may only be a few inches high. The tsunami wave may come gently ashore or may increase in height to become a fast moving wall of turbulent water several meters high. Although a tsunami cannot be prevented, the impact of a tsunami can be mitigated through urban/land planning, community preparedness, timely warnings, and effective response.

19.2.2 Terrorism/Explosive Threats

Explosive threats tend to be the criminal and terrorist weapon of choice. Devices may include stationary and moving vehicle-delivered, mail bombs, package bombs or large amounts of explosives that require delivery by a vehicle. Normally the best defense is to provide defended distance between the threat location and the asset to be protected. This is typically called standoff distance (Figure 19.2). If standoff is not available or is insufficient to reduce the blast forces reaching the protected asset, structural hardening may be required.

Effective secure building design involves implementing countermeasures to deter, delay, detect, and deny attacks from human aggressors. It also provides mitigating measures to limit hazards and prevent catastrophic damage should an attack occur. The design of blast-resistant structures and their subsystems is a long-established discipline practiced mostly by the military; however, these structures are usually located below grade. It is impractical to design conventional, above grade structures to be blast resistant because the potential risk cannot often be defined, nor can the potential threat be quantified because we are unaware of the type of weapon to be used, its capacity, or the proposed mode of delivery. In addition, as the general impact of blast pressures is far greater than that of gravity or wind loads (Figure 19.3) the resultant impact on cost, function, and appearance of blast-resistant design features can be enormous and therefore, unacceptable. Nevertheless, major improvements in susceptibility to a car bomb attack can be achieved by simply incorporating common sense, good structural systems, effective countermeasures, and a well developed contingency or security plan.

19.2.3 Biochemical Terrorism

The potential for a bioterrorism attack on a building's air-handling system is daunting. Increased attention is now being paid to mechanical systems in terms of security and access, as well as filtering and detection (Figure 19.4A,B). This includes the consideration of impacts to the facility HVAC systems in general, and those systems interacting with the building envelope specifically. Of particular concern are airflow patterns

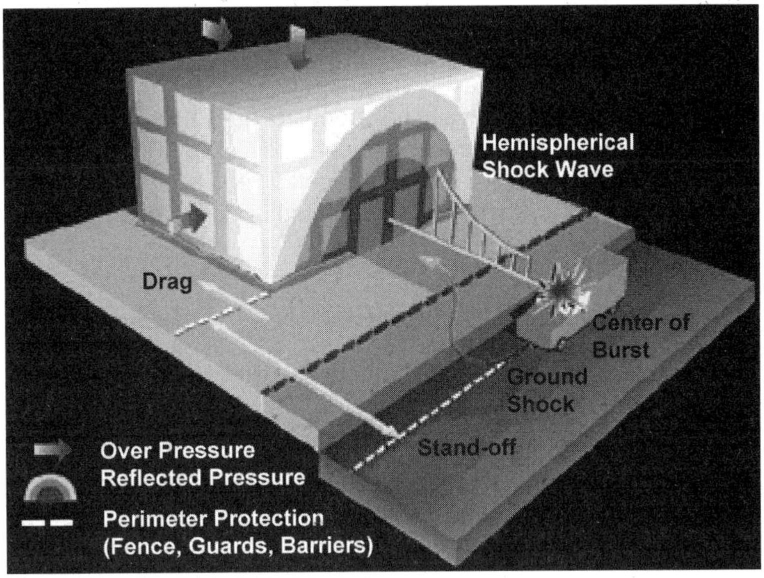

Figure 19.2 Vehicle weapon threat—appropriate building setback required *(Courtesy Hinman Consulting Engineers)*.

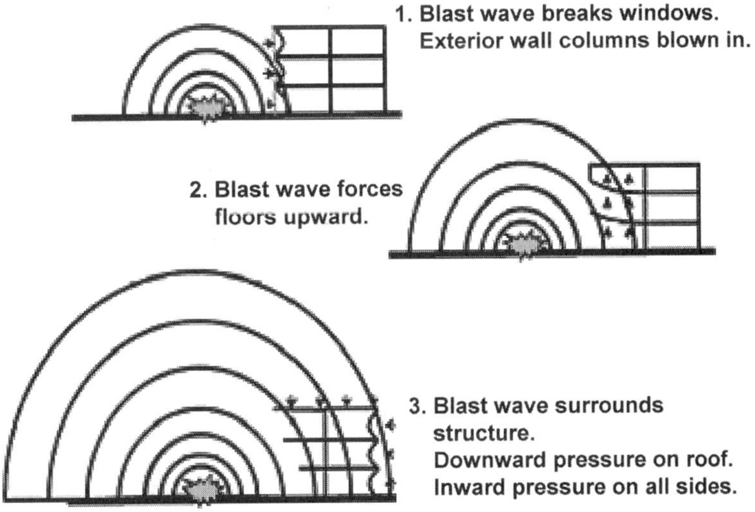

Figure 19.3 Sequence of air-blast effects. The drawing illustrates damage caused by the high-intensity pressures of the air-blast close in to the explosive source. These may induce the localized failure of exterior envelope components, depending on several factors *(Courtesy Hinman Consulting Engineers)*.

and dynamics both inside and outside of buildings, especially pertaining to the internal release or external release of chemical, biological or radiological contaminant, and the measures necessary to limit airborne contamination.

Exposure of building occupants to potentially hazardous chemical, biological, and radiological (CBR) agents negatively impacts the indoor environment and can pose serious health threats. To help maintain good indoor air quality and protect occupants' health, dedicated ventilation and exhaust systems should be installed as well as dedicated HVAC systems to serve perimeter zones and to maintain positive pressurization with respect to the building envelope.

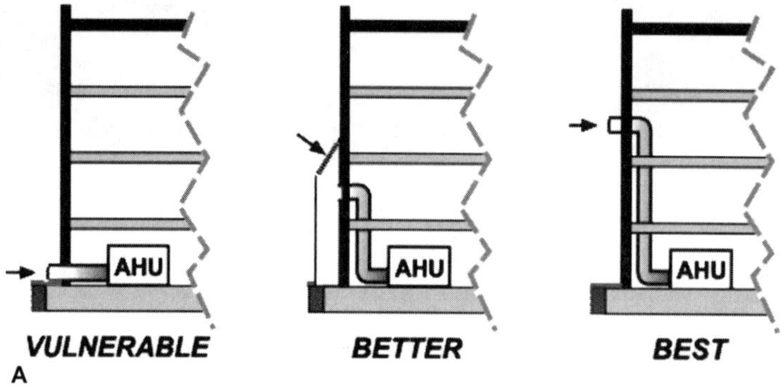

Figure 19.4 Protecting outdoor air intakes *(Courtesy Guidance for Protecting Building Environments from Airborne Chemical, Biological and Radiological Attacks, National Institute for Occupational Safety and Health (NIOSH)).*

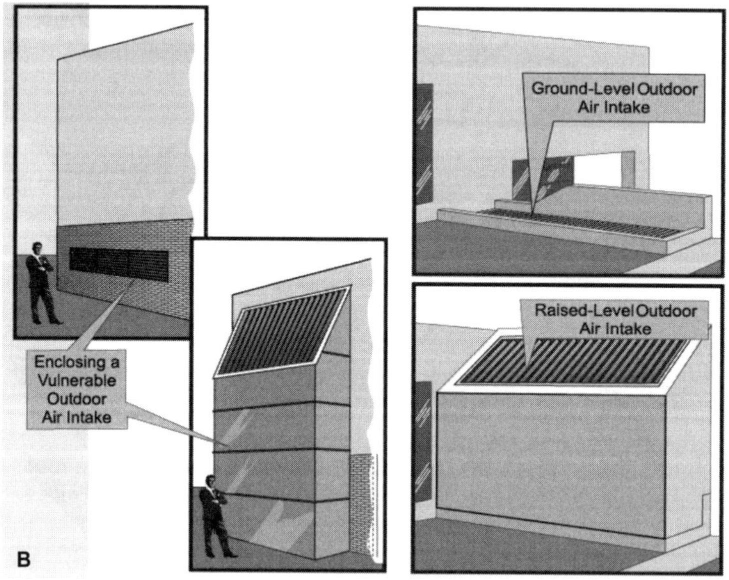

Figure 19.4 Vulnerable outdoor air intakes *(Courtesy Guidance for Protecting Building Environments from Airborne Chemical, Biological and Radiological Attacks, NIOSH).*

19.3 DEFINING SECURITY NEEDS

Security in the built environment is for the protection of people, information, and property. Security determinations are therefore essential in defining security needs prior to designing new facilities or retrofitting existing facilities. Attempting to overlay security strategies and measures after a design concept is in place can be very counter productive, causing delays and cost overruns. Moreover, while the scope and level of assessments within each facility will vary, the ultimate goal will remain the same—to decide upon an acceptable minimum level of security protection.

One expert on physical security and terrorism avoidance, Ross D. Bulla, president of Charlotte, NC-based The Treadstone Group Inc., offers the following 10 procedures for private-sector and government facilities, which he says can deter or mitigate terror attacks:

1. **Enforce a standoff zone:** A standoff zone is a secure area in which only pre-screened vehicles, bicycles, etc. are allowed to enter. A 100- to 300-foot standoff zone is ideal, but the effects from a blast are decreased in direct correlation to the increase in distance between a blast and its intended target. Therefore, even a 10-foot standoff zone is better than no standoff zone. Bollards, barriers, and barricades (natural and man-made) are used to enforce the integrity of the standoff zone (Figure 19.5A,B).
2. **Implement surveillance detection:** Nearly every major terrorist attack has been preceded by months or years of surveillance. Initial surveillance is usually conducted by amateurs or unwitting accomplices (children, taxi drivers, delivery/service persons, etc.) paid to take photographs, provide facility descriptions, or obtain other information (or information is surreptitiously elicited from them). Once a target list is narrowed, comprehensive surveillance is conducted by "professional"

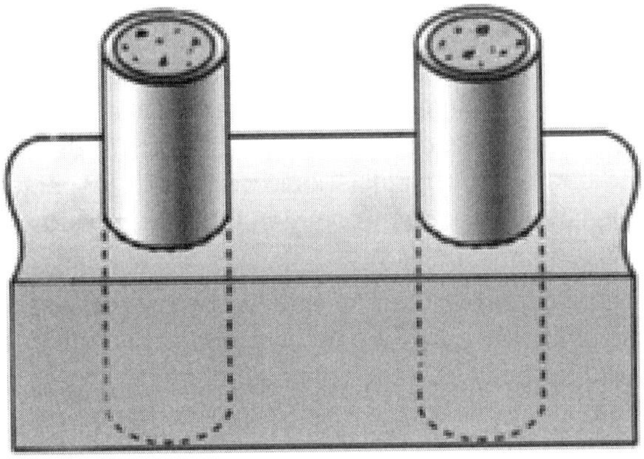

A

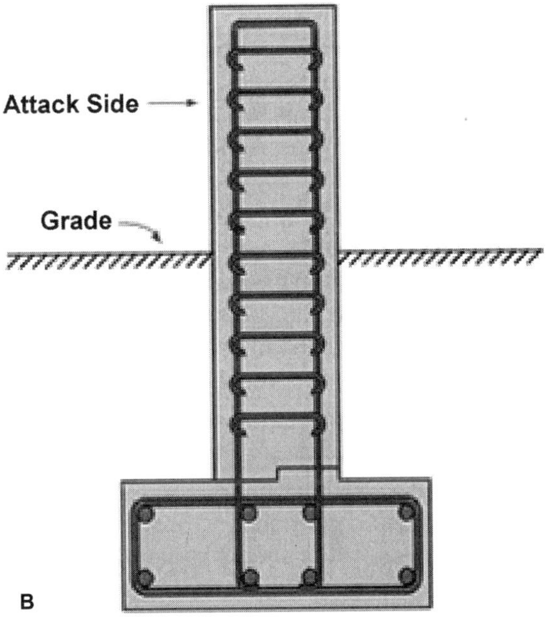

B

Figure 19.5 A. Anti-ram bollards detail. B. Anti-ram knee wall detail.

operators. Security personnel should be trained to observe and report unusual interest in a facility or activities that are out of context for the environment (e.g., a taxi driver photographing a service entrance).

3. **Screen deliveries:** All delivery, service, and courier vehicles and their contents should be screened using the following procedures: a) deliveries, other than courier services, should be scheduled in advance, and drivers should be required to present a bill of lading that reflects the driver's name and a password issued by the receiving department; b) all drivers, including couriers, and their assistants should present photo identification and their presence should be documented; c) all license tags should be documented; d) ideally, cargo areas should be inspected by security at a remote location and sealed by security or a receiving clerk/dock master; e) all incoming parcels should be x-rayed or physically inspected; f) no parcels should be accepted anywhere other than at the designated receiving areas.
4. **Stagger security:** The number of security personnel on-duty, as well as the times during which shifts change, should vary each day to eliminate a discernable pattern. When conducting patrols, security personnel should use random start and finish times and vary their routes (at times, even suddenly changing direction or backtracking). If possible, vary the methods of patrol (vehicle, bicycle, walking). The use of both uniformed and "plain clothed" security personnel is advantageous.
5. **Facilitate evacuation:** During non-business hours, facility management personnel, including the property manager, chief engineer, and security director, should conduct an evacuation drill using only emergency lighting in the emergency exit stairways. This enables them to mimic, as closely as possible, a real life emergency scenario. Often, these "evacuees" identify critical needs in stairways, such as: a) the need for additional emergency lighting on each landing; b) the benefit of luminous paint, decals, and/or signs, at floor and eye levels, to highlight primary and secondary escape routes; c) the need for public address speakers in the stairways, so evacuees can hear important announcements. Where possible, stairways should be widened, and separate stairways should be provided for exclusive use by emergency personnel. Stairways should never exit into public lobbies.
6. **Screen visitors:** Where possible, screen visitors at a remote location, distant from any facilities. Visitors should be scheduled in advance by their hosts, and hosts should be required to escort visitors at all times. Visitors should present government-issued photo identifications, which should be held until their visitors' passes are returned. Hand-carried belongings should be visually inspected or x-rayed, and persons should be required to pass through a magnetometer. Outerwear, such as jackets and coats, should be opened and/or removed for inspection.
7. **Screen employees:** All employees should be required to wear facility-issued photo identification at eye level on their outermost garments. The use of access cards are recommended and are best when used in conjunction with biometric or keypad systems. Always verify either electronically or visually that the card holder is the person to whom the card is issued; and never assume that an employee with whom you are acquainted is still employed at the facility.
8. **Review your emergency procedures:** Know what to do and when to do it. Review and, if necessary, update your security, evacuation, and life safety procedures and policies.
9. **Make security the responsibility of all users:** Everyone that works at your facility should be reminded continuously to observe and report unusual behavior. Users should challenge those who appear lost or are not known to them.

10. **Assess your security:** Retain a security consultant to assess your physical, technical, and operational security. Where possible, their involvement early in the architectural, engineering, landscape design, and construction phases can help to avoid costly rectification later.

The designer and facility manager must recognize and evaluate the nature of security threats to the corporation and the built environment and the relative risks associated with those threats. To improve safety and security, steps should be taken, including the following:

Asset Analysis: The space planner/designer must identify and prioritize the assets that require protection. These include people, operations, vital data and property. People are essentially the chief asset of any organization as they have the operational and technical know-how. Prioritizing assets can be achieved by examining the importance of various organizational functions to the survival of the organization.

Threat Analysis—Identify and Fortify Security Weaknesses: This step includes understanding the real role of security in your organization and increasing security's importance in the day-to-day running of the business, and the understanding that security is a continuous process and not an end state. An evaluation should be conducted on the impact of inadequate security on the company's bottom line. An action plan should be in place with countermeasures for security breach prevention. Contingency plans should be developed to counter various forms of security threats in the organization.

Determine what needs to go into your security plan, and put your plan into action with a minimum of headaches. Also define which areas of your property comprise the greatest safety and security risks. The owner must decide whether to contract out the company's security or to use in-house security staff.

Vulnerability Assessments and Appropriate Response: A vulnerability is any weakness that allows the realization of a threat. Once vulnerable points are identified, corrective countermeasures can be put in place. Your vulnerability assessment and a cost-benefits analysis determine whether a passive or active response is appropriate. Indeed, one of the most beneficial actions a facilities manager can take is authorizing a top-to-bottom security survey conducted by a qualified industry professional.

Active systems include electronic entry controls, closed circuit TV, intrusion detection, and many other technology solutions. Scanners, turnstiles, and cameras are expensive but human labor costs even more. Effective passive systems like landscaping, bollards, lighting, physical barriers, and evacuation and response plans, can be incorporated in place of or in addition to active systems. Many designers are also now considering the use of explosion-resistant glass in important structures. There would be a premium of possibly 20 percent or more for features like two-inch (5 cm) thick glass, Kevlar panels and special fireproof fabrics. It is unlikely that typical new construction will incorporate these changes without further drastic events. Nevertheless, "we can make effective changes through common sense threat assessment, responding appropriately, and using good design to ensure that solutions are effective and lasting," says Kate Kirkpatrick of Gensler.

Risk Analysis and Threat Assessment: Risk potential can be determined from the findings of asset, threat, and vulnerability analyses. These results can help determine the security measures that need to be put in place to effectively counteract a potential threat. Threats must be gauged in the context of the existing facilities. For example, are the facilities a likely target for workplace violence or a car bomb or for some other threat between these extremes? We need to examine the vulnerability of our infrastructure systems. Ira Winkler, author of *Corporate Espionage* uses the risk equation shown below to define an organization's specific level of risk.

$$\text{RISK} = \frac{\text{Threat} \times \text{Vulnerability} \times \text{Value}}{\text{Countermeasures}}$$

Methods for improving safety and security: The most common methods and approaches practiced today to improve safety and security of building environments are outlined below:

Access control: According to security expert Jeffrey Dingle, the basic concept of access control is simple: "Decide who can come in, and keep everyone else out." Dingle defines access control as "the use of barriers and recognition devices to restrict access into a controlled area." Access control systems can provide an enhanced level of security. But as with all security systems, any increase in the level of security brings with it a potential increase in the level of inconvenience.

Although access control can be overt and obvious, in most applications, it makes better sense to be low key and unobtrusive. Building occupants and visitors often experience a certain level of discomfort when physical barriers are present, particularly if they appear obtrusive. Safety and security measures should be balanced and integrated into the design so as to give the appearance of "art," or to blend into its surroundings so as to become inconspicuous. Better control of entrances can be achieved through integrated bollards and standards that act as barriers to protect entrances from vehicles.

Access control systems typically consist of two main parts: equipment and hardware, and policies and procedures.

A successful access control system must achieve two principle objectives: First, the building or area must be secured to prevent all unauthorized persons from gaining access except by going through a control point; second, there must be a specific list of persons that have authorized access.

In multi-tenant facilities, many forms of additional controls can be established to prevent unauthorized access. A very common form is the use of card-controlled elevators, in which an access card is needed to stop the elevator on the desired floor. However, in new high-rise construction, garage and basement level elevators are typically located in a different area from those serving tenant floors. This is a conscious design decision and necessitates a person first exiting the garage or basement elevator in order to re-enter a tenant floor elevator, passing through the lobby area on the way.

In many applications it is pertinent to install a single-door access system, even if the cost is high. When retrofitting existing facilities, high costs can be mitigated by the use of a single-door system or an off-line reader—a single-door system that operates independently and is not tied into the control system.

19.4 TYPES OF ACCESS CONTROL SYSTEMS

Access control systems basically rely on one or a combination of four basic operating concepts:

1. **Personal recognition:** This depends on the ability of an individual to recognize employees and authorize access. A facility with a small employee base and a low turnover rate can make personal recognition very secure. The main disadvantages are that security staff turnover wipes out the access control database, and turnover of employees can make it difficult for the security staff to keep track of who is and isn't allowed in.
2. **Unique Knowledge:** Unique knowledge requires a person to have special information or knowledge to gain access, as with a push-button combination lock. The advantage is that there is nothing to lose. The disadvantage is that it is possible for an authorized user to give a code or combination to an unauthorized user.

   Keypad access systems also require a person to have knowledge of the correct numerical access code to gain access. The combination or code is entered into a four-, six- or 10-digit keypad. Keypad systems can be electronic and tied into a system, or mechanical and stand-alone like a single-door, push-button door access system.

3. **Unique possession:** Systems based on unique possession require a person to possess something that allows access. The most common unique possession system is a key and lock. A weakness in a unique possession system is that it will allow access to anyone who is in possession of the item, whether or not they are allowed access.

   One increasingly common way to control access is through card readers. Each person who will require access receives a card. Each access card leaves an audit trail—a record of who enters and when. Most systems allow access time windows to be created, so that the time when each person has access can be limited. Remember, the system records what card opened the door, not who opened the door. Employees must be discouraged from loaning their cards to others, and it is very important for the user to protect his or her card. To overcome this problem, smart cards have been developed with embedded microchips that contain an encoded biometric description of the cardholder, so that when the card passes through a reader, the machine would verify that the card belonged to the person who presented it.
4. **Biometric devices:** Today, biometric security techniques are in use in multiple applications. In the U.S., fingerprint scans are used to crack down on persons claiming welfare benefits under different names and several jails have introduced iris scans to ensure the correct people are relocated or released. A number of universities have integrated fingerprint scanners into ATMs to eliminate the need for bankcards. These examples are only a brief illustration of the various biometric techniques deployed today, and the use of biometrics continues to increase on a daily basis.

Biometric systems are generally considered the most secure method, and the biometrics industry is showing continuous and sustained growth. These systems grant or deny access to buildings, information, and benefits by automatically verifying the identity of people through their unique physical characteristics, such as thumbprints, palm scans, voiceprints or iris checks. The information received is translated algorithmically into a complex string of numbers and is compared with a stored template of that person in a central database. These techniques have varying degrees of accuracy, ease of use, failure to enroll, failure to acquire, and universality.

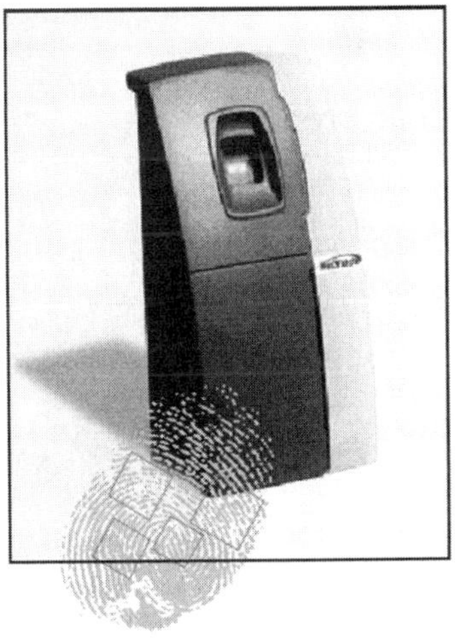

Figure 19.6 Plug and play fingerprint readers can confirm whether people are who they claim to be by matching fingerprint templates stored in a central database.

Such systems are based on digital analysis using cameras or scanners of biological characteristics, such as facial or palm structures, fingerprints (Figure 19.6), and retinal and iris patterns, which are then matched with profiles in available databases of people such as suspected terrorists (Figure 19.7, 19.8). Facial recognition techniques show promise and are already being used at several airports.

Typically, a combination of more than one of these methods offers the soundest security solution. One method is the use of a card access system with a PIN number: access is achieved by both having the card as well as knowing the PIN number. Modern photo ID cards can contain a combination of measures, such as unique possession (the card), unique knowledge (PIN), and personal identification (a person's photo on the card). According to the International Biometric Group (2003), a majority of biometric studies (about 74 percent) fall into the categories of fingerprint, facial, and symbol analysis and recognition.

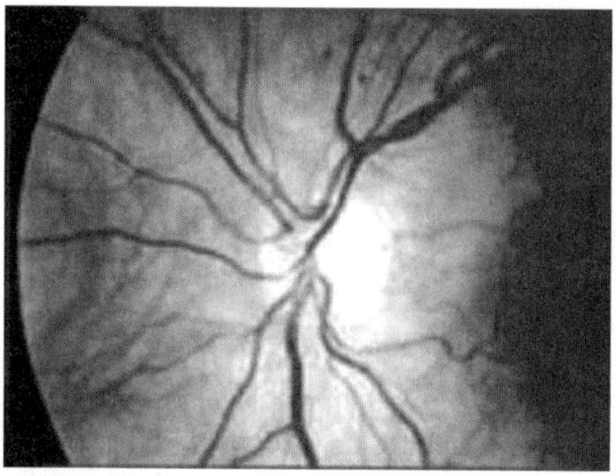

Figure 19.7 Retinal scanning.

Choosing the right system: Before making a determination on what system is right for a particular facility, many issues need to be considered, including access time, imposter resistance, reliability and error rate, ease of use, user acceptance, input time and effort, storage, and cost.

Access time and imposter resistance are critical factors when selecting access control systems. Access is the time taken by someone to use the system and for the system to respond positively. Access can take from a few seconds to a few minutes. Access time (sometimes called throughput) becomes critical in situations where large numbers of people require simultaneous passage, such as during a shift change.

Imposters gain access by convincing the system that they are authorized. Thus, a simple key and lock has no imposter resistance, while biometric systems have a high level of imposter resistance. The level of imposter resistance relates directly to the level of security required. It is obviously better from a failure rate and security standpoint to keep out people who should get in than to let people in who should be kept out.

Security technology is evolving at a rapid pace and recent developments include intelligent software that generates real-time alert alarming, thus allowing for the appropriate proactive action to be taken immediately.

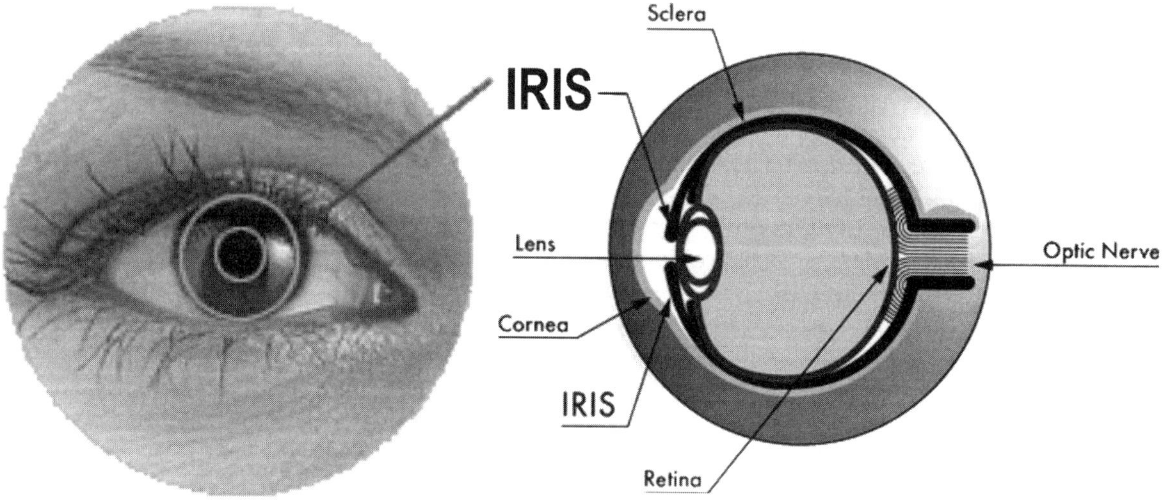

Figure 19.8 Iris scanning is one of the promising biometric techniques being developed. At the heart of the iris scanning system is a simple CCD digital camera. It uses both visible and near-infrared light to take a clear, high-contrast picture of a person's iris. With near-infrared light, a person's pupil is very black, making it easy for the computer to isolate the pupil and iris.

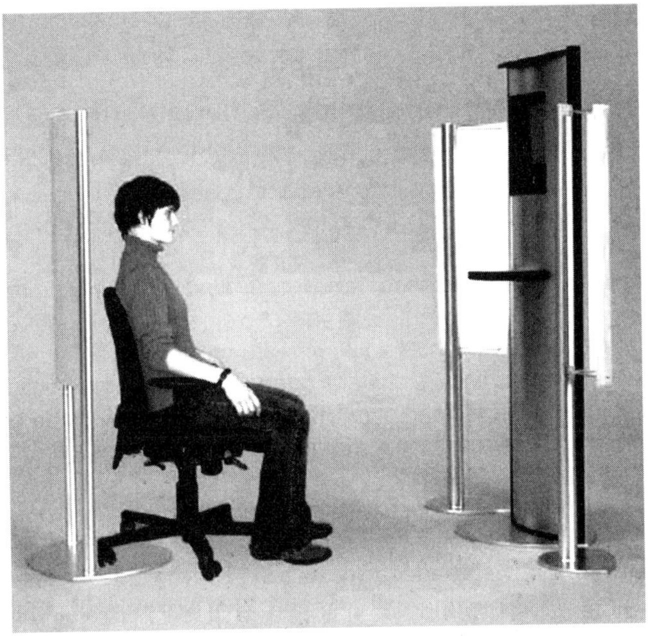

Figure 19.9 Face recognition continues to advance and shows considerable promise *(Source Cognitec Systems GmbH)*.

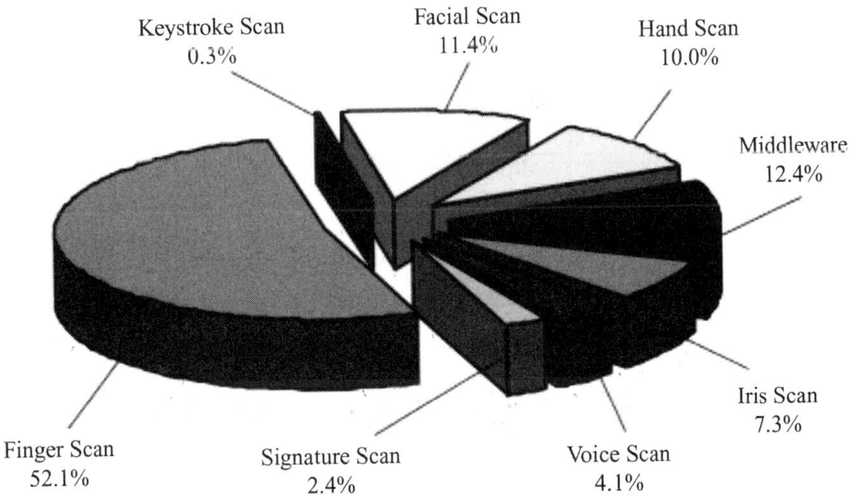

Figure 19.10 Percentage of biometric applications in real life, in which biometrics are defined as automated methods of recognizing a person based on physiological or behavioral characteristics *(Courtesy Int. Biometric Group)*.

19.5 MISCELLANEOUS ISSUES

19.5.1 Egress Planning and Emergency Management

Confusion often contributes to the loss of life at times of emergency, partly due to the issuing of conflicting instructions on where to go, unclear exit signs, etc. A survey conducted by the Society for Human Resource Management after the September 11 attacks found that 35 percent of American companies had no emergency plans in place.

The education of owners and tenants about emergency systems of buildings should go hand in hand with engineering and design. Corporate clients are now showing a heightened awareness concerning the security of their buildings and sites. Enlightened clients are more frequently asking architects and space planners to explore increasing the width of exit stairs over code minimums to allow firefighters to travel up while still permitting the building occupants to exit. During an emergency, good communication is vital. An evacuation response to a bomb threat will differ significantly from that of a fire. One calls for a controlled exit while the other necessitates a speedy exit.

Perimeter and access control: Equipment that enhances perimeter and access control security is a major consideration once you start weighing your technology options and budget.

"In an ideal world, you would have 360-degree coverage," says Gee Cosper, President and CEO, Gee Cosper & Associates. "This means anyone entering your grounds or building would be monitored. You would have an outer perimeter of security that ensures only authorized people get in, whether they are employees, patients, or visitors using a visitor pass." Exterior camera protection is therefore important, both to act as a deterrent and for monitoring purposes.

19.5.2 The Parking Problem

The World Trade Center experience has clearly highlighted the fact that a public parking garage located within a target building is a likely location for a car bomb. To eliminate this potential threat, one can implement one of two strategies: restrict the garage to building occupants and inspect every car that enters, or eliminate parking in the building altogether. These options obviously raise serious practical issues, particularly in urban areas, and the inconvenience may not be acceptable.

Potential solutions include requiring employee badges for garage entry, limiting self-parking to badge holders, and restricting large vehicles to controlled areas. Some local parking companies are assessing the situation and making changes as needed, but the majority feel that they have the situation under control.

A strong perimeter fence around a building offers better protection against a car bomb attack than a building allowing a car to be parked directly next to it. Furthermore, a strong perimeter fence located some distance from the building is likely to marginalize the effect of a car bomb, unless the bomb is massive in size.

19.5.3 New GSA (General Services Administration) Standards

Planners can find federal government standards for security requirements for their buildings online, providing a good resource on the subject.

Security areas and lobby functions are interdependent. Security screening should occur at entry and lead directly to the lobby and other areas. A lobby's internal circulation should not impede security processing. Further, the lobby should function freely and logically, and not compromise the circulation pattern.

Research continues for ways and means to improve safety and security in high-rise buildings. These include examining the impact resistance of structural fire protection materials, additional protection to escape routes, as well as 'hardening' escape stairs and corridors to provide impact resistance and protection against extreme fire events. Likewise, the industry is undertaking a more detailed analysis of the risk of severe damage to structural elements in the event of fire, increasing the number or capacity of stairs, upgrading lifts with emergency power, and employing or training fire evacuation marshals.

The consulting firm Arup Ltd., of London, proved that properly protected elevators can assist rapid evacuation. Their study on a 50-story building in London showed that the use of elevators nearly halved the escape time compared to using stairs only. Arup believes that building owners and tenants should be informed of relative risks from different sources. Reconfiguring the core can provide cost-effective refuge areas with a dedicated elevator and stairwell for emergency egress without increasing core square footage. The system bundles a service elevator for use by firefighters, a lobby, and a stairwell in a pressurized shaft.

The National Fire Protection Association has commenced with the development of a security code that will mandate minimum levels of protection.

19.5.4 Legal & Liability Issues

Due to the complexity of the matters involved, this chapter cannot possibly address the many legal concerns that may arise with regard to liability issues, and designers are strongly advised to consult their attorneys and professional liability insurance carriers for advice on these matters. While building owners and managers are not expected to guarantee the safety of their tenants, visitors, and guests, they are required to exercise reasonable care to protect them from foreseeable events. The number of liability lawsuits filed against American companies has increased dramatically over the last decade.

Building owners and facility managers wishing to be proactive toward security issues and to minimize liability should address the following issues:

- Adopt written security policies and procedures that get communicated throughout the property.
- Develop policies that address protection of all assets, including people, property information systems, and the building environment. Include a professional crime risk analysis and a building security vulnerability assessment.
- Procedures should include the review of all security incidents, including theft, vandalism, harassment, and breaches of information. Programs should be reviewed and validated by professionals as effective, economical and legally sound.
- Be sure to compare your security measures with buildings of similar type and against others in your marketplace.

Though specific law governing security considerations varies from state to state, the following common issues, when present, generally form the basis of proving liability in lawsuits regarding security:

- Owners owe a legal duty of care to anyone invited onto the property. These are defined as "special relationships" and each state defines which relationships are special to an owner.
- The crime should have been foreseeable. Most crimes are judged foreseeable unless the victim has exhibited gross negligence.
- The owner failed to use a reasonable standard of care in warning or protecting the victim.
- The owner's breach of duty in taking reasonable precautions was the cause of the injury.

Planners need to understand the measures that can be taken to reduce an organization's legal liability within the building, the parking lot, and beyond. Planners must also understand and address scope of work, disclaimers, and other essential elements of premises liability lawsuits with respect to how the law defines an owner's responsibility to protect facility users. In addition, planners should identify the interaction between OSHA and organizational security and should check whether the client is compliant under OSHA's General Duty Clause. The client should be made aware of the safety and security requirements relating to ADA.

Finally, since increased security is going to be with us for the foreseeable future, designers need to take advantage of advances in technology to make security stations less imposing and more acceptable. The psychological and functional requirements for increased security and defensible space should be achieved through the use of integrated security solutions that are balanced, pleasing, and do not disrupt a building's efficiency. Where an inspection of the security systems is required, reputable security professionals should be called in.

CHAPTER

20

Indoor Air Quality (IAQ), Environmental & Pest Control

20.1 INDOOR AIR QUALITY AND ENVIRONMENTAL ISSUES

Studies show that humans spend as much as 90 percent of their time indoors. Moreover, we expect our indoor environment to be free of effects that will damage or compromise our health. However, year after year, cases are documented of building related illness and sick building syndrome. This is because we live in a contaminated environment.

What triggers an investigation for mold contamination: An investigation for indoor air quality contamination can be triggered by adverse health concerns of occupants, observations of growing mold, unusual odors, or events of water intrusion. A variety of symptoms or observations, such as respiratory problems, headaches, nausea, irritation of eyes, nose, or throat, tiredness, fatigue, etc. may trigger an investigation into potential mold contamination. Mold may be observed on walls, pipes, ceiling tiles, window ledges, books, files, documents, etc. Musty odors and other unusual smells may indicate potential mold contamination. Also, any indication of water intrusion, flooding, condensation, or high humidity, especially if chronic and or severe, suggests potential mold contamination.

Air sampling requires the use of a device to implant organisms from a specific volume of air onto a sterile agar growth medium. The sample is then incubated for a specified period of time (say, 7 days). The colonies are then counted and the results recorded. When testing the air of a potentially contaminated area, it is best to have comparative samples of air from both the contaminated area and the air outside of the potentially contaminated building.

Environmentally regulated materials: The field of general building diagnosis and evaluation has in more recent times been expanded to include environmental evaluations. In the past several years an environmentally regulated material (ERM) evaluation has become a critical part of both the condition assessment and due diligence efforts. Evaluation strategies and methods can vary widely among consulting firms, and in some cases, even the regulatory agencies themselves. However, there are numerous experienced consultants with standardized procedures for providing assessment services.

There are several types of basic environmental assessments. The industry generally refers to Level I (Phase I) and Level II (Phase II) assessments. Level I is basically an overall view of the facility, and tends to be relatively general in nature. During the Level I assessment, the information gathered is preliminary and qualitative. A plan is then generated, which includes an identification of specific issues that need further investigation. The Level II assessment to further assess the facility when necessary is quantitative and typically includes site sampling and characterization activities when contaminants are suspected. Measurements are taken and the extent of environmental hazard, contamination, and liability at the property are identified. The assessor should submit recommendations to mitigate any problem issues.

Indoor air quality (IAQ): The quality of indoor air has become an area of increasing concern within the past decade. During the energy crisis of the 1970s and the conservation emphasis of the 1980s, buildings were designed to save energy. In designing and constructing for this, it has become increasingly apparent through the past few years that many of these buildings lack adequate ventilation or fresh air. More and more building users have experienced health problems due to the poor quality of indoor air. Also termed "sick building syndrome," IAQ issues are often dependent on the building function, the design of the HVAC system, and the quality of maintenance at a building.

Technology breakthroughs are making facility monitoring systems more affordable for a wider range of building types. The list of benefits continues to expand as access to indoor environmental data and the knowledge it imparts is applied to building performance. Benefits related to IAQ include improved indoor air quality, a complaint response mechanism, meeting LEED™ certification requirements, construction and renovation monitoring, more marketable tenant spaces, and verifying effectiveness of maintenance programs.

Until recently, it has been both prohibitively expensive and impractical to monitor indoor air on a periodic or continuous basis for typical commercial buildings. The cost of populating an entire facility with high-quality, very accurate sensors is only part of the challenge. Sensors, including those that monitor very common air quality parameters (i.e. carbon dioxide [CO^2]), have traditionally been a maintenance burden due to the sensor's need for repeated calibration and its tendency to drift over time. The result is that indoor environmental quality measurements or tests are usually conducted on a reactive basis, and even then, only when the situation is extreme enough to warrant the expense. One-time environmental testing can easily cost thousands of dollars and often requires a week or more to receive results.

Recent technological advances have removed many financial and maintenance obstacles, making permanent monitoring systems a consideration for a broader range of facilities managers. Schools, healthcare facilities, and general office buildings can benefit from measuring a host of environmental conditions; they can use that information to respond to occupant complaints, optimize facility performance, and keep energy costs in check. In addition, feedback from the indoor environment can be used to establish baselines for building performance and to document improvements to indoor air quality.

Parameters useful for evaluating indoor environmental quality and energy efficiency may be classified into three categories:

- Comfort and ventilation
- Air cleanliness
- Building pollutants

Within these categories, facility-wide monitoring systems can provide independent measurement of a range of parameters, including temperature, humidity, carbon dioxide (CO_2), carbon monoxide (CO), total volatile organic compounds (TVOCs), and airborne particulates. While useful for reducing investigative time and expense in responding to occupant complaints, the data and analysis from continuous monitoring can also be used proactively to optimize building performance. For example, particle counts can be used to indicate the effectiveness of the ventilation system.

Buildings are dynamic environments, and while the original basis for design may have been sound, after they are operational, the reality is that mechanical system controls drift, building use changes, and occupancy rates fluctuate. These changes can have a significant impact on the ability of the HVAC system (as designed) to maintain a balance between occupant comfort, health, productivity, and operating costs.

A facility monitoring system can be a valuable tool for improving indoor air quality, identifying energy savings opportunities, and validating facility performance. Automating the process of documenting and analyzing key parameters and providing facilities managers access to the results can better equip them to meet the challenge of maintaining healthy, productive environments.

Many factors have contributed to poor indoor air quality, including energy conservation, "least cost" design and construction, changes in office layout and furnishings, technical advances in office equipment, changes in materials used for construction, poorly designed ventilation and/or its operating after hours, the "no maintenance" mentality, cheap air filtration, and the tendency to down play complaints.

Conditions as diverse as dust or bacterial build-up in ductwork to second-hand smoke or the off-gassing of paint solvents can all become significant health hazards. IAQ deficiencies can oftentimes be very complex and are building-specific. A typical IAQ study consists of interviews with the building users as well as environmental measurements for the presence of various potential contaminants.

Fungi and Mold: Fungi are primitive plants that lack chlorophyll and therefore must live as parasites or feed on organic matter that they digest externally and absorb. The true fungi include yeast, mold, mildew, smut, and mushrooms. They usually grow best in dark moist habitats, and are found wherever organic matter is available. Some fungi can grow under extremely difficult conditions. In Figure 20.1, if the peeling of paint at the wall's base is lifted, it would probably reveal fungal amplification under the paint/paper. There is also a high probability that extensive fungal growth will appear inside the wall cavity and under the carpet.

The first step in every mold remediation project includes determination of the root cause of the mold growth. The next step is to delineate the order of magnitude of the mold growth via thorough visual examination. Since old growth may not always be visible, investigators may use instruments such as moisture meters, thermal imaging equipment, or borescope cameras to identify moisture in building materials or "hidden" mold growth within wall cavities, HVAC ducts, etc. Mold assessments and inspections should always include HVAC systems and their air-handler units, drain pans, coils, and ductwork. In addition, depending on the age of the building, the inspection should include sampling of building materials, such as ceiling tiles, drywall joint compound, and sheet floor to check for the presence of asbestos.

Four Essential Elements for Fungi Growth:

1. **Acceptable temperature range:** Each fungus has an optimal temperature range that allows for its growth.
2. **A nutrient source:** Fungi consume organic (carbon-based) matter. This includes paper and wood products, carpet, wall coverings, organic dust particles, paint, adhesives, plastics, fabrics and many other building products.
3. **Presence of a consistent moisture source:** Excessive humidity ratios within the walls of the building and furnishings, and the moisture produced in the form of condensation in HVAC systems can support mold growth.

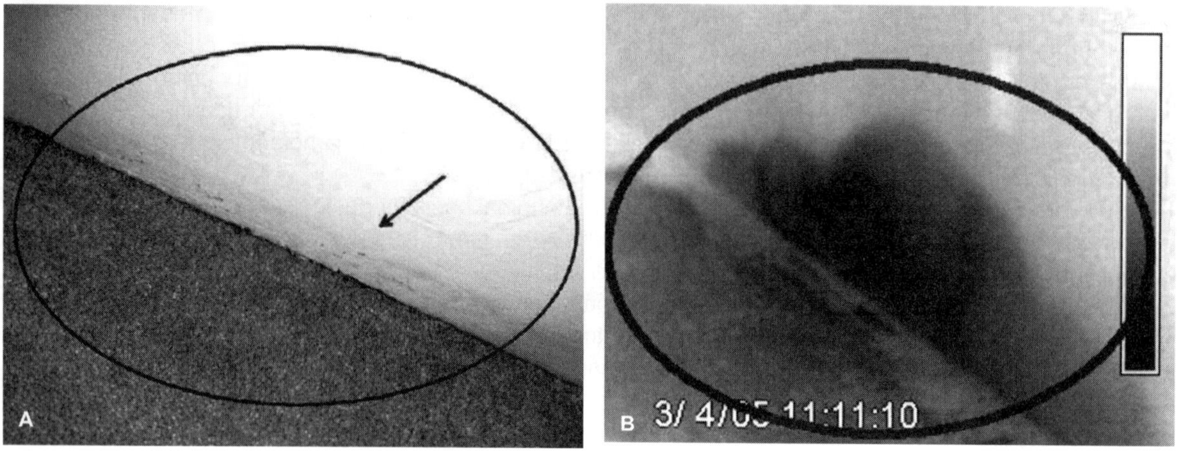

Figure 20.1 A. View at base of wall indicates presence of moisture at base of wall and carpet area. B. Thermal image shows extent of moisture saturation (darker areas) in both wall and carpet. Moisture levels were verified using Delmhorst electronic moisture meter. Both carpet and wall are saturated *(Courtesy Closer Look Inspections)*.

4. **Viable spores:** Spores are present in all buildings and systems. Remove one of the four elements and the growth process will be inhibited or nonexistent.

These organisms may contribute to poor indoor air quality and can cause health problems. Fungi in indoor environments comprise microscopic yeasts and molds, known as micro fungi, while plaster and wood-rotting fungi are referred to as macro fungi because they produce sporing bodies that are visible to the naked eye. Apart from single-celled yeasts, fungi colonize surfaces as a network of filaments, and some produce numerous aerially dispersed spores and other chemical substances such as volatile organic compounds (VOCs). The naturally occurring substances produced by fungi that bring about a toxic response are called mycotoxins, and are usually contained in the spores. Toxicity can arise from inhalation or skin contact with toxigenic molds. The mold investigator should check the following:

Building exterior

- Windows, doors, air conditioning units, dormers, etc.—check for peeling or blistering paint, rot, or other damage that might allow water to penetrate.
- Roof—check for damage that could allow water penetration.
- Exterior walls—check for breaks, cracks, or other openings.
- Check joints at corners, top sills, side jambs, and where different claddings meet to ensure continuous caulking that seals the joint properly.
- Check basement window wells for proper drainage (gravel and drain tube to base of wall is normal) and to be sure they don't leak.
- Basement walls should be examined for cracks or other damage that could indicate water intrusion sites.

- Drainage pipes (e.g., rain-trough down spouts) should be examined for damage or blockages that might lead to water entering the building.
- Pipes that penetrate the basement wall (e.g., utilities) should be checked for proper seals.
- Slope of ground around basement wall should be adequate to provide proper drainage.
- Drainage holes and pipes for water that might collect behind exterior veneer must not be blocked.

Building interior:

- Inspectors should examine the following in basements: renovations that might trap condensation, evidence of leaks around pipes that penetrate the wall, leaks around windows, condensation around cold spots or on plumbing pipes, plumbing leaks (water and sewage pipes, appliances), HVAC system components, standing water (e.g. sewers, sumps, and puddles), active ventilation of the area, leaks from the floor above, relative humidity, materials that might sustain growth in high humidity, and expansion joints at floor-wall junctions.

The medical community appears to be divided regarding the threat of mold, but seems to agree that some people with allergies are sensitive to mold and that mold can lead to respiratory diseases in sensitive individuals. The issue with mold then is not to prevent any mold growth, or to eliminate any existing mold growth, but to control it within acceptable limits.

Toxic molds and fungi are a significant source of airborne volatile organic compounds (VOCs) that create indoor air quality (IAQ) problems. Toxic mold growth produces dangerous mycotoxins and infectious airborne mold spores, which often cause serious health problems to residents and workers.

To grow, or to establish itself, mold requires at least four elements: mold spores, organic matter (like wood, paper, and drywall), moisture, and warmth. Note that the mere presence of humid air does not necessarily promote mold growth, except where air with a relative humidity (RH) level at or above 80 percent is in contact with a surface. Carried by air currents, mold spores can reach all surfaces and cavities of buildings. If these surfaces and/or cavities are warm, and contain the right nutrients and amounts of moisture, the mold spores will grow and gradually destroy the things they grow on. To control mold growth, designers should focus on controlling moisture indoors and on the temperatures of all surfaces, including interstitial surfaces within walls.

Asbestos: Asbestos is the name given to a number of naturally occurring, fibrous silicate minerals mined for their useful properties, such as thermal insulation, chemical and thermal stability, and high tensile strength. Asbestos is commonly used as an acoustic and thermal insulator, for fire proofing and in other building materials. Many products are in use today that contain asbestos. Asbestos is made up of microscopic bundles of fibers that may become airborne when asbestos-containing materials are damaged or disturbed. When these fibers get into the air they may be inhaled into the lungs, where they can cause significant health problems.

Asbestos is the most widely recognized ERM considered during building evaluations. It is a natural fire-retardant mineral fiber that has been used in a variety of construction materials in the past 70 years. Asbestos-containing building materials are grouped as either surfacing materials (including pipe, tank and other equipment insulation) or miscellaneous materials that can also cause respiratory diseases when the fibers are inhaled. If the asbestos-containing material is in good condition and not likely to become disturbed, there is no requirement to remove or replace the material. A typical asbestos survey involves the sampling and laboratory analysis of suspect building materials as well as air sampling for airborne fibers.

Many materials containing asbestos are located in concealed areas, such as wall cavities, below ground level, and other hidden spaces. In order to provide a sufficient asbestos survey, the inspector must perform destructive testing (i.e., opening walls, etc.) to inspect these areas for suspect materials.

Polychlorinated biphenyls (PCBs): PCB oils have been used mainly as a coolant in electrical transformers. Despite the fact that production and sale of PCB was banned by the Environmental Protection Agency (EPA) in 1979, an estimated 150,000 PCB-filled transformers remain in use nationwide. Also, it is estimated that another 2,000,000 mineral oil transformers contain some percentage of PCB. PCBs can also be found in light ballasts and elevator hydraulic fluids. Although they are a suspected carcinogen, properly sealed or contained PCBs will not pose a hazard. PCBs become a hazard when they catch fire, creating carcinogenic by-products. These by-products can contaminate the air, water, finishes, and contents of a building. Leaking PCB can also contaminate building materials and soil. PCB evaluations typically involve identifying the existence of, or potential for, PCB leakage, measuring the level of PCB concentrations, and identifying the presence of combustible materials adjacent to PCB-containing equipment.

Lead: Lead was added to paint to improve its durability and drying characteristics. In 1955 the industry adopted a voluntary standard limiting lead content in paint to no more than one percent by weight. This was gradually reduced and lead was eliminated altogether in 1978. Many homes built before 1978 still contain high levels of lead-based paint. In commercial buildings, lead has been used mainly as a paint preservative. Ingestion of lead has been proven to cause several neurological disorders.

The hazards of lead-containing paint have come into the news predominantly within the last decade due to the hazards associated with lead-based paint in public low-income housing. As the paint peels and chips with age, children have eaten the paint, causing irreparable neurological problems and learning disorders.

Lead piping has also been used in some older buildings. While not required to be replaced, in many cases the piping is deteriorating and leaching into the building's drinking water. In some buildings lead solder has also been used in the installation of copper pipes. This has been banned in many jurisdictions due to the deterioration of the solder resulting in water contamination. In an evaluation for lead contamination, the content of the water is analyzed by a laboratory for lead concentrations. Actions mitigating the hazards should be taken to reduce contamination if lead content is in excess of regulated limits. The majority of the time, the potential for water contamination can be eliminated by chemical treatment of the water. If this cannot be accomplished, the piping may require replacement.

Lead paint may be detected by several means. The most commonly accepted method is through use of an X-Ray Fluorescent lead-in-paint analyzer (XRF). The XRF analyzer is held up to the surface being tested for several seconds. The analyzer emits radiation, which is absorbed and then fluoresces (is emitted) back to the analyzer. The unit breaks down the signals to determine if lead is present and in what concentration. An XRF analyzer is generally able to read through many (up to about 20) layers of paint. XRF analyzers are expensive, and must be used by trained professionals.

Radon (Rn): Radon is a natural, odorless, tasteless gas that is emitted from soil as a carcinogenic by-product of decaying uranium. The by-product can cling to dust particles and when inhaled, lodge in bronchial airways. The gas can enter through floor slab and wall cracks, as well as openings for piping in building spaces coming in close contact with uranium-rich soil. If there is insufficient ventilation, radon can accumulate in the building space and pose a health hazard. A radon survey measures the concentrations of radon in the air and determines whether actions will be necessary to reduce the contamination. Radon levels can vary from one building to another and from season to season. It is located everywhere and at various levels. The reason that it is harmful in a building is that it can become trapped and grow to hazardous levels.

The United States Environmental Protection Agency states that radon causes an estimated 14,000 lung cancer deaths each year. It is the earth's only naturally produced radioactive gas and comes from the breakdown of uranium in soil, rock, and water. Although you cannot see or smell radon, it can become a health hazard when it accumulates indoors. When radon decays and is inhaled into the lungs, it releases energy that can damage the DNA in sensitive lung tissue and cause cancer. However, elevated radon levels should not necessarily keep an investor from buying a building because the problem can normally be easily fixed, even in existing buildings.

Site contamination issues: Within the past few years, underground storage tank (UST) evaluation and soil and groundwater contamination evaluation have increasingly been added to the scope of work of a typical facility evaluation. In the past, both above and below ground storage tanks were constructed using single wall containment. As a result, many older tanks have become damaged or deteriorated to the point of leaking a variety of chemicals, from oil to chlorinated hydrocarbons. The leaking tanks can contaminate both the soil and the groundwater at the property. As is typical in the Level I assessment, in addition to a review of the existing conditions at the site, a thorough review of the past and present public records of the property is performed to determine the historical uses of the site. If the site was used for operations extensively employing chemicals, the property should be reviewed carefully.

20.2 INSECT, RODENT AND PEST CONTROL

Cockroaches, rats, termites, and other pests have plagued commercial facilities for far longer than computer viruses. Increasingly, research has confirmed and pinpointed pest infestation as the trigger or cause of a host of diseases. In fact, according to the National Pest Management Association, pests can cause serious threats to human health, including diseases such as rabies, salmonellosis, dysentery, and staph infections. But in addition to pests presenting a serious health concern to a building's occupants, they also distract from a facility's appearance and value.

20.2.1 Rodents

Animals that may come indoors during winter include rats, mice, squirrels, and sometimes even raccoons. Rodents may come in through almost any opening—pet doors, holes in walls, missing vent screens, openings around pipes, dryer ducts, vents, etc. Rats and mice are likely to enter buildings during any time of the year. However, fall and winter are considered the "rodent season" as these pests crawl into homes and other structures searching for a new food supply, now that their natural supply of seeds outside is no longer available. Once inside, rodents can be very destructive. They chew through wallboards and can eat through cardboard boxes, wood, and plaster. Rodents also gnaw on electrical wiring and could potentially cause an electrical fire.

Various species of rodents, such as the Norway rat and roof rat, have become problematic in the U.S. According to the U.S. Centers for Disease Control, rats bite more than 45,000 people a year. They can burrow three feet straight into the ground, chew through building materials such as cinderblock, wire, aluminum, and lead, and can climb inside pipes with diameters between one-half and four inches (Figure 20.2A,B). Rats primarily rely on smell, taste, touch, and hearing; they typically eat and urinate on human and animal food, and support many ectoparasites.

By far, the most effective way to stop rodent invasions is to exclude them from the building. Buildings under good repair with few openings for rodents to enter experience few rodent invasions. "Rodent proofing" is a process where potential entry points are identified and steps taken to permanently close them or otherwise prevent rats or mice from gaining access.

Mice, like rats, can also pose serious problems. For example, under ideal conditions and no mortality, mice can produce up to 2,500 heirs in six months. Moreover, mice can fit through an opening the size of a nickel. Effective rodent proofing requires finding and closing as many such openings as possible. In some cases, because rodents can gnaw their way inside, doors may require metal plates along the bottom or fitted around the corners.

Doors should be kept closed, except if screen doors are present, and should have tight-fitting weatherstrips along all edges, especially the bottom. Large overhead doors and rail doors, if present, require specialized weatherstrips to seal out rodents. All foundation and attic vents need to be equipped with tight-fitting screens and 1/4-inch hardware cloth to exclude both insects and rodents.

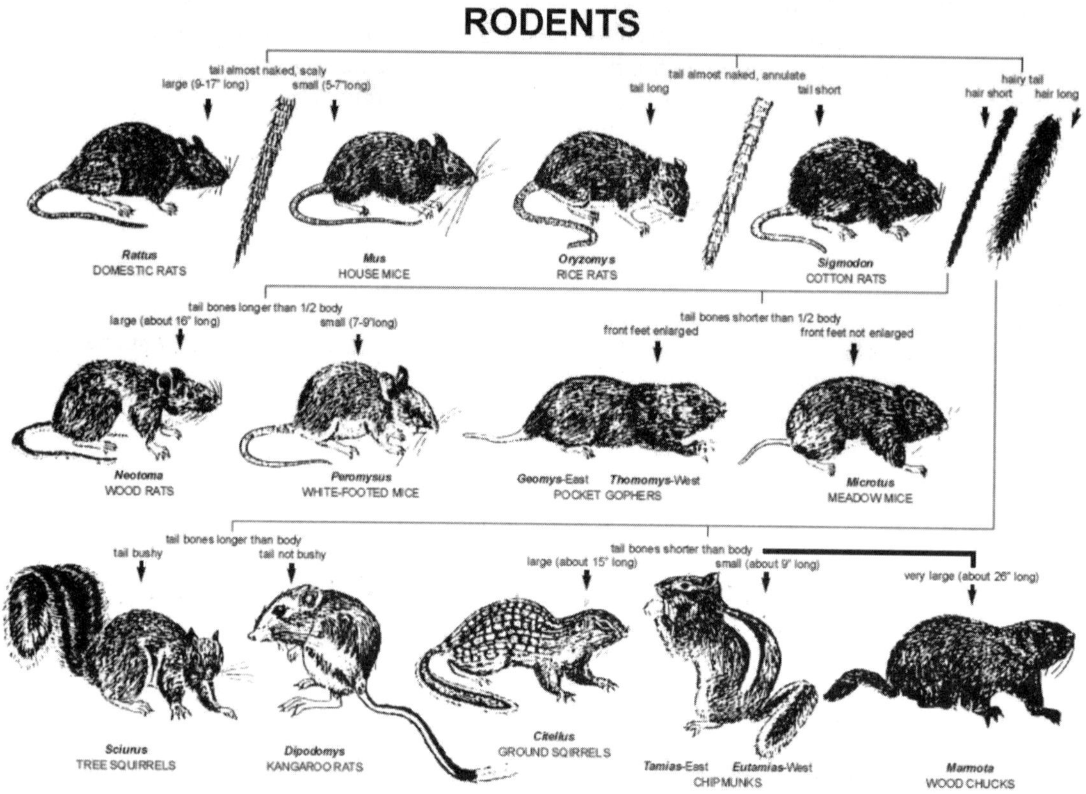

Figure 20.2 A. Types of common rodents found in the United States *(Courtesy Harold G. Scott)*.

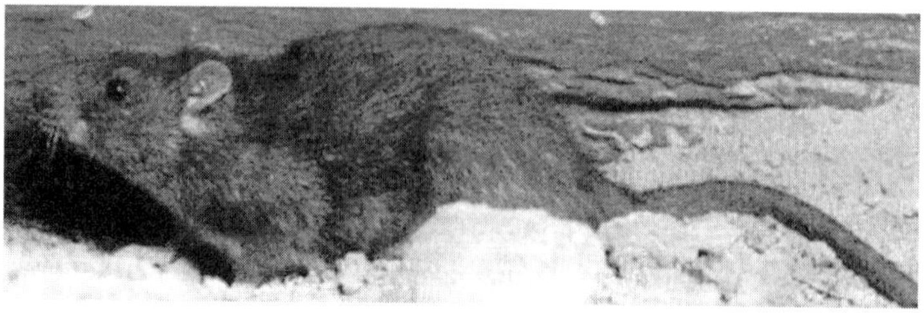

Figure 20.2 B. Photo of a Norway rat, which has become problematic in the United States.

Diseases associated with rodents: Rodents carry disease and fleas and leave waste. Wild and domestic rodents have been reported to harbor and spread as many as 200 human pathogens. Diseases include the deadly Hantavirus and arena virus. Hantavirus is contracted primarily by inhaling airborne particles from rodent droppings, urine or saliva left by infected rodents, or through direct contact with infected rodents.

20.2.2 Insects

More than 900,000 species of insects exist and additional species are identified every day. The following are some of the insects commonly encountered in today's living and commercial environments:

Cockroaches have been reported to spread at least 33 kinds of bacteria, six kinds of parasitic worms, and at least seven other kinds of human pathogens. They can pick up germs on their bodies as they crawl through decaying matter and then carry these onto food surfaces (Figure 20.3).

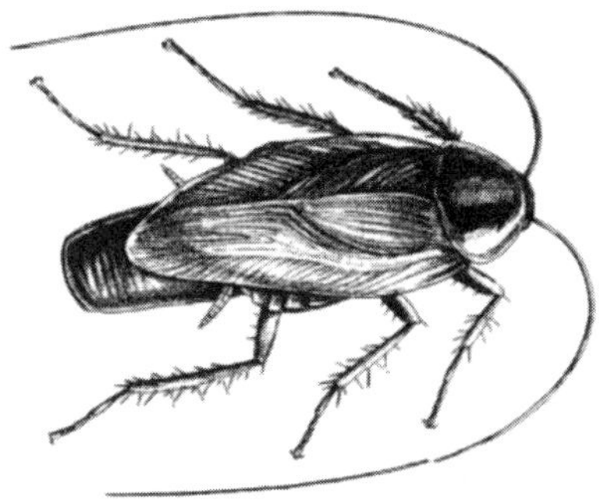

Figure 20.3 Illustration of an American cockroach.

Termites can pose a major threat to structures, so the sooner a termite infestation is addressed with a qualified termite control company, the better. The field observer should look for the tell-tale signs of termites: small holes in wood, crumbling drywall, termite insect wings, straw shaped mud tubes, and sagging doors or floors (Figure 20.4).

The most relevant and common termite species include:

1. **Formosan termites:** This species originally came from China and are the most voracious, aggressive, and devious of over 2,000 known termite species. Formosan termites are found in about 10 states across the country, particularly in the south. They organize into huge underground colonies and construct intricate mud nests inside a building's walls. Because of their devious and voracious nature, Formosan termite control is difficult once they've infested a property, so prevention is the best cure.
2. **Subterranean termites:** Found in all 50 states, subterranean termites live underground or in moist secluded areas above ground, and their colonies can contain up to two million termites. Subterranean termite infestation can be pinpointed by the characteristic mud tubes they construct to

Figure 20.4 Illustration of a winged ant and termite.

gain access to food and protect themselves from the open air. They can also build these mud tunnels through cracks in concrete.

3. **Drywood termites:** Unlike subterranean termites, which like moisture, drywood termites prefer to feast on dry wood. Although they are similar to subterranean termites in size and color, drywood termites do not have a worker termite in their caste. Rather, they rely on immature drywood termites (called nymphs) to do the work before they reach adulthood. Drywood termites form colonies of about 2,500 members, and they infest dry wood areas, such as attic framings and door frames.
4. **Dampwood termites:** Like the subterranean termites, dampwood termites love wood with high moisture content. For this reason, dampwood termites are not often found in structures. However, when they find a moist wooden structure to inhabit, dampwood termites can still do significant damage, which is why their control is important.

Ants: There are more than 20 varieties of ants invading homes throughout the United States during the warm months of the year. Worldwide, there are more than 12,000 species, but of these, only a limited number actually cause problems. All ants share one trait: they are unsightly and contaminate food. Ants range in color from red to black (Figure 20.5).

Destructive ants include fire and carpenter ants. Others ant types include the honey, Pharaoh, house, Argentine, Carpenter, and the thief ant. Fire ants are vicious, unrelenting predators with a powerful, painful sting. At least 32 deaths in the U.S. can be attributed to severe allergic reactions to fire ant stings.

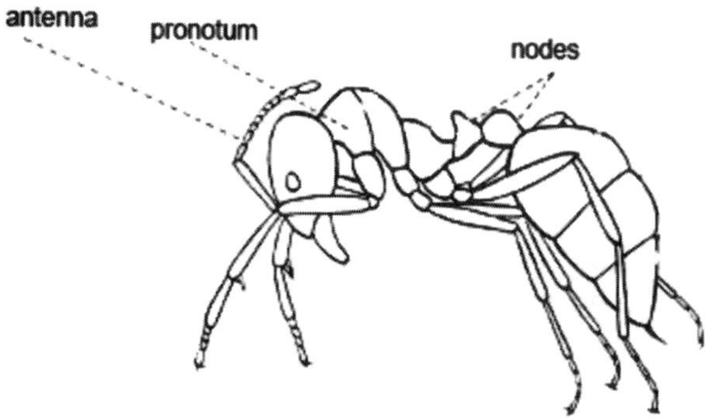

Figure 20.5 Drawing showing the identifying features of an ant.

Survey methodology: Normally, a field observer would require a bright flashlight and a magnifying glass to conduct a survey. Evidence of pests is typically found in different forms, such as droppings (especially from cockroaches and rodents) and frass (from wood borers), gnawing, tracks, and grease marks (from rodents), damage (such as powderpost beetle exit holes), and shed insect skins. The presence of feeding debris or frass is an indication of infestation.

Window sills should regularly be examined as many pests fly or crawl towards light. Pests may also be found behind baseboards, under furniture, behind moldings, in floor cracks, behind radiators, and in air ducts. The inspector should check around door jambs for cockroaches and spider webs. Conditions that would invite pest problems should be checked out, like the presence of moisture, both indoors and out, which may lead to moisture-related pests such as carpenter ants, termites, or mold. Damaged screens, doors, and walls, which could allow pest entry, should be fixed. Any sanitation problems should be noted. Heavy landscaping near the foundation and plants such as ivy growing on walls increases the risk of outdoor pests moving inside and need to be controlled or avoided. Moisture problems around the foundation, gutters, or air conditioning units should be monitored and rectified as they can favor moisture-related pests entering a facility. Bright exterior lights attract insects to the outside of the building, and these insects may then find their way indoors. Poor trash management may be attracting rodents, which could also find their way inside through utility lines or other openings.

CHAPTER 21

Business Development

21.1 GENERAL

Many skilled and experienced senior professionals are finding themselves on their own, seeking employment for the first time after being forced to abandon the safety of an organization that regularly delivered their paychecks each month. As a result of this, an increasing number of senior professionals are re-thinking their employment strategy. Cash flow, health insurance, and retirement concerns dominate this strategy. For seasoned veterans, there are also growing concerns over job satisfaction, location, and stress. When asked what they are doing in this new world of uncertainty they often respond, "Some consulting." But saying it and successfully doing it are not the same.

Nevertheless the decision has been made to incorporate and move into new offices. There are seductive attractions to being an independent consultant, like being your own boss, having flexible hours, and seeing the family whenever you like. You bill your clients for services you are good at and like to do. Many due diligence professionals appear to head toward consulting with these implanted visions. The reality, however, is often somewhat different. We should not confuse being a consultant with operating an independent consulting firm—whether on our own or with others.

The industry is very competitive and firms cannot afford to keep anyone who is not doing billable work. These firms respond quickly to business cycles, and job security can be tenuous at best. Add all the usual company politics and one can see that this type of consulting career may offer little change from the prior job. Second, the freedom that comes with independent consulting comes with a heavy price, including the potential loss of security. While there is greatly diminished security in today's corporate world, being employed in someone else's organization still carries a degree of stability that many desire. One suddenly attains an illusion of freedom being independent, but where the next dollar is coming from is often in question. One needs to be mentally prepared for this reality, and this fact can be particularly disturbing to family members.

21.2 PREPARING A BUSINESS STRATEGY AND PLAN

A written business strategy and plan should be prepared that incorporate the following components:

Introduction: Give a brief and comprehensive summary of how the company came into existence, the ideas it was based upon, and the people linked to it.

Mission and vision: In any organizational venture, the vision and mission are the first things to clearly define. The vision and mission statements shall reflect the direction of the company's business, as well as its goals and expected achievements. Define both the short-term and long-term goals and the factors that are to be focused on in achieving them.

Management biography: A business plan should also include a short biography of principals and senior personnel as well as their backgrounds, positions, and responsibilities.

The successful business plan: A business plan is basically a written document that describes the business, its objectives, its strategies, the market it is in and its financial forecasts. Proper planning is the key to the success of any business and its importance cannot be overemphasized. The process of putting a business plan together, including the thought necessary before beginning to write it, forces one to take an objective, critical, unemotional look at the business project in its entirety. Doing so will identify areas of weakness and strength, pinpoint needs that might otherwise be overlooked, and spot opportunities early. An effective plan must also show the marketing strategy that shall be implemented. A business plan is thus an operating tool that, if properly used, will help manage the business and work effectively toward its success.

Although a business plan serves many functions, from securing external funding to measuring success within the business, its main purpose is twofold. First, it helps ensure you have researched and thought through the various aspects of running the business so you don't encounter any sudden unpleasant surprises. Second, lenders require one and it can help convince banks or potential investors that your firm is worthy of receiving financial assistance for funding the new venture. The concept here is to communicate ideas to others while providing the basis for a financial proposal.

A business plan is therefore an important working document that should be used—not filed and forgotten. Setting up a business is never easy; statistics show that over half of all new businesses fail within the first 10 years. A major reason for such failure is lack of planning. The best way to enhance the chances of success is to plan and follow through on that plan. Also, because of the great difficulty for new startup businesses in finding capital, it is prudent for new business owners to expect to have to supply required startup capital from their own funds initially or from a bank loan linked to income or security other than the business.

It is also strongly advised to consider seeking legal counsel to be sure the plan and business venture are legal and meet your requirements. In addition, the service of an experienced accountant is important. Unless you are prepared to construct spreadsheets and graphs explaining how you intend to use your money and what projections you have for the future, you might want to hire someone who knows all the financial ins and outs of a business.

The executive summary: Typically, investors will not spend more than a few minutes reviewing a business plan to determine whether they should read it in detail or go on to another plan. Normally, if the investor reads any part of the plan, it will be the executive summary. It is therefore essential to prepare an appealing and convincing executive summary to capture the investor's attention and imagination and to make them more likely to read the remainder of the plan. In essence, the executive summary is the most important part of the business plan, as it will determine whether the remaining pages are read. Although the executive summary appears as the first part of the plan, it should be written only after completion of the whole document.

Success factors: Many factors will impact the chances of a new company's success. These include:

1. **Extensive network:** A single contact may yield a lucrative contract, but it takes a strong network to yield a continuing stream of work. What you might consider to be a well-developed network may be seen as just a starter list by successful consultants. Sometimes a very successful consultant, who is virtually unknown, has been brought on board by one or two clients immediately after leaving a prior employer. Sometimes it is the former employer that immediately brings them back as a consultant because of their knowledge of the operations.
2. **Excellent communication skills:** Most senior and especially executive-level professionals have excellent verbal skills, since this competency is one of the primary determinants for moving up the corporate ladder. Writing skills are an entirely different matter. Many consulting projects end in some form of written report and this can be a major challenge to those who depended on others to put pen to paper.

   Building a network depends on access to potential clients. Face-to-face contacts are the best, but they are also the most time-consuming and expensive. Independent consultants rarely have the marketing budget or the time required to build quality face-to-face networking relationships. Publishing quality articles that attract attention is another, potentially more cost-effective approach to getting the word out.
3. **Intelligence and people skills:** Managers may have been able to dictate orders to employees inside the industry, but dealing with clients takes skill. Consultants have to respond to a much greater array of personalities with little background information on their likes and dislikes. Techniques such as bullying and intimidation that bosses seem to get away with inside companies will not get much favorable response in consulting. Likewise, independent consultants may find themselves quickly dropped if they appear to be less than top-notch. Having phenomenal people skills will bring in the work, but will not necessarily help you hold onto it or get repeat business.
4. **Willingness to work hard:** There is some flexibility in the work hours, but this is no eight-to-five job; hard work and effort will be needed to build the practice. Some may have fallen immediately into client work and have become complacent. Others may be straddling the fence and have not made the full commitment as they continue to seek a suitable position. They fail to prepare the marketing materials, to obtain a Web domain and to aggressively build a presence. Even if this is the case, there is no real excuse for not projecting a professional image while seeking alternative employment.
5. **Self directed:** Some people have great difficulty in working on their own initiative and need a structured environment to perform. Independence can be freeing, but it can also be lonely; some people require daily, face-to-face interaction. This is especially true of individuals who work out of their home office instead of renting space in some corporate office park. Again, much of consulting is about self-awareness, self-confidence and the ability to go it alone.
6. **Marketing skills:** Some people are shy and introverted; others are oblivious to where the new client work may come from. If you are not willing to engage in relentless self-promotion, you may not be able to bring in sufficient new business to succeed. Identify your target market. There

should be specific target markets that will need your services and be willing to pay for them. Outline a marketing strategy with a competitive edge that draws customers to you and your company rather than to the competition. List the main competition and provide an honest appraisal of their strengths and weaknesses and how you expect to successfully compete against them.

If the market appears to be saturated with consultants in your areas of expertise, you may be in for a challenge. Many new consultants have expectations of what they will do and usually that centers on what they want or like to do. However, clients can come from a number of different, unanticipated directions. One has to be flexible.

7. **Financial security:** The independent consulting business can be feast or famine. Unless you have resources to survive the dry periods, which could easily last a year or more, it may be prudent to reconsider the decision to be an independent consultant. One of many challenges that face the independent consultant is the need to be a sort of "jack of all trades" who is responsible for all aspect of the project. People who are exceptionally strong in one area, such as building systems, but very poor in marketing may be wise to team up with others who can compensate for these weaknesses.

In addition to the various bureaucratic and legal hurdles that an entrepreneur must overcome to incorporate and register a new firm, there are other procedures as well as time and costs involved in launching a consulting firm. These need to be examined before attempting to launch such a venture.

21.3 START-UP COSTS AND SETTING THE BUDGET

You cannot hope to start, operate and succeed in setting up a business without sufficient capital. A lack of cash is one of the primary reasons that a large number of small businesses fail within the first year of operation. Many first-time business owners don't consider, or they greatly misjudge, the amount of money needed to get their small business off the ground. Consequently, they don't secure enough financing to carry their business through the period before the business starts to make money.

To avoid being "undercapitalized" you will need to do adequate cost planning during your pre-launch phase. It is likely that you will end up spending more money than planned, so better to err on the side of caution. Most experts recommend that start-up funding be adequate to cover operating expenses for six months to a year. At the very least you will need several months to find customers and get established. But to determine how much in financing to seek, you will need to develop detailed cost projections. Experts suggest a two-part process. First, develop an estimate of your one-time start-up costs. Second, put together a projection of your operating expenses for at least the first six months of operation. Performing these two exercises will help to ensure that you put into place the necessary financial cushion to start and stay in business.

Start-up costs estimates: Estimating how much will be needed to start a new business requires a careful analysis of several factors. Put together a list of realistic expenses of one-time costs for opening your doors. For example, determine what furniture, fixtures and equipment is needed. List the cost, the down payment or cash price, and if purchased on an installment plan, the amount of each monthly or periodic payment. Record them in the costs table that follows.

Down Payment $_______
Amount of each payment $_______

The furniture, fixtures, and equipment required may include such things as desks, moveable partitions, storage shelves, file cabinets, tables, safe, special lighting, and signs.

Typical start-up costs items to be paid only once:

Furniture, fixtures, and equipment:
Interior decorating $_______
Installation of fixtures and equipment $_______
Starting inventory $_______
Deposits with public utilities $_______
Legal and other professional fees $_______
Licenses and permits $_______
Advertising and opening promotion $_______
Advance on lease $_______
Other miscellaneous cash requirements $_______

TOTAL ESTIMATED CASH NEEDED TO START = $__________

Estimated monthly expenses:

$_______Salary of owner-manager
$_______All other salaries and wages
$_______Payroll taxes and expense
$_______Rent or lease
$_______Advertising
$_______Delivery expense
$_______Office Supplies (Figure 21.1A,B)
$_______Telephone
$_______Other utilities
$_______Insurance
$_______Property taxes
$_______Interest expense
$_______Repairs and maintenance
$_______Legal and accounting
$_______Miscellaneous

TOTAL ESTIMATED MONTHLY EXPENSES = $________
$______ Multiply by 4 (4 months)
$______ Add: Total Cash needed to start above
TOTAL ESTIMATED CASH NEEDED = $______

When the approximate amount of cash needed to start is determined, one can then estimate how much money is actually available or can be made available to put into the business, and where the rest of the money required to start the business will be coming from.

ABC Corp International
155 Any Place Lane, Herndon, VA 50170
(703) 742-0000 (tel) (703) 742-0001 (fax)

Ordered Through:
World Class Business Products
21-33 44th Drive, Long Island City,
New York 11101-4709
(718) 482-0408 (tel) (718) 482-0535 (fax)
Contact Person:

P.O. No. ________
Order Date:________
Ordered by:________
Delivery Date:________

QUANTITY	PRODUCT	TYPE	PRICE	NOTE
Paper				
	White Copy Paper	8½ x 11 (letter)		
	White Copy Paper	8½ x14 (legal)		
	White Copy Paper	11x17 (ledger)		
	Post-its (Yellow)	1½"x2", 3"x3"		
	Yellow Pads	Ltr Size 8x11 RO811C		
	Purchase Order Books			
Binders				
	1½" 3-ring clear view binders (Equitable Due-Dil Reports)			
	¼" White 3-Wring clear view binders (Site Visit Reports)			
Writing Utensils				
	Red Felt Tip Pen	Pmop 862-11		
	Blue, Black Felt Tip Pen	Pmop 861-11, 863-11		
	Red Metal Point Roller Pen	Uni-ball 60102		
	Black, Blue Roller Point Pen	Uni-ball 60101, 60103		
	Highlighter (yellow)	Eberhard Faber 4009		
	Highlighter (blue)	Major Accent 25010		
	Pencil (wooden)	No 2 American		
Labels				
	Brother P-Touch Tape Cassette	Black on White		
	Address Laser Labels (white)	Avery 1"x4" 5161		
	File Folder Labels (white)	Avery 1/3 cut 5366		
	Laser Labels	Avery 3 1/3x4 6464		
	White Liquid Paper	Pmop 28411		
	Correction Tape	Universal 65416		
	Ring Binder Insertable Indexes	8 Dividers		
Envelopes				
	#10 Plain White			
	Inter Office Manila			
	Tyveck Survivor White (no green edging)w/release strip	11x15 Stock No. R1790		
	Tyveck Survivor White (no green edging) w/release strip	9½x12½		
	Tyveck Survivor White (no green edging)w/release strip	8 1/2x11		

Figure 21.1 Typical office supplies need to be considered when setting up a new business *(continued on next page)*.

QUANTITY	PRODUCT	TYPE	PRICE	NOTE
Batteries				
	Double AA			
	Triple AAA			
	3-Volt, 6-Volt, 9-Volt	DL123A		
Folders				
	Letter Size Green Hanging Folders			
	Legal Size Green Hanging Folders			
	Letter Size Manila File Folders	3rd Cut		
	Legal Size Manila File Folders			
Clips				
	Paper Clips Regular	LEO201E		
	Paper Clips Jumbo	LEO301E		
	Binder Clips			
	Large Binder Clips			
	Standard Staples	SW135109		
	Heavy Duty Staples			
	Fasteners Self Adhesive	1" Capacity 70011		
	Fasteners	3" Capacity 70723		
Miscellaneous				
	CD-R 700MB-80 Min Rewritable			
	Rubber Bands			
	Sheet Protectors (3-hole Punch)	Top Loading		
	Calculator	TEX-TI-17955V P-9274		
	Staple Remover	BOS-4000		
	Clear Packing Tape 2"	MMM3750260CR		
	Scotch Tape			
	Bubble Wrap			
	Banker Boxes	EEL00704		
	Report Covers	Dark Blue 25973		
	Blue Ink	X-Stamp SHA22113		
	Red Ink	X-Stamp SHA22111		
	Black Ink	X-Stamp SHA22112		
	Velcro-Backed Key Organizer	22tag MJM201502203		
	Plastic Utility Knife			
	Refill Utility Blades	5 Pack		
	Gluesticks	Large Size AVE00196		
Audio/Visual				
	Mini-Micro Cassettes (audio)	MC-60 minutes		
	VHS 30-60 minute Tapes			
	8 mm Video Tapes (for cam corder)			

Figure 21.1 Typical office supplies need to be considered when setting up a new business *(continued from previous page)*.

Employees and required forms: If you intend to hire yourself or others as a full or part-time employee of the company, then you may have to register with the appropriate state agencies or obtain Workers Compensation insurance or unemployment insurance (or both). Of note, many major firms now allow (or prefer) some of their employees to work from home and only come into the office say, once a week.

It can take hundreds of hours annually to prepare and file the various payroll reports and other necessary governmental forms—an unacceptable burden for a person trying to keep up with everything on his own. When you have expanded to the point you can afford good employees and/or managers, don't hesitate to hire them. Properly trained and advised personnel can significantly improve a company's performance.

Personnel files are necessary for each person you hire. At a minimum an I-9 form, an IRS form W-4 and the state equivalent form for employee income tax withholding need to be included in the file. If independent subcontractors are used, they should sign IRS form W-9. You may also need to get a copy of the contractor's workers compensation insurance. Check whether state law requires subcontractors to be included on the firm's policy.

Utilities: Upon deciding to establish your own business, find out when the next issue of the telephone book will be printed and the deadline for getting listed so that you can place a display ad in the yellow. It could be a catastrophe if you miss the deadline for the next issue by a few days and have to wait nine months to a year for a listing in the permanent directory. Advance deposits are usually required when you sign up for electricity, gas, water, and sewer service.

Expense report: Many firms have developed standardized expense report forms for their employees so that they can request reimbursement for their business expenses. However, even if the consultant has just started doing business, it is vital to monitor expenditures, and a standard form is perhaps the best way to do so. The expense report should be neatly typed and organized, identifying each location, project name and number, and applicable dates. All original receipts and supporting documentation should be attached in date order to the report. It should then be given to accounting to process and record in a timely manner before filing.

Office equipment: Each business is different and no two businesses will need the same fixtures and equipment. It is also sometimes much better to preserve cash for inventories or working capital and purchase good used fixtures and equipment at a much lesser price. Get quotes on the equipment and furniture you will need. With the recent changes in the income tax laws you will have to do extra analysis to determine whether a lease program or direct purchase is the best way to proceed. Whether to buy or lease depends on many facts, which can only be determined by observation and computation. It could be better to lease electronic equipment, computers, copiers, printers, fax machines, copier machines, telephone and telephone systems, and certain other products due to the rapid advances continuously taking place in these fields. Record the cash down payment if you will be purchasing the equipment on contract.

Furniture: If you need office furnishings (desks, credenzas, file cabinets, bookcases, sofas, chairs, end tables, lamps), record the cost of each. If you're paying cash in full, enter the full retail price. If you are going to pay by installments, make note of the down payment as your start-up cost.

Decorating and remodeling: If your office space will need to be reconfigured, or you will need to redecorate, anticipate what you will spend to do so. Talk to suppliers with whom you plan to purchase these services, and record in this category the cash price of such services. If you are renting office space, sometimes you can negotiate with the landlord to include renovations in your base rent.

Phone and Internet Service: Get a phone number and domain name (for your Internet site) for your new business. When you get the phone number, look into a yellow page advertisement (or at least listing), and consider whether to be listed in several headings, or just the most appropriate heading.

Suppliers: Suppliers are reluctant to ship their goods to new businesses. That is one reason you should get to know your banker as he can offer credit references acceptable to most suppliers. You will have to convince your proposed suppliers that you are honest and hard working and that your business has a good chance for success. You may have to pay C.O.D. while getting started, so take this fact into account when preparing your financial planning and start-up requirements. After you have become established with your suppliers send your financial data to *Dun and Bradstreet* so your company will be listed in their files. Most firms in the country recognize Dun and Bradstreet as a reliable organization for obtaining correct credit information.

Bookkeeping and accounting: Set up your accounting and record-keeping system and learn about the taxes your new company is responsible for paying.

You are generally required to keep company documents for three years, including the following: a list of all owners and addresses, copies of all business formation documents, financial statements, annual reports, amendments, or changes to the company. All tax and corporate filings should be kept for at least three years.

There is probably no reason you cannot do your own record keeping, at least in getting started. Just use a separate check book and bank account for your business. Use a columnar check register with several "headed up" columns and distribute the amount of each check written to the proper columns. List your deposits on the check register and carry across a continuous bank balance.

With just the above two records of original entry plus a "General Journal" to record any extraneous transactions, and a "General Ledger" to which accounts from the three records are posted at the end of each month, you have all that is necessary for a simple "cash" accounting system. This cash system can be easily converted to the accrual method of accounting by simply journalizing accounts receivable, payable, accruals, prepaid insurance, etc. After posting these entries the balance sheet and income statement can be readily completed.

After preparing the financial statements, reverse the accruals and you will be ready for entries the following month. You can enter your gross payroll, payroll deductions, and the net amount in your check register. Give your employees a payroll slip showing all the facts, and maintain subsidiary payroll sheets with all the information for each employee. With these individual payroll records and the control accounts in the General Ledger, you have all the information necessary to complete the various payroll tax reports and returns as they come due. At the end of each annual accounting period all the information for filing your income tax returns will be right at your fingertips.

If you know nothing about bookkeeping, have an accountant set up your books on the basis of the above simple method. Let him "keep the books" the first few months while you learn how, and then, if you prefer, take them over yourself. Use your accountant as your advisor. After a short time you probably will be able to do all the accounting without outside help. The next step would be to invest in an appropriate accounting software package. Your accountant can advise you on this.

Miscellaneous issues to consider: You'll want to consider both business and personal living expenses when determining how much cash you will need. If you are leaving a salaried job to start your business, you should include in your expense projection an estimate of your and your family's living costs for the months it will take to build your business. Talk to family members about the minimum amount of money your household will need each month to function.

Once you add up start-up costs to your six-month tally of recurring costs, the total may amaze you and spur you to consider ways to economize. It probably makes sense to review certain categories, like equipment, office supplies, or advertising/promotions, with cost-control in mind. As a new business owner, you may be tempted to overbuy or insist on purchasing brand new items; these practices could rapidly put you out of business.

Review your list of projected expenses and decide if used office equipment or furnishings might make sense. Perhaps you could look for items at tag sales or used goods sales. Newspaper classified ads can lead you to house sales, bankruptcy auctions and furniture resellers. Shopping on the Internet can make it easy to search for new or used products and comparison shop for the best prices.

You've estimated your start-up costs to the best of your ability, but chances are, you've never owned or operated a business before. It's probably wise to talk to an established or experienced business owner to determine whether you've made the correct assumptions in projecting your costs. Finally, you can ask your attorney or accountant for referrals to business owners who have relevant experience in evaluating start-up costs.

The U.S. Department of Commerce Minority Business Development Agency (www.mbda.gov) has articles that discuss how much money you will need to start your business, includes helpful checklists, and provides referrals to other resources. The U.S. Small Business Administration (www.sba.gov) was created specifically to assist and counsel small businesses. Its publication, Small Business Start-up Kit, includes a checklist for calculating start-up costs. The SBA's Online Women's Business Center at www.onlinewbc.gov includes a helpful section on evaluating start-up costs.

21.4 LICENSES, PERMITS AND INSURANCE

Having made the decision to start a new business, you may now need to obtain a number of licenses and permits from federal, state, and local governments. Since licensing and permit requirements for small businesses can vary from one jurisdiction to another, it is critical that you contact your state and local government to determine the specific obligations of your new business. Consider the following as you explore the different federal, state, and local licenses and permits you may need to acquire prior to opening for business:

- **A basic business operation license** is required from the city in which your business will operate, or from the local county (if the business will be operated outside of any city's limits). Most cities or counties require you to obtain a business license, even if you operate a home-based business. This is a license granting the company the authority to do business in that city/county, after you pay a fee, of course.

Contact your city's business license department to learn about getting a business license. When you file your license application, the city planning or zoning department will check to make sure your area is zoned for the purpose you want to use it for and that there are enough parking spaces to meet the codes.

You can't operate in an area that is not zoned for your type of business unless you first get a variance or conditional-use permit. To get a variance, you'll need to present your case before your city's planning commission. In many cases, variances are quite easy to get, as long as you can show that your business won't disrupt the character of the neighborhood where you plan to locate.

- **A federal employer identification number** (EIN), also called a tax identification number is required for almost all types of businesses. Note: your business may also need to acquire a similar tax identification number from your state's department of revenue or taxation. When you get your corporate charter back (if a corporation) then you must apply for a federal Employer Identification Number (EIN). To do so, first go to the IRS website at www.irs.gov and download form SS-4, and fill it out. Then call toll-free (866) 816-2065 to get your EIN in 15 minutes or less.

Once you get the EIN number, download Form 2553 (S-election, if you want to avoid double taxation on your company earnings), and fill it out. Be sure to sign in BOTH places (as a shareholder in the middle of the page, and as an officer at the bottom). We strongly urge you to mail this form via certified mail, return receipt requested, since the IRS misplaces this important tax election frequently, and the burden of proof is solely on you to prove you sent it within the first 75 days. If you cannot find in the form instructions the appropriate IRS address to which you should mail the form for your location, then simply call your local IRS office and ask them.

If you chose to form a limited liability company, or LLC, you will also need to decide how you want to be taxed (as a sole proprietorship, partnership, S-corporation, or C-corporation), and make that election on IRS Form 8832.

- **A fictitious business name permit,** also called "dba" or "doing business as" permit, is required for almost all types of businesses. To make the public better aware of just what your firm offers, it is generally good practice to choose a business name that describes your product or service. Apply for a fictitious business name with your state or county offices when you plan on going into business under a name other than your own. Also, the bank will require a certificate or resolution pertaining to your fictitious name at the time you apply for a bank account. Your county clerk can tell you where to apply for the name.

Name and legal structure: You basically have 4 choices when selecting a legal structure: 1. Sole proprietorship, 2. Partnership, 3. Limited Liability Company (LLC), 4. Corporation or S-Corporation.

Determine whether you are going to do business as an individual proprietorship, partnership, corporation, or a Limited Liability Company (LLC). The individual proprietorship is the form of entity frequently used by small businesses at start up. If you need additional capital or expertise, a partnership may be the best entity. You can always incorporate later if practical. The expense to incorporate a small business is nominal, but unless incorporating increases your chances of success or better protects your investment, there is not much benefit in forming a corporation. Even though there is limited liability as to your personal assets with a corporate entity when obtaining outside financing, or in the event funds are misused, you can still be personally liable.

Before deciding, consult with an attorney and check with your Secretary of State—almost all departments now are online—and look for the Corporations Division to find the form for either Articles of Incorporation (to form your own corporation) or Articles of Organization (to form a Limited Liability Company). Many entrepreneurs today prefer forming a LLC since it requires less paperwork to maintain. While waiting for the Secretary of State to send you the charter, you should contact each of the relevant city, county, and state tax departments.

The strict laws, higher state income taxes in some states, the legal work involved, and the heavier accounting and tax reporting requirements are some of the disadvantages of running your business as a corporation. Also, if you decide later to close out your corporation, the paperwork involved, especially to conform to the provisions of the Internal Revenue Code, is difficult and often creates more problems than the initial incorporation.

The Limited Liability Company is the new business entity that every entrepreneur should understand. It combines the best aspects of incorporation with the tax advantages of partnership without the red tape of either structure. This combination of benefits has never existed before in such a simple and effective way. Anyone starting a new business must separate their personal assets and life from their business ventures. A limited liability company is personal protection in its purest form.

Business or occupational licenses: When you're embroiled in the excitement of starting a new business, it's easy to ignore the need for licenses and permits. Persons entering into certain kinds of business will have to obtain an occupational license through state or local licensing agencies. These include real estate brokers, those in the engineering profession, electricians, plumbers, building contractors, insurance agents, and many others. Often, they have to pass state examinations before they can get these permits and conduct business. Contact your state government offices to get a complete list of occupations that require licensing.

If you are planning to run the business from home, you should carefully investigate zoning ordinances. Residential neighborhoods tend to have strict zoning regulations preventing business use of the home. Even so, it's possible to get a variance or conditional-use permit; and in many areas, attitudes toward home-based businesses are becoming more supportive, making it easier to obtain a variance.

Other licenses: Federal regulations control many kinds of interstate activities with license and permit requirements. In most cases, you won't have to worry about this. However, a few types of businesses do require federal licensing, including investment advisory services. The Federal Trade Commission can tell you if your business requires a federal license.

County governments often require essentially the same types of permits and licenses as cities. If your business is outside any city or town's jurisdiction, these permits apply to you. County regulations are usually not as strict as those of adjoining cities.

Some cities and suburbs have sign ordinances that restrict the size, location, and sometimes the lighting and type of sign you can use outside your business. To avoid costly mistakes, check regulations and secure the written approval of your landlord (if you rent the space where you will conduct business) before you go to the expense of having a sign designed and installed.

Insurance: Don't forget about insurance. The premiums are expensive, especially business liability, but you cannot operate with peace of mind without full coverage. There are many types of insurance for businesses, but they are usually packaged as "General Business Insurance" or a "Business Owner's Policy." These policies can cover everything from service liability to company vehicles. It is imperative to have adequate liability insurance and anyone contemplating offering due diligence services is strongly advised to consult with an attorney. In any case, check with a good agent regarding insurance for fire, liability, Workmen's Compensation, business interruption, burglary, glass, extended coverage, vehicles, etc. Have two or three agents submit estimates. If you plan to offer your employees health insurance, talk to your agent about the up-front fee. Record the premium payment you will need to make before opening your business.

Office space: If you are not working from your own home, then find appropriate office space and sign a lease. Secure the lease in the name of the corporation rather than your personal name to limit your liability exposure should the business not succeed.

People can work in a cramped space for a while, especially during the exciting start-up phase of a company or project. But over time, the best way to support productivity and encourage employee retention is to offer appropriate space that supports the work being done.

The location of your business will of course vary depending on the kind of business or service you offer. Adequate parking space is always a plus. Is your lease a Net-Net lease, requiring the tenants to pay all expenses, including utilities, signs, lighting, taxes, insurance, garbage, maintenance, etc.? If you're going into an office business or an unproven venture, get a month-to-month rental agreement. In the event your venture is unsuccessful, you will not be stuck with future rent as you would if you were under a long term lease. The landlord is in control in long-term leases. You must get his approval in the event you want to sub-lease to another, and even if he agrees you are still secondarily liable for the term of the lease.

Bank account: With the federal EIN number in hand, you can now also open a corporate checking account. Get to know the manager of your bank. He will be one of your best references. Ask his advice and get his help on financial matters. The more he advises you the better he will come to know you. Develop a line of credit so it will be there when you need it. The banks can't exist without making loans, so don't hesitate to apply. Try and get a corporate American Express, Diner's Club, Visa card, etc. as you will need it when entertaining or buying office supplies, and for other things.

To establish your bank account you will need a Federal ID number or social security number along with your certificate of assumed (fictitious) business name. If you are incorporated, the bank will want a copy of the minutes and a corporate resolution authorizing the account.

Contact the bank prior to opening the account to see what their specific requirements are to open a business checking account; some banks' requirements are fairly simple while other banks' requirements are extremely complex.

Tax strategies: Tax planning is a year-round process if you want to minimize your business's tax bill. Whether it's surviving an audit, capitalizing on business deductions, or finding tax-friendly ways to run your business, a good accountant can help reduce tax obligations and make paying taxes less anxiety provoking.

One of the first things to do when starting your new business is to get Federal and State application forms for ID numbers. Request "business start-up" application forms from the Internal Revenue Service and from your state Tax Commission. After you send in your applications, you will be notified of your number and get a packet of information. Depository forms, quarterly report forms, W-4-As, W-2s, estimated tax forms, etc., will then be mailed to you periodically as needed.

Payroll taxes and expenses will range from 13 to 17 percent of your gross payroll, depending on workmen's compensation rates for the various job classifications. Payroll expenses include FICA taxes (Social Security) FUE taxes (Federal Unemployment) SUE taxes (State Unemployment) WC or SDI (Workmen's Compensation). Also, you will be required to withhold income tax from your employees' wages and pay them quarterly to federal and state tax authorities.

If you are a sole proprietorship business or a partnership, you will have to file and pay federal estimated tax reports each quarter based on estimated annual income. Partnerships file an annual information return and each partner's share of profits is included in their individual personal income tax returns. Corporations must also pay regular estimated taxes.

Deductions and write-offs: Maximize what you can deduct, and discover what you can write off by knowing what constitutes legitimate business expenses.

21.5 BASIS FOR PROPERTY CONDITION ASSESSMENT (PCA) FEES

The inspection fee you will charge is determined by the size, age, value, and location of the property, and by the service level the client requests. In addition, PCA fees are quoted on an individual basis contingent upon a number of variables, such as HVAC and electrical systems, which can vary considerably from one commercial property to the next. As such, it is imperative to at least know and understand the concept of a baseline PCA—what most inspection services provide—as opposed to a more detailed and comprehensive property condition assessment.

It is obvious yet important to note that a cursory or baseline PCA usually costs much less because it takes considerably less time to do. Moreover, if the PCA fee is based entirely upon square footage, or a percentage of the appraisal value or selling price of the property, it will consist of a cursory or baseline PCA. Once more, what's probably least understood is that such methods are hardly a basis to determine, let alone justify a fee for a more thorough PCA being correctly carried out.

It is difficult to structure a formula for quoting an exact fee because it is highly uncommon for two properties to be exactly alike in all variables that need to be considered. In the real world it becomes a guessing game in attempting to quote a PCA fee on a cost-per-square-foot basis without having all the information up front. As for appraisal value or selling price, they have absolutely no bearing whatsoever and should not be used to quote a PCA fee.

If the assignment is not a baseline PCA, it would be customary to visit the site beforehand (at no cost to the client) to obtain information needed to prepare and submit a proposal that outlines the consultant's scope of services and methodology. This in turn helps to avoid surprises down the road since the client already knows what to expect up front. Sometimes it may not be necessary to visit a site to prepare a quote for, say, a small commercial property, but such a decision is contingent upon the consultant being comfortable with the information in hand (e.g. obtained from the client or other reliable source). When additional work is required, a separate invoice should be presented (Figure 21.2).

BILLING FORM
ADDITIONAL WORK PERFORMED

EMPLOYEE NAME:

DATE:

PROJECT NO.

JOB NAME:

FOR PERIOD UP TO AND INCLUDING: ____________________

DESCRIPTION OF WORK PERFORMED, INCLUDING WHO WAS INVOLVED, DATES, ETC.

HOURS: ____________________

EXPENSES: ____________________

____

____

APPROVED: SIGNATURE:

Figure 21.2 Typical form for additional work done.

CHAPTER

22

Selling Yourself—Sample Letters, Brochures, and Websites

22.1 GENERAL

Professional performance means much more than doing your job effectively. The way you conduct yourself in a business environment not only reflects your position within a company but impacts your chances for career growth.

Many people are unsure of the proper protocol for various situations in a business setting. Most potential clients decide within minutes whether to trust you or your employees. Trust is pivotal in establishing relationships that can ultimately lead to business partnerships.

Awkward introductions, weak handshakes, poor communication, ineffective meetings, and lack of consideration can negatively affect your career and business relationships. When all else is equal, good manners can be your greatest strength.

22.2 CREATING A PROFESSIONAL IMAGE—SAMPLE LETTERS AND BROCHURE

Owning your own business is one of the better ways to gain wealth and personal satisfaction, provided you know what is required. Starting a business is risky but your chances for success increase if you understand the challenges you will face and work out as many of them as possible before beginning.

Develop a business identity: It is imperative that you create a good corporate image and business identity that reflect confidence and efficiency. One of the first things to organize is a professionally designed logo, business card, letterhead and promotional material for the business. A professionally created logo and letterhead can go a long way to giving clients the desired image.

Advertising and promotion: Many new businesses start operating with a grand opening announcement, giving press releases to local papers and relevant business publications. It may also be prudent to print out a few hundred circulars to distribute to potential clients. Alternatively, grand opening circulars can be placed in the newspaper to be distributed to subscribers. In any case, the dollar cost of any planned advertising and marketing initiative to announce the launch of the new business should be recorded and should include the cost of flyers, sales letters, phone calls, signs, brochures, and other promotional items.

Study the ads of the competition and check their websites. Also check out the various promotional materials of similar businesses on the Internet and in specialized journals. Record them for future use when preparing your own ads or brochures. There are all kinds of promotional ideas and gimmicks to keep your business out in front of the competition. Search the library, book stores and mail order media for such publications. Choose the ones that fit your promotional programs or those that can be modified to fit your needs.

Marketing yourself: Develop professionally designed brochures and other marketing materials. As you are essentially selling a specialized service, be sure to know how to market it, which means a marketing plan and strategy is necessary to target your ideal customer. Now that you've set up the company for success, you need to get the word out. Figure 22.1 is a typical letter to let customers and potential clients know you are ready for business.

Time management: A secretary/office manager could help make the operational aspect of the business as automated and efficient as possible to allow you to concentrate on growing the business. This will free you from having to process orders, pay bills, pay employees, pay taxes, maintain your permits, etc. The more organized you are, the more efficient you are and the less time you waste.

22.3 IDENTIFY SOURCES FOR LEADS

There are many methods to identify potential sources and project leads, depending on whether your business is a one-person organization or a well organized firm with several employees. These methods include the following:

1. Send out flyers, brochures, emails, and other materials to potential clients. That would be an excellent starting point.
2. Scan the Internet. Typically all major due diligence firms have websites, and some of these firms have client lists (to build up potential customer confidence) on their websites (Figure 22.2A,B). These lists can be researched to see if any names are worth following up on.
3. A general drive around the area can often highlight possible leads. One such example of a potential lead is Figure 22.3. Note that even if it is too late to be commissioned for this particular project, the lender or property owner may have other projects to offer you.
4. The consultant should also visit the various neighborhood commercial real estate agents to see what commercial properties are on the market. Make a list of all these possible leads and follow up with letters and brochures offering the company's services (See sample letter).

March 24, 2007

Mr. John Doe
Sales Manager VA1945
First Union Bank
1070 Chain Ridge Road,
Mclain, VA 22101

(Tel) (703) 760 0000
(Fax) (703) 760 0001
Email: jdoe@abc-asses-intl.com

Re: Due-Diligence Services

Dear Mr. Doe:

I am taking this opportunity to apprise you of our engineering consulting services that we offer for lending institutions.

ABC Assessments International has recently been formed to provide construction and due diligence consulting services on behalf of private and institutional lenders and investors. Although ABC is a newly formed company, its principals have over twenty five years of experience in design, construction, property condition assessments and litigation support. For further information and an overview of our services, please view our website at: www.abc-assess-intl.com.

Our services can be tailored to your specific requirements and can include:

- Project Management Oversight
- Project Condition Evaluations & Surveys
- Phase I Environmental Assessments
- Litigation/Expert Witness support

We are able to travel anywhere within the United States to provide services to meet your requirements.

I'll give you a few days to look things over, and then I'll call you to set-up a time to discuss your requirements.

Sincerely,

Sam A.A. Kubba,
Principal
ABC ASSESSMENTS INTERNATIONAL

SAK/bs
enclosures

cc: General Files

ABC/PROMO/LETTERS/First Union/ promo.doc

Figure 22.1 An example of a typical promotional letter that can be sent to clients to inform them that your company is ready for business. Promotional material should accompany the letter.

A

Commercial Real Estate

Beacon Capital Partners, Boston, MA
Boston Scientific Corporation, Watertown, MA
CB Richard Ellis, Boston, MA
Ciba Corning Diagnostics, Walpole, MA
Citicorp/Citibank, New York, NY
Clark Construction Group, Bethesda, MD
David Nassif Associates, Wellesley, MA
DSF Advisors, Boston, MA
Fidelity Properties, Boston, MA
Forest City Management Company, Cambridge, MA
Genuity, Burlington, MA
HallKeen Management, Inc., Norwood, MA
Harris County Sports and Convention Corporation, Houston, TX
Honeywell Bull, Norwood, MA
Keyspan, Boston, MA
Nortel, Billerica, MA
Proctor & Gamble, Cincinnati, OH
Raytheon Corporation, Waltham, MA
Reliance National, New York, NY
Scudder Investments, Boston, MA
Shawmut Design and Construction, Boston, MA
Sordoni Skanska, Cambridge, MA
Spaulding & Slye, Boston, MA
The Gillette Company, Boston, MA
TJX Company, Framingham, MA
Trammell Crow Company, Boston, MA
Winthrop Management, Miami, FL

Law Firms

Baron & Budd, P.C., Dallas, TX
Beall, Pelton, O'Brien & Brown, Albuquerque, NM
Carroll, Kelly & Murphy, Providence, RI
Choate, Hall & Stewart, Boston, MA
Conn Kavanaugh Rosenthal Peisch & Ford LLP, Boston, MA
Cremer, Kopon, Shaughnessy & Spina, Wheaton, IL
Davis, Polk & Wardell, New York, NY
Doresey & Whitney, Minneapolis, MN
Foley, Hoag & Eliot, Boston, MA
Goodwin Proctor LLP, Boston, MA
Gordon & Rees, San Francisco, CA
Governo Law Firm, Boston, MA
Hale & Dorr, Boston, MA
Harris, Karstaedt, Jamison & Powers, P.C., Englewood, CO
Hill & Barlow, Boston, MA
Holland & Knight, Boston, MA
Jaffe, Raitt, Heuer &Weiss, P.C. , Detroit, MI
Kelsch Kelsch Ruff & Kranda, Mandan, ND
Kirkpatrick & Lockhart, Boston, MA
Mahoney, Hawkes & Goldings, Boston, MA
Martin, Magnuson, McCarthy & Kenney, Boston, MA
Massery & Gillis, LLP, Boston, MA
McDermott, Will & Emery, Boston, MA
Mintz, Levin, Cohn, Ferris, Glovsky and Popeo, P.C., Boston, MA
Morrison, Mahoney & Miller, Boston, MA
Nutter, McClennen & Fish LLP, Boston, MA
Palmer and Dodge, Boston, MA
Quarles & Brady, Milwaukee, WI
Richardson, Stoops, Richardson & Ward, Tulsa, OK
Roetzel & Andrews, Akron, OH
Sarrouf, Tarricone & Flemming, P.C., Boston, MA
Smith & Duggan, Boston, MA
Swidler & Berlin, Washington DC
Waystack & King, Colebrook, NH

B

Figure 22.2 A. Examples of a Satisfied Customer List *(Source VFA)*. B. Client Lists *(Source Environmental Health Engineering)* found on competitor websites.

Figure 22.3 Photo of property under construction *(The Point at Beaumeade—Sterling, VA. 50,000 SF office building)* taken while driving in author's neighborhood, suggesting a potential lead.

5. Since many of the clients will be lenders (e.g., banks and other lending institutions) and attorneys (if expert witness and litigation services are offered), it would be prudent to make a potential client list from the yellow pages, the Internet, and from research in the public library.

Typical Lead:
David Orr—Developer/Owner Tel. 703 761 9882 see Photo
The Orr Company—Development & Project Management
Developing 50,000 SF Office Building on Waxpool Rd, Sterling, VA.
At Beaumeade Corporate Park.
Architect: Hughes Group Architects 703 437 6600
Contractor: TUCON Construction

22.4 SELLING YOURSELF

Dress for success: One's appearance is a very powerful form of communication and an effective strategic tool when used properly. Selecting professional attire today is not as simple as the "dress for success" formula of a few decades ago. Proper dress might seem like common sense for some, but it does not come naturally to everyone. Whether a person's work dress code is business attire, business casual or plain casual, that person will typically be taken as seriously as their dress. It is that simple.

For women, clothing should not be too revealing. Great basics for any work environment include collared shirts, pencil skirts and good slacks. If you remain unsure of what to wear to work, look at some of the successful women in your industry. They usually provide a good example of what is acceptable in your particular environment (Figure 22.4).

Figure 22.4 Example of acceptable professional female attire in the office.

When attending a business meeting with a client, start off with a firm hand shake and then go for eye contact. Remember, first impressions can make a tremendous difference in how we are perceived. Obviously, it is not necessary to wear a business suit every day if you are an engineer on site.

Different companies and industries have different norms in regard to business dress. For example, a financial analyst at an investment firm may not wear the same work attire as a computer engineer at a small start-up Internet company. The majority of organizations in all industries, however, have very similar expectations when it comes to business meeting attire. The standard protocol is professional dress, which means a conservative, well-tailored suit. Although a business suit is not always the everyday work attire for an organization, potential clients expect consultants to look their most professional during a project meeting.

It is always prudent to err on the side of conservative dress. Your clothing and accessories should not draw so much attention that they distract from the true purpose of the meeting.

Introductions: Introductions and mingling can be uncomfortable experiences in the business world, especially for shy people. If attending an event where there are likely to be introductions, such as a conference, be sure to carry business cards and perhaps some literature about the company.

Correspondence: Correspondence is a tricky subject since there are numerous ways to communicate today. The decision to communicate with a client via telephone, email or face-to-face depends largely on one's personality. Introverts tend to prefer email because it is efficient and avoids direct contact; extroverts on the other hand prefer direct face-to-face communication.

When sending an email or letter, make sure it is sent to the correct person. Also, review correspondence for accuracy, and use spell check before sending it. It is advisable to put the email address in last to avoid accidentally sending an incomplete email.

Confidence: If you are confident, you will appear as an accomplished professional to others. Confidence is attained by being organized and prepared and having the necessary knowledge to execute the job successfully. Being confident doesn't mean never asking questions or succumbing to challenges. Paradoxically, confident people know the importance of questions. Remember to be cool, calm, and collected, and, above all else, think before you speak. Whether you are entering a new work environment or are attempting to reinvent yourself professionally, know that you can do it. The corporate world can be rough, but, with the aforementioned skills, you are already on a path for success.

Dining etiquette: To avoid confusion, you should arrive 10 minutes before your reservation. You can give the server your credit card, or simply inform the server the bill should come to you. Prior to this, you can make a few restaurant suggestions and ask the client to select amongst them. Be familiar with the restaurants' atmospheres and menus to avoid unpleasant surprises. If a restaurant accepts reservations, be sure to make them. On the day of your lunch, call your client in the morning and confirm the time and place.

Defer to your client about smoking. If the client smokes and you don't, you should sit in the smoking section if you can tolerate it. If you smoke but the client doesn't, request a nonsmoking table. Smokers should wait until the meal is completed and should ask permission from others at the table before lighting up.

Before ordering, your client may ask you for some recommendations. By doing this, they are often trying to get a sense of the price range with which you're comfortable. When your server takes orders, allow the client to go first.

Mealtime is more about bonding than business. Unless your client brings it up first, you should wait until the entrees are removed and dessert and coffee have been offered before you discuss business.

If the client seems eager to discuss business sooner, do so. But if the discussion will require you to litter the table with folders and papers, suggest waiting. Meanwhile, focus on getting to know your client, but avoid subjects that are too personal. Sports, movies, literature, travel, and current events that won't incite political debates are appropriate topics of conversation.

Regardless of rank or gender, typically, whoever extended the invitation to lunch or dinner pays. If the check accidentally is given to a client, inform him or her that the meal is your company's treat. Refrain from saying, "It's my treat." It's much easier for a person to accept a free meal from a company than from a person.

Meetings: Meetings are another area where success is largely dependent upon good organization and adequate preparation. It is a time when you will meet people who are busy and often inaccessible to you. Compile questions you want to ask or topics you want to cover, and know in advance what you hope to accomplish.

Business etiquette is essentially about building relationships with colleagues, clients, or customers. In the business world, it is these people that can influence your success or failure. Etiquette, and in particular business etiquette, is simply a means of maximizing your business potential by presenting yourself favorably.

Business meetings are one arena in which poor etiquette can have negative effects. By improving your business meeting etiquette you automatically improve your chances of success. Comfort, trust, attentiveness, and clear communication are examples of the positive results of demonstrating good etiquette.

Informal meetings: Informal meetings are generally more relaxed affairs and may not necessarily take place in the office or meeting room. Even so, a sense of professionalism and good business etiquette are still required.

Consider the following points with informal meetings:

- Business etiquette typically requires that the person calling the meeting (henceforth 'the chair') should be the most senior or the one with the most direct or urgent interest in the topic at hand.
- The chair should decide (in consultation with the other participants) the time, place, and agenda.
- The chair must make the purpose of the meeting clear to the attendees, how long it is expected to last, and what is required of them, i.e., particular information or preparation of documents. Failing to relay the proper information is bad business etiquette as it could cause embarrassment and undermine the meeting's objectives.
- Punctuality is important. Keeping people waiting is considered the height of poor taste as it abuses their time.
- The chair should strive to ensure that the meeting remains within the agreed agenda so that it is kept as short and effective as possible.
- The chair should (pre-) appoint someone to take minutes of the proceedings, documenting major decisions or action points. This record can later be typed and distributed to the attendees for reference.

Formal meetings: The business etiquette of formal meetings such as departmental meetings, management meetings, board meetings, negotiations and the like can be puzzling. Such meetings usually have a set format.

Business etiquette guidelines for formal meetings include the following:

- Prepare well for the meeting, as your contribution may be integral to the proceedings. If statistics, reports, or other information are to be used, it should be handed out prior to the meeting with sufficient time to be studied.
- Arrival on time appropriately dressed is important to reflect professionalism.
- Mobile phones should be switched off.
- If there is an established seating pattern, accept it. If you are unsure, ask.
- Acknowledge any introductions or opening remarks with a brief recognition of the chair and other participants.
- When discussions are under way, it is good business etiquette to allow more senior figures to contribute first.
- Refrain from interrupting anyone—even if you disagree strongly. Note what has been said and return to it later with the chair's permission.
- When speaking, be brief and to the point and ensure what you say is relevant.
- Always address the chair unless it is clear that others are not doing so.
- It is a serious breach of business etiquette to divulge information to others about a meeting. What has been discussed should be considered confidential.

22.5 THE WEBSITE

"When I took office, only high energy physicists had ever heard of what is called the Worldwide Web . . . Now even my cat has its own page."

Bill Clinton, announcement of Next Generation Internet initiative, 1996

Why a website is imperative: First, decide (and understand) why a web site is necessary and what can be achieved from it. At a minimum, a web site can market your company to the world. Additionally, it is an excellent vehicle to sell the company's services over the Internet. Remember to consider what information you want prospects to gather from visiting your web site. A well designed website can typically be used to:

- Attract inquiries from potential customers
- Provide a better service to customers
- Provide more information about the firm and its services
- Obtain feedback from customers on the company's services
- Recruit staff
- Improve efficiency

Using your website to provide a user with better access to your company can reap great benefits.

Clients are happier and receive resolutions to problems quickly, and you can devote more of your time to other critical issues. The list of services you can offer via your website is enormous.

For example, it can include project facts and figures, including condition assessments, survey results, etc. It can also include clarification regarding your firm's structure—who does what and the tasks that facilities management is (and isn't) responsible for. The site can be used to draw attention to upcoming events or time-sensitive information.

Many facilities management companies and consultants also use their websites to communicate with general contractors, subcontractors, and other building team members to explain bidding guidelines, standards, etc. They also offer downloadable forms, building fact sheets, and equipment procedures for field workers or contractors who may be accessing the site remotely. This information (along with any other information you choose) can be password-protected or located on an intranet site vs. your Internet site (which is available to anyone with an Internet connection) so that only certain individuals can access the information.

Phase One—plan your approach: The Internet and your web site is just another channel to your target audience. You have already been implementing all the necessary steps in your day-to-day business. You now need to translate this to the new medium. Think about the image you want to convey to site visitors, and make sure everything on your site contributes something toward that image. Developing and maintaining a website is no small accomplishment.

But whether you are creating a concept for your website for the very first time, or you are trying to update a current site, make sure you look at your site from the user's point of view. For example, what will site visitors want to know when they log on? If you're working with an existing site, ask clients and prospects what they think of the information offered there. What else would they like to see featured on the site? Know your visitors (or future visitors) and what they want and need. If you're starting from scratch, a quick survey may help determine the answers to these questions. Check out other due diligence and facilities management websites to discover additional services that your peers are providing to users.

Thus, for each of the objectives you have set for the company website and yourself, you need to decide:

- Who is the target audience
- What you are trying to get them to do or obtain from your site
- What you need to have on your site to attract prospects to the site in the first place and to come back again. Website content and design are both vital for market success.
- What service do you need to provide on or off-line to back up your 'promise' to your visitors?
- How you are going to promote your website and contents to your target audience

Phase Two—setting up the website: To set up an acceptable commercial website (as opposed to a personal home page) the following would be needed:

- A domain name, such as www.mysite.com
- Server space—a home for your website's files, provided by a hosting company
- The website itself—a collection of pages and images, linked together to make a complete site.

Registering a domain name: First, a web address, called a domain name, is needed. Scores of companies let you register a domain name online and offer search tools to check whether the name desired is available. Domain registration is not expensive: you need not pay more than 20 dollars per year. Often the domain name will be registered with the same hosting company that provides the server space.

Server space: Server space is space on a computer owned by a hosting company. It is set up so that anyone who types your domain name into their browser will be connected to your website. You should be able to rent enough space for a good-sized site for around 300 dollars per year. There are numerous hosting companies, and some online research will help you find one that best serves your needs.

Anyone can put a website together, and it seems that just about everyone does, with greater or lesser success. If you can use a word processor, you can create a web site. However, creating a good website is an entirely different matter, and requires a lot of thinking and preparation. And while you can certainly design your own website, it is usually wiser to bring in a competent professional to do the job.

Phase Three—website components and details:

1. Website overview and contents: The website should articulate the services offered. This may be outlined in a mission or vision statement. When you are starting out on the Internet you are starting with something close to a clean sheet. With a few international exceptions, the majority of Internet users probably won't actually know who you are. You can project any kind of image that you wish, and moreover, you can emphasize any particular aspect of the organization that you wish to.

Sit down with some colleagues and some paper and brainstorm until you come up with a series of points that match your organization and what you do, or wish to do. Next, you need to match that to the kind of image you want to portray on your site. Consequently, when it comes time to actually put the site together you can ignore the flashy graphics and animations and concentrate on guiding the user quickly and effectively to the information that they need. Use your site to display your particular abilities to their best advantage; in other words, play to your strengths.

Corporate image comes into play here as well. You will probably want to make sure that the image on the web pages matches that of the image displayed in other formats and media. However, don't forget you are starting from scratch here, so you have a free hand. It might actually make sense to have some subtle changes on the web site; if your corporate color is blue, think about changing to another shade, or be radical and go for red! Decide on a theme and stick to it. Use the same logo on your pages, in the same position, in the same size.

Today, it is easier than ever to create a website; you can even do it overnight. With a wealth of tools and options available on the web today, you don't need to be a graphic designer or web developer to capture the basics. Templates are a great way to get started in developing your own website, and you can choose from a variety of simple but attractive designs. There's always room to upgrade, and it's easier than ever to find a unique template so you're not simply imitating another site. No coding involved—you don't even need to learn HTML.

Nevertheless, the website should be inviting and reflect your vision and objectives. It can be a great marketing tool, and enable you to develop your services and launch multiple marketing campaigns in a few simple steps. Consider your website as a platform to feature your professional services and expertise, or just share commentary. Developing this portal to your world is important; you can set up your own website in no time!

One of the best ways to add to your own website is to download a website template that you like (using "Save As" on your browser), and then editing it with an html editing program. It is illegal to copy another company's webpage, but tracking down a free template is simple; just download it from the Internet, and you'll have the framework ready to go. Once you've found the right match, take a look at your options for upgrading and customizing it. Not everyone needs a customized website; if you're looking for standard functions and presentation, you'll find plenty of attractive options on the Internet. After installing the templates using your favorite website builder, you can publish to the web immediately. Microsoft Frontpage, Dreamweaver, and BlueVoda are the most popular choices for html editors and web page creators. Figure 22.5A,B shows two examples of designs you can find on the Internet. These websites offer free web tem-

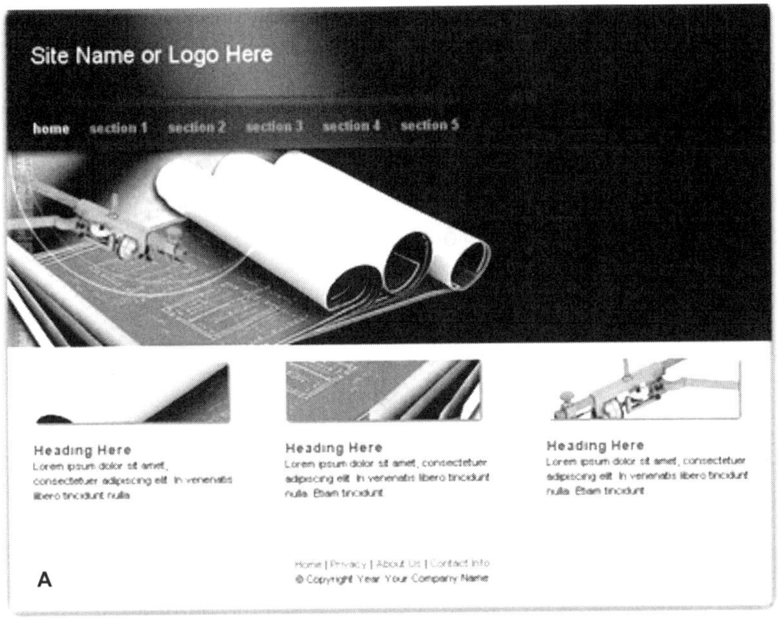

B

Figure 22.5 A. Example of sample home page template, free from *www.steves-templates.com*, showing the link buttons on the upper part of the page. B. Typical sample of landscape home page template from *www.freesitetemplates.com*, with the link buttons on the left of the page.

plates as well as design services. In Figure 22.5A the link buttons are on the top whereas in the landscape template, they are on the left side of the page. Both easily take you to where you want to go (e.g. to the mission statement, jobs in progress, services offered, firm principals and qualifications, etc.). It is largely a matter of preference and how the page is composed and designed. However, as previously stated, for a professional looking website it is strongly recommended that you hire a professional web designer (if your budget permits).

2. Who do you want to visit your site? This depends very much on the answers that you have already come up with. Existing customers and clients, potential customers, people interested in your subject area who may never have heard of you, organizations, individuals, different groups, and so on. If you are a due diligence firm, your list of target groups might look a little like this:

- Facility managers and property owners
- Lenders
- Investors
- Attorneys
- Architects and engineers
- Contractors

Create your list and then prioritize it. For example, if you want to promote an image of a due diligence firm that specializes in litigation work, attorneys may well take higher priority than casual users. This should be emphasized in the structure of the site's pages and the weighting that you give to it in your proposal.

To let users know you are to be trusted, remember what was mentioned earlier—you cannot take it on trust that your viewer knows who you are. The message must be hammered home at every opportunity. Use your company logo, university crest, and so on to reinforce this. If you have won an award, make sure everyone who visits knows this! Your viewers need to be reassured that your firm is to be trusted, and that its information is reliable. This must be emphasized on every single page that you publish—there is no telling which page a user will go to first, so be consistent on the positioning of your logo, and place it on every page.

3. Get them there and keep them: You've got less than 15 seconds to make an impact before visitors to your site are gone. You have to work very hard in this small window of opportunity. Don't let them go quite yet! Refrain from huge flashy graphics that take forever to load. Get some information up there immediately for them to read while your graphics are loading. Also, make the purpose of your site very clear. If you don't know, your viewers won't. This is where the image business is vital. Give viewers enough guidance to let them work their own way(s) through your site.

A website's success is not measured by its attractiveness or its use of the latest web technology. It is not even usually how many people visit it. Rather, it is measured by how many visitors come back again and by how much business it generates.

It is vital to keep your site current. Update it periodically (at least once a month) if you can afford the staff time. If the site is old or carries outdated information, it shows that you don't care. If you don't care, why should one expect the user to care? Use graphics to show that something is new, revised, or updated. Decide who is to be the webmaster, who will have the authority to update the site, to request and receive new copy, and so on.

4. Miscellaneous website issues: As mentioned earlier it may be easy to set up a website, but it is not easy to do it well. The webmaster should take into account security issues, creating firewalls and other measures to protect your content. Also, whoever is going to keep the site up to date must be able to write the pages and keep abreast of new and breaking technologies in order to keep the site fresh and interesting. The issue of cost must not be forgotten for setting up and maintaining the site.

The secretary/office manager will be required to answer any email inquiries or to transmit them to a principal for reply.

5. Getting traffic: Much time and money has been spent, and you wait for the inquiries to come in but they don't, because no one knows your site is out there. The site must be publicized. Potential customers need to know the website exists. Moreover, all letterheads, brochures, cards, and other advertising should mention the web site address and email address.

Submit your site to all the search engines. For a small fee your site could be submitted to some 500 search engines and directories by software packages, or you could use one of the free submission services on the Internet. Generally speaking, it often takes at least a few months for a website to become recognized and start to generate responses. That's how long it usually takes the big search engines, especially Google, to index a new site. Of course, the popularity of your site and the speed at which it becomes popular really depends on what is being offered and how it is promoted.

Key issues to remember: Good business websites are based on doing simple things well. These include:

- Understanding who you are trying to reach and what you want to achieve
- Getting the message and service right and keeping them right over time
- Delivering these to the target audience in a manner they can understand and that will motivate them
- Ensuring first class service to the customer wherever and whenever required
- Integrating the website into the business operations for efficiency and good service levels
- Marketing the website well to ensure it is used and understanding what works for the business
- Being prepared to develop and change the site and its content as the business and customer needs change
- Keep to the basics whenever possible and learn what works best for your business
- Prioritize your investment of time and money in the development of the content, the website design, and the marketing aspects; don't spend everything just on the design
- Integrate your website into your marketing and operations so it is a normal part of your business.

Appendix

Miscellaneous Sample Forms, Templates, and Resources

PRE-SURVEY QUESTIONNAIRE

ABC INTERNATIONAL

Building Inspection Division
ABC Due Diligence Center • 155 Anywhere Lane • Los Angeles, California 91303
(310) 000-1900 (tel) • (310) 000-1901 (fax)

Pre-Survey Questionnaire

To the best of your knowledge, please provide written responses to this questionnaire and upon completion fax it to ABC at (310) 000-1901 (fax). For those questions, which are not applicable to the Subject, please respond with a "N/A". This document is to be signed below by the owner or his representative. If you have any questions about how to answer any of the questions, please call ABC. If additional pages for response are necessary, please attach hereto and reference same to the appropriate question number. Of importance, if any of the items completed by ABC are incorrect, please make the appropriate correction. This document along with your written responses will be an exhibit within ABC's Property Condition Report.

Name of Property:		**ABC Project No.:**	
Address:		**ABC Project Manager:**	
		ABC Property No.:	
Age of Property:		**Tax I.D. # (Sec, Lot, Block):**	
SFG:		**Size of Parcel (Acres):**	
Number of Buildings:		**Property Management Co.:**	
Number of Stories:		**Tel:**	
Ownership Entity:		**Fax:**	
Borrower's/Owner's Representative:		**Duration of Current Management:**	
Tel:		**Prepared and Submitted by:**	
Fax:		**Signature:**	
Site Contact :		**Date:**	
Tel:	(310) 231-1900	**Date Forwarded to Recipient by ABC:**	
Fax:	(310) 231-1901		

1. What is the current occupancy, as a percentage, of the building and what is the annual turnover rate?

2. Who provides the following utilities to the Subject?

Water:	
Sanitary Sewer:	
Storm Drainage:	
Electric:	
Gas/Oil:	
Steam:	
Chilled Water:	

3. How many parking spaces are available to the site?

	At Grade	Garage	Carport	Off Site
Standard				
Handicap				

4. To the best of your knowledge, is the contractor that installed the Subject's roof still in business? Yes ☐ No ☐ U/K ☐

5. To the best of your knowledge, does the building have any of the following conditions or have any repairs or replacements been made within the last three years to alleviate same?

a. Roof or sidewall leakage? Yes ☐ No ☐

b. Structural problems such as excessive floor framing deflection, sidewall or foundation cracks? Yes ☐ No ☐

c. Cellar/Basement water/moisture infiltration? Yes ☐ No ☐

d. Heating capacity, distribution or equipment deficiencies? Yes ☐ No ☐

e. Air conditioning capacity, distribution or equipment deficiencies? Yes ☐ No ☐

f. Inadequate domestic water pressure, discolored potable water, or drain line problems? Yes ☐ No ☐

g. Inadequate electrical capacity or distribution? Yes ☐ No ☐

h. Asbestos insulation, fireproofing or Transite panels? Yes ☐ No ☐

If "Yes", please state where:

i. Presence of phenolic roof insulation? Yes ☐ No ☐ U/K ☐

j. Aluminum branch or distribution wiring? Yes ☐ No ☐ U/K ☐

k. Polybutylene water supply piping? Yes ☐ No ☐ U/K ☐

l. Fire retardant treated plywood roof sheathing? Yes ☐ No ☐ U/K ☐

m. Omega or Star sprinkler heads? Yes ☐ No ☐ U/K ☐

If "Yes", have the Omega heads been replaced prior to January 1, 1999? Yes ☐ No ☐ U/K ☐

n. On-site septic system? Yes ☐ No ☐ U/K ☐

If "Yes", any problems?

What is the date of the last septic tank pumping/cleaning?

6. Are you in receipt of, or have you solicited, any proposals to perform any repairs or replacement work to the building(s) or any of its components that will exceed an aggregate cost of $5,000? Yes ☐ No ☐

If "Yes", please explain:

7. Are the elevators, if any, fitted with a "firemen's" return? Yes ☐ No ☐ U/K ☐

8. To the best of your knowledge, has the building(s), or any portion thereof, been subject to a property condition survey during the last three (3) years to opine on the subject's physical condition? Yes ☐ No ☐

If "Yes", who conducted such a survey and when was it performed?

9. Has any portion of the site incurred flooding as a result of backup of municipal stormwater system, levee, stream/creek/lake overflow, tidal conditions, etc.? Yes ☐ No ☐

If "Yes", please explain and identify location.

10. Is any portion of the site located in a flood plain? Yes ☐ No ☐

If "Yes", please provide any information as to the extent of historical flooding.

11. Is any portion of the site encumbered by wetlands? Yes ☐ No ☐

If "Yes", please provide any information as to the size and location of these areas.

12. Has there been any additions made to the property? Yes ☐ No ☐

If "Yes", please explain and identify location and the date of the improvements.

13. Has there ever been any written or verbal complaints regarding the building's indoor air quality? Yes ☐ No ☐

14. Have any ADA related improvements been made to the property? Yes ☐ No ☐

If "Yes", please identify the improvements.

15. Are you in receipt of any notices of code violations from the municipality's building department, zoning and/or planning department, fire department, or health department? Yes ☐ No ☐

If "Yes", please disclose the nature of the violations, attach copies of the violations to this statement and explain what actions are being undertaken to comply.

16. Are you aware of notice from any government agency regarding potential condemnation or right-of-way widening? Yes ☐ No ☐

If "Yes", explain.

17. Please identify the following components or systems where **tenants are solely responsible** for repair, servicing/maintenance, and replacement under the terms of their lease:

a. Domestic Hot Water Heaters ☐
b. Rooftop Air Conditioning Units ☐
c. Air-cooled DX Condensers/Compressors ☐

18. Please fill-out the following schedule as to the replacement status of the stated components, equipment or systems, which are applicable to the Subject:

Item or System	Approximate Quantity Replaced Thus Far	Quantity or $ for Historical Replacements			Average Unit Cost For Replacement or Total Cost Incurred or Contract Amount
		2003	2004	2005	
Asphalt Pavement Sealant					$ /SY
Asphalt Pavement Overlay/Repairs					$ /SY
Roofing					$ /SF or $ /Bldg
Exterior Painting					$ /Bldg.
A/C Compressors					$ /Each
A/C DX Condensers					$ /Each
Roof Top Units (HVAC)					$ /Each
Chillers					$ /Each
Cooling Towers					$ /Each
Individ. Domestic Hot Water Heaters					$ /Each

19. Please provide a tenant schedule detailing the name of tenant and the SF of space occupied.

DOCUMENT & INFORMATION CHECKLIST

ABC INTERNATIONAL

Building Inspection Division
ABC Due Diligence Center • 155 Anywhere Lane • Los Angeles, California 91303
(310) 000-1900 (tel) • (310) 000-1901 (fax)

Document & Information Checklist

Borrower: Your written response to this checklist is to be completed prior to the ABC's site visit and faxed to ABC at (310) 000-1901. For those questions, which are not applicable to the Subject, please respond with a "N/A". This document, and your written response to same, will be an exhibit in ABC's Property Condition Assessment.

Property Name: ____________________ **ABC Project No.:** ____________________

Project City, State: ____________________ **Date:** ____________________

DOCUMENT	N/A	DATE RECEIVED	COMMENT
A. As-Built Plans & Specifications			
1. Survey			
2. Site Plans			
3. Structural			
4. Architectural			
5. Mechanical			
6. Electrical			
B. Municipal Department Documents			
1. Certificate of Occupancy			
2. Building Permit			
3. Schedule of Building Code Violations			
4. Zoning Variances or Restrictions			
5. Site Survey			
6. Zoning Determination			
C. Promotional/Leasing Information			
1. Copy of the Most Recent Appraisal			
2. Promotional Leasing Literature			
3. Tenant Rentable Square Footage("SFR") Schedule			
4. Location Map			
D. Building Maintenance History			
1. Number of Phases			
2. Age of the Building(s)			
3. Schedule of Capital Expenditures for Previous Five (5) Years.			

DOCUMENT	N/A	DATE RECEIVED	COMMENT
E. Miscellaneous Certifications/Studies			
1. Roof Condition Survey			
2. Elevator Inspection Certificate			
3. Boiler Inspection Certificate			
4. Certificate of Electrical Compliance			
5. Asbestos Survey			
6. Asbestos Abatement Approvals & Sign-offs			
7. Phase I Environmental Assessment Rpt			
8. Flood Zone Identification & Delineation			
9. Previously Prepared Due-Diligence Condition Survey Reports			
10. Sprinkler System/Standpipe Survey Prepared by Insurance Company			
11. Tenant Complaint Log			
12. Schedule of Floor Area Measurements: Gross, Usable and Rentable SF			
13. Schedule of Operating Expenses			
14. Schedule of CAM Expenses, if applicable			
15. Previously Prepared Replacement Reserve Studies			
16. ADA Survey & Compliance Report			
17. Verification of Local Law 5 Compliance, if applicable			

Completed By:_____________
Signature:________________
Date:____________________

Page 2

PROJECT REVIEW CHECKLIST

PROJECT REVIEW CHECKLIST

Project Name
Project City, State

ABC Project No. P______ Date		
DOCUMENT	**DATE RECEIVED**	**COMMENT**
A. Plans, Specifications, Technical Back-up & Reports		
1. Two (2) complete sealed and signed sets of the following plans and specs. Plans are to be an exact duplicate set of those submitted to the Dept. of Buildings and the permanent lender, if any. If one of the sets is not stamped "Approved" by the Building Department, a letter should then accompany the plans from the architect's office stating that these documents are an exact duplicate set of those approved by the Building Department. Copies of all revised drawings (with revisions indicated) and specification addenda should be forwarded as issued.		
• Off-Site Plans, if any		
• Site Plans		
• Landscape Plans		
• Zoning Sheets		
• Architectural		
• Interior Design		
• Structural		
• Structural Calculations		
• Plumbing		
• Fire Protection		
• HVAC		
• Electrical		
• Specifications/Project Manual		
2. Parking structure plans and specifications.		
3. A drawing list from the architect's office should accompany the drawings forwarded to ABC International which references each drawing as to the date of preparation and last revision date.		
4. One (1) complete set of the existing building plans and specs (as-builts if available).		
5. Site survey sealed and certified to the Lender/Investor.		
6. Copy of the Property Improvement Plan or other guidance document issued by the Client for this project.		
7. Evidence that the Client has approved the project's construction documents, including a list of the approved plans and specifications.		
8. Certifications from the designers-of-record that the drawings comply with all local and state building construction codes, zoning requirements, and the Americans with Disabilities Act.		

ABC Project No. P_____ Date		
DOCUMENT	**DATE RECEIVED**	**COMMENT**
9. Certifications from the designers-of-record that the project as designed will meet Year 2000 Compliance Standards.		
10. A copy of the Offering Plan or Prospectus for the project in draft or final form.		
11. A written description of the building, the exterior height, number of stories, and the existing and proposed gross and net leasable areas.		
12. A copy of the affordable housing grant awarded to the project, if any. Any documentation related to the city, state or federal government or private participation in the project as well as tax credit application packages.		
13. Soils investigation data and soils engineer's report with foundation recommendations.		
14. Elevator Study, including calculations, weight, speed, round trip time and 5-minute passenger capacity.		
15. Copies of all testing reports prepared to date (if any) including but not limited to: soil compaction, reinforcing steel placement, concrete test reports, structural welding and bolting, and spray fireproofing. Reports are to be sent throughout the construction phase.		
16. Copies of all inspection reports prepared to date (if any) by the Architect's office and the Engineers-of-Record.		
17. A statement from the structural engineer that the existing building is adequate for the construction of the proposed improvements and the remedial work required, if any.		
18. Copies of the following reports:		
• Asbestos Survey		
• Lead Based Paint Survey		
• Roof Condition Survey		
• Building Condition Survey		
• ADA Survey & Compliance Report		
19. A statement prepared by the civil engineer-of-record as to whether a 100-year (or less) storm frequency flood plain area encroaches upon the site. If it does, the survey is to show the high water contour line of same and the proposed F.F. elevations are to be provided.		
20. A statement prepared by the civil engineer-of-record as to whether the site is encumbered by wetland areas and whether any mitigation work will be completed. If wetlands are present, they are to shown on the site plans		
21. Phase I Site Assessment Report that is to include a historical search of the property's use and physical on-site survey to determine if there is or has been any presence of hazardous wastes and/or toxic materials on the site.		
22. Copy of the Environmental Impact Statement (original and final), if any, and final acceptance letter of same by the lead agency or, certification of a negative declaration.		
23. Copy of the Quality Control/Controlled Testing Program.		

ABC Project No. P______ Date		
DOCUMENT	**DATE RECEIVED**	**COMMENT**
24. Seismic Evaluation Report of proposed improvements.		
25. Life Safety/Code Compliance report, if any.		
B. Contracts, Budgets, & Schedules		
1. Copy of the CM or GC agreement. The names of the project manager and superintendent and their telephone numbers.		
2. Copy of Architect/Owner Agreement. Indicate which designers will be retained by the architect directly, if any, and if architect has field inspection and requisition review responsibility.		
3. Copies of the remaining design agreements, the names of the project's designers-of-record and their telephone numbers.		
4. Evidence of professional liability insurance acceptable to the Lender from each of the designers of record.		
5. Copies of all subcontracts and major purchase orders executed to date.		
6. Copies of all change orders executed to date, including back-up information (field orders, etc.) prior to commencing the work.		
7. A list of all contractors, subcontractors and major material suppliers along with the proposed contract amounts, as available.		
8. Copy of the proposed Anticipated Job Cost Report prepared by the CM, GC or developer which will be used to track executed and pending contracts and approved and pending change orders.		
9. Copies of all subcontractor trade payment breakdowns in detail (also referred to as schedules-of-values), which have been approved by the CM or GC. If not provided by the subs, copies of the trade payment breakdowns prepared by the CM or GC for requisition review purposes.		
10. Copy of the project's indirect and direct cost budgets.		
11. Schedule of Capital Expenditures for Previous Five (5) Years.		
12. Furniture, Fixtures and Equipment ("FF&E") estimate.		
13. Project's direct cost estimate prepared by the borrower, his cost consultant, and/or the CM or GC complete with quantities and unit costs.		
14. A breakdown of the tenant workletter and estimated costs.		
15. Copy of the project's direct cost disbursement schedule.		
16. Copy of the trade-by-trade construction schedule noting all long lead items and milestone dates.		
17. Copies of the CM's or GC's and major subcontractors' performance and payment bonds, if any.		

C. Permits & Approvals		
1. All zoning information: copy of ordinance under which project was approved; copies of all variances, approvals and declarations; and any other zoning information or approvals pertinent to the project. Include a print of the Zoning Sheet showing all calculations along with evidence that the zoning computations have been approved by the Planning Board. If the project was not designed "as-of-right," please provide a brief written description of the variances and/or bonuses received and a letter copy of the Zoning Board of Appeals' letter granting approval.		
2. A comprehensive list of all agreements between the borrower and any governmental agencies for the construction of the proposed improvements and copies of all agreements.		
3. A comprehensive list of all permits necessary to construct the proposed improvements prepared by the designers-of- record.		
4. Copies of all permits secured to-date with the remaining provided as they are available.		
5. Copies of all approvals/permits from the appropriate Landmarks Commission, Historical Preservation Group and/or other agency for historical renovation and restoration work.		
6. Statement of Certificate of Occupancy ("CO") procedures (whether on a building-by-building, unit-by-unit, etc.) and any special requirements to obtain same upon completion of the work. Also note if temporary COs are issued for partial or phased completion.		
7. Confirmation from appropriate authority of availability, adequacy and intent to provide the following utilities for the proposed project:		
• Water		
• Gas		
• Steam		
• Sanitary Sewers		
• Storm Sewers		
• Electricity		
8. Copies of the utility load calculations prepared by the engineers-of-record and confirmation that existing services will or will not be adequate to serve the proposed project.		
9. Existing Certificate of Occupancy		
10. Schedule of Building Code Violations		

D. General		
1. Contractor's Qualification Statement, AIA Document No. A305.		
2. Architect's Qualification Statement, AIA Document No. B431.		
3. Resumes of the CM's or GC's project manager and superintendent.		
4. A statement as to whether this is a non-union, union or open shop project.		
5. 8"x 11" renderings of the project, descriptive or promotional information for the review of governmental agencies and/or investors		
E. Promotional/Leasing Information		
1. Copy of the Most Recent Appraisal		
2. Promotional Leasing Literature		
3. Tenant Rentable Square Footage("SFR") Schedule		
4. Location Map		

SAMPLE APARTMENT CHECKLIST

Typical Apartment Unit

Living Areas

Floors:	☐ Carpeting ☐ Vinyl Tile ☐ Wood
Walls:	☐ Painted ☐ GWB ☐ CMU ☐ Stucco ☐ VWC
Ceilings:	☐ ACT ☐ Painted GWB ☐ Textured GWB ☐ Stucco

____

____

Bathrooms

Floors:	☐ Ceramic Tile ☐ VCT ☐ Vinyl Flooring	
Walls:	☐ Ceramic Tile ☐ Painted ☐ GWB ☐ Stucco ☐ VWC	
Ceilings:	☐ ACT ☐ Painted GWB ☐ Textured GWB ☐ Stucco	
Vanities:	Frame:	☐ Wood ☐ Metal ☐ P-Lam
	Countertop:	☐ Wood ☐ Metal ☐ P-Lam
	Sink:	

____

____

Kitchens

Floors:	☐ Ceramic Tile ☐ VCT ☐ Vinyl Flooring	
Walls:	☐ Ceramic Tile ☐ Painted ☐ GWB ☐ Stucco ☐ VWC	
Ceilings:	☐ ACT ☐ Painted GWB ☐ Textured GWB ☐ Stucco	
Cabinets:	☐ Good ☐ Fair ☐ Poor	
	Box:	☐ Wood ☐ Particle Brd ☐ Metal
	Face Frame:	☐ Wood ☐ Metal ☐ P-Lam
	Countertop:	☐ Wood ☐ Metal ☐ P-Lam
Fixtures:	☐ Single Basin Sink ☐ Double Basin Sink	
	☐ Dishwasher Make:___________	
	☐ Refrigerator ___________CF Frost Free? ☐ Yes ☐ No	
	☐ Range Electric/Gas Self Clean? Yes ☐ No ☐	
	☐ Garbage Disposal	
	☐ Microwave ☐ Microwave w/Vent Hood ☐ Yes	
	☐ Washer/Dryer Stacked ☐ Side by Side ☐	

PCA ASSIGNMENT DATA SHEET

PCA Assignment Data Sheet

Project Information:

Project Name: Address: City, State & Zip: Client Proj. I.D. No. Report Update:	ABC Proj. Number: P0000000 ABC Property No. Date of Proposal: Primary ABC Project Mgr. (PPM): Secondary ABC Project Mgr. (SPM):	Date: ABC Enviro?:

Project Description:

General: Building Use: Size: No. of Buildings Basement, Cellar & Crawl Space: No. of Parking Spaces: Construction Type:	Client Protocol: Year Built: Year Renovated: No. of Stories: Occupied: Type of Parking: Site Area:

Format, Purpose & Costs	**Schedule**
Report Type: Photos per Page: Report Use: Draft Required? Verbal Required? Reserves?: Reserve Term: Inflation Rate: Cost Categories: Insurable Value: No. of Copies + Original: Specialty Consultants: None of the Above	Delivery Time (Days): Site Visit Date: PM's Completion: Report Due Date: PPM Units: SPM Units: **Mobilization Information** Red Rope File: Checklist/Pre-Survey: Bldg Dept. Fire Dept. FOIA: Flood Zone Info: Template File Transfer:

Borrower or Site Rep Contact	**Client Information**
Borrower Rep: Title: Company: Address: City, State & Zip: Borrower Rep Tel: Borrower Rep Fax: Site Contact: Site Contact Tel: Site Contact FAX:	Client: Client Contact: Title: Street Address: City, State & ZIP: Telephone: FAX: Email

Comments?	

PCA Assignment Invoice Data

Billing Information	
Approved for Billing	**Base Fee:**
	Lump Sum:
Submitted for Billing	**Hourly:**
	Not-to-Exceed Amount:
	Travel Included in Fee:
	No. of Copies + Orig.:
	Copies Included in Fee
	Overnight Mail or Msgr:
	TOTAL FEE
	Retainer Required?:
	Retainer Received?:
	Amount of Retainer:
	Invoice w/ Report?:

Special Forms and Documents

PCA RESEARCH LOG

PCA Research Log

Project Name: **Address:** **City, State and Zip:**		**ABC Project No.:** **ABC Project Mgr:** **PCR Format:**	

Description & Site Contact **General:** **Building Use:** **Size:** **No. Of Buildings:** **No. of Stories:** **Site Contact:** **Site Contact Telephone:** **Site Contact FAX:** ***Contacted?:*** ☐	**Schedule** **Site Visit Date:** **PM's Completion Date:** **In Client's Hand:** **Elevator Research Letter** **Is the Subject over 3 stories in height and does it have an elevator?** **Did you send Elevator Research Letter?:** **Sent:** ☐ **Received:** ☐
Building Dept FOIA **Sent:** ☐ **Received:** ☐	**Fire Dept FOIA** **Sent:** ☐ **Received:** ☐
Mobilization Documents **Flood Plain Data:** ☐ **Site Location Map:** ☐ **Pre-survey Quest. Docs:** ☐ **Red Rope Folder Prepared:** ☐	**Client Information** **Name:** **Contact:** **Title:** **Street Address:** **City, State & ZIP:** **Telephone:** **Fax:**

ELEVATOR INSPECTION FORM

ELEVATOR INSPECTION FORM

PROJECT NAME: ______________________

PROJECT NO. ______________________

DESCRIPTION:

Quantity Type: ______________________

Manufacturer: ______________________

Date Installed: ______________________

Capacity: ______________________

Rated speed:

____

Landings: ______________________

Openings: ______________________

Doors: ______________________

Machine: ______________________

Operation:

____

NOTES: ______________________

____

____

____

HVAC SYMBOLS

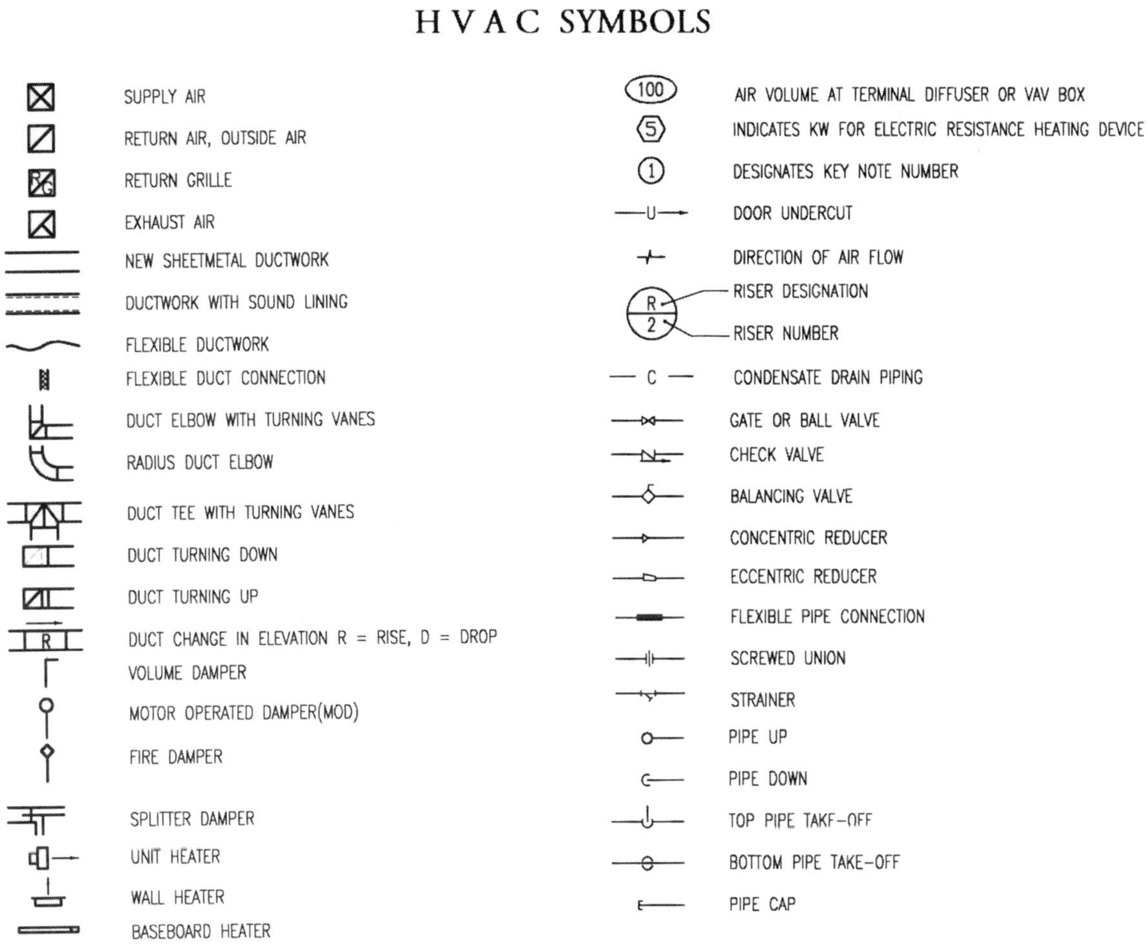

SAMPLE CLIENT DEBRIEFING LETTER

ABC INTERNATIONAL

Building Inspection Division
ABC Due Diligence Center • 155 Anywhere Lane • Los Angeles, California 91303
(310) 000-1900 (tel) • (310) 000-1901 (fax)

To:	Mr. John Doe, Vice President
Firm:	Union Bank
Tel:	(212) 000 3000
Fax:	(212) 000 3001
Date:	November 25, 2007
From:	Sam A.A. Kubba, R.A.
Re:	Property Condition Assessment 7000 Anywhere Drive Building 335,000 SF One (1) 2-Story Office Building Woodland Hills, California ABC Project No. P311

Dear Mr. Doe:

Today, we completed our site visit, and are prepared to provide you with a preliminary debriefing as to the property's general physical condition. During our site visit, the weather consisted of light drizzle and the temperature was about 45 degrees F.

Salient Points:

- Overall, the Subject was considered to be in very good condition.
- It was evident that preventive maintenance has been exercised. Based upon our observations and the limited information reviewed to date, maintenance can best be characterized as proactive.
- Only minor physical deficiencies were observed and consist of: isolated loose asphalt shingles, distribution panels were missing the front covers, and isolated cast-in-place concrete pavement cracks. These will reportedly be attended to by the new tenant during renovation.
- Property management was helpful and very cooperative with our requests for information. They have produced some of the information requested on the Pre-survey Questionnaire and Disclosure Form that we faxed to their offices, which we are to review on Union Bank's behalf.

We have yet to complete our research with the service companies, nor have we prepared any opinions of probable costs to remedy the physical deficiencies observed. Furthermore, we are still awaiting information from the owner. However, should you wish to discuss our observations prior to completing our Property Condition Report, please call me.

TYPICAL PCA REPORT COVER AND LETTER

PROPERTY CONDITION ASSESSMENT REPORT

Name of Property
One-Line Description of Property
City, State

PHOTO OF PROPERTY

Prepared for:
Client Name
City, State

Date
ABC Project No. P______

Date

Client Name
Title
Client Company Name
Street Address
City, State, Zip Code
(___) ___-____ (tel)
(___) ___-____ (fax)

Method of Delivery if
Other than US Mail

Re: ABC Project No. P______
Summary Property Condition Assessment
Name of Property
One Line Description of Property
City, State

Dear Mr./Ms.__________:

Pursuant to your request, attached is ________ copies of our Report outlining the general physical conditions observed on __________, 200__ complete with remedial cost estimates for deferred maintenance and existing deficiencies along with a ___ year term Replacement Reserve Schedule.

We certify that we have no undisclosed interest in the property, and that our employment and compensation are not contingent upon our findings or our estimated costs to remedy the deficiencies noted. The scope of this assessment, methodology and limiting conditions are outlined within the Report.

We appreciate the opportunity to assist you. If you have any questions, please contact me at extension _____.

Sincerely,

ABC INTERNATIONAL, INC.
Building Inspection Division

Reviewed by:____________________

Sam A.A. Kubba, R.A.
Senior Project Manager

John B. Doe, R.A.
Senior Project Manager

SAK/sk

TYPICAL OFFICE TRANSMITTAL FORM

ABC Branch Office Transmittal

DATE: 20 August 2007	**ABC PROJECT NO.: P000000**
TO: John Doe	**ABC PROPERTY NO.: 100**
FROM: Michael A. Smith	**PROJECT NAME: Anywhere Apts.**

From the Branch Office in:

☐ **New York** ☐ **Chicago** ☐ **Los Angeles** ☐ **Washington DC** ☐ **Dallas**

The following documents are contained within this package:

☐ Assignment Data Sheet ☐ Debriefing Letter

☐ Site Confirmation Letter ☐ PCA Checklist Booklet

☐ Report Body ☐ Remedial Cost Estimates

☐ Replacement Reserves ☐ Photos

☐ Exhibits: ☐ Pre-Survey ☐ Site Location Map ☐ Building FOIL
☐ Fire FOIL ☐ Seismic Location Map ☐ Elevator Research
☐ Plot Plan ☐ Rent Roll ☐ Typ. Floor Plans
☐ Other ______________________________

Copy on Enclosed Diskette: ☐ Yes ☐ No

Items to E-Mail: ☐ Report Body ☐ Costs ☐ Reserves

☐ Photos ☐ All

Comments/ Instructions: ______________________________
____
____
____
____
____

Branch Office Manager Signature: ______________________________

REPRESENTATIVE SAMPLING OF POTENTIAL CLIENTS

- AAA Mortgage Equity Service
- AMBAC Assurance Corporation
- Amcor Network Mortgage
- Anglo-American Financial
- Archon Group
- ASB Capital Management, Inc.
- Atlas Capital LLC
- Babylon Funding Group
- Bank of America
- Bankers Trust Company
- Barclays Bank PLC
- Bowery Savings
- C.B. Richard Ellis, Inc.
- CIBC World Markets
- Citicorp/Citibank
- Clark Construction Group
- Cohoes Savings Bank
- Columbia Equities, Ltd.
- CommerzBank
- Cornerstone Realty Advisors
- Custom Capital Corporation
- David Nassif Associates
- Deloitte & Touche
- Deutsche Bank Capital Corporation
- Emmes Capital
- Ensign Bank, FSB
- Fairmont Funding, Ltd
- Federal Deposit Insurance Corporation
- Federal Standard Mortgage Banking
- Fidelity Properties
- First Union National Bank
- Gefen Financial Corp
- Goldman, Sachs & Co.
- Great American Insurance
- Guardian Mortgage Capital Corp.
- Home Life Insurance Company
- HSBC Bank
- HSH-Nordbank
- Hudson Bay Mortgage
- Integrated Funding, Inc.
- Irving Trust Company
- J.P. Morgan Chase Bank
- J.P. Morgan Investment Management, Inc
- John Hancock Insurance Co.
- Key Bank
- Key Mortgage Funding, Inc.
- Kleinwort Benson Limited
- Knight-Ridder Financial Information
- Lehman Brothers
- Lend Lease Real Estate Investments
- Levein, Rich & Company
- Liberty Mortgage Banking, Ltd.
- Liberty Mutual Insurance
- Long Island Savings Bank, FSB
- Meridian Capital Group LLC
- Merrill Lynch Real Estate Investment
- Metropolitan Life Insurance Co.
- Moody's Investors Service
- National Institutes of Health
- New York Life Insurance Company
- New York State Teachers Retirement System
- Northern Home Funding Corp
- Northwest Mutual Life Insurance Co.
- One Beacon Insurance Group
- Oppenheimer Government Securities
- Park Terrace Properties
- Perri Funding Corp
- Prudential Mortgage Capital Corp.
- Prudential Insurance
- Related Mortgage Corporation
- Reliable Financial Services
- Richland Equity Resources Corp
- Rosenberg & Rosenberg, P.C.
- Russell Financial Corporation
- SAFECO Insurance Company
- Salomon Brothers Inc.
- Salomon Smith Barney, Inc.
- Security Mutual Life Insurance Co.
- Sibley Mortgage Corporation
- Statewide Funding Corp.
- Sterling National Mortgage Corp.
- Teachers Insurance & Annuity Association
- The Bank of New York
- The Union Labor Life Insurance Co.
- Ticor Title Guarantee Company
- Tokyo-Mitsubishi Bank
- Trammell Crow Company
- TransAmerica Realty Services, Inc.
- UBS Securities, Inc.
- University of Georgia
- U.S. Department of Justice
- U.S. Environmental Protection Agency
- Valcon Construction Consultants, Inc.
- Washington Mutual
- Westdeutsche Immobilien Bank
- Worldwide Capital Mortgage
- Zurich North America

Note: Contact details regarding the above can be found on the Internet, yellow pages, etc. A letter (see Promotion Template Letter—Chapter 22) offering professional services can be sent to those considered to have the most potential.

DUE DILIGENCE FIRMS

1. **Inspection & Valuation International, Inc. (IVI)**
   55 West Red Oak Lane, White Plains, NY 10604
   Mr. Carl de Stefanis, PE, President
   914-694-1900; www.ivi-intl.com
   Corporate Office
2. **Eckland Consultants, Inc.**
   Three Parkway North, Suite 100, Deerfiled, IL 60015
   Mr. Joe Chittenden or Frank Hennessey,
   Executive VP; 847-948-0100; www.eckland.com
3. **EMG**
   11011 McCormick Road, Hunt Valley, MD 21031
   Mr. Patrick Jarosinski, A&E Director
   Mr. James M. Hulbert, Env. Services Director
   410-785-6200; 888-364-8258; www.emgbalt.com
4. **Building Diagnostics, Ltd.**
   1738 Elton Road, Suite 318, Silver Spring, MD 20903
   Phil Ulzheimer; 301-317-8400; www.bdlmain.com
5. **Property Solutions, Inc.**
   501 Delran Parkway, Unit C, Delran, N.J. 08075
   Mr. Edward Gallagher, Timothy Downes, Principals
   856-813-3000; bids@propertysolutionsinc.com;
   www.propertysolutionsinc.com
6. **VFA, Inc.**
   266 Summer Street, Boston, MA 02210-1112
   617-451-5100; www.vfafacility.com
7. **Project Resources Inc. (PRI)**
   3760 Convoy Street, Suite 230, San Diego, CA
   92111
   Mr. Joseph Boyer, PE, VP
   619-505-1000; 858-505-1000; www.priworld.com
8. **Criterium Engineers**
   22 Monument Sq. Suite 600, Portland, ME
   Mr. Peter E. Hollender, Executive VP
   800-242-1969; 207-828-1969;
   phollander@criterium-engineers.com;
   www.criterium-engineers.com
   Each office is independently owned & operated
9. **ENSR Headquarters**
   35 Nagog Park, Acton, MA 01720
   978-635-9500; 877-222-2260; 800-722-2440;
   info@retec.com; www.ensr.aecom.com
   North American HQ-Offices throughout U.S. &
   abroad
10. **Construction Insight, Inc.**
    270 Farmington Avenue, Suite 357,
    Farmington, CT 06032
    John W. Thompson Jr., PE, President
    860-676-8282; www.constructioninsightinc.com
11. **Terracon**
    16000 College Boulevard, Lenexa, KS 66219
    Kevin Langwell, VP, Client Development
    913-599-6886; 800-593-7777;
    kflangwell@terracon.com;
    corporate@terracon.com; www.terracon.com
12. **Building Analytics**
    528 State Street, Glendale, CA 91203
    Mr. Jan H. Schutze, VP
    818-500-1898; www.buildinganalytics.com;
    www.baenvironmental.com
13. **Merrit & Harris, Inc.**
    110 E. 42nd Street, 12th Floor,
    New York, NY 10017-5685
    Mr. Thomas C. Richard, AIA, President & CEO
    212-697-3188; trichard@mharrisinc.com;
    www.merrittandharris.com
14. **C.L.I. Group, LLC**
    34090 Roberts Road, Eastlake, OH 44095
    Mr. Al Tibbs, CIEC, Principal
    440-946-7191; office@closerlookinspection.com;
    www.closerlookinspections.com
15. **Dames & Moore Group**
    911 Wilshire Boulevard, Los Angeles, CA 90017
    Mr. A.C. Darrow, President & CEO
    213-996-2200; www.dames.com
    Now part of URS
16. **Marx-Okubo & Assoc. Ltd.**
    150 Paularino Avenue E., Suite 192,
    Costa Mensa, CA 92626
    Mr. Mark Haddix, AIA, Executive VP
    714-545-6220; www.marxokubo.com

Acronyms & Glossary

ACRONYMS

TERM	ACRONYM
Actual Age	ACT AGE
ADA Architectural Guidelines	ADAAG
Americans with Disabilities Act	ADA
American EC Association	AECA
American Society of Mechanical Engineers	ASME
American Society for Testing and Materials	ASTM
Ampere	A or AMP
Asbestos Containing Material	ACM
Association of European Building Surveyors	AEEBC
British Thermal Unit per Hour	BTUH
Building Officials and Code Administrators	BOCA
Building Owners and Managers Association	BOMA
Built-up Roofing	BUR
Business Co-operative Centre	BCC
Business Co-operation Network	BC-NET
Business and Industry Advisory Committee	BIAC
Business and Information Centers	BIC
Commission of the European Communities	CEC
European Committee for Standardization	CEN
Commercial Mortgage Backed Securities	CMBS
Collateralized Mortgage Obligations	CMOs
Concrete Masonry Unit	CMU
Debt Service Coverage Ratio	DSCR

Directive	Dir
Ductile iron pipe	DIP
Each	EA
Effective Age	EFF AGE
European Council	EC
European Development Fund	EDF
European Economic Community	EEC
European Free Trade Association	EFTA
Environmental Protection Agency	EPA
European Standards Institute	ESI
Electro Magnetic Fields	EMF
Energy Management System	EMS
Etheylic-Propalene Dian-Molomer	EPDM
Expected Useful Life	EUL
Exterior Insulation & Finish System	EIFS
Federal Emergency Management Agency	FEMA
Fair Housing Act	FHA
Federal Fair Housing Act	FFHA
International Real Estate Federation	FIABCI
Finishes, Furniture (fixtures) & Equipment	FF&E
First Union National Bank	FUNB
Flood Insurance Rate Maps	FIRM
Freedom of Information Letter	FOIL
Freedom of Information Act and similar state statutes	FOIA
Factory Mutual	FM
Funds from Operations	FFO
General Agreement on Tariffs and Trade	GATT
Ground Fault Circuit Interrupter	GFCI
Hazardous Materials	HAZMAT
Heating, Ventilation, Air Conditioning	HVAC
Horse Power	hp
Indoor Air Quality	IAQ
Internal Rate of Return	IRR
International Chamber of Commerce	ICC

Inverted Roof Membrane Assembly (Application)	IRMA
International Standards Organization	ISO
Kilovolt-Ampere	kVA
Kilowatt	kW
Loan to Value	LTV
National Fire Protection Association	NFPA
Net Operating Income	NOI
Official Journal	OJ
Pounds Per Square Inch	psi
Probable Maximum Loss	PML
Project Management Oversight	PMO
Property Condition Assessment	PCA
Property Condition Report	PCR
Protected Membrane Roofing System	PMRS
Real Estate Investment Trust	REIT
Real Estate Mortgage Investment Conduit	REMIC
Reduced Pressure Zone	RPZ
Remaining Useful Life	RUL
Request for Proposal	RFP
Rooftop Package Unit	RTU
Secretariat-General	SG
Securities and Exchange Commission	SEC
Special Directive	SD
Slab-on-Grade	SOG
Special Floodway Hazard Area	SFHA
Square Foot	SF
Square Foot Gross	SFG
Standard & Poor's	S&P
Statement of Work	SOW
Ton	T
Underground Storage Tank	UST
Uniform Building Code	UBC
Volt	V
Water Heater / Domestic Hot Water Heater	DHWH

GLOSSARY

Accessible Describes a site, building, facility, or portion thereof that complies with these guidelines.

Accessible Route A continuous unobstructed path connecting all accessible elements and spaces of a building or facility. Interior accessible routes may include corridors, floors, ramps, elevators, lifts, and clear floor space at fixtures. Exterior accessible routes may include parking access aisles, curb ramps, crosswalks at vehicular ways, walks, ramps, and lifts.

Addendum A written or graphic instruction issued by the architect prior to the execution of the contract which modifies or interprets the bidding documents by additions, deletions, clarifications or corrections. An addendum becomes part of the contract documents when the contract is executed.

Agency (1) Relationship between agent and principal. (2) Organization acting as agent. (3) Administrative subdivision of an organization, particularly in government.

Agent One authorized by another to act in the other's stead or behalf.

Agreement (1) A meeting of minds. (2) A legally enforceable promise or promises between two or among several persons. (3) On a construction project, the document stating the essential terms of the contract between owner and contractor which incorporates by reference the other contract documents. (4) The document setting forth the terms of the contract between the architect and owner or between the architect and a consultant. Agreement and contract are frequently used interchangeably without any intended change in meaning.

Alligatoring A pattern of rough cracking on a coated surface, similar in appearance to alligator skin.

All Risk Insurance Insurance against loss arising from any cause other than those perils or causes specifically excluded by name. This contrasts with the ordinary type of policy which names the peril or perils insured against.

Amortization The liquidation of a financial debt through regular periodic installment payments for tax purposes, the periodic deduction of capitalized expenses such as organization costs.

Applications For Payment Contractor's certified request for payment of amount due for completed portions of the work and, if the contract so provides, for materials or equipment delivered and suitably stored pending their incorporation into work.

Appraisal See Cost Appraisal.

Approval Written or imprinted acknowledgement that materials, equipment or methods of construction are acceptable for use in the work, or accepting a contractor's or owner's request or claim as valid.

Approved Equal Material, equipment or method approved by the architect for use in the work as being acceptable as an equivalent in essential attributes to the material, equipment or method specified in the contract documents.

As-Built Drawings See Record Drawings.

Assumed Liability Liability which arises from an agreement between people, as opposed to liability which arises from common or statutory law. See also Contractual Liability.

Balloon Frame A wooden building frame composed of closely spaced members (studs) which are continuous from the sill to the top plate of the roof line; also called eastern frame; compare platform frame.

Base Building The core (common areas) and shell of the building and its systems that typically are not subject to improvements to suit tenant requirements.

Base Flashing Flashing that covers the edges of a membrane.

Baseline The minimum level of observations, due diligence, inquiry/research, documentation review, and preparation of opinions of probable costs to remedy material physical deficiencies for conducting a PCA as described in this guide.

Bearing Wall A wall which supports any vertical loads in addition to its own weight.

Bond See (1) Bid Bond; (2) Completion Bond; (3) Fidelity Bond; (4) Labor and Material Payment Bond; (5) Performance Bond; (6) Statutory Bond; (7) Surety Bond.

Boundary Survey A mathematically closed diagram of the complete peripheral boundary of a site, reflecting dimensions, compass bearings and angles. It should bear a licensed land surveyor's signed certification, and may include a metes and bounds or other written description.

BTU British Thermal Unit; the energy required to raise the temperature of one pound of water by one degree fahrenheit.

Budget, Construction The sum established by the owner as available for the entire project, including the construction budget, land costs, equipment costs, financing costs, compensation for professional services, costs of owner-furnished goods and services, contingency allowance, and other similar established or estimated costs.

Builder's Risk Insurance A specialized form of property insurance which provides coverage for loss or damage to the work during the course of construction. See also (1) Property Insurance; (2) All Risk Insurance.

Building Department Records Records maintained by or in possession of the local government authority with jurisdiction over the construction, alteration, use, or demolition of improvements on the subject property.

Building Envelope The enclosure of the building that protects the building's interior from outside elements, namely the exterior walls, roof and soffit areas.

Building Inspector A representative of a governmental authority employed to inspect construction for compliance codes, regulations and ordinances.

Building Loan Trust Account A separate non-interest bearing bank account with the lender which is not drawn upon except to pay direct and indirect costs approved by the lender.

Building Permit A permit issued by an appropriate governmental authority allowing construction of a project in accordance with approved drawings and specifications.

Building Systems Interacting or independent components or assemblies, which form single integrated units, that comprise a building and its site work, such as, pavement and flatwork, structural frame, roofing, exterior walls, plumbing, HVAC, electrical, etc.

Build-Out The interior construction and customization of a space (including services, space and stuff) to meet the tenant's requirements; either new construction or renovation (also referred to as fit-out or fit-up).

Capital Markets Public and/or private markets where businesses or individuals can raise or borrow capital.

Capitalization Rate The rate at which net operating income is discounted to determine the value of a property. It is one method that is utilized to estimate property value. When two of three values are known (annual net operating income, cap rate, property value estimate) the calculations are as follows: Value = NOI/Cap Rate; NOI = Value × Cap Rate; Cap Rate = NOI/Value.

Caulking The soft, putty-like material used to fill joints, seams, and cracks.

Certificate For Payment A statement from the architect to the owner confirming the amount of money due the contractor for work accomplished or materials and equipment suitably stored, or both.

Certificate of Insurance A document issued by an authorized representative of an insurance company stating the types, amounts and effective dates of insurance in force for a designated insured.

Certificate of Occupancy Document issued by governmental authority certifying that all or a designated portion of a building complies with the provisions of applicable statutes and regulations, and permitting occupancy for its designated use.

Certificate of Substantial Completion A certificate prepared by the architect on the basis of an inspection stating that the work or a designated portion thereof is substantially complete, which established the date of substantial completion; states the responsibilities of the owner and the contractor for security, maintenance, heat, utilities, damage to the work, and insurance; and taxes the time within which the contractor shall complete the items listed therein.

Change Order A written and signed document between the owner and the contractor authorizing a change in the work or an adjustment in the contract sum or time. The contract sum and time may be changed only by change order.

Circulation Path An exterior or interior way of passage from one place to another for pedestrians, including, but not limited to, walks, hallways, courtyards, stairways, and stair landings.

Clear Floor Space The minimum unobstructed floor or ground space required to accommodate a single, stationary wheelchair and occupant.

Codes See Building Codes.

Coinsurance An insurance policy provision which requires the insured to carry insurance equal to a named percentage of the value of the property covered, or share in the loss proportionately in the event of a claim.

Collapse Insurance Insurance to cover building and contents loss or damage caused by collapse.

CMBS—Commercial Mortgage Backed Securities Securities collateralized by loans on commercial real estate. All principal and interest from the mortgages flow through to the investors, less a service charge by the issuing organization.

Commercial Real Estate Improved real property, except a dwelling or property with four or less dwelling units exclusively for residential use. This term includes, but is not limited to, improved real property used for industrial, retail, office, hospitality, agriculture, other commercial, medical, or educational purposes; property used for residential purposes that has more than four residential dwelling units, and property with four or less dwelling units for residential use when it has a commercial function, as in the operation of such dwellings for profit.

Commercial Real Estate Transaction A transfer of title to or possession of improved real property or receipt of a security interest in improved real property, except that it does not include transfer of title to or possession of improved real property with respect to an individual dwelling or building containing four or less dwelling units.

Common Use Refers to those interior and exterior rooms, spaces, or elements that are made available for the use of a restricted group of people (for example, occupants of a homeless shelter, the occupants of an office building, or the guests of such occupants).

Compensation (1) Payment for services rendered or products or materials furnished or delivered (2) Payment in satisfaction of claims for damages suffered.

Completion Bond Bond of the contractor or the owner in which a surety guarantees to the lender that the project will be completed free of liens.

Completion Date See Date of Substantial Completion.

Component A fully functional portion of a building system, piece of equipment, or building element.

Comprehensive General Liability Insurance A form of liability insurance covering a wide range of claims for bodily injury and property damage which are combined under one policy coverage for all liability exposures except those specifically excluded on a blanket basis and automatically covers new and unknown hazards that may develop. Comprehensive general liability insurance automatically includes contractual liability coverage for certain types of contracts.

Conditions of the Contract Those portions of the contract documents which define the rights and responsibilities of the contracting parties and of others involved in the work. The conditions of the contract include general conditions, supplementary conditions and other conditions.

Consent of Surety Written consent of the surety on a Performance Bond and/or Labor and Material Payment Bond to such contract changes, change orders or reductions in the contractor's retainage, or to final payment, or to waiving notification of contract changes. The term is also used with respect to an extension of a time in a Bid Bond.

Construction Documents A term used to represent all drawings, specifications, addenda, and other pertinent construction information associated with the construction of a specific project.

Construction Inspector See Inspector.

Construction Loan The direct costs loan and indirect costs loan, collectively, and in the amount initially equal to the loan amount.

Consultant The entity or individual that prepares the PCR and that is responsible for the observance of and reporting on the physical condition of commercial real estate in accordance with this guide. The consultant generally is an independent contractor; however, the consultant may be an employee of the user. The consultant may be an individual that is both the field observer and PCR reviewer.

Contingency Allowance A sum included in the project budget designated to cover unpredictable or unforeseen items of work, or changes in the work subsequently required by the owner. See Budget, Project.

Contingent Liability (1) Liability which is not absolute and fixed, but is dependent upon the occurrence of some uncertain future event or the existence of an uncertain specified condition. (2) Particularly in insurance law, liability imposed upon an individual or entity because of injuries or damages caused by persons or entities, other than employees, for whose acts or omissions the first party may be legally responsible.

Contract A legally enforceable promise or agreement between two or among several person. See also Agreement.

Contract Documents A term used to represent all executed agreements between the owner and contractor; any general, supplementary or other contract conditions; the drawings and specifications; all addenda issued prior to execution of the contract; and any other items specifically stipulated as being included in the contract documents.

Contractor (1) One who contracts. (2) In construction terminology, the person or entity responsible for performing the work and identified as such in the owner-contractor agreement.

Cost Appraisal Evaluation or estimate (preferably by a qualified professional appraiser) of the market or other value, cost, utility or other attribute of land or other facility.

Cost Estimate A preliminary statement of approximate cost, determined by one of the following methods. 1. Area and volume method; cost per square foot or cubic foot of the building. 2. Unit cost method; cost of one unit multiplied by the number of units in the project; for example, in a hospital, the cost of one patient unit multiplied by the number of patient units in the project. 3. In-place unit method; cost in-place of a unit, such as doors, cubic yards of concrete, and squares of roofing.

Curb Ramp A short ramp cutting through a curb or built up to it.

Dangerous or Adverse Conditions Conditions which may pose a threat or possible injury to the field observer, and which may require the use of special protective clothing, safety equipment, access equipment, or any other precautionary measures.

Date of Agreement The date stated in the agreement. If no date is stated, it could be the date on which the agreement is actually signed, if this is recorded, or it may be the date established by the award.

Date of Commencement of the Work The date established in a notice to the contractor to proceed or, in the absence of such notice, the date of the owner contractor agreement or such other date and may be established therein.

Date of Substantial Completion The date certified by the architect when the work or a designated portion thereof is sufficiently complete, in accordance with the contract documents, so the owner can occupy the work or designated portion thereof for the use for which it is intended.

Deferred Maintenance Physical deficiencies that cannot be remedied with routine maintenance, normal operating maintenance, etc., excluding de minimis conditions that generally do not present a material physical deficiency to the subject property.

Deficiency See Physical Deficiency.

Detectable Warning A standardized surface feature built in or applied to walking surfaces to warn visually impaired people of hazards on a circulation path.

Direct Costs (Hard Costs) The aggregate costs of all labor, materials, equipment and fixtures necessary for the completion of construction of the improvements.

Direct Costs Loan; Indirect Costs Loan That portion of the loan amount applicable and equal to the sum of the loan budget amounts for direct costs and indirect costs, respectively, shown on the borrower's project cost statement.

Dismantling To take apart or remove any component, device or piece of equipment that is bolted, screwed, secured, or fastened by other means.

Due Care A legal term indicating the requirement for a professional to exercise reasonable care, skill, ability and judgment under the circumstance. Performance of duties and services must be consistent with the level of reasonable care, skill, ability and judgment provided by reputable professionals in the same geographical area at the same period of time. Failure to exercise DUE CARE constitutes NEGLIGENCE.

Due Diligence The process of conducting a walk-through survey and appropriate inquiries into the physical condition of a commercial real estate's improvements, usually in connection with a commercial real estate transaction. The degree and type of such survey or other inquiry may vary for different properties and different purposes.

Egress, Means of A continuous and unobstructed way of exit travel from any point in a building or facility to a public way. A means of egress comprises vertical and horizontal travel and may include intervening room spaces, doorways, hallways, corridors, passageways, balconies, ramps, stairs, enclosures, lobbies, horizontal exits, courts and yards. An accessible means of egress is one that complies with these guidelines and does not include stairs, steps, or escalators. Areas of rescue assistance or evacuation elevators may be included as part of accessible means of egress.

Elastomeric A material having characteristics which allow it to expand or contract its shape and still return to its original dimensions without losing stability.

Element An architectural or mechanical component of a building, facility, space, or site, e.g., telephone, curb ramp, door, drinking fountain, seating, or water closet.

Employer's Liability Insurance Insurance protection for the employer against claims by employees or employees' dependents for damage which arises out of injuries or diseases sustained in the course of their work, and which are based on common law negligence rather than on liability under workers' compensation acts.

Epicenter The point of the earth's surface directly above the focus or hypocenter of an earthquake.

Expected Useful Life (EUL) The average amount of time in years that an item, component or system is estimated to function when installed new and assuming routine maintenance is practiced.

Extended Coverage Insurance An endorsement to a property insurance policy which extends the perils covered to include windstorm, hail, riot, civil commotion, explosion (except steam boiler), air craft, vehicles and smoke. See (1) Property Insurance; (2) Boiler & Machinery Insurance.

Facility All or any portion of buildings, structures, site improvements, complexes, equipment, roads, walks, passageways, parking lots, or other real or personal property located on a site.

Field Observer The individual that conducts the walk-through survey; also known as the assessor.

Final Completion Term denoting that the work has been completed in accordance with the terms and conditions of the contract documents.

Final Inspection Final review of the project by the architect to determine final completion, prior to issuance of the final certificate for payment.

Final Payment Payment made by the owner to the contractor, upon issuance by the architect of the final certificate for payment, of the entire unpaid balance of the contract sum as adjusted by change orders. See also Final Acceptance.

Fire Barrier A continuous membrane such as a wall, ceiling, or floor assembly that is designed and constructed to a specified fire-resistant rating to hinder the spread of fire and smoke. This resistant rating is based on a time factor. Only fire-rated doors may be used in these barriers.

Fire Compartment of Fire Zone An enclosed space in a building that is separated from all other parts of the building by the construction of fire separations having fire resistance ratings.

Fire Department Records Records maintained by or in the possession of the local fire department in the area in which the subject property is located. These records should be practically reviewable and readily accessible for use by the consultant by exercising an appropriate inquiry within the time frame required for production of the PCR.

Fire Resistance Rating Sometimes called fire rating, fire resistance classification, or hourly rating. A term defined in building codes, usually based on fire endurance required. Fire resistance ratings are assigned by building codes for various types of construction and occupancies, and are usually given in half-hour increments.

Fire Wall 1. A wall constructed of solid masonry units, faced on each side with brick or reinforced concrete, used to subdivide a building or separate buildings, to restrict the spread of fire. 2. A wall with adequate fire resistance used to subdivide buildings to restrict the spread of fire.

Flashing A thin, impervious sheet of material placed in construction to prevent water penetration or to direct the flow of water. Flashing is used especially at roof hips and valleys, roof penetrations, joints between a roof and a vertical wall, and in masonry walls to direct the flow of water and moisture.

Immediate Costs Opinions of probable costs that require immediate action as a result of any of the following: (1) material existing or potential unsafe conditions, (2) material building or fire code violations, or (3) conditions that, if left unremedied, have the potential to result in or contribute to critical element or system failure within one year or will result most probably in a significant escalation of its remedial cost.

Indemnification A contractual obligation by which one person or entity agrees to secure another against loss or damage from specified liabilities. See also Contractual Liability.

Indemnification, Implied An indemnification which is implied by law rather than arising out of a contract to provide indemnification.

Indirect Costs (Soft Costs) Certain costs (other than direct costs) of completion of the improvements, including but not limited to, architects', engineers' and lenders' attorneys' fees, ground rents, interest on and recording taxes and title charges in respect to building loan mortgages, real estate taxes, water and sewer rents, survey costs, loan commitment fees, insurance and bond premiums and other such non-construction costs as are part of the "cost of improvements," as defined in the applicable state's lien law.

Indirect Cost Statement A statement by the borrower in a form approved by the lender of indirect costs incurred and to be incurred.

Initial Advance The first advance of the loan proceeds made to the borrower.

Inspection Examination of work completed or in progress to determine its conformance with the requirements of the contract documents. The architect ordinarily makes only two inspections of work, one to determine substantial completion and the other to determine final completion. The term is also used to mean examination of the work by a public official, owner's representative, or others.

Labor and Material Payment Bond A bond of the contractor in which a surety guarantees to the owner that the contractor will pay for labor and materials used in the performance of the contract or any subcontractor. A Labor and Material Payment Bond is sometimes referred to as a Payment Bond.

Liability Insurance Insurance which protects the insured against liability on account of injury to the person or property of another. See also (1) Completed Operations Insurance; (2) Comprehensive General Liability Insurance; (3) Contractor's Liability Insurance; (4) Employer's Liability Insurance; (5) Owner's Liability Insurance; (6) Professional Liability Insurance; (7) Property Damage Insurance; (8) Public Liability Insurance; (9) Special Hazards Insurance.

Lien See Mechanic's Lien.

Limit of Liability The maximum amount that an insurance company agrees to pay in case of loss.

Live Load A temporary and changing load superimposed on structural components by the use and occupancy of the building, not including the wind load, earthquake load, or dead load.

Loan Budget Amounts The portion of the loan amount, as set forth on the project cost statement, to be advanced by the lender for each category of direct and indirect costs.

Loss of Use Insurance Insurance protecting against financial loss during the time required to repair or replace property damaged or destroyed by an insured peril.

Major Leases Any leases for space in excess of the lease percentage of the rentable area of the improvements.

Major Subcontractor Any subcontractor or supplier engaged by the general contractor and any contractor or supplier engaged by the borrower, under one or more contracts or work orders aggregating the subcontract amount.

Mechanic's Lien A lien on real property created by statute in all states in favor of a person supplying labor or materials for a building or structure for the value of labor or materials supplied by them. In some jurisdictions a mechanic's lien also exists for the value of professional services. Clear title to the property cannot be obtained until the claim for the labor, materials or professional services is settled.

Minor Changes in the Work Changes of a minor nature in the work not involving an adjustment in the contract sum or an extension of the contract time and not inconsistent with the intent of the contract documents.

Mortgage A legal document by which real property is pledged as security for repayment of a loan. The pledge is canceled when the debt is repaid in full.

Mortgage Clause/Mortgagee Clause A provision in a fire or other damage insurance policy covering mortgaged property which states that, in the event of loss, the mortgagee shall be paid to the extent of the mortgagee's interest in the property. No violation of the policy conditions by the insured voids the policy as to the mortgagee. The clause also gives the mortgagee other rights and privileges.

Mortgaged Property The premises and other property constituting the "Mortgage Property."

Multi-family Dwelling Any building consisting of more than two dwelling units.

Negligence Failure to exercise due care under the circumstances. Legal liability for the consequences of an act or omission frequently depends upon whether or not there has been negligence. See also Due Care.

Non-conforming Work Work that does not fulfill the requirements of the contract documents.

Observation The visual survey of items, systems, conditions, or components that are readily accessible and easily visible during a walk-through survey of the subject property.

Observation of the Work A function of the architect in the construction phase, during visits to the site, to become generally familiar with the progress and quality of the work and to determine in general if the work is proceeding in accordance with the contract documents.

Occupancy Permit See Certificate of Occupancy.

Opinions of Probable Costs Estimate of probable costs to remedy a physical deficiency; a preliminary budget for a suggested remedy.

Owner The entity holding the title to the commercial real estate that is the subject of the PCA.

Partial Occupancy Occupancy by the owner of a portion of a project prior to final completion. See Final Completion.

Patent Defect A defect in materials or equipment of completed work which reasonably careful observation could have discovered; distinguished from a latent defect, which could not be discovered by reasonable observation.

PCR Reviewer The individual that both exercises responsible control over the field observer and reviews the PCR prior to delivery to the user.

Performance Bond A bond of the contractor in which a surety guarantees to the owner that the work will be performed in accordance with the contract documents. Except where prohibited by statute, the Performance Bond is frequently combined with the Labor and Material Payment Bond.

Permanent Commitment The commitment of the permanent lender and the commitment of any other person to provide funds for the permanent closing, including any three party agreement between the lender, the borrower and the permanent lender supplemental thereto.

Physical Deficiency Conspicuous defects or significant deferred maintenance of a subject property's material systems, components, or equipment as observed during the field observer's walk-through survey. Included within this definition are material life-safety/building code violations and material systems, components, or equipment that are approaching, have reached, or have exceeded their typical EUL or whose RUL should not be relied upon in view of actual or effective age, abuse, excessive wear and tear, exposure to the elements, lack of proper or routine maintenance, etc. This definition specifically excludes deficiencies that may be remedied with routine maintenance, miscellaneous minor repairs, normal operating maintenance, etc., and excludes de minimis conditions that generally do not constitute a material physical deficiency of the subject property.

Plans All final drawings, plans and specifications prepared by the borrower, borrower's architects, the general contractor or major subcontractors, and approved by the lender and the construction consultant, which describe and show the labor, materials, equipment, fixtures and furnishings necessary for the construction of the improvements, including all amendments and modifications thereof made by approved change orders (and also showing minimum grade of finishes and furnishings for all areas of the improvements to be leased or sold in ready-for-occupancy conditions).

Premises The real property as described and located in the BLA to the mortgage upon which all or part of the improvements are to be constructed.

Primary Commercial Real Estate Improvements The site and building improvements that are of fundamental importance with respect to the commercial real estate. This definition specifically excludes ancillary structures that may have been constructed to provide support uses such as maintenance sheds, utility garages, pool filter and equipment buildings, etc.

Private Facility A place of public accommodation or a commercial facility subject to title III of the ADA and 28 CFR part 36 or a transportation facility subject to title III of the ADA and 49 CFR 37.45.

Progress Payment Partial payment made during progress of the work on account of work completed and or materials suitably stored.

Progress Schedule A diagram, graph or other pictorial or written schedule showing the proposed and actual starting and completion dates of the various elements of the work.

Project (1) The total construction of which the work performed under the contract documents may be the whole or a part. (2) The total furniture, furnishings and equipment and interior construction of which the work performed under the contract documents may be the whole or a part.

Project Application for Payment Certified requests for payment from individual contractors on a construction management project, assembled for certification by the architect and submitted to the owner.

Project Cost Total cost of the project including construction costs, professional compensation, land costs, furnishings and equipment, financing and other charges.

Project Cost Statement A statement in a form approved by the lender setting forth, by category, the costs of completion of the improvements and the loan budget amounts in respect to the direct costs loan and indirect costs loan.

Project Manual The volume(s) prepared by the architect for a project which may include the bidding requirements, sample forms and conditions of the contract and the specifications.

Property Condition Assessment (PCA) The process by which a person or entity observes a property, interviews sources, and reviews available documentation for the purpose of developing an opinion and preparing a PCR of a commercial real estate's current physical condition. At the option of the user, a PCA may include a higher level of inquiry and due diligence than the baseline scope described within this guide or, at the user's option, it may include a lower level of inquiry or due diligence than the baseline scope described in this guide. Such deviations from this guide's scope should be disclosed in the PCR's executive summary.

Property Condition Report (PCR) A written report, prepared in accordance with the recommendations contained in this guide, that outlines the consultant's observations, opinions as to the subject property's condition, and opinions of probable costs to remedy any material physical deficiencies observed.

Property Damage Insurance Insurance coverage for the insured's legal liability for claims for injury to or destruction of tangible property including loss of use resulting there from, but usually not including coverage for injury to or destruction of property which is in the care, custody and control of the insured. See also Care, Custody & Control.

Public Facility A facility or portion of a facility constructed by, on behalf of, or for the use of a public entity subject to title II of the ADA and 28 CFR part 35 or to title II of the ADA and 49 CFR 37.41 or 37.43.

Public Use Describes interior or exterior rooms or spaces that are made available to the general public. Public use may be provided at a building or facility that is privately or publicly owned.

Punch List See Inspection List.

Ramp A walking surface which has a running slope greater than 1:20.

Readily Accessible Describes areas of the subject property that are promptly made available for observation by the field observer at the time of the walk-through survey and do not require the removal of materials or personal property, such as furniture, and that are safely accessible in the opinion of the field observer.

Record Drawings Construction drawing revised to show significant changes made during the construction process, usually based on marked-up prints, drawings and other data furnished by the contracts to the architect. Preferable to As Built Drawings.

Remaining Useful Life (RUL) A subjective estimate based upon observations, or average estimates of similar items, components, or systems, or a combination thereof, of the number of remaining years that an item, component, or system is estimated to be able to function in accordance with its intended purpose before warranting replacement. Such period of time is affected by the initial quality of an item, component, or system, the quality of the initial installation, the quality and amount of preventive maintenance exercised, climatic conditions, extent of use, etc.

Requisition A statement prepared by the borrower in a form approved by the lender setting forth the amount of the loan advance requested in each instance and including, if requested by the lender, a complete draw request which is to include all documents and information as stipulated in the agreement with the lender.

Retainage A sum withheld from progress payments to the contractor in accordance with the terms of the owner-contractor agreement.

Running Slope The slope that is parallel to the direction of travel (see Cross Slope).

Schedule of Values A statement furnished by the contractor to the architect reflecting the portions of the contract sum allocated to the various sections of the work and used as the basis for reviewing the contractor's applications for payment.

Securitization The process of converting an illiquid asset, such as a mortgage loan, into a tradable form, such as mortgage-backed securities.

Seismicity The worldwide or local distribution of earthquakes in space and time; a general term for the number of earthquakes in a unit of time, or for relative earthquake activity.

Shear Distribution Distribution of lateral forces along the height or width of a building.

Short-Term Costs Opinions of probable costs to remedy physical deficiencies, such as deferred maintenance, that may not warrant immediate attention, but require repairs or replacements that should be undertaken on a priority basis in addition to routine preventive maintenance. Such opinions of probable costs may include costs for testing, exploratory probing, and further analysis should this be deemed warranted by the consultant. The performance of such additional services are beyond this guide. Generally, the time frame for such repairs is within one to two years.

Shutdown Equipment, components or systems that are not operating at the time of the field observer's walk-through survey. For example, equipment, components, and systems that may be shutdown as a result of seasonal temperatures.

Site A parcel of land bounded by a property line or a designated portion of a public right-of-way.

Site Improvement Landscaping, paving for pedestrian and vehicular ways, outdoor lighting, recreational facilities, and the like, added to a site.

Special Hazards Insurance Insurance coverage for damage caused by additional perils or risks to be included in the property insurance at the request of the contractor or at the option of the owner. Examples often included are sprinkler leakage, collapse, water damage, and coverage for materials in transit to the site or stored off the site. See Property Insurance.

Specifications A part of the contract documents contained in the project manual consisting of written requirements for material, equipment, construction systems, standards and workmanship. Under the uniform construction index, the specifications comprise 16 divisions.

Standard As used by ASTM, a document that has been developed and established within the consensus principles of the society and that meets the approval of the ASTM procedures and regulations.

Statute of Limitations A statute specifying the period of time with which legal action must be brought for alleged damage or injury, or other legal relief. Ordinarily, the period commences with the occurrence of the damage or injury, or discovery of the act resulting in the alleged damage or injury. In construction industry cases, many jurisdictions define the period as commencing with completion of work or services performed in connection therewith.

Structural Frame The components or building systems that support the building's nonvariable forces or weights (dead loads) and variable forces or weights (live loads).

Subcontractor A person or entity who has a direct or indirect contract with a subcontractor to perform any of the work at the site.

Subsurface Investigation (Sometimes called Geotechnical Investigation) The soil boring and sampling program, together with the associated laboratory tests, necessary to establish subsurface profiles and the relative strengths, compressibility and other characteristics of the various strata encountered with depths likely to have an influence on the design of the project.

Superintendent Contractor's representative at the site who is responsible for continuous field supervision, coordination, completion of the work and, unless another person is designated in writing by the contractor to the owner and the architect, for the prevention of accidents.

Survey Observations made by the field observer during a walk-through survey to obtain information concerning the subject property's readily accessible and easily visible components or systems.

System (a process) A combination of interacting or interdependent components assembled to carry out one or more functions.

Thermal Resistance (R) A unit used to measure a material's resistance to heat transfer. The formula for thermal resistance is: R = Thickness (in inches)/k.

Time of Completion Date established in the contract, by a calendar date or by number of days, for; substantial completion of the work. See also (1) Date of Substantial Completion; (2) Contract Time.

Timely Access Entry provided to the consultant at the time of the site visit.

Title Insurer The issuer(s), approved by the interim lender and permanent lenders, of the title insurance policy or policies insuring the mortgage.

Topographic Survey The configuration of a surface including its relief and the locations of its natural and man-made features, usually recorded on a drawing showing surface variations by means of contour lines indicating height above or below a fixed datum.

Toxicity A reflection of a material's ability to release poisonous particulate.

Transient Lodging A building, facility, or portion thereof, excluding inpatient medical care facilities and residential facilities, that contains sleeping accommodations. Transient lodging may include, but is not limited to, resorts, group homes, hotels, motels, and dormitories.

Vehicular Way A route intended for vehicular traffic, such as a street, driveway, or parking lot.

Waiver of Lien An instrument by which a person or organization who has or may have a right of mechanic's lien against the property of another relinquishes such right. See also (1) Mechanic's Lien; (2) Release of Lien.

Walk-Through Survey Conducted during the field observer's site visit of the subject property, and consists of non-intrusive visual observations, survey of readily accessible, easily visible components and systems of the subject property. Concealed physical deficiencies are typically excluded.

Warranty Legally enforceable assurance of quality or performance of a product or work, or of the duration of satisfactory performance. Warranty guarantee and guaranty are substantially identical in meaning; nevertheless, confusion frequently arises from supposed distinctions attributed to guarantee (or guaranty) being exclusively indicative of duration of satisfactory performance or of a legally enforceable assurance furnished by a manufacturer or other third party. The uniform commercial code provisions on sales (effective in all states except Louisiana) use warranty but recognize the continuation of the use of guarantee and guaranty.

Zoning The legal restriction that deems that parts of cities be for particular uses, such as residential, commercial, industrial and so forth.

Bibliography

Adaptive Environments Center, Inc. & R.S. Means Engineering Staff, *Means ADA Compliance Price Guide*, R.S. Means Company, Inc., 1994.

Apgar, M., *The Alternative Workplace: Changing Where and How People Work*, Harvard Business Review, pp.121–135, May–June, 1998.

Armer, G.S.T., *Monitoring and Assessment of Structures*, Spon Press, New York, 2001.

ASTM, *Standard Guide for Property Condition Assessments: Baseline Property Condition Assessment, Designation: E2018-01.*

Ballast, David K., *Interior Design Reference Manual*, Professional Publications, Inc., Belmont, California, 1998.

Calow, P., *Handbook of Environmental Risk Assessment and Management*, Blackwell Science Ltd, Oxford, 1998.

Carmody, John; Christian, Jeffrey; Labs, Kenneth, *Builder's Foundation Handbook*, Oak Ridge National Laboratory, Oak Ridge, Tennessee, May 1991.

Chromow, S. & Little, T.G., *CDOs Impact the Dept Markets*, New York Law Journal, September 19, 2005.

Cuzzi, R. & Warr, W.G., *Elevator Basics & Evaluations*, VDA (Van Deusen & Associates), Presentation to Inspection & Valuation International, Inc., 2000.

Day, Robert W., *Forensic Geotechnical & Foundation Engineering*, McGraw-Hill Professional, New York, 1998.

De Chiara, Joseph; Panero, Julius, *Time-Saver Standards for Interior Design and Space Planning*, McGraw-Hill, New York, 2001

Deasy, C.M., *Designing Places for People: A Handbook for Architects, Designers, and Facility Managers*, Whitney Library of Design, New York, 1985.

Duffy, Francis, *The New Office: With 20 International Case Studies*, Conran Octopus, 1997.

Dworkin, Joseph F., "Waterproofing Below Grade," The Construction Specifier, March 1990.

Edwards, Sandra, *Office Systems—Designs for the Contemporary Workspace*, PBC International Inc., New York, 1986.

Federal Emergency Management Agency, FEMA 426, *Reference Manual to Mitigate Potential Terrorist Attacks in High Occupancy Buildings*, 2004.

Feld, J. and Carper, K.L., *Construction Failure, 2nd Edition*, John Wiley & Sons, New York, 1006.

Geldermann, D. & Sapp, D., *Streamlined Facilities Condition Assessments and Parametric Modeling for Deferred Maintenance Cost Estimates*, Plexus Scientific Corporation, October 2006.

Giesecke, Frederick E. et al, *Technical Drawing*, MacMillan Publishing Co., Inc., New York, 1974.

Goldsmith, Selwyn, *Designing for the Disabled—The New Paradigm*, Architectural Press, An imprint of Butterworth-Heinemann, Oxford, 1999.

Griffin, C.W.; Fricklas, Richard, *The Manual of Low-Slope Roof Systems, Third Edition*, The McGraw-Hill Companies, Inc., 1996.

Gunn, R. A., & Burroughs, M. S., *Work spaces that work: Designing high-performance offices*, The Futurist, pp.19–24, March–April 1996.

Harmon, Sharon Koomen, & Kennon, Katherine E., *The Codes Guidebook for Interiors, 2nd Edition*, John Wiley & Sons, New York, 2001.

Henshell, Justin, The Manual of Below-Grade Waterproofing Systems, John W. Wiley & Sons, Inc., 2000.

Hess-Kosa, K., *Environmental Site Assessment Phase I, 2nd Edition*, CRC, 1997.

Hinks, John, *Technology of Building Defects*, Spon Press, 1998.

Iano, E. A and J., *Fundamentals of Building Construction: Materials and Methods, 4th Edition*, John Wiley & Sons, Inc., New York, 2003.

Kearney, Deborah, S., *The ADA in Practice*, R.S. Means Company, Inc., Kingston, MA., 1995.

Koomen-Harmon, S., & Kennon, K. E., *The Codes Guidebook for Interiors, 2nd Edition,* John Wiley & Sons, New York, 2001.

Kubal, Michael T., *Construction Waterproofing Handbook*, The McGraw-Hill Companies Inc., 2000.

Kubba, Sam, A.A., *Space Planning for Commercial & Residential Interiors*, McGraw-Hill, New York, 2003.

Architecture and Linear Measurement During the Ubaid Period in Mesopotamia, BAR International Series 707, Oxford, 1998.

Kubba, Shamil, *Mesopotamian Architecture and Town Planning*, BAR International Series 367(i), Oxford, 1987.

Lewis, B. T. and Payant, R. *Facility Inspection Field Manual: A Complete Condition Assessment Guide*, McGraw-Hill, New York, 2001.

Lstiburek, J. and Carmody, J., *Moisture Control Handbook*, Oak Ridge National Laboratories, Oak Ridge, Tennessee, October 1991.

MacDonald, Susan (Editor), *Concrete Building Pathology*, Blackwell Publishing Ltd., 2002.

Mendler, Sandra & Odell, William, *The HOK Guidebook to Sustainable Design*, John Wiley & Sons, New York, 2000.

Piper, J. E., *Handbook of Facility Assessment*, Fairmont Press, 2004.

Propst, Robert, *The Office—A Facility Based on Change*, The Business Press, Elmhurst, Illinois, 1968.

Ratay, R. T., *Structural Condition Assessment*, John Wiley & Sons, New York, 2005.

Rayfield, Julie K., *The Office Interior Design Guide: An Introduction for Facility and Design Professionals*, John Wiley & Sons, Inc., New York, 1994.

Redstone, Louis G., *New Dimensions in Shopping Centers and Stores*, McGraw-Hill Book Company, New York, 1973.

Reznikoff, S. C., *Specifications for Commercial Interiors*, Whitney Library of Design, New York, 1989.

Richardson, Barr, *Defects and Deterioration in Buildings: A Practical Guide to the Science of Material Failure, 2nd Edition,* Taylor & Francis, 2001.

Riley II, Charles A., *High-Access Home, Design and Decoration for Barrier-Free Living*, Rizzoli International Publications, Inc., New York, 1999.

Sampson, Carol A., *Estimating for Interior Designers*, Watson-Guptill Publications, 2001.

Sara, M. N., *Site Assessment and Remediation Handbook*, 2nd Edition, CRC, 2003.

Smith, William D.; Smith, Laura H., *McGraw-Hill On-Site Guide to Building Codes 2000: Commercial and Interiors*, McGraw-Hill Professional Publishing, New York, 2001.

Steven Winter Associates, *Accessible Housing by Design*, McGraw-Hill, New York et al., 1997.

Tilton, Rita; Jackson, Howard J; Rigby, Sue Chappell, *The Electronic Office: Procedures & Administration, 11th Edition,* South-Western Publishing Co., Cincinnati, Ohio, 1996.

Vukovich, S.M., *Secure Commercial Real Estate: The Investor's Guide to Control the Physical Realm*, Prescriptive Diagnostic Publishers International, Massachusetts, 2000.

Wakita, Dr. Osamu A; Linde, Richard M., *The Professional Handbook of Architectural Working Drawings*, John Wiley & Sons, New York, 1984.

Zelinsky, Marilyn, *New Workplaces for New Workstyles*, McGraw-Hill, New York, 1998.

Index

E

F